E M P I R E · S I B E R I A

Tobolsk

Ob' River

Irtysh River

Omsk

Ishim River

Akmolinsk (Astana)

···STAN

Lake Balkhash

Turkistan

···ymkent

Tashkent

Kokand

Samarkand

KYRGYZSTAN

Pishpek (Bishkek)

Verniy (Almaty)

TAJIKISTAN

Dushanbe

Pamirsky Post

Pamir

WAKHAN

Balkh

Hindu Kush

Chitral

Gilgit

Kabul

Peshawar

···STAN

Ghazna

Indus River

Quetta

Lahore

Karachi

B R I T I S H
I N D I A

Delhi

Agra

NEPAL

Kathmandu

SIKKIM

BHUTAN

Calcutta

Bombay (Mumbai)

Yenisei River

Sayan Mountains

Lake Baikal

Kyzyl

TUVA

Irkutsk

Nerchinsk

Altai Mountains

Dzungarian Desert

Ürümqi

Turfan

Hami

Tian Shan

Kashgar

Yarkand

Taklamakan Desert

Khotan

M O N G O L I A

Karakorum

Urga (Ulaan Baatar)

Gobi Desert

C H I N E S E   E M P I R E

Dolon Nor

Hohhot

Beijing

Tengger Desert

Xining

Himalaya

Lhasa

The major empires of Central Asia and neighbouring regions in 1907, and the main historical sites in the Age of Decline and Revival

- ● Cities and sites
- ● Modern capitals

- ▢ Russian Empire 1907
- ▢ British India, including the princely Indian states, 1907
- ▢ Chinese Empire, including Tibet, Mongolia and Tuva, 1907
- ▢ Ottoman Empire, including autonomous Bulgaria, excluding Qatar, Cyprus and Crete, 1907

Scale (km)

0   250   500   750   1000

M000073057

THE HISTORY OF
CENTRAL ASIA

VOLUME **FOUR**

THE HISTORY OF
CENTRAL ASIA

The Age of Decline and Revival

CHRISTOPH BAUMER

LONDON · NEW YORK

Published in 2018 by
I.B.Tauris & Co. Ltd
London • New York
www.ibtauris.com

Translated by Christopher W. Reid, Academic Translation and Proofreading,
Hamburg, Germany.
Photographs © Christoph Baumer 2018

ISBN: 978 1 78831 049 9
ISBN: 978 1 78831 351 3 (*The History of Central Asia*, 4-volume set)

A full CIP record for this book is available from the British Library
A full CIP record is available from the Library of Congress

Library of Congress Catalog Card Number: available

Designed by Christopher Bromley
Project managed by Carolann Young, ITS

Image editing and processing by Sturm AG, 4132 Muttenz, Switzerland

Printed and bound in Italy by Printer Trento

Contents

1. Aerial view of the 77-km-long Fedchenko Glacier, extending in a north–south direction in the Pamir Mountains, Tajikistan. It is named after the Russian researcher Alexei Fedchenko (1844–73). The Pamir Mountains were the scene of intense Anglo-Russian rivalry in the 1880s and 1890s.

Introduction

'It must never be forgotten that geography, despite popular views to the contrary, is not something fixed and unalterable, but, like history, is something which is essentially dynamic.'

CLIFFORD KINVIG in his review of Halford Mackinder's *The Scope and Methods of Geography and the Geographical Pivot of History*[1].

The history of Central Asia from the sixteenth to twenty-first century bears out Kinvig's underlying critique of Halford Mackinder, who posited that mastery of Eurasia's heartland, i.e. the control of Central Asia, was the key to world domination. Certainly, in view of the development of new weapons systems and means of transport, the advent of modern logistics, and the different interests of the neighbouring major powers, a static understanding of geography proved increasingly less useful to understanding Central Asia. Instead, a dynamic interpretation needed to take precedence. In terms of longitude and latitude, Central Asia, of course, remained the heartland of Eurasia. But as far as its political, economic and cultural importance is concerned, in the course of the fifteenth century the region lost the political centrality it had acquired from the beginning of the thirteenth century. Beginning in the sixteenth century, it found itself more and more on the periphery of world political and economic events. It was not until the British-Russian conflicts of interest in the nineteenth century that Central Asia became the focus once again of the Eurasian continent. The region then 'disappeared' behind the Iron Curtain in 1920 and degenerated into a kind of 'backyard' of the Soviet Union. Only in the last quarter of the twentieth century did the dynamism of Central Asia's geography gain momentum again. First, the world's two superpowers, the US and the Soviet Union, clashed via their surrogates on the southern edge of Central Asia, the Hindu Kush. And when the Soviet Union collapsed in 1991, also as a consequence of the failed war in Afghanistan (1979–89), the Central Asian states and Mongolia won back their sovereignty. In particular, the resource-rich countries Kazakhstan, Turkmenistan and Uzbekistan managed, at least to some degree, to regain control of their own history. But their room to manoeuvre continued to be constrained by the interests of the regional superpowers Russia and China as well as the logistical challenges that are still posed today by their landlocked geography.

As explained in the third volume of the present study, the Mongols overran large parts of the Eurasian realm with their tenacious horsemen at the beginning of the thirteenth century. They created their own empire that extended almost from the Yellow Sea to the Mediterranean and on to Moscow. The instruments of their former world domination included a bow-equipped and extremely mobile cavalry, an unprecedented degree of military planning and organisation, and innovative leadership. Two of the most significant limitations were climatic and geographic in nature: their sphere of influence stopped where their horses could no longer graze and where a humid climate made their glued reflex bows inoperable. At the turn from the fifteenth to the sixteenth century, firearms began to challenge the previous superiority of the bow riders. The maritime trade between Europe and India also gradually replaced the traditional trade routes through Central Asia, depriving the local states of a substantial source of revenue. These factors, and the rapidly growing headstart of Europe in the field of the exact sciences and technologies, caused Central Asia to fall behind. This was exacerbated by the simultaneous emergence of two powerful, expanding nation-states along the borders of Central Asia: Russia under the Romanov dynasty and China under the Qing. Increasingly, they restricted the room of Central Asia's rulers to manoeuvre. Emblematic of the power-political decline of the proud descendants of Genghis Khan is China's destruction of the Dzungar nomadic empire in the middle of the eighteenth century.

The rivalry between the major maritime power Britain and the terrestrial superpower Russia that emerged after the Napoleonic Wars was played out – whether through direct warfare or skirmishes or proxy wars – in an area that extended from Constantinople in the west to the Amur River in the east. Russia's strategic goal was the acquisition of a warm-water port and the conquest of Constantinople; for Britain, it was to defend India and maintain its maritime supremacy. Immediately after the Crimean War (1853–56), Russia began to advance into Central Asia and, until 1873, to subdue the still independent Khanates of Bukhara, Kokand and Khiva. As a consequence, the Russian Empire appeared to be a direct threat to British India. Although Central Asia was not a strategic priority for either Britain or Russia, the region was of great concern to the major powers for half a century, until the Anglo-Russian Entente of 1907. It was almost paradoxical: in political and economic terms, the impoverished Central Asian region had long been a peripheral concern of the major European powers and yet, from a military standpoint, it was crucial for London and St Petersburg. The Anglo-Russian rivalry was put to an end due to the maritime superiority of Britain and Japan, who had been allies since 1902. At the time, Russia had yet to exploit the strength of a transcontinental railway.

After the fall of the tsarist regime in 1917 and the outbreak of the Russian Civil War, the Emirate of Bukhara and several provisional governments tried to regain their independence. Nevertheless, the Bolsheviks re-conquered the breakaway regions of Central Asia as successors of the tsars. Apart from the brief interlude at the end of World War I, the period from 1865/73 to 1991 was a political nadir for Central Asia. For the Mongols, the low point had already begun in 1691. After all, there was no longer a single true sovereign state but only nominal republics without authority. Central Asia stood under Moscow's control from 1920/21 and, in the course of the 1920s and 1930s, was brought into line culturally with the *homo sovieticus*. Afghanistan, which had enjoyed sovereignty again since 1919, also seemed to fall victim to the Soviet empire with the communist coup in 1978. It appeared as though the Kremlin would soon realise the old dream of the tsars of securing a warm-water port on one of the world's oceans. Yet exactly the opposite happened: at the southern corner of Central Asia, a bloody guerrilla war flared up between the Soviet Union and its Afghan client government, on the one hand, and a heterogeneous grouping of Afghan, Pakistani and Arab mujahideen, on the other. The latter were coordinated by Pakistani intelligence and armed and funded by the US and Saudi Arabia. The Soviet Union lost the nine-year-long war and even broke apart itself two years later. From its ruins emerged, *inter alia*, the states of Kazakhstan, Uzbekistan, Kyrgyzstan, Tajikistan, Turkmenistan and Mongolia. Finally, there were sovereign states once again in Central Asia.

The nascent states succeeded in escaping from their previous peripheral regional status thanks to their coveted raw materials such as natural gas, oil, uranium, copper, gold and silver. The landlocked geography, coupled with a traffic and transport network aligned towards Moscow, forced the new republics to sell their raw materials on Moscow's terms. As a southern neighbour to Central Asia, Iran offered itself as an alternative to the Russian pipeline and rail network. However, the American blockade against Iran initially prevented such a solution. This logistical 'Gordian knot' was first severed by Turkmenistan with the construction of a small natural gas pipeline and a railway line to Iran; it was then followed by Kazakhstan with its oil and gas pipelines to China.

Despite this breakthrough, the Central Asian states today are at a major disadvantage compared to producers of raw materials that have access to the oceans. It remains to be seen if they can maintain their independence or whether, as raw material suppliers to China, they will become more and more economically dependent on their main customer and, by extension, its surrogates. How a resurgent Islam will evolve is equally uncertain. Its further development as a private concern or as the only political alternative to the authoritarian regimes will depend on both the region's economic progress and the domestic political climate. In any event, the Muslim countries of Central Asia do not belong to Putin's 'arc of instability'.[2]

Descendants of the Genghis Khanids

'The king of Boghar [Abdullah Khan of Bukhara] hath no great power or riches. (...) There is a yeerely great resort of Marchants to this Citie of Boghar, which trauaile [travel] in great Caravans from the Countries thereabout adioyning, as India, Persia, Balke, Russia...and in times past from Cathay,...but these Marchants are so beggarly and poor, and bring so little quantitie of wares..., that there is no hope of any good trade there to be had worthy the following.'

ANTHONY JENKINSON agent of the English *Muscovy Company* and envoy of Tsar Ivan IV, winter 1558–59.[1]

In the period from about 1470 to 1560, the groundwork was laid throughout Eurasia for important developments that would influence the region's history well into the twentieth century. In Western Europe, expansive nation-states emerged however that were shaken by violent religious conflicts. In East Asia, apart from the earlier emperors of the Qing Dynasty, Kangxi and Qianlong, China was in the thrall of a Confucian-based hubris and, accordingly, isolated itself. South-west of Central Asia, two new major regional powers arose: the Persian Safavids and the Ottoman Turks. While the boundaries between Persia and the neighbouring Central Asian states remained disputed until the late nineteenth century, the Ottoman Empire increasingly attracted the attention of the leading maritime power, Great Britain, and the largest empire by surface area, Russia, because of its strategically important geographical location. In the nineteenth century, this had a direct impact on Central Asia. It was the Portuguese navigators who strategically bypassed the empires of the Ottomans, Persians, and Central Asia during the transition from the fifteenth to the sixteenth century, clearing the way for European colonies with the establishment of port bases. In 1498, Vasco da Gama landed at the southern Indian port city of Calicut and, in 1515, Afonso de Albuquerque annexed the Persian Hormuz Island, which not only controlled access to the Persian Gulf, but was also a gateway to Central Asia. The growing superiority of European military technology in the form of muskets and especially cannons, along with the latter's industrial production, gave the colonial powers superior strength. At the same time, the Central Asian mounted armies lost their previous advantages over infantry divisions. Gradually, the Central Asian states lost their initiative and the ability to control their own history. It was not until the collapse of the Soviet Union that the new states of Central Asia regained their political independence.

The seizure of power in Iran by Ismail (r. 1501–24), the sheikh of the Shiite Order of Safaviyya, turned out to be probably the most momentous event of the period around 1500. In 1501, he founded the Persian dynasty of the Safavids (1501–1736), established an Iranian national state for the first time since the Sassanids (224–651), and elevated the Islamic faith of Twelver-Shia to the state religion. With the enforcement of Twelver-Shia within his realm, Ismail gave his newly formed kingdom of Iran and his dynasty of the Safavids an unmistakable national-religious identity. It contrasted sharply with that of his fiercest opponents, the Sunni Ottomans in the west and the Uzbeks in the east. Shah Abbas I (r. 1587–1629) completed the enforcement of Twelver-Shia in Iran and stressed the demarcation from the hated Sunni. Their ancestors had allegedly ignored the legitimate claim to power of the descendants of the Prophet Muhammad and usurped the leadership in the Islamic world.[2] The forced divide between Shiites and Sunnis after 1501 not only influenced relations between southern Central Asia and Iran for centuries, but it also rearranged the geography of the Islamic world, especially the Middle East. The opposition between Twelver and Sunna continues to shape politics in this region in the twenty-first century, as many of the local conflicts run along these confessional boundaries between Sunna and Shia.

In the fifteenth century, the once-mighty Golden Horde dissolved under the rule of the descendants of Jochi, the eldest son of Genghis Khan, into regional khanates. In the sixteenth century, they found themselves increasingly pressured by Moscow's princes. First, some Genghis Khanids managed to achieve a remarkable restoration, expelling the Timurids, the descendants of Timur-e Lang, from Mawarannahr, i.e. Transoxania. Because of the influx of mounted warriors with Turkish Kipchak roots from the Uzbek confederation, Timurid Transoxania became the country of Uzbekistan. The Uzbek steppe horsemen also brought their traditional power structures of land distribution in appanages and a gathering of leading nobleman and military leaders, the so-called *kuriltai*. Each leading male member of the ruling clan had a right to a share of the dominated territory. The *kuriltai* ruled over the territorial division in appanages and confirmed the succession of a khan. The last Timurid to govern in Transoxania, Babur, fled south and established the Mughal Empire (1526–1858) in the Indian subcontinent.[3]

1. The Uzbek Khanate

1.1 The Dynasty of the Abu'l-Khayrids

In the literature, members of the Uzbek dynasty of the Abu'l-Khayrids are also imprecisely referred to as 'Shaybanids'. This is due to the fact that Shayban, the fifth son of Jochi, was not only the precursor of the Transoxian Abu'l-Khayrids (1500–98), but also of another dynasty, namely the Arabshahids, who ruled in Chorasmia from 1511 to 1804, and also of the Shaybanid Kuchum of Sibir (r. 1563–82, d. 1598). In the sixth generation of Shayban's heirs, the following bifurcation occurred: Arabshah bin Fulad founded

the line of the Arabshahids, and Ibrahim Oghlan bin Fulad of the Abu'l-Khayrids, named after his grandson Abu'l Khayr.[4] In the first quarter of the fifteenth century, the two lines of descent vied for supremacy over the steppe dwellers of the Dasht-i Kipchak steppes between the Central Asian Yaik (Ural) and Sary Su rivers, who referred to themselves as 'Uzbeks'. At the time, it was customary for tribes of the steppe to take the name of a famous leader, in this case Özbek Khan (r. 1313–41), who had once and for all Islamised the Golden Horde.[5] The designation 'Uzbeks' was initially political, not ethnic, in nature.

After the two rivals Jumaduq and Barak Oghlan were killed in action around 1428 fighting for the title of Uzbek Khan, the barely

2. The Abdullah Khan Mosque built by the Uzbek Abu'l-Khayrid ruler Abdullah Khan II (r. 1583–98) in Bukhara, Uzbekistan, in 1590. Photo: 2004.

3. The Mir-i Arab Madrasah in Bukhara, which was completed in 1535/36 and stands opposite the Kalyan Mosque. Image taken from the Kalyan minaret, 2004.

17-year-old **Abu'l Khayr Khan** (r. 1429–68/69) was elected as the new khan over the Ulus-e Uzbek by a *kuriltai* in the Siberian city of Chimgi-Tura (today's Tyumen). Following numerous campaigns, the young khan succeeded in bringing most of the *ulus* (dominions) of Shayban under his rule. In the years 1431 and 1435/36, he marched south and plundered Chorasmia, which belonged to the realm of the Timurid Shah Rukh. In 1446, the Uzbek khan penetrated the lower reaches of the Syr Darya River (Iaxartes River) to the south-east, where he conquered major trading centres and made Sighnaq his winter capital. At the same time, the focus of his steppe empire shifted to the south. When Ulugh Beg (r. 1447–49) fought near Herat for the legacy of his deceased father Shah Rukh, Abu'l Khayr took advantage of the absence of the Timurid army to attack the area around Samarkand and to raid Transoxania. In 1451, the Uzbek again had an opportunity to invade Transoxania and even to conquer the wealthy region when the Timurid Abu Said (r. 1451–69) asked him for help against his rival Abdallah ibn Ibrahim (r. 1450–51). Abu'l Khayr and Abu Said defeated Abdallah near Samarkand, but the Timurid duped the Uzbek by quickly occupying the heavily fortified city and closing its gates before him. As compensation, Abu Said presented Abu'l Khayr with precious gifts and a daughter of Ulugh Beg. Abu'l Khayr then withdrew.[6]

Around 1457, Abu'l Khayr suffered a first serious setback when Uz Temür Tayishi,[7] ruler of the Western Mongolian Kalmyks (Oirat), dealt him a devastating defeat south of Sighnaq. As a result of this reversal, the allied Manghits switched sides and henceforth supported his opponents, the Arabshahids. Soon after, from 1458 to 1461, Abu'l Khayr suffered a third, even more severe blow, when a part of his *ulus* seceded and adopted a hostile posture. The two leaders Giray and Jani Beg, whose lineage went back to Togha Timur, the thirteenth son of Jochi, took advantage of the khan's weakness and relocated with their followers south-eastward to the region located between Chuy Valley and Lake Balkhash, i.e. Moghulistan's western territory. These renegade Uzbeks called themselves Uzbek-Kazakhs, whereby the ethnonym *kazakh* basically means 'vagabond' or 'freebooter'.[8] As the near-contemporary leader and historian Mirza Muhammad Haidar Dughlat (1499 or 1500–1551) stated: 'Since they [Giray Khan and Jani Beg] had first of all separated from the mass of their people, and for some time had been in an indigent and wandering state, they got the name of Kazak, which has clung to them.'[9] Abu'l Khayr died around 1468. His son and successor **Shaikh Haydar** (r. *ca.* 1469–?) failed to assert himself and, after 1469, fell in the fight against the Togha-Timurids Ibaq and Ahmad Khan of the Great Horde. The Uzbek *ulus* subsequently disintegrated into warring parties.[10]

Abu'l Khayr's grandson **Muhammad Shahi Beg**, called Shah Bakht, the future **Shaybani Khan** (b. 1451, r. 1500–10), tried in vain for about 20 years to revive his grandfather's realm. With his followers, he was only able to occupy a smaller area along the northern shore of central Syr Darya because the Uzbek-Kazakhs ruled over the central and eastern part of the Dasht-i Kipchak steppe. This pressure by Uzbek-Kazakhs coerced him to test his luck in an attack on Samarkand, where a power vacuum had prevailed since the death of the Timurid Mahmud (r. 1494–95).[11] In conquering Samarkand and Bukhara in 1500, Shaybani Khan allowed the empire of the Abu'l-Khayrids to resurrect itself in Transoxania. Although in the winter of 1500/01 he lost Samarkand for several months to the Timurid Zahir al-Din Muhammad Babur, he nevertheless reclaimed the city soon afterwards. Surrendering in rapid succession to Shaybani Khan were Fergana and Tashkent (1502), Kunduz, Gurganj (today's Konye-Urgench) and Khiva (1504–05), Balkh (1506), Herat and Kandahar (1507). The fall of Herat and Kandahar compelled Babur to retreat to Kabul, which he had conquered in 1504. Difficulties in the hinterland of Kandahar, however, forced Shaybani Khan to refrain from undertaking a further advance to Kabul.[12] Shortly afterwards, Shaybani Khan invaded Khorasan and, in 1508, captured the cities of Mashhad (where he destroyed the Shiite sanctuary around the grave of Imam Reza), Nishapur, and Sabzavar and Bastam.[13] The destruction of the major Shiite pilgrimage site in Mashhad stoked the animosity of Shah Ismail I, the founder of the Shiite Safavid dynasty, toward the Sunni Uzbeks. As Mirza Haidar Dughlat reports, in the same year Shaybani Khan had his former patron Mahmud Khan of Moghulistan (r. 1487–1508) and his five sons murdered, when Mahmud Khan asked him for his support.[14] As a result of all of these conquests, it appeared as though Shaybani Khan would be able to restore the Timurid Empire.

Although Khorasan soon went to Persia and the Khanate of Moghulistan dwindled away, Shaybani Khan not only laid the foundation for the formation of a national state of Uzbeks, corresponding more or less to today's Uzbekistan, but deepened the turkification of Transoxania that had begun with the Old Turks, the Oghuz, the Seljuks and the Karakhanids. Today's Uzbek language is a Turkic language and belongs to the group of southeastern Turkic languages, which also includes the related Uyghur language. The Uzbek language originated from the Kipchak-Uzbek dialect and the Chagatai language, which was prevalent in the Chagatai Khanate and in the Timurid Empire. Shaybani Khan also set up a different kind of administration in his newly conquered empire. He tried to combine elements of traditional ruling

mechanisms with those of a theocratic approach and contemporary urban management. This soon proved impractical, however. From the steppe tradition, he adopted the principle of dividing land into hereditary appanages and the aforementioned *kuriltai*. In this meeting of the royal princes, the khan was little more than a *primus inter pares*. Shaybani Khan thus chose Samarkand as his capital, but handed over major cities and the surrounding regions, such as Bukhara, Tashkent, Turkistan and Andijan as hereditary appanages to his next of kin or to deserving military leaders. This territorial structure fragmented the Uzbek state from the beginning and sowed the seeds for the internal feuds that took root in 1512 after Shaybani Khan's death.[15] Simultaneously, the khan tried to follow the example of Shah Ismail I by establishing a theocracy. He appointed himself at its head as the '*imam al-zaman wa khalif al-rahman*', i.e. the 'Imam of the Age and Caliph of the Merciful', i.e. God.[16] Finally, Shaybani Khan strove to repair the neglected irrigation canals and to recover abandoned agricultural land, as well as to institute monetary reform that would curb the galloping inflation which had been triggered by the last wars.[17]

The triumphant military advance of Shaybani Khan was abruptly halted by the Kazakhs and Shah Ismail. Since the Kazakhs had taken advantage of Shaybani's absence from Transoxania to plunder the regions around Samarkand and Bukhara in 1508, the khan conducted a campaign against the Kazakhs in the beginning of 1509. After an initial Uzbek success, the Uzbek main army was caught off-guard towards the end of 1509 (or very early 1510) by the future ruler Qasim Khan and retreated with heavy losses. This caused Shaybani Khan to order the campaign to be abandoned, whereupon part of his army dissolved in Samarkand.[18] The khan spent the winter of 1509/10 in Herat, where another campaign, this time against the Hazaras in central Afghanistan, also ended unsuccessfully. Mirza Haidar reported: 'As it was winter, and the two armies in succession had fared thus badly [against the Kazakhs and the Hazaras], he gave his soldiers a general leave of absence to return . . . home. [. . .] At this juncture, news came that Shah Ismail was advancing on Khorasan.'[19] Shaybani's demobilisation of his army had proved disastrous.

Coinciding with Shaybani Khan's conquests, Ismail bin Haydar al-Safavi (r. 1501–24) – the sheikh of the militarily organised Shiite Sufi order *Safaviyya* – founded the Shiite dynasty of the Safavids (1501–1736). He did this after conquering the northern Iranian city of Tabriz of the Turkmen Aq Qoyunlu. The Safaviyya were descended from Sufi Sheikh Shafi al-Din Ishaq (1252–1334) from Ardabil. It is uncertain when the originally Sunni religious order accepted the teachings of the Twelver-Shia, which it adopted along with popular religious elements such as the belief in miracles and the veneration of saints. Sheikh Khwaja Ali (d. 1439) may have been the first Shiite order leader. In any event, Ismail's grandfather Sheikh Junaid (d. 1460) and father Sheikh Haydar (d. 1488) tried to assert themselves militarily and to exploit the Shia faith as a means of extending their power. Both fell in combat, however. It was Sheikh Haydar who founded the Qizilbash ('red heads'), an elite Shiite troop of Turkmen origin named after the red turbans they wore. Within a decade, Ismail used his Qizilbash to bring to heel all of Iran and the current areas of Azerbaijan up to Derbent in present-day Russian Dagestan, parts of Mesopotamia, and eastern Anatolia.[20] As simultaneous leader of Safaviyya and ruler over Iran and Mesopotamia, Ismail singlehandedly tried to merge religious and political power in a theocratic form of government. He inflated the position of Muhammad's son-in-law Ali by calling him 'a manifestation of God'. He designated himself a descendant of Ali and Fatima, the Prophet's daughter, and representatives of the Twelve Imams.[21] As a kind of divine Imam-king, he enjoyed the reputation of being invincible.

4. *Cuerda seca* tile made of stone paste, showing the figure of an archer. Safavid dynasty, early seventeenth century. British Museum, London, Object no: 1878.1230.732.a.

In 1510, Ismail attacked Khorasan because Shaybani Khan's successful campaigns of 1507/08 against Herat, Nishapur, Sabzevar and Bastam endangered his eastern flank. Moreover, the desecration of the mausoleum of Imam Reza in Mashhad and Shaybani's appointment as caliph were two provocations that he could not possibly ignore. Ismail's attack caught Shaybani Khan, who had demobilised his army, completely by surprise. Shaybani Khan marched with a small army to Merv, where he defeated the Shiite vanguard. Instead of staying put in the mighty fortress of Merv to await further reinforcements, he fell into a trap set by Ismail, who made a feigned retreat. He followed the supposedly disorderly retreating Persians, until he ran into Shah Ismail's army lying in wait. Thanks to its superior firepower and greater numbers, Ismail's Qizilbash annihilated the Uzbek army in early December 1510. Shaybani Khan fell in battle. The Uzbeks fled and Shah Ismail occupied Merv, where he committed a massacre against the Uzbeks. As the contemporary historian Mir Ghyas ad-Din Muhammad Husayni, called Khwandamir (*ca.* 1475–1535), reported: 'The heads of the slain [of Merv] were piled into towers.'[22] The Shah also subsequently occupied Herat.

After Shaybani Khan's death in the Battle of Merv, a *kuriltai* chose **Söyünch (Suyunjuq) Muhammed Khoja** (r. 1511–12), the second oldest sultan (prince) of the dynasty as Khan *ad interim*, since the oldest Abu'l-Khayrid, sultan **Köchkünji Muhammed**, was leading a campaign against Qasim Khan's Kazakhs. Two other candidates for the khan's title, Shaybani's son Muhammed Timur Sultan (d. 1514) and Shaybani's nephew Ubayd Allah assumed commander responsibilities.[23] But when the Timurid Babur heard of the defeat and death of Shaybani Khan at the end of 1510, he immediately commenced the reconquest of his heritage and formed a coalition directed against the Uzbeks. He sent envoys to the Moghul prince Muhammed Mirza of Andijan. After a first victory, he told Shah Ismail he would convert to Twelver-Shia and enforce it in his future empire, if the Shah would provide him with troops. The contemporary historian Khwandamir recorded Babur's proposal as follows: 'If you send one of your great Amirs with a detachment of warriors to me, it is hoped that soon the rest of the kingdom of Transoxania will be taken, the Khutba and coinage will be in your royal name, and an end will be put to the Uzbek sultans.'[24] In the meantime, Ismail Shah marched from Herat to Balkh. Given Ismail's military superiority, the Uzbek commanders Timur Sultan and Ubayd Allah concluded a peace agreement with the Shah, without waiting for Khan Söyünch's consent. They ceded Balkh to Ismail and accepted the Oxus (Amu Darya) as a border with Iran. As a consequence, they relinquished all of Khorasan. Shah Ismail returned to Iran, but left troops to Babur as his future vassal.[25]

5. Courtyard of the Kalyan Mosque in Bukhara, Uzbekistan, completed in 1514. A mulberry tree stands in the middle of the courtyard. Photo: 2004.

Thanks to these reinforcements, Babur conquered Bukhara and occupied Samarkand, which did not show any resistance. He declared himself Ismail's vassal and propagated the Twelver-Shia: 'The khutba was read and coinage was issued with the names of the Twelve Imams and the shah's name and title.'[26] Further beneficiaries of the Uzbek defeat were the two sultans Ibars and Balbars from the line of Arabshahids. They conquered Chorasmia.

The fact that Babur promoted the Twelver-Shia alienated him from the people of Samarkand and Bukhara, who were beginning to prefer the rule of the Uzbeks over that of Babur. The Uzbeks took advantage of this change of mood to counter-attack, and in spring 1512 Ubayd Allah defeated Babur at Kul-i Malik near Bukhara. Babur consequently had to leave Samarkand for the third time in May, withdrawing to Hissar, 30 km west of the present-day capital of Tajikistan, Dushanbe.[27] In the autumn of 1512, a powerful Persian army advanced under General Yar Ahmad Khuzani, called Najm-i Thani, to Transoxania. There, in the city of Qarshi south-east of Samarkand, he carried out a bloodbath, despite

Babur's pleas for mercy. The situation for Babur was now hopeless. Najm's massacres in Qarshi and his avowal to completely destroy Samarkand after its conquest alienated the local population from Babur even further. Babur must also have feared being relegated to a mere tool of the Persians or simply cast away. Babur therefore took a wait-and-see approach in the Battle of Ghijduvan north-east of Bukhara on 12 November 1512. Ubayd Allah, however, destroyed the Persian army and beheaded the captured Najm.[28] Babur had to flee, first to Hissar, then to Kunduz, and subsequently returned to

Kabul. However, he did not abandon hope of retaking Transoxania or Khorasan until 1514. Then, as the historian and vizier Abu'l Fazl ibn Mubarak (1551–1602) observed in ornate prose: 'He was led by divine inspiration to turn his mind to the conquest of Hindustan.'[29]

As for Shah Ismail, things took a turn for the worse after the defeat of Ghijduvan. In March 1514, the Ottoman Sultan Selim I (r. 1512–20), a staunch Sunni, suggested to Ubayd Allah that they encircle and simultaneously attack the despised Shiites. Ubayd Allah welcomed the Ottoman initiative, but assessed his position in Transoxania as being too uncertain to attack. Despite this rejection, Selim attacked Persia and on 23 August 1514 decimated Shah Ismail's army near Chaldiran in north-eastern Anatolia. This outcome was due not least to his modern artillery and a strong infantry division with matchlock rifles, along with tactical mistakes by Ismail, who had now lost the aura of divine invincibility.[30] Ismail's defeat simultaneously averted the threat of another Safavid invasion in the khanate of the Uzbeks.

In 1512, a *kuriltai* appointed Uzbek prince **Köchkünji Muhammed ibn Abu'l Khayr Khan,** also called **Kuchum Khan** (r. 1512–*ca.* 1530), as the supreme khan of the Uzbek Empire and apportioned the four main regions to representatives of the four

major lineages of Abu'l-Khayrids: Ubayd Allah received Bukhara; Samarkand went to Köchkünji and Muhammed Timur, who died in 1514; Janibeg received Miyankal, the valley of Zeravshan west of Samarkand, and after its conquest in 1526, the city of Balkh; finally, Söyünch eventually received Tashkent. Given this division of the empire's territory, the authority of the supreme khan was merely nominal. There was also no fixed capital. The 'capital' was identical to the seat of the supreme khan or the supreme commander.[31] Between 1510 and 1539, Ubayd Allah was the supreme commander and the most powerful man of the Uzbek Khanate. He succeeded in convincing the other sultans to adopt a common foreign policy. In this role, Ubayd Allah undertook five campaigns in Khorasan

6. The Kukeldash Madrasah in Tashkent, Uzbekistan, built in the 1570s, was one of the few historic buildings to survive the devastating earthquake of 1966. Photo: 2004.

7. Upper part of the pishtak (monumental portal) of the Divan Begi Madrasah in Bukhara, Uzbekistan, built around 1620–22. The restored entrance is adorned with a sun with a human face and two fantastical birds in flight. The latter represent phoenixes or the mythical Persian bird Simurgh, holding a boar in its claws. Photo: 2004.

between 1524 and 1538. Aside from the conquest of Balkh in 1526, they resulted in no lasting successes – probably due to lack of efficient artillery. The only decisive battle took place in 1528 near Jam, where Ubayd Allah was defeated by Shah Tahmasp I (r. 1524–76).[32] The efforts of the two Sunni opponents of the Shiite Safavids – the Ottomans and Uzbeks – to coordinate their attacks also failed. Throughout the sixteenth century, the border was established between the Sunni khanate of the Uzbeks and Shiite Iran roughly along the middle reaches of the Oxus. The river therefore not only became a national and cultural border, but also a denominational border between Sunna and Shia.[33] This fundamental religious, linguistic and cultural boundary later shifted nearly 400 km to the south, since the Turkmen who had immigrated from the north had never been conquered by Persia and remained Sunnis.

Köchkünji Khan, who died *ca*. 1530, was succeeded by his eldest son **Abu Said Khan** (r. 1530–33), who was followed by the veteran commander **Ubayd Allah Khan** (r. 1533–39). Under his successors **Abdullah Sultan I** (r. 1539–40), **Abd al-Latif** (r. 1540–52), **Nawruz Ahmad**, called **Buraq Khan** (r. 1552–56), and **Pir Muhammad**

(r. 1556–61), the khanate crumbled into five warring principalities.[34] As a consequence, the irrigation systems wasted away, agricultural land dwindled, and interregional trade atrophied. The English diplomat Anthony Jenkinson (1529–1611) – who was also an agent of the English Muscovy Company established in 1555 – travelled to the khanate in this chaotic, civil-war-like period. He was commissioned to conclude an Anglo-Russian trade agreement with Tsar Ivan IV and to explore a trade route from Moscow to Central Asia and China. Like the Portuguese, who had circumnavigated the major Islamic powers of the Ottomans and Safavids via the Cape of Good Hope, English merchants wanted to discover a maritime north-east passage to China which would follow the as-yet undiscovered north coast of Russia. Since in those days the Spanish and Portuguese fleets dominated the southern sea route around the Cape of Good Hope and in the Indian Ocean, the English traders needed to find an alternative route. In 1553 the Company of Merchant Adventurers to New Lands, founded in 1551 and from which would emerge four years later the Muscovy Company, dispatched two captains with three ships. Captain Willoughby and two ships were

8. Covered bazaar with central dome in Bukhara. Photo: 2004.

lost at sea in the northern circumnavigation of Norway and Sweden, but Captain Chancellor was able to penetrate into the White Sea and to land near the modern port of Arkhangelsk. He then met Tsar Ivan in Moscow, who promised him that English merchants could trade freely in Russia.[35] It is likely that Tsar Ivan was himself keen to open a trade route from Russia to China.

Unlike his predecessors Jenkinson didn't search for a sea route far north but for a land route. He left Moscow in the spring of 1558 and travelled on the Volga via Kazan to Astrakhan, and then crossed the Caspian Sea and landed at the Mangyshlak Peninsula. He struggled to cross the peninsula, which was inhabited by steppe horsemen of the Nogai Horde and infiltrated by bandits. He reached Bukhara on 23 December.[36] In his travelogue, he not only commented on the bad drinking water, which caused tapeworms, but also on the weakness of the ruler (presumably the later Abdullah Khan II) and his limited revenues. Jenkinson also noticed that although the Bukharians spoke Persian, they still conducted brutal wars against the Persians because of their Shiite confession and cursed them as 'infidels'.[37] As mentioned above, Jenkinson was disappointed by Bukhara's trading opportunities. In addition, having to barter as a result of a monetary crisis only made doing business

more difficult. Finally, it was already obvious by the mid-sixteenth century that sea trade had seriously hurt traditional trade on land via camel caravan. As a consequence, the revenues of the affected countries declined: 'But gold, silver, precious stones and spices they [the Indians] bring none. I enquired and perceived that all such trade passeth to the Ocean Sea, and the veins where all such things are gotten are in the subjection of the Portingals [Portuguese].'[38] The armed conflicts between the Uzbek rulers and their inability to safeguard trade caravans against raids from nomadic tribesmen did further irreparable damage to interregional trade. Jenkinson witnessed how the newly discovered sea routes began to isolate Central Asia geopolitically. By ship it was possible to transport much larger loads than by caravan, and the sea route was not subject to the same countless tolls and high tariffs as the transit trade over land. Still a trading hub among the Mongols and Timurids, Central Asia gradually degenerated to a hinterland of the transcontinental trade. The decline of traditional transit trade also led to the isolation of Transoxania from the intellectual and technological developments of Europe. Over time, the region lost its technological link-up and closed itself off from threatening strangers by means of religious ideas such as the superiority of Islam.

Central Asia's slow decline accelerated in the eighteenth century, when one of its major inexhaustible resources, the horse, became less important among neighbouring sedentary empires as a result of the growing domination of firearms. Jenkinson left Bukhara on 8 March 1559 (18 March per Gregorian calendar) and, as the wars between Kazakhs and Tashkent as well as between the Western Mongols and Moghulistan (Kashgaria) made an onward journey to China impossible, he returned to Moscow.[39] Jenkinson was lucky, for ten days later the Sultan of Samarkand attacked Bukhara and seized the city.[40]

Abdullah Khan II (r. 1583–98) prevailed as the winner in the first twelve-year period of the 30-year civil war. The de facto ruler of Bukhara since 1557, he was strong enough in the winter of 1560/61 to depose his unpopular uncle Pir Muhammad and enthrone his pious father **Iskandar Khan** as the nominal supreme khan (r. 1561–83). However, the internal Uzbek clashes continued unabated, as the sultans of Tashkent and Samarkand refused to recognise Abdullah's supremacy. Only after 20 years of further wars did Abdullah Khan manage to again unite the appanages in 1582: Qarshi and Hissar in 1574; Samarkand in 1578; Khujand and Andijan in 1579; and Tashkent and Turkistan in 1582. The

empire of Shaybani Khan was thus nearly restored.[41] Abdullah was appointed the new khan after the death of his father, Iskandar Khan. He affirmed Bukhara as the capital of a reunified khanate.

Domestically, Abdullah undertook measures to boost the ailing economy. He carried out a currency reform, had irrigation canals repaired, and built madrasahs, caravanserais and covered marketplaces in Bukhara. He also revived international trade, with the Indian subcontinent as well as with Russia, which had access to the Caspian Sea via Astrakhan. In foreign policy, Abdullah took advantage of the Safavids' temporary weakness in order to expand. He occupied Balkh in 1573 and Badakhshan in 1584, and conquered Herat in 1589 after a nine-month siege during which he perpetrated a massacre against the local garrison and population. He subsequently dispatched his hot-headed and infamously cruel son Abd al-Mumin to Mashhad. There, Abd al-Mumin seized and thoroughly plundered the city in 1589, including the library of the Imam Reza mausoleum. He also did not hesitate to desecrate the grave of the late Shah Tahmasp I.[42] Before the campaign, Abdullah ordered a leading jurist to give him a *ferman*. According to this binding decree, Khorasan, the land of the infidel Shiite, belonged to Dar al-harb, the 'House of War'. Conducting war against the

9. The Chor-Bakr complex west of Bukhara, Uzbekistan, built in 1560–63 and extensively restored from 1999 to 2001, consists of a mosque, a madrasah, and a khanaqah, a hostel for pilgrims and Sufis. Photo: 2004.

infidels was accordingly meritorious for Sunnis.[43] In 1593, Abdullah annexed Chorasmia and put down a revolt there in 1595/96. He had sent an army to Moghulistan in 1594/95, which penetrated into Kashgar and Yarkand. However, it achieved no lasting gains. After the conquest of Chorasmia in 1593, Abdullah commissioned three of his nephews with the conquest of Kandahar in southern Afghanistan. But the Mirzas of Kandahar employed a ruse, claiming that their city was under the protection of Akbar, the emperor of Mughal India (r. 1556–1605), who had annexed Kabul in 1585. Since Abdullah feared an alliance between Akbar and Shah Abbas I of Persia (r. 1588–1629) directed against him, he abandoned Kandahar, which was considered a gateway to India, and proposed to Akbar that the Hindu Kush be established as the boundary between their empires. After Akbar had occupied Kandahar in 1595, he consented to making the Hindu Kush the border.[44] In a letter to Abdullah Khan dated 15 June 1596, he wrote: 'What you have written with a pen perfumed with brotherhood on the subject of our mutually exerting ourselves to strengthen the foundations of Peace, and to purify the fountains of concord, and of making this Hindu Koh the boundary between us, has most fully commended itself to us.'[45]

Abdullah's final years were overshadowed by the conflict with his ambitious son Abd al-Mumin, who openly rebelled in 1597 and was preparing for war against his father. The Kazakh Tevekkel (Tauekel) Khan (r. 1582–98) recognised the opportunity to intervene and marched into the khanate with an army that had Russian firearms.[46] He conquered Tashkent and destroyed an Uzbek army in 1598 that obstructed his path. Abdullah then placed himself at the head of the remaining troops, but soon fell seriously ill and died. As Abu'l Fazl surmised, the khan was probably poisoned.[47] Soon thereafter, **Abd al-Mumin** (r. 1598) hurried from Balkh to Bukhara, had himself appointed as the new khan, and forced Tevekkel to retreat. He then launched a brutal purge of his uncles and cousins and liquidated several of his father's military leaders, all of whom he saw as possible rivals. During the subsequent war against the invading Safavid Abbas I, several Uzbek commanders murdered their khan in the summer of 1598. Since Abd-al Mumin had murdered the entire elite of the Abu'l-Khayrids, the dynasty collapsed and Shah Abbas reconquered Khorasan.

10. Registan Square in Samarkand, Uzbekistan. On the left, the Ulugh Beg Madrasah built from 1417–21; in the centre, the Tilla Kari Madrasah built from 1646–60; and on the right, the Shir Dor Madrasah built from about 1616–36. The latter two were built by the governor of Samarkand, Yalangtush Bagadur (d. 1665/66). Photo: 2008.

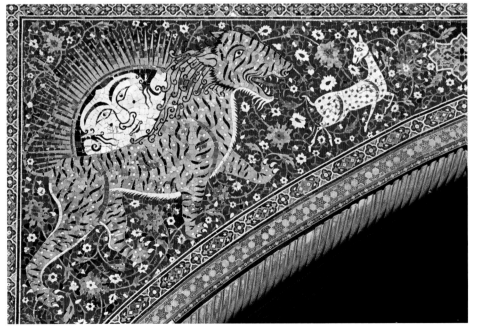

11a. The Shir Dor Madrasah, 'the one with the tiger', in Registan Square, Samarkand, Uzbekistan. Photo: 2004.

11b. Each of the two tympana of the Shir Dor Madrasah shows a tiger chasing a fallow deer; behind each tiger's back is a radiant sun with a human face. As reported by the Castilian envoy Ruy Gonzales de Clavijo, who visited Timur-e Lang in Samarkand in 1404, the motif was already familiar at that time. When visiting Timur's palace in Kesh (present-day Shahr-i Sabz), he observed that 'on the top of this [second] doorway there was the figure of a lion and a sun, which are the arms of the lord of Samarcand'.[1] Photo: 2004.

1.2 The Dynasty of the Togha-Timurids (Astarkhanids)

The dynasty of the Togha-Timurids, which followed that of the Abu'l-Khayrids, traced its descent back to the thirteenth son of Jochi, Togha Timur. This new dynasty was also called the Astarkhanids or Janids, after the name of its first ruling khan in Samarkand **Jani Muhammad** (r. 1599–1603), whose son Din Muhammad fell in the defence of Herat against Shah Abbas I in 1598. As with the previous dynasty, Jani Khan divided up the now smaller khanate among his nearest male relatives in appanages, which led to the partitioning of the khanate a few years later. When Jani's son and successor **Baqi Muhammad** (r. 1603–5) died, his oldest brother **Wali Muhammad** (r. 1605–11) claimed the title of khan and entrusted Samarkand and Balkh, respectively, to his nephews Imam Quli and Nazr Muhammad. But the two brothers revolted against their uncle Wali and divided the khanate between themselves: **Imam Quli Khan** (r. 1612–41/42) ruled in Samarkand and Bukhara, while the younger **Nazr Muhammad** (r. in Balkh 1612–41/42, 1645–51; as the supreme Khan 1641/42–45) ruled independently in Balkh.[48] For most of the seventeenth century, the Uzbek Khanate existed as the double khanate of Samarkand/Bukhara and Balkh. The two brothers cultivated a relatively peaceful relationship, which brought the double khanate three decades of prosperity.

During the reign of Imam Quli there were contacts between Russia and the khanates of Bukhara and Chorasmia. In 1620, the Bukharian envoy Adam Biy arrived in Moscow and informed Tsar Mikhail Romanov (r. 1613–45) that two opponents of Russia, the Crimean Tatars and the Nogai, had sold a large number of Russian prisoners to Bukhara. He further indicated that Imam Quli would be willing to negotiate their release with an envoy of the tsar. The tsar dispatched Ivan Danilovich Khokhlov, who arrived in Samarkand and Bukhara in the summer of 1621, after he had been attacked in Khiva by Turkmen gangs and suffered ill-treatment. After difficult negotiations, Khokhlov returned with only 31 prisoners, whose freedom was purchased. Imam Quli had quickly realised that Russian prisoners and slaves constituted excellent leverage for extorting ransom from Russia. This business model – whereby Bukhara and Khiva bought Russians who had been kidnapped by the Nogai, Turkmens and Kazakhs in order to resell them to private individuals or to extort ransom from Russia – remained in place until the conquest of the khanate in the mid-nineteenth century. Chorasmian prince Awgan Mirza (d. 1648), who had accompanied Khokhlov to Moscow in 1622, was responsible for setting a second precedent. He offered to become the

Tsar's vassal, with the understanding that the latter would intervene militarily on his behalf in Khiva.[49] It was the first time that a Central Asian prince had personally asked the tsar to intercede against the rulers of his homeland.

Due to blindness, Imam Quli abdicated in favour of his brother Nazr in 1641 or 1642. Nazr immediately instituted land reform, which aimed to put the large estates of the amirs and khojas (an honorific title for pious Muslims) under government control and to compensate the dispossessed through annual monetary gifts. The amirs and khojas, threatened with expropriation, resisted, however. Led by the powerful military commander and governor of Samarkand, Yalangtush Bagadur (d. 1665/66), who built the magnificent madrasahs Shir Dor and Tilla Kari at Samarkand's Registan Square (figs. 10–12), Nazr's eldest son **Abd al-Aziz** (r. 1645–81) forced his father to step down. Nazr returned to Balkh and abdicated in 1651. Henceforth, Abd-al-Aziz ruled in Bukhara and his brother **Subhan Quli** in Balkh (r. in Balkh 1651–81; as the supreme khan 1681–1702). The two brothers were fairly hostile towards each other. The khanate was consequently divided into two parts from 1651 to 1681, so that Yalangtush Bagadur governed in Samarkand from about 1641 to 1665/66 de facto independently. When Abd al-Aziz surrendered his throne to Subhan Quli in 1681, the khanate was again nominally united.[50]

The instability of the khanate that had been caused by the internal tensions of 1641–45 prompted neighbours to the west and south to attack. The Chorasmian Khans Abu'l Ghazi (r. 1643–63) and Anusha Muhammad (r. 1663–85) initiated four campaigns against Bukhara, and Shah Jahan (r. 1628–58), the Mughal Emperor, instructed his two sons Murad Baksh and Aurangzeb in 1646/47 to capture Balkh. Although the brothers commanded a strong army with superior firepower, they were helpless against the guerrilla resistance of the Uzbeks and Afghans and therefore retreated. This was not the last time that a strong invader in Afghanistan was forced to surrender to enemy guerrillas.[51] On the death of Subhan Quli there was a re-partitioning of the khanate, for his son **Ubayd Allah Khan II** ruled in Bukhara (r. 1702–11) and a grandson of Subhan Quli, **Muhammad Khan Muqim**, ruled in Balkh (r. 1702–07).[52] Ubayd Allah, however, failed in his attempts to curb the growing autonomy of the tribes by way of reform and was murdered in 1711. Under his successor **Abu'l Fayz Khan** (r. 1711–47), the khanate disintegrated completely into several chiefdoms: amirs of the Ming tribe reigned from 1709 or 1710 in Fergana and laid the foundation for the Khanate of Kokand. Further amirs of the Ming ruled in Urgut south of Samarkand and in Balkh and Maimana. The Keneges dominated in Shahr-i Sabz; the Yuz in Ura

Tube and Hissar; the Qataghan in Kunduz; and in Bukhara the strongman from 1714 was Muhammad Hakim Bey, leader of the Manghit and 'ataliq' (chief adviser of the khan).[53]

From the 1720s, the political and economic crisis in Transoxania worsened. In the north, the Kazakhs came under military pressure from the expanding Western Mongolian Dzungars under Tsewang Rabtan, beginning in 1698. They suffered heavy defeats in 1709–11, 1718, and especially 1723–25. The Kazakhs were expelled from the basin of the Syr Darya River. They escaped to the south, where they devastated Mawarannahr and repeatedly besieged Bukhara, plundered villages, and inflicted serious damage on the agricultural infrastructure.[54] As Tsar Peter's envoy Florio Beneveni reported: 'Samarkand, the former capital of the celebrated Timur, is a large city, but now stands empty and ruined.' He further noted that only two quarters were inhabited in Bukhara.[55] The once flourishing region of Mawarannahr was in danger of suffering the same fate as the Chu Valley in today's Kyrgyzstan and regressing from a wealthy combined urban/agricultural economy to a poor grassland economy. Paradoxically, Transoxania was saved from precisely this fate by the two victories of its Kazakh enemy over the Dzungars around 1726 and 1730. The Kazakhs returned to their homeland, where, in the western half of their domain, they partly stood under Russian protection.[56]

In 1737, the Uzbek Khanate again became the focus of the resurgent Persians under Nader Shah Afshar (r. as regent from 1732; as shah 1736–47). Nader Shah belonged to the Turkmen tribe of the Afshars of Khorasan and, towards the end of 1736, after expelling the Afghan dynasty of the Persian Ghilzai Hotaki (1722–29) ruling in Isfahan,[57] he commenced a military campaign against Afghanistan, Punjab and the Mughal Empire. While Nader Shah besieged Kandahar for fourteen months in 1737/38 and pillaged Delhi in early 1739, his eldest son, Reza Quli, conquered Balkh, Kunduz and Badakhshan. Without the permission of his father he then crossed the Oxus and besieged the Uzbek Abu'l Fayz Khan in Qarshi. Nader Shah, however, feared that the Uzbeks might close ranks against Reza Quli, whom he began to distrust, and ordered his withdrawal.[58] In 1740, Nader Shah himself attacked the khanate, which offered no resistance. Abu'l Fayz Khan, Ataliq Muhammad Hakim Bey and his son Muhammad Rahim surrendered, avoiding the siege and occupation of Bukhara. Bukhara was forced to cede the territories to the south of the Oxus and Nader Shah confirmed Muhammad Hakim as ruler of Bukhara. Soon after Nader Shah defeated the ruler of Chorasmia, Ilbars Khan II, and had him executed.[59]

Nader's campaign from 1740 made the two khanates vassals of Persia. After Nader's retreat, Muhammad Hakim Bey (d. 1743)

declared himself *amir-i kabir*, 'Great Amir'. His son and successor Muhammad Rahim (r. 1743–58) assumed this title and appointed himself khan in 1756, thereby founding the dynasty of Manghit Bukhara (1756–1920). In doing so, he broke with the five centuries of unwritten law in Central Asia, according to which only a Genghis Khanid, a descendant of Genghis Khan's paternal lineage, had the right to be the legitimate ruler and khan of a sovereign people. Muhammad Rahim had Abu'l Fayz executed in 1747, then his son **Abd al-Mumin** (r. 1747–48) a year later and **Ubayd Allah III** (r. 1748–56) in 1756.[60] After Muhammad Rahim's death in 1758, riots broke out. His uncle Danial Bey assumed power as 'ataliq' and placed **Abu'l Ghazi** (r. 1758–85) on the throne as a puppet khan. Danial Bey's son and successor Shah Murad took over as amir in 1785.[61]

Although the Abu'l-Khayrids expelled the Timurids from Central Asia, in terms of the architecture of public buildings such as mosques and madrasahs, they were oriented towards the concepts of their Timurid predecessors. They thus erected magnificent monumental buildings with huge domes. To the extent that funds were available, the Togha-Timurids followed suit. However, the rulers of both dynasties decided against establishing their own magnificent standalone mausoleums, presumably because they sympathised with the orthodox Sunni aversion to excessive veneration of the dead. The mausoleums of the Sufi masters represent an exception. Both in Bukhara and Samarkand the rulers had their own splendid buildings constructed on the sites of former showpiece structures, which were either dilapidated or which they had torn down for this purpose. In Bukhara, the Friday Mosque, which had been started earlier by the Timurids, was completed in 1514 with the preserved Kalyan minaret from 1127 (fig. 5). Opposite the mosque, the Mir-i Arab Madrasah was finished in 1535/36 (fig. 3). To the east of the covered and domed bazaars built from 1562 to 1587 (fig. 8) is the Qul Baba Kukeldash Madrasah from 1568/69. To the south of this is the *Lab-i Hauz* complex, whose name means 'edge of the basin' and which was funded in the early 1620s by Imam Quli's vizier Nader Divan Begi. West of the basin is the Nader Divan Begi Khanaqah, a refuge for pilgrims and sufis which is combined with a mosque, and east of the water reservoir is the Divan Begi Madrasah (fig. 7). The latter was designed by the vizier as a caravanserai, but the khan allegedly converted it arbitrarily into a madrasah. In the area of Bukhara, two complexes were built around the tombs of Sufi masters. As with the Kukeldash Madrasah, the pilgrimage site Chor Bakr[62] (fig. 9) west of the city went back to Abdullah Khan II. He had had a mosque, a madrasah and a khanaqah built between 1560 and 1563. The complex, which served as a family tomb for Juybari sheikhs of the Naqshbandi Sufi

12. The prayer niche, called mihrab, indicating the direction of prayer to Mecca in the Friday Mosque of the Tilla Kari Madrasah, Samarkand, Uzbekistan. Photo: 2008.

Order, was heavily restored from 1999 to 2001. A similar complex was built from 1544 to 1720 north-east of Bukhara around the mausoleum of Baha al-Din Naqshband Bukhari (1318–89), the founder of the Naqshbandi Order.[63] The pilgrimage site was further expanded in 1870 and 1993.[64]

In Samarkand, the Registan public square, whose Persian name means 'sandy place', stood out as the most magnificent medieval square in Central Asia (fig. 10). It was with good reason that the future viceroy of India, George Nathaniel Curzon, wrote in 1888: 'I have hazarded the statement that the Registan of Samarkand was originally, and is still even in ruin, the noblest public square in the world. I know nothing in the East approaching it in massive simplicity and grandeur; and nothing in Europe, save perhaps on a humbler scale – the Piazza di San Marco at Venice – which can even aspire to enter in competition … [There is] no open space in any Western city that is commanded on three of its four sides by Gothic cathedrals of the finest order.'[65] While the Ulugh Beg Madrasah soars upward in the west, the Khanaqah of Ulugh Beg opposite it was replaced by the Shir Dor Madrasah built around 1618 to 1636. Its name essentially means 'The one with the tiger'. In the tympanum of the entrance portal two Aral tigers chase after a female deer. Behind the doe's back shines a sun with a human face (figs. 11a–11b). In the north, finally, Yalangtush Bagadur had the 'gold-adorned' Tilla Kari Madrasah built between 1646 and 1660. The interior of the mosque incorporated into the madrasah is in fact mostly decorated with golden paint.[66] Although the three madrasahs were built in different eras, the Registan has an impressive and harmonious unity.

13. In the old town of Khiva: On the left, the 43-m-high minaret of the Friday Mosque; in the centre, the mausoleum of the furrier, wrestler and poet Pahlavan Mahmud (1247–1325). The current buildings were erected by Muhammad Rahim Khan I (r. 1806–25) and Khan Isfandiyar (r. 1910–18). On the right is the 57-m-high minaret of the Islam Khodja Madrasah, built in 1910. At the beginning of the twentieth century, Islam Khodja was a grand vizier, who pushed through a number of social reforms, including opening public secular schools, health clinics and a hospital. This aroused the anger of some mullahs and bazaar merchants, who had him assassinated in 1913; Khan Isfandiyar (r. 1910–18), who knew of the conspiracy, did not intervene. Photo: 2004.

2. The Khanate of Chorasmia under the Arabshahids and Russia's First Advance

Although Abu'l-Khayrid Shaybani Khan had conquered Chorasmia in 1505, after his death in 1510 and a brief occupation by the Safavids, **Ilbars Khan I** (r. 1511–25) seized power and founded the dynasty of the Arabshahids (1511–1804), also called 'Yadigarids'. Their lineage likewise dated back to Jochi. After Ilbars' death, he was succeeded by his brother **Sultan Hajji** (r. 1525–?). Vezir, east of Sarygamysh Lake, initially served as the capital, and then Urgench (Gurganj) became the capital from about 1518. As Jenkinson observed in 1558, the drying up of the Daryaliq River, a major tributary of the south-western arm of the Oxus and a feeder of the Uzboy, threatened the very existence of Urgench.[67] As **Abu'l Ghazi Khan I** (r. 1643–63), who also acted as a historian, reported, the Uzboy began to dry up in 1575 and the area around Urgench gradually turned into a desert.[68] For this reason, **Arab Muhammad Khan** (r. 1602–23) moved the capital to Khiva, which is 50 km south-west of the current course of the Oxus.[69] The small khanate was even more exposed to pressures from rapacious and conquest-hungry neighbours than the Uzbek Khanate – specifically from the Kazakhs, the semi-nomadic, quarrelling Turkoman tribes, the Uzbek Transoxanians, the Safavids, and sometimes Russian Cossacks. The Uzbeks thus occupied Chorasmia in 1538, but were defeated a year later by Din Muhammad Sultan at the Battle of Hazarasp and driven back. Later, in 1593, the Uzbek Abdullah Khan II overran Chorasmia, which was only liberated by **Hajji Muhammad Khan I** (r. 1558–1602) after Abdullah's death in 1598.[70]

On the death of Arab Muhammad Khan a fratricidal war broke out, in which **Isfandiyar Khan** (r. 1623–43) prevailed against his brother Ilbars. Another brother of Isfandiyar, **Abu'l Ghazi Khan I,** then seized power himself (r. 1643–63). Abu'l Ghazi carried out destructive raids into the Uzbek Khanate. His son and successor **Anusha Muhammad Khan** (r. 1663–85) continued this policy and even briefly occupied Bukhara and Samarkand. After a new but unsuccessful and costly campaign against Bukhara in 1684, Anusha was deposed and blinded by his amirs. This was followed by a 30-year period of instability with eleven or thirteen khans, each of whom reigned only briefly and who were enthroned and deposed by the tribal chiefs. The last ruling Arabshahid was **Shir Ghazi Khan** (r. 1714 or 15–28), for he was usually succeeded by Kazakh Jochids who were mostly simply nominal khans.[71]

Shir Ghazi Khan was confronted by a Russian advance in 1717. In Chorasmia, as in Siberia, the Cossacks had already made inroads a century earlier. In 1603 Nechai Starenskoi, the ataman (leader) of the Yaik Cossacks, invaded the khanate after a forced ride on horseback and looted Gurganj, before Arab Muhammad Khan then surrounded and massacred the invaders.[72] Although Starenskoi's foray was motivated by the prospect of plunder, he fitted into the strategic concept of the Russian tsars. Indeed, following up on Jenkinson's report on the abandonment of direct trade links between China and Transoxania, Tsar Ivan's successor Boris Godunov (r. 1585–98 as regent, 1598–1605 as tsar) decided that Russia had to establish a land route to China itself. Therefore, he refused to allow British trade expeditions through Russia and entrusted this task, *inter alia*, to the Cossacks.[73] In the years 1605 and 1606, they set off from the city of Tomsk, founded in 1604, to discover a route to China in the grass steppes of Central Asia.[74] Until the nineteenth century, Russia's primary interest in its advance to Central and East Asia lay in its resources and direct trade routes to China and India – not in either religious proselytising, like the Spanish and Portuguese, or territorial gains. The latter aspect only became relevant from the 1820s onward in the context of the geopolitical confrontation between the leading maritime power, Britain, and the largest land power, Russia.

The strategic objectives of Tsar Peter I (r. 1682–1725) were the modernisation and reorientation of Russia to the West, and secure access to the Baltic Sea and the Black Sea, which were controlled by Sweden and the Ottomans respectively. As a result of the ensuing Great Northern War (1700–21) and the war against the Ottomans, Tsar Peter not only needed new iron deposits for Russia's armouries, but also massive revenue, which he sought to generate in Siberia and Central Asia through the development of new resources like gold and iron, and direct trade contacts with India and China. From 1699, he commissioned Nikita Demidov to prospect new mines beyond the Urals. In 1715, he sent Lieutenant Colonel Ivan Buchholz with a small army from Tobolsk southward, through the territory of the powerful Dzungars (Oirat), to search for purported gold mines near Yarkand. Buchholz did not reach Yarkand, but was halted by the Dzungars in the Baraba steppe between the Ob and Irtysh rivers and forced to retreat. He subsequently established the city of Omsk in 1716. At the time, the Swedish officer J.G. Renat experienced a peculiar fate: captured by the victorious Russians in the Battle of Poltava in 1709 and sent to Siberia, he participated in Buchholz's expedition, only to then fall into the hands of the Dzungars in 1716. He was held captive until 1733. While among the Dzungars, he set up an artillery regiment, and taught them

14. The western city walls of Khiva, Uzbekistan. Photo: 2004.

how to cast cannons, print books and draw maps. On his return, he brought with him a detailed map of Central Asia.[75]

Also in 1715, Tsar Peter heard that the Oxus had once flowed via the Uzboy into the Caspian Sea and that the Uzbeks had diverted the river into the Aral Sea by means of a dam. The tsar undertook the bold plan to feed the water back into the dried-up bed of the Uzboy, which would open up a water route across the Volga from Moscow to Astrakhan and then across the Caspian Sea to Khiva and onward to Balkh. This would result in a combined water and land route to the Indian Mughals. He sent Prince Alexander Bekovich-Cherkassky to Khiva with 4,000 men. His task was to first convince the khan of Khiva and then the khan of Bukhara to become Russian vassals; to explore the reaches of the Uzboy; and to send a trade caravan to India. After a gruelling march of 1,500 km in 65 days, the Russians arrived at the oasis

of Khiva in the summer of 1717. Khan Shir Ghazi, however, had been forewarned about the Russian advance by the khan of the Kalmyks, Ayuka (r. 1669–1724), a supposed ally of Russia. He then lured Prince Bekovich into a trap. After a three-day battle in which Khiva cavalry suffered heavy losses, the khan made an appeal for peace and invited the prince to come into the city with a limited number of troops. Under the pretext that the soldiers could not be quartered in a single location, he asked Bekovich to divide up his protection force into smaller groups. Despite the vehement protest of his deputy Major Frankenberg, Bekovich agreed to the shrewd khan's request. No sooner had the Russians been divided into five small divisions than Bekovich was captured and the isolated soldiers were massacred.[76] Tsar Peter, however, was still preoccupied with the Great Northern War and decided to forgo a retaliation campaign. Russia concluded from the setback that without control of the vast Kazakh steppes, advances into the Central Asian khanates were pointless. To this end, the Cossacks and regular vanguard began to build a series of fortifications on the southern border – the so-called 'lines' that gradually shifted southward until they collided with the northern boundary of the khanate of Kokand.[77] Nevertheless, the next Russian campaign against Khiva under General Perovsky in 1839–40 failed miserably due to poor planning.[78]

Unlike in Bukhara, Shir Razi's successor **Ilbars Khan II** (r. 1728–40) made a desperate stand in two battles against Nader Shah, who afterwards had him beheaded. After Nader Shah's assassination in 1747, infighting erupted between the long-established urban and Turkic-speaking Sarts and the Kazakh, Karakalpak and Turkmen tribes, which allowed the khanate to sink into chaos. This feud reached its peak in the conquest and looting of Khiva by the Turkmen tribe of Yomut in 1770. In the same year, the *inaq* (chief minister) Muhammad Amin from the Qungrat clan (r. 1770–90) drove out the Yomut and established himself as the de facto ruler behind a puppet khan. Avaz Inaq (1790–1804) also maintained a puppet Genghis Khanid, but his son and successor **Iltüzer** (r. 1804–6) abolished this custom. He elevated himself to khan and in doing so officially founded the Qungrat dynasty (1804–1920).[79]

3. The Khanate of Moghulistan and the Naqshbandi Khwajas

Moghulistan's history is as complex as its geography. While the steppes in the relatively humid north-west between Tashkent and the Dzungarian basin favour semi-nomadic horse breeding, an extremely arid climate prevails to the south of the Tian Shan mountain range. Deserts predominate here, yet the fertile but small oases of Turfan and the Tarim Basin enable urban-commercial and agrarian economies. A similar geographic–economic and social fault line had already divided the khanate of Chagatai into the pastoral region in the north-east and the urban–agrarian Transoxania in the south-west around 1347.[80] Without a strong standing army, it was difficult to govern the freedom-loving tribes of the steppe horsemen and the urban centres. In the case of Moghulistan, there was the added difficulty that the oasis towns – Kashgar, Yarkand, Khotan, Aksu, Kucha and Turfan – in today's southern Xinjiang, then called *Altishahr* ('Six Cities') or *Yetishahr* ('Seven Cities')[81] could not support standing armies. Mirza Haidar Dughlat (1499 or 1500–51) concluded from personal experience in his *Tarikh-i Rashidi* that: 'In Kashgar [one of the city-oases of Altishahr] it is impossible to support an army upon the produce of the country; …with regard to productiveness and its capacity to support an army, it cannot be compared to those steppes.'[82] This limitation tied to Xinjiang's geography, and the resulting tendency toward political fragmentation, shaped the history of the region until its integration into the People's Republic of China in the autumn of 1949 and the construction of efficient motorways.

Moghulistan, not to be confused with the empire of Mughal in the Indian subcontinent, arose as a result of the partitioning of the Khanate of Chagatai in 1347, when the traditionally Mongolian-dominated steppe broke away from the Turkic-dominated cities.[83] At the time, Amir Bolaji, the leader of the Mongol tribe of Dughlat, installed as khan **Tughlugh Temür** (r. 1347–63), who instituted a radical Islamisation of the elite for political reasons. Like previous rulers of heterogeneous tribal societies, Tughlugh Temür recognised Islam's integrating force, rooted in the idea of a homogeneous religious community or *umma*. He also saw its value as an ideology of military expansion under the aegis of *jihad* (holy struggle).[84] When Tughlugh Temür's son and successor **Ilyas Khwaja** (r. 1363–65) failed in the siege of Samarkand, the younger brother of Amir Bolaji, named **Qamar al-Din Dughlat** (r. 1365–ca. 1390), seized power in Moghulistan and usurped the title of khan. This, in turn, provided Timur-e Lang (r. 1370–1405) with a pretext to wage six military campaigns against him. After Qamar's

escape into the Altai Mountains, Amir Khudaidad Dughlat placed **Khizr Khwaja** (Khoja, r. *ca.* 1383/90–99), Tughlugh Temür's son, on the throne. Khizr Khwaja extended his domain to the east and conquered the oases of Turfan and Qarashahr. Towards the end of the fifteenth century, Moghulistan stretched from Tashkent in the west to Turfan in the east, and from Lake Balkhash in the north to Khotan in the south. However, the realm remained plagued by power struggles and rapidly changing political alliances. After the reign of **Sham-i Jahan** (r. 1399–1408), his brother **Muhammad Khan** (r. 1408–16) forcibly pushed through Islamisation, including among the non-noble population. As Mirza Haidar reported: 'During his [Muhammad's] blessed reign most of the tribes of the Moghuls became Musulmans. […] If…a Moghul didn't wear a turban [*dastar*], a horseshoe nail was driven into his head.'[85] The succeeding rulers **Uways Khan** (r. 1418–21, 1425–28) and **Esen Buqa** (r. 1428–62) were often involved in struggles with the Western Mongolian Oirats in the north and the Timurids in the west.[86]

The splintering of Moghulistan occurred for the first time under **Yunus Khan** (r. 1462–87), when **Mirza Abu Bakr Dughlat** (r. in Yarkand *ca.* 1481–1516) declared his independence in the Tarim Basin in Kashgar, Yarkand and Khotan. After losing Kashgar to Said Khan in 1514, he fled from his capital Yarkand two years later.[87] While Yunus Khan conquered Tashkent in the early 1480s, his son **Ahmad Alaq Khan** (r. 1487–1503 in Turfan) rebelled against him shortly before his death. In 1502, he rushed to help his brother **Mahmud Khan** (r. in Tashkent 1487–1508), who was ruling in western Moghulistan, in the fight against the Uzbek Shaybani Khan. The brothers were defeated, and Tashkent fell to the Uzbeks. At the same time, a massive migration of Kyrgyz began into the territory of modern Kyrgyzstan, which caused the Moghul to gradually lose control of it. Later, in the late seventeenth and early eighteenth century, the Kyrgyz on the Yenisei River were pushed into Dzungaria by Russian immigrants.[88]

Ahmad's son and successor **Mansur Khan** (r. 1508–43 in Turfan) established himself in the east and was nominally khan of all Moghulistan from 1508 to 1514, until his brother **Said Khan** (r. 1514–33 in western Moghulistan) conquered western Moghulistan from Abu Bakr Dughlat. Instead of fighting each other, the two brothers Mansur and Said concluded a treaty so that peace would prevail within Moghulistan.[89] In the east, towards the end of his reign, Mansur Khan wrested the Hami oasis away from the Chinese Ming dynasty, which **Shah Khan** (r. 1543–1560 in Turfan) then incorporated. In the west, Said Khan and his military leader Mirza Muhammad Haidar Dughlat looked to the south: a raid of Badakhshan in 1529, deemed a 'holy war', was followed in

1532 by looting expeditions to Ladakh and Kashmir. The khan died from a high-altitude oedema during a failed attack on central Tibet in 1533. **Abdu'l Rashid** (r. 1533–60 in Yarkand) decimated the Dughlats, and Mirza Haidar fled to Emperor Humayum in Lahore.[90] Abdu'l Rashid's sons **Abd al-Karim Khan** (1560–91) and **Muhammad Sultan** (1591–1609) managed to politically unite Moghulistan again, if only nominally.[91]

During the reign of Muhammad Sultan, a rare visitor arrived in Moghulistan. The Portuguese Jesuit Bento de Goes (1562–1607) was sent to Beijing by his superiors in Goa via a land route to investigate whether Marco Polo's 'Cathay' was really identical to China, where the Jesuit Matteo Ricci had been residing in Beijing since 1601. De Goes travelled from Agra via Lahore, Kabul and the Pamir Mountains, reaching Yarkand in November 1603, where he had to wait for a whole year before continuing his journey. He witnessed how Muhammad Sultan sold to the highest bidding trader the right to organise a trade caravan to Beijing. He also saw how the buyer, who was appointed an envoy, in turn sold the right to participate in his caravan to a further 72 dealers. In Chinese jargon, these trade caravans were called 'tribute bringers', but they were actually highly profitable for the respective foreign rulers and their merchants. The traders presented as a 'gift' to the emperor quality jade, diamonds or horses, while he gave them goods and gold, which greatly exceeded the value of the gifts. Ricci also saw through this stratagem: 'Every five years seventy-two persons in the quality of ambassadors shall bring tribute to the king [the Chinese emperor]. . . . All this is an immense burden on the treasury, but the Chinese, who are well aware of the fraud, want by such devices to flatter their sovereign and make him believe that the whole world pays tribute to China, while it is the Chinese themselves who pay tribute to those countries.'[92] This policy of self-deception was used not only to flatter the emperor, but primarily in order to buy peace from restless neighbours – a policy that China had utilised since the conflict with the Xiongnu in the second to first century BCE.[93] At the end of 1604, De Goes set out from Yarkand to Aksu and then travelled from there, via Turfan and Hami, to Suzhou (today's Jiuquan), which he reached in late 1605. In the meantime, he had recognised that Cathay must be identical with China. The caravan was held up in Suzhou, however, and De Goes died in March 1607. It is likely he was poisoned by his travelling companions, to whom he had loaned money.[94]

During the transition from the sixteenth to seventeenth century, influential leaders of the Naqshbandi Sufi Order, who had participated in the Islamisation of Moghulistan, increasingly gained clout and power and, with few exceptions, supplanted

the khans. Between Muhammad Sultan, who died in 1609, and the death of the last Chagataiids in 1694, several khans ruled in Yarkand and Turfan for only short periods. The power of the Naqshbandi leaders, called khojas (*khwajas*), traced back to Ahmad Kasani (1461–1542), called *Makhdum-i Azam*, 'supreme master', who settled in Altishahr at the beginning of the sixteenth century. Two of his sons later gave rise to two rival factions. His fourth son, Ishaq Wali (d. 1599), instructed Muhammad Sultan and supported him in the seizure of power. He founded the Order of Ishaqiyya, also called Qarataghliq ('residents of the Black Mountains'), which was based in the capital Yarkand. Some time later, Khoja Muhammad Yusuf (d. 1653), the fourth son of Makhdum-i Azam's eldest son Ishan-i Kalan, began preaching with great success in Moghulistan. A supporter of Ishaqiyya poisoned him out of envy, whereupon his son Hidayetullah (d. 1694), called Khoja Afaq, 'master of horizons' established the rival Afaqiyya order, also called Aqtaghliq ('residents of the White Mountains'), which was based in Kashgar.[95]

The political situation in Moghulistan became even more complex during the reign of **Abdullah Khan** (r. *ca.* 1636–67), as the pressure from Sengge Khong Tayishi (r. 1653–71), ruler of the Buddhist Dzungars, increased considerably. A war conducted between Abdullah and Sengge ended in a standoff and a truce, and so Sengge incited Abdullah's son Yolbars to rebel against his father and the leaders of the Ishaqiyya who supported him. In 1667, **Yolbars Khan** (r. 1667–70) occupied the capital Yarkand with the aid of Khoja Afaq from the Afaqiyya and forced his father Abdullah to flee into the empire of the Mughal. Khoja Afaq of the 'White Mountains' immediately purged the religious and secular centres of power of representatives from the 'Black Mountains'. Threatened by another attack from Sengge, Yolbars was forced to bow down to him. In 1670, Yolbars Khan was murdered, and the Afaqiyya designated Yolbars' son **Abdu'l Latif II** (r. 1670) as his successor. After a few months, however, he was assassinated by the Qarataghliq, who elevated **Ismail Khan** to the throne (r. 1670–78). Ismail and leaders of the Ishaqiyya now persecuted the representatives of Afaqiyya. Khoja Afaq thus fled to Kashmir and from there to Lhasa, Tibet.[96]

Khoja Afaq met with the Fifth Dalai Lama (r. 1642–82), the leader of the ruling Buddhist Gelugpa monastic order, in Lhasa. The Dalai Lama owed his reign to Gushri Khan, the leader of the Western Mongolian Khoshut, one of the four major subgroups of Oirats. Both orders, the Islamic Naqshbandiyya of Turkestan and the Buddhist Gelugpas, aimed at theocratic forms of government and were thus quite similar in their objectives. This resemblance probably explains why the Fifth Dalai Lama called on the new

15. The Id Khah Friday Mosque in Kashgar, Xinjiang, China, founded in 1442, at the end of the prayer service. Photo: 2009.

ruler of the Dzungars, Sengge's brother and successor Galdan (r. 1671–97), to intervene militarily. Galdan seized the opportunity to extend his power to the south and to allow his domain to border on that of the Fifth Dalai Lama, who was well disposed towards him. He sent an army in 1678 that captured Ismail Khan, installed Khoja Afaq as tributary vassal of the Dzungars, and appointed the Chagataiid **Abdu'l Rashid II** (r. 1679–82) as a puppet khan.[97] With the conquest of Turkestan, Galdan not only controlled the gold and jade deposits around Yarkand, but also China's foreign trade with Central Asia and India. The concept of indirect governance, which Russia would also employ vis-à-vis the Emirate of Bukhara as of 1868, was very beneficial for the Buddhist Dzungars. They received income and resources, without having to bear the cost

and responsibility for ruling the heterodox Muslims of Altishahr. Finally, the common border with Tibet opened up the possibility of attacking arch-rival China by way of Tibet.

A power struggle between Abdu'l Rashid's successor **Muhammad Amin Khan** (r. *ca.* 1682–*ca.* 94), a younger brother of Ismail Khan, and Khoja Afaq (d. 1694) led to the overthrow of the latter. Muhammad Amin Khan then tried – with active diplomacy and envoys to China, Bukhara and India – to free himself from the Dzungars' stranglehold. He even undertook a campaign against the Dzungars, capturing 30,000 of them. But in 1694 he was killed by supporters of Afaqiyya and replaced by **Khoja Yahya** (r. *ca.* 1694–95), a son of Khoja Afaq. A short time later, after Khoja Afaq's death, his widow **Jallad Khanum** (r. 1695), the 'Butcher

16. The Kul-Sharif Mosque, completed in 2005, inside the Kazan Kremlin in Tatarstan, Russia. Photo: 2013.

Queen', launched a reign of terror which even claimed the life of her son Khoja Yahya.[98] Even after her assassination, the fighting continued undiminished between Ishaqiyya, Afaqiyya, Chagataiids and invading Kyrgyz. Only Galdan's successor Tsewang Rabtan (r. 1697–1727) was able to restore political order through his intercession in 1713. Several years later, Tsewang Rabtan installed representatives of Ishaqiyya again in Altishahr as tributary vassals. The last two khojas of Kashgar, Burhan al-Din and Jahan of the Afaqiyya, were defeated by Emperor Qianlong and killed while taking flight in Badakhshan in 1759.[99] Other descendants of the khojas fled to Kokand, from where they made several attacks on

Kashgaria in the nineteenth century.[100] The likely last descendants of the Chagataiids were able to survive in the semi-autonomous khanate of Kumul (Ch. Hami) in the east of Xinjiang. The khanate lasted from 1697 to 1930, seven centuries after the death of its progenitor Genghis Khan.[101] The Hami Khanate originated as a Chinese vassal state, after the Kangxi Emperor (r. 1661–1722) had wrested it from the Dzungars in 1696.[102]

4. The Descendants of the Golden Horde

Between 1240 and 1550, the area between the Volga and Ural rivers belonged politically, ethnically and linguistically to Central Asia or at least to its north-western sphere of influence. Ultimately, the rulers of the Golden Horde who, at its peak, dominated the region from the lower Danube to the middle reaches of the Ob were Mongols and Kipchaks. But the Golden Horde had already begun to dwindle on its western border in the first half of the fourteenth century under pressure from the Grand Duchy of Lithuania and from Hungary. Internal power struggles and the outbreak of the 'black death' weakened the horde further. After the campaigns of Timur-e Lang in the 1390s, when he deliberately destroyed the commercial cities and transport hubs of the horde, its demise accelerated, giving way to a process of fragmentation.[103] Parallel to this decline, the Grand Duchies of Lithuania and Moscow became stronger. Yet while the Lithuanian-Polish Kingdom had to deal with the neighbouring rivals Moscow, Crimea and several German military orders, Moscow turned to the south-east – to the Volga and the Caspian Sea, and, to the east, to Siberia. Towards the end of the sixteenth century, the political border between Europe and Central Asia had already moved from the Volga to the Urals. In this time of upheaval, the Tatar khanates of Kazan, Kursk, Crimea, Astrakhan, Kasimov, Sibir, the Nogai Horde and the Great Horde emerged.[104]

4.1 The Khanate of Kazan and the Small Khanates of Kursk and Kasimov

When the Jochid **Khan Ulugh Mohammad** of the Golden Horde (r. 1419–21, 1428–33, in Kazan in 1437/38–45) was expelled from Sarai for the second time in 1433, he first fled to Crimea. He then conquered the city of Kazan in the winter of 1437/38 and founded the khanate of the same name[105] (figs. 16, 20). The conquest was successful despite the military resistance of the Moscow Grand Duke Vasily II, who wanted to prevent him from taking over this strategically important trading city. In the same year, 1438, the small Tatar **Khanate of Kursk,** also called Jagoldai, similarly emerged south-west of Moscow. It soon subordinated itself to the Grand Duchy of Lithuania and was conquered by Moscow in 1508.[106] Kazan replaced Bolghar, which lay 90 km further south on the Volga. Both cities controlled trade on the Volga, which connected Moscow with the Caspian Sea via the Moskva and Oka rivers. Bolghar's decline had already begun in the second half of the fourteenth century, and

the city was further depopulated after the Russian invasion of 1432. Numismatic finds dating from 1408 show that Kazan overtook Bolghar as the new commercial and administrative centre no later than the beginning of the fifteenth century. At that time, the city was called New Bolghar.[107] The khanate of Kazan bordered on Moscow to the west; on Sibir to the east; on the Nogai Horde and its Bashkir vassals to the south-east; on the Golden Horde, and from about 1466 the Great Horde, to the south-west; and, finally, to the south, on the steppe between Astrakhan and Don, an area of dispute for the Nogai and Crimean Tatars. The Muslim khanate was ruled by a khan from the house of Genghis Khan, but his power had been severely limited by the Tatar nobility.[108] Unlike the Golden Horde, the khanate was not a steppe empire, but it had an urban-mercantile capital and its population included farmers and woodland hunters. Kazan's culture was also a hybrid, because the steppe culture of the Golden Horde in the khanate had been enriched with Volga Bulgarian[109] elements. In ethnic terms, the rather small khanate was likewise varied, consisting of urban Turkic-speaking Kazan Tatars and, in the countryside, of Turkic-speaking Chuvash, Finno-Ugric-speaking Mordvins and Cheremis, and of Udmurts (Votyaks), whose Udmurt language belongs to the Permian group of the Finno-Ugric language family.[110]

Kazan's central location caused the khanate, from the sixteenth century, to be drawn into the clash between two emerging powers – Moscow and the Tatar khanate of Crimea, an Ottoman protectorate since 1478. As a consequence, Kazan experienced a turbulent history. In the 114-year history of the khanate, there were fourteen different khans and 21 periods of rule, as some khans intermittently ruled two or even three times. Towards the end of the khanate, pro-Muscovite rulers often took turns with anti-Muscovite khans who belonged to the Crimean Tatar Giray dynasty. For Moscow, which had no ice-free access to the sea and thus was excluded from the evolving world trade, the Volga was of paramount importance as a waterway. The successful liberation of the Grand Duchy of Moscow (from 1547 the Russian Tsarist Empire) from its unfavourable landlocked geographical position began with the sovereignty it gradually acquired over the Volga and hence access to the Caspian Sea. By moving the border south, Moscow also gained strategic depth.

Ulugh Khan Mohammad initiated the first conflict with Moscow. His goal was to compel the Grand Duchy, which had stopped regularly paying tributes to the Golden Horde in the early 1370s, to submit again to Tatar rule.[111] In 1439, he occupied the commercial city of Nizhny Novgorod, located at the confluence of the Volga and the Oka. Then, five years later, along with his son and successor **Mahmud bin Ulugh Mohammad** (r. 1445–66), he again attacked the Grand Duchy in a battle near Suzdal and took Grand Duke Vasily II (r. 1425–62) prisoner. Instead of continuing on to Moscow, Ulugh Mohammad released Vasily after the payment of a high ransom. Vasily, on the other hand, was forced in 1452 to surrender the city of Meshchersky Gorodets as a Tatar khanate to Ulugh Mohammad's son **Kasim bin Ulugh Mohammad** of Kasimov (r. 1452–69). As the city lay to the south-east of Moscow along the middle reaches of the Oka River, it was strategically important for Moscow. The Grand Duchy of Moscow, however, was able to downgrade the **Khanate of Meshchersky Gorodets** or **Kasimov** to its own vassal and to promote agreeable khans who could be appointed to other khanates under Genghis Khanid rule.[112] In Kasimov (which is called 'Kirman' in Muslim sources) in 1512, a new Tatar dynasty from Astrakhan superseded that of the Great Horde, which was destroyed in 1502.[113]

In 1467, Grand Duke Ivan III (r. 1462–1505) seized the initiative when he supported the claim of his vassal Kasim to the throne of Kazan and marched against Khan **Ibrahim bin Mahmud**

(r. 1467–79). After two unsuccessful Muscovite campaigns, Kazan had to capitulate in the autumn of 1469. But Ibrahim was able to hold on to power, and the tiny khanate of Meshchersky was renamed the **Khanate of Kasimov**. In the last quarter of the fifteenth century, Ivan III gained the Crimean Tatar Khanate as a tactical ally, as both pursued the same objective in the short term, albeit with different long-term goals. Ivan III wanted to finally be free from the sovereignty of the Great Horde and, in the medium term, to expand Moscow's sphere of influence to the west and south. The Crimean Tatar Mengli Giray perceived the alliance of Poland-Lithuania with Khan Ahmad of the Great Horde as an acute threat, which in turn drove him into the arms of Moscow. Over the long term, however, Mengli Giray (r. 1468–69, 1471–74, 1475, 1478–1514) not only strove for independence from the Great Horde, but also claimed nothing less than its heritage.[114] The alliance from around 1470 to 1509, though, enabled Moscow to finally shake off the Tatar yoke at the so-called 'Great Stand on the Ugra River' in 1480.[115]

17. The small town of Sviyazhsk west of Kazan. Tsar Ivan IV had in 1551 a prefabricated fortress rebuilt here which served as a base for the conquest of Kazan in 1552. In 1955, Sviyazhsk was turned into an island as a result of the downstream Kuibyshev reservoir; a road connects Sviyazhsk to the riverbank. Tatarstan, Russia. Photo: 2013.

18. The Assumption of the Blessed Virgin Mary Monastery on the island of Sviyazhsk, Tatarstan, Russia. On the left is the St Nicholas Church, founded in 1555/56; on the right, the Dormition Cathedral, founded in 1560, which contains the murals from the founding period. Photo: 2013.

Grand Duke Ivan now had sufficient room to manoeuvre and to establish a protectorate over Kazan. Major rivals in Kazan included **Ali bin Ibrahim** (r. 1479–84, 1485–87), who enjoyed the support of the Nogai Horde, and **Muhammad Amin bin Ibrahim** (r. 1484–85, 1487–95, 1502–18), the client of Moscow. In 1487, Ivan's army sailed on the Volga to Kazan and occupied the city on 9 June. Ali was brought as a prisoner to Moscow and Muhammad Amin was installed on the throne as Ivan's vassal. In 1495, the native of Sibir **Mamuq Khan** (r. 1495–96) attacked Muhammad Amin with support from the Nogai. He was ousted a year later, however, by the pro-Russian faction. Ivan now put Muhammad Amin's brother **Abd al-Latif** (1496–1502) on the throne. On his death, Muhammad Amin assumed his third period of rule. Although Muhammad Amin rebelled in 1505 and won a spectacular victory in June 1506 against the Russian troops outside of Kazan, he preferred to make peace again and to subordinate himself to Ivan's successor, Vasily III (1505–33). Vasily enthroned the designated heir of the Kasimov dynasty, **Shah Ali bin Allah Yar** (r. 1518–21, 1546, 1551–52), after Muhammad's death in 1518.[116]

Meanwhile, there was a change of alliances in the power struggle over north-eastern Europe: Moscow's dominion in Kazan and success against Poland-Lithuania made Mengli Giray fearful that the Grand Duchy could next target the Pontic steppe and reach the Black Sea. And when Vasily III wrested control of the city of Smolensk from Poland-Lithuania in 1514, King Sigismund I joined forces with Khan Mehmed Giray I (r. 1514–23), Mengli Giray's son and successor, in an anti-Moscow alliance.[117] The battle for Kazan now intensified, and, after staging his own revolt of the nobility, Mehmed Giray I placed his brother **Sahib Khan Giray** (r. 1521–24) on the throne of Kazan in 1521. The two Giray brothers coordinated an attack with two armies against the Grand Duchy of Moscow, in which they took tens of thousands of people into slavery. Besides this, Vasily had to recognise the dynastic union of Kazan and the Crimean Tatar Khanate created by the Tatar Giray dynasty. Mehmed Giray's efforts to revive the Great Horde under his leadership foundered two years later, however, when he was defeated and killed by the Nogai during an attack on Astrakhan. Several years earlier, in 1509, Mehmed Giray's father Mengli had already failed woefully outside of Astrakhan.[118]

then prepared a new major attack on Moscow to bring the Grand
Duchy under Tatar control once again. He advanced in 1541 – at a
time when leading boyars were fighting over the regency for the
ten-year-old Grand Duke Ivan, the future Tsar Ivan IV. Thanks to
the support of **Shah Ali** of Kasimov (r. 1516–18, 1535–46, 1546–51,
1552–67), the attack could be averted. This renewed push to
Moscow left a lasting impression on the young Ivan. He understood
that Moscow's security was at risk as long as it could not bring
Kazan and Astrakhan under its control. The pro-Muscovite party
in Kazan made **Shah Ali** its leader. The party staged a revolt in
1546, but it failed after just one month and Safa Giray ascended the
throne for the third time. He held on to it until his death in 1549.
He was succeeded by his underage son **Ötemish Giray** (r. 1549–51),
whose mother Söyembikä exercised the regency in his stead.
Shah Ali's third accession (r. 1551–52) also failed to bring about a
permanent solution for Moscow, as he had been forced into exile
in February 1552 and replaced by a prince from Astrakhan named
Yadgar Muhammad (r. 1552).

Soon after his ascent to the throne, Tsar Ivan IV (r. as Grand
Duke of Moscow 1533 to 1547, as Tsar of Russia 1547–84) decided
to finally eliminate the danger posed by Kazan. After two unsuccessful demonstrations of military power in the years 1547–48 and
1549–50, Ivan renewed the alliances with the tribal leaders of the
Nogai and had the basic structure of a strong wooden fortress built
to the north of Moscow in the city of Uglich on the Upper Volga.
In 1551, Ivan shipped the premanufactured fortress along the Volga
River to the south, where it was rebuilt on the hill of the Sviyazhsk
Peninsula, at the confluence of the Volga and Sviyaga. Pieced
together within four weeks, the fortress stood deep inside Kazan
territory and was only 30 km from the capital city (fig. 17). The
following year, it served as a base of operations for the attack on
Kazan. On 2 October 1552 the Russian army conquered Kazan.[120]
To commemorate this landmark achievement, Tsar Ivan built
St Basil's Cathedral in Moscow (fig. 19).

Tsar Ivan seized the opportunity to advance further to the
Caspian Sea and forged an alliance with the steppe warriors of
the Nogai Horde. The Nogai wanted to get rid of the Khanate
of Astrakhan, which repeatesdly allied itself with their Crimean
Tatar rivals. In 1554, Ivan's troops occupied the khanate, which lay
approximately 1,500 km south of Kazan. The tsar encountered no
resistance and appointed Dervish Ali (r. 1554–56) as a puppet ruler.
But when Dervish Khan allied himself in 1556 with the Crimean
Khanate against Moscow, Ivan's Cossacks and Streltsy[121] conquered
the then capital Hajji Tarkan, which they burned down, and
annexed the khanate to the Russian Empire. Now the 3,530-km-long

19. St Basil's Cathedral in Moscow, Russia, built by Ivan IV from 1555 to 1561 to
commemorate the conquest of Kazan. The leading architect Postnik Yakovlev
was also instrumental in the construction of the Annunciation Cathedral of
Kazan (fig. 20) and the two main churches of the Assumption of the Blessed
Virgin Mary Monastery of Sviyazhsk (fig. 18). Photo: 2002.

When Sahib Giray abdicated in Kazan in 1524, he was
succeeded by his nephew **Safa Giray Khan**. He ruled three times
(r. 1524–32, 1535–46, 1546–49) and pursued a policy that was hostile
to Moscow. In the interim, after staying in Istanbul for several
years, Sahib Giray established himself as the khan of the Crimean
Tatars (r. 1532–51) and brought Astrakhan under his rule in 1533.[119]
Although Vasily III succeeded in putting the khan of Kasimov
Jan Ali bin Allah Yar on the throne (r. in Kasimov 1519–32, in
Kazan 1532–35) in 1532, the pro-Crimean fraction of the Kazan
nobility killed him three years later. He was followed again by
Safa Giray (second reign 1535–46). The Crimean Tatar Sahib Giray

course of the Volga – from its source to its estuary in the Caspian Sea – was in Russian hands. Tsar Ivan thus pushed open the gateway to Central Asia and gained direct trade opportunities with Persia and the Uzbek khanates. Moreover, with the possession of Astrakhan, Moscow could block, or at least severely limit, the caravan routes of the Crimea through the southern steppe of Kipchak to Central Asia. In any case, this partial victory in the fight for the heritage of the former Golden Horde elevated Ivan's prestige and substantiated his further territorial claims. While Lithuanian and Muscovite rulers managed in the late fourteenth and fifteenth century to free themselves from the sovereignty of the Golden Horde and the subsequent Great Horde and to slowly expand their territory, Tsar Ivan IV set about making preparations for the conquest of Genghis Khanid successor states. He could boast of having reversed power imbalances from east to west that had existed since the thirteenth century and of having subjugated, or at least put on the defensive, the former Central Asian rulers. This megatrend relating to Europe's dominant position compared with Central Asia, and even Asia in general, was

not challenged until the twentieth century – first by the Russian defeat by Japan in 1904–05, then by the seizure of power by the Communist Party in China in 1949 and the collapse of the Soviet Union in 1991.

To protect the newly acquired territory and the tribes of the Bashkirs, who joined Russia more or less voluntarily, from the raids of the rebellious Nogai and Crimean Tatars, in 1574 Ivan had the Ufa fortress built 450 km east of Kazan. Additional fortresses were then built along the Volga: Samara in 1586, Tsaritsyn (Stalingrad, Volgograd) in 1589, and Saratov around 1590. These fortresses not only safeguarded navigation on the Volga, but also formed a fortress line, which prevented the steppe horsemen of the Nogai from crossing the river. However, for the Crimean Tatars who claimed they were descendants of the Great Horde, the fall of Kazan and Astrakhan was unacceptable – not least because Russia could hinder Crimea's trade contacts with Central Asia from Astrakhan. In addition, the Ottomans were concerned that the city could serve as a springboard for a Russian military operation in the north-eastern

20. The Annunciation Cathedral in the Kazan Kremlin in Tatarstan, Russia. In the first phase from 1555–62, the two architects Postnik Yakovlev and Ivan Shiryay built the cathedral (seen on the right) in the rather simple Pskov style with five crossed domes and three apses. In the eighteenth century, the helmet-shaped domes were replaced by onion domes. Photo: 2014.

21. Orthodox crucifixes carved from ice at the Raifa monastery, constructed for the Epiphany on the adjacent lake. Cross-shaped holes are cut out of the ice and believers jump into the icy water three times as a symbolic imitation of Christ's baptism. The Raifa Monastery, located to the north-west of Kazan, dates back to the hermit Philaret of Moscow, who first built a wooden chapel here in 1613. The Bolsheviks closed the famous pilgrimage site in 1918 and the buildings were misappropriated as a penal camp from 1933 to 1954. The complex was returned to the Church in 1991. Photo: 2014.

Caucasus. Although an Ottoman attack on Astrakhan failed in 1569, Tsar Ivan allowed the Russian fortress, which he had built in 1567 along the Terek River, to be razed in 1571/72. Furthermore, in the years 1555, 1562, 1564, 1565, 1571, 1572 and 1592, Moscow continued to be exposed to Crimean Tatar attacks. In 1571 and 1592, the Moscow suburbs were set in flames.[122] In spite of all military efforts Russia was forced to pay tribute to the Crimean Tatar till 1700.[123]

As for the political integration of Kazan, Tsar Ivan was initially influenced by the Orthodox clergy and the crusade mentality. He agreed to an aggressive conversion policy of Tatar Muslims and rural followers of nature religions. Mosques were destroyed and Orthodox churches were built in their place. People were also forcibly baptised, and those who refused were drowned. But in 1555, Ivan underwent a radical change. He decreed that priests and monasteries were not allowed to baptise newly won subjects. Instead, the conversions were to take place as a result of exemplary

behaviour and charity. Ivan's pragmatic integration policy shielded the Muslims along the Volga against aggressive proselytising efforts until the 1680s. At the same time, Moscow guaranteed the non-Russian upper classes of the khanate that they could continue to own their possessions and integrated Muslim-Tatar nobles as equal members of a landowning military aristocracy in the Russian nobility. To boost trade with Central Asia again, Moscow granted Tatar traders within the Russian Empire numerous privileges, allowing the Muslim Tatars from Kazan to soon build an extensive trading network. Finally, Russian landowners were prohibited from downgrading non-Russian Muslims to serfs.[124] Tsar Ivan's policy towards non-Russian ethnic groups and religions differed

▶ **22.** The procession from Raifa Monastery to the frozen lake during the Epiphany celebration on 6 January as per the Orthodox calendar and 19 January of the Gregorian calendar. Photo: 2014.

fundamentally from the one that Catholic Spain and Portugal pursued in their overseas colonies. Ivan was hardly driven by missionary zeal; he was instead interested in Russia's security and the additional commercial benefits that the conquered territories brought to his landlocked empire. Spain and Portugal, on the other hand, were guided by the principles of the Catholic Church and its Inquisition and tried to convert the people in their remote colonies – by force if necessary. This even affected non-Catholic Christians such as the Nestorian St Thomas Christians of South India.[125] In the Russian land power, there were also significantly fewer socio-politically relevant differences between Russians and non-Russian Muslims than in the case of the maritime powers of Western Europe and their distant colonies. This disparity was not only a function of different geography, but also of a pragmatic view of the world, which was not guided by religious proselytising ideas and strove instead for a supra-ethnic and supra-religious empire. The integration policy towards non-Russian communities introduced by Ivan IV remained, with some qualifications, groundbreaking for the Russian conquests in Central Asia in the nineteenth century.

Kazan's special status ended with Tsar Peter the Great (r. nominally 1682–89, in real terms 1689–1725), who made the city into a shipbuilding centre for the Caspian fleet because of its neighbouring large forests. At the same time, he pursued the goal of rebuilding Russia into a centrally managed, uniform and absolutist state along Western European lines. The coordination of all subjects included the forced conversion of all non-Christians to Russian Orthodoxy. In 1713, Tsar Peter ordered Kazan's Muslim landowners to be baptised. Noncompliance carried with it the threat of the expropriation of all lands which were inhabited by Christian peasants. A year later, he rescinded the privileges of the non-Russian peasants (i.e. Tatar, Chuvash, Mordovian, Cheremis and Udmurt) and incorporated them into the class of state peasants bound to community and land. This included having to pay significantly higher taxes and to do compulsory labour. In the 1740s, the oppression continued to increase, and Tsarina Elisabeth (r. 1741–62) issued an order in 1742 to demolish all mosques built after 1552. By 1744, 418 of the 536 mosques of the former khanate had been destroyed. For the rural population, strong financial pressure and the unequal treatment of Christians and non-Christians in matters of taxes and conscription were accompanying measures. This repressive religious policy did not achieve its aims, however, as the conversion of traditional shamanists remained superficial, and the Muslim institutions were forced into the anti-Russian underground. Even worse, the crackdowns drove the non-Russian and non-Orthodox minorities on the Volga into the arms of the Don

Cossack rebel Yemelyan Pugachov (*ca.* 1742–75), who rallied to his side the dissatisfied peasants, serfs, Tatars, Bashkirs[126] and members of other minority groups.

The assassination of Tsar Peter III (r. 1762) was the starting point of the rebellion that rapidly grew into a large-scale peasant war from 1773 to early 1775. On 17 July 1762, he was killed by Grigory Orlov, the lover of his power-hungry wife Catherine, née Sophie von Anhalt-Zerbst. Along with the assassination, there was a coup. Shortly before this, Tsar Peter III had announced significant reforms, including the abolition of serfdom, and Catherine was wary of implementing them. Yemelyan Pugachov posed as Tsar Peter III, having escaped being killed himself, and quickly won a large following. He founded a rival government in the Urals. His troops captured Samara in 1773, and in the attack on Kazan in July 1774 the city went up in flames. But the Kremlin remained in the hands of pro-government troops. Pugachov fought an undecided battle near Kazan in the same month against the regular army and then suffered two defeats, after which he fled to the south on the Volga River. After a heavy defeat at Tsaritsyn, his closest collaborators handed him over to the tsarist authorities. He was then executed in Moscow on 21 January 1775. But soon after coming to power, Tsarina Catherine (r. 1762–96) overturned several discriminatory commands and, in 1775, after suppressing the Pugachov Rebellion, she permitted the reconstruction of the city of Kazan with its mosques. In 1784, finally, Catherine prohibited the Orthodox proselytising of Muslims. Four years later, she recognised the Tatar Muslims as a community with equal rights by establishing the 'Orenburg Muslim Spiritual Assembly' administrative office, headed by a mufti.[127]

4.2 The Great Horde, the Astrakhan Khanate, the Nogai Horde and the Khanate of Sibir

The histories of the Great Horde, the small Khanate of Astrakhan and the Nogai are closely interwoven. Above all, they are linked together in the person of Amir Edigü, the forefather of all three political entities. In the first two decades of the fifteenth century, the non-Genghis-Khanid commander **Edigü** (d. 1419) from the Mongolian Manghit tribe controlled the southern areas of the Golden Horde by means of puppet khans. They included the cities of Sarai, Astrakhan and Derbent in the eastern Caucasus. After his death, eight khans followed in rapid succession in nine periods of rule, until the Jochid **Küchük Mohammad** (r. *ca.* 1435–59), who had ruled in Astrakhan since 1433, seized power.[128] But Küchük and his sons and successors **Mahmud** (r. 1459–65) and **Ahmad** (r. 1465–81)

23. The Astrakhan Kremlin built by Ivan IV from 1582–89. On the left, the Assumption Cathedral with the free-standing bell tower; to the right of centre, the Trinity Cathedral. Photo: 2014.

could neither prevent nor undo the defection of Kazan and Crimea. As a result, the remaining remnant of the khanate was no longer 'Golden', but rather referred to as the '**Great Horde**' (*ca.* 1466–1502). At that time, Astrakhan probably still belonged to their sphere of influence, which is why the beginning of the khanate of the same name is estimated to be in 1502, not 1466.[129] Ahmad Khan, together with the Siberian Shaybanid Ibak Khan, in or shortly after 1469, killed the Uzbek Khan Shaikh Haydar (r. *ca.* 1469–?).[130] Ahmad then made another attempt to force Moscow to recognise his sovereignty. But at the 'Great Stand on the Ugra River' in 1480, he did not risk attacking the Muscovites without his Polish-Lithuanian ally Casimir IV, who had left him in the lurch. He subsequently retreated. A year later, he was killed in action against the Nogai and Ibak Khan, a grandson of Hajji Muhammad Khan, the founder of

the Khanate of Sibir.[131] By that time the Great Horde was severely threatened since it was menaced in the north-west by Moscow, in the south-west by the Crimea and in the east by the Nogai. Succeeding Ahmad were **Murtada Khan** (co-ruler 1481–98, r. 1499) and **Sheikh Ahmed** (co-ruler 1481–98, r. 1499–1502).

After a deterioration of relations between the Great Horde and Poland-Lithuania, which led to the armed conflict of 1487 and the defeat of the Horde,[132] Sheikh Ahmed renewed the alliance with Alexander Jagiellon, Grand Duke of Lithuania and future King of Poland, in 1501. But when in the winter of 1501/02 Ahmed immediately attacked Moscow, which was allied with the Crimean Tatars, his Lithuanian ally let him down once again, and he was forced to withdraw in a weakened state. The Crimean Tatar khan Mengli Giray seized the opportunity to deliver a fatal blow to the

24. The bell tower and Assumption Cathedral in the Astrakhan Kremlin, Russia. The cathedral, founded in 1602, assumed its present form a century later, 1698–1710. The bell tower is located on unstable ground, as branches of the Volga flowed passed the east and south sides of the Kremlin until the end of the seventeenth century. The first tower was replaced by a second in 1809–13; this then had to give way to a third tower, the current one, in 1908–12, which is also tilted slightly. Photo: 2014.

Great Horde. He defeated Sheikh Ahmed and destroyed his capital city New Sarai in June 1502. The Great Horde ceased to exist and the small **Khanate of Astrakhan** (1502–54/6) formed as a successor state.[133] For Moscow, the situation had relaxed only temporarily. Now Mengli Giray, who saw himself as the heir of the Great Horde, demanded that Vasily III pay tribute. It was thus of the utmost importance to Moscow that Astrakhan could hold its ground thanks to the help of the Nogai Horde. The first two khans – **Abd al-Karim Khan bin Mahmud Khan** (r. 1502–14), who had probably played a pivotal role since the early 1490s in Astrakhan, and his brother **Jani Beg Khan bin Mahmud Khan** (r. 1514–21) – enjoyed the support of Yaghmurchi, the Nogai prince. Thanks to the military support of the Nogai, Crimean Tatar attacks on ancient Astrakhan (Hajji Tarkhan) in the years 1509 and 1523 both failed. It was not until 1533 that the khan of Crimea, Sahib Giray, managed to force Astrakhan into the Crimean Tatar sphere of influence. It appears that Jani Beg was succeeded by his son Husayn and later only briefly and nominally ruling khans, who were alternately dependent on the goodwill of the Nogai or Crimean Tatars.[134] Nearly 250 years after the visit of

the German botanist Samuel Gottlieb Gmelin in Astrakhan in the years 1770 and 1772–73, his resigned statement remains relevant: 'He who wants to get involved with historical uncertainties can nowhere better indulge in his conjectures than in the old and middle history of Astrachan.'[135] As discussed above, Astrakhan was annexed by Russia between 1554 and 1556.

After the conquest of the city of Hajji Tarkhan, Tsar Ivan's voivode (military commander) Ivan S. Cheremisinov had a wooden Kremlin constructed 12 km downriver on a long island in the Volga in 1558. As a result, the fortress blocked upstream access to the Volga. After the wooden fortress successfully withstood a joint Crimean Tatar and Ottoman attack in 1569, it was decided in 1582 to build a fortress of stone and brick (fig. 23). Although the wooden fortifications had the advantage that their walls did not collapse over a large area in the face of cannon fire, they were less robust and, especially, highly inflammable. The construction of the stone and brick wall with its seven towers was completed in 1589.[136] The building materials were taken from the ruins of the former Tatar city of New Sarai. Over time, the city spread to the west of the

Kremlin. It was also surrounded by a white brick wall, now missing. The threat posed to the Ottoman Empire by the Russian conquest of Astrakhan and Tsar Ivan's newly built fortress along the Terek River prompted Sultan Selim II in 1569 to send out an army under Kasim Pasha to capture Astrakhan. He also commissioned the pasha to set about building a canal between the Don and Volga in order to create a waterway from the Black Sea to the Caspian Sea.[137] But Kasim Pasha's attack by sea and land failed, not least because the Crimean Tatar Khan Devlet Giray (1551–77), a vassal of Istanbul, sabotaged the campaign. With his troops, he suddenly abandoned the Ottoman army near the Volga. As Gmelin reported, the majority of the Ottoman army was killed.[138] A century before Gmelin's visit, Astrakhan succumbed to the vortex of the Cossack and peasant uprising from 1667–71 led by Stepan (Stenka) Razin, who seized the cities of Samara and Astrakhan and, as a consequence, controlled the lower Volga.[139] Later, at the beginning of the nineteenth century, the city suffered an economic downturn, which was halted again thanks to oil prospecting at the beginning of the 1870s in Baku, Azerbaijan. In the Second World War, German units advanced to about 100 km west of Astrakhan, and the city was bombed several times in late summer of 1942. The Soviet victory in the winter of 1942–43 at Stalingrad (today Volgograd), lying just under 400 km to the north, eliminated the German threat.

The term 'Nogai Horde' referred to the mighty Amir Nogai (d. 1299), whose name in Mongolian means 'dog' – considered a distinction because of the animal's fighting power.[140] In fact, the horde went back to the non-Genghis Khanid Amir Edigü (d. 1419) of the Mongolian Manghit tribe.[141] At the time, the pastures of the Nogai extended between the Ural (Yaik) and Emba rivers in the west of present-day Kazakhstan. Although Edigü had a strong following, the Nogai did not form an independent horde either in his own lifetime or in that of his sons Mansur bin Edigü (r. ?) and Nur al-Din bin Edigü (ca. 1426–ca. 1440). It was not until the second half of the fifteenth century that the Nogai Horde emerged under its leader Musa bin Waqqas as an independent political entity. At this time, the pastures of the Nogai stretched from the Irtysh in the east across the area north of the Aral Sea to the Middle Volga in the north-west and the Caspian Sea in the south-west. The urban centre of the Nogai was Saraichik ('little Sarai') on the lower reaches of the Ural River, about 50 km north of the current western Kazakh city of Atyrau. The loosely structured tribal confederation was a considerable force thanks to its rich grass pastures, which provided it with a large reservoir of horses. Until the 1630s, it was Russia's most important supplier of mounts. In numerous conflicts between Moscow, the Great Horde, the Khanate of Kazan, the Khanate of Astrakhan and

the Crimean Tatars, the sides they took were decisive. After a setback in 1519 when the Kazakh Khan Qasim bin Jani Beg penetrated deep inside the territory of the Nogai (and even occupied Saraichik from 1519 to 1521), three descendants of Musa bin Waqqas led the horde to renewed prominence. It extended its reach all the way to the Bashkirs, who lived east of the Volga.[142]

Around the mid-sixteenth century, the Nogai under the leadership of Yusuf Bey bin Musa (r. ca. 1536–ca. 1555) were no longer able to withstand the pressure from the two emerging regional great powers, Russia and the Ottoman Empire (the Crimean Tatars had been the latter's vassals since 1478). Firstly, the horde weakened itself from within in an internal power struggle, which Ismail Bey bin Musa (r. ca. 1554–63) won. But partisans of the defeated Khan Yusuf and the Nogai living in the lower reaches of the Volga who rejected the supremacy of Russia migrated south-west to the steppes of Azov and into the Kuban region. There, they soon formed the backbone of the Crimean Tatar army and were called the 'Lesser Nogai Horde'. The Nogai who remained in the area around Saraichik formed the Greater Nogai Horde. Two other lesser hordes were the Jemboyluq Horde (also called Altiuli), who nomadised along the Emba River and the Bujaq Horde on the lower Don.[143] While Ismail's son Din Achmad (r. 1563–78) managed to preserve the unity of the Greater Horde, it subsequently collapsed following raids by the Cossacks, who plundered Saraichik in 1581, and by the immigrant Kalmyks (bands of Oirats). From the late 1570s, Nogai of the Greater Horde began to cross the Don and penetrate into the steppes of the Crimea, where they encountered resistance from the Lesser Horde. Especially after the death of Ishterek Bey ibn Din Achmad (d. 1618), the pressure from the Kalmyks intensified. After reaching the Emba River in 1608 and the Urals five years later, they advanced to Astrakhan in 1633, where they defeated the Nogai and the Russian governor. The Kalmyks continued their raids in the delta of the Volga in 1634–35. The Nogai then left the Volga region due to the lack of Russian support and sought protection near the Ottoman fortress of Azov. Around 1637, they crossed the Don and invaded the Crimea, where they were welcomed by the Crimean Tatar princes as much-needed reinforcement to their private armies.[144]

When the Golden Horde started to dissolve at the beginning of the fifteenth century, three new tribal groups gradually emerged in its north-eastern region. The Nogai settled between the Volga and the Ural rivers and the Uzbeks settled in the steppe east of the Urals. And to the north of the latter, the forest regions of Western Siberia (1000 km north-east of Kazan) was under the control of a tribe that described itself as the 'Taybugids'. The Taybugids spoke a Turkic language and derived their descent from the semi-mythical leader Taybuga.

The power centre of the resulting **Khanate of Sibir** was located on the Tura River and called Chimgi-Tura. In close proximity, the Cossacks founded the city of Tyumen in 1586. **Hajji Muhammad Khan** (d. 1428 or 1429) probably established the capital around 1427. He was then killed in a battle along the Tobol River in 1428/29 by the Shaybanid **Abu'l Khayr Khan** (r. 1429–68/69). Upon the death of Abu'l Khayr, **Ibak Khan** (r. *ca.* 1468/69–*ca.* 1494) seized power in 1468 with support from the Nogai. Ibak and the Nogai appear to have remained allies, for together they defeated Ahmad, the khan of the Great Horde, in 1481. In the last decade of the fifteenth century, the Taybugid **Mamuq (Mamat, Muhammad) Khan** (r. *ca.* 1494–95, 1496–?), who was also briefly khan of Kazan, managed to kill Ibak Khan and seize power for himself. Mamuq moved the capital to Sibir, which lay at the confluence of the Irtysh and Tobol rivers, near the present city of Tobolsk.¹⁴⁵

Around the mid-sixteenth century, the Taybugid **Yagidar Bey** (r. ?–1563), who probably governed Sibir jointly with **Bey Bulad**, was exposed to two different threats: in the west, Tsar Ivan had conquered Kazan, and in the south the Shaybanid Küchüm Khan enjoyed the support of the Nogai and perhaps also of the Kazakhs. Yagidar opted for the far-flung tsar and in 1555 or 1556 sent a legation to Moscow, who offered to Tsar Ivan Sibir's subordination and to pay tribute in return for military protection against Küchüm. Ivan responded enthusiastically, though he was particularly eager to use West Siberian resources like salt, metals and furs. But when **Küchüm Khan** (r. 1563–82, as a guerrilla leader 1582–98) attacked Yagidar, Ivan, who was busy with the consolidation of his power in Kazan and Astrakhan, deserted him and Küchüm conquered the Khanate of Sibir in 1563. Impressed by the Russian advance, Küchüm first offered the tsar his obedience and paid tribute to Moscow. After the major attack of the Crimean Tatars on Moscow in 1571, however, Russia's vulnerability was obvious. Küchüm, for whom the encroachments of Russian hunters and settlers in areas east of the Urals was a constant irritation, subsequently ceased paying tributes in 1572 and insisted on his independence. Although Tsar Ivan was consumed with the Livonian War of 1558–83, in which Russia fought against Poland-Lithuania, Denmark and Sweden for supremacy in the Baltic Sea, Küchüm's disloyalty could not be tolerated for economic reasons. In addition, Küchüm started to attack and burn down the Russian settlements in the area around Perm, which amounted to a declaration of war on the trading empire of the Stroganov family.

The wealth of the Stroganov family of entrepreneurs was based on the extraction of salt (at the time food could only be preserved by salting), trade in valuable animal skins such as sable and ermine,

and the mining of iron ore and gold. Tsar Ivan had transferred the exploitation of resources in the region of Perm – between the Volga and Ural, along the banks of the River Kama – to Grigory Stroganov in 1558. Since the Kama flows south of Kazan into the Volga, goods could easily be shipped to Moscow. Ivan delegated the task to the Stroganovs to tap into, 'pacify', and develop resource-rich areas east of Kazan. He gave them a 20-year tax exemption and the right to raise their own taxes among the locals, to build fortresses and fortified settlements there, as well as to maintain a private Cossack army equipped with firearms. In a second step, Russian officials and soldiers arrived in 1585 to incorporate the exploited areas into Russia, where they were managed by voivodes. Russian trading companies, hunters, adventurers and Cossacks were the tip of the spear for Russia's conquests in Asia.

The business and conquest model set up by Tsar Ivan and the Stroganovs anticipated that of the British East India Company, founded in 1707, by more than a century. When the Stroganovs struck rich deposits of silver and iron ore east of the Urals, Ivan also granted them (around 1568) a huge area comprising half of the Khanate of Sibir. Conflict with Küchüm was therefore inevitable. Küchüm swiftly intensified his attacks on the advancing Russian settlers in 1573 and also killed Ivan's envoys. In response, the tsar allowed the Stroganovs to attack the khanate with their private army of Cossacks led by Yermak Timofeyevich (d. 1585). Although the tsar backed down at the end of the 1570s and ordered the Stroganovs to retreat back behind the Urals, Grigory's sons Nikita and Maxim ignored the command.¹⁴⁶ Yermak's small force numbered only 550 Cossacks and 300 mercenaries, but thanks to the superior firepower of their muskets, he defeated Küchüm in 1582/83 and conquered Sibir. Although Küchüm succeeded in luring Yermak into a trap in the summer of 1585, causing him to drown in the Irtysh River, he was nevertheless unable to recapture the khanate. As the Livonian War was now over, the tsar sent reinforcements and incorporated the khanate into the Russian Empire. Küchüm, however, conducted an unsuccessful guerrilla war in the West Siberian forests until 1598. After another defeat, he fled to the Nogai, who killed him out of fear of possible Russian reprisal. The regent appointed by Ivan, Boris Godunov, consolidated the newly acquired Asian areas by building fortified settlements: Ufa (1574) and Tyumen (1586) were followed by Tobolsk in 1587 and Tomsk in 1604.¹⁴⁷ Only 57 years after Yermak had conquered Sibir, the Cossack captain Ivan Moskvitin reached the Sea of Okhotsk, a marginal sea of the Pacific Ocean, in 1639. The port of Okhotsk was built there in 1647.¹⁴⁸

4.3 The Khanate of the Crimean Tatars

Of the successor states of the Golden Horde, the Khanate of the Crimean Tatars (1441–1783) endured by far the longest, not least because it had been an Ottoman protectorate since 1478 and had close economic ties with the Ottoman Empire.[149] All 49 khans who split among them 71 periods of rule belonged to the family of Giray and descended from the Togha-Timurid Tash Temür, who had his name minted on coins in the Crimea around 1395.[150] In the traditionally organised khanate, the power of the Giray khans rested on the four major tribes of Shirin, Barïn, Arghïn, and Kipchak, with the Manghit joining later. It was the first khan Hajji Giray who had invited these powerful clans of the Golden Horde to the Crimea to spread his power base. Following the death of a khan, the leaders of these clans chose his successor, although not in a vertical line, e.g. from father to son, as with the Ottomans. It was instead done horizontally, with the eldest male descendant claiming the title of khan.[151] These four, later five, clans possessed the most fertile pastures and lands in Crimea – except for the south coast, which a governor administered as an Ottoman wilayah (province) – as hereditary possessions and they maintained their own private armies. This strong position of the tribes forced the khan to align his foreign policy with their interests, which mainly consisted in looting and kidnapping.

Hajji Giray (r. *ca.* 1441–*ca.* 1466), a descendant of Tash Temür, was elected the first khan of Crimea in 1441 or 1443 by the tribal leaders and immediately had his name minted on coins.[152] He secured his position against the Golden Horde by entering into an alliance with Casimir IV of Poland-Lithuania. Together, the allies thwarted the attacking Golden Horde in 1452. The next year, the political geography around the Black Sea changed fundamentally when the Ottoman Sultan Mehmed II (r. 1444–46, 1451–81) conquered Constantinople on 29 May 1453. The Byzantine Empire was thus wiped off the map permanently. Sultan Mehmed continued his conquests not only to the west – in the Balkans, Wallachia, and against Venice – but also to the north against Trebizond, which he captured in 1461, and against the Genoese outposts in the Crimea. Mehmed wanted to make sure that the Genoese, who had allied themselves with Poland, did not extend their sovereignty over the entire Crimea. He also wanted to bring the lucrative trade across the Black Sea under his control. Even though a first joint attack by Hajji Giray and Mehmed II over land and sea in 1454 on Caffa (present-day Feodosia) failed, the city

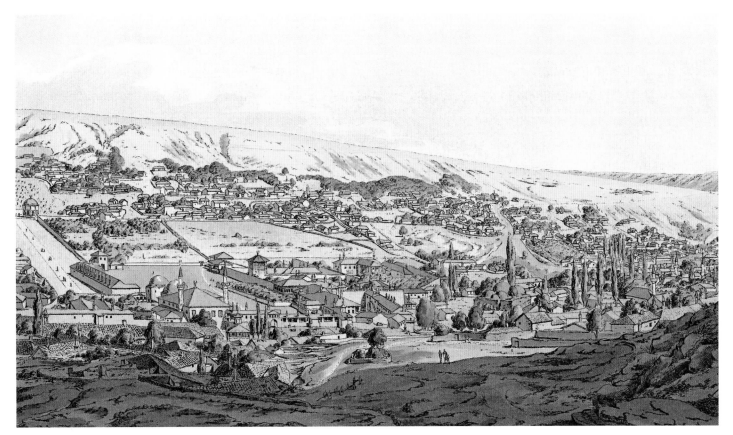

25. The capital of the Crimean khans, Bakhchisarai, in the south-west of Crimea, Russia. Subsequently coloured copper engraving. Peter Simon Pallas, *Bemerkungen auf einer Reise in die südlichen Statthalterschaften des Russischen Reichs in den Jahren 1793–1794* (Leipzig: G. Martini, 1799–1801), vol. III, fig. I/2.

26. The palace of the Crimean khans, probably built after 1533, in Bakhchisarai, Crimea, Russia. Photo: 2011.

The Ottomans made the newly conquered territories into an independent wilayah of Kefe. It was administered by a governor appointed in Istanbul and not subordinated to the khan in any way. The wilayah also included Kerch in the east of the Crimea and the fortress of Azov, built in 1471 (near the ancient city of Tanaïs) in the delta of the Don.[154] Between 1699 and 1706, the Ottomans secured the strategically important Kerch Strait by building the Yeni-Kale fortress.[155]

In the late autumn of 1477, the leading clans of the Crimea appealed to Ottoman Sultan Mehmed II to dethrone Nur Devlet, who ruled since 1476 as a puppet khan of the Great Horde, and to install Mengli Giray I again. The sultan dispatched his fleet, which put Mengli Giray in place as an Ottoman vassal in early 1478. The khan was obliged 'to be the enemy of the enemy and the friend of the friend [of the sultan], to contribute troops when the sultan called for them, and pay tribute gifts'.[156] The khan thus had to align his foreign policy with that of the Ottomans. Otherwise, he retained his sovereignty and was allowed to mint his own coins and levy tributes from Moscow, Poland-Lithuania and the Nogai. He also received extensive subsidies from Istanbul. From this point forward, three axes determined the fate of the Crimea: the khan, the leaders of the powerful tribes, and the Sublime Porte. Also, the economic potential of the khan and his khanate were limited because the south coast and the lucrative trade were under Ottoman control and the clans held many of the fertile pastures and farmlands. The Crimean economy depended on the tributes from Poland-Lithuania and Moscow (the latter were only rescinded under Tsar Peter with the Treaty of Constantinople in 1700), the Ottoman subsidies, and especially the kidnapping and sale of Christian slaves from the Danubian principalities, Poland-Lithuania, Russia and the north-western Caucasus. The khan and tribal leaders undertook annual military campaigns for the purpose of kidnapping. Of the abductees, those of higher social standing were released in exchange for high ransoms, which was a heavy burden on the state coffers of Moscow and Poland. The rest were sold on the Ottoman slave markets, which slowed down Muscovy's population growth.[157] The economic model of the Crimea was distinctly predatory in nature. When Poland and Russia became stronger towards the end of the seventeenth century and ceased paying tribute, the khanate lost its main source of income. This heralded its decline.[158] From the perspective of Istanbul, the Crimea served as a buffer state against the north and as a profitable supplier of slaves. From the Russian point of view, the Crimea constituted a check on further economic growth. Its strong cavalry not only extorted tributes and ransom payments, but they also blocked the

nonetheless had to pay tributes to the Sultan from then on.[153] In return, the Genoese of Caffa induced some clans to depose Hajji Giray in favour of his son **Haydar Khan** (r. 1456). Hajji Giray, however, very soon took back power. Upon the death of Hajji Giray around 1466, a twelve-year power struggle broke out between his eldest son **Nur Devlet** (r. 1466–68, 1469–71, 1474/75, 1476–78) and his sixth son **Mengli Giray I** (r. 1468/69, 1471–74, 1475, 1478–1514). It was only finally settled when the Ottoman military intervened on behalf of Mengli Giray. Three years earlier, the Ottomans had used a powerful fleet to transform the Black Sea into an Ottoman lake. In 1475, they first conquered the Genoese outposts on the southern coast of Crimea like Caffa, Soldaia (Sudak) and Cembalo (Balaclava), and then subjugated the Principality of Theodoro, also known as Gothia, and seized its port Kalamita (today's Inkerman).

economic use of the lower reaches of the Don River, as well as the immigration into today's Eastern Ukraine and the development of its fertile soil. As historian Alan W. Fisher recognised, Russian agriculture in the sixteenth and seventeenth centuries remained limited to climatically unfavourable northerly zones that required labour-intensive cultivation. This, in turn, necessitated serf labour. This development meant that impoverished peasants and serfs tended to flee to Siberia, either as settlers or hunters.[159]

After Mengli Giray's death, he was succeeded by his son **Mehmed Giray I** (r. 1514–23), who lost his life in the failed attack on Astrakhan, **Ghazi Giray** (r. 1523–24) and **Saadet Giray** (r. 1524–32). The Ottoman Sultan Suleiman I (r. 1520–66) decided to designate the next khan himself, going over the heads of the tribal leaders. He appointed as new khan **Sahib Giray** (r. 1532–51), the former Khan of Kazan. In response, the tribes named **Islam Giray** (r. 1532–34) as an alternative khan; however Sahib Giray defeated him two years later.[160] Sahib Giray's attack on Moscow in 1541 had convinced the young Tsar Ivan IV to dissolve the Khanate of Kazan, which

was often governed by the Crimean Tatars. As for the Palace of Bakhchisarai in south-west Crimea (fig. 26), although an inscription on the 'golden gate' indicates 1503 as the founding year, it is suspected that it was Sahib Giray who moved the capital here from Solkhat and had a palace built, after 1533.[161] The next ruler **Devlet Giray** (r. 1551–77) was the last khan to enjoy a relatively high degree of independence from the Sublime Porte. He thus undermined the Ottoman campaign of 1569 to capture Astrakhan, preferring instead to attack Moscow in 1571 and 1572 and reap a rich 'harvest' of slaves.

Under the khans **Mehmed Giray II** (r. 1577–84) and **Islam Giray II** (1584–88), an era of greater dependence on the Ottoman Sultan began. There was a realignment in foreign policy. These khans and their successor **Ghazi Giray II** (1588–96, 1596–1608) and the four-time sovereign **Selim Giray I** (r. 1671–78, 1684–91, 1692–99 and 1702–4) pursued fewer military expeditions to the north. On the other hand, there was an increase in the number of campaigns to the south in the Caucasus and Iran and to the south-west in the

27. The south-eastern gate of the Ottoman fortress, Yeni-Kale, which was built with the help of French engineers from 1699 to 1706. Since the waterway in the Cimmerian Bosphorus, i.e. the Kerch Strait, was very close to the western shoreline during this time, the Turkish artillery was able to control the strait until 1771. Photo: 2011.

Lower Danube territories and, on Ottoman orders, against Anatolia's Jelali rebels. By the same token, the khans' loss of authority caused the tribal leaders to undertake unauthorised incursions into today's Ukraine and against southern Russia, where they clashed with semi-autonomous groups of Cossacks. The period of relative prosperity under Ottoman sovereignty ended with the Ottoman defeat in the Great Turkish War of 1683–99 against a Habsburg-led coalition also involving Poland and Russia. The Ottomans were not only forced in the Peace of Karlowitz from 1699 to cede large territories to Habsburg and Venice, but in the Treaty of Constantinople from 1700 they also had to recognise the loss of the fortress of Azov which Tsar Peter had captured in 1696.[162] After Prince Vasily Golitsyn's two failed campaigns against the Crimea in 1687 and 1689 – in which he was defeated in each case by the Crimean Tatar cavalry personally led by Selim Giray – the Russian conquest of Azov represented a geopolitical turning point.[163] Russia now had a naval base on the Azov Sea and could attack the khanate on its north-eastern coast. However, the Ottomans were able to maintain the Yeni-Kale fortress until 1771 and – in tandem with fleet support – to prevent Russian warships from passing the Kerch Strait and entering the Black Sea.

In the eighteenth century, no less than 20 different khans in 31 periods of rule split up the remaining 83 years of Crimean Tatar independence. They were repeatedly enthroned and dethroned by the Ottoman Sultan. In the first three decades of the eighteenth century, the Crimea was fortunate in that Tsar Peter was preoccupied in the west with the Second Northern War (1700–21) and that after his death in 1725 civil unrest broke out in Russia. But after Tsarina Anna (r. 1730–40) had stabilised her rule thanks to the support of the boyars, she approved the plan of the German-born Count Burkhard Christoph von Münnich to eliminate Crimea's status as an independent state. Beginning in 1736, his troops broke through the Tatar defence at the Isthmus of Perekop and set the capital Bakhchisarai on fire. The greatly weakened khanate was rescued by supply difficulties on the part of the Russians and the outbreak of an epidemic in the Russian army, which then had to retreat. Khans **Mengli Giray II** (r. 1724–30, 1737–40) and **Selamet Giray II** (r. 1740–43) – who succeeded the deposed Khan **Kaplan Giray I** (r. 1730–36) and Khan **Fatih Giray II** (r. 1736–37) – realised that Crimea had to orient itself economically and politically towards Russia in view of the Ottomans' chronic weakness. Tsarina Elizabeth (r. 1741–62) recognised the enormous strategic benefit to Russia if it possessed a warm-water port: a protectorate in the Crimea would open up access for Russia to the Mediterranean. She thus opened a consulate in Bakhchisarai, from where the Russian consul could monitor and direct the Crimean policy.[164]

At the beginning of 1765, Khan **Selim Giray III** (r. 1765–67, 1770–71, 1778) dared to close the Russian consulate. The Russian-Turkish War (1768–74) broke out soon thereafter, and the Ottoman fleet was destroyed in the Battle of Çeşme in 1770. This Ottoman defeat was devastating for Crimea, because the Yedisan-Nogai, who lived on the Black Sea coast between the Dnieper and Dniester rivers and were nominal subjects of Crimea, placed themselves under the protection of Russia. Russia now controlled southern Ukraine and severed the land connecting the Ottoman Empire and Crimea. The Crimea's only connection to the Sublime Porte was by sea, but the Ottomans no longer had a significant fleet.[165] This political and geographical isolation of Crimea offered Tsarina Catherine II (r. 1762–93) the opportunity to occupy the Crimea from 1771 to 1783 by means of four campaigns and to annex it in April 1783. The last khan **Sahin Giray** (r. intermittently 1777–83) was executed in 1787 as a potential troublemaker while in Ottoman exile.[166]

The Russian incorporation of the last successor state of the Golden Horde and the southern Ukraine was more than the conclusion of a 400-year effort on the part of Moscow, as a descendant of orthodox Kiev, to acquire the former territories of Kievan Rus and to gain a warm-water port. It also served as a base for the imperial vision of a conquest of Constantinople and unimpeded access to the Mediterranean via the Bosphorus and the Dardanelles. Russia began to set its sights on this new geopolitical goal in the late eighteenth century with the strategy of advancing into the southern Caucasus and, at the same time, of neutralising Persia. This geostrategic goal, whose realisation the British opposed with increasing determination, guided the policy of the Russian Empire until its demise in 1917. The clashes between the world's largest land power, Russia, and the world's mightiest naval power, Britain – subsumed under the name 'the Great Game' – had a critical impact on the history of Central Asia.[167]

II

The Descendants of the Timurids: the Dynasty of the Mughal in India and Afghanistan

'Therefore I thought good at present to advertise Your Highness [Mughal Emperor Jahangir] that if it shall please you to have a care of your subjects and their goods, that you would bee pleased to send to the Kinges Majestie of England to entreate of peace, before hee send his armadas and men of warre to be revenged of the wronges that to His Majestie and his subjects hath been offred within your dominions unjusttlie.'

A threatening letter from sea captain **SIR HENRY MIDDLETON** (d. 1613) to Emperor Jahangir dated 18 May 1612, requesting his recognition of the East India Company's rights to establish a commercial branch at the harbour of Surat.[1]

28. The mausoleum in Delhi, India, completed in 1571 for the second emperor of the Mughal Humayum (r. 1530–40, 1555–56). Constructed without minarets, the mausoleum stands in the middle of the Chahar Bagh garden, which is divided by four water channels. The architects Mirak Sayyid Gyath-al-Din and his son Sayyid Muhammad, who originated from Herat, combined Central Asian-Timurid and Persian architectural elements, establishing the basic forms of the grand architectural style of the Mughal.[2] Photo: 2005.

1. The Build-up of the Empire: from Babur to Akbar

Just as the Crimean Tatar dynasty of the Giray lasted for centuries due to the extraordinary prestige of their progenitor Genghis Khan outside of Central Asia, the dynasty of the Mughal also survived for several hundred years. The dynasty founder **Zahir al-Din Muhammad** (r. as Mughal 1526–30), called **Babur** ('tiger'), descended from Genghis Khan on his mother's side and from Timur-e Lang on his father's side.[2] Like his cousin Mirza Muhammad Haidar, Babur was not only a military leader, but also a historian. He wrote a detailed autobiography, *Bāburnāma,* in the Turkic language Chagatai.[3] Babur, who was born in 1483 in Andijan, Fergana, led an erratic existence on both sides of the Hindu Kush: he was both refugee and conqueror and sparked a cultural transfer from Central Asia to India. The refined Babur was completely rooted in the Perso-Timurid culture, its architecture and literature, and also brought it with him to India. The contact and exchange with Central Asia persisted for as long as his descendants were able to hold on to the cities in southern Afghanistan like Kabul and Kandahar, which were influenced by the Timurid culture.

Babur was the great-great-grandson of the Timurid dynasty founder, Timur-e Lang (r. 1370–1405), and his last descendant in Samarkand (r. 1497, 1500/01, 1511/12). Babur conquered and lost Samarkand three times: first in 1497, when a revolt broke out in his power base Andijan, to where he was forced to return; then, in 1501, to the Uzbek Shaybani Khan; and, finally in 1512, when he succumbed to the Uzbek military leader Ubayd Allah in the battle at Kul-i-Malik near Bukhara. He stayed for two years north of the Hindu Kush and bided his time, before returning to Kabul in 1514.[4] Babur had already conquered the cities of Kabul and Ghazni in 1504, which he developed into his new, second power base.[5] As Babur had determined, four passes led from Kabul to the plains of India. In January 1505, he undertook a first looting expedition to Peshawar and from there to Multan.[6] Then, Babur entered into an alliance with the Timurid Sultan Husayn Bayqara (r. 1469–1506), the ruler of Herat, to organise a united defence against their common enemy Shaybani Khan. But Babur's initiative showed no results because Husayn Bayqara died shortly afterwards. This led to the mutual paralysis of the joint government of his two warring sons, Badi al-Zaman Mirza and Mirza Muzaffar Hussain. In this context, the contemporary historian Khwandamir cited the proverb that 'two swords cannot fit into one scabbard'.[7] Balkh fell when the brothers, fearing a third brother residing in Mashhad, refused to rush to the

city's aid after it was besieged by Shaybani Khan. Babur realised that the threatened city of Herat was also lost. He returned to Kabul, prompting Shaybani Khan to capture Herat and Mashhad in 1507 and 1508, respectively.[8] Babur was now the last ruling Timurid.

After his return to Kabul in 1514, Babur decided to turn once and for all to India. He prepared carefully for his mission by setting up a new army, which consisted of Afghans, Persians and Turko-Mongols, who had fled with him. Babur's military genius was that he did not simply depend on heavy and light cavalry – the traditional armed branches of Turko-Mongolian steppe warriors – but also tried to acquire and utilise firearms in a modern fashion. Impressed by the resounding victory at Chaldiran of the Ottoman Sultan Selim I over the Safavid and former patron of Babur, Ismail I, in 1514, Babur asked Selim for cannon foundry and artillery experts, which he also received. Babur mentions two of them in his memoirs: Ustad Ali Kuli and 'Mutafa Rumi [the Ottoman], the cannoneer'.[9] Babur had these specialists build several gun types: heavy mortars mounted on a four-wheeled cart (*kazan*); lighter field guns and culverins mounted on a two-wheeled carriage (*zarbzan*); and light swivel guns mounted on a revolving base. Babur also adopted the Ottoman operational doctrine concerning firearms. The artillery stood behind an obstacle such as interconnected wagons, or the guns were bundled together themselves, and it was protected by infantrymen armed with matchlock rifles, standing just behind and to the side. The cavalry, armed with bows and arrows and sabres, waited on the flanks to surround the enemy, which was bewildered by the cannon fire. Once the cavalry attacked the enemy on the flanks, the rifle-carrying infantry also moved up, so that the enemy found itself surrounded on all three sides.[10] After Selim, Babur was the second ruler of Asia not only to use cannons statically for siege purposes, but to manoeuvre them in pitched battles.

After several smaller campaigns in the Punjab, Babur received invitations around the end of 1523 from Daulat Khan Lodi, the rebellious governor of Punjab, and the Hindu Prince of Mewar in the current province of Rajasthan, to topple the despised Sultan Ibrahim Lodi (r. 1517–26). Ibrahim originated from the Pashtun (i.e. southern Afghanistan) Lodi dynasty.[11] Babur's relatively small army with its 12,000 soldiers crossed the Indus in December 1525 and on 21 April 1526, in the First Battle of Panipat north of Delhi, destroyed the 40,000-strong force of Ibrahim Lodi, which had 100 war elephants and an additional 60,000 followers. Ibrahim died in battle. The victorious Babur positioned his army as follows: 'I directed that, according to the custom of Rûm [the Ottomans], the gun-carriages should be connected together with twisted bull-hides or with chains. Between every two gun carriages were six or seven *tûras*, breast-works. The matchlock-men stood behind these guns [and cannons] and *tûras*, and discharged their matchlocks.'[12] Babur further reported that he had lined up his army so that the suburbs of the city of Panipat were on his right. To protect his left flank, he had trenches dug. This funnel-shaped formation forced Ibrahim Lodi to attack head-on and to expose his troops to the lethal fire of the enemy artillery. Babur's cavalry encircled Lodi's army.[13] Babur then occupied Delhi and Agra, which he chose for his formal capital, and laid the foundation for the **Mughal** dynasty (1526–1858), as the Mongols were called in Persian. In the following year, Babur used the same strategy to defeat the rebellious Rajput ruler of Mewar named Rana Sangha in the Battle of Khanwa. Like his great-great-grandfather Timur-e Lang, Babur built a macabre memorial: 'On this hillock, I directed a tower of the skulls of the Infidels to be constructed.'[14]

Babur's empire stretched from southern Afghanistan in the west to Bihar in the east and Kabul in the north to Mewar (central India) in the south. However, just as Babur established the Mughal Empire, which was later similar in size to the realms of the Safavids and Ottomans, a development began that would fundamentally change the balance of power in Asia in the centuries that followed. The Western European maritime powers arrived on the scene, and, due to their mobility and technological superiority, as well as a novel, quasi-state concept of rule, soon put the sovereignty of Asian countries in question. After the Portuguese explorer Vasco da Gama landed in Calicut in 1498, the second Portuguese governor Afonso de Albuquerque (in office 1509–15) captured the port city of Goa and its hinterland. It remained in Portuguese hands until 1961. The English East India Company, founded in 1600, followed the Portuguese. In the small but important Battle of Swally near Surat, Gujarat, the main port city of the Mughal Empire, it won a decisive victory over the Portuguese in 1612. This marked the beginning of the British Indian colonial empire. The ships of the Dutch East India Company, founded in 1602, used Surat from about 1608 as a transit port on the way to Java. English ships also began to dock at Surat around 1608.[15] The English East India Company opened its first independent trading post on the Indian subcontinent in 1611 in the port city of Machilipatnam on the south-east coast, where their Dutch competition had been active since 1606. In the years 1616–19 English warships demonstrated their superiority in two battles against the Portuguese and Sir Henry Middleton attacked foreign merchant ships in the Red Sea. After this the English ambassador Sir Thomas Roe obtained the concession to establish an exclusive commercial settlement in Surat from the fourth Mughal

Emperor Jahangir (r. 1605–27). Further settlements followed in Madras in 1639, in Bombay in 1668, and in Calcutta in 1690.[16] These foreign trading posts were not limited to trade, but also organised the production of textiles on Indian soil. These textiles were intended for export to Europe, and the East India Company even had a monopoly on this trade. But the Mughal Empire remained purely a land power, in contrast to the Ottomans, despite its thousands of kilometres of coastline. Therefore, it was hardly in a position to oppose the Europeans' armed trade companies. As a result of the slow, continuous progress of the East India Company to the interior and of the political fragmentation of the subcontinent, the dominion of the Mughal emperors shrank at the beginning of the nineteenth century to their royal seat, the Red Fort in Delhi.

In the four years that remained to him, Babur travelled constantly to consolidate his new empire, which is why the government and court were located at the same place as his camp. Since Babur planned to go back and forth between the large and strategically important cities, he laid spacious gardens there to serve as campsites. In Kabul alone he created ten gardens. Several of Babur's gardens and those of his successors corresponded to the Perso-Timurid type of a Chahar Bagh, a quadrilateral garden with two intersecting axes. These axes formed four channels arranged at right angles, emanating from a pool of water in the centre of the compound. Babur ascribed great importance to such gardens, which he designed himself: 'It always appeared to me, that one of the chief defects of Hindustân is the want of artificial watercourses. I had intended, wherever I might fix my residence, to construct water-wheels, to produce an artificial stream, and to lay out an elegant and regularly planned pleasure-ground.' After describing the Chahar Bagh of Agra, whose construction began in 1526, Babur observed: 'I, however, produced edifices and gardens which possessed considerable regularity.'[17] Such geometrically arranged gardens were often part of the grave sites of the Mughal rulers, as, for example, at the mausoleum of Humayum in Delhi (built *ca.* 1562–71, fig. 28); at the mausoleums of Akbar in Sikandra near Agra (*ca.* 1605–13), of Itimad al-Daula in Agra (*ca.* 1622–28), and of Jahangir in Lahore (*ca.* 1627–37); at the Taj Mahal in Agra (*ca.* 1632–43; fig. 32); and at the grave of Bibi Ka Maqbara in Aurangabad (*ca.* 1753–54). These Chahar Bagh gardens, which were located in front of or around a mausoleum, probably symbolised Paradise: the four channels hinted at Paradise's four rivers,[18] and the central, slightly raised water tank, at Paradise's abundance. The mausoleum itself can be understood as the throne of God on the Day of Resurrection, and, in the case of the Taj Mahal, the minarets as its four supporting columns.[19]

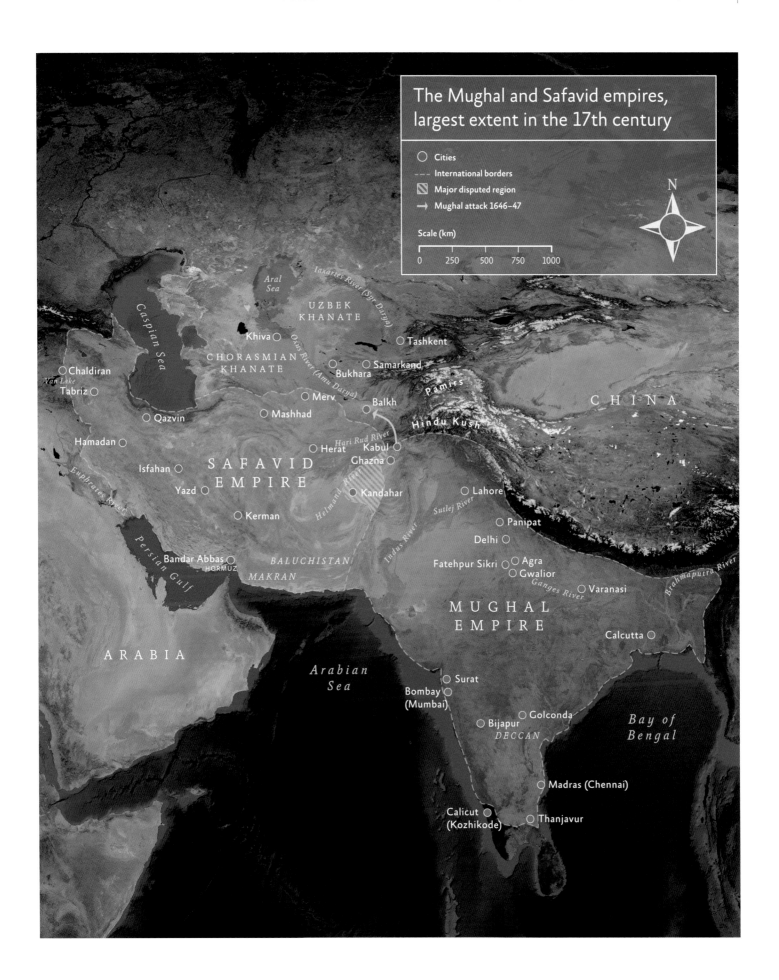

The Mughal and Safavid empires, largest extent in the 17th century

○ Cities
--- International borders
▨ Major disputed region
→ Mughal attack 1646–47

Scale (km)
0   250   500   750   1000

N

Aral Sea

UZBEK KHANATE

Caspian Sea

Iaxartes River (Syr Darya)

Khiva ○
Oxus River (Amu Darya)

○ Tashkent

CHORASMIAN KHANATE

○ Samarkand

Bukhara ○

○ Chaldiran
Van Lake
Tabriz ○

Merv ○

Balkh ○

Pamirs

CHINA

○ Mashhad

Hindu Kush

Hamadan ○

Hari Rud River

○ Herat Kabul ○
Ghazna ○

Isfahan ○

SAFAVID EMPIRE

Helmand River

○ Kandahar

○ Lahore

Sutlej River

Qazvin ○

Yazd ○

○ Kerman

Euphrates River

Persian Gulf

Bandar Abbas ○
HORMUZ

BALUCHISTAN
MAKRAN

Indus River

○ Panipat

Delhi ○

Fatehpur Sikri ○ ○ Agra
○ Gwalior
Ganges River ○ Varanasi

MUGHAL EMPIRE

Brahmaputra River

Calcutta ○

ARABIA

Arabian Sea

Surat ○
Bombay ○
(Mumbai)

Bijapur ○ ○ Golconda
DECCAN

Bay of Bengal

Madras (Chennai) ○

Calicut ○
(Kozhikode) ○ Thanjavur

29. Resting on a mountain ridge, Gwalior Fort is located in Madhya Pradesh, India, south of Agra; it was seized by Emperor Babur in 1527 and Emperor Akbar in 1558.[3] Photo: 2006.

Babur's son and successor **Humayum** (r. 1530–40, 1555–56) inherited a still unconsolidated empire. In the east, Afghan commanders waited for the opportunity to restore the rule of the Pashtun Lodi; within the empire, Humayum was the victim of the Timurid government system, in which a realm was divided into more or less autonomous appanages. The four brothers of Humayum thus possessed important regions: Sulaiman had Badakhshan, Kamran had Kabul and Kandahar, and Askari and Hindal had large tracts of land at their disposal in Punjab. In 1537, Hindal made an unsuccessful coup attempt. All four brothers challenged Humayum's authority more or less openly and denied him any access to the resources and commercial revenues of Punjab and Afghanistan. In the years 1539 and 1540, the Afghan Sher Khan (d. 1545) attacked Humayum from his power base of Bihar, dealing him two crushing defeats. Humayum fled to Lahore and continued on to Herat, which belonged to the Safavids. At the same time, he left all of northern India to Sher Khan, who established the short-lived Sur dynasty (1540–55). After Humayum had converted to Shia under pressure from the Persian Shah Tahmasp,

the latter provided him with Persian troops. Thanks to the Persian support, Humayum managed to prevail in the eight-year fratricidal war against Kamran and to occupy Kabul in 1553. When a succession dispute broke out the following year between the sons of Islam Shah Suri (d. 1554), Sher Khan's successor, Humayum sent his general Bairam Khan, who defeated the Afghans and put Humayum on the throne in the summer of 1555. A short time later, Humayum took a fall in his library in Delhi and died.[20]

Unlike Humayum, his son and successor **Akbar** (r. 1556–1605) was an excellent general, a cunning diplomat, and a far-sighted planner. First, Humayum's general Bairam Khan took over the regency for the just thirteen-year-old emperor. On 5 November 1556, he secured the continuation of the dynasty in the Second Battle of Panipat, when he defeated the superior army of the rebellious Hindu general Hemu, who called himself Vikramaditya.[21] In the years 1557–58, Bairam Khan subjugated Ajmer, Lahore and Multan in the west, Gwalior in the south, and Jaunpur in the east. In 1560, the now-adult Akbar exploited the dislike of his Sunni circles for the Shiite prime minister Bairam Khan, and forced his abdication. Bairam Khan was assassinated soon thereafter. One of Akbar's greatest achievements was to build a close-knit, centrally managed administration, headed by four ministers who were responsible for revenue and finance, military and intelligence, judicial and religious matters, as well as public buildings and the imperial court. The same structures were built in each province, where the provincial governor stood directly under the emperor. In order to keep the finances under control, each administrative unit had to report its balance twice a month in writing.[22] Finally, Akbar created a new nobility to reduce the influence of the commanders and nobles originating from Central Asia, who were inclined to revolt. Also, to minimise the gulf between the Muslim conquerors and Hindu subjects, he allowed Hindus, and especially the Rajputs, to join a new military aristocracy. For the same reason, in 1579 he abolished the Jiziya, a special wealth tax imposed on all non-Muslims.[23] Akbar laid the foundation for an empire that later nearly united the entire Indian subcontinent in 1700 and numbered around 135 million people – a tremendous achievement for a small

community originating from Central Asia. Akbar's empire was by no means inferior to the 1,500-year-older empire of the Kushans, who also came from Central Asia.[24]

In keeping with the Timurid tradition of magnificent architecture, Akbar emulated his illustrious ancestors Timur-e Lang, Shah Rukh and Ulugh Beg by ordering the construction of the new capital Fatehpur Sikri, 30 km south-west of Agra, in 1570. His contemporary biographer Arif Kandahari confirmed that Akbar was driven by the same expectation as his ancestor Timur-e Lang,[25] who thought that monumental architecture should reflect the greatness of the ruler: 'Through majestic buildings a king establishes a reputation … That is, the worth of their buildings suggests the size of the men and the grandeur of their buildings the state of the royal house.'[26] As the building site, Akbar decided on the village of Sikri, where Sheikh Salim Chishti (d. 1572) from the moderate Sufi Order of Chishtiyya lived. It was Chishti who had foretold the birth of Akbar's first son Salim, the future Emperor Jahangir. Sikri's nickname Fatehpur, 'City of Victory', recalled Akbar's conquest of

30. On the right of the image stands the Diwan-i-Khas in the city of Fatehpur Sikri, the private audience chamber of Emperor Akbar, built from 1570 to 1582; on the left is the Ankh Micholi Treasury; Uttar Pradesh, India. Photo: 2005.

Gujarat.[27] The association of his person with the most popular Sufi order underlined Akbar's adherence to Islam. In 1571, Akbar moved to his capital (still under construction). He left fourteen years later, however, in favour of Lahore due to problems with the water supply and the uncertain political situation in Rajputana (Rajasthan) and at the border with the Uzbek Khanate of Bukhara. Akbar's reverence for Sheikh Salim did not prevent him, though, from introducing a sun cult at his court in the 1580s, aimed at deifying the monarch. He gathered a small circle of nobles around himself who swore their unquestioning obedience to him, as disciples to their master. Together, they introduced rituals honouring the sun and light that Akbar designed himself.[28] Finally, the members of this chosen group even worshipped the deified emperor himself, which was blasphemous in an Islamic context.

In 1585, Akbar moved to Lahore because of the looming threat from the north-west.[29] A year earlier, the Uzbek Abdullah Khan had occupied Badakhshan. Then, Akbar's half-brother Mirza Muhammad Hakim had died in 1585; he had ruled in Kabul independently for 29 years and Akbar had to drive him out of Lahore in 1566. To prevent Abdullah Khan from taking advantage of the resulting power vacuum in Kabul, Akbar ordered Kabul to be quickly occupied. As a result, he secured the control of trade with Central Asia all the way to the Hindu Kush, along with the vital supply of horses for the army. After the city of Kandahar, which had belonged to Persia, put itself under Akbar's protection in 1595, Abdullah recognised the Hindu Kush as a border to the Mughal. Since the Persian Shah Abbas I (r. 1587–1629) was preoccupied with consolidating his power, he did not react immediately to this disloyalty and waited for a favourable opportunity to regain Kandahar without risking a war with the Mughal. This opportunity arose when Akbar's opium-addicted successor, Jahangir, became seriously ill in 1620, and the inner circle of power vied to take control. In March 1622, Shah Abbas recaptured Kandahar. When Abdullah Khan died in 1598 and power struggles broke out in Bukhara, the situation on the north-west border of the empire calmed to such an extent that Akbar left Lahore and moved his court to Agra.[30] It is also possible that the ongoing conflict with his eldest son Salim persuaded Akbar to return to the centre of the empire. Salim in fact rebelled in 1600 and 1602, whereupon Akbar put him under house arrest in Agra. On his deathbed – despite everything – Akbar appointed Salim his successor.[31]

2. Stagnation and Decline: from Jahangir to Bahadur Shah II

During Akbar's final days, his son Salim – who named himself **Jahangir**, 'world conqueror' (r. 1605–27) – nearly lost his throne to his own rebellious son Khusrau, who instigated a first insurrection among the nobles. In the following two years, Khusrau also attempted an armed uprising. In suppressing the revolt, Jahangir impaled the captured followers of his son right before his son's eyes. Khusrau then organised an assassination plot against his father. Jahangir was warned in time, however, and had his treacherous son blinded.[32] As Jahangir discovered again in 1622/23, and his son Shah Jahan would learn later, the militarily capable adult sons of Mughal emperors were a serious threat to their ruling fathers, which often led to open-ended wars. The fact that these brutal power struggles did not permanently damage the empire speaks to the quality of the administrative structures that Akbar established. The adage about the Roman Empire, that it was so strong that it could even survive bad emperors, was also true for the Mughal Empire until the beginning of the eighteenth century. In the case of Jahangir, one could add that the empire also withstood drug-addicted emperors. Jahangir was a serious opium addict and alcoholic. He soon left government affairs to four individuals from his immediate circle: his wife Nur Jahan, whom he married in 1611, her father Itimad al-Daula, his brother-in-law Asaf Khan and crown prince Kamran, the future emperor Shah Jahan. The crucial position of Nur Jahan was also expressed by the silver rupees that she had minted: Jahangir's titles could of course be read on the front, but on the back was the inscription 'minted on behalf of the Queen Begum, Nur Jahan'.[33] When Jahangir fell dangerously ill in 1620, Nur Jahan tried to seize power completely. She had Jahangir's youngest son Shahryar married to her own daughter from a previous marriage in order to position herself as regent in the event of a future birth of a son. These and other intrigues failed, however. Following the death of Jahangir, vizier Asaf Khan took sides with crown prince Kamran and turned against his sister. He put Nur Jahan under house arrest, ordered the execution of Shahryar and in January 1628 set Kamran on the throne as Emperor Shah Jahan. His name means 'king of the world'.

Jahangir was less active as an originator of monumental buildings, even if he finished the mausoleum of his father in Sikandra at Agra and created some splendid gardens, such as the Shalimar Bagh in Srinagar, Kashmir. In fact, he was an expert in and promoter of miniature painting. The art of elaborate books, written in fine

31. Emperor Jahangir, whose head is encircled by a luminous aureole, sits on a throne in the shape of an hourglass. He hands Sheikh Husayn Chishti a book and ignores the three smaller figures standing before the hourglass: an Ottoman Sultan, King James I of England and VI of Scotland, and the painter Bichitr himself, who produced the painting around 1616–20. The image symbolises Jahangir's understanding that all creation is transitory and his devotion to the spiritual world of the Sufi orders. Opaque watercolour, ink, and gold on paper. Freer Gallery of Art and Arthur M. Sackler Gallery, Smithsonian Institute, Washington DC. Purchase Charles Lang Freer Endowment, F1942.15a.

calligraphy and decorated with exquisite miniature paintings, were especially favoured by the Timurids – the much-admired ancestors of the Mughal – since the times of Shah Rukh, Gyath al-Din Baysunghur and Ulugh Beg.[34] Babur was himself not only a historian, but also a calligrapher who developed his own writing – *khatt-i baburi* – around 1504/05.[35] When Humayum, who owned a large library, returned to Delhi in 1555, he brought Persian miniature painters and calligraphers with him in his entourage, and they then trained local artists. Akbar's library reportedly counted 24,000 volumes. He promoted illustrated books that represented the Islamic traditions and stories such as the *Hamza nameh*, which includes the stories of Hamza, the uncle of the Prophet Muhammad, and Persian translations of Hindu epics like the *Ramayama* or *Ramzenameh*, the 'Book of Wars'. There were also dynastic chronicles, in which the ruler was the focal point, as in the illustrated *Babur nameh* and the *Akbar nameh*. Here, the realistic reproduction of portraits was central. When Akbar organised theological debates to be held in Fatehpur Sikri, which were not only attended by Islamic theologians, but also representatives of the Hindus, Parsi and Jains, he invited three Jesuits from Goa called Monserrate, Henriques and Aqua Viva, who stayed at his court in 1580–82.[36] They brought as gifts a multilingual illustrated bible,[37] small paintings, engravings, and altar paraphernalia. Many of the biblical images such as depictions of the Madonna and Child were then copied by court artists in the Mughal style.[38] Under Jahangir, portraiture and depictions of nature that were incorporated in large albums gained in prominence. Jahangir was fascinated by Akbar's collection of European paintings and dedicated to expanding it. The English paintings brought by the English ambassador Sir Thomas Roe in 1616 gave further impetus to Mughal portrait painting. In a famous allegorical painting from Bichitr from *ca.* 1616–20, the larger-than-life Jahangir, whose head is surrounded by a luminous halo, sits on an hourglass, which serves as his throne. He hands over a book to the venerable-looking Sheikh Husayn Chishti, while he ignores three smaller figures cowering before the throne. They are an Ottoman sultan, King James I of England and VI of Scotland, and the painter Bichitr himself (fig. 31). The painting illustrates how Jahangir, aware of the transience of all created things, including himself, turns away from earthly power and the world toward the spiritual realm.[39] Painting under

Jahangir's successor Shah Jahan lost its joy in experimentation and began to ossify into specified forms, and the orthodox Islamic Emperor Aurangzeb stopped promoting illustrated chronicles and closed the imperial scriptoria and painting studios.[40]

Under **Shah Jahan** (r. 1628–58, d. 1666) a counter-movement arose against the liberal attitude of his predecessors Akbar and Jahangir in religious matters. The new emperor promoted Naqshbandi, which was dominant in Central Asia Sufi orders, and Muslim orthodoxy, as taught by the four accepted legal schools of Sunni Islam. From 1633, he intensified religious repression and issued laws to regulate the construction and repair of temples and churches.[41] In terms of foreign policy, Shah Jahan undertook the last attempt by the Mughal to reclaim the ancestral homeland of the Timurids north of the Hindu Kush. The opportunity presented itself in the mid-1640s, when the Uzbek Abd al-Aziz forced his father Nazr Muhammad Khan to abdicate and the latter appealed to Shah Jahan for support. He sent an expeditionary force under the direction of his son Murad with a mandate to either once again enthrone as khan Nazr, as a vassal of the Mughal, or to annex the khanate. While Murad managed to occupy the city of Balkh in the summer of 1646 and to plunder the state treasury, the prince felt overwhelmed and returned to India. Shah Jahan then sent his war-tested second son Aurangzeb to Balkh. But even Aurangzeb was unable to contain the Uzbek-Afghan guerrillas led by Nazr, who had fled from his supposed allies. After negotiations with Aurangzeb, the latter withdrew with heavy losses to Kabul, while Nazr only nominally recognised the supremacy of the Mughal.[42] In the war against the Safavids over Kandahar, Shah Jahan was also denied a victory. The city, conquered in 1622 by Shah Abbas, actually fell to the Mughal in 1638 due to the treachery of the Persian governor. This, in turn, gave the Mughal control of the two 'gateways to India', Kabul and Kandahar, for the last time. Shah Abbas II. (r.1642–66), however, exploited the failure of the Mughal in northern Afghanistan by recapturing Kandahar in a daring winter campaign in 1648/49. In the years 1649, 1652 and 1653, the emperor launched three major campaigns against Kandahar. All failed miserably. Kandahar remained in Persian hands until 1709.[43] Jahangir and Shah Jahan were now paying the price for not being interested in infantry firearms and guns, unlike Babur and Akbar. They had wantonly neglected their further development and left the production to European and Ottoman emigrants. The former, however, were often deserters from European ships and garrisons and had only limited technological know-how. As evidenced by the siege of Kandahar, the artillery of the Mughal was no longer competitive by international standards.[44] The lack of interest of the Mughal in the

---

◀ **32. The Taj Mahal in Agra, India, is most likely the work of the Herat architect Ustad (master) Ahmad Lahori (1570/75–1649), who constructed the mausoleum for Shah Jahan's wife Mumtaz Mahal (d. 1631) between 1632 and 1643; the entire complex was completed in 1653.** Photo: 2005.

33. The Badshahi Mosque in Lahore, commissioned by Mughal emperor Aurangzeb (r. 1658–1707), was completed in 1673/74; it is the largest mosque of the Mughal. Photo: 2007.

European development of weapons technology was part of a general unwillingness to look to and learn from the advances in technology, production methods and economic systems in Europe. In fact, the Mughal interest in Europe was primarily limited to painting.

The most lasting legacy of Shah Jahan was architectural in nature. He not only built the mausoleum for his father in Lahore and renewed the fort, but also erected the new capital Shahjahanabad near Delhi from 1639 to 1648. The most significant building was the palace complex, known today as Red Fort. Here stood the famous Peacock Throne that was stolen by Nader Shah in

1739. The other building of particular note was the Friday Mosque completed in 1656, the Jama Masjid. As the largest mosque in India, it served as a counterpoint to the palace (fig. 35). The palace takes its name from the 3-km red sandstone wall surrounding it. The main pavilions were brick structures, whose interior and exterior walls were completely covered with white marble slabs. The pinnacle of the Perso-Indian architecture of the Mughal is undoubtedly the Taj Mahal in Agra. Shah Jahan had it built from 1632 to 1643 for his deceased wife Mumtaz Mahal, who died in childbirth (fig. 32). The fact that the mausoleum was actually conceived as an allegory of Paradise and the Last Day of Resurrection is indicated by the marble-engraved verses from the Qur'an by the Persian calligrapher Abd al-Haqq Shirazi, called Amanat Khan ('Lord of Trust'). These include Sura 89 ('The Dawn'), which concerns the Last Judgement.[45]

When Shah Jahan fell seriously ill in 1657, a violent struggle for power broke out between his four sons Dara Shikoh, Aurangzeb, Shah Shuya and Murad Bakhsh that only one could survive. The French doctor François Bernier, who was in India from 1656 to 1668, witnessed the civil war first hand as the doctor of Dara Shikoh and Aurangzeb. He described the initial situation as follows: 'The four Princes openly declared their settled purpose of making the sword the sole arbiter of their lofty pretensions. It was, in fact, too late to recede: not only was the crown to be gained by victory alone, but in case of defeat life was certain to be forfeited. There was now no choice between a kingdom and death.'[46] The victor Aurangzeb took his father captive in the summer of 1658 and held him in the fort of Agra, under strict house arrest, until his death.[47] According to the Venetian traveller Niccolò Manucci, who lived in India from 1656 to ca. 1717 and served Dara Shikoh as an artilleryman, Aurangzeb did not hesitate to torture his father: as a special 'present', he had the severed head of his father's favourite son Dara Shikoh served to him for dinner.[48]

Aurangzeb (r. 1658–1707), who took the name Alamgir ('conqueror'), was the last Mughal with a link to Central Asia. This became manifest in Aurangzeb's response to the uprising of the Pashtun Afridi between Peshawar and the Khyber Pass in 1672/73. In 1674, the emperor personally led an army into difficult, mountainous terrain where the British in the nineteenth century would suffer several defeats to the same Afridi and other Pashtun tribes, and endeavoured to pacify the region. He then appointed as governor the Persian Amir Khan, who kept the province of Kabul under control until his death in 1698. Domestically, the devout emperor decided in the medium term to transform his realm into an Islamic state. To this end, he promoted leading Muslims and sought to steer the 'infidel' majority, especially the Hindu nobility,

34. The 'Lahore Gate', also known as the 'Amar Singh Gate', is the main entrance to the Red Fort in Agra, India. Emperor Akbar had the original military fort built from 1565–73; it was later reconstructed by Jahangir and Shah Jahan into a palace and expanded. Shah Jahan spent the last eight years of his life here as a prisoner of his son Aurangzeb. Photo: 2005.

35. Shah Jahan had the Masjid-i Jahan Numa (Persian 'World-Reflecting Mosque'), also called the Friday Mosque, built in Delhi from 1644–56. Photo: 2005.

towards conversion through rewarding and repressive measures. The latter included the ordered destruction in 1669 of recently built Hindu temples; the execution of the ninth Nanak (master) of the Sikh, Tegh Bahadur, in November 1675; and the reintroduction of Jiziya, a special tax for non-Muslims, in 1679.[49] Aurangzeb not only saw himself as a champion of Islam, but also as a conqueror in the spirit of his heroic ancestors Babur and Akbar. He devoted the last quarter-century of his rule to the conquest of the Deccan Plateau; that is, central and southern India. He managed to curb the rising power of the Hindu Marathas and to subdue the two sultanates of the Deccan, Bijapur (1685) and Golconda (1687), allowing the Mughal Empire to reach its greatest territorial expansion. Nonetheless, the continuous wars were a heavy burden on the state administration and budget.[50] Aurangzeb's forced Islamisation efforts increasingly alienated previously loyal Hindu nobles and commanders from the empire and his ruling dynasty. Finally, the resistance extended in the face of forced Islamisation to a rejection of the Timurid Empire.

Two incidents announced the coming loss of authority and the empire's decline: in 1687, the rebellious Jats – a predominantly peasant people of semi-nomadic origin, whose members often banded together to form robber gangs – succeeded in taking the suburb of Agra Sikandra. There, they plundered the mausoleum of Akbar and desecrated his remains.[51] Furthermore, Aurangzeb's attempts to crush the growing autonomy of European trading companies, particularly the East India Company, and to avert the dangers posed by European naval blockades and piracy, failed. Between 1686 and 1690, a dispute escalated with the fortified port city of Bombay (present-day Mumbai), which Charles II, King of England and Scotland had obtained as a dowry from the Portuguese in 1661. He subsequently transferred the city to the East India Company, which began to mint its own coins. A war ensued. While Aurangzeb's vassal Siddi Yaqut Khan managed to besiege the island, he could not capture the citadel and drive out the English, as the emperor ordered. As a compromise, the East India Company paid an indemnity, but retained its fortified port.

Similarly unsuccessful were the attacks that Aurangzeb ordered in 1701/02 on the heavily fortified trading post of Madras (Chennai), established by the Company in 1639, and on the French settlement of Pondicherry. In both cases, reparation payments to Aurangzeb's warring vassal halted the conflict in favour of the Europeans.[52] The East India Company had successfully defended its three heavily fortified outposts: Bombay, Madras and Calcutta. Compared to Aurangzeb, the Persian Shah Abbas had had greater success 80 years earlier. In 1622, he actually forced the East India Company to help the small Persian navy to capture the port of Hormuz being held by the Portuguese. Shortly thereafter, Shah Abbas relocated the trade from the island of Hormuz to the neighbouring port city of Bandar Abbas, which he had already wrested from the Portuguese in 1614.[53] The fact that a parastatal trading company, whose head office was more than 13,000 km from India's west coast by ship, could hold its own against the resistance of the Mughal, demonstrated that the latter had two fundamental weaknesses. First, Western European weapons technology was far superior to the Mughals' own. Secondly, a land power with maritime borders, but without a naval force, was virtually defenceless against attacks from modern naval powers. This was a painful experience that India would also endure in the eighteenth century and China in the nineteenth.

In the twelve years from 1707 to 1719, four emperors, whose ascents to the throne were each preceded by bloody fratricidal wars for power, assumed the Peacock Throne. The unity of the empire, which was already fragile under Aurangzeb, broke apart and the provinces claimed their independence. Over the following decades, the former empire degenerated into the prey of aggressive neighbours. In 1737, the Marathas plundered Delhi, and two years later the Persian Nader Shah thoroughly ransacked the city and set it ablaze. Nader Shah's former commander and later ruler of Afghanistan, Ahmad Abdali, then plundered the tormented city again in 1757 and 1761. In September 1803, General Gerard Lake finally occupied Delhi. The last two nominal emperors of the Mughal lived out their lives under British protection at the Red Fort. But when the Indian uprising, also called the Sepoy Mutiny, broke out in May 1857, insurgents put the aged **Bahadur Shah II** (r. 1837–58, d. 1862) at the nominal head of their rebellion. The reconquest of Delhi sealed the end of the uprising, which claimed two prominent victims when all was said and done: the dynasty of the Indian Timurids was abolished, and the East India Company was transformed into a crown colony. Bahadur Shah, who was deported to Rangoon, wrote shortly before his death in 1862:

> 'I am the light of no one's eye
> The balm of no one's heart
> I am of no use anymore
> A handful of dust, that's all.'[54]

A Reorganisation of Geography: North Central Asia Becomes a Periphery

'The construction of a single temple spares the nourishment of one hundred thousand soldiers stationed in Mongolia.'

EMPEROR KANGXI, who purposely promoted Buddhism among the Mongols[1]

36. Erlig-jin Jarghagchi (Vajrabhairava) is a wrathful manifestation of the transcendent Bodhisattva Manjushri. Here, he is represented with 34 arms, 16 legs, and 9 heads, of which the uppermost head represents Manjushri himself. Vajrabhairava is in sexual union with his companion Vidyadhara, who has the third eye in her demonic face. Both deities trample upon various animals and Hindu deities. Thangka painting, nineteenth century, Zanabazar Museum, Ulaan Baatar, Mongolia.

A REORGANISATION OF GEOGRAPHY: NORTH CENTRAL ASIA BECOMES A PERIPHERY

With their withdrawal from China to Mongolia in 1368, the Mongols did not entirely disappear from the historical record, even if their political fragmentation makes it difficult to historically trace certain events.[2] East Central Asia soon became the scene of a battle between Eastern Mongolian Genghis Khanids, Western Mongolian Oirats and the Chinese Ming dynasty, which sought to prevent a reunited Mongolian Empire through any means necessary. In fact, no Mongolian leader ever succeeded again in rallying all the tribes, let alone in seriously threatening the Ming – the sole exception being the Oirat Esen Khan in the autumn of 1449. Around the mid-seventeenth century, two new actors emerged: in the north of Central Asia, Dzungars of Oirat origin created a powerful steppe empire, while Russian Cossacks simultaneously appeared east of Mongolia along the Amur River. This second three-way struggle between the Dzungars, the Chinese dynasty of the Qing of Manchu origin, and Russia ended with the integration of the Eastern Mongols in the Qing's vassal system and the destruction of the Oirat state and people. From about 1760, the northern half of Central Asia became just the peripheral regions of China and Russia.

1. The Legacy of the Yuan: the Western Mongolian Oirats and the Genghis Khanid Eastern Mongols

The last emperor of the Yuan dynasty **Toghon Temür** (r. 1333–68, 1368–70) was also the first of the **Northern Yuan dynasty** (1368–1634). He and his successors regarded themselves as the legitimate successors of Genghis Khan and claimed dominion over all Mongols. The young Chinese dynasty of the Ming (1368–1644) found itself confronted with the question of how to deal with the threat of new Mongol aggression. Over time, they applied three different strategies: first, there was an offensive in which the Chinese armies crossed the Gobi Desert to break the fighting power of the Mongols and to prevent the re-emergence of a united Mongol Empire. At the same time, they tried to pit the Mongols against each other by supporting the respective weaker party in internal Mongol clashes. At the end of the 1420s, the Ming adopted a defensive strategy by setting up larger military garrisons and, from about 1470, by means of the stone construction of the Great Wall. They also established a trade boycott against their northern neighbours, which the latter countered with increased raids in the Chinese border regions. In 1571, the Ming finally abandoned the trade boycott. They won

peace by offering generous gifts to Mongol commanders and began to promote Buddhism among the Mongols.

While Toghon Temür's successor **Ayushiridara** (r. 1370–78) suffered a crushing defeat against the Ming in 1370, his general Kökö Temür scored a resounding victory two years later when the Chinese attacked Karakorum. However, in the west, the Ming succeeded in conquering the oasis city of Khara-Khoto, which traditionally served as a gateway from south-west Gobi to Gansu. They also annexed Gansu, which gave them control over the bottleneck of the Silk Road, the Hexi Corridor. In 1404, the Ming consolidated its supremacy over the Hexi Corridor, as the neighbouring principality of Hami in the west declared itself a Ming vassal. In 1388, Ayushiridara's brother and successor **Tögüs Temür** (r. 1378–88) suffered a crushing and decisive defeat against a strong Chinese army in eastern Mongolia at Buir Lake. This shattered the supremacy of the Northern Yuan and split up the Mongols into Eastern Mongols and Western Mongols. Soon after this defeat, **Yesüder** (r. 1388–92), a descendant of Arik Böge, murdered the fleeing khan and allied himself with the Western Mongolian Oirats.[3] From this point on, the Genghisid khans of Mongolia were little more than puppets of non-Genghisid Eastern Mongol or Oirat leaders; the latter bore the Chinese honorific *tayishi* ('great master'). The home of the Oirat confederation was at the upper reaches of the Yenisei in Tuva and belonged to the forest peoples. Genghis Khan had bequeathed the region to his son Jochi in 1207/08 as an appanage.[4] The first quarter of the fifteenth century was marked by the three-way struggle between the powerful Eastern Mongol Arughtai (d. 1434), the Oirat Mahmud Tayishi (Batula, d. 1416) and his son Toghan Tayishi (d. 1438/39), and the battle-tested Ming emperor Yongle (r. 1402–24), who deliberately moved the capital from Nanjing to Beijing in order to launch military offensives against the Mongols. Both Mongolian parties had puppet khans from the family of Genghis Khan, which they dethroned or murdered as necessary. Khan **Elbeg** (r. 1393–99) was killed by the Oirats and Khan **Gung Temür** (r. 1400–02) by Arughtai. The khans who stood in Arughtai's good graces were **Örüg Temür** (r. 1402–08), **Öljey Temür** (Bunyashiri, r. 1408–12), who had converted to Islam in his previous exile at the court of Timur-e Lang in Samarkand, and **Adai** (r. 1426–38). The khans of the Oirats Mahmud and Toghan were **Delbeg** (r. 1412–14), **Oyiradai** (r. 1415–25) and **Toghtoa Bukha** (r. *ca.* 1438–53).[5]

The fact that no party was able to prevail in Mongolia was the result of the active intervention of the Yongle Emperor. He deliberately weakened the respective stronger faction by supporting the weaker one. He also sowed discord and envy in the camp of the

37. The Great Wall of China near Badaling from the 1570s, about 60 km north of Beijing. This section guards the Juyong Guan Pass. It is one of the most important passes along the Great Wall, for it leads from the southern reaches of Inner Mongolia directly to the lowlands of Beijing. Thus, if the enemy could manage to get through the Juyong Pass, there were no other natural obstacles along his way to Beijing. The fortifications consist of two complexes: the southern *Juyong Guan* and the northern *Badaling*. The name roughly means 'eight (Ba) big (da) mountain paths (ling)'. Photo: 2015.

superior party through the targeted giving of gifts and honours. In addition, the emperor himself undertook five campaigns in Mongolia. After Arughtai had defeated a Chinese army at the Kherlen River in 1409, Yongle launched his first campaign in the spring of 1410. He twice defeated Arughtai, who nominally subordinated himself. But after the Oirat Mahmud defeated Arughtai, killed his puppet khan Öljey Temür, and advanced to the Kherlen River in north-east Mongolia, Yongle began a second campaign in 1414, this time against the Oirats. Thanks to the use of lighter guns, he won out in the end. However, he suffered heavy losses, not least because Arughtai stayed away from the battle to spare his own troops. The now stronger Arughtai exploited the weakened condition of the Oirat Mahmud, whom he defeated and killed in 1416. He subsequently advanced to the south of Mongolia to Kalgan (Zhangjiakou). As Kalgan is located just 160 km north-west of Beijing, Arughtai threatened the safety of the capital – especially given that he had conquered the Eastern Mongolian Uriyangkhad

tribes, who protected the north-eastern border as China's ally. In 1422, Yongle penetrated all the way to Dolon in today's Inner Mongolia. Arughtai, however, fled to the north. Even during Yongle's fourth (1423) and fifth (1424) offensives, Arughtai managed to avoid getting caught up in a pitched battle. Yongle, on the other hand, died at Dolon in 1424.[6] The relative failure of Yongle's campaigns was due to the fact that the fast-moving Mongolian troops were able to escape his grasp on a regular basis. Nearly two centuries later, Emperor Kangxi (r. 1661–1722) adopted the Mongolian tactic of employing several armies simultaneously in a coordinated manner: while the main army and a minor division marched towards their target striving for a decisive victory, one or two more divisions ensured that the enemy's retreat or escape route was cut off.

Yongle's campaigns, each with more than 100,000 soldiers, presented a huge logistical challenge. In 1414, the imperial army covered more than 3,000 km in hostile terrain that could not sustain the army. All the supplies thus had to be transported. The fourth campaign, for example, brought with it 340,000 donkeys, 117,000 carts, 235,000 draft animals and 24,000 tons of flour.[7] Yongle's successors were neither able nor willing to continue this costly strategy (with the disastrous exception of 1449). Not only did it not decisively weaken the Mongol tribes, but it also did not prevent them in the medium term from threatening the northern Chinese border. Nonetheless, Yongle's campaigns, which brought the war to Mongolia, compensated for the lack of strategic depth north of the capital. The Juyong Pass (the 'North Gate' south of Zhangjiakou) was just 60 km north of the capital. The alternative to Yongle's strategy was to withdraw the Chinese armies behind the Great Wall, which had increasingly deteriorated since the thirteenth century.

In Mongolia, where the Ming had not intervened since Yongle's death, there were three power centres in the later 1420s and 1430s: the Oirats in the west; Arughtai and the Chahar Mongols in the south-east; and the Uriyangkhad in the north-east. Mahmud's son and successor Toghan Tayishi (r. 1415–38/39) destroyed this delicate balance. He united the Oirats, and, in 1434, killed Arughtai, his

main rival for domination of the Mongol tribes. Toghan's successor Esen Tayishi (r. de facto 1438/39–53, as khan 1453–55), who retained the Genghis Khanid Toghtoa Bukha (r. *ca.* 1438–53) as nominal khan, began to rapidly expand his territory. He conquered the Uriyangkhad tribes and, between 1443 and 1448, wrested the oasis city of Hami from the Ming. At the same time, Yongle's successors wantonly neglected the defence of the northern border: deserters were not replaced, drills and training were abandoned, and the soldiers were misappropriated for non-military menial labour. In addition, the military colonies settled along the border, called *tuntian*, fell into decline, as the officers became landowners and the soldiers were relegated to serfs. Esen, however, needed ever-greater revenue to secure his dominion over the newly conquered territories, which extended from Hami in the east of today's Xinjiang region to the Korean border, and to finance the 'loyalty' of his followers. He therefore demanded that the Ming pay increasingly higher tributes in exchange for peace. These were presented each year at court as 'imperial gifts' to his arriving legations. When

38. The so-called 'White Palace' Tsagaan Baishing of Tsogtu Khong Tayishi (1581–1637), Bulgan Aimag, Mongolia. South-west of the palace, a stone stele in Tibetan and Mongolian reports that the 'White Palace' was not a palace, but a fortified Buddhist monastery called Samye, which most likely belonged to the Tibeto-Buddhist school of the Sakyapa. As founder of the monastery, built in the Iron-Ox Year (1601), the inscription mentions the Khalkha prince Tsogtu Khong Tayishi and his mother Tsin Taihu Khatun. The monastery consisted of a main temple and five smaller shrines and was built on the ruins of a much older building, probably from the time of the Khitan (907–1125).[5] Single photo: 2012.

China refused to meet Esen's demands in the winter of 1448/49, he declared war, not least because he knew that the Chinese troops were unfit for battle.

He attacked with three columns in the summer of 1449, while the division under his command rode against Datong. The young emperor Zhengtong (r. 1435–49, 1457–64), who was ill advised by chief eunuch Wang Chen, personally headed up a nearly 400,000-strong army against Esen Tayishi. The campaign, however, was poorly planned, while the unprepared army was miserably equipped and even more incompetently commanded. After a futile march to Datong, Wang Chen and Zhengtong decided to return to the capital. Esen observed the disorderly withdrawal of Chinese troops and destroyed them in the three-day Battle of Tumu (30 August – 1 September 1449). All high-ranking Chinese officers were killed in action and the emperor was taken prisoner. Esen was by no means prepared for this success – he demanded a large

ransom for the captive emperor, whereas he could have quickly taken Beijing instead, before it had organised a defence. When the majority of the court, the eunuchs, and the ministers in the capital expressed a preference for either paying the ransom or escaping to the south, the vice minister of war, Yu Qian (1398–1457), threatened to execute anyone who wished to escape. He prevailed in the end, denying any ransom payment and providing fresh troops from the provinces. In a brilliant move, he then eliminated Esen's imperial pawn by putting Zhengtong's brother Zhu Qiyu on the throne as Emperor Jingtai (r. 1449–57) on 23 September. At a single stroke, Esen's hostage Zhengtong was not only worthless, but even became a risk, as the immensely high ransom demand had sparked the greed of the Mongol leaders. When Esen realised that Yu Qian would neither negotiate nor pay, he decided to march on Beijing after all, on 27 October. The city now had its defences ready, however. Esen Tayishi's 70,000 mounted warriors, on the other

hand, were not sufficient to besiege the city, let alone occupy it. He therefore quickly withdrew and, in 1450, released the now useless former emperor without having received a ransom. In response, Jingtai immediately put Zhengtong under house arrest.[8]

Esen's inability to capitalise on his resounding victory at Tumu or his imprisonment of the emperor was the beginning of the end for him. In 1453, he murdered his nominal khan Toghtoa Bukha and proclaimed himself khan. Nonetheless, according to the unwritten law of the Turko-Mongol peoples, only the descendants of Genghis Khan could claim for themselves the title of khan. This move exacerbated the discontent of Esen's commanders so much that they killed him in 1455. The young empire of the Oirats later collapsed. Esen's attempt to consolidate his domain did not fail solely because of the unexpected resistance of the Ming. It was also due to the lack of new, cross-tribal structures, like the ones Genghis Khan had introduced in his decimal-based division

of all Turko-Mongols and the creation of a new military aristocracy.[9] From the Chinese perspective, assertive leaders such as the Yongle Emperor or Yu Qian proved to be an equal match to the Mongol warlords. At the same time, however, the governments led by Confucian-inspired ministers and eunuchs, who were hostile to the military, undermined the capacity of the state and dynasty to defend themselves. The governor of Datong, Wang Yue, was another capable official: in the 1470s, he claimed several victories against invading Mongols such as Khan Mar Körgis and Bolai Tayishi. Beyond this, he took the initiative from 1471 to compensate for the lack of strategic depth north of Beijing by rebuilding the Great Wall out of stone. He built the first section on the southern edge of the Ordos. This gave way in the 1540s and 1570s to the construction of additional sections, from Datong to Beijing and then to the Gulf of Bohai in the Pacific. The Great Wall thus emerged as we know it today[10] (fig. 37).

39. Three of the four monumental painted and gilded Buddhist brass figures, which the Swedish explorer Sven Hedin acquired in 1930 from the owner of the abandoned and dilapidated Efi monastery in Chahar, north-eastern Inner Mongolia. On the left, the 180.3-cm-tall figure of Manjushri, the Bodhisattva of Wisdom; in the middle, the also 180.3-cm-tall figure of the Bodhisattva Avalokiteshvara Shadakshari; and, on the right, the 184.5-cm-tall figure of the protector deity Vajrapani. The three bodhisattvas often appear together, representing the fundamental values of strength (Vajrapani), compassion (Avalokiteshvara), and wisdom (Manjushri). The fourth 129.5-cm-tall figure represents the founder of the Gelugpa Order, Tsong Khapa. The four figures are ascribed to the atelier of Zanabazar (1635–1723) and dated around the year 1700.[6] Folkens Museum Etnografiska, Stockholm, Sweden.

40. The outer wall of the Erdene Zuu Buddhist monastery, founded in 1586 by Abatai Khan and renovated in 1796, in Övörkhangai Aimag, Mongolia. The wall, which is 420 m long on each side, was not built until the early nineteenth century.[7] Photo: 2001.

With the collapse of the Oirat confederacy, the pendulum swung again in Mongolia in the Eastern Mongols' favour. After the rather insignificant khans **Mar Körgis** (r. 1455– *ca.* 1465), whose name hints at his Christian-Nestorian roots,[11] **Molon** (**Tögüs** r. *ca.* 1465–66), and **Mandughul** (r. *ca.* 1473–78/79)[12], the Eastern Mongol **Batu Möngke Dayan Khan** (r. *ca.* 1480– *ca.* 1524) managed to temporarily unite the Mongols again.[13] Dayan Khan's early life is not well documented. According to the Mongolian chronicle *Erdeni-yin tobči* of 1662, Khan Mandughul's widow Mandukai Sechen Khatun (d. *ca.* 1510) adopted a boy whom she claimed was a great-grandson of the younger brother of Khan Toghtoa Bukha. She remained regent in office and title until he reached adulthood. She then married him in the late 1480s and thus remained involved in the exercise of power.[14] It cannot be determined whether Dayan Khan was actually a Genghis Khanid. Dayan Khan and Mandukai first defeated Ismayil Tayishi and, in a second step, conquered the Oirats. The remaining Mongol commanders then recognised Dayan Khan as khan in the hope of gaining plunder and wealth under his leadership. For the khan, these expectations meant that he had to force the Chinese Ming dynasty to finance his young, embryonic state. Although militarily

weak, China refused to receive his envoys. It also rejected the possibility of buying peace through payments and lifting the trade boycott. Although his rule was not yet well established, Dayan Khan went on the attack and advanced on Beijing three times. But his relatively small armies suffered a number of defeats and had to be content with pillaging. The result was that the loyalty of his followers began to disintegrate.[15] After Dayan Khan's death, probably around 1524, the fragile Mongolian unity rapidly fell apart. On the other hand, his division of Eastern Mongolian tribes into six socio-military units called 'tümen', which was based on older structures, proved sustainable. The left, eastern, and dominant flank consisted of the tümen of the Chahar, the appanage of the crown prince, the Uriyangkhad, and the Khalkha. The right and western flank was made up of the Ordos, the Twelve Tümed, and a group that included the Asud and the Karachin. But Dayan Khan decided not to integrate the Western Mongols and maintained their division into the Four Oirat-Tümen of the Choros (Olot, Dzungars), Torghut, Dörbet and Khoshut.[16] The four khans who followed Dayan remained local tribal leaders: **Bodi Alagh** (r. ? –1547) **Daraisung Gudeng** (r. 1547–57), **Tümen Jasaghtu** (r. 1557–92), and **Buyan Sechen** (r. 1592–1604).[17] Only the last khan of the Northern Yuan, **Ligdan** (r. 1604–34), was able to extend his influence over his tümen of Chahar.

The Genghis Khanid **Ligdan Khan** (r. 1604–34) was one of nine tribal leaders of the Chahar-Eastern Mongols and nominally Great Khan of all Mongols. He tried to transform the nominal title of Great Khan into an actual sovereign position, which brought him into conflict with the other Eastern Mongolian leaders. To finance his wars, he settled a treaty with the Ming dynasty in 1618 to protect its northern border against the rising Manchus for a fee. The founder of the Manchu dynasty (1616–1911), China's future Qing dynasty (1644–1911), was Nurhaci (1559–1626). From 1619, he attacked China in the north-east and began to occupy territory. When his son and successor Hung Taiji (Abahai, r. 1626–43) recognised that the Chinese stronghold on the eastern end of the Great Wall near the strategically important pass of Shanhai was invincible, he changed his tactics. He chose Inner Mongolia instead as the basis for a future attack on Beijing. Ligdan's aggressive approach against the other Eastern Mongolian princes benefited him, as many fled in his direction with their mounted warriors and were incorporated into the Manchurian army. Ligdan Khan and Hung Taiji were now on a

collision course – particularly as Ligdan had Nurhaci's envoy, who proposed an anti-Ming alliance, beheaded in 1620. After several attacks between 1626 and 1632, Hung Taiji – who possessed artillery, unlike his opponent – expelled Ligdan from Mongolia. The khan fled into the territory of Kokonor (today's Qinghai Province) and died in 1634. With the incorporation of Chahar into his sphere of influence, the Manchurian Hung Taiji separated the southern Eastern Mongols from the Northern. In doing so, he anticipated the future separation of Inner Mongolia from Outer Mongolia. Hung Taiji integrated the southern Mongols into the territorially defined Manchurian banner system. By prohibiting them from leaving their assigned banner, he ended their traditional mobility.[18] Ligdan's death effectively put to an end the dynasty of the Northern Yuan, as his son Ejei Khan (d. 1661) never actually governed.[19] However, Hung Taiji – who renamed his Jurchen people the Manchus in 1635, and bestowed his dynasty with the name Qing in 1636 – was recognised by the Dalai Lama (who was constantly on the lookout for potential patrons) as the embodiment of Bodhisattva Manjushri in 1640.[20]

41. On the left, the whitewashed Altan (golden) Stupa; on the right, the again active Laviran (Tibetan: Labrang) temple in the Erdene Zuu Monastery, Mongolia. Photo: 2001.

2. Altan Khan and the Revival of Buddhism: an Alliance between Mongol Rulers and Tibetan-Buddhist Hierarchs

The weakness of the four Great Khans who succeeded Dayan Khan offered other regional rulers the opportunity to extend their power. The most successful and historically significant of these was a grandson of Dayan Khan called Altan (Altyn) Khan (1507–82) from the Twelve Tümed, whose name means 'golden khan'. In the 1540s, he expanded his power to the entire right flank of the Eastern Mongols, and he drove the Oirats from Karakorum in 1552. With regard to China, he continued the policy of his grandfather by regularly attacking the adjacent territories. In 1550, he even advanced to the gates of Beijing, with the aim of bringing an end to the Chinese trade boycott. The military weakness of China, whose

troops were 'unfit to combat, but able to loot',[21] forced the government to change its thinking. Wang Chonggu, governor of Shaanxi Province, convinced Emperor Longqing (r. 1567–72) that Altan Khan's actual goal was a trade agreement with China and regular tribute payments. The raids were merely a means to this end. In 1571, China bought peace by ending the trade boycott and settled a treaty with the khan that guaranteed him and his tribal leaders predictable tribute payments and marketplaces, where China had to buy inadequate horses at inflated prices.[22] The price that China paid to secure the peace was not only monetary, but also political in nature. After all, the Middle Kingdom financed the budget and continued existence of a threatening opponent. But as Wang Chonggu had probably recognised, Altan Khan was interested in the continuation of the Ming dynasty insofar as he needed a steady source of income.

Shortly after the treaty was concluded, Wang Chonggu issued another sage piece of advice: he recommended promoting the spread of Buddhism among the Mongols, so as to make the bellicose and

42. Sakyamuni Buddha flanked by his disciples Sariputra and Maudgalyayana; standing in front are Suryaprabha, the Bodhisattva of Sunlight, and Chandraprabha, the Bodhisattva of Moonlight. The middle temple of the Erdene Zuu three-temple complex, Mongolia. Photo: 2001.

brutal Mongols softer and more pliable.[23] In addition, the construction of monasteries in Mongolia and in the Kokonor territory would tempt young men to become monks instead of warriors. This strategy, which was aimed at weakening the military might of the Mongols and was also pursued by the subsequent Qing dynasty (1644–1911), was ultimately successful from the Chinese point of view. Nonetheless, it carried the risk that a leading Buddhist figure, such as a Dalai Lama, could be incarnated again in the family of a ruling Genghis Khanid. This could give rise to a Buddhist-Genghis-Khanid theocracy that would rally together all the Mongols. Such a figure would combine in his own person the two most prestigious lineages – that of the Buddha and that of the world conqueror – and could even surpass the standing of the Chinese emperor.

Altan Khan had probably encountered Buddhism on several occasions. It can be deduced from archaeological finds, for instance, that it survived the fall of the Yuan dynasty in Mongolia.[24] Moreover, Altan Khan's campaigns into the region of Kokonor – where the Tibeto-Buddhist school of the Gelugpa was established with its monasteries – brought him into contact with Tibetan Buddhism. Around the year 1574 (the *Erdeni-yin tobči* cites the year 1576), Altan Khan decided to revive the old politico-religious alliance between a Tibetan-Buddhist hierarch and a secular Mongolian patron, as it had existed between Chögyel Phagspa and Kublai Khan in the 1260s.[25] This alliance, called *khoyar yosun* in Mongolian, was aimed at a world order in which the hierarch, as Buddha's representative, legitimised the rule of the Mongol ruler and gave it a religious dimension. On the other hand, the ruler, who was considered a contemporary embodiment of the Buddhist ideal ruler Cakravartin Raja, would protect and promote Buddhism. The chronicle *Erdeni-yin tobči* reports how Khutukhtai Sechen Khong Tayishi (1540–86), Altan Khan's great-nephew, who had visited Tibet, advised the khan to invite Sonam Gyatso (1543–88), the highest incarnation of the Gelugpa order and abbot of the Tibetan Drepung Monastery, to a meeting in Kokonor: 'You have taken revenge on the Chinese ... and you have avenged yourself on the Oirats ... But now your years have increased, and you are approaching old age. [...] Would it not be wonderful if we were to invite him [the corporeal form of the Bodhisattva Avalokiteshvara], and re-establish the relations between Church and State as they once existed between Emperor Khubilai and the lama Phagspa?'[26]

After a second invitation around 1577, Sonam Gyatso consented and met Altan Khan in Kokonor in 1578. There, they formed a *khoyar yosun* alliance and exchanged honorary titles: Altan Khan gave the head of the Gelugpa the title 'Wonderful Vajradhara, Good and Splendid Ocean of Merit', in short Dalai Lama, and

43. The wrathful Buddhist protector Gombo Gur (Panjara-Mahakala) is the patron deity of Mongolia, especially the yurts of pastoral nomads. He stands on a corpse and holds a wand in front of his chest, decorated at both ends with jewels. The middle temple of the Erdene Zuu three-temple complex, Mongolia. Photo: 2001.

the Third Dalai Lama[27] called the khan the 'Perfect Brahma, Supremely Powerful Cakravartin Dharmaraja'.[28] In addition, the khan pledged to ban animal sacrifices at funerals (the animals were to be given to a monastery instead), to arrange hunting-free fasts, and to free the Buddhist clergy from taxes and forced labour.[29] Thanks to this alliance, the Mongolian khan won a unique legitimacy for his claim to rule. The Dalai Lama acquired not only a militarily strong ally in the political dispute with the other Tibetan orders, but he opened the vast missionary field of Mongolia for the Tibetan Gelugpa. Altan Khan thus laid the foundation for the secular rule of the Dalai Lama (1642–1951). Immediately after the meeting, Ming emperor Wanli (r. 1572–1620) invited the Third Dalai Lama to Beijing, presumably because he was unsettled by this Tibeto-Mongol alliance. The Dalai Lama refused, however, and returned to Tibet. From now on, there was an unpredictable

44. Gushri Khan (1582–1655), the ruler of Oirat Khoshut, and the regent of Tibet Desi Sangye Gyatso (1653–1705). The mural in the Great Courtyard (Khyamra Chenmo) of the Tsuglagkhang (Jokhang) Temple in Lhasa was created after the death of the Fifth Dalai Lama in 1682; Tibet, China.[8] Photo: 1996.

three-way relationship between the Mongolian rulers, Tibet, and China. Emperor Kangxi stabilised it in China's favour in 1720 by occupying Lhasa and downgrading Tibet to a protectorate.

Altan Khan's son and successor Dügüreng Sengge (r. 1582–86) and his wife Jönggen Khatun (d. 1612), the former third wife of Altan Khan, invited the Third Dalai Lama to southern Mongolia. He arrived there in 1585 and evangelised diligently until his death in 1588, which later gave the Gelugpa a religious monopoly. The visit of the prince of Eastern Mongolian Khalkha helped lay the foundation for the spread of Buddhism in Central Mongolia: Abatai Khan (d. 1588) was a great-grandson of Dayan Khan and met with the Dalai Lama in 1586 in the capital city of Köke Qota, the 'blue city' (today's Hohhot). The Dalai Lama gave him the honorary title 'Incarnation of the Bodhisattva Manjushri' and thereby gained the protection of a second Mongolian tribal leader. A short time earlier, Abatai had followed the example of Altan Khan by founding a small Buddhist temple in Karakorum. When he returned, he expanded it into the large Erdene Zuu ('Precious Lord') Monastery. The building material was taken from the ruins of Karakorum. (Figs. 40–43) The monastery standing over the destroyed palace of the Great Khan Ögödei was last renovated and expanded between 1780 and 1799.[30]

The alliance between the emerging Gelugpa order and the Mongol rulers was soon deepened further. When the Third Dalai Lama died in Mongolia in 1588, his reincarnation was not 'discovered,' for example, in Tibet, but in Mongolia – in the person of a great-grandson of Altan Khan and grandson of Dügüreng Sengge, born in the beginning of 1589. With the selection of a Mongol from the lineage of Altan Khan, the Gelugpa were able to ensure the continuation of the *khoyar yosun* alliance. The Fourth Dalai Lama, Yontan Gyatso (1589–1617), was a Genghis Khanid on his mother's and his father's side. He was simultaneously the leader of the Gelugpa. The Dalai Lama was not escorted to Lhasa until 1602, where he received the monk ordination in 1603. His early death under suspicious circumstances and the disintegration of the supremacy of the Tümed after 1612[31] prevented him or his Mongolian patrons from taking advantage of this unusual situation. Yontan Gyatso was the only non-Tibetan Dalai Lama.

Twenty years after Yontan Gyatso's death, the Fifth Dalai Lama, Ngawang Lobsang Gyatso (1617–82), gained the powerful ruler of the Oirat Khoshut, Gushri Khan (1582–1655), as protector of the Gelugpa (fig. 44). In a six-year war, Gushri Khan defeated the political opponents of the Gelugpa and established the theocracy of the Dalai Lama in Lhasa. As a result, Tibet became a focus of Mongolian (and later Chinese) policy. In the mid-1630s, the Dalai Lama asked for military aid against the competing order of the Karmapa and the non-Buddhist Bönpo church, along with their mutually allied patrons: the Tibetan king of Tsang based in Shigatse and the king of Beri in eastern Tibetan Kham, Donyo Dorje. The opponents of the Gelugpa also included the Khalkha prince Tsogtu Khong Tayishi (1581–1637), who supported Gushri Khan's rival Ligdan Khan and resisted the spread of the Gelugpa (fig. 38). In 1635/36, Gushri Khan occupied Kokonor. The following winter he defeated Tsogtu Khong Tayishi, and between 1639 and 1642 he destroyed the kings of Beri and Tsang. He then transferred rule over Tibet to the Fifth Dalai Lama, who awarded him the title 'King of the Dharma'. But Gushri Khan retained control of the Tibetan forces and appointed a Tibetan regent, a so-called Desi, to run

government affairs. The Dalai Lama took advantage of the opportunity to convert monasteries of the Kagyüpa, Sakyapa, Nyingmapa and Bönpo into Gelugpa monasteries and to consolidate the supremacy of the Gelugpa.[32] Depending on one's point of view, Tibet was a united, theocratic state under the leadership of the Gelugpa, or a Mongolian protectorate. Eighty years later, Emperor Kangxi ended a power struggle over the true Seventh Dalai Lama and occupied Lhasa in 1720. From then on, Tibet belonged to China's sphere of influence.

The Mongolian identity was now based on the identification with the legacy of Genghis Khan and his descendants, as well as on Buddhism. In the seventeenth century, the link between the Mongol ruling families and Buddhist institutions of the Gelugpa was further strengthened. Here, Mongolian princes exploited Buddhism to protect their power, and the order of the Gelugpa

45. The northern Buddhist Barun-khit monastery, also called Zsun khit, was founded at the beginning of the eighteenth century and is located in the Ala-Shan (Helan) Mountains, Inner Mongolia, China. Here, the mummy of the Sixth Dalai Lama, who died under mysterious circumstances, was allegedly preserved in a gilded stupa.[9] The complex has been under reconstruction since 1991; photo 1995.

46. Gilt bronze figure of Shadakshari Avalokiteshvara from the atelier of Zanabazar (1635–1723). Rossi & Rossi, London.

found ways, despite celibacy, to establish dynasties with their own deified hierarchs by means of the system of rebirths.[33] In 1639, the ruler of Middle Khalkha, Tushiyetu Khan Gombodorji (1594–1655), possibly a Genghis Khanid and a grandson of Abatai Khan, managed to have his son, born in 1635, recognised by an assembly of leading princes of Khalkha as the reincarnation of Târanâtha (1575–1634), the famous philosopher and teacher of the Tibetan school of the Jonangpas. Gombodorji probably hoped that if his son was equipped with the prestige of a high Buddhist incarnation, he could end the political divisions between the leaders of Khalkha and ultimately rally all the Mongols behind him. By around 1616, all the princes of the Oirats had converted to Buddhism themselves.[34] The Fifth Dalai Lama confirmed this reincarnation contrived by Mongol princes, bestowing it with the title Jebtsundamba ('Holy, Precious Master'). He named the boy Zanabazar (Sanskrit Jnanavajra, 'Thunderbolt of Wisdom'). The Mongols called him Bogda Gegeen ('Holy Incarnate Lama'). Because the Dalai Lama condemned the rival order of Jonangpa as heretical, he integrated the young Zanabazar (1635–1723) into his Gelugpa order. And since Târanâtha had founded many monasteries among the Khalkha, this move automatically put them into the Gelugpas' possession.[35] Because Emperor Kangxi recognised the equal standing of this new reincarnation as the supreme authority of the Gelugpa in Mongolia, he restricted the Dalai Lama's influence to Tibet.

Although Zanabazar – who also created wonderful Buddhist metal figurines and invented the ornate Soyombo alphabet in 1686 – enjoyed the highest reputation as head of the Gelugpa in Mongolia and as the undisputed spiritual leader of the Khalkha Mongols and as a descendant of the lineage of Genghis Khan, he did not succeed – unlike the Fifth Dalai Lama – in unifying all Mongols under his leadership. On the one hand, the Oirat Galdan Khan (r. 1671–97) was not willing to compromise in regard to his claim to leadership. On the other hand, the formation of a Genghis Khanid-Buddhist theocracy on the northern border with China was in no way consistent with Emperor Kangxi's strategy to eliminate the risk of a strong, reunited Mongol Empire by incorporating the Mongolian tribal organisations into a future Chinese protectorate. Nonetheless, the institution of Jebtsundamba at least preserved the identity of the Khalkha. In 1686, Zanabazar's effort to reconcile the Oirats and the Khalkha failed. Galdan Khan subsequently attacked with full force. Followed by tens of thousands of Khalkha Mongols in 1688, Zanabazar and his brother the Tushiyetu Khan fled to Inner Mongolia, where they asked Emperor Kangxi for aid and protection. With this appeal,

Zanabazar and the Khalkha presented Emperor Kangxi with an opportunity to realise his strategic goal. In 1690, he halted Galdan's advance. He also forced the Khalkha princes, the Jebtsundamba Zanabazar, and 550 nobles, to become vassals of the Chinese Qing emperors by swearing an oath of allegiance at Dolon Nor in the early summer of 1691. Some four centuries after Kublai Khan's rule, the Genghis Khanids of Mongolia had been degraded to supplicants and vassals of China.[36] In this way, Kangxi greatly restricted Zanabazar's political independence. He further claimed sovereignty over the successors of Genghis Khan and, along with it, the title of Cakravartin Raja.

In 1696, three Chinese armies invaded Mongolia. They decimated Galdan and, in the process, strengthened the protectorate of the Qing over the territories of today's Outer and Inner Mongolia.[37] As an emperor of Manchurian origin, Kangxi continued the policy of his grandfather Hung Taiji (r. 1626–43). The latter regulated Buddhism in the territories under his control and restricted its dissemination, while promoting the religion among the Mongols for political reasons.[38] If the statement from the Jesuit Gerbillon, who lived at Kangxi's court from 1687 to 1707, is to be believed, the emperor deplored the Tibetan monks for being

47. Erlig-jin Jarghagchi (Vajrabhairava) combats death and rebirth and is revered as an important meditational deity by the Gelugpa order. Maidari-yin Juu monastery, Tümed Right Banner, Baotou, Inner Mongolia, China. Photo: 1995.

uncivilised. Thus, while he supported the Lamas 'to maintain the Tatars [Mongols] obedience . . . he actually despised them for their coarseness, as they knew nothing about science nor the visual arts. It was for political reasons that he hid his true feelings and gave them outwards signs of his appreciation and favour.'[39] Kangxi confirmed in a bon mot that he supported the Tibetan Buddhism among the Mongols for political reasons: 'The construction of a single temple spares the nourishment of one hundred thousand soldiers stationed in Mongolia.'[40] Zanabazar lived from 1691 to 1701 at the court of Emperor Kangxi until the protectorate of the Qing was firmly established.

Although Emperor Kangxi promoted the Jebtsundamba religiously, while severely limiting his political scope, he established a counterweight in the form of the Changkya Khutukhtu of the Gelugpa, Ngawang Lobsang Choeden (1642–1714). Kangxi had met him at the oath of allegiance of Dolon Nor.[41] Emperor Qianlong (r. 1735–96, de facto until 1799) continued Kangxi's policy. He also made every effort to support his ally the Second Changkya Khutukhtu Rölpai Dorje (1717–86) from the small nation of the Mongolian-speaking Monguor, who glorified him as the incarnation of Manjushri, the Bodhisattva of Wisdom.[42] With this strategy, the Qing emperor purposely limited the spiritual authority of the four highest Gelugpa hierarchs along territorial lines: The Dalai Lama and Panchen Lama, who had been Chinese vassals since 1720, were responsible for the Tibetans and Kalmyk;[43] the Jebtsundamba for Outer Mongolia; and the Changkya Khutukhtu for Inner Mongolia. Qianlong's displeasure with the Jebtsundamba's disloyalty was revealed when the second incarnation (1724–58) of Genghis-Khanid descent hesitated during the revolt of the Khalkha princes in 1756–57 to declare his support for the existing order and his opposition to the rebels. By all appearances, Qianlong had him poisoned in 1758.[44] In response to the suspect loyalty of the religious leader of Mongolia, who enjoyed the prestige of being a descendant of Genghis Khan, Qianlong decreed that all future supreme Khutukhtus would have to be born in Tibet as Tibetans. He consequently severed the familial ties between leading hierarchs and the Mongolian nobility.[45] Just over 30 years later, in 1792, he nullified the competence of the leading lamas of Mongolia and Tibet to determine the reincarnations of their leaders. He ordered that they would have to be determined by lottery from a circle of acceptable candidates. In this way, he also prevented the development of hereditary dynasties.[46] Now, the Gelugpa incarnations of Avalokiteshvara (that of the Dalai Lama) and Manjushri (that of the Jebtsundamba Khutukhtu and Changkya Khutukhtu) stood under the authority of the Cakravartin Raja

emperor of the Qing. Even though Emperor Kangxi liked to have himself painted on Buddhist scroll paintings as a Bodhisattva Manjushri[47] (fig. 54), he said in a proclamation from 1792: 'In patronizing the Yellow Church [Gelugpa], we maintain peace with the Mongols. [. . .But in doing this,] we do not in any way give preference to or adulate the Tibetan priests, as was done under the Yuan.'[48] The Thirteenth Dalai Lama (1876–1933) and the Eighth Jebtsundamba Khutukhtu (1870–1924) were the first to successfully exploit the weaknesses of the Qing Dynasty, shake off its sovereignty, and free the short-lived, more or less autonomous states of Tibet (1912–51) and Mongolia (1911–19, nominally 1921–24) from the Chinese yoke. But both countries were heavily dependent on major foreign powers: Tibet on British India and Mongolia on Russia, and later on the Soviet Union.[49]

3. Russia Advances to the East

While China dealt with its northern neighbour for security reasons, Russian hunters, traders, and Cossacks penetrated into the northeast of Central Asia out of commercial motives. They looked for salt deposits, furs and metals and, on behalf of the tsar, explored a possible direct trade route to China.[50] At the end of this process, the Russians and Chinese clashed along the Amur River in the mid-seventeenth century. The greatest impulse behind the Russian eastward expansion was to capture valuable furs, especially sable, ermine, black fox and marten, which were called 'soft gold'.[51] In Russia, a veritable fur fever broke out. And, as soon as the hunters and trappers had killed off all fur-bearing animals in a region, they moved onward to the east. The rapid conquest of Siberia was driven by the greed for furs and the desire for trade, not missionary zeal. The Cossacks followed on the heels of the hunters. They erected fortresses and fortified settlements in strategic locations that were commanded by voivodes, who were under the tsar's control. Tsar Ivan IV had already declared Siberia an Imperial possession and the wholesale trade of furs a state monopoly.[52] On the march eastward, Ufa was founded in 1574, Tyumen in 1586, Tobolsk in 1587 (fig. 48), Tomsk in 1604, Yakutsk in 1632, the port of Okhotsk on the Pacific in 1647 and Irkutsk on Lake Baikal in 1652/61.[53] The advance of Russians with their superior arms had catastrophic consequences for the approximately 140 tribes of Siberia. They were not only relegated to tribute-paying subjects, who were at the mercy of voivode tax collectors, but the extermination of fur-bearing animals deprived them of their livelihood. Those who could not pay taxes in the form

48. The Tobolsk Kremlin founded in 1587, Tyumen Oblast, Russia; in the background, the Irtysh River.

of furs or the debts accrued on the purchase of alcoholic beverages were forced to hand over young women, who were then sold to the surrounding garrisons. Furs, women and spirits were accordingly the most profitable trade goods for the Russians.[54]

As the Russians were determined to find a direct trade route to China, they pushed on to the south-east, into the Baraba steppe south of Tobolsk. Instead of fur-bearing animals, they encountered the Turkic people the Teleuts, who were subjects of the up-and-coming Oirat leader Khara-Khula (r. *ca*. 1600–34). As a result of Khara-Khula's military strength, the Russians ruled out the possibility of a violent incursion. Instead, they entered into negotiations with the khan. This, however, did not prevent Khara-Khula from attacking the Russian settlers of southern Siberia from 1628–34.[55] When the voivode of Tomsk sent Cossack expeditions south

into the Central Asian steppes between 1604 and 1606, they ran headlong on the Upper Yenisei into one of the then four khans of Khalkha, Sholoi Ubashi Khong Tayishi (1567–1623), a bitter enemy of the Oirat Khara-Khula. The Russians realised that there was a potential route to China from the khanate of Sholoi Ubashi, whom they called 'Altan Khan'.[56] The political situation was complicated: some tribal leaders of the Oirats who lived on the border of the khanate of Sholoi Ubashi had sworn an oath of allegiance to the tsar around 1607/08. In return, Russia promised military support.[57] For Russian transit rights, however, Altan Khan demanded military aid against the same Oirats who had placed themselves under Russian protection. When Sholoi's envoy, the Lama Tarkhan, tactlessly appeared in Moscow in 1620, demanding not only Cossacks, but also gunsmiths, Tsar Mikhail I Romanov (r. 1613–45)

RUSSIA

Ob River

Yenisei River

Yenisei
1619

Tobolsk
1587

Tara
1594

Tomsk
1604

Krasnoya
1628

Tyumen
1586

Tobol River

Ishim River

Irtysh River

Kuznetsk
1618

Kazan

Ufa
1574

Omsk
1716

Ob River

Barnaul
1739

Volga River

Astana

Semipalatinsk

Altai Mountains

ALTYN KHA

Orenburg
1743

Ural River

Orsk
1734/35

DÖRBET

KAZAKHS

TORGHUT

DZUNGAR
EMPIRE

*Lake
Balkhash*

Raimskoe/Aralsk
1847

CHOROS

Ürümqi

Bar

*Aral
Sea*

DÖRBET

Perovsky (Ak Mejet)
1853

Verny
1854

Tian Shan

Turfan

Hami

Syr Darya River

Issyk Kul

Tarim River

KHOSHUT

Tashkent

*Caspian
Sea*

Amu Darya River

Kashgar

Tarim Basin

Yarkand

Khotan

Karakorum Mountains

Kunlun Mountains

TIBET

Himalaya

Lhasa

N

Yakutsk
1632

Okhotsk
1647

Lena River

gara River

Ust
1630

Nikolaevsk
1850

Bratsk
1630

BURIYAT

Lake Baikal

Irkutsk
1652

Albazin
1665-89

Argun River

Amur River

JURCHENS

Selenginsk
1666

Nerchinsk
1658

Argunsk
1681

Kyakhta
1727

Khabarovsk
1665

Selenge River

Urga (Ulaan Baatar)

JURCHENS

iyasutai

Erdene Zuu

MANCHURIA

KHALKHA MONGOLS

Gobi Desert

CHAHAR MONGOLS

Hohhot

Beijing

ORDOS

Huang He (Yellow River)

Lake
Kokonor

Xining

Lanzhou

HOSHUT

CHINA

Nanjing

The Russian advance into northern Central Asia and the Dzungar Empire, late 16th to early 18th century

○ Cities

● Towns

🔔 Temple

– – Ming Empire boundary

– – Qing Chinese–Russian border according to the Treaty of Kyakhta 1727

Scale (km)

→ Main routes of Russian colonisation

→ Route of the Torghut to the Volga River
ca. 1605–32

→ Occupation of Lhasa 1717–20

1xxx Date of Russian settlement

▪ Dzungar Empire 15th–16th century

▪ Dzungar Empire end of 17th century

0   250   500   750   1000

49. The city of Nerchinsk established in 1658 in Transbaikalia, Russia. It was here that the border in Transbaikalia was determined between Russia and China in 1689 and trade relations were defined. E. Ysbrants Ides, *Three years travels from Moscow over-land to China: thro' Great Ustiga, Siriania, Permia, Sibiria, Daour, Great Tartary, &c. to Peking* (London: Printed for W. Freeman et al., 1706), opposite p. 42.

replied that Russia would not fight against its own Oirat vassals. He thus refused any form of military aid. The transit route through Sholoi's khanate, accordingly, remained off limits to the Russians, which forced them to look for an alternative further to the east.[58] The failure to obtain transit rights through Sholoi's khanate was all the more painful for Moscow later on, when the Cossacks Ivan Petlin and Andrey Madov were able to prove the feasibility of this trade route in the course of their trip to Beijing in 1618. Since the two Cossacks did not have diplomatic accreditation from the tsar, they were forbidden to see the emperor. They received a letter for the tsar written in Chinese, which stated that the emperor never sent his own envoys to foreign powers and that if the tsar wished to have diplomatic and commercial relations with China, he would first have to send a tribute-bearing delegation. In any event, as no one in Moscow understood Chinese, the letter remained unread until 1675.[59]

The next two options for a possible transit route to China were in Buryatia, south of Lake Baikal, and in Transbaikalia, also called Dauria. The second compelling reason to explore these southern

areas was the logistical need for Russian settlements to be able to sustain themselves east of the Urals. When the Cossacks heard that there were fertile and agriculturally viable regions in south-eastern Transbaikalia, along the Amur River, they moved there under the leadership of Vasily Poyarkov in 1643–46 and, in the early 1650s, under Yerofey Khabarov. This led to the establishment of the fortress of Nerchinsk (1654; the settlement was completed in 1658; fig. 49) on the Nercha River, one of the headwaters of the Shilka, and of the forts of Khabarovsk (as a camp in 1652, as a fortress in 1665) and Albazin (as a camp in 1651, as a fortress in 1665) on the Amur itself. At the same time, the Cossacks built the fort of Selenginsk (1666) in southern Buryatia.[60] Owing to the brutality of the Cossacks, the native Daurs turned to Qing emperor Shunzhi (r. 1644–61) for help. Since the Manchus considered Dauria to be part of their northern safety zone, they sent a small army with artillery. A defeat in 1652 was followed in 1658 by the overwhelming victory of a powerful Manchurian flotilla which freed the middle Amur of Russians, east of Nerchinsk.[61] Since the Cossacks, who returned between 1665 and 1672, posed a threat,

Emperor Kangxi demanded that Moscow destroy the fortresses, especially that of Albazin. The negotiations were unsuccessful, prompting a Manchurian army to destroy the Albazin fortress in June 1685. Also in June, Khalkha Mongols laid siege to Selenginsk, but failed to conquer the fortress there.

The Cossacks, however, returned to the Amur and rebuilt the fortress of Albazin. Kangxi, in turn, also sent back his army. The Cossacks held out under the renewed siege for months until Kangxi ordered a ceasefire in early 1687. The reason for this surprising turn of events was a letter from Moscow that announced the arrival of the envoy Prince Fedor Golovin, who was authorised to resolve all border disputes between Russia and China. In fact, the negotiations culminated in the Treaty of Nerchinsk, which not only regulated the north-eastern border between Russia and China, but also severely undermined the long-term survival of a Central Asian steppe empire.[62] Northern Central Asia had thus become the scene of an armed conflict between two non-Central Asian great powers for the first time.

The Treaty of Nerchinsk: the Jesuits Jean-François Gerbillon and Thomas Pereira as Intermediaries between China and Russia

The starting point in the negotiations was lopsided: Russia was primarily interested in trade with China, yet was neither willing nor able to send more troops to the region, which was 6,000 km from Moscow. At the time, Russia's interest in Siberia and the Amur region was purely economic: the tsars sought the highest possible revenue with minimal administrative expenditure to realise their strategic objectives in the west. China, conversely, did not want trade, but only security on its northern border. In particular, Emperor Kangxi feared an anti-China alliance between the Dzungar Khan Galdan and Russia following his decision to expel Galdan from the territories of the Khalkha Mongols. For Galdan, an alliance with Moscow would have given him access to Russian firearms and strategic depth in Siberia. Emperor Kangxi, who was kept informed of Russia's disputes with Sweden and Poland thanks to the Jesuits residing at court,[63] was therefore prepared to drive the Russians from the Amur militarily. Kangxi instructed his envoy and minister Songgotu that the Russians would have to clear out of the Amur and that military pressure could be exercised, if necessary. Ideally, it would be possible to neutralise the Russians politically in western Transbaikalia through concessions. Golovin, on the other hand, was directed to avoid a war with China at all costs.[64] The Chinese delegation could therefore proceed from a position of strength, which was demonstrated by the differently-sized escorts of the envoys. As the Jesuit and interpreter Gerbillon reported, where Golovin was accompanied by 500 soldiers, Songgotu arrived with an army of 10,000.[65]

A first round of negotiations had failed in 1687/88 when a delegation of Khalkha Mongols allied with Kangxi and a delegation from Jebtsundamba Zanabazar arrived in Selenginsk. They issued an ultimatum to Prince Golovin to transfer dominion over the Buryat to them. Golovin categorically refused. An 8,000-strong Khalkha army then began to besiege Selenginsk in January 1688 – a negotiating tactic that Songgotu also threatened to use a year later in Nerchinsk. Nevertheless, the Khalkha suddenly withdrew in late March after Galdan launched a major offensive against them.[66] The continuation of the negotiations was postponed to the following year. In view of the Dzungar offensive, Golovin proposed that they take place further to the east in Nerchinsk. Kangxi decided to go along with the proposal, firstly because of the Dzungar–Khalkha war that erupted and secondly because Galdan had announced he would go to war on behalf of the tsar. Kangxi now had to immediately neutralise Russia. Although the Manchus had Russian-speaking interpreters and the Russians had Mongolian speakers, the parties agreed to use the Latin and Chinese-speaking Jesuits Jean-François Gerbillon (1654–1707) and Thomas Pereira (1645–1708) as interpreters. Both Jesuits were mathematicians and resided in Beijing. Gerbillon, moreover, undertook eight trips to 'Tartary' between 1688 and 1698 on behalf of Kangxi.[67] As a reward for their efforts, the Jesuits hoped that Kangxi would give them permission to proselytise. This, in fact, occurred with the tolerance edict from 1692.[68]

Right at the beginning of the highly charged negotiations on 22 August 1689, Songgotu issued his highest demand: the Russians were to withdraw from Selenginsk and all areas further east. This prompted Golovin to suggest maintaining the status quo, i.e. a border demarcation along the Amur River all the way to the Pacific. The talks faltered. When Golovin refused to give up Albazin, Songgotu, who was under considerable pressure to force a rapid settlement, began to surround the Russian fortress of Nerchinsk on 27 August and establish a blockade. Given his military inferiority and the order to avoid war at all costs, Golovin yielded the next day and offered to destroy the Albazin fortress (as Gerbillon reported).[69] The standoff was broken and the treaty, drafted in Latin, was signed by both agents on 7 September. It went into force immediately.[70] Russia destroyed the Albazin fortress and moved the border with China to a course that ran about 120 km north of the Amur River. It retained, however, the fortresses of Argunsk along the Argun River and Nerchinsk as well as Buryatia. China dispensed with Buryatia and most of Transbaikal and granted Russia trading rights. It held on to Mongolia, however. In return, Russia committed to not supporting

Galdan and his Dzungars. Both parties agreed to return refugees and deserters, so that Dzungar refugees would not be able to escape the clutches of the imperial armies, and nor would Buryat subjects be able to flee to the south. The treaty was beneficial for both sides: Russia won trading rights[71] and Kangxi was free to wage war against Galdan. Indeed, Galdan was the loser of the agreement, which he must have quickly realised when Golovin rebuffed his proposal of an anti-Khalkha alliance in early 1690.[72] Galdan also lost strategic depth, for the agreement robbed him of the opportunity to seek temporary refuge in southern Siberia if the war took an unfavourable turn. The Treaty of Nerchinsk and the subsequent Treaty of Kyakhta of 1727 defined the Russian-Chinese border as having a length of more than 4,000 km, which sealed off the steppe to the north.[73] Another attack by the Manchurian hammer would have caused fleeing Dzungars to collide with the Russian anvil. These two agreements thus paved the way for the division of Central Asia between Russia and China. At the same time, Central Asia, which in the age of the Mongols was a centre of power and trading hub of the Eurasian continent, was relegated to the periphery of foreign powers.

The border north of the Amur drawn in 1689 remained in place until 1854. But when the explorer Alexander von Middendorf, who had traced the course of the river in 1843, reported in St Petersburg that the Chinese had never occupied the border awarded to them in 1689 and, moreover, that there was a risk that British or American ships would sail up the Amur and take possession of Albazin, the governor of Eastern Siberia, Infantry General Nikolay Muravyov-Amursky (1809–87), seized the initiative. First, he sent Lieutenant Colonel Gennady Nevelskoy, who established Fort Nikolaevsk in 1850 along the lower reaches of the Amur. In light of the exploration of the Lower Amur by British agents and the outbreak of the Crimean War in 1853, where Russia faced an Ottoman-British-French alliance, Muravyov was convinced that Russia needed to occupy the Middle and Upper Amur as quickly as possible. Otherwise, the British would advance there and, in a second move, threaten Irkutsk. The circumstances were propitious. Because of the Taiping Rebellion of 1851–64, China was unable to send troops to the north. In May 1854, Muravyov again occupied Albazin and repulsed an Anglo-French attack on the port city of Petropavlovsk on the Kamchatka Peninsula. In the following year, he fended off another allied attack on Nikolaevsk, and the left bank of the Amur River remained Russian – which China was forced to accept in the Treaties of Aigun (1858) and Beijing (1860).[74]

50. The small Tubten Chokhorling monastery in Kyzyl, Tuva, Russia, consecrated in 1992 by the Fourteenth Dalai Lama. Photo: 2002.

4. The Dzungars: The Last Powerful Steppe Empire of Central Asia

In the wake of the death of Esen Khan in 1455, the first confederation of Oirats had collapsed. Four main Oirat branches then formed – Torghut, Dörbet, Khoshut and Choros – which, however, were severely pressured in the second half of the sixteenth century. In the east, the Eastern Mongol Altan Khan expelled them from Central Mongolia to the west into the region of Khobdo (Khovd). Under pressure from the Khalkha in the years 1619–21, they continued from there to flee westwards. In the south-west, however, the Uzbeks advanced to the north; and in the west, they were beset by the Kazakh Tevekkel (Tauekel) Khan (r. 1582–98). As a result, from around 1627/28, the Torghut migrated westward in droves, all the way to the Lower Volga, where they were known as Kalmyks. Around the year 1635/36, the Khoshut wandered into Kokonor and Amdo (north-eastern Tibet).[75] But the Choros, called 'Eleuths' by older European sources; the Dörbet; and a sub-tribe of the Khoit established the khanate of the Dzungars in the territory of Tarbaghatai (eastern Kazakhstan and northern Xinjiang).[76] In the 1630s, three Oirat confederations emerged: the khanates of the Kalmyks, the Khoshut and the Dzungars. Of these, only the last had embryonic state structures.

The founder of the Dzungar confederation was **Khara-Khula Tayishi** (r. *ca.* 1600–34). He expanded the rule of the Dzungars and, in 1618, also settled a first treaty with Russia, which had destroyed the khanate of Sibir and pushed forward to the south-east. This agreement regulated the affiliation and tax liability of the tribes living along the common border. Khara-Khula's son and successor **Erdeni Batur Khong Tayishi** (r. 1634–53) defeated the Kazakhs in the years 1635 and 1643. Further, he participated in Gushri Khan's campaign in Tibet which led to the establishment of the theocracy of the Fifth Dalai Lama. Erdeni Batur engaged in lively diplomatic exchanges with Russia, sending 33 Dzungar legations and receiving 19 Russian ones. As during the time of Khara-Khula, questions of trade and the taxation of border tribes predominated in Russian-Dzungar relations. In a dispute over the tax liability of the Kyrgyz living along the Yenisei in 1641, the two powers arrived at a compromise whereby the Kyrgyz had to pay tributes to both parties. Civilian trade with the Russians flourished: the Dzungars exchanged horses, cattle and furs for raw materials and handicraft products made of leather, as well as ivory, silver and other metals. Although Moscow severely punished the export of firearms and gunpowder,[77] the Dzungars managed to acquire them. After 1713,

51. Buddhist carvings from Tamgaly Tas, the 'painted stone', on the right bank of the Ili River in the south-east of Kazakhstan. The petroglyphs were carved at the time of the Dzungars around 1710. Appearing in the centre is Bodhisattva Avalokiteshvara; to his right, Buddha Sakyamuni, and to his left, Manla, the medicine Buddha. Photo: 2005; the petroglyphs have since been vandalised.[10]

the Swede Renat instructed them how to cast small lightweight field guns, which were carried into battle by camels.[78]

Erdeni Batur's efforts to secure hegemony over other Oirat tribes, and also probably over Eastern Mongols, failed, however. In 1635/36, many Khoshuts fled to Kokonor and Amdo. In 1648, further Khoshuts wandered westward into the regions of the Upper River Tobol and between the Urals and Volga, from where they expelled the Torghut-Kalmyks.[79] The large pan-Mongolian conference of 1640, involving leaders of the Dzungars, Kalmyks, Amdo Khoshuts and Khalkhas, was politically unsuccessful. Although the conference, convened by Erdeni Batur, the Khalkha Jasaghtu Khan, and the Buddhist monk Zaya Pandita, declared Tibetan Buddhism the official religion of all Mongols and procedures were agreed upon for dealing with inner-Mongolian conflicts, it did not achieve a political consensus. The Khoshut and Kalmyks wanted to preserve their independence and the Khalkha, threatened by the Manchus, were not willing to submit to the hegemonic claims of the Dzungars.[80] Zaya Pandita (1599–1662), however, developed the *todo* or so-called 'Clear Script' in 1648 for the Oirat language from the Mongolian-Uyghur script and from the Galik script developed by Lama Zordji Osir in 1587. It was written in vertical columns, from left to right, and was used by the Kalmyks until 1924, when it was replaced by a modified Cyrillic alphabet.[81] The reign of Erdeni Batur's son and successor **Sengge Khong Tayishi** (r. 1653–71) was overshadowed by the power struggles with two half-brothers, who murdered him in 1671 with the intent of succeeding him. Although Sengge was absorbed by these conflicts, he nonetheless managed to annex the khanate of Altan Khan in Khobdo in 1667. Ultimately, the plot of the two half-brothers failed, as Sengge's younger brother Galdan killed them and put himself on the throne.[82]

Galdan Boshughthtu Khan (r. 1671–97) had studied as a young monk in Tibet with the Fifth Dalai Lama. The Dalai Lama bestowed upon him the title Boshughthtu Khan ('legitimate khan') in 1678, even though he was a descendant of Esen Khan and thus not a Genghis Khanid.[83] Galdan was determined to bring all the Mongol tribes, except for the Kalmyks, under his rule – not by means of a conference as in 1640, but by war. He first conquered the Khoshut in 1676 and occupied the Kokonor. He then conquered the Muslim oasis towns of Hami, Turfan, Kashgar, Yarkand and Khotan in 1678–80.[84] Galdan's next target was the Eastern Mongolian Khalkha, who served the Manchu Qing in the north as a protective barrier against the Cossacks. A successful attack on the Khalkha by Galdan would make military conflict with Emperor Kangxi unavoidable. Despite this danger, Galdan intervened in a dispute between the Jasaghtu Khan and Tushiyetu Khan (both names were titles) of the Khalkha in 1686, which Zanabazar tried to mediate. He sent his brother to help the Jasaghtu Khan, but both were killed in battle with the Tushiyetu Khan. Galdan then unleashed an all-out attack. Galdan not only wanted to avenge his brother, but above all to conquer the Khalkha and to destroy the rival of the Dalai Lama, the Jebtsundamba. Galdan's army decimated the troops of the Khalkha and the survivors fled to the border with China. As discussed above,[85] Kangxi feared a Russian-Dzungar alliance, which is why he neutralised Russia in the Treaty of Nerchinsk and personally took to the field of battle against Galdan the following year in 1690. Kangxi won a victory at Ulaan Butung, 350 km north of Beijing, but was unable to destroy Galdan. Kangxi's top ally, however, was a Dzungar

– specifically Galdan's nephew and Sengge's son Tsewang Rabtan. He had rebelled in the same year in Dzungaria and proclaimed himself the new khan. Galdan was forced to retreat to Khobdo.[86] Yet Kangxi wanted to eliminate Galdan as a threat once and for all. After the forced submission of the Khalkha princes at Dolon Nor, he ordered an economic blockade around Galdan's base, Khobdo, and sent gifts to Galdan's rival Tsewang Rabtan. When Galdan moved his camp eastward to the Kherlen River, Emperor Kangxi personally led three army columns into the fray. Thanks to artillery, his general Fiyanggû completely destroyed Galdan's troops on 12 June 1696 at the Battle of Jao Modo, about 50 km east of the present-day city of Ulaan Baatar. Galdan fled with a few followers to Khobdo, where Kangxi tracked him down the following year. As he was severely threatened by Kangxi and unable to escape to the west, where Tsewang Rabtan ruled, Galdan committed suicide. That same year, Hami and the Khoshut of Kokonor asked Kangxi for protection.[87] In general, it can be said that Galdan's impetuous attack in 1688 drove the Khalkha into the arms of China. Until 1911, China retained its supremacy over Mongolia.

Tsewang Rabtan (r. 1697–1727), who severely defeated the Kazakhs in 1698,[88] avoided a conflict with Russia sometime around 1703. Instead of offering military protection to the Kyrgyz living on the Upper Yenisei against invading Russian Cossacks, he asked his Kyrgyz vassals to leave their homes and settle south of Lake Balkhash in the valley of the Ili. Shortly thereafter, the Russians began to exploit the rich natural resources. Russia's hunger at the time for metal ore is explained by Tsar Peter's efforts to modernise the Russian army and switch to muskets and cannons. Russian peasants soon flowed into the region. In 1739, the city of Minusinsk and the Barnaul fortress were established.[89]

In the face of the military strength of the Qing, Tsewang Rabtan adopted a wait-and-see attitude with regard to China. Kangxi, for his part, did not want to attack the empire of the Dzungars head on, but rather waited for an opportunity to free subordinated Tibet from their control. Tibet had moved to the forefront of Kangxi's concern when he learned from Oirat prisoners-of-war in 1696 that the Fifth Dalai Lama had already been dead for fourteen years. The Dalai Lama had appointed Desi Sangye Gyatso (r. 1679–1705), his alleged son, regent in 1679. When he died in 1682, the regent, who pursued a pro-Dzungar policy, kept the death a secret and continued to rule. Enraged, Emperor Kangxi demanded that the regent enthrone the Sixth Dalai Lama, Tsangyang Gyatso (1683–1706). This occurred on 8 December 1697.

But as the new Dalai Lama was more interested in mundane things like poetry, archery, wine and young women than his

52. The Potala Palace, located on the Marpori Mountain in Lhasa, Tibet, was the main residence of the Dalai Lama from 1649 to 1959. The Fifth Dalai Lama (1617–82) built the Potrang Karpo, the 'White Palace', in 1645–48; the Potrang Marpo, the 'Red Palace', was completed by the Regent Desi Sangye Gyatso in 1694.[11] Photo: 1996.

monastic obligations, the Desi remained in control.[90] In 1702, the Dalai Lama renounced his monastic vows, while retaining his temporal authority. For Kangxi and his nominal vassal Khoshut Lazang Khan (r. 1703–17), this political constellation was unacceptable because it solidified the supremacy of the Dzungars in Tibet. With Kangxi's encouragement, Lazang Khan, a descendant of Gushri Khan, captured Lhasa in 1705 and killed the regent. Now, Lazang Khan was the ruler of Tibet, and the country was part of the Qing's zone of influence.[91] At Kangxi's behest, Lazang sent the deposed Sixth Dalai Lama to Beijing, but he died along the way near Kokonor.[92] Lazang then enthroned a new 'true' Sixth Dalai

Lama called Ngawang Yeshe Gyatso, who was rumoured to be his own son. Lazang's intervention was met with resistance among the Tibetans. This resistance stiffened further after a rebirth of the Sixth Dalai Lama, that is a future Seventh Hierarch, had supposedly been discovered in Kham (eastern Tibet). Kangxi recognised the explosive nature of this alternate Dalai Lama, and had him brought to the Kumbum Monastery in Qinghai.[93]

The displeasure of the Tibetans continued to grow, which provided Tsewang Rabtan with an opportunity to intervene in Lhasa and to restore Dzungar sovereignty. But before Kangxi could launch a preventive attack on the Dzungars, he had to assure himself of Russia's neutrality. At the same time, he wanted to clarify whether the Kalmyk khan Ayuka (r. 1669–1724) – who had tried in vain after Galdan's death to become a Dzungar ruler in place of Tsewang Rabtan – could be won as an ally to attack the Dzungars by means of a pincer movement.[94] Kangxi's envoy Tulishen (1667–1741), whose report has been preserved, met Ayuka Khan in July 1714 east of the Volga. However, the khan of the Kalmyks, who owed his throne to Tsar Peter, could not pursue an independent foreign policy and had to take the tsar's instructions into account. In fact, Tsar Peter warned Ayuka in no uncertain terms against an attack on the Dzungars, as it would embroil Russia in the conflict, at a time no less when Russia was at war with Sweden. Despite Ayuka's cautious attitude, Tulishen's delegation was successful insofar as it was able to confirm Russia's neutrality in a Sino-Dzungar war. Kangxi thus had free rein to move against Tsewang Rabtan.[95] On his return, Tulishen had a remarkable conversation with the governor of Siberia, Prince Gagarin. When the governor asked about Chinese warfare, Tulishen answered: 'As soon as the enemy are within the range of our shot, we fire at them with great guns; when they are nearer, we shoot at them with bows and arrows, and musketry.' Gagarin replied that the Russian army had until recently fought with the same weapons. Now, however, Tsar Peter ordered that conventional weapons such as bows and arrows and spears be done away with and that war should now only be conducted with firearms.[96] But neither Tulishen nor Emperor Kangxi took Tsar Peter's military reform and its possible consequences for Chinese warfare seriously. Just like the Mughal in India, China was not sufficiently prepared to learn about Europe's military technology or its operational doctrine.

Tsewang Rabtan was most likely aware of Tulishen's delegation and decided to take the initiative. But the attack on Hami in 1715 failed, prompting Tulishen to comment sardonically in his report: 'The rats have accordingly returned to their holes.'[97] Two years later, however, Tsewang Rabtan sent a powerful army to Tibet under Tsering Dondub. The attack on Kumbum, which was aimed at abducting the young Seventh Dalai Lama, did not

53. Detail of a painting of the Battle of Qurman, in which the Chinese general Fude won a victory over Khoja Burhan al-Din on 3 February 1759. Like the Dzungars, the troops of the Qing had camels carry light field guns into battle. Library of Congress, Prints and Etching Division. LC USZ62-44377. Palace Museum Beijing, 6336-7-16.

succeed. Nonetheless, it resulted in Lhasa's capture and the death of Lazang Khan. The city and the surrounding monasteries subsequently suffered heavy looting by the Dzungars. Tsewang Rabtan now controlled Lhasa, but the Seventh Dalai Lama was in Kangxi's hands. After the failure of a first army that Emperor Kangxi had sent to Lhasa in 1718, he now sent two armies that advanced on Lhasa – one from Sichuan, the other from Kokonor. The Kokonor army, which largely consisted of Khoshut warriors, defeated Tsering Dondub, who fled to Dzungaria, and the Sichuan army occupied Lhasa without a fight. The Kokonor army, for its part, reached Lhasa on 24 September 1720 and immediately enthroned Kelsang Gyatso as the Seventh Dalai Lama.[98] From this point forward, Kangxi and his successors controlled not only Tibet, which served China as a bulwark against attacks from the West, but also the institution of the Dalai Lamas, who enjoyed the highest standing among all Buddhist Mongols. Kangxi clearly settled the dispute with Tsewang Rabtan over control of the two highest authorities of Tibetan-Mongolian Buddhism in his own favour. Kangxi and his successor Yongzheng (r. 1722–35) secured their dominion over Tibet by installing two senior civilian officials called *amban* above the Dalai Lama and his council of ministers. They had a 2,000-strong force at their disposal[99] and Tibet was now a Chinese protectorate. In the campaigns of 1669–97 and 1720, the combination of field artillery, muskets and Mongolian cavalry proved highly effective in the fighting against the Dzungar federations. The biggest challenges were still the logistics of the enormously long approach routes and the fact that several target regions could not support larger armies (e.g. Mongolia, northern Tibet, the oases of Altishahr). For this reason, Kangxi refrained from directly attacking Dzungaria.[100] But when the Mongolian Khoshut launched an uprising after the death of Kangxi, Emperor Yongzheng quickly put it down. He then abolished the previous autonomy of the Khoshut princes and severed their political connections to Tibet by annexing the Kokonor (Amdo) and Kham to the neighbouring Chinese provinces. This division of the Tibet region from 1724 corresponds almost exactly to the present provincial borders of the People's Republic of China.[101]

Tsewang Rabten managed to compensate for his losses: he undertook a massive offensive against the Kazakhs in the west in 1723–24 and advanced to the cities of Turkistan and Tashkent.[102] The khan died in 1727 from poisoning, probably administered by his wife or his son and successor **Galdan Tsering** (r. 1727–45).[103] The latter's victories against the Khalkha, who had been vassals of the Qing since 1691, motivated Emperor Yongzheng to send troops to Luntai (East Turkestan) in 1731. He also sent a larger army to Khobdo, where they fell into a Dzungar trap and were slaughtered. At the same time, the Qing had to evacuate from Luntai again. Galdan Tsering then tried to win the Khalkha over to his side, but they remained loyal to the emperor and dealt a devastating blow to the advancing Dzungars under the leadership of the Genghis-Khanid Sayin Noyan in 1732. The war was now in a stalemate, which led to the peace agreement of 1739. Galdan Tsering had to relinquish Tuva and the Great Lake Depression in today's Western Mongolia, though he obtained trading rights with China.[104] Galdan Tsering also tried to take maximum advantage of his numerous foreign prisoners of war, including the Swede Johan Gustaf Renat, who was held captive from 1716 to 1733. Renat and his fellow prisoners taught the Dzungars the production of cannons and mortars, the processing of ore, letterpress printing and paper making, and the drawing of maps. Following the outbreak of power struggles after Galdan Tsering's death, all of these manufacturing skills fell again into decline.[105]

The death of Galdan Tsering in 1745 gave way to bloody in-fighting among the Dzungars. This presented Emperor Qianlong with the long-awaited opportunity to destroy the Central Asian empire of the Dzungars and to eliminate for good the threat posed by mounted nomadic steppe warriors to agrarian China. Galdan Tsering's successor **Tsewang Dorje Namgyal** (r. 1746–50) was a cruel and poor khan, who was overthrown and blinded by his elder brother **Lama Darja** (Dorji, 1750–52). The internal power struggle then immediately flared up again. His rivals were Amursana, a descendant of Tsewang Rabtan, and Dawachi, a grandson of Tsering Dondub. In December 1752, Lama Darja was killed by mutinous soldiers and **Dawachi** (r. 1753–55), who was appointed Tayishi, promptly expelled his ally Amursana. In his distress, the latter committed the fatal mistake of requesting military aid from Emperor Qianlong and offering, in return, his subservience. The emperor did not hesitate to agree, sending two armies to the west to capture Dawachi. Qianlong, however, had decided to divide the empire of the Dzungars into four tribal groups and to appoint four equal khans. **Amursana** (r. as khan of the Khoit 1755–57) rejected this power-sharing and successfully rebelled in late summer 1755, as Qianlong had already withdrawn his victorious armies. Amursana's resistance motivated the Khalkha prince Chinggunjav to also rebel against Qianlong in July 1756. Faced with the threat of Dzungars and the Khalkha closing ranks, Qianlong decided to wipe out all of the Dzungar population. In January 1757, he defeated Chinggunjav and then conducted a genocidal war against the Dzungars. Simultaneously, a smallpox epidemic broke out among the Dzungars. Ultimately, the Dzungar people and their state

54. Portrait of the Qianlong Emperor (r. 1736–96, de facto until 1799) as the Bodhisattva Manjushri and as high Tibetan Lama. The emperor's face may have been painted by the Italian Jesuit Giuseppe Castiglione (Lang Shining, 1688–1766), who lived in China from 1715.[12] Thangka, ink and colour on silk, around or before 1766. Like his grandfather Kangxi before him, Qianlong promoted Buddhism among the Mongolians and the Tibetans for political reasons. By spreading the idea that he was an incarnation of Bodhisattva Manjushri, he linked to himself the Buddhist Mongols and Tibetans, who themselves felt no particular allegiance to the Qing dynasty. Freer Gallery of Art and Arthur M. Sackler Gallery, Smithsonian Institute, Washington DC; Purchase: Charles Lang Freer Endowment, F2000.4.

were wiped off the map. Of the approximately 600,000 to 800,000 Dzungars, about 40 per cent died from disease, 20 per cent fled to the Kazakhs and Russians, and 20 per cent were killed or died of starvation. Only 20 per cent survived. Amursana, furthermore, fled to Russia, where he died in 1757. That same year, with Dzungaria almost completely depopulated, Qianlong settled in the region Han Chinese, Manchus, and Turkish oasis dwellers from Altishahr, along with the Kalmyks who had fled there from the Volga in 1771/72.[106] The destruction of the Dzungars not only eliminated a 2,000-year threat, which had endangered China since Chanyu Modu (r. 209–174 BCE),[107] but also brought to an end the glorious history of Central Asia's steppe empires.

The strategic foreign policy goal of Emperors Kangxi and Qianlong with regard to Central Asia was the long-term protection of China's northern and western borders. Before 1757, the major milestones toward achieving this objective had been the two border agreements with Russia in 1689 and 1727, the integration of Mongolia in 1691, the subjugation of Tibet, and the extermination of the Dzungars. The only remaining weakness was East Turkestan, which regularly attracted Muslim conquerors from the west. There was concern that they might provoke unrest among their coreligionists in western China, in particular the Huizú (Dungans) living in Gansu, Qinghai and Ningxia, who were ethnically and linguistically Chinese. What's more, Mongolia could be easily attacked from Turkestan. Since Mongolia was critical to the security of Beijing, and since its stability depended on the control of East Turkestan,[108] Qianlong decided to pursue two measures.

First, in December 1759, his troops conquered all of East Turkestan – to the Ili Valley in the north-west and Kashgar, Yarkand and Khotan in the south-west. The Qing armies managed this logistical feat with relative ease, not least because there was neither a Uyghur state nor a Uyghur nation, or even a Uyghur identity, at that time. East Turkestan rather consisted of various oasis states, and there was no overarching ethnonym. People called themselves Kashgarlik ('person from Kashgar'), Khotanlik, Kuchalik or Loplik.[109] The ethnonym 'Uyghur' to indicate the Turkic Muslims of Xinjiang is a creation of Russian Orientalists of the late nineteenth century. It was recorded at a socialist 'Workers and Peasants Congress' that convened in Tashkent and then officially adopted in 1934 by the warlord Sheng Shicai.[110] Under Qianlong, East Turkestan became China's 'new frontier' – which is the precise meaning of the current province name Xinjiang, introduced at the end of the eighteenth century.[111]

Second, the imperial armies moved far to the west, as far as Taraz and even Tashkent, where no Chinese army had penetrated for more than a thousand years,[112] and to Kokand and the mountain region of Pamir.[113] The emperor had no aims here of further territorial expansion. With this show of force, he rather wanted to make clear to his western neighbours that they were always within range of Chinese artillery. The ruler of Badakhshan, Mir Sultan Shah, received the message: he had the last two khojas of Kashgar, Burhan al-Din and Jahan,[114] who had fled to him, executed. Other Muslim princes tried, with the help of Ahmad Shah Durrani, the ruler of Afghanistan, to forge an alliance directed against the 'infidels'. But Ahmad Shah was not interested in a military confrontation with the Qing. He was content to invade, together with his ally Bukhara, Badakhshan in 1765 and to kill the 'traitor' Mir Sultan Shah.[115] However, because the Chinese commander Fu Tajen had a trilingual stone stele erected at the site of his victory over the elusive khojas in 1759, which celebrated the Chinese success in the Chinese, Manchu and East Turkic languages, China

later claimed the area between Alichur Pamir and Lake Yashil Kul as state territory. This claim was contested in the late 1880s and early 1890s by both Afghanistan and tsarist Russia, which in the course of the 'Great Game' moved ever closer to the Upper Oxus and thus the Hindu Kush.[116]

With the Chinese triumph over the Dzungars, the Mongolian steppe warriors of the Khalkha, who had provided the bulk of the Qing armies used against the Dzungars, rapidly lost in importance. They were demobilised and, as a result, the number of Buddhist monks under the Mongols exploded, not least because the Qing dropped the existing restrictions on the number of monasteries and monks. At the same time, immigration of Chinese peasants in Inner Mongolia was allowed, and in Outer Mongolia the restrictions on Chinese traders to conduct business were gradually loosened. As a consequence, in Inner Mongolia, land was developed and pastures were converted into farmland;[117] in Outer Mongolia, the Mongolian

55. The 44-m-high Emin Minaret and the Friday Mosque of Turfan with the modern sculpture of Emin Khoja, Xinjiang, China. The minaret was built in 1777–78 in honour of the local ruler and military leader Emin Khoja, who took sides with China in the Sino-Dzungar War of 1755–59. Photo: 2009.

56. The medieval stone figure of a sheep called *koshkartas*, which stands over the grave of a mounted warrior. Necropolis of Masat Ata, Mangyshlak Peninsula, West Kazakhstan. Photo: 2005.

clan leaders and nobles gradually went into debt, obtaining credit from traders by putting up the possessions under their banner as collateral. These three factors – demilitarisation, the large increase in the number of unproductive monks, and the predominance of credit-giving Chinese traders – strongly contributed to the impoverishment of the Mongol population in the nineteenth century.[118]

As for the newly acquired territories in East Turkestan, Emperor Qianlong decided in 1760 against integrating them into the Chinese Empire and instead converted them into a military colony. The supreme authority had a military governor in northern Xinjiang, located in the Prefecture of Ili, today's Yining. The Manchurian cavalry was stationed in the north, because of the lush pastures there. The oasis towns of the Tarim Basin in the south, however, were unable to support larger numbers of troops. The garrisons functioned according to the 'tuntian' system of self-sustaining, agricultural production units, introduced by the Han Dynasty in the second century BC.[119] To increase the productivity of the now so-called 'bingtuan' local military colonies and to resettle the depopulated Dzungaria, thousands of Turkic farmers of the Tarim Basin, the Taranchi, were relocated to the north. Living there as military serfs, they were not permitted to leave the land that was allotted to them. There were also exiled criminals and impoverished farmers from the neighbouring Gansu Province. On the other hand, Han Chinese remained prohibited from unregulated settlement in Xinjiang until 1830. In the large districts, senior officials, called 'amban', supported the military governor in the administration. At the same time, individual ethnic groups such as the Kazakhs and the Kalmyks who returned to Dzungaria in 1771, along with the urban oases Turfan and Kashgar, were governed according to the yasak system by their own hereditary princes. In the other southern oases, local Muslim officials called Begs managed the Turkic population. Their main tasks lay in maintaining public order and in collecting taxes to finance the northern garrisons.[120] After the destruction of the Dzungar Empire the Kazakh hordes were the only remaining buffer between Russia and China, so that their strategic importance increased for St Petersburg.

5. The Kazakh Hordes

Unlike the Dzungar Empire, the khanate of the Kazakhs (*ca.* 1465/70–1718) never formed a stable state.[121] The establishment of the khanate began with the Jochids **Giray Khan** (d. *ca.* 1480) and **Jani Beg Khan** (d. 1480), the putative sons of Baraq Khan (r. 1422–27), a ruler of the Golden Horde. Around 1458–61, they left the federation of Uzbeks led by Abu'l Khayr and, with their 200,000-strong entourage, went to Moghulistan.[122] The two separatist leaders rejected Abu'l Khayr's sole claim to power and his strict Islamic codes of conduct. The efforts of Abu'l Khayr, who died around 1468,

to force the Uzbek-Kazakhs' return failed, which is why the beginning of the Kazakh Khanate is dated 1465–70.[123] Although the next two khans, **Burunduq Khan** (r. 1480–1511), a son of Giray Khan, and **Qasim Khan** (r. 1511–19/21), a son of Jani Beg, were able to extend the realm of the Kazakhs in the northern steppes between the Urals and western Altai, the khanate remained unstable. Following in quick succession were **Muhammad Husain (Mumash) Khan** (r. 1519/21–23) **Tahir Khan** (r. 1523–*ca.* 29/33) **Birilash (Buydash) Khan** (r. 1529/33–34) and **Tughum Khan** (r. 1534–38), all of whom were only recognised by minority Kazakh groups.[124] **Haqq (Aq) Nazar Khan** (r. *ca.* 1538–80) was the first to succeed in restoring the unity of the khanate. He also made peace with the Uzbek Khanate

57. The rebuilt city wall of Turkistan, Kazakhstan, overlooking the mausoleum of Khoja Ahmed Yasawi (1094–1166) constructed by Timur-e Lang in 1396/97. Photo: 2005.

and wrested control of the eastern pastures from the Nogai in 1568, which allowed the Kazakh Khanate to extend all the way to the Yaik (Ural) and Irtysh rivers. The short reign of **Shighay Khan** (1580–82) gave way to that of **Tevekkel (Tauekel) Khan** (r. 1582–98), who counted the Uzbek Khanate, Küchüm Khan of Sibir, and the Dzungar tribes among his rivals. In these conflicts, the bow-and-arrow carrying Kazakhs were outmatched by the Uzbeks, who possessed firearms. For this reason, Tevekkel Khan sent a delegation in 1594 to Tsar Feodor I and regent Boris Godunov to obtain guns. Godunov interpreted Tevekkel's delegation as a request to be recognised as a Russian vassal. The diplomatic exchange was continued and in early 1598 khan Tevekkel penetrated deep into the Uzbek Khanate thanks to his newly acquired weaponry. He conquered Tashkent and Samarkand, but came up short against Bukhara. His death ended the campaign. Tashkent and Turkistan, though, remained intermittently in Kazakh possession until 1723 although the Astarkhanid Imam Quli Khan also claimed a rather nominal sovereignty over Tashkent.[125]

The fragmentation of the khanate began again under Tevekkel's successors. While Tevekkel's brother **Ishim (Esin) Khan** (r. 1598–1628) resided in the city of Turkistan, which served as the capital of the khanate, **Tursun Mohammad** (r. before 1613–28)

58. The three Kazakh sages, from left to right Kasybek Biy (leader of the Middle Horde), Töle Biy (poet and leader of the Senior Horde) and Aiteke Biy (judge and leader of the Junior Horde), who, according to tradition, contractually regulated the relations between the Kazakh tribes in the beginning of the eighteenth century. Monument in Astana, Kazakhstan. Photo: 2005.

reigned virtually autonomously in Tashkent. The dissolution of the khanate and Dzungar attacks continued under **Jahangir Khan** (r. 1628–52), **Batyr** (a title, r. 1652–80?),[126] and **Tavke (Tauke) Khan** (r. 1680–1718). Although Jahangir Khan still won a victory in 1643 against the Dzungars, Batyr and Tavke suffered several defeats, respectively in 1680 and between 1709 and 1718. After Tavke's death, the khanate finally broke apart into three hordes, the zhuz. In the west and closest to Russia, there was the **Junior Horde** (Kishi Zhuz), whose pastures stretched from the lowland north-east of the Caspian Sea to the delta of the Syr Darya; in the centre, there was the **Middle Horde** (Orta Zhuz), which occupied the area of modern Central Kazakhstan to Lake Balkhash; finally, there was the **Senior Horde** (Ulu Zhuz), whose territory ranged from the lower reaches of the Syr Darya to around Semirechie (Zhetysu) in today's Kyrgyzstan, including Turkistan and Tashkent.[127] The latter horde was most exposed to Dzungar attacks and suffered a brutal attack at the hands of Tsewang Rabtan in 1723/24.[128] At the same time, numerous clans of the Middle Horde fled to Samarkand and those of the Junior Horde to Bukhara and Khiva. There, they proceeded to carry out repeated devastating onslaughts of their own. Threatened with the extinction of the Kazakh identity, the clans of the Middle and Junior Hordes combined their forces and won a first victory in 1726. In a second important step, the two hordes agreed to a shared command, which they bestowed upon **Abu'l Khayr**, the khan of the Junior Horde (r. 1718–48). Shortly thereafter, in 1730, Abu'l Khayr Khan claimed a resounding victory over Galdan Tsering's Dzungars. He forced them to more or less evacuate the territories of the two hordes, allowing the clans to return to their homeland.[129]

But no sooner had the two hordes driven out the Dzungars than the 'Kazakh disease' of internal dissension broke out again. Abu'l Khayr's command was thus called into question. At the same time, Galdan Tsering was gearing up for a counter-attack. Given this dismal starting position, Abu'l Khayr was forced to seek protection for his approximately 100,000-tent-strong horde from its powerful neighbour Russia.[130] After brief negotiations, Tsarina Anna (r. 1730–40) recognised the Junior Horde as Russian vassals on 19 February 1731. On 10 October 1731, the khan and his leaders concluded the oath of allegiance. As a consequence, a Muslim community[131] sought protection from a Christian state against a Buddhist enemy. In the following year, khan Semeke (r. 1719–34) likewise expressed the desire of the Middle Horde to become Russian vassals. Also following suit between 1734 and 1742 were Jolbarys Khan and some of his followers from the Senior Horde.[132] The Kazakhs committed to paying nominal tributes; to neither attacking Russians nor Russian vassals; and to protecting Russian

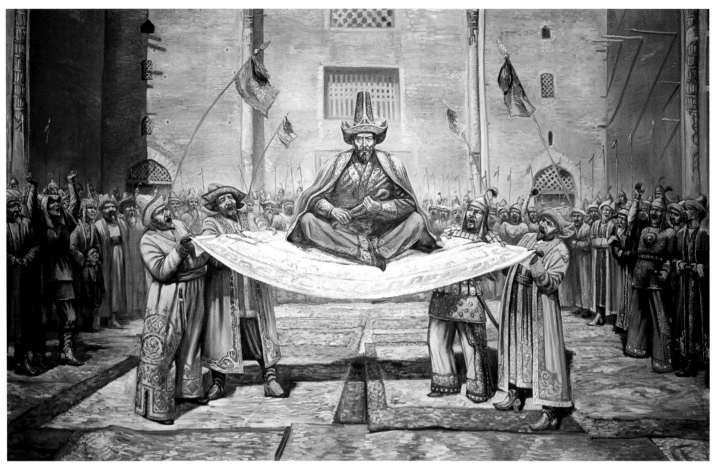

59. On the occasion of the enthronement of an Uzbek or Kazakh khan, the new ruler was lifted into the air while sitting on a felt rug to demonstrate his exalted position. Painting in the municipal museum of Turkistan, Kazakhstan. Photo: 2005.

trade caravans. In return, they expected military protection against their Dzungar rivals. Russia used the opportunity to expand to the south-east. It built the Orsk fortress in 1734/35 at the confluence of the Ural and Or rivers, which was called Orenburg until 1743. In the same year it also erected present-day Orenburg, lying about 250 km downstream. At the same time the Russian military built a chain of small, but cannon-fitted fortresses, which connected to the east Samara on the Volga via Orenburg on the Ural, all the way to Omsk on the Irtysh River. This effectively separated the Bashkir vassals from the Kazakhs. As the Russian officer Nikolai Petrovich Rytchkov, who travelled the Kazakh steppe from 1769 to 1771, reported, this new 'Orenburg line' replaced the older 'Tsaritsyn line'. The latter, described by Rytchkov as the 'Szakam line', protected the area of Kazan against the Bashkirs.[133] Emerging along the new Orenburg line was a first Trans-Siberian route, which facilitated the immigration of Russian settlers into the Bashkir and the Kazakh steppe, while also serving troop movements.[134] But the Bashkirs revolted in response to the construction of the new fortress line and tried to win the Kazakhs of the Junior Horde over to their side. An

eyewitness to this tumultuous time was John Castle, who had been commissioned by the Russians. He was a member of the Orenburg expedition from about 1734 and set out as an unofficial envoy from Orsk to Abu'l Khayr Khan's camp in 1736. On the way, he learned that about 40,000 Kazakh mounted warriors were preparing, together with the Bashkir rebel Kilmyak, to attack Orenburg; that is, Orsk, Ufa and Kazan. In a face-to-face meeting with the khan, Castle emphasised the might of Russia in hopes of dissuading the khan from participating in the Bashkir rebellion. Castle's efforts bore fruit, for the Kazakhs stayed away from the uprising.[135]

Due to the geographical distances, Russia was only able to militarily support and politically influence the Junior Horde. The Middle and Senior Horde quarrelled among themselves and remained exposed to Dzungar raids. The insignificance at the time of Russian sovereignty over the two geographically distant hordes became apparent after Galdan Tsering had made peace with Emperor Qianlong. In 1741/42, his troops devastated the regions of the Middle and Senior Horde and came within a four-day march of the fortified Orenburg line. Russia, for its part, failed to come to

60. The wooden Russian Orthodox cathedral of Karakol, Kyrgyzstan. During the Soviet period, it served as club premises and sports hall, which saved it from destruction. The church was restored in 1989 and has again been in use since 1995. Photo: 2004.

the aid of its new vassals. Instead, it avoided a military conflict with the Dzungars and remained passive. For this reason, both hordes remained subjects of the Dzungar Empire until it collapsed. The then leading Kazakh ruler was **Ablai (Ab'il Mansour)**, sultan of the Middle Horde (d. 1781). He recognised the Chinese supremacy around 1757 and subsequently expelled the remaining Dzungars from his territory. Ablai was appointed khan of all thee hordes in 1771 by a *kuriltai*, which Russia also recognised.[136] But the withdrawal of the Dzungars did not bring renewed independence to the Kazakhs, as increasing numbers of Russian settlers populated the fertile regions and numerous pastures were converted into arable land. This strongly limited the Kazakhs' freedom of movement. The ever-diminishing role of the cavalry in the Russian army also lowered the demand for imported horses, which caused the living standards of the Kazakh herders to fall even more. The varying factors of the Russian colonisation, the restriction of movement, impoverishment, and an intensified Islamisation provoked numerous Kazakh revolts. This began with the Kazakh

participation in the Pugachov Uprising of 1773–75[137] and did not end until the 1850s.[138] Regarding the Islamisation of the Kazakhs, the initiative stemmed from Russia: from the 1740s, it had promoted the construction of mosques and Islamic proselytising by imams from the Volga-Ural region of Kazan.[139] These measures served to undermine the authority of the khans and to forestall missionaries from Bukhara, who had a stricter interpretation of Islam and were hostile towards the Russian 'infidels'.[140]

In the early nineteenth century, the Kazakh uprisings led to administrative adjustments. In 1801, the Russian government had allowed a part of the Junior Horde led by Sultan Bukey to settle between the Ural and Volga rivers, an area that had only been sparsely populated since the exodus of the Kalmyks in 1771.[141] The allocation of new pastures eased the plight of the Junior Horde, whose pastureland had shrunk due to the colonisation of Russian settlers. This splinter group of the Junior Horde was called the 'Inner Horde' and in 1812 Sultan Bukey received the title of khan. However, from the Russian point of view, the growing number of Russian settlers and Cossacks, along with the rebellious Kazakh khans and sultans, made the traditional structures obsolete. As a result, the Russian government gradually disbanded the hordes: the Middle Horde in 1822, the Junior Horde in 1824, the Inner Horde in 1845, and the Senior Horde in 1848.[142] The territories were then incorporated into the Russian Empire.[143] The colonisation by Russian settlers, which the Kazakhs considered a land grab, was extended further as a result of Tsar Alexander's (r. 1855–81) abolition of serfdom in 1861. At first, the liberated serfs were forbidden from settling in the Kazakh steppes. However, once the new Steppe Statute of 1891 declared the steppes to be state property, hundreds of thousands of Russian peasants flocked to the fertile northern region of Kazakhstan. The boundary for arable farming, accordingly, shifted southward.[144] The Russian southward advance from the 1820s, though, soon led to conflicts with the khanates of Khiva and Kokand expanding northward. Khiva tried to penetrate areas of the former Junior Horde,

and regularly plundered Russian trade caravans, which gave rise to General Perovsky's failed winter expedition in 1839.[145] Kokand, however, conquered the cities of Tashkent, Shymkent and Sairam in 1809, which put the khanate on a collision course with Russia. In 1847, the Russian army erected the fortress of Raimskoe (later Aralsk) in the delta of the Syr Darya. From this position, the Russians posed a threat to Khiva, Shymkent and Tashkent. The first major military confrontation with the Kokand Khanate occurred in 1852. Here, Colonel Blaramberg unsuccessfully attacked the Kokand fortress Ak Mejet (Ak Masjit), located in southern Kazakhstan at the site of the present city of Kyzyl Orda. In the following year, General Perovsky conquered Ak Mejet, prompting Russia to establish the fortress of Verny in 1854 in Semirechie. Later, it would become the city of Almaty.[146] The peace over the ensuing decade in the unstable Kokand Khanate was merely due to the fact that Russia's military resources were tied up in the Crimean War from 1853 to 1856.

61. The *Burkhan Bakshin Altan Sume*, the Golden Abode of Buddha Shakyamuni, in Elista, Kalmykia, built in 2005, is the largest Buddhist temple in Europe and has 27 monks (as of February 2017). The spiritual leader of the Buddhists of Kalmykia is the 20th Shadjin Lama, who was born in the United States as Erdene Basan Ombadykow in 1972. He is in charge of the 27 reconstructed Buddhist temples and prayer houses of Kalmykia. Photo: 2017.

6. Migration and Exodus of the Kalmyks

The migration of the ethnically Oirat Kalmyks,[147] which occurred in several waves between 1606 and the 1680s, was the last great migration of Central Asian nomadic horsemen to the west. In early 1771, however, it experienced a surprising turn, for the majority of the Kalmyks of the Volga wandered back to Central Asia. There were several drivers of this multi-stage migration. To begin with, the Oirat tribes in the sixteenth century were severely pressured, first by the Eastern Mongol Altan Khan and then by the Kazakh Khan Tevekkel from the south. As a result, they sought safe haven in the north and west. In the seventeenth century, the leadership claims of the two founders of the Dzungar confederation, Khara-Khula Tayishi and Erdeni Batur Khong Tayishi,[148] prompted other Oirat groups to migrate to the Volga. The first to emigrate to the north was **Khoo-Örlög Tayishi** (r. before 1604–44) of the Torghut tribe, whose camp was on the Upper Irtysh. Its trade links with Mawarannahr had been severed by the Kazakhs. The hope was that Khoo-Örlög and his followers could settle in the territory of the former khanate of Sibir. In 1606, however, he encountered the Russian Tara fortress, founded in 1594. In 1607, the nomads of Dörbet, led by Dalay Bagatur Tayishi, also arrived on the scene. Both groups asked for permission to graze in Sibir and to trade with Russia. Moscow agreed in principle, but demanded that the two Tayishis recognise Russian sovereignty and pay yasak (tribute). The Tayishis, however, steadfastly refused. This led to a series of skirmishes in the 1610s between the Russian garrisons and the Oirat immigrants, all of which the garrisons won thanks to their firearms. Faced with this stalemate, the Tayishis decided to flee to the south-west, namely to the lush pastures of the Nogai surrounding the Emba, Ural and Volga rivers. They sent cavalry with the mission to survey the territories, to attack the camp of the nomadic Nogai, and to send them running. Oirat warrior units thus emerged along the Emba River in 1608. These bands then crossed the Urals in 1613 and reached the Volga in 1632. These heavily armed cavalry units left devastation everywhere in their path.[149]

The migration to the west, which swelled to a mass emigration around 1627/28, could finally not be reversed from 1630–32. This is when Khoo-Örlög, his son Daichin, and the Torghut Louzang Tayishi overran the Caspian lowlands and the northern steppes with more than 10,000 mounted Kalmyk warriors. They drove the Nogai – who were unable to coordinate a resistance – before them like cattle. The latter, for their part, appealed to the

Russian governor for protection. But Louzang Tayishi defeated Astrakhan's musketeers in 1633. At the same time, the persistent Kalmyk attacks forced the defeated Nogai to flee again to the Ottoman fortress of Azov in 1635, and then even further into the Kuban region and the Ottoman protectorate of the Crimea in 1637. After an invasion lasting only five to seven years, the Kalmyks dominated the vast Caspian steppe between the Don and Ural rivers. Consequently, the Buddhist Kalmyks comprised a veritable Buddhist-Mongolian island between the Muslim-Turkic peoples of the Bashkirs, Kazakhs, Nogai, Crimean Tatars and the Orthodox Russians.[150] Now, the once pro-Russian Nogai began to take part in the Crimean Tatar raids against Russian cities. Simultaneously, the Don Cossacks took advantage of the withdrawal of the Nogai to conquer the Azov Fortress (Azak) in 1637.[151] Around the year 1641/42, however, groups of the Dörbet and Khoshut who refused to recognise Erdeni Batur's claim to leadership began to pressure Khoo-Örlög's Torghuts, causing him to flee to the south-west. There, he met his death in 1644 when he attacked the Circassian tribe of the Kabardians in the North Caucasus. Since Khoo-Örlög's son **Daichin Tayishi** (r. 1647–61) was staying in Tibet on pilgrimage at the time, he did not assume the leadership of the Kalmyks until three years later. He immediately faced an invasion of hostile Dörbet and Khoshut who had lost a power struggle with Erdeni Batur. The newcomers occupied the steppe between Tobol and Ural, while Daichin's Kalmyks now nomadised between the Ural and Volga.[152]

Around the mid-seventeenth century, there was a strategic rapprochement between the Kalmyks and Russia. After the Zaporozhian Cossacks of today's Ukraine had a successful uprising against Poland-Lithuania in 1648, they took an oath of allegiance to the Russian Tsar Alexei I at the Pereyaslav Council in January 1654. Afterwards, Poland-Lithuania allied itself with the Crimean Tatars against Moscow, which immediately looked for an ally with a strong cavalry. The Kalmyks, who were rivals of the Nogai and Crimean Tatars, had a strong cavalry, and an inexhaustible supply of horses, formed a perfect complement to the musket- and cannon-armed Russian foot-soldiers and the slow Russian cavalry. The first three Russian-Kalmyk treaties of 1655, 1656 and 1657 were more or less ineffective. While the Kalmyks interpreted them as a purely military alliance between two equal generals, the Russian side understood them as a commitment between vassal and monarch.[153] Only the fourth Russian-Kalmyk treaty between Moscow and Daichin Tayishi and his son and successor **Puntsuk Tayishi** (r. 1661–69) had beneficial results for both sides: the Kalmyks, who were allied with the Zaporozhian Cossacks, dealt

62. More than 80 per cent of ethnic Kalmyks consider themselves practising Buddhists; the affiliation to Buddhism is a strong element of Kalmyk national identity. Prayer drums in the Golden Abode of Buddha Shakyamuni in Elista, Kalmykia. Photo: 2017.

the Crimean Tatars several more devastating defeats. In return, the Russians allowed the Kalmyks to nomadise along the Don, erecting for their defence against Dzungar attacks a fortification line along the Ural River manned with 2,000 musketeers.[154] This strategy, which the Russians pursued from 1661 until about 1722/23, aimed at establishing a single powerful ruler among the Kalmyks, who, in return, would defend the south-eastern edge of the Russian Empire. Puntsuk's successor **Ayuka Khan** (r. 1669–1724) attempted to implement his own policy, but internal Kalmyk conflicts and threats from Khoshut tribes forced him to seek Moscow's help. On four occasions (1672/73, 1697, 1699 and 1701), he owed his throne to Russia's continued military presence. Despite his loyalty oath from 1673, he cultivated an anti-Russian policy from 1680 to 1697. He sabotaged the Russian siege of the fortress of Azov in 1695, which had belonged to the Ottomans since 1642. The following year, Ayuka suffered a defeat against the Nogai and Kuban Tatars, while Tsar Peter I conquered the fortress of Azov. This broke the

connecting line between the Ottoman and Crimean Tatars, on the one hand, and the Tatars still inhabiting the Caspian steppe and the Nogai and the Kalmyks, on the other. In his weakened position, Ayuka recognised both the regional power shift in favour of Russia and the growing relevance of firearms, in particular field artillery. For this reason, he signed a mutual assistance pact with Prince Golitsyn in July 1697.[155] Despite the alliance, Russian sales of firearms to the Kalmyks were prohibited. If they nevertheless obtained cannons for a limited time in the case of war, the cannons had to be operated by Russian artillerymen.

The treaty from 1697 was beneficial for both parties: Russia saved Ayuka's throne three times; the latter, for his part, put down uprisings of the Bashkirs and Don Cossacks on Tsar Peter's behalf in 1708/09. He also caused widespread devastation in the Kuban in 1711. And during the visit of Emperor Kangxi's Manchu envoy Tulishen in 1714, he at least took a neutral stance as per Russian instructions.[156] On 22 June 1722, Ayuka met his monarch

63. The Sherning Dyundok ceremony in honour of the female Bodhisattva Green Tara. The ritual is aimed at removing and overcoming external and internal obstacles with the help of Green Tara. It is held on the second day of the four-day celebration of the Mongolian New Year, *Tsagaan Sar*, which is also celebrated by the Kalmyks as the start of spring. Tsagaan Sar, the 'White Moon', falls on the first day of the Mongolian lunar calendar. Around 600 people took part in the three-hour prayer; the four men standing in the centre of the image read aloud from a list the names of those believers who want to personally entreat the Green Tara for help. Photo: 2017.

Tsar Peter near the modern city of Saratov on the Volga. Tsar Peter had decided to take advantage of the disintegration of the Persian Safavid Empire for conquests along the west coast of the Caspian Sea. He then continued on to Astrakhan. According to the contemporary Voltaire (1694–1778), Peter's goal was to dominate the Caspian Sea with a powerful fleet in order to establish a direct trade route to India.[157] Scottish doctor and traveller John Bell of Antermony, who had travelled from 1715 to 1722 on behalf of Russia to Persia and China, was a member of Tsar Peter's Russian military expedition and therefore witnessed the meeting between the Tsar and Ayuka. He commented: 'The Ayuka-Chan came on horseback, attended by two of the princes his sons, and escorted by a troop of about fifty of his officers and great men, all exceedingly well mounted. About twenty yards from the shore [of the Volga] the King alighted from his horse, and was received by a privy-councellor and an officer of the guards. When the Emperor saw him advancing, he went on shore, saluted him, and, taking him by the hand, conducted him on board the galley. [...] The Emperor intimated to the Ayuka-Chan, that he would be desirous of ten thousand of his troops to accompany him to PERSIA. The King of the KALMUCKS replied, that ten thousand were at the Emperor's service, but that he thought that one half of that number would be more than sufficient to answer all these purposes.'[158] Then Tsar Peter sailed for Astrakhan and conquered the ports of Derbent and Baku, and the Caspian provinces of Dagestan, Mazandaran, Gilan and Astarabad (Gorgan). Ayuka, however, was double-dealing: He provided only 3,727 unusable cavalrymen, among whom there was a Nogai spy. Presumably, this convinced Tsar Peter to change his strategy in 1723. Instead of supporting a single strong Kalmyk ruler, a 'divide-and-conquer' philosophy prevailed. It was propagated by Artemy Volynsky, the governor of Astrakhan, who was also responsible for the relations with the Kalmyks.[159]

Ayuka was succeeded by his son **Cheren Donduk Khan** (r. 1724–35). His power, however, was increasingly restricted by his mother Darma Bala and her lover Donduk Ombo, a grandson of Ayuka. Following the new strategy, Russia reduced its financial support of the Kalmyks after Tsar Peter's death. It further divided up the khan's reduced financial support to him and his mother Darma Bala, which suited well the 'strongman' Donduk Ombo. In addition, the Russian authorities systematically favoured Kalmyks who allowed themselves to be baptised.[160] On the basis of these two tactical manoeuvres, Russia split both the Kalmyks' leadership and their community. In 1730, Darma Bala and several Tayishis attempted to pursue an independent foreign policy once again. For this purpose, they sent a delegation that was supposed to travel to

Tibet, but in reality went to Beijing. The envoys were to propose a military alliance to Emperor Yongzheng directed against the Dzungars. They also were to suggest the replacement of Cheren Donduk with Galdan Danjin, another son of Darma Bala, who would then return the Kalmyks to their ancient homeland. The latter proposal presented China with a compelling opportunity to make the Kalmyks into its vassals. The government thus sent its own delegation to the Kalmyks in 1731. In the meantime, the Russian authorities had become suspicious: fearing a China-supported putsch in favour of Galdan Danjin, they arrested four Kalmyk envoys during their return journey and confirmed Cheren Donduk as khan. Simultaneously, they forcefully reminded the khan that the Kalmyks were Russian vassals and that he could not enter into any treaties without Russia's consent. When Cheren Donduk and Darma Bala received the Chinese delegation in the presence of the Russian governor of Saratov in June 1731, the khan adhered to the Russian instructions. He decided that he could not send troops against the Dzungars without the express orders of Tsarina Anna. This put to an end the plan for a Kalmyk-Chinese alliance.[161]

Nonetheless, when the rivalry between Cheren Donduk and Donduk Ombo degenerated into a bloody civil war, Russia dropped the khan. It then recognised **Donduk Ombo Khan** (r. 1735–41) as the new ruler. Under him and his successors **Donduk Dashi Khan** (r. 1741–61) and **Ubashi Khan** (r. 1761–71, d. 1774/75) the economic situation of the Kalmyks worsened dramatically. As a result of the resettlement of the Don Cossacks on the Volga, the local population swelled rapidly. In the process, the number of pastures converted into arable land also increased. The situation was further exacerbated when Tsarina Catherine II (r. 1762–96) called for and accordingly promoted the settlement of German immigrants along the Volga. The extensive land use of the nomads was further restricted, and the impoverished Kalmyks had to look for work in the Russian fishing industry. A similar development had taken place after the Russian reconquest of the Azov fortress in 1739, with thousands of Russian peasants settling along the Don River. The rapid expansion of fortified border lines continued to worsen the Kalmyks' economic situation, making it impossible for them to continue their traditional nomadic way of life. In the south-west, the Dnieper line (from the Dnieper to the Donets) sealed off Crimea, while in the south the Mozdok line, finished in 1762,[162] shielded the Northern Caucasus from the steppe between the Don and Astrakhan. In the north-east, the new Orenburg line threatened to limit the freedom of movement to the east, and in the north-west the Tsaritsyn line forced the Kalmyks to ask for permission to use their pastures west of the Volga.[163] The Kalmyks were effectively trapped between the fortress lines.

Faced with this impasse, the Kalmyks decided under Ubashi Khan's leadership to return to Dzungaria, which had been depopulated since the Dzungars were wiped out.[164] Although Tsarina Catherine was warned by the governor of Astrakhan of the Kalmyks' imminent escape, she ignored the warning. She also reprimanded the governor for wanting to take leading Tayishis hostage: 'The empress was convinced that the Kalmyks could not possibly leave Russia because they had nowhere to go.'[165] In the autumn of 1770, Ubashi was able to freely gather the majority of the Kalmyks – according to Emperor Qianlong about 170,000 people[166] – on the eastern bank of the Volga, while about 60,000 Kalmyks remained to the west of the Volga. Vasily Mikhailov,[167] who was an inadvertent eyewitness to the Kalmyk exodus, reported that in order to appease suspicious border posts Ubashi maintained he was preparing for a conflict with attacking Kazakhs.[168] On 5 January 1771, the Kalmyks' exodus east began. As the Kalmyks moved forward quickly without regard to losses, they were able to escape the Russian divisions of Major General von Traubenberg (1722–72), who was pursuing them. Officer Rytchkov, who participated in the chase, reported that the Russian cavalry was too slow, barely had food, and lacked useful maps.[169] When the Kalmyks reached Lake Balkhash, they were repeatedly attacked by Kazakhs. The Kazakhs did not want to miss out on such an opportunity to plunder. They moreover feared that the fleeing Kalmyks might establish a strong state again. The exodus cost the Kalmyks more than 85,000 lives.[170] The survivors were initially allowed to settle in Dzungaria. After 1774, however, many were moved inland and assigned to various military units.[171] Catherine's lack of foresight and the exodus had serious consequences for Russia: Rytchkov reported that trade collapsed and major riots broke out in the province of Orenburg as a result.[172] The unhindered flight of the Kalmyks had revealed the weaknesses of the Russian border troops, which emboldened the Circassians to attack the Russian border fortresses and cities. The riots in Orenburg that erupted in 1771 gave way to a Cossack uprising in the Urals in 1771/72. This culminated shortly after in the bloody Pugachov Uprising of 1773–75.

The Kalmyks who remained in Russia were placed under the rule of the governor of Astrakhan in 1771 and the title of the Kalmyk Khan was abolished. Although the Kalmyk mounted warriors continued to fight with bows and arrows and spears, they were used on the Russian side during the Napoleonic Wars as scouts and guerrillas.[173] Like many other non-Russian ethnic groups, the Kalmyks who lived south-west of Astrakhan suffered woefully under the Stalin dictatorship. From 1930, its Buddhist temples and monasteries were destroyed, and as a new large-scale collectivisation began in 1935, herders who owned more than 500 sheep were deported to Siberia.[174] Although many Kalmyks fought loyally on the Soviet side in World War II, a significant minority welcomed the German *Wehrmacht* as liberators from the Soviet yoke when it occupied the capital of Elista without a fight in August 1942. However, the German occupiers left Kalmykia a few months later in January 1943, after the failed attack on Astrakhan in autumn 1942. The Red Army then advanced once again. On 27 December 1943, a decree proclaimed the dissolution of the Autonomous Soviet Socialist Republic of Kalmykia and ordered the deportation of all Kalmyks to Central Asia and Siberia. In all, 120,000 Kalmyks were deported. Khrushchev finally revoked the deportation in 1956. On 7 January 1957, the Kalmyk Autonomous Oblast was then established, which allowed the Mongolian Kalmyk people to return to their homeland in far-eastern Europe.[175]

IV

Afghanistan until 1837 and the Khanates of Central Asia until the Russian Conquest

'In all other parts of the world light descends upon earth, from holy Bokhara it ascends.'

Proverb from Bukhara, nineteenth century.[1]

As in northern Central Asia, there were also significant upheavals in the south in the mid-eighteenth century. The new state of Afghanistan was formed south of the Hindu Kush and, to the north, the three Uzbek khanates of Khiva, Bukhara and Kokand were consolidated after the military expedition of Nader Shah.[2] From an economic point of view, these countries were of little importance, not least because of the uncertainty and high transit duties on trade routes. In political terms, on the other hand, they became a primary concern of the two rival great powers, Russia and Great Britain.

1. The Emergence of Afghanistan as a Tribal Alliance

Hardly any country is as strongly influenced by its geography as Afghanistan:[3] 'Afghanistan is a term of geography combined with an own mindset, barely a country at all.'[4] Indeed, in this extremely craggy mountain landscape, with its steep mountain slopes and deep canyons, a tribal society is the most suitable form of organisation for larger groups of people. Recent history has shown that this observation does not need to be qualified even in the twenty-first century, despite the opportunities offered by air transport and electronic communications. Each fertile valley offers tribes and sub-tribes the opportunity to exist independently of one another. Unless the tribes make an effort to come into contact, they remain separate from each other and from a central government. In an environment that greatly separates people from each other, the common characteristics that remain include, first, the affiliation to a particular ethnicity and language, such as Pashto, Tajik, Uzbek or Hazaragi; second, the different manifestations of the Muslim identity; and, third, the respective mindset. South of the Hindu Kush, the latter is particularly pronounced among the Pashtuns in the code of ethics, the so-called 'Pashtunwali'. The Pashtunwali includes hospitality, which ends at one's own doorstep or at the border of the clan; a pronounced sense of honour or of the violation of one's own honour or that of family members; retaliation, hereditary blood feuds, conciliation and consensus through meetings of the distinguished elders; and an unrestrained pride in the freedom and independence of one's own tribe.[5] Such a cocktail of values was and is the breeding ground for a strong warrior culture, which radically rejects any form of foreign intervention. Such a mindset makes the work of any central government difficult, which must continually seek balance and compromise. The British officer

and philologist Sir Henry Rawlinson rightly maintained in 1874: 'Afghanistan never has had, and never can have, the cohesion and consistency of a regular monarchical government. The nation consists of a mere collection of tribes.'[6]

When a local government was open to compromise, and refrained from interfering in the affairs of the tribes, the latter remained in their mountains. But when a foreign power penetrated into the country, for example into the Kabul Basin, the tribal warriors rushed to fight the intruder. If the occupier was an 'infidel', the liberation war assumed the character of a jihad, a holy war. Thus, the Persian Safavids, British, Soviets, Americans, and NATO troops experienced the same painful reality – that it is easy to invade Afghanistan, but impossible to control the country in the long run. However, as soon as they claimed their victory, the unity of the Afghans came to an immediate end. Given this complex situation, a central government could only function as a kind of feudal state. The great tribal leaders, the Sardars, needed financial resources to assure themselves of the 'loyalty' of their subordinates. For its part, the government needed troops to maintain internal and, above all, external security, as the monarch only had authority over his own tribe. For this reason, the monarch transferred the revenues from state agricultural property, called Jagir, to the Sardars. In return, the Sardars were obliged to provide armed warriors.[7] Afghanistan's most important ethnic groups are the Pashtuns, Tajiks, Uzbeks, Hazara, Baloch and Turkmen. The Pashtuns, who since the early eighteenth century have mainly lived south of the Hindu Kush, speak a north-eastern Iranian language. Of the approximately 49 million Pashtuns in the world today, around 16 million live in Afghanistan and 30 million in Pakistan. Two million of these are Afghan refugees. They are divided into four large tribal federations, the Ghilzai, Durrani (Abdali), Karlani and Ghurghusht, with the first two being the largest. The power of the Durrani, who predominated politically from 1747 to 1978, rested on four subgroups: the Popalzai, whose Sadozai tribe held power from 1747 to 1818; the Alikozai; the Achakzai; and the dominant Barakzai, whose Muhammadzai tribe determined policy from 1818 to 1978.[8] In Afghanistan, clan, tribe and tribal federation were the relevant social units and not the nation, composed of at least six different ethnic groups. Despite the poverty of the landlocked country, and even though it was cut off from the important trade flows, Afghanistan became the focus of the major powers from the end of the 1830s – a circumstance that would shape the history of its northern neighbours.

Modern Afghanistan is a creation of Abdali-Pashtun Ahmad Khan (*ca.* 1722–72). At the beginning of the eighteenth century, the southern half of Afghanistan was divided between the kingdom of the Mughal and that of the Safavids. The border ran approximately between Ghazna and Kandahar, near Moqor.[9] The two most important cities of southern Afghanistan, Herat and Kandahar, which formed the gateways to India, were under Safavid sovereignty. At the same time, the Ghilzai dominated in Kandahar and the Abdali (Durrani) in Herat. When the bigoted Safavid Shah Sultan Husayn (1694–1722) pushed the Sunni Pashtuns to convert to Shia Islam, it stirred resistance. Among the protagonists of the resistance in Kandahar was Mir Ways, the leader of the tribe of the Hotaki, who belonged to the Ghilzai federation. Gurgin Khan – the former Georgian King Giorgi XI of Kartli, who had converted to

Islam and was appointed Safavid governor in 1704 – arrested Mir Ways and sent him to Isfahan, but there he was set free. When **Mir Ways** (r. 1709–15) – who allegedly called himself 'God's Shadow on Earth'[10] – returned to Kandahar, he succeeded in killing Gurgin Khan in 1709 and established the short-lived **Hotaki dynasty** (1709–38). Since Mir Ways' brother and successor **Abd al-Aziz** (r. 1715–17) wanted to submit again to Shah Husayn, against the will of the Hotaki, Mir Ways' son **Mir Mahmud** (r. 1717–25) overthrew him. At the same time, the Abdali of Herat liberated themselves under Abdallah Khan Sadozai (r. 1717–19/20), who – after the defeat of his son Asad Allah at the hands of Mir Mahmud Hotaki – was overthrown by Muhammad Zaman Khan Sadozai,

64. Camel caravan in south-eastern Afghanistan. Photo: 1980.

the father of the future King Ahmad Khan Abdali.[11] Muhammad Zaman's seizure of power after Asad Allah's defeat nullified the rare victory of a Ghilzai leader over an Abdali clan and stabilized the latter's position.

As soon as Mir Mahmud Hotaki cemented his rule in Kandahar, he turned west to fight the 'infidel' Shiites and Zoroastrians of Kerman. There, he carried out a massacre in 1720. The next year he returned to Kerman, from where he marched on Isfahan, the capital of the Safavids. On 22 October 1722, he conquered Isfahan and took the title of shah. Shah Husayn abdicated and of all his sons only Tahmasp Mirza was able to escape. He first fled to Qazvin, where he declared himself Shah Tahmasp II (r. 1722–32). When the Afghan Ghilzai conquered Qazvin in December 1722, he fled to Mazandaran. The Ghilzai dominated a large part of Iran, but only briefly. Shah Mahmud's reign was marked by numerous arbitrary executions, which is why some of his followers invited **Ashraf**

65. Cheerful rider next to the busy road between Herat and Kandahar. Photo: 2002.

Khan (r. 1725–29, d. 1730), the oldest son of Abd al-Aziz, to Isfahan. Immediately after his violent seizure of power, Ashraf Khan was confronted with Ottoman and Russian invaders. Like birds of prey swooping in for the kill, the Ottomans and Russia overthrew the moribund Safavid Empire in 1722.[12] When the Ottomans attacked the province of Azerbaijan in the spring of 1726, Ashraf Khan first ordered the imprisoned Shah Husayn to be executed. He next defeated the superior Turkish army near Korramabad, south of Hamedan. In the Treaty of Hamedan concluded in 1727, Ashraf surrendered western Iran, and the Ottomans recognised him as the Shah of Iran. While Ashraf Khan suffered a defeat at Langarud against the Russians stationed in Gilan, the Peace of Rasht signed in February 1729 effectively recognised his rule.[13] Although Ashraf Khan succeeded in keeping the two great powers in check, General Nader Quli Beg Afshar now emerged as a superior rival. The local warlord, Nader Shah, had offered his support to Tahmasp II at the beginning of 1726, and conquered the city of Mashhad in November. At the beginning of 1729, Nader neutralised the Abdali at Herat and then proceeded to defeat Ashraf Khan twice, on 29 September at Mihmandust near Damghan, and in November at Murchakhur, north of Isfahan. This ended Afghan rule in Iran. While fleeing to Kandahar, Ashraf Khan was murdered by Balochis, presumably at the behest of **Husayn Hotaki** (r. in Kandahar 1725–38). This fifth and last ruler of the Hotaki was overthrown and killed in March 1738 by Nader Shah on the occasion of the conquest of Kandahar. Nader Shah, on the other hand, had Tahmasp II deposed in 1732 and declared himself to be the new shah in 1736. In Kandahar, Nader Shah liberated the sixteen-year-old Ahmad Khan Abdali of the Sadozai tribe and took him into his service.[14]

Ahmad Khan soon rose under Nader Shah to command a 4,000-strong division of Abdali mounted warriors, who accompanied the shah everywhere as his guard. When Nader Shah was murdered by his own officers in 1747, the Abdali returned to Kandahar. On the way, they plundered a caravan from India with treasure destined for Nader Shah. This gave Ahmad the means to buy the followers of other sub-tribes. Since the leading Ghilzai had been decimated after the fall of Kandahar in 1738, the Abdali seized power and, in October 1747, chose **Ahmad Shah Durrani** (r. 1747–72) as their ruler. He took the title of Pâdshâh, Durr-i-Durran ('King, Pearl of Pearls'). From this point onward, the Abdali called themselves 'Durrani'. But even then, rivalry already manifested between the two leading subgroups of the Abdali: the Popalzai and the Barakzai. Since Ahmad Shah was a Sadozai of the Popalzai, Hajji Jamal Khan, a Muhammadzai of the Barakzai, was appointed vizier in compensation.[15] Ahmad seized the advantage and captured Ghazna,

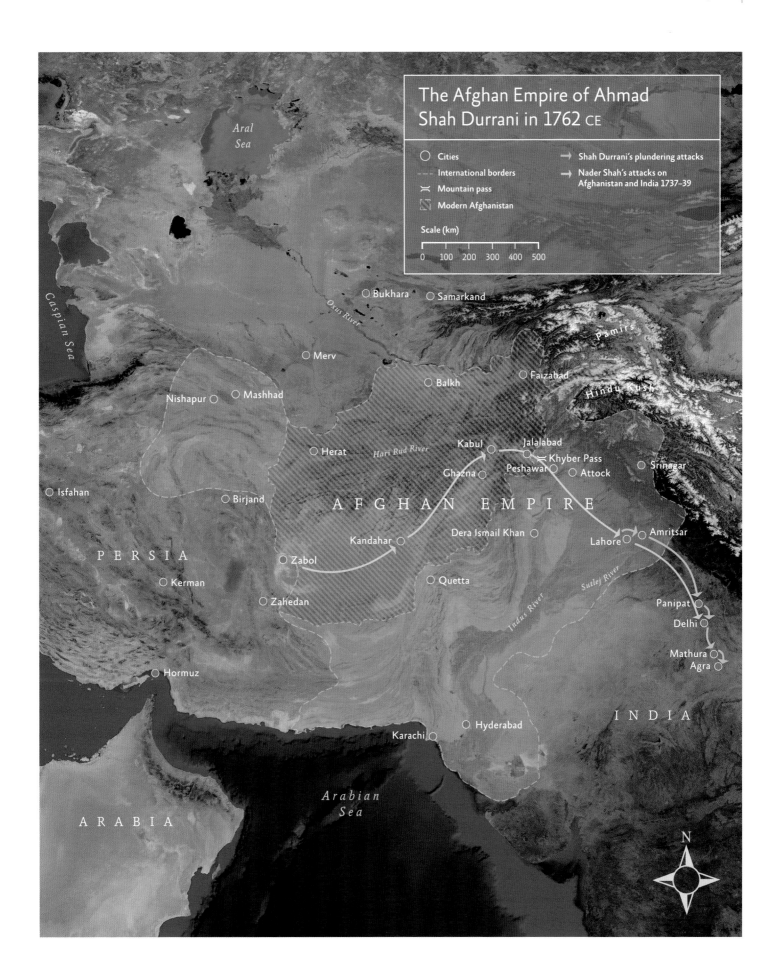

The Afghan Empire of Ahmad Shah Durrani in 1762 CE

- ○ Cities
- --- International borders
- ⤬ Mountain pass
- Modern Afghanistan
- → Shah Durrani's plundering attacks
- → Nader Shah's attacks on Afghanistan and India 1737–39

Scale (km)

0 100 200 300 400 500

Kabul, Peshawar and Lahore by January 1748. Despite his military success, Ahmad Shah faced the classic dilemma of a leader who presided over an alliance of tribal federations. To maintain such an ad hoc coalition over the long haul and to defend its territory, he needed an army. But the army had to be paid for and the tribal chiefs financially supported. To paraphrase a dictum by General Nicolls (1778–1849): 'An Afghan king is certain of the allegiance of his people only within the range of his guns and of his gold.'[16] As taxes could not be imposed, Ahmad Shah decided to plunder and coerce tributes. Between 1748 and 1769, he attacked the Indian subcontinent seven times on the path of previous invaders such as the Ghaznavids, Ghurids, and Nader Shah. There, the weak Mughal were unable to make a stand, except in the year 1748. Ahmad Durrani plundered Delhi in 1757 and 1761, and Amritsar in 1757 and 1762. Agra and Mathura also suffered fierce plundering. Sir Alexander Burnes (1805–41), who visited Kabul three times, assessed the Afghan invasions of India as follows: 'The Afghan invasions of India were not made by open warfare: they were as the prowling of wild beasts after their prey; and, like them, the invaders were contented secretly, and by surprise, to obtain their spoil and drag it back into their dens.'[17]

The Afghans, however, were unable to control North India, not least because they had two new adversaries, the Hindu Marathas and the Sikhs, who followed the teachings of Guru Nanak (1469–1538). Although Ahmad Durrani managed to crush the supremacy of the Marathas in the Third Battle of Panipat, his victory had unexpected consequences: the destruction of the Marathas paved the way for the military advancement of both the Sikhs and the East India Company, Afghanistan's two strongest opponents. Ahmad Shah's triumphs against the Sikhs between 1762 and 1767 were a Pyrrhic victory, as Punjab also escaped the control of the Afghans. In particular, the growing strength of the Sikh state in Punjab on Afghanistan's eastern frontier meant that the access route to further plundering in India was blocked and that Ahmad Shah's predatory economic model could not be sustained much longer. Ahmad Durrani, however, not only waged wars for the sake of looting, but also to establish a new empire. He therefore also conquered Herat, Mashhad, Bamiyan, Balkh, Mazar-e Sharif and Kunduz.[18]

Ahmad Durrani did not leave behind a consolidated state, but at best the outline of a state whose territorial delimitation he had marked out. Afghanistan had no institution that was superior to tribal structures and was little more than a tribal coalition, whose continued existence depended on the personality of the leader. As the Scottish diplomat Mountstuart Elphinstone (1779–1859) observed, the Afghan king controlled at most only the Durrani,

while the other tribal federations merely recognised him as an army commander. Accordingly, they would not tolerate any royal interference in their internal affairs.[19] State formation was also made difficult by the fact that Ahmad Shah's kingdom was an initiative of the Pashtuns, and he had to either buy or coerce the loyalty of other ethnic groups. Thanks to British financial support, Amir Abdur Rahman (r. 1880–1901) finally succeeded in building a national administration, which restricted the tribal leaders' autonomy.

The process of territorial contraction and the decline of Afghanistan began immediately after the death of Ahmad Durrani. His second son and successor **Timur Shah** (r. 1772–93) attempted to free himself from the dominance of the Durrani tribal leaders soon after ascending to the throne. He moved the capital from Kandahar to Kabul in 1775/76, and designated Peshawar as his summer residence. At the same time, he created a 12,000-strong troop of bodyguards, consisting of Shiite Qizilbash ('red heads'). The Qizilbash were Turkic warriors who had converted to Shia. In foreign affairs, Timur Shah was engaged in defensive wars against Bukhara, the Sikhs and Sindh, which was largely liberated from Afghan supremacy. Timur, who may have died of poison, had 24 sons. Of these, **Zaman Shah** (r. 1793–1800) owed his throne to the leader of the Muhammadzai Sardar Payenda Khan, a son of Ahmad Shah's vizier Hajji Jamal Khan. Zaman had his brother Humayum, residing in Kandahar, blinded, but he left his brother Mahmud, who governed in Herat and had rebelled against him, in office. This later proved to be a fatal mistake. Zaman Shah then planned a campaign against the British in India at the prompting of Tipu Sultan of Mysore (r. 1782–99), the East India Company's arch-enemy. Since Tipu Sultan had also proposed a military alliance to France on several occasions, British fears of a Franco-Afghan-Indian alliance prevailed. For the first time, London realised that the British territories in India were vulnerable to attack from the north-west. When General Napoleon Bonaparte, who had landed in Egypt in July, and foreign minister Talleyrand declared in 1798 that the road to India went through Egypt, this possibility seemed to gain traction. Afghanistan thus became a central policy concern of the major European powers for the first time.[20] But in his campaigns to India, Zaman never made it past Lahore and had to return to Afghanistan each time because of rebellions. When Zaman tried to break the dominance of Durrani leaders, especially the Barakzai, they conspired together to overthrow Zaman. Zaman, however, beat them to the punch and executed the ringleader Sardar Payenda Khan. As the Afghan diplomat and historian Mohan Lal (1812–77) reported, Fateh Khan, the oldest of Payenda Khan's 21 sons, persuaded Zaman's brother Mahmud to rebel against Zaman. Zaman was captured and blinded in 1800, which led to **Shah Mahmud** (r. 1801–3) taking the throne.[21] During Mahmud's first short period of rule, Mashhad was lost to the Persians in 1802. Soon afterwards, street battles broke out in Kabul between Sunnis and Shiites, which offered Mahmud's younger half-brother **Shah Shujah** (first rule 1803–9) the opportunity to seize power himself. As the shah was almost constantly preoccupied with the suppression of Durrani and Ghilzai tribes, the region was hardly ever at peace.

The meeting in Peshawar between Shujah and the envoy of the East India Company, Mountstuart Elphinstone, was unprecedented from a foreign policy perspective. The treaty concluded on 17 June 1809 stipulated that neither France nor any other foreign power could open up a diplomatic office, let alone a military base, in Afghanistan.[22] It was directed against both Napoleon and Tsar Alexander I, and was intended to thwart a possible Franco-Persian or French-Russian attack on India via Afghanistan.[23] Elphinstone already pointed out at this time to the governor-general of the

East India Company, Lord Minto (in office 1807–13) that the military frontier of India would have to be shifted northwards to the Indus if Great Britain hoped to stave off the Russian advance into Central Asia.[24] Even earlier, in March 1801, the British envoy in Tehran, John Malcolm (1769–1833), outlined the only possible approach for a Russian advance to India: given the topographical conditions, he presumed that Russian troops would land in Astarabad (today's Gorgan) on the south-east of the Caspian Sea, and continue from there to Mashhad, Herat and Kabul or Kandahar. Malcolm's hunch was surprisingly realistic. He also pointed out that it was unlikely the Afghan shah would ever enter into a military alliance with Russia.[25] The British ambassador in Baghdad, Harford Jones (1764–1847), offered a similar assessment: he considered the passage of a French army from Syria to the Caspian Sea feasible, where it could then unite with a Russian expeditionary corps. But in contrast to Malcolm, Jones assumed that the greed for plunder might motivate Afghanistan to join the French-Russian invaders.[26]

66. Sketch of the fortress of Ghazna, Afghanistan. In the foreground, the two Ghaznavid victory towers from the twelfth century.[13] James Atkinson, *Sketches in Afghanistan* (London: Graves, 1842), pl. 15.

The renewed fears of the British stemmed from two treaties concluded by Napoleon: in the Treaty of Finkenstein of 4 May 1807, France guaranteed Persia's territorial integrity and promised arms and military instructors. Napoleon, furthermore, sent General Gardane as an envoy to Tehran. In return, Persia agreed to declare war on Britain, to give French troops free access to India, and to persuade the Afghans to attack the British possessions in India together with France.[27] The Treaty of Tilsit signed with Russia on 7 July 1807 largely annulled the Treaty of Finkenstein,[28] but left room for a joint French-Russian attack on India, as Napoleon and Tsar Paul had already contemplated in 1800/01.[29] Great Britain secured the vulnerable west flank of its Indian possessions in the Anglo-Persian Agreement of 12 March 1809, which annulled all previous treaties between Persia and a European power, and obligated the shah to prevent the passage of European troops to the best of his ability.[30] From the Persian point of view, however, the three Anglo-Persian treaties of 1809, 1812 and 1814 were worthless, since Great Britain, which had been allied with Russia against Napoleon since 1812, did nothing to stop the Russian advance into the south-eastern Caucasus.[31]

While Shah Shujah was still negotiating with Elphinstone, his half-brother Mahmud rebelled with the help of Fateh Khan and occupied Kabul. The two rebels then defeated Shah Shujah in the Battle of Nimla (between Kabul and Peshawar), and **Shah Mahmud** (1809–18) ascended the throne for the second time. After unsuccessful attempts to reclaim power, Shah Shujah fled to Ranjit Singh (r. 1801–39) in Lahore in 1813. There, the Maharajah of the Sikhs seized the famous Koh-i-Noor diamond from the refugee. The diamond had been stolen in Delhi by Nader Shah in 1739 and had fallen into Ahmad Durrani's hands after 1747.[32] Also in 1813, Ranjit conquered vizier Fateh Khan in the Battle of Attock. However, Shah Mahmud and his sadistic son Kamran were jealous of Fateh Khan, who had the real power. They therefore blinded him in 1818 and cruelly tortured him to death. But this proved to be a grave error. As Mohan Lal writes: 'The end of the Vazir Fatah Khan was the end of the Sadozai realm.'[33] In fact, the 20 brothers of the murdered Fateh Khan mobilised the Barakzai tribal warriors, forcing Shah Mahmud and Kamran to flee to Herat, where a small realm of Sadozai rule existed until 1863. Outside of Herat, a fratricidal war raged on among Fateh Khan's

---

67. The Hazrat Ali Mosque in Mazar-e Sharif, Afghanistan. The mosque was rebuilt in 1481 by the Timurid Sultan Husayn Baqara and later renovated several times. The alleged tomb of the fourth caliph Ali ibn Abi Talib (r. 656–61) is highly revered by both Shiites and Sunnis from northern Afghanistan. Photo: 2002.

68. Winter landscape between Kunduz and Farkhar in northern Afghanistan. Photo: January 2008.

20 brothers until 1826, which Ranjit Singh exploited to conquer Multan and Kashmir. In 1826, the situation stabilised, as **Dost Muhammad Khan** (first rule 1826–39), fourth youngest brother of Fateh Khan, seized power in Kabul, Ghazna and Jalalabad, while his brother Kohandil Khan ruled in Kandahar. As a consequence, the Muhammadzai-Barakzai dynasty replaced that of the Sadozai-Popalzai.[34]

In 1834, Shah Shujah made another attempt to regain power in Kabul. In return for troops and financial support, he offered to officially transfer to Ranjit Singh the city of Peshawar, which, however, he did not even control. Armed with the unofficial support of the British diplomatic agent at Ranjit Singh's court, Captain Claude Wade, and the tacit understanding of governor-general Lord Bentinck, Shah Shujah attacked Kandahar in the summer. There, he suffered a severe defeat against Kohandil Khan and Dost Muhammad and had to flee. Ranjit Singh, however, annexed Peshawar, and Dost Muhammad henceforth called himself Amir al-Muminin ('Leader of the Faithful'). In April 1837,

Amir Dost tried to recapture Peshawar and sent out his son Akbar Khan for this purpose. He defeated and killed the Sikh governor of Peshawar at Jamrud, at the southern end of the Khyber Pass. Instead of exploiting the victory by making an advance, the Amir Dost ordered a retreat – possibly because he feared direct confrontation with Ranjit Singh, or because he did not want to provoke the interference of Great Britain, Ranjit Singh's ally.[35] He chose the path of diplomacy and sent a letter to the new British governor-general Lord Auckland (in office 1836–42). In it, he complained about the aggression of the Sikhs and proposed making the Indus River a border to them. Peshawar thus would have belonged to Afghanistan again. The question of who possessed Peshawar forced Great Britain to choose either between its present ally Ranjit Singh or Dost Muhammad, who would provide a bulwark against possible invaders from the north and west. The third possibility was direct interference by deposing one of the two rivals in favour of a submissive successor who would not make any claim on the disputed city.[36]

2. The Khanate of Chorasmia under the Qungrat and the Prelude to the Anglo-Russian Rivalry

The reign of the Qungrat dynasty began in 1770, when **Muhammad Amin** (r. 1770–90) expelled Yomut Turkmen from Khiva and took power as chief minister, or atiq.[37] His successor **Avaz** (1790–1804) was content to maintain the title of atiq. However, **Iltüzer Khan** (r. 1804–6) called himself khan and established the **dynasty of the Qungrat** (1770/1804–1920).[38] After only two years of rule, Iltüzer fell in battle against Bukhara. His successor **Muhammad Rahim Bahadur I Khan** (1806–25) was much more successful. He managed to subdue various nomadic tribes of the Uzbeks, Turkmen and the Karakalpaks living on the eastern bank of the Aral Sea, whom he resettled in the delta of the Amu Darya. In 1822, he wrested the oasis of Merv from Bukhara, which was lost to the Turkmen tribe of the Sariq from 1843 to 1854. Relations with the Turkmen tribes of Tekke, Sariq and Yomut were tense: on the one hand, the Turkmen, who were active as kidnappers, supplied the slave market of Khiva, the largest in Central Asia. The khan levied a tax of 20 per cent on the trade in slaves, who also constituted the backbone of the army.[39] On the other hand, the Turkmen were inclined to rebel, and resisted the efforts of the government to increase the amount of arable land by expanding the irrigation system.[40] Muhammad Rahim's third successor – after **Allah Quli** (1825–42) and **Rahim Quli** (1842–46) – was **Muhammad Amin** (1846–55). He died in the fighting against the Tekke near Sarakhs, at which point Khiva finally lost control of Merv. The death of the khan set off further Turkmen revolts, in which two other khans, **Abdallah** (r. 1855) and **Qutlugh Murad** (r. 1855–56) lost their lives. **Sayyid Muhammad** (1856–65) was the first to stabilise the situation, especially in the areas north of the Amu Darya. His successor **Sayyid Muhammad Rahim II** (r. 1865–1910, Russian vassal from 1873), however, had to recognise the Russian supremacy in 1873.[41]

The economy of the khanate was parasitic: while it is true that agriculture flourished in the oases, the main source of income came through abductions. Turkmen invaded Iran and kidnapped defenceless Persian peasants, and Kazakhs in the north kidnapped Russian settlers, selling them on the slave market of Khiva and, less frequently, to Bukhara. Russia itself sometimes bought the freedom of Russian slaves. According to the Russian captain Nikolay N. Muravyov, who visited Khiva in 1819, 3,000 Russian and 30,000 Persian slaves languished in captivity.[42] Their owners were allowed

to kill or mutilate them, and if a slave repeatedly tried to escape, 'the unfortunate soul was nailed by his ear to a stake or the door of the house of his master, where he had to remain without food for three whole days'.[43] For Russia, the regime in Khiva was a nuisance in many respects: first, it was a disgrace to know that their own citizens were enslaved; second, the khanate allowed raids on Russian merchant caravans; and, third, Khiva isolated itself, which made transit trade to the south impossible. Chorasmia, however, remained protected for a long time by its geography; namely, the

69. The 'short minaret' Kalta Minar in Khiva, Uzbekistan. The unfinished 26-m-high minaret was commissioned by Muhammad Amin Khan (r. 1846–55); construction was stopped after his death, however. Photo: 2004.

deserts Kyzyl Kum in the north and Kara Kum in the south-west, as well as the semi-desert peninsula of Mangyshlak in the north-west. Despite this, Russia undertook measures early on to subdue the disruptive khanate. After the failed expeditions of the Starenskoi Cossacks in 1603 and of Prince Alexander Bekovich-Cherkassky in 1717,[44] the governor of Orenburg had the opportunity in 1793 to explore the secluded khanate when a delegation from Khiva requested that he send an eye specialist to heal an eye complaint of the khan's uncle. The governor sent the doctor and later Major General Blankennagel, who stayed in Khiva from 5 October 1793 to 12 March 1794. Blankennagel, who could not heal the completely blind man, escaped death only because Avaz Atiq feared Russian reprisals should he kill its envoy. The doctor recognised the potential here for cotton cultivation and trade and recommended conquering Khiva, also in part to open a trade route to India.[45]

In 1819, General Aleksey Yermolov, the Russian supreme commander in the Caucasus, attempted to establish trade relations with Khiva in order to then, in a second step, annex the khanate. A short time earlier, Georg Stepanovich Vinsky, adviser to the Russian Foreign Ministry, had recommended conquering Khiva to secure trade routes and to promote trade with Bukhara and ultimately with India: 'Khiva, I conclude, would in time become a Russian Gibraltar in Great Tartary. She would serve the traders of all lands as a peaceful wharf . . . She would become a gateway through which our own merchants could import the rich wares of India.'[46] Yermolov dispatched Captain Nikolay Muravyov to Khiva with the additional secret commission of finding an approach route and spying on the khanate's military strength. Muravyov embarked in Baku, crossed the Caspian Sea and landed in the area of the former delta of the Uzboy River. He then followed its dried-up course.[47] His Turkmen travelling companions, however, noticed that Muravyov recorded the distances between the wells and their depths, so they denounced him as spy to the khan. Like Blankennagel, Muravyov escaped death only because of Muhammad Rahim Khan's fear of Russian retaliation. The khan received him after 48 days of imprisonment, but rejected trade with Baku via Krasnovodsk (today's Turkmenbashi) and over the Caspian Sea.[48] Muravyov also recommended the conquest of Khiva as it blocked a possible trade route to India.[49] Muravyov, and presumably Yermolov, hoped to divert India's trade with Europe via Khiva, Baku and Astrakhan to Russia, and to disrupt the British trade monopoly between India and Europe by way of India's back doors, the cities of Herat and Kandahar. Yermolov, however, was unpopular with Tsar Alexander, and Alexander's successor, Tsar Nicholas I (r. 1825–55), soon dismissed him after taking power. Khiva consequently remained safe for another 20 years.

By the end of the 1830s, the geopolitical situation on the Eurasian continent had changed dramatically. The former allies against Napoleon from 1812–15 were now bitter rivals. Since the Treaty of Turkmenchay of 1828, Russia had established a de facto protectorate over Persia, annexed the southern Caucasus, and sought to gain control of Constantinople, the Bosphorus and the Dardanelles. For London, this was not acceptable. With the opening of the Suez Canal in November 1869, this issue became much more explosive, as the canal would have allowed a Russian fleet, having passed the Bosphorus and Dardanelles unhindered, a further advance to India or South Persia. Already Napoleon's first ambassador in Persia, Antoine-Alexandre Romieu, had pointed out in 1805 that Russia's real aim in advancing into the Caucasus was not the conquest of Persia, but the destruction of the Ottoman Empire and the conquest of Constantinople.[50] The British foreign minister George Canning (1770–1827, in office 1822–27) and prime minister Arthur Wellesley, 1st Duke of Wellington (1769–1852, in office 1828–30), expressed their concern about Russia's intentions in the course of the Greek War of Independence (1821–32). Canning and Wellington were determined to ensure that the Ottoman Empire remained independent: 'The independence of the Porte is important to all powers of Christendom. Its maritime independence, and particularly the independent exercise of sovereign authority in its own waters, is important to all Powers of the Mediterranean, and to all maritime Powers.'[51] After the Crimean War, it appeared that several offensive Russian campaigns directed against India were aimed at getting a free hand against Constantinople.

In the 1820s, Russia had also begun its advance to the southeast and dispersed two of the four Kazakh hordes by 1824. Great Britain, on the other hand, had brought India largely under its rule, and was allied with Ranjit Singh, the powerful ruler of the Sikhs.[52] Moreover, in 1837–38, Persia had laid siege to Herat for nine months with active Russian support.[53] The city's defence had been organised by the British lieutenant Eldred Pottinger. The Persian-Russian advance on Herat was all the more menacing to British India given that the officer Arthur Conolly (1807–42) had already shown in 1830 that there was a route from the fertile oasis of Herat via Kandahar and Quetta to the Indus that could be easily negotiated by a large army. This was just as John Malcolm had outlined in 1801. The only geographical obstacle was the narrow Bolan Pass.[54] The British governor-general Lord Auckland forced the Persian Shah to withdraw by sending a small flotilla. The fleet occupied the Persian island of Kharg on 19 June 1838 and threatened war.[55] At the same time, the British envoy Alexander Burnes, who had visited Bukhara in 1832,[56] and the Russian captain Ivan Vitkevich,[57] who had already been to Bukhara three times, courted the favour of Dost Muhammad. When the latter decided to enter into an alliance with Russia in April 1838, Lord Auckland moved to depose the amir militarily and replace him with Shah Shujah. On 6 July 1839, the British army occupied Kabul.[58] From the Russian point of view, the question arose as to whether British India would use the newly established protectorate over Afghanistan to force the three Uzbek khanates into its sphere of influence. This suspicion was all the more justified as Colonel Charles Stoddart (1807–42) had arrived in Bukhara in December 1838 to assure Nasrallah Khan (r. 1827–60) that the impending British attack on Kabul was by no means directed against him.[59] In view of Great Britain's offensive strategy, Russia also decided to adopt a similar approach, specifically in its conquest of Khiva and the liberation of Russian prisoners.

In the late summer of 1839, General Vasily Perovsky (1794–1857), military governor of Orenburg, was ordered to annex Khiva. The timing was especially auspicious as the British were caught up in Afghanistan. As the route from Orenburg to Khiva crosses the arid Ustyurt plateau, Perovsky opted for a winter campaign to avoid the summer heat. The expedition was ill-prepared, however, especially since the 5,300-strong army consisted mainly of recruits, condemned criminals, exiles, and only few experienced Cossacks. The troops left Orenburg in mid-November and were soon surprised by extraordinarily heavy snowfall. As more and more soldiers fell victim to the cold and various diseases, and the transport camels fell by the dozen, General Perovsky had to order a retreat halfway to Khiva on 1 February 1840. It was the only way to avert the demise of the entire expeditionary corps.[60] The retreat was a disgrace – not a single Russian slave was liberated and Khiva was never at risk. The failure was all the more painful as Great Britain had apparently achieved a brilliant victory in Afghanistan. Great Britain did not remain inactive in the face of the Russian preparations for invasion, however. It sent Captain James Abbott (1807–96) to Khiva to convince Khan Allah Quli of the necessity of freeing the Russian slaves and thus preventing an impending Russian assault. Allah Quli received Abbott at the beginning of 1840 and was disappointed

70. The courtyard of the harem of the khans of Khiva in the palace Tash Hauli, the 'stone house', decorated with majolica tiles, built in 1830–38. Khiva, Uzbekistan. Photo: 2004.

71. The reception hall of the Khan of Khiva called Ichrat Hauli inside the Tash Hauli Palace; in the middle is the silver throne of the khans. Khiva, Uzbekistan. Photo: 2004.

72. A carved wooden column on a marble pedestal. Tash Hauli Palace, Khiva, Uzbekistan. Photo: 2004.

that the British would not promise him military support against the Russians. In March, he dismissed Abbott without giving him a positive answer.[61] Three months later, a second British officer, Lieutenant Richmond Shakespear (1812–61), appeared in Khiva with the same task. Shakespear's effort proved extremely successful: on 15 August he left Khiva in the direction of Orenburg together with 416 Russian slaves. General Perovsky was delighted, even though Shakespear had achieved single-handedly what he, Perovsky, had failed to accomplish with his army: to liberate some of the slaves. He released the 600 traders from Khiva, who were held in retaliation in Orenburg and Astrakhan. While Tsar Nicholas officially congratulated him on his success, he was privately furious that, in going it alone, the young Briton had eliminated the pretext for a second Russian invasion.[62] Two years later, Russia sent a peaceful delegation headed by Colonel Denilevsky to Khiva, which included the botanist Theodor Basiner, and signed a trade agreement with Khan Rahim Quli.[63]

A short time later, the priorities of the Russians changed, and they decided on a new strategy. In the North Caucasus, local resistance to the Russian occupation intensified, and in view of the catastrophic British defeat against the rebellious Afghans in the winter of 1841–42, Russian fears of a British intervention north of the Oxus were greatly reduced. The war in Dagestan and Chechnya, which lasted until 1859, and the lost Crimean War, gave the three Uzbek khanates a 20-year respite. Russia, moreover, had changed its tactics in Central Asia. Instead of undertaking risky military expeditions with long marches, Perovsky's successor, General Obruchev, pursued the ongoing pacification of the Kazakh steppe and the construction of small fortresses. The goal over the long term was to use the steppe as a springboard for conquering the khanates.[64] The establishment of the fortresses of Raimskoe (1847), Ak Mejet (1853) and Verny (1854) marked the most important stages of this new, more cautious strategy.[65] Russia maintained the goal of an annexation of Central Asia – not just for geopolitical, but also for economic, reasons. Although Russia's industry grew, its products were not competitive against those from Western Europe. As a result, they urgently needed new markets, not least because the purchasing power of the Russian population was still low due to widespread serfdom.[66] In 1826, Major General Alexander Vergin had already recommended in a memorandum to Tsar Nicholas I that a captive market be created in Central Asia for Russian goods, which could not keep up with Western European products.[67]

3. The Emirate of Bukhara and the Manghit Dynasty

As in the neighbouring Khiva, tribal leaders who served as ataliq displaced the khans from power and degraded them to interchangeable puppets. Since **Muhammad Hakim Bey** (as ataliq 1714–43) rose to chief minister in 1714, the leaders of the Manghit held power with brief interruptions until 1920.[68] Hakim Bey's successor **Muhammad Rahim** (r. as ataliq 1743–56, as khan 1756–58) appointed himself khan in 1756. However, due to the unrest following his death, **Danial Bey** (r. as ataliq 1758–85) settled on the title of ataliq. His son and successor **Shah Murad** (r. as amir 1785–99), on the other hand, called himself 'amir' and did away with nominating a Genghis-Khanid puppet khan. The pious Shah Murad not only sought to revitalise the emirate economically, but he also promoted tax-free Islamic foundations (*vaqf*) and conquered the oasis city of Merv around 1798. He then proceeded to deport its Shiite population to Bukhara and to impose the adoption of Sunni Islam. His son and successor **Amir Haydar Töre** (r. 1800–26) continued the conversion policy of his father in favour of Sunnism, as well as keeping up his efforts to extend the emirate's territory. In 1822, he lost Merv to Khiva, but conquered the territories of Balkh, Maymana, Kunduz and Badakhshan, south of the Amu Darya River (Oxus) in 1817. His son and

73. As Arminius Vámbéry, who visited Khiva in 1863 dressed as a Dervish, reported, the tribal warriors who presented severed heads of defeated enemies to the treasurer were rewarded with different types of valuable honorary dress.[14] Vámbéry, *Voyages d'un faux derviche* (1865), opposite p. 132.

successor Nasrallah, however, forfeited them once again between 1850 and 1855 to the Afghan ruler Dost Muhammad.[69]

Since Amir Haydar was interested in trade contacts with Russia, an embassy led by M. de Negri – protected by a strong military escort from attacks by Kazakhs and robbers from Khiva – reached Bukhara in 1820. Taking advantage of the opportunity to explore the enigmatic city and to map the region east of the Aral Sea were three scientists: officer and cartographer Georg von Meyendorff (1795–1863), who is responsible for one of Bukhara's earliest descriptions;[70] the botanist and zoologist Eduard F. Eversmann (1794–1860); and the zoologist Christian H. Pander (1794–1865). Five years later, the English veterinarian and horse breeder William Moorcroft (1767–1825) had less success. He reached Bukhara in February 1825, together with his companions George Guthrie and George Trebeck. Moorcroft intended to sell select British goods

74. The Chor Minor in Bukhara, built in 1807 and whose name in Persian means 'four minarets', was never a mosque, but rather the gatehouse to a now-vanished madrasah. Photo: 2004.

in Bukhara and to acquire horses for breeding with the proceeds. But he quickly recognised that the Bukhara market was flooded with cheap Russian bulk goods and that good horses were in short supply because the amir had confiscated them for a campaign. Amir Haydar, for his part, expected his guests to assist him in the operation of siege artillery. Moorcroft refused, however, and the disappointed amir dismissed him. Six weeks later, the three Britons died on their way home near Balkh without any signs of external injury. The amir presumably had them poisoned.[71] As Moorcroft's biographer Garry Alder emphasises, Moorcroft, who had been informed in detail about the armed Russian legation of 1820, predicted in his notes the military advance of Russia into the Uzbek khanates. He had also anticipated the Russian threat from Herat and Chinese Turkestan, where he additionally suspected the outbreak of Muslim revolts against China – events that took place between 1865 and 1914.[72]

Amir Nasrallah (r. 1827–60) was infamous for his cruelty and bore the nickname Amir-i Qassab ('Amir the Butcher').[73] The eloquent diplomat Alexander Burnes, who also mastered the required etiquette in his contact with Central Asian despots and respected local customs, reported: 'The King of Bokhara rules, as in other Asiatic nations, a sovereign despot; nevertheless, he is controlled in every action by the authority of the Moolahs or priests.... The constitution of the monarchy, which is exclusively based on the laws of the Koran, [is] here more strictly enforced than in any other Mahommedan country. [...] The reigning king ...appears, indeed, to be gradually sinking into the bigoted habits of his father. [...] There is no shadow of popular government, but still there is no evidence of discontent under such a system of rule, though people cannot be more thoroughly enslaved than the Uzbeks. [...] The most trivial offences are punished with death.'[74] Other travellers who visited Bukhara and Khiva also confirmed Burnes' impression of a rigid, backward and brutal society marked by pious bigotry. For example, Theodor Basiner in 1842 and the Hungarian Orientalist and British spy Arminius Vámbéry (1832–1913), who had travelled to Khorasan, Khiva and Bukhara in 1863–64 disguised as a Turkish Dervish, reported of how women in Khiva, rightly or wrongly accused of adultery, were stoned to death. They further told of how warriors returning from a raid were rewarded according to how many severed heads and useful slaves they handed over to the authorities. 'I actually looked at 100 horsemen covered with dust arriving from their camp. Each one of had several captives to tow, including children and women, who were either bound to the tail of the horse or the saddle-knob; [the rider also] had a large open sack, which contained the cut-off

75. The gateway to the 'Ark' citadel of Bukhara; the structure that is visible today dates from the eighteenth and early nineteenth centuries. Photo: 2004.

heads of the enemy. Once arriving at the square, he surrendered the prisoners ... and then untied the sack, grabbed a hold of it at both ends, and as if pouring out potatoes, these bearded and beardless heads rolled out in front of the clerk, whose servant thrust them together with his feet until a great mound of a several hundred had piled up. Each warrior got a receipt of the heads he handed over, and the payout took place a few days later'[75] (fig. 73). In Bukhara, on the other hand, Vámbéry was struck by the religious conceit according to which Bukhara and its native inhabitants were the 'true bearers of Islam' and the spy network of the mullahs and the government. 'Every trace of cheerfulness or exhilaration has been banished from circles where religion and the government's system of surveillance are so tyrannizing.'[76]

Less fortunate than Alexander Burnes were the two Britons Stoddart and Conolly a few years later. Lieutenant Colonel Stoddart (1807–42) was arrested in Bukhara shortly after his arrival at the end of 1838 and thrown into a miserable dungeon. Unlike Burnes, Stoddart lacked tact. He had already offended Amir Nasrallah at the first encounter. Nasrallah, moreover, suspected him of spying.

To save his own life, Stoddart had to convert to Islam, though he remained in detention. The amir probably stopped short of carrying out an execution due to the fact that Kabul was occupied by the British. Three years after his arrest, Stoddart welcomed a fellow sufferer in the person of Captain Conolly. He had followed the utopian plan of reconciling the three Uzbek khanates with each other in order to form an anti-Russian bloc. When the two rulers of Khiva and Kokand, Allah Quli and Muhammad Ali, received Conolly, they made it clear that they had no interest in an anti-Russian alliance. In addition, both khans warned Conolly against travelling to Nasrallah. Despite all the warnings, however, he arrived in Bukhara in November 1841, where the amir also quickly sent him to prison. Nasrallah was irritated that his letter, sent months earlier to Queen Victoria, remained unanswered. Foreign minister Palmerston, furthermore, informed him that his letter had been passed on to the governor-general of British India. Nasrallah interpreted this as contempt on the part of London and, what is more, as a sign that Stoddart and Conolly were not official envoys, but mere impostors. Nor did the Russian legation, led by Major

76. The rebuilt entrance of the mighty fortress of Hissar, Tajikistan. The fortress stood on a natural hill that had been inhabited since the Stone Age, and it controlled the ancient trade route that linked Termez on the Oxus with Kashgar. In the late Middle Ages, Hissar was the capital of a smaller, more or less independent khanate, which Russia allotted to Bukhara in 1873.[15] Photo: 2008.

Butenev in the winter of 1841/42, manage to obtain the release of the two Britons.[77] However, when Nasrallah learned of the British catastrophe in Afghanistan, he no longer had to fear retribution. He had the two prisoners decapitated in June 1842. A year later, Nasrallah showed a gentler side when he permitted the Christian missionary Joseph Wolff, who had travelled to Bukhara to investigate the fate of Stoddart and Conolly, to leave the city unmolested.[78]

In 1858, Sayyid Muhammad, the khan of Khiva, and Nasrallah, the amir of Bukhara, were confronted by the arrival of a powerful Russian delegation. They had both sent legations to Russia a year earlier in 1855 on the occasion of Tsar Alexander II's ascension. The tsar, who was humiliated by the Crimean War, took the opportunity to regain the initiative lost in Central Asia after General Perovsky's debacle of 1839–40. He sent a delegation under the leadership of the young officer Count Nikolay Ignatyev (1832–1908) and protected by Cossacks, that arrived in Khiva in July 1858. Ignatyev's commission was to open up the markets of both khanates for Russian products, to explore the navigability of the Oxus, and to spy on the military strength of both khanates.

In Khiva, Sayyid Muhammad, who was still angry about the appearance of the Russian flotilla on the lower reaches of the Oxus, was not very accommodating.[79] He rightly feared that regular shipping from the Aral Sea through his khanate and onwards to Bukhara would unsettle his dominion. Ignatyev's last audience with the khan on the night of 24 to 25 August was all the more terrifying, as he had to appear without his Cossacks: 'Near the gates of the Palace protruded two enormous stakes upon which were impaled tortured victims of this barbarous government to scare me personally.' The audience ended in turmoil, and Ignatyev owed his life to a troop of armed Cossacks, who entered the palace without instructions to ensure his safety.[80] Amir Nasrallah, who at the time was at war with the neighbouring khanate of Kokand, received Ignatyev cordially, but remained non-committal. He refused free navigation on the Oxus, yet proposed attacking the khanate of Khiva and dividing it between Russia and Bukhara.[81]

Nevertheless, the legation was successful from the Russian perspective, since it had revealed the military weakness of the two khanates and the unreliability of the two khans.[82] Ignatyev was convinced that the only way to eliminate the danger of British interference was a conquest of the khanates. In his report, Ignatyev programmatically defined the essential cornerstones of Russian foreign and military policy: 'In case of an explosion with Great Britain, only in Asia can we expect to win and harm Turkey [which stood under British protection]. [...] I felt that Asia was the only area remaining for our trade activities and development of our industry because we were too weak to enter into successful competition with Great Britain, France, Belgium, and the United States of America. [...] I continually showed the necessity ...to subordinate Central Asia to Russian influence, gain control of the Amu Darya...for the use of our military ships and finally to threaten Great Britain in order to force it to value our friendship.'[83] A short time later, in 1859–60, Ignatyev pulled off a masterstroke of diplomacy. By playing off a Franco-British military alliance, which occupied Beijing, against the weakened Chinese government, it was possible to secure once and for all the possession of the territories conquered by General Muravyov on the Amur River.[84] Nasrallah, however, was the last independent ruling khan of Bukhara, as his son and successor **Muzaffar al-Din** (r. 1860–85) had to recognise the supremacy of Russia after three defeats suffered in 1868.[85]

4. The Khanate of Kokand and the Dynasty of the Ming

The origins of the khanate of Kokand go back to the early eighteenth century, when the khanate of Bukhara had begun to collapse. The chief **Shah Rukh** (r. 1709–21) from the Uzbek tribe of the Ming allegedly defeated his rivals in the Fergana Valley, including the Naqshbandi khojas of Chadak, and built a first fortress in Kokand. He was followed by his eldest son **Abdu'l Rahim** (r. 1721–33), who was killed in a conspiracy in 1733 due to an alleged mental disorder. His brother **Abdu'l Karim Bey** (r. 1733–46 or 1750) succeeded him. He rebuilt the citadel of Kokand, which had been destroyed in the previous power struggles, and expanded the surrounding city. Abdu'l's successor **Abdu'l Rahman** (r. *ca.* 1750–51) was deposed after only one year. **Irdana Bey** (1751–70) then asserted himself following a power struggle. As a consequence of Emperor Qianlong's destruction of the Dzungar Empire in 1757, Irdana Bey was confronted with foreign invaders. First, he had to repel fleeing Dzungars, who invaded the Fergana Valley. Chinese troops then began to close in on Kokand. When a Chinese envoy asked

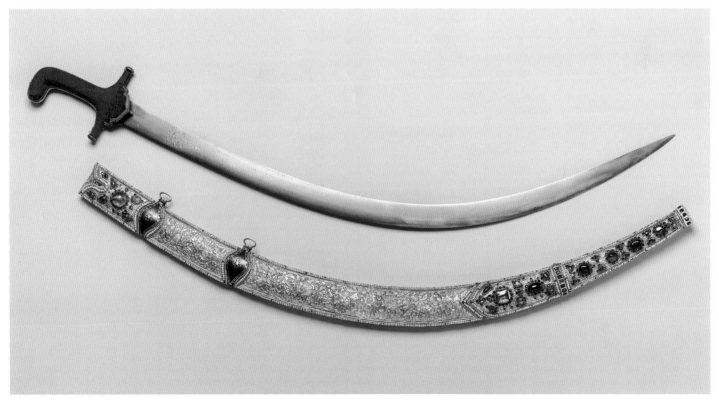

77. Sabre with a scabbard. The Persian-made sabre dates from the late eighteenth century, the scabbard, manufactured in Khiva, from the middle of the nineteenth century. The total length of the sabre is 92.5 cm; it was presented by the Khan of Kokand Muhammad Khudayar Khan (3rd reign 1865–75) in 1868 to Tsar Alexander II (r. 1855–81). Inv. No. B.O.-1848. The State Hermitage Museum, St Petersburg, Russia.

78. Late medieval petroglyphs of riders and modern scrawlings of names at Langar II, Tajikistan. Photo: 2008.

Irdana Bey for assistance in the search for the two fleeing khojas from Kashgar, Irdana preferred to offer China the nominal subjugation of his khanate. This, in turn, gave him commercial advantages in trade with Kashgar. Afterwards, an Afghan army appeared around 1763/65 in the vicinity of Kokand: some Muslim rulers of the region, and allegedly also Irdana Bey, had called on Shah Ahmad Durrani for help against the 'infidels'. Ahmad Durrani contented himself with the intimidation of Bukhara and the plundering of Badakhshan, and withdrew his troops in 1765. Meanwhile, Irdana succeeded in conquering the important trading city of Osh in 1762. Irdana's successor **Sulayman Shah** (r. 1770) was murdered after a few months and the plotters put **Narbuta Bey** (r. 1770–98/99) on the throne. He succeeded in consolidating his rule over the entire Fergana Valley. During his reign, early tensions developed with Kokand's nominal overlord, when he refused to hand over Sarimsaq – the son of Burhan al-Din, one of the last two khojas of Kashgar[86] – to the Chinese authorities. A second source of conflict concerned trade policy. In 1785, China declared a trade boycott on Russia and closed the Kyakhta border market. Kokand, which bordered on Kashgaria, filled the void by buying and selling Chinese goods to Russia. In the dispute with China, Narbuta stood firm, for Sarimsaq,

who continued to claim Kashgaria, was a valuable means of applying pressure to China. The Chinese military presence in Kashgaria was weak. What is more, an attack by Sarimsaq, supported from Kokand, likely would have appealed to the local Muslims.[87] Many Kokand merchants took advantage of the Chinese vulnerability and settled in Altishahr, the 'six cities'.[88] Kokand consequently requested permission as early as 1813 to send a political agent to East Turkestan, who would be responsible for the Kokand people. Although the request was made repeatedly, it was rejected until 1832.[89]

Narbuta's successor **Alim Khan** (r. 1798/99–1810) became the first ruler of Kokand to take the title of khan[90] and built up a strong army of standing mercenaries. Next, he extended the khanate far north, and conquered the cities of Tashkent, Shymkent and Sairam in 1809. As a result, the khanate controlled a part of the trade between Russia and Mawarannahr. These cities in the catchment area of the Syr Darya River were later secured by the construction of an advanced series of fortresses such as Ak Mejet (today's Kyzyl Orda) in the west and Karakol, later Przhevalsk, in the east. The latter was nominally located on Chinese territory. These fortresses also served as a starting point for advances into the Kazakh steppe. Here, conflict with Russia was essentially predestined once the tsar's empire expanded southwards.[91] The next khans, **Umar Khan** (r. 1810–22) and **Muhammad Ali** (Madali, r. 1822–42) continued the expansionist policy of Alim Khan, initially towards the south in the direction of the Pamirs and Badakhshan. This gave Kokand access to the Indian opium market and soon it operated a lucrative opium trade with West China.[92] Kokand then turned eastward and, from 1820, began to use its trump card from Kashgar: the descendants of the khojas living in exile. In the years 1820 and 1825, Sarimsaq's son Jahangir launched two unsuccessful attacks on Kashgar with the help of Kyrgyz mounted warriors, which Kokand benevolently tolerated. In the third expedition of 1826, in which Muhammad Ali participated personally, the invaders suffered two devastating defeats. Muhammad Ali was able to return to Kokand, but Jahangir was taken prisoner and executed through dismemberment. The fourth attack of 1830 under Muhammad Ali – Jahangir's son, Yusuf Khwaja, merely played a secondary role – did not result in any military success. Nevertheless, China had to accept that the mobilisation of larger armies to defend against Kokandian attacks was too costly and agreed to negotiate. In the treaty concluded in 1832, China conceded all three contentious points: first, the tax on goods imported by foreign traders (except those from Kashmir and Badakhshan) to Kashgaria was no longer owed to the Chinese authorities, but to Kokand. Second, in every city of Altishahr a Kokandian agent was now to collect this import tax. And, third, all the Kokandian merchants of Kashgaria would be subordinate to these agents in administrative and legal matters. The khanate in Kashgaria thus received tariff autonomy and extraterritorial jurisdiction within China, which anticipated the later concessions of the colonial powers. Despite the Chinese concessions, the attacks from Kokand continued in 1847, 1852, 1855 and 1857. Now, they were led by Khoja Wali Khan, a son of Jahangir. In his fourth campaign, Wali Khan managed to capture the city of Kashgar, but not the citadel. Nevertheless, this did not prevent him from killing innumerable Muslim Kashgarliks during his almost three-month reign of terror.[93] Adolf Schlagintweit, a German explorer, also fell victim to his tyranny on 26 August 1857.[94] Ultimately, these events were by no means uprisings of local Muslims of East Turkestan (let alone of Uyghurs) against Chinese domination. The descendants of the overthrown dynasty of the khojas had rather attempted to regain power in Kashgaria, which was tolerated or actively supported by Kokand.

79. The 7,135-m-high Ibn Sina Peak (right) in the Trans-Alai mountain range soars upward along the border of north-east Tajikistan and south-west Kyrgyzstan. From 1871 to 1928, the summit was called Mount Kaufmann in honour of the first Russian governor-general of Turkestan, Konstantin Kaufmann, and then until 2006, Lenin Peak. Photo taken from Sary-Mogol, Kyrgyzstan, 2008.

When unrest broke out in Kokand in 1842 and the khan abdicated in favour of his brother **Sultan Mahmud** (r. 1842), Amir Nasrallah took advantage of the situation from Bukhara to take the city, raze the palace, and execute the khan as well as his predecessor. Although a popular uprising was able to expel the occupying force from Bukhara after a few months, the three decades that remained for Kokand were marked by instability and ethnic clashes between the nomadic Kyrgyz and Kipchaks and the settled Tajiks and Uzbeks. **Sher Ali Khan** (1842–45), whom the Kyrgyz and Kipchaks enthroned, was deposed and killed by Alim Khan's son **Murad Bey Khan** (r. 1845). He met a violent end, however, at the hands of the Kipchak commander Musulman Quli after a mere eleven days. The new strongman Musulman Quli appointed **Muhammad Khudayar Khan** (r. 1845–58, 1862–63, 1865–75), the underage son of Sher Ali, to the throne. Musulman Quli reigned as an all-powerful regent until the year 1853, when Khudayar Khan joined a rebellion against the Kipchak rule, killed Musulman Quli, and took power. At the same time, a first Russian attack on the khanate took place, in which the Ak Mejet fortress was conquered. The Verny fortress was built in 1854, but the Crimean War subsequently interrupted the Russian advance for ten years.[95] But after a revolt broke out in Tashkent in 1858 and the khan sent his older brother **Mallya Khan** (r. 1858–62) there, the latter put himself on the throne. With Kyrgyz support, he forced Khudayar to go into exile in Bukhara. Real power, though, resided with the Kyrgyz Alim Quli until 1865. In 1864, Russia resumed its advance to the south and that same year wrested from the khanate the cities of Turkistan and Shymkent. While the first attack on Shymkent had been repulsed by Alim Quli in July, Alim Quli was forced to leave Shymkent when the khan of Bukhara Muzaffar al-Din took advantage of the Russo-Kokandian War to invade the Fergana Valley. This enabled Major General Mikhail Chernyayev (1828–98) to seize Shymkent in September. Chernyayev's first attack on Tashkent also failed. The second in May/June 1865 proved successful, however, with Alim Quli falling in battle from a defensive position.[96]

Again Muzaffar al-Din exploited Kokand's weakened condition to launch a new invasion and placed **Khudayar Khan** (3rd reign 1865–75) back on the throne. Russia now had to fear that Bukhara and its vassal Kokand would try to reconquer Tashkent. After Chernyayev failed once again – this time in taking Bukhara's fortress of Jizzakh – he was recalled and replaced by Major General D. Romanovsky. Romanovsky defeated Muzaffar al-Din in May 1866, and subsequently conquered the towns of Jizzakh, Khujand and Ura Tyube (Istaravshan) belonging to the emirate of Bukhara. This resulted in the geographic separation of Kokand

and Bukhara. These cities, as well as Tashkent, were then annexed by Russia and made into the General Government of Turkestan in 1867 with Tashkent as the capital. The khanate of Kokand was thereby reduced to the Fergana Valley.[97] In the meantime, Russia renounced the annexation of Kokand in deference to Great Britain, since Kokand bordered on Badakhshan, which had belonged more or less nominally to Afghanistan since the late 1850s. Khudayar Khan acknowledged the informal sovereignty of Russia, and, in January 1868, granted the Russian governor-general of Turkestan, Konstantin Petrovich von Kaufmann, comprehensive trading rights. The loss of Tashkent, however, struck Kokand's economy hard. It caused a steep drop in revenues, which Khudayar tried to offset with massive tax increases. The resentment of the population, especially the Kyrgyz and Kipchaks, gave way to a general uprising in July 1875. Led by the Kyrgyz pretender, **Pulad Khan** (r. 1875), it was directed against both the khan and his Russian rulers. Khudayar fled to Tashkent and, to accommodate Pulad Khan's explicit request, the rebels appointed Khudayar's son **Nasir al-Din** (r. 1875–76) as the new khan. Governor von Kaufmann now dispatched General Mikhail Skobelev (1843–82) to Fergana, where the latter was able to quell the insurrection by January 1876. On 19 February 1876, Tsar Alexander II dissolved the remaining khanate and annexed it as the Fergana Oblast to the General Government of Turkestan. The principalities of Karategin and Darvaz were allocated to Bukhara to reward Muzzafar al-Din's neutrality during the war with Kokand.[98] Russia had already pacified the rebellious region of East Bukhara with the cities of Shahr-i Sabz and Hissar (fig. 76) on behalf of the amir Muzzafar al-Din in the years 1870–73.[99] Now, the General Government of Turkestan bordered on Badakhshan, which Afghanistan claimed. Russia, moreover, took advantage of the fact that Kyrgyz cattle breeders allowed their herds to graze in the Pamirs in the summer in order to also claim these mountain regions.[100] In fact, Russia had established a protectorate over Bukhara with the peace treaty of 30 June 1868, which meant that Russia had essentially bordered on Afghanistan since that date. The border was ill defined, however, due to conflicting local demands and a lack of geographical knowledge on the part of Russia and Great Britain. Darvaz also included territories on the left bank of the Panj River, whereas the principalities of Shugnan and Roshan, which the Afghan Amir Abdur Rahman occupied in 1883, likewise had areas on the right bank of the Panj.[101] The absence of a clear border between Russia and Afghanistan led to severe tensions between the two major powers, which were not resolved until the joint border demarcation of 1895.[102]

V

The 'Great Game': Central Asia as a Pivot of Russian and British Expansion Policy

'[The Russian's] object is not Calcutta, but Constantinople; not the Ganges, but the Golden Horn. He believes that the keys of the Bosphorus are more likely to be won on the banks of the Helmund [near Herat] than on the heights of Plevna [Russian victory over Turkey in today's Bulgaria in 1877]. To keep England quiet in Europe by keeping her employed in Asia, that, briefly put, is the sum and substance of Russian policy.'

GEORGE NATHANIEL CURZON, MP and later Viceroy of India 1899–1905[1]

'To my mind the whole Central Asian Question is as clear as the daylight. If it does not enable us in a comparatively short time to take seriously in hand the Eastern Question, in other words, to dominate the Bosphorus, the [Central Asian] hide is not worth the tanning.'

Russian **GENERAL MIKHAIL SKOBELEV** after his successful conquest of the Turkmen fortress Geok Tepe in January 1881[2]

While the horse people and tribal confederations in the north of Central Asia came under the pressure of the centrally administered expanding states of Russia and China from the eighteenth century onward, the countries in the south went through a similar development a century later. Here, however, it was not two land powers that came into conflict, but the largest land power in the world, Russia, and the greatest naval power in the world, Great Britain.[3] Due to their different starting positions from a military point of view, the clashes were occasionally asymmetrical. Britain, specifically, did not necessarily respond militarily to a Russian advance in Central Asia in the same region, but rather with its fleet in the Baltic Sea or off the coast of Vladivostok. At same time, British India, which eventually grew into its own realm within the British Empire, was also exposed as a land power to the threat of internal revolts. While the British Isles remained safe behind the bulwark of

the then invincible British navy, India also needed a strong army to ward off threats or to pre-empt them.

This rivalry between Great Britain and Russia was initiated by the Franco-Russian Treaty of Tilsit in 1807 and fought out in proxy battles, beginning with the Persian-Russian siege of Herat in 1837/38. It lasted exactly 100 years, until the Anglo-Russian Convention of 1907, but continued to unfold in Persia, the Caucasus and especially Transcaucasia until 1921. This 'cold war' is subsumed under the name the 'Great Game'. As indicated in the secondary literature, the term was coined by Arthur Conolly to convey a 'big game' or 'competition'. In July 1840, he wrote Major Rawlinson a letter in which he congratulated him on his appointment as a political agent in Kandahar: 'You've a great game. A noble game before you.'[4] However, as Malcolm Yapp has shown, Sir Arthur Wellesley, later Duke of Wellington, had used the

80. The upper Bala Hissar fortress located south of Kabul and overlooking the city from its dominating position; in the foreground lies a small cemetery. Photograph taken by John Burke (*ca.* 1843–1900) in 1879 during the Second Anglo-Afghan War. National Army Museum, London.

expression long before Conolly, albeit not with reference to Central Asia. On 2 May 1804 he wrote to Colonel Murray, the commanding officer against the Marathas: 'You have now a great game on your hands.'[5] In the context of the competition of the two imperial colonial powers Russia and Britain, the officer and historian John William Kaye (1814–76) was the first to use the term.[6] On the Russian side, foreign minister Count Nesselrode (in office 1816–56) referred to this diplomatic and military chess as 'a Tournament of Shadows'.[7] The playing field of this 'Great Game' was first and foremost Afghanistan, and then Crimea, Persia, Xinjiang and Tibet. Developments and events taking place in Central Asia were thus directed from outside Central Asia.

1. The Setting of the 'Great Game' from Constantinople to Kabul

At the end of the Napoleonic Wars, it became clear to a number of Britain military strategists like General Robert Wilson and General George De Lacy Evans that Great Britain would have to pay a very high price for its victory over the pan-European hegemonic power, France. Russia was on the cusp of becoming a continental hegemon itself, with ambitions ranging from the Mediterranean to the Indian Ocean.[8] Russia, after all, did not have a year-round port, since the ports of the Baltic Sea and of Odessa in the Black Sea were only free of ice for seven and nine months, respectively.[9] This severely limited the scope of both Russia's weak navy and its merchant navy. Since regional expansion to Western Europe did not come into the equation, Constantinople, which controlled the Bosphorus, presented an alternative. As the French diplomat Romieu had recognised in 1805, Russia's strategic goal in the Caucasus consisted less in conquering Persia than in seizing control of the Bosphorus.[10] For Russia, the push south meant the realisation of Tsar Peter I's vision of continual access to the world's oceans – a vision, however, that had been interrupted by his death in 1725 and domestic strife. With the conquest of the Crimea in 1771–83[11] and the gradual annexation of Kartli-Kakheti (East Georgia) in the years 1783–1801 and Imereti (West Georgia) in 1810,[12] Russia established two bases of operation against Constantinople: one by sea from Crimea, and one over land from Georgia. The Treaty of Gulistan on 24 October 1813, which ended the Russo-Persian War from 1804–13, confirmed Russia's possession of Georgia and the khanates of the present state of Azerbaijan. This underlined Russia's supremacy in the north of the Ottoman Empire and Persia.[13] With

Napoleon's final defeat, Russia could deploy the forces that had become available on its western border in the south. The second motivation for Russia's involvement in the Caucasus and Persia was the hope of attracting part of the European trade with India towards land routes controlled by Russia instead of the existing sea routes controlled by Britain.[14]

But for the dominant naval power, Britain – which had destroyed France as its remaining maritime rival in the naval victories of Aboukir (1798) and Trafalgar (1805) – a Russian advance into the Mediterranean was unacceptable. After all, a Russian protectorate over the Ottoman Empire or its destruction would have massively disrupted the European balance of power. From the time of the Greek Revolution of 1821–29 and the Russian intervention from 1828–32 at the latest, the Britain diplomats Canning and Wellington and their successors had set about the difficult task of curtailing Russian support for the Greek insurgents. They sought, specifically, to limit it in a way that allowed the Greeks to achieve their goal, while preserving the Ottoman Empire at all costs and avoiding armed engagement with Russia.[15] Edward Law, Earl of Ellenborough (1790–1871) and recurring President of the Board of Control of the East India Company, was convinced that both the security of British India and the balance of power in Europe depended on the preservation of the Ottoman Empire.[16] Over the course of the next six decades, Britain deployed its navy no less than four times against Russia, just as General Wilson had advised: 'England must … attend to her naval power, and negotiate with the trident in her hand.'[17] In 1829, a partial mobilisation of the navy prevented the conquest of Constantinople by Russian troops, who had just occupied Edirne.[18] In 1853, a British-French fleet blocked the mouth of the Dardanelles to prevent Russia from establishing a protectorate over the Ottoman Empire, which led to the Crimean War.[19] And, in 1878, the British Mediterranean fleet stopped a Russian army off the coast of Constantinople and barred the establishment of a large Bulgarian principality which would have nominally stood under the sultan's control, but in fact have given Russia access to the Mediterranean.[20] As the Austrian Major General Alois Ritter von Haymerle realised, Britain, which already had strong military bases in Gibraltar and Malta, had reinforced in 1878 its supremacy in the Mediterranean by gaining control over Cyprus. From here, the British could control both the Dardanelles and the Suez Canal. Since the British fleet could shut down the Strait of Hormuz, the only strategically attractive port for Russia was one lying directly on the Indian Ocean. To obtain it, however, Russia needed to conquer the western Afghan city of Herat.[21] Russia took this step in March 1885, when it wrested the oasis of

Panjdeh from Afghanistan and severely threatened Herat. Only the global mobilisation of the British navy and the threat of an all-out war forced Russia to suspend its advance.[22] Britain managed to force Russia to retreat three times solely by means of making a threat, just as the Chinese military strategist Sun Tzu (*ca.* 544–496 BC) had recommended: 'Those who render others' armies helpless without fighting are the best of all.'[23]

While in absolutist Russia, political leadership was concentrated in the person of the tsar, who presided over both the government and the military, in the parliamentary monarchy of Great Britain setting goals and priorities and decision-making responsibility fell under the purview of the elected government. In India, Britain pursued primarily commercial purposes – first in the form of tributes and then, from the nineteenth century onward, as a supplier of raw materials and an export market for British capital and industrial goods. The semi-private East India Company served as a vehicle for this undertaking, which, when necessary, received military support. It was not converted into a royal colony until 1858. The East India Company, which was supported militarily and diplomatically by the superior naval power of Great Britain, can be viewed as a kind of forerunner of the United States' global business empire today. The Company was headed by the governor-general, commonly called the viceroy. He, in turn, was subordinate to the President of the Board of Control, and, from 1858, to the Secretary of State for India, a cabinet minister. Until an undersea telegraph line with London was put into operation in 1870, the governor-general enjoyed a high degree of autonomy. Great Britain was both a European and an Asian power – in other words, a bipolar empire that occasionally pursued two mutually divergent foreign policies. A key factor in the British India policy was the composition of parliament, which was dominated by the Tories or the liberal Whigs and, from 1859, the Liberals. With regard to India, the Liberals preferred a prudent, tight financial strategy, the Tories one that was aggressive.

While Great Britain managed to preserve the sovereignty of the Ottoman Empire in the 1820s, this was not the case with Persia. The Treaty of Turkmenchay of 22 February 1828, which ended the Russo-Persian War of 1826–28, transformed Persia gradually into a de facto Russian protectorate. Persia not only had to cede the khanates of Yerevan and Nakhchivan, but also to renounce its military maritime rights in the Caspian Sea, grant extraterritorial rights to Russian citizens, allow the stationing of Russian consuls in Persian cities, and accept Russian-dictated trade agreements.[24] Britain had long neglected to support Persia's independence, and, in the words of Harford Jones, 'Persia was delivered, bound hand

and foot, to the court of St. Petersburgh'.[25] Persia was deeply disappointed by Great Britain, as Russia's sphere of influence was extended in one fell swoop to the Afghan border. The reason for this failure lay in the fact that Persia was considered of secondary importance from London's European perspective.[26] From India's point of view, however, it was extraordinarily important. This dichotomy of strategic priorities with regard to Persia persisted 40 years later. In his memorandum of 1868, Sir Henry Rawlinson complained: 'Every measure of defence, referring either to Persia or Afghanistan, must be organised in India and executed from India.'[27]

2. A Two-pronged Russian Attack on Afghanistan and the Siege of Herat

As a result of the Russian annexation of the Caucasus and the Treaty of Turkmenchay, the spectre of a Russian invasion of India, posited by Wilson and De Lacy Evans, seemed to take shape. This consequently forced prime minister Wellington and Lord Ellenborough to fundamentally rethink the situation. While Wellington was confident of being able to destroy a Russian army attacking from Persia on the other side of the Indus, he feared that Indian revolts might follow. Ellenborough, however, considered a direct Russian attack on India unlikely, expecting instead Russian advances against the Uzbek khanates. Both politicians were advocates of a 'Forward Policy', according to which British India needed strategic depth to the west and north. Along these boundaries, officially neutral but de facto pro-British buffer states would have to be set up, whose external borders would then be ensured by Great Britain.[28] Viceroy Sir John Lawrence (in office 1864–69), who rejected the Forward Policy as unnecessarily risky and expensive, was exemplary as a representative of the opposite strategy of 'Masterful Inactivity'. Instead of moving towards the enemy geographically with a Forward Policy, while moving away from their own base of operations, the British armed forces should instead await the enemy on its own border. The enemy – exhausted following a long march and weakened by guerrilla attacks by Afghan tribes – would thus run headlong into their own fresh troops. As for the risk of rebellion, this could be avoided with good governance.[29] To counter the threat, Ellenborough took two measures. First, he sought to acquire geographical knowledge of the unknown frontier areas in the north-west of India like Punjab, Sindh, Afghanistan, Baluchistan and the Uzbek khanates and scouted the local approach routes; second, he strove to expand trade relations to gain political influence in these border regions.[30]

81. Afghan tribal warriors with jezail rifles, which had more than three times the effective range of the British 'Brown Bess' rifles thanks to their long barrel. Burnes, *Kabul* (1843), opposite p. 61.

In 1830, Captain Arthur Conolly agreed to travel from England to India not by ship but by land, and in this manner to advance on Khiva. Although he was attacked and plundered near Astarabad (today's Gorgan), he survived and reached Herat in September, where he met Sadozai Kamran Shah.[31] His further journey then took him to Kandahar, Quetta, and through the Bolan Pass to the Indus. On this ride on horseback from the Caspian Sea to the Indus via Herat, Conolly recorded the simplest approach route for a Russian invasion. However, he also mentioned a second route, which he had not used, from Khiva to Balkh, and then over the Hindu Kush to Kabul and on through the Khyber Pass to Peshawar and Attock along the Indus. Conolly emphasised in his report to governor-general Lord Bentinck that both routes led through the territory of the Afghans, who would fanatically defend themselves and decimate any intruder, and also the hated Shiite Persians. Therefore, it would be advantageous for British India to restore the Afghan political unity, lost in 1818, with a strong leader, with whom the British could maintain good relations. Conolly recommended supporting Kamran Shah in the battle for supremacy in Afghanistan, not least because he controlled Herat.[32] Conolly thus outlined the British policy in Afghanistan until 1919. It consisted in forming a united Afghanistan into an upstream bulwark that would protect India and which, by excluding Russia, would fall within the British sphere of influence. Just as Russia had converted

Persia into its own protectorate, British India was to direct the foreign policy of Afghanistan.

After Conolly had explored the remote western edge of British India, Governor Bentinck (in office 1828–35) commissioned the 25-year-old Alexander Burnes to explore the Indus. He was also to spy on the military strength of the principalities of Sindh and the Sikh state of Ranjit Singh, which was allied with the East India Company. Setting out in January 1831, Burnes proved the navigability of the Indus river system with flat-bottomed boats to Lahore. Ships, conversely, needed to be steam-operated due to the lack of wind.[33] In Lahore, Burnes was received by Ranjit Singh (1780–1839) with great ceremony. He then visited the exiled Shah Shuja,[34] who did not make a favourable impression on him: 'I do not believe the Shah possesses sufficient energy to seat himself on the throne of Cabool; and that if he did regain it, he has not the tact to discharge the duties of so difficult a situation.'[35] Burnes' critical assessment was completely borne out ten years later.[36] And just as he predicted, the Sikh Empire collapsed after Ranjit's death.[37] It was annexed by the Company in 1849, six years after the annexation of Sindh. After Burnes had made good contact with the unpredictable Ranjit Singh, he suggested that Governor Bentinck carefully take up diplomatic relations with Dost Muhammad Khan in Kabul to spy on his military strength, and then establish contact with Nasrallah Khan in Bukhara. Burnes' goal of winning Dost Muhammad for an

82. The British Indian 'Indus Army' marches through the 90-km-long Bolan Pass in March 1839. Sketch by James Atkinson (1780–1852), Superintending Surgeon of the 'Indus Army'. James Atkinson, *Sketches in Afghanistan* (London: Graves, 1842), pl. 5.

informal alliance against Russia would soon, as of 1835, turn out to be like squaring a circle. While Dost Muhammad expected the return of the city of Peshawar, disputed since 1818 and which Ranjit Singh would finally annex in 1834, Britain was not willing to risk putting a nearby ally under pressure in favour of a potential ally further away.[38] In March 1832, Burnes left for Kabul, along with the officer James Gerard, the land surveyor Mohammed Ali, and the multilingual diplomat Mohan Lal, whose two-volume biography of Dost Muhammad is a primary resource for the First Anglo-Afghan War.[39] Burnes was warmly received in Kabul by Dost Muhammad, who hoped for the Company's support in his confrontation with Ranjit Singh. He even offered Burnes the post of Afghan commander-in-chief.[40] Burnes' group travelled on to Bamiyan, where they admired the two giant Buddhas, and then to Balkh, where they tracked down the graves of Moorcroft, Trebeck and Guthrie.[41] In late June 1832, they reached Bukhara. Here, too, the vizier received Burnes cordially. Yet he refused him access to Amir Nasrallah.[42] Burnes intended to visit Khiva next, but the vizier strongly discouraged him from doing so. Burnes thus decided to return to Bombay via Merv, Mashhad and Tehran, where he met Shah Qajar Fath'Ali (r. 1797–1834)[43].

Conolly and Burnes completed their missions and provided Lord Bentinck and the Board of Control with a wealth of invaluable geographical knowledge. But whereas Conolly advised aiding Kamran Shah of Herat in the fight for supremacy in Afghanistan, Burnes recommended backing the energetic and popular Dost Muhammad. Conversely, he noted that Kamran and Shah Shuja would not enjoy any support from the Afghans and could only be placed on the throne by a foreign power: 'It is evident, therefore, that the restauration of either Shooja ool Moolk, or Kamran, is an event of the most improbable nature. The dynasty of the Sudozyes has passed away, unless it is propped up by foreign aid; and it would be impossible to reclaim the lost provinces of the empire, without a continuation of the same assistance.'[44] Burnes, accordingly, formulated an insight that remains valid to this day: any regime that is inserted by an external power is likely to be rejected and resisted by the local population as a foreign presence and therefore cannot survive without continuous financial and military support. In the words of military historian Stephen Tanner: then comes the choice whether 'to support it [the regime] in perpetuity or to abandon it with more dire consequences than would have come before'.[45] This painful reality is especially true for tribal societies like those in Afghanistan – as the British learned twice in the years 1839–42 and 1878–80, the Soviet Union experienced in 1979–89, and as the alliance led by the United States has come to recognise since 2001.

Alexander Burnes, though, would act against his better judgement a few years later and pay for it with his assassination in Kabul in the autumn of 1841.[46]

It was revealed in 1837 at the latest that the warnings from British diplomats, officers and spies of a future Russian push towards India were not the chimeras of alleged Russophobes. That year, in a coordinated pincer attack of both military and diplomatic dimensions, Russia started the project to gain control over both gateways to India: Herat and Kabul. It is not known whether Governor Lord Auckland (1784–1849, in office 1836–42) knew of Dost Muhammad's discreet establishing of contact with Russia in October 1835.[47] In any event, in the autumn of 1836, his superiors instructed him to send a special envoy to Kabul to counteract the Persian-Russian machinations. At the same time, he received carte blanche to intervene in Afghanistan (including militarily): 'The time has arrived at which it should be right for you to interfere decidedly in the affairs of Afghanistan.'[48] A game of chess now began with at least six players. Ranjit Singh wanted to keep Peshawar and to preserve the British alliance; British India hoped to neutralise the Afghan princes, especially Dost Muhammad, but without putting pressure on Ranjit Singh regarding the return of Peshawar; Persia sought to compensate for the loss of territory in the north-west through conquests in the east, particularly in Herat; and Russia strove to further expand its own sphere of influence in the direction of India. In Afghanistan, Dost Muhammad was looking for an ally who would help him to recapture Peshawar. As a result, he established open contact with Lord Auckland,[49] but also secretly approached Russia and even his arch-enemy Persia.[50] And the exiled Shah Shuja still hoped to finally find an ally who would put him on the throne in Kabul. As for the alliance possibilities: both the great powers as well as Dost Muhammad and Ranjit Singh were implacable enemies; Persia was a Russian satellite; the Sikhs counted on their friendship with the Company; and the two Afghan rivals were willing to enter any alliance as long as it was strong militarily. Two protagonists here faced a particularly painful dilemma. Specifically: if Lord Auckland decided in favour of Dost Muhammad, he would lose the goodwill of Ranjit Singh, while if he opted for the Sikhs, Dost Muhammad would open the door to the Russians. As for Dost Muhammad, if he chose an alliance with the Company, he would permanently lose Peshawar, whereas if he went with the Russians, he would have to renounce Herat.

The Russian strategy was on the table in the late summer of 1837, when a strong Persian army marched on Herat. It was personally led by Mohammed Shah Qajar (r. 1834–48) and also included 2,000 Russian troops headed by the generals Berowski and Samson.[51] The Russian envoy and general Count Simonich, who had repeatedly urged Mohammad Shah Qajar (r. 1834–48) to attack Herat,[52] accompanied the army. At the same time, the young lieutenant Henry Rawlinson discovered by chance in East Persia that a Russian envoy named Ivan Vitkevich (1806–39) was on his way to Dost Muhammad in Kabul with a personal message from Tsar Nicholas.[53] Now, it became clear that Russia intended to simultaneously establish a foothold in Herat, Kandahar[54] and Kabul, and to bring the supposed bulwark Afghanistan under its control in a single stroke. This represented a serious threat to the security of British India. British India was fortunate, however, that a capable officer and spy named Eldred Pottinger (1811–43) was in Herat, and at the beginning of the siege of the city on 23 November he offered to help defend it. Shah Kamran and his vizier Yar Mohammed enthusiastically enlisted the support of the young artillerist. The ten-month siege, which lasted from 23 November 1837 to 9 September 1838, subsequently developed into a duel between Pottinger and Count Simonich, who personally oversaw the Persian attacks. Lord Auckland forcefully compelled the abandonment of the siege, when he sent a small flotilla which occupied Kharg Island in the Persian Gulf.[55] At the same time, Lieutenant Colonel Stoddart openly threatened the shah with war if the siege did not immediately end. Towards the end of their exchange, the shah said to Stoddart: 'The fact is, if I don't leave Herat, there will be war, is not that it?' 'It is war,' Stoddart responded, '[it] all depends upon your Majesty's answer.'[56] Shah Mohammad wanted in any case to avoid a two-front war against Britain and withdrew his army. Thus, thanks to the initiative of a lieutenant and skilful gunboat diplomacy, Great Britain won a strategic victory without any losses – and humiliated its Russian enemy in the process.[57]

Coinciding with the start of the Siege of Herat, Lord Auckland's special envoy Alexander Burnes arrived in Kabul to negotiate with Dost Muhammad.[58] While the amir preferred an agreement with the Company over a deal with Russia, Burnes' negotiations were doomed from the start. The amir insisted on the return of Peshawar and Lord Auckland absolutely refused to put pressure on the Sikhs for this reason. Shortly after Russian envoy Ivan Vitkevich likewise arrived in Kabul on 19 December 1837,[59] Auckland instructed Burnes that Dost Muhammad would have to renounce Peshawar. Auckland had probably already decided to forcefully replace Dost Muhammad with Shah Shuja on the recommendation of Captain Claude Wade, the British envoy at the court of Ranjit Singh.[60] He sent a final ultimatum on 20 January 1838. The amir had to immediately expel Vitkevich, otherwise Auckland would break off negotiations. And if the amir entered into a political agreement

with Russia, 'the act will be considered a direct breach of friendship with the British Government'; this was an indirect threat of war.[61] A month later, on 21 February, Auckland confirmed that Peshawar belonged to Ranjit Singh and that Vitkevich needed to be expelled. When Dost Muhammad responded to these two ultimatums with an official, ceremonial reception of the Russian ambassador, Burnes yielded to Vitkevich and left Kabul on 25 April.[62] Meanwhile, foreign minister Lord Palmerston (1784–1865, in office 1830–34, 1835–41, 1846–51) unconditionally demanded Russia's dismissal of Simonich and Vitkevich and the nullification of the agreements concluded with Dost Muhammad and the leaders in Kandahar.[63] Tsar Alexander relented in May 1838, whereupon Count Nesselrode made the two men into scapegoats. Simonich, he claimed, had acted on his own and Vitkevich was merely an adventurer and intriguer. The forsaken Vitkevich subsequently committed suicide.[64]

With the abandonment of the Siege of Herat and the cancelling of the recently concluded Russian-Afghan agreement, Great Britain scored a brilliant dual victory without losing a single soldier. But Auckland and the Board of Control did not appreciate that Dost Muhammad was now completely isolated and that, if he wanted to keep his throne, he had to be prepared to compromise with regard to Peshawar. Instead of continuing to exploit Great Britain's success through skilful diplomacy and to put the war preparations on hold, Auckland signed the Tripartite Treaty of Simla with Ranjit Singh and Shuja on 25 June 1838. The Company undertook to put Shuja on the throne of Kabul, even though he had not achieved a single success in 30 years. The latter, in turn, definitively renounced the Afghan claims to Peshawar, Kashmir and Sindh as well as his rights to an independent foreign policy. He also pledged to fight any enemy who attacked the Sikhs or the Company. The treaty thus effectively downgraded Afghanistan to an Anglo-Sikh protectorate.[65] Auckland then proceeded to make a public declaration of war in the infamous Simla Manifesto of 1 October,[66] despite the serious reservations expressed by experts on India. For example, 'The Duke of Wellington said that our difficulties would commence where our military successes ended' and 'spoke of the folly of occupying a land of rocks, sands, deserts and snow.' Mountstuart Elphinstone wrote almost prophetically: 'If you send 27,000 men up the Durra-i Bolan [Pass] to Candahar ... I have no doubt you will take Candahar and Caubul and set up Sooja; but for maintaining him ... among a turbulent people like the Afghans, I own it seems to me to be hopeless.... I fear you will weaken the position against Russia.'[67] Auckland stubbornly held fast and turned the fresh diplomatic victory into one of Great Britain's most bitter military defeats of the nineteenth century.

3. Dost Muhammad and the First Anglo-Afghan War: British Victory Transformed into Defeat

From a military standpoint, the invading army, called the 'Indus Army', was under the command of Lieutenant General Sir John Keane (1781–1844). From a political standpoint, it fell under the purview of envoy Sir William Macnaghten (1793–1841). Macnaghten's deputy was the now knighted Sir Alexander Burnes, who took part in the expedition against his better judgement. Although Britain was a war-tested colonial power, its army was not equal to the task. It consisted of 15,000 British and Indian soldiers and 6,000 followers of Shah Shuja, along with a dispro-portionately large baggage train of 38,000 men. The Indus Army thus resembled one of the huge military campaigns dating back to the Mughal in the seventeenth century. While Keane proved to be an able strategist, his two successors – Sir Willoughby Cotton (1783–1860) and William Elphinstone (1782–1842) – turned out to be incompetent, and, indeed, in the case of Elphinstone, senile. Both the light firearms of the British and their battle tactics dated back to the Napoleonic Wars. The standard rifle was the 'Brown Bess', a muzzle-loading smoothbore flintlock musket with an effective range of 135 m. It was hopelessly inferior, however, to the Afghan *jezail*, a long-barrelled matchlock that fired slowly, but had an effective range of 450 m (fig. 81). The Afghan snipers fought with several jezail guns that were loaded continuously by their young assistants, or they rode with several loaded guns into battle. Until General Pollock's counter-offensive in the spring of 1842, the British also refrained when marching through the mountain passes to occupy the ridges in advance. In pitched battles, the

83. Baluchi sharpshooters aiming in spring 1839 at British Indian troops passing through the Kajur Pass south-east of Quetta while being attacked by Indian sepoys from above. The picture illustrates the need to secure the crests of passes while one's own troops march through. James Atkinson, *Sketches in Afghanistan* (London: Graves, 1842), pl. 6.

infantry fought in densely crowded squares, making them an easy target for the Afghan snipers who stood outside the range of their Brown Bess rifles. In the words of eyewitness Vincent Eyre: 'All have heard of the British SQUARES at Waterloo, which defied the repeated desperate onsets of Napoleon's choicest cavalry. At Beymaroo [Kabul, 23 November 1841] we formed squares to resist the distant fire of infantry, thus presenting a solid mass against the aim of perhaps the best marksmen in the world.'[68] To the extent that the Afghan foot-soldiers sat behind horsemen and were thus carried into the battle, the Afghan infantry also enjoyed a tremendous mobility advantage.[69] The British defeat at Beymaroo reflected the mismatch between a Napoleonic operational doctrine and the precursor of a motorised infantry. In the end, the invaders faced white-clad Ghazi, fanatical jihadists, and forerunners to contemporary mujahideen who could only be stopped with cannon and gun salvos.[70]

As Ranjit Singh prohibited the British army at the last moment from marching through Punjab, it had to invade Kandahar via Sindh, the Bolan Pass and Quetta. When it arrived in Kandahar on 25 April 1839, the British immediately realised that Shah Shuja enjoyed no support from tribal leaders and the population. He was despised as a puppet of the invaders.[71] The storming of the solid fortress of Ghazna on 22 July succeeded thanks to Mohan Lal, who convinced an Afghan to reveal which of the gates had not been walled up. A mine was affixed there, causing the gate to collapse and the fortress to fall.[72] Lieutenant Colonel Wade (1794–1861) then defeated Dost Muhammad's son Akbar (1816– *ca.* 1845/47), and, on 7 August, the army and **Shah Shuja** (second reign 1839–42) marched into Kabul after Dost Muhammad's troops had deserted. In Kabul too, Shah Shuja was met with contempt: 'there was no popular enthusiasm. [. . .] It was more like a funeral procession than the entry of a King into the capital of his restored dominions.'[73]

84. Amir Dost Muhammad Khan surrenders to the British ambassador Macnaghten on 3 November 1840. James Atkinson, *Sketches in Afghanistan* (London: Graves, 1842), pl. 18.

Macnaghten immediately recognised that Shah Shuja would never survive without British bayonets. Auckland, however, ruled out deploying such a large army outside of India, especially given that Kabul could not sustain it. Therefore, General Keane left Kabul with the bulk of the army in October. He handed over command of the 8,000 remaining soldiers to General Cotton, who was replaced in December 1840 by the senile and completely overwhelmed General Elphinstone.[74] In his choice of camp for the remainder of the army, the inept Cotton put in place the first cornerstone for the disaster that followed in the late autumn of 1841. Instead of occupying the robust and spacious fortress of Bala Hissar that commanded Kabul and the surrounding area, Cotton had the cantonment built outside the city in marshy areas that were dominated on all sides by hills and three Afghan strongholds. Moreover, the camp lay within reach of the jezail rifles from two of these fortresses; conversely, these same fortresses were out of reach for the obsolete Brown Bess rifles. The marshes also prevented the use of the cavalry. Worse still, the ammunition depot and the food reserves were *outside* the camp, while the army treasury was within the city. Cotton, supported by Macnaghten, ignored all the advice of his officers and flagrantly violated several basic military principles.[75]

The year 1840 was relatively quiet, not least because Macnaghten possessed sufficient funds to buy peace with leading tribal leaders. News of the failed Russian expedition to Khiva in winter 1839/40 was auspicious, as was the surrender of Dost Muhammad on 3 November 1840. In the wake of this, Macnaghten and Burnes allowed themselves to ignore the local warning signs in the summer of 1841 and to imagine themselves in safety.[76] The accomplished Major General William Nott (1782–1845), stationed in Kandahar, had a much more realistic view of the situation. In a private letter of 29 September 1840, he wrote: 'We are become hated by the people. [. . .] The conduct of 10,001 politicals has ruined our case and bared the throat of every European in this country to the sword and knife of the revengeful Affghan and bloody Belooch and, when [i.e. unless] several regiments be quickly sent, not a man will be left to note the fall of his comrades.'[77] A change of government in London ultimately lit the powder keg's fuse. At the end of August, the Whig government of Lord Melbourne fell and the new Conservative prime minister, Sir Robert Peel, promptly decided to cut in half the financial resources that had been made available to Shah Shuja and Macnaghten and to withdraw the troops. By the end of September, Macnaghten was forced to halve the payments to the eastern Ghilzais, who dominated the passes to Jalalabad. In response, they rebelled. This was the signal for a general uprising against the hated shah and the British, which first erupted in

Charikar north of Kabul. The 300-strong garrison was completely massacred, except for Major Pottinger and another officer.[78]

Although between November 1841 and mid-January 1842 only about 40 officers and soldiers survived of the 6,000-strong army, scholars are well informed about these tragic weeks thanks to the diary of Major General (at the time Lieutenant) Sir Vincent Eyre (1811–81).[79] The uprising in Kabul – coinciding with the one in Charikar – began on 2 November with the murder of Alexander Burnes and the looting of the army treasury. Two days later, the supply depot was lost, sparking an immediate lack of food.[80] General Elphinstone remained agonised by indecision and was unable to deploy his still-powerful army, while his deputy, Brigadier John Shelton (1791–1845) sulked and gave free rein to his contempt for his superior. Instead of requisitioning supplies in Kabul and occupying the fortress of Bala Hissar, as Macnaghten and various officers insisted,[81] or fighting his way to Jalalabad, Elphinstone did nothing and let Burnes' murder go unpunished. As a result of the general's blatant lack of leadership, discipline began to fall by the wayside, and on 13 November, Muslim gunners from the Punjab were the first to mutiny. Then, during a sortie under Shelton, the infantrymen ignored the attack orders and retreated in chaos.[82] The ultimate disaster struck the besieged on 23 November, when, in a desperate attack on the elevated Afghan position of Bemaru (Beymaroo), Brigadier Shelton committed several grave errors. Instead of taking the surrounding peaks in a night attack and securing the positions with stone walls, he attacked with half the army during the day. He then ignored the general command to always use guns in pairs, and took only one gun, which promptly overheated and repeatedly could not fire for an extended period of time. When the Afghan cavalry appeared on the battlefield, he formed his infantry into two squares. Since they were immobile, they were ideal targets for enemy snipers. And as the Afghan infantry divisions were advancing, the Indian foot-soldiers refused to follow their officers in a counter-attack. The front square broke up first, and the second soon followed. The survivors flocked haphazardly back to camp. But the victorious Afghan commander Osman Khan refrained from pursuing the fleeing soldiers. If he had gone after them, as Vincent Eyre maintains, not a single soldier would have survived the day, and the cantonment would also have been lost.[83]

Instead of pulling back with the remaining soldiers to the fortress of Bala Hissar, Elphinstone ordered the envoy to negotiate a withdrawal with Dost Muhammad's son Akbar. Akbar lured Macnaghten into a trap and killed him personally on 23 December. Before this, Elphinstone had refused to provide Macnaghten with a bodyguard.[84] In Mohan Lal's judgement, this was 'the loss of the British honor in Central Asia'.[85] Since neither Elphinstone nor Shelton were capable of responding, only a coup attempt by Major Pottinger – who wanted to fight all the way to Jalalabad with the guns, but without the baggage train – would have saved the expedition.[86] But Pottinger was not a mutineer and he noted with resignation in his diary: 'I was obliged [by Elphinstone] to negotiate for the safety of a parcel of fools who were doing all they could to ensure their destruction.'[87] The now clearly senile Elphinstone delivered most of the guns to the treacherous Akbar and received in return the vague promise of a unhindered withdrawal. On 6 January 1842, in snow and bitter cold, the death march of 4,500 soldiers and officers and 12,000 camp servants began. A week later, all were dead, except the doctor William Brydon.[88] Shah Shuja was recklessly left to his own fate. The Afghan tribal warriors, who had been fanaticised by the mullahs, tasted blood and fell like hungry wolves upon the disorderly fleeing soldiers. The army was destroyed on 12 January 1842 at the Jugdulluk Pass, south-east of Kabul. The next day, the final stand took place near Gandamak, where the remaining 65 soldiers and officers fell.[89] On 5 April Shah Shuja was assassinated and his son **Fateh Jang** (r. 1842) was installed as an impotent and merely nominal khan. His vizier was none other than Akbar Khan, the arch-enemy of his father.[90]

Blame for the disaster went, first of all, to Lord Auckland, who wanted to impose an unpopular ruler on the Afghans and had appointed the weak generals Cotton and Elphinstone as commanders, rather than, for example, the capable generals Pollock, Nott or Sale; second, to the stingy financial policy of the new Peel government; third, to the blind optimism of Macnaghten and Burnes; and, fourth, the incompetent officers Elphinstone, Cotton and Shelton. General Nott in Kandahar and Brigadier Sir Robert Sale (1782–1845) in Jalalabad both demonstrated that Kabul could have been held on to with intelligent planning and warfare. They each ignored Elphinstone's orders to vacate their strongholds and abandon Afghanistan and instead successfully defended their positions. On 7 April 1842, Sale even launched a victorious attack and blasted apart Akbar Khan's circumvallation.[91] Meanwhile, in February, Auckland had been replaced by Ellenborough. He wanted to pull out of Afghanistan entirely, but first had to free Sale in Jalalabad. For this task, he commissioned General George Pollock (1786–1872), who arrived in Jalalabad in mid-April, after occupying the ridge of mountains at the Khyber Pass. He and Nott, however, refused to pull back without having freed the British hostages being held north of Kabul. Wellington intervened and wrote to tell Ellenborough that abandoning the

hostages was unacceptable. He further remarked: 'It is impossible to impress upon you too strongly the notion of the importance of Restoration and Reputation in the East.'[92] Ellenborough relented, and Pollock reached Kabul on 15 September. Nott arrived two days later. The prisoners were freed, and as retribution for Macnaghten's murder, they burned down the bazaar of Kabul.[93] On 12 October, the British and Fateh Jang, who did not want to experience the same fate as his father, left Kabul and evacuated Afghanistan. Now, **Shapur** (r. 1842), another one of Shah Shujah's sons, ascended the throne as an impotent ruler. Soon thereafter, however, he was forced to flee to exile in Peshawar. Despite the victories of Pollock and Nott, British policy in Afghanistan was an utter failure – not least because **Dost Muhammad** (second rule 1842/43–63) took power once again in Kabul, with his son Akbar (d. *ca.* 1845/47) as vizier, after being released by the British.[94] The only upshot of this unnecessary war was that, instead of forming an anti-Russian bulwark, the Afghans now had a passionate hatred for the British. What is more, the myth of British invincibility was in tatters. The British had to accept that, while it was easy to occupy this poor and barren land, it was virtually impossible to hold on to it. Afghanistan's geography is ideal for guerrilla warfare: 'No European troops . . . are any match whatever for the Afghan troops as mountaineers.'[95] In addition, Auckland's wilfully initiated war and Elphinstone's incompetent leadership caused a deep rift between the Indian soldiers and the British elite. As Pottinger noted in 1842: 'If the Government does not take some decided steps to recover the affections of the Army, I really think a single spark will blow the sepoys into mutiny.'[96] His prediction would come true fifteen years later in the 'Sepoy Mutiny'.

Dost Muhammad's most urgent task was to recapture those areas which had slipped from Kabul's control since the war in 1839–42. Between 1850 and 1855, he reconquered Balkh, Kunduz and Badakhshan to the north of the Hindu Kush, and then Kandahar in 1856.[97] His entry into the war in 1848 on the side of the Sikhs for the purpose of claiming Peshawar failed, however. In February 1849, the Sikhs suffered a crushing defeat against the British, and the amir just barely escaped. Afghanistan and the British now had a common border, established in the Treaty of Peshawar on 30 March 1855. Dost Muhammad recognised Peshawar as a British possession and vowed 'to be the friend of the friends and enemy of the enemies of the Honorable East India Company'.[98] According to the second Baron Montagu of Beaulieu (1866–1929), India now shared, from a strategic point of view, a common border with Central Asia: 'India is left behind and Central Asia is entered when the Indus is crossed.'[99]

85. Courtyard of the 'Gazar Gah' mausoleum in the north-east of Herat. On the left, the base is visible of the tomb of the Hanbali scholar and Sufi Mawlana Khwaja Abdullah Ansari (1006–89); behind on the right stands the stele at the head of the tomb of Amir Dost Muhammad Khan (1793–1863). Shah Rukh founded the mausoleum in the first half of the fifteenth century; the white marble panels and broken balustrades are said to have originated from the Musalla complex.[16] Photo by Rudolf Stuckert, 1942, RS 406. Foundation Phototheca Afghanica, Bubendorf, Switzerland.

The amir's decision to back down soon paid off. The following year, Persia, encouraged by renewed calls from Russia, occupied the city of Herat, whereupon Britain declared war on Persia on 1 November 1856. British troops landed in Kharg and Bushehr and marched inland to Ahvaz. In the Peace of Paris of 4 March 1857, Persia had to renounce Herat and evacuate the town, which was handed over to a governor of the Afghan Barakzai. During the war, British-Afghan relations were strengthened by the Treaty of Friendship of 26 January 1857.[100] Dost Muhammad showed his gratitude for Great Britain's support by remaining neutral during the Sepoy Mutiny of 1857–58, also known as the Indian Mutiny. He had rightly anticipated that Britain would make every effort to put down the revolt.[101] On the other hand, Russia was left in such a weakened state by the lost Crimean War that it could not actively exploit the Indian uprising. In May 1863, Dost Muhammad finally succeeded in reclaiming Herat. Here, he more or less established the boundaries of the modern state of Afghanistan that exist today. The Afghan ruler was able to successfully confront a militarily superior colonial power and compel it to seek his friendship. Dost Muhammad died in June during the victory celebrations. A six-year civil war then broke out.

FORMER INNER
KAZAKH HORDE
(Bukey Zhuz)

R U S S I A N

FORMER JUNIOR
KAZAKH HORDE
(Kishi Zhuz)

1839-40

● Raimskoe (Aralsk) 1847

*Aral
Sea*

1833

Ak Mejet
(Fort Perovs
1853
○

1864

1873

K H I V A   K H A N A T E
(before Russian attacks)

○ Khiva

O L D   K H I V A

Bukhara ○

Samarka

*Caspian
Sea*

Amu Darya (Oxus River)

○ Krasnovodsk

1879

1868/73

1716   1869

1881

T U R K M E N   T R I B E S
and   M E R V

B

1877

○ Asghabat

○ Merv

1884

1885

○ Mashhad

P E R S I A

● Panjdeh

● Kushk

A F G H A N

in 1895

○ Herat

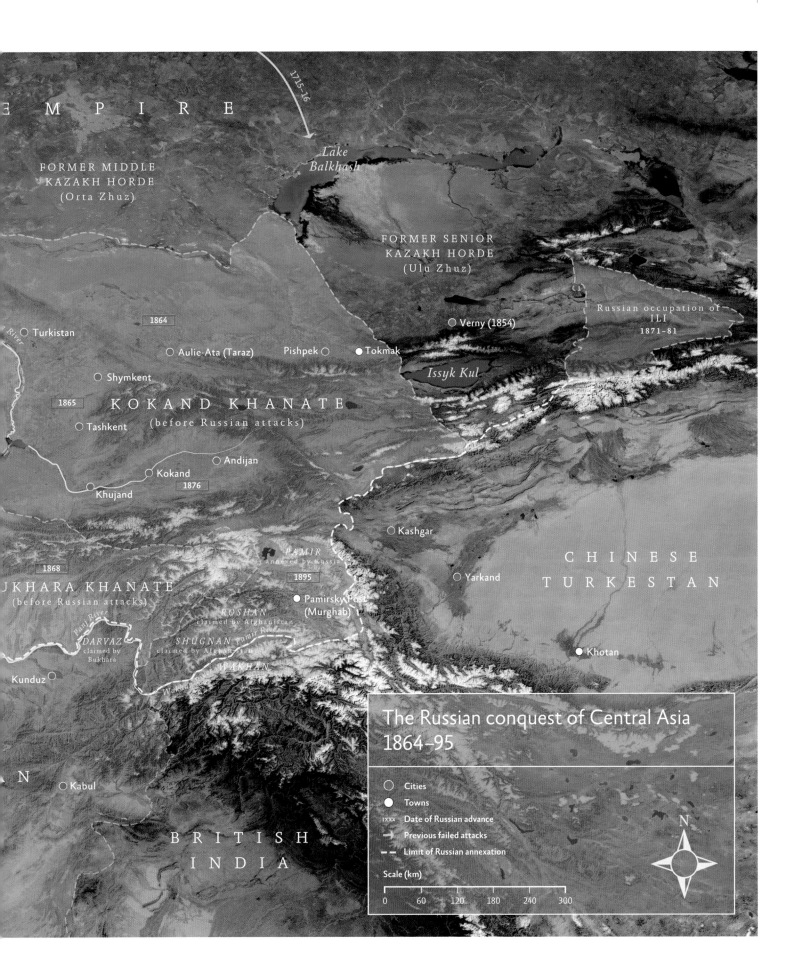

E M P I R E

1715-16

FORMER MIDDLE
KAZAKH HORDE
(Orta Zhuz)

*Lake
Balkhash*

FORMER SENIOR
KAZAKH HORDE
(Ulu Zhuz)

Russian occupation of
ILI
1871–81

○ Turkistan

1864

○ Aulie-Ata (Taraz)

Pishpek ○

● Tokmak

○ Verny (1854)

○ Shymkent

Issyk Kul

1865

K O K A N D   K H A N A T E
(before Russian attacks)

○ Tashkent

○ Andijan

○ Kokand

○ Khujand

1876

Kashgar ○

*PAMIR
annexed by Russia*

C H I N E S E

1868

1895

● Pamirsky Post
(Murghab)

○ Yarkand

T U R K E S T A N

BUKHARA KHANATE
(before Russian attacks)

Panj River

*ROSHAN
claimed by Afghanistan*

*DARVAZ
claimed by
Bukhara*

*SHUGNAN
claimed by Afghanistan*

Pamir River

WAKHAN

● Khotan

Kunduz ○

Wakhan River

N

○ Kabul

B R I T I S H
I N D I A

The Russian conquest of Central Asia 1864–95

○ Cities
● Towns
1xxx Date of Russian advance
⟍ Previous failed attacks
╍╍ Limit of Russian annexation

Scale (km)

0   60   120   180   240   300

N

4. The March to the Oxus: the Russian Conquest of the Uzbek Khanates

After Russia and Britain had suffered grave defeats in Central Asia, the tensions between the two great powers regarding Central Asia subsided somewhat. Indeed, when Tsar Nicholas visited Great Britain in 1844, he assured the British Foreign Secretary, Lord Aberdeen, that Russia recognised the independence of the three Uzbek khanates.[102] Nevertheless, as may be surmised by Russia's capture of the fortress Ak Mejet (Fort Perovsk, today's Kyzyl Orda) in 1853 and the erection of the fortress of Verny (Almaty) in 1854,[103] Russia did not lose sight of its long-term goal of advancing to the Oxus. Fort Perovsk formed the south-eastern stronghold of the Orenburg–Syr Darya fortress line, and Verny the end of the West Siberian line, beginning at the Ishim River and running through Semipalatinsk. As Major General Romanovsky reported, there was a gap between the two forts of 930 km, which is why 'it was resolved by a Special Committee [as early as 1854] and confirmed by the Emperor, to connect the then established Syr-Daria line with the newly advanced Siberian line of frontiers'.[104] The Crimean War of 1853–56 prevented Russia from realising the imperial command – only the two Kokandian fortresses of Tokmak and Pishpek (Bishkek) in today's Kyrgyzstan were taken.[105] After the war, the pacification of the Northern Caucasus and the securing of Russian dominance in south-east Siberia had first priority, and absorbed all Russian military resources. As Tsar Alexander II stressed in a directive to General Alexander Baryatinsky (1814–79) in the late 1850s: 'Only after Russia has subjugated the Caucasian nations and established her preponderance in the Amur Basin [will she] be able to go ahead in Central Asia.'[106] In 1859, the leading North-Caucasian resistance fighter Imam Shamil surrendered and, in the following year, Russia secured her possessions in the Amur region through the Convention of Peking.[107] The last major uprising in the Caucasus came to an end in 1864, thus clearing the way for a march to the Oxus.

On 20 December 1863, Tsar Alexander issued the order to close the gap between Fort Perovsk and Verny by means of a military offensive against Kokand. As the military historian and later minister of war General Alexey Kuropatkin (1848–1925) emphasised however, a further aim was to conquer Shymkent and Tashkent.[108] Underlying this offensive directive was a strategic memorandum from War Minister Dmitry Milyutin (1816–1912, in office 1861–81) to the tsar on 7 July 1863, which stated: 'In case

86. The Russian General Konstantin Petrovich von Kaufmann (1818–82) was the governor-general and commander-in-chief of the Russian troops in Turkestan, 1867–82. He was the architect of the continuous Russian dominion over vast areas of West Central Asia until 1991. *Turkestan Album*, commissioned by General von Kaufmann in 1872.

of a European war we ought particularly to value the occupation of that region, which would bring us to the northern border of India . . . By ruling Kokand we can constantly threaten England's East-Asian possessions. This is especially important, since only in that quarter can we be dangerous to this enemy of ours.'[109] Russia wanted to coerce Great Britain to abandon the hated London Straits Convention of 1841. This convention (which was confirmed by the Treaty of Paris of 1856) prohibited all warships other than those of the sultan and his allies from passing through the Dardanelles and the Bosphorus. As a consequence, Russia was denied access to the Mediterranean.[110] The two imperial decrees of 1854 and 1863 leave no doubt that the ultimate and long-term strategic goal of Russia in Central Asia was to finally put pressure on Britain's Achilles heel – British India. Britain's maritime supremacy was thus to be challenged at the borders of Afghanistan. The countless assurances sent to London that there was no intention to conquer Tashkent, Bukhara, Khiva and

Merv were mere smokescreens, for this is exactly what happened. As the former foreign minister and future prime minister Lord Palmerston (1784–1865) aptly stated in 1853: 'The policy and practice of the Russian Government has always been to push forward its encroachments as fast and far as the apathy or want of firmness of other Governments would allow it to go, but always to stop and retire when it met with determined resistance, and then to wait for the next favourable opportunity to make another spring on the intended victim. In furtherance of this policy, the Russian Government has always had two strings on its bow – moderate language and disinterested professions at St. Petersburg and at London; active aggression by its agents on the scene of operation.'[111] The Russian plans to invade India of 1854, 1855, 1869, 1877 and 1878 demonstrate precisely what Russia had in mind.[112] In the view of the present author, the Russian annexation of Crimea in the spring of 2014 and the outbreak of fighting in eastern Ukraine show that Palmerston's assessment is still valid today.

Of course, it was not just geopolitical considerations that triggered Russia's southward advance, but also economic ones. The abolition of serfdom in 1861 liberated about 20 million peasants, but they did not receive any land – instead, they had to buy it themselves on credit. As a result, landless peasants gradually penetrated into the Kazakh steppes. Second, the expanding Russian industry needed new markets, as the purchasing power of the domestic market was too small and the products were not competitive on the world market. Russia identified these markets in Central Asia, which for the time being was shielded from the British India export economy due to the Hindu Kush. In contrast to the maritime power Great Britain, which advocated free trade, the land power Russia pursued a protectionist economic policy: high import duties impeded foreign imports, which, in turn, determined the political control of the markets. In addition, the cotton-producing Uzbek khanates became increasingly important to

Russia in the early 1860s, as the American Civil War of 1861–65 severely hampered American cotton exports. Russia consequently became dependent on cotton imports from Central Asia. Since cotton was vital for the textile industry, Russia had to ensure that the Central Asian cotton market did not fall under the control of its arch-enemy Great Britain. As General Romanovsky reported, high-quality American cotton was also cultivated in Central Asia, where it replaced local short-fibre cotton.[113] Cotton became even more important in the 1880s when it found its way into ammunition production.

In the early summer of 1864, moves were made to implement the imperial directive of 20 December 1863. Starting from the Syr Darya line, Major General Verofkin conquered the city of Turkistan, and Major General Chernyayev, starting from the Siberian line, conquered Aulie-Ata and Shymkent, and, in May–June 1865, the important city of Tashkent.[114] The military objective of closing the gap between the two fortress lines was thus achieved, though not the political and economic objectives. Russia was determined to prevent Bukhara from taking advantage of Kokand's defeats for the purpose of territorial expansion and acquiring control itself of Kokand and its cotton plantations. General D. Romanovsky therefore continued with the war, capturing the Bukharan border fortress of Jizak, claiming victory at Irdjar, and conquering the cities of Khojand and Ura Tyube.[115] Russia annexed the northern half of the khanate of Kokand (including Tashkent) and made the southern half into a protectorate in January 1868. To counteract the British fears, foreign minister Alexander Gorchakov (1798–1883) had written a memorandum in November 1864 to explain the Russian policy. He justified the Russian advance on the grounds that all 'civilised' countries needed to secure their borders with a 'half-savage nomad population' by subduing it. This simply displaced the problem, however, for the pacified nomads bordered themselves on other half-savage tribes. 'The United States

87. Sabre with gilt scabbard decorated with pearls, diamonds, emeralds and rubies. Manufactured in Bukhara in the 1880s. Gift to Tsar Alexander III (r. 1881–94) from an embassy of Bukhara. Inv. No. B.O.-172. The State Hermitage Museum, St Petersburg, Russia.

of America, France in Algeria, Holland in her colonies, England in India – all have been irresistibly forced, less by ambition than by imperious necessity, into this onward march, where the greatest difficulty is to know when to stop.'[116] The logic of this Asian policy implied that Russia would continue to subdue tribes and small states until it was hindered by a major power. In November, Gorchakov affirmed that the border near Shymkent would be drawn along the northern edge of Kokand's densely populated and agricultural areas. As early as the following June, however, Russia conquered Tashkent, located further south.

This strategy behind Russian foreign policy was based on the experience of the Mongol invasions in the thirteenth century and the corresponding conviction that borders with tribal and mobile societies would always be vulnerable. There was an unbridge-able chasm between agrarian Russia and its pastoralist neighbours in the south-east: Russia wanted secure borders and trade routes, the pastoralists free access to pastures. Furthermore, the latter respected state boundaries and the integrity of trading caravans only against tribute payments. Since Tsar Ivan IV, Russian policy had aimed at pacifying its south-eastern neighbours and making them sedentary, a process which was accelerated by the settlement of Russian Cossacks and peasants.

With the appointment of General Konstantin Petrovich von Kaufmann (1818–82) as governor-general of Turkestan in July 1867, the conquest of the Uzbek khanates continued as planned. Kaufmann was given far-reaching powers: He could conduct diplo-matic negotiations in Central Asia, declare war, and conclude binding contracts with neighbouring countries.[117] When Muzaffar al-Din (r. 1860–85) of Bukhara succumbed to the pressure of the mullahs and declared 'holy war' on Russia in April 1868, Kaufmann defeated his army and seized Samarkand on 2 May. In doing so, he controlled the Zeravshan River and thus Bukhara's water supply.[118] The amir capitulated on 30 June and surrendered to Kaufmann's conditions: he had to forfeit Samarkand, open access to the Bukhara market to Russian traders, and pay a war indemnity. He was allowed to keep his throne and remained nominally a sovereign ruler, but soon became a vassal of Russia. However, after the amir indepen-dently resumed negotiations with Afghanistan, Khiva and the Ottoman Empire from 1870 to 1872 without informing Kaufmann, Kaufmann forced him in 1873 to relinquish his foreign policy to Russia. It was then delegated to the governor-general. While Muzaffar al-Din retained domestic sovereignty, he nevertheless was forced to abolish slavery.[119] Abd al-Malik, the amir's oldest son, and the city of Shahr-i Sabz revolted after the signing of the peace treaty in 1868, but Kaufmann quashed the insurgency in 1870. Kaufmann

then returned the territories to the amir. In the same year, the amir occupied the regions of Hissar and Kulyab in southern Tajikistan, with Russian support. Six years later, during the dissolution of the khanate of Kokand in the spring of 1876, Russia gave the areas of Darvaz and Karategin to Bukhara. It wanted to compensate the amir for the previous loss of Samarkand.[120]

The conquest of Bukhara put Russia directly on the border of the khanate of Khiva, which General Kaufmann defeated in 1873. In preparation for this, the port and the fortress of Krasnovodsk were established in 1869 on the eastern shore of the Caspian Sea in the former delta of the Uzboy.[121] Now, Russia had the opportunity to ship troops to Krasnovodsk and, from there, to threaten not only Khiva, but also Herat, the gateway to India. Viceroy Lawrence, who had rejected a Forward Policy till late 1867 but was impressed by Rawlinson's memorandum of 1868,[122] wrote to Foreign Secretary Lord Clarendon that the Court of St Petersburg should 'understand, that it cannot be permitted to interfere in the affairs of Afghanistan, or these of any state which lies contiguous to our frontier. [. . .] Failing that, we might give that power to understand that an advance towards India, beyond a certain point, would entail on her war, in all parts of the world, with England.'[123] With his recommendation to send an unmistakable threat of war to Russia, the 'dove' Lawrence suddenly mutated into a 'hawk'. The question of where this red line should be drawn, moreover, defined Russian-British relations regarding Afghanistan until 1895 and the neighbouring states until the Anglo-Russian Convention of 1907. Lord Clarendon accepted Lawrence's recommendation to obtain a territorial agreement with Russia. At the same time, he aimed less at a sharp line of demarcation which would define the two zones of influence than at a neutral zone between the two empires. Gorchakov welcomed the initiative and proposed Afghanistan as such a neutral zone. London, however, could not agree to the neutralisation of Afghanistan. Clarendon, therefore, recommended the Oxus as a demarcation line, which Gorchakov promptly rejected. Although no agreement could be reached, the importance of defining the northern border of Afghanistan, in particular the status of small principalities in the Upper Oxus of Badakhshan and Wakhan, quickly became apparent. Great Britain claimed them for Afghanistan and Russia for Bukhara.[124]

In 1872, Foreign Secretary Lord Granville (1815–91) presented another proposal regarding Afghanistan's northern border. On 17 October, he sent the following message to Gorchakov: 'The right of the Ameer of Kabul (Sher Ali) to the possession of the territories up to the Oxus as far down as Khoja Saleh is fully estab-lished. [. . .] For Your Excellency's more complete information I state the territories and boundaries which Her Majesty's Government consider as fully belonging to the Ameer of Kabul, viz:

1. Badakhshan with its dependent district Wakhan from the Sarikal (Wood's Lake)[125] on the east to the junction of the Kokcha River with the Oxus (or Panjah), *on the west, the stream of the Oxus* forming the northern boundary …

2. Afghan Turkestan, comprising the districts of Kunduz, Khulm and Balkh, the northern boundary of which would be the line of the Oxus from the junction of the Kokcha River to the post of Khoja Saleh, inclusive, on the high road from Bokhara to Balkh. Nothing to be claimed by the Afghan Ameer on the left bank of the Oxus below Khojah Saleh.

3. The internal districts of Aksha, Seripuul, Maimana, Shibberjan and Andhui, the latter of which would be the extreme Afghan frontier possession to the north-west, the desert beyond belonging to independent tribes of Turkomans.

4. The western Afghan frontier between the dependencies of Herat and those of the province of Khorassan is well known and need not here be defined.'[126]

Contrary to what is often written, Granville's message and Gorchakov's answer did not represent a contract – there were only two letters, and Gorchakov's agreement remained decidedly vague. In addition, the British proposal had serious flaws: it was not sufficiently thought out, and was poorly formulated and founded on erroneous geographical assumptions. First of all, at point (1) in the official version, which sought to define the eastern half of the northern border, the secretary erroneously omitted the words in italics, making the passage difficult to understand. Second, rivers only form useful natural boundaries on plains, not in the mountains, where members of the same community sometimes live on both banks of a river; real natural boundaries are watersheds and mountain ridges, as General Gerard, commander of the British Pamir Boundary Commission emphasised in 1895.[127] Third, the small principalities of Wakhan, Shugnan and Roshan, to which Amir Sher Ali laid claim, also extended along the right bank of the Oxus/Panj, while Darvaz, which belonged to Bukhara, also possessed lands on the left bank.[128] The designation of the Oxus as a northern border of Afghanistan therefore did not correspond to the actual situation. Fourth, equating the Oxus and the Panj implied that the latter is the head stream of the former. Lieutenant Colonel T.E. Gordon contradicted this, however. He explored the Pamirs in the spring of 1874, and identified the River Murghab, lying 120 km further north, as the major tributary of the Oxus,[129] which would have granted Afghanistan a large area up to the north

of the Alichur Pamirs. Fifth, as Gordon observed,[130] between Lake Zorkul (Wood's Lake) and the Chinese border there was a 100-km-long gap that Russia exploited in the early 1890s. Sixth, regarding the western northern border (2), the Russian-British Boundary Commission from 1886 was forced to conclude that the Fort Khoja Saleh no longer existed, if it ever had.[131] Seventh, (4) the western border near Herat was anything but distinct, as revealed in the course of the calamitous 'Panjdeh incident' of 1885.[132] Eighth, Granville ignored the question of the borders of the Russian sphere of influence. Ninth, he failed to even consult the Afghan amir, who only learned of the agreement through a letter from General Kaufmann.[133] And finally, Granville did not respond to the Russian proposal to designate the border on-site by means of a commission. Somewhat surprisingly, Gorchakov agreed to the British proposal on 31 January 1873 with reservations: 'The English cabinet includes within them [the dominions of Sher Ali] Badakhshan and Wakhan, which, according to our views, enjoyed a certain independence.' But 'we do not refuse to accept the boundary line laid down by England.'[134] Probably Russia agreed to the British proposal only to gain time until Khiva and the Turkmens were conquered.[135]

Russia, however, understood Granville's failure to address the demarcation of the Russian zone of influence west of Khoja Saleh as a licence to cross the lower reaches of the Oxus and to attack Khiva. On 19 December 1872, the tsar issued an order to seize the city.[136] The British omission was all the more surprising given that **Sayyid Muhammad Rahim II** (r. 1865–1910) had earlier requested help from British India, Persia and the Ottoman Empire with regard to the Russian ultimatum.[137] Within a few months, London's supposed diplomatic victory transformed into a Russian triumph and Great Britain's humiliation. Khiva provided the pretext for the invasion in 1871, when a cavalry detachment attacked a Russian unit from Krasnovodsk and stole its camels.[138] In the spring of 1873, three columns from Tashkent, Orenburg and Krasnovodsk attacked, and supreme commander Kaufmann rode into Khiva on 29 May.[139] Exercising his powers, Kaufmann decided to leave the khan on his throne, but established a protectorate over the khanate. In addition, Khiva had to cede the areas lying on the Oxus' right bank, release all its slaves, and pay a large indemnity. With the conquest of Khiva, Russia dominated the eastern coast of the Caspian Sea and navigation on the lower reaches of the Oxus up to Termez. Moreover, its troops were moved to within 800 km of Herat. In late 1874, Sir Henry Rawlinson warned: 'Russia in possession of Herat would have a grip on the throat of India.'[140]

While Russia annexed Kokand, it left domestic political sovereignty to Bukhara and Khiva. This had the great advantage that

88. Alichur Lake in the Alichur Pamir, over which Afghanistan, China and Russia all laid claim from the early 1870s until 1893. Photo: 2007.

the khans still remained responsible for the administration, the collection of taxes, the judiciary and sensitive religious affairs within their dominions. This autonomy spared Russia substantial administrative costs and shielded it from the hostility of the local populations, which would not have accepted a foreign government of 'infidels'. Even Russian efforts to efficiently combat the annual locust plagues and to improve health care met with strong opposition. Mullahs and shamans 'denounced Russian solicitude as a subterfuge destined to further subjugate the Muslims'.[141] For these reasons, the settlement of Russian peasants in the khanates was prohibited, as was Orthodox Christian proselytising.[142] Russia had achieved its dual strategic objective: a monopoly over the resources of Central Asia and a closed market for Russian products. The inclusion of Bukhara in the Russian customs system in 1895 deepened the economic integration of the khanate into the

empire.[143] Although the economic link of the khanates to Russia sparked economic growth, it also entailed serious disadvantages: the accelerated expansion of the cultivation of cotton caused a significant reduction in food production, so that the former selfsufficient populations of Bukhara, Fergana and Khiva became food importers. This would have catastrophic consequences in World War I when Russia neither paid for the cotton deliveries nor supplied food.[144] Second, the large-scale irrigation of cotton plantations in Semirechie and in the region of Samarkand took so much water from the Syr Darya and Oxus rivers that the territories at the rivers' lower reaches were threatened with water shortage and dehydration. The astronomer and meteorologist Franz von Schwarz had already warned of this in 1893.[145] Third, with its exorbitant interest rates, the credit system drove the farmers, who were 'paid' for their crops with overpriced payments in kind, into poverty

and de facto slavery.[146] Fourth, the Russian industrial enterprises wanted to retain value creation in western Russia and sell only finished products in the east. As a result, no industrial processing took place in Russian Central Asia, which downgraded the Uzbek khanates to Russian colonies. And, fifth, the import of cheap Russian commodities by train ruined local handicrafts, beginning in the 1890s. In the absence of industrialisation, the region degenerated into a supplier of raw materials, anticipating a process which has developed in trade between Central Asia and China since the mid-1990s. Here, Central Asia sells raw materials, fuels and metals and China exports cheap goods, which destroy the local artisanal and post-Soviet enterprises.[147]

The next step in the Russian expansion was the annexation of Kokand in February 1876, which moved the borders of the empire closer to Afghanistan and Kashgaria. Within twelve years, Russia had shifted the 1,600-km-long military border an average of 450 km to the south, representing a territorial extension of 720,000 km², an area slightly larger than Texas. Since Russia had occupied the city and region of Kuldja (today's Yining) in the north-west of Xinjiang in 1871, Kashgaria found itself facing the threat of a Russian invasion.[148] From Kashgaria, however, it was possible to control the northern side of the passes leading to Kashmir and Ladakh. The Balkan crisis that broke out in April 1877 and the entrance of a British fleet squadron into the Sea of Marmara in February 1878, however, prevented the next Russian gambit in Central Asia.[149]

5. Yaqub Beg's Emirate of Turkestan in Xinjiang

In the early 1870s, the remote and economically poor region of East Turkestan was pulled into the wake of the 'Great Game'. The trigger for this was the Emirate of Turkestan (1866–77), which seceded from China as a result of Muslim revolts. Until the mid-1850s, there was little resistance from the Turkic-speaking Muslim population in the Tarim Basin against the government of the Qing dynasty. The revolts that broke out among the ethnically Chinese and Chinese-speaking Dungans were sparked by the Taiping Rebellion (1851–64) in China, which severely affected its financial situation. In response, the central government was forced to cut the subsidies to the western regions and to massively raise taxes. The first riots took place in Gansu and Shaanxi in 1862, and then in Ili in 1863,

and in Kucha in June 1864. When the order was issued to disarm the Dungan soldiers in East Turkestan, the uprising expanded to the whole of East Turkestan. As the Chinese garrisons either only existed on paper or were opium-addicted and unfit for battle, the Dungan met little resistance. Soon, the Kyrgyz and the Muslim city dwellers, who also fought each other, also rebelled.[150] The ruler of Kokand, Alim Quli, wanted to take advantage of the opportunity to once again intervene militarily in Kashgaria. In early 1865, he sent Khoja Buzurg with a small army that was commanded by the Kokandian **Yaqub Beg** (1820–77, r. 1866–77). Yaqub Beg conquered Kashgar and Yarkand; he then got rid of Khoja Buzurg and in the spring of 1866 took power for himself. Over the next six years, Yaqub Beg conquered the cities of the Tarim Basin, whose Turkic-speaking residents resisted him until he managed to occupy Ürümqi in the winter of 1870/71.[151] At the same time as Yaqub Beg's conquest, the Taranchis in the north-west of Xinjiang drove out

89. Taifoochees of the Army of the Amir of Kashgar. The painter Captain Chapman explained: 'The armament of the Tungane and Chinese troops in the service of the Amir consist of what in European parlance would be called a wall-piece, but is here known as Taifoo. This is a cumbrous weapon about 6 feet long in stock and barrel. The taifoo throws a bullet of no more than 1 ½ ounces... Against an enemy not armed with rifle arms, a large number of taifoos ... must be sufficiently formidable. [...] In the actual working of these pieces, strictest attention is paid to the minutiae of drill, and, the positions of the performers are in the highest degree studied.' Watercolour drawing by Captain E.F. Chapman, 1873–74. Private Collection.

90. The Valley of the Shyok in northern Ladakh. The second mission of Sir Thomas D. Forsyth marched in the autumn of 1873 from Leh to the Shyok Valley, crossed the 5,575-m-high Karakoram Pass, and reached Yarkand in today's Xinjiang on 7 November 1873. Captain (later General Sir) Edward Francis Chapman was in charge of the logistics of the expedition and documented it in watercolour drawings and photographs. Private Collection.

both the Qing troops and the Dungans and established the small sultanate of Kulja (1866–71) under **Ala Khan** (Abul Oghlan).[152] After Ala Khan had rejected the stationing of a Russian consul in Ili in late November 1870, Russia attacked in the next summer. It occupied the region of Ili and unlawfully appropriated Chinese territory.[153] Russia simultaneously made sure that the Dungans, who had plundered Uliasutai in 1870 and Khobdo in 1871, could not advance to Ili.[154] Yaqub Beg, for his part, escaped the same fate in 1872, only because he consented to a trade agreement favourable to Russia, which was making preparations in Verny (Almaty) for an invasion.[155] Yaqub Beg now tried to find support among Russia's enemies – British India and the Ottomans – and in the autumn of 1872 sent Yaqub Khan as an envoy to Calcutta and Istanbul. Sultan Abdulaziz (r. 1861–76) sent weapons and instructors to Kashgar, and Yaqub Beg announced on 28 January 1874 that East Turkestan had become an Ottoman protectorate. He, furthermore, took the title of an Amir al-mu'minin (Commander of the Faithful) and ordered the Friday prayer to be introduced in the name of the sultan and to have his name minted on the coins.[156]

Yaqub Beg's secession from China posed a dilemma for British foreign policy: while London supported the Chinese government and the territorial integrity of China and thus did not recognise Yaqub Beg's rule, British India feared that Yaqub Beg could fall under the Russian sphere of influence. Russia's area of control would then have reached the Karakoram Mountains. Therefore, India advocated a strong East Turkestan as a buffer state with Russia.[157] When Yaqub Beg decided to send an envoy to Viceroy Lord Mayo (1822–72, in office 1869–72) in 1870 with the request for a British official to come to Kashgar, he commissioned Sir Thomas D. Forsyth (1827–86). This first Forsyth mission in 1870 failed because of intrigues in Kashmir and Yaqub Beg's absence from Kashgar.[158] However, the tea merchant Robert Shaw and the explorer George Hayward – who was commissioned by Henry Rawlinson to survey the passes between Ladakh and Kashgaria – had already separately visited Yarkand and Kashgar in 1868.[159] Lord Mayo was alarmed by Hayward's assertion that the Chang-Lang Pass, which had an elevation of 5,742 m and connected Leh in Ladakh with the Yarkand Valley, was 'quite practicable for laden horses and camels, and would offer no great impediment to the passage of artillery'.[160] When Yaqub Beg sent another envoy to British India in 1873, Viceroy Lord Northbrook (1826–1904, in office 1872–76) seized the opportunity to confront Russia with a strong diplomatic offensive for the first time in 30 years. The second Forsyth mission of 1873/74 numbered 350 men, including officers, cavalry, infantry, and surveyors as well as one geologist, ethnologist, historian, and a watercolourist, who also took photographs[161] (figs. 89, 90). The expedition stayed in Kashgar from 4 December 1873 to 17 March 1874 and was highly successful in terms of trade and making new geographical discoveries. Forsyth and the amir concluded a comprehensive trade agreement, which even provided that a British agent be stationed in Kashgar. A political agent thus would have been posted outside of the red line from 1873 for the first time. But London hesitated to accredit a resident since Kashgar would be easy for Russia to conquer and represented an outpost for British India that it could not defend. The amir, in turn, refrained from ratifying the treaty out of fear of Russia, which is why the designated resident, Shaw, returned to India in 1875. As Sir Henry Trotter remembered, there were also surprising encounters: 'The punishment of theft was the loss of a hand, and on one occasion at Kashgar an unfortunate individual come to Dr. Bellew's dispensary, and, after some natural hesitations, pulled his severed hand out of his pocket, and asked the Doctor to affix it to its proper place.'[162]

On the other hand, the geographic knowledge that Lieutenant Colonel Gordon, captains Biddulph and Trotter, Dr Stoliczka and four so-called 'Pundits' gathered in the spring of 1874 in the Pamirs, a stronghold of the Ismailis, was critically important. The Pundits were specially trained local surveyors disguised as pilgrims, mullahs, or traders. They explored regions of the Hindu Kush, Pamirs, Karakoram and the Himalayas that were unfamiliar to the British and in reports were simply referred to by code names or letters.[163] The discoveries made in 1874 were worrying for British India. Granville's boundary definition of October 1872 was wrong in numerous respects. First of all, Afghanistan and East Turkestan did *not* share a common border in the Pamirs. There was in fact a gap that the Russians could penetrate. Gordon stated in a confidential report: 'It will be very easy for her [Russia] . . . to take possession of the Little Pamir Lake, and thus insert a very narrow wedge of actual Russian territory between Afghanistan and Kashgar.'[164] Eleven years later, in the autumn of 1885, the explorer and diplomat Ney Elias (1844–97) confirmed the existence of this gap in the Wakhan and recommended encouraging Afghanistan and China to close it.[165] By the same token, the Russian officer Lev Kostenko had already

written after 1876 that the Pamirs were a no-man's land that had not been claimed by any country.[166] The group led by Gordon also discovered a practicable route from the Russian fortress of Osh across the Alai Mountains to the Little Pamir in the north-eastern Wakhan, and from there to Sarhad on the Wakhan River, the southernmost major tributary of the Oxus. Second, Trotter recognised that Roshan, Shugnan and Darvaz extended on both sides of the Oxus and that the Murghab River, lying far north of the Panj, is the Oxus' longest tributary.[167] Finally, Gordon's confidential report assessed the Karakoram Mountains to be impassable for an army with artillery, which contradicted Hayward. By contrast, two passes to the west in the southern Wakhan were quite negotiable for an army and also provided sufficient pastures: the Ishkoman Pass led to Yasin and Gilgit while the Baroghil Pass led either on an easy route to Chitral and further to Peshawar, or to Yasin and Gilgit via the difficult Darkot Pass.[168] Thus, from the mid-1870s, three approach routes theoretically came into question that put India at risk:

1. from the Caspian Sea to Herat and through the Bolan Pass to Quetta or to Kandahar and through the Khyber Pass to Peshawar,
2. from Termez to Balkh, Bamiyan, Kabul, and through the Khyber Pass to Peshawar,
3. from Osh to the Little Pamir, to Sarhad, and through the Baroghil Pass to Chitral and Peshawar.

Ultimately, the information that Gordon's team collected led to the realisation that the Sarikol Mountains, running from north to south, form the watershed between the Oxus to the west and Tarim to the east and, as Younghusband would confirm later, that the Hindu Kush divides the water systems of the Oxus to the north from those of the Indus to the south.[169]

In 1874, Russia responded to the Forsyth mission by dispatching Captain Reintal to Kashgar, who called for further trade concessions. Yaqub Beg refused, and it was only the outbreak of the revolt in Kokand that saved Yaqub Beg from a Russian invasion. Since Russia and Kashgaria shared a common border from February 1876, Yaqub Beg was forced to yield in early 1877, leaving three additional border posts to Russia.[170] His days, in any case, were numbered, for China, contrary to Russian and British expectations, had successfully started to recapture the breakaway region. General Zuo Zongtang (1812–85) reconquered Hami in 1875, Ürümqi in 1876, and Turfan in April 1877. Yaqub Beg died in Korla in May, probably from a stroke or poison. By the end of the year, Zuo occupied Kashgar, which enabled China to win back Xinjiang, with the exception of the Ili region occupied by Russia.[171] The three empires, Russia, Great Britain and China, now encountered each other in the Pamirs, where there was also a piece of unclaimed no-man's land. China demanded from Russia the immediate return of Ili. After completing a first round of negotiations in 1879, Beijing refused to ratify the unfavourable Treaty of Livadia and threatened war. In the Treaty of St Petersburg of 1881, China regained most of Ili, but had to pay an indemnity to Russia, grant painful trade concessions, and allow for the opening of seven consulates in Xinjiang.[172] Russia had no interest in annexing Xinjiang with its restless Muslim population, but was rather interested in its raw

materials and in using the region as a market for Russian industrial goods. It also sought further strategic advantage over British India. The treaty, accordingly, corresponded with all of Russia's intentions. Not only did it provide Russia with most of Xinjiang's resources, but the opening of consulates with extraterritorial powers seriously undermined Chinese sovereignty. As the later British consul Percy Etherton (1879–1963, in office 1918–22) observed, the new Russian consul general Nikolai Petrovsky (1837–1908, in office 1882–1903) established himself as 'virtual ruler of Kashgar' thanks to his ruthlessness and his Cossack escort.[173] The

91. The approach to the 4,336-m-high Kyzyl Art Pass, leading from north-eastern Tajikistan to south-western Kyrgyzstan; in the background stand the Trans-Alai Mountains. Photo: 2008.

92. Guards of the artillery and officers assembled in the courtyard of the urda (palace) of the Dadkhhawah (governor) of Yarkand. Forsyth, *Report of a mission to Yarkund in 1873* (1875), photo facing p. 106.

province, moreover, became an 'unofficial [Russian] colony'[174] – a situation that would persist until the October Revolution.

China wanted to bind Xinjiang more strongly to the empire and gave the region the status of a province in 1884. It then undertook efforts to sinicise the population by promoting the immigration of Han Chinese, not least to promote agriculture and thereby achieve a wider tax base. At the same time, Beijing tried to transfer Han Chinese administrative methods to Xinjiang and to introduce Confucian school curricula. Wealthy Muslim families circumvented these arrangements by paying poorer families to send their children to the Chinese schools instead of their own.[175] But Beijing's efforts soon failed and the two communities and worldviews remained apart. The Han Chinese built their own walled cities a few kilometres from the existing Muslim walled cities. Beijing's efforts proved futile since the local Muslims rejected any assimilation, there was a lack of transport infrastructure which made trade with Han China impossible, and Russia had unimpeded access to the region's resources. The poor province remained dependent on substantial subsidies from the central government.

6. Sher Ali and the Second Anglo-Afghan War

Tensions in Xinjiang had barely subsided following Yaqub Beg's death when a war threatened to break out between Russia and Britain 4,000 km to the west. The crisis was triggered in 1875 by an uprising of Christians in Bosnia-Herzegovina against the Ottomans, which the Bulgarians joined. Since the revolt was brutally suppressed by the Ottomans, Russia saw an opportunity. On the pretext of coming to the aid of their co-religionists as a protecting power of Orthodox Christians, the Russians declared war on the Ottoman Empire in April 1877. When the Russian army marched on Constantinople at the beginning of 1878, it ran headlong into a British naval fleet moored in the Sea of Marmara. Russia avoided direct confrontation, however, and the Russo-Turkish Treaty of San Stefano of 3 March 1878 forced Istanbul to establish a Greater Bulgarian kingdom. This would have become a de facto Russian protectorate. It would also have given Russia access to the Mediterranean and to India via the Suez Canal.[176] London was unwilling to go along with this and continued its preparations for war, including in Asia. Prime minister Disraeli had already explained to Queen Victoria in July 1877: 'Russia must be attacked from Asia, troops should be sent to the Persian Gulf, and the Empress of India should order her armies to clear Central Asia of the Muscovites, and drive them into the Caspian Sea. We have a good instrument for this purpose in Lord Lytton, and indeed he was sent there with that view.'[177] After Viceroy Northbrook's refusal to pursue a tougher policy towards the Afghan Amir Sher Ali, Disraeli chose the pretentious, impulsive, and unstable Lord Lytton (1831–90, in office 1876–80) as the new viceroy.

In 1863, Dost Muhammad had appointed his son **Sher Ali Khan** (first rule 1863–66) as his successor, but his two brothers Mohammad Afzal and Mohammad A'zam challenged him for the throne. At first, Sher Ali had the upper hand. But in 1866, Afzal's son Abdur Rahman Khan, the future amir from 1880–1901, prevailed over Sher Ali and placed his father **Mohammad Afzal** (r. 1866–67) on the throne; he died a year later, however. **Mohammad Khan A'zam** (1867–69) then followed, though **Sher Ali** (second rule 1869–79) overthrew him in 1869. Sher Ali pushed through a number of reforms: he removed the governors' authority to collect taxes and transferred it to the central government, which allowed for the financing of a standing army.[178] His initially positive relations with British India took a decided turn for the worse when General Frederic Goldsmid (1818–1908) was supposed to mediate a dispute between Afghanistan and Persia over the province of Sistan. He attributed the western half of Sistan, including the fertile oasis of Zabol, to Persia, while leaving the eastern, more arid half for Afghanistan. Conversely, the common Hamun Lake was now one-third in Persia and two-thirds in Afghanistan, from where it is also fed. Afghanistan had thus lost a fertile oasis, and Persia had to rely on water from Afghanistan. Colonel Sir T.H. Holdich (1843–1929), who was involved in five border commissions, observed laconically: 'Here we have an object-lesson on the lasting disadvantages of a boundary which cuts an irrigation system into two.'[179] Barely after arriving in India, Lytton began to implement both Disraeli's public and secret instructions. His public mission was to force Sher Ali to allow British Political Agents in Herat, Kandahar and later Kabul. His secret mission was to undertake the first assessments and preparations for an attack on Russia in Central Asia and, in the absence of cooperation from Sher Ali, to plan the break-up of Afghanistan. Towards the end of 1876, Lytton then compelled the khan of Khelat to hand over the city of Quetta, north-west of the strategic Bolan Pass. When in the spring of 1877 Sher Ali expressed to a British agent willingness

93. Amir Yaqub Khan (r. 1879–80) with his leading commanders and officers. The Amir is seated in the centre and at his right the Ghilzai Daoud Shah, commander-in-chief of the Afghan army. Photograph by John Burke in late spring 1879, when Yaqub Khan was forced on 26 May 1879 by the British envoy Sir Pierre Louis Napoléon Cavagnari to sign the humiliating Treaty of Gandamak, handing over foreign policy to British India. National Army Museum, London.

to compromise on the issue of the stationing of diplomats, Lytton suspended the talks, seeking a pretext to attack. London, however, still refused him permission to initiate the war.[180]

Russia was also making preparations for an offensive in Central Asia. On the military level, General Kaufmann mobilised three columns in April 1878, and on the diplomatic level, he sent General Nikolay Stolyetov (1834–1912) to Kabul. The first column was supposed to advance from Samarkand, via Kabul, to the Khyber Pass; the second to advance from Krasnovodsk via Merv to Herat; and the third to attack from Samarkand via Kokand, the Pamirs, the Wakhan, Chitral and Peshawar.[181] However, if operations had started, the first and third columns would have failed due to the topography, and even the second column might have quickly stalled because of a lack of adequate logistical planning. On 25 July, Stolyetov arrived in Kabul, where Sher Ali received him with great ceremony. The amir faced a dilemma: on the one hand he was being threatened by Lytton, and on the other hand Kaufmann could support his nephew Abdur Rahman, who was living in exile in Bukhara, militarily in a coup attempt. Kaufmann had instructed Stolyetov to obtain Sher Ali's permission for the free passage of Russia's armies and to convert Afghanistan into a Russian protectorate in exchange for the promise of Russian military aid. Tsar Alexander, however, had rejected the idea of a protectorate. Stolyetov, nonetheless, ignored the imperial directive and settled a military

alliance with Sher Ali, promising to rush to his side with a 30,000-strong army in the event of British intervention.[182] Meanwhile, a revised peace treaty was signed between Russia and the Ottomans on 13 July at the Berlin Congress convened by Chancellor Bismarck. Here, the sultan recovered almost 70 per cent of the lost territories, Bosnia-Herzegovina was now ruled by Austria, and Russia was denied access to the Mediterranean. Thus, a reason for war in Central Asia no longer existed either for Great Britain, which had reached its strategic goal, or for Russia, which did not want to risk a global war against Britain. Lytton was aware of this and ignored London's instruction to delay the planned deployment of a militarily protected legation to Kabul that had been refused by the amir. On 21 September, it was halted by Afghan troops at the Khyber Pass, prompting Lytton to issue a 20-day ultimatum to Sher Ali on 2 November. Confident about his treaty with Stolyetov, Sher Ali did not respond. On 21 November, Lytton declared war on Afghanistan.

This Second Anglo-Afghan War, for which there was no longer a *casus belli* as in 1838/39, had a similar outcome to the first and proved futile. The British attacked Kandahar, Jalalabad and the Kurram Valley south of the Khyber in three columns. The troops now had the new Martini-Henry breech-loading rifle with an effective range of 550 m (but which tended to overheat in strong sunlight); a powerful light mountain artillery; and heliographs to communicate.[183] Sher Ali quickly called upon

94. British envoy and resident in Kabul Sir Pierre Louis Napoléon Cavagnari (1841–79) and Amir Yaqub Khan. F.l.t.r: William Jenkyns who spoke Pashtu and mainly negotiated the Treaty of Gandamak; Sir Cavagnari; Amir Yaqub Khan; Afghan commander-in-chief Daoud Shah and Mustafi (Prime Minister) Habibullah Khan.[17] Photograph by John Burke in late spring or summer 1879. National Army Museum, London.

95. Soldiers from a British Indian regiment, Peshawar Fieldforce, during the Second Anglo-Afghan War 1878–80. In the centre sits the then Lieutenant Robert Warburton (1842–99), whose father was Lieutenant-Colonel Richard Warburton and whose mother was a niece of Amir Dost Muhammad. Speaking Persian and Pashtu, he served for eighteen years as Political Agent for the Khyber District.[18] Photograph by John Burke; Collection of the J. Paul Getty Museum, Los Angeles.

General Kaufmann for help, who immediately ruled out a Russian intervention. Left in the lurch by Russia, the amir fled to Mazar-e Sharif, where he died on 21 February 1879. Given the rapid advance of the British, his successor **Yaqub Khan** (r. 1879–80) had no alternative but to take up negotiations with the victor. The treaty signed on 26 May 1879 in Gandamak, the site of the last stand in January 1842, committed Afghanistan foreign policy to Great Britain, which promised in return to defend the territorial integrity of the country with arms and troops. Moreover, Yaqub Khan had to agree to a resident British envoy in Kabul and to cede to Great Britain the Khyber Pass and the Michini Pass, and the districts of Kurram, Pishin, Shibi and the enclaves in Quetta. In response, Kandahar and Jalalabad were returned to him.[184] Now, British India controlled the three main passes that led from Afghanistan to India: the Khyber Pass, the Kurram Valley, and the Bolan Pass.[185] Lytton appeared to have won an easy victory and appointed Major Sir Pierre Louis Napoléon Cavagnari (1841–79) as British resident in Kabul (fig. 94). Major General Sir Frederick Roberts (1832–1914), who had commanded the Kurram column, had a more realistic assessment of the situation: 'I thought that peace had been signed too quickly, before, in fact, we had instilled that awe of us in the

Afghan nation which would have been the only reliable guarantee for the safety of the Mission. [...] I could not help feeling ... that the chances were against the Mission ever coming back.'[186] Roberts' foreboding soon became reality, for Cavagnari, who had arrived in Kabul in July 1879, was killed on 3 September with his small escort, like Macnaghten and Burnes before him.[187]

In September 1879, Russia also suffered a humiliating defeat near Ashgabat, now the capital of Turkmenistan. Russia had taken advantage of the international focus on Istanbul to penetrate into the territory of the Turkmen steppe nomads. After General Lomakin had been driven back to the coast by the Turkmen horsemen in 1877 and 1878, he launched a third attack in September 1879 on the fortress of Geok Tepe, halfway between Krasnovodsk and Merv. The assault failed, and Lomakin had to retreat back to the coast.[188] Meanwhile, General Roberts had been ordered to occupy Kabul and to punish Cavagnari's murderers. The order read as follows: 'Your object should be to strike terror, and striking it swiftly and deeply; but to avoid a Reign of Terror.'[189] Lytton's instruction seems to have come straight from Machiavelli's *Il Principe*: 'The conqueror who seizes power should weigh carefully all acts of violence which he must commit and perform them at a single stroke. [...] Violent acts

96. General Frederick Roberts with Afghan officers and leaders in Kabul, *ca.* 1879/80. Photograph by John Burke; National Army Museum, London.

must all be committed at once. [. . .] If [the ruler], namely, makes a few examples for the sake of deterrence, he is more merciful than those who as a result of too much leniency allow disorder to arise, giving rise to murder and plunder.'[190] Lytton's instruction also corresponded to the British 'hit and run' strategy used in tribal areas, in which a military expedition burned down villages in a tribal area in retaliation and immediately withdrew again. Despite Lytton's martial command, Roberts had only 89 ringleaders executed. After Roberts' victory near Charasia, 11 km south of Kabul – in which heliographs played an important role and two Gatling machine guns were used for the first time in Afghanistan[191] – he occupied Kabul on 13 September, one day after Yaqub Khan's abdication (fig. 94). But Roberts had learned the lesson of 1841–42 and selected as camp a strategic location with an unobstructed field of fire. Roberts' caution had been warranted, as the siege of his camp began on 14 December 1879. At first, it appeared as though the disaster of 1841–42 would repeat itself. Roberts was not Elphinstone, however, and he prepared scrupulously for the next attack. It took place in the early morning of 23 December, and about 50,000 Afghans stormed the camp of the 6,500-strong British army. As the Afghans rushed in the dark

towards the apparently sleeping garrison, they were hit by a swarm of flares and dense artillery and gunfire. The British cavalry then demolished them even further. On 24 December, Brigadier Charles Gordon's column, which Roberts had urgently summoned by heliograph, arrived from Jagdalak, 40 km east of Kabul.[192]

In the interim, Disraeli and Lytton had taken the decision to divide Afghanistan into three kingdoms: Kabul, Kandahar (which was held by Lieutenant General Primrose) and Herat (where Yaqub Khan's brother Ayub Khan ruled). The situation became even more confused when Kaufmann sent Abdur Rahman to Kabul to enforce his demand. Abdur, however, did not trust Kaufmann in view of his 'betrayal' of Sher Ali and quickly came to an understanding with the British. On 22 July 1880, they put him on the throne as king of northern Afghanistan. Abdur was willing to leave foreign policy to the viceroy, but he also ensured that no British envoy would be stationed in Kabul, but instead an Indian Muslim representative or 'vakil'. The Lyall Agreement of July 1880 stated: 'it is plain that your Highness can have no political relations with any foreign power except with the British Government.'[193] In return, Great Britain promised to guarantee the territorial integrity of Afghanistan against a hostile third country. This meant that the Indian army could no longer counter a Russian attack on the Indus, but was forced to fight in Afghanistan.

Abdur Rahman (r. 1880–1901) proved to be a capable and energetic ruler. Moreover, 'he was neither pro-Russian nor anti-British, but pro-Afghan'.[194] Abdur Rahman also had the good fortune that on 21 April the Disraeli government had been overthrown and the Liberal Gladstone became prime minister. He replaced Lytton with Lord Ripon (1827–1909, in office 1880–84), who put an end to the 'Forward Policy' of his predecessor. But the war was not over yet: Ayub Khan began to march on Kandahar, where he crushed the army led by Brigadier George Burrows near Maiwand on 27 July. He then laid siege to Kandahar and dealt a devastating blow to Primrose, who ventured a careless attack. In this critical situation, General Roberts was accordingly asked not only to stop Ayub Khan, but also to restore British prestige in Afghanistan and northern India. He advanced in forced marches to Kandahar, where, thanks to superior tactics, he decisively defeated

Ayub Khan and victoriously ended the war. As recognition, Roberts later received the noble title 'Earl Roberts of Kandahar' and became one of the most successful and highly decorated military leaders of Britain. The Second Anglo-Afghan war was over, and Gladstone decided in November 1880 to return Kandahar to Abdur Rahman, to finally refrain from dividing Afghanistan, and to support Abdur Rahman financially.[195] After all, as Stephen Tanner explains: 'Afghanistan was too troublesome to be annexed but too dangerous to be ignored.'[196] Furthermore, as in 1842, a military victory was also achieved in 1880 through superior military leadership – but at the price of heavy losses and very modest gains. In the end, British India essentially left the administration of the Khyber Pass region and the Kurram Valley to the local Pashtun tribes. The actual benefit was the stable government of Abdur Rahman and the understanding that Britain was prepared to answer threats and provocations with war, while Russia appeared to shy away from a direct confrontation with Britain.

97. Russian forces under General Skobelev storm the Turkmen fortress Geok Tepe on 24 January 1881. Based on a painting by Russian war painter Vasily Vereshchagin (1842–1904), who accompanied Russian military campaigns in Turkestan. Vereshchagin, *Turkestan. Etyudy s natury. Études d'après nature. Studien nach der Natur.* Published *on behalf of the governor-general of Turkestan* (St Petersburg: Hofkunstbuchhandlung A. Beggrow, 1874), Part II, panel 13.

7. Abdur Rahman, the Crisis of Panjdeh and the Anglo-Russian Agreement of 1895

Although Russia had lost any influence with the accession of Abdur Rahman in Afghanistan, it continued unabated with its strategic advance along Afghanistan's western border. After General Lomakin had failed to take Geok Tepe, General Mikhail Skobelev (1843–82) launched another campaign in the following year, which he capped with the storming of the fortress of Geok Tepe on 24 January 1881. Afterwards, he seized Ashgabat without a fight.[197] Russia then imposed upon Persia the secret Russian-Persian border agreement dated 21 December 1881, which allowed Russian troops to freely advance along its attack route against the Turkmen.[198] The conquest of Geok Tepe was of high military importance for Russia, since it made possible the prolongation of the railway to Ashgabat and Sarakhs, the springboard to Herat. For this reason, the military engineer Pavel Lessar was ordered to extend the Transcaspian railway, constructed up to Kizil Arvat in 1881, to Ashgabat and to prepare a further line to Sarakhs and Herat. Second, Lessar was to explore the feasibility of a diversion of the lower Amu Darya to the dry riverbed of the Uzboy. The Russian leadership wanted to set up a waterway from the Baltic via the Volga and the Caspian Sea to Bukhara and Termez.[199] Lessar did a thorough job in 1882. He reported that while a diversion of the Amu Darya to the Uzboy was impossible, a canal might be excavated from Chardju via Merv to Ashgabat to irrigate the desert-like territory and make it fertile. Lessar outlined here the future Karakum Canal. He also found out that the railroad could easily continue from Ashgabat to Sarakhs and that there were no insurmountable geological obstacles between Sarakhs and Herat for an army, including artillery. Lessar thus opened the way for Russia to Sarakhs and Herat.[200] He 'proved that the Key of India was more within the keeping of Russia than of England, that, in a word, Herat, by his newly discovered road, was completely at the mercy of the Cossack'.[201] Colonel Holdich, member of the British Boundary Commission from 1884–86, confirmed that British journalist Charles Marvin was not exaggerating when he said: 'Lessar had already disposed of the myth of an impassable range north of Herat to some extent, but we were hardly prepared to find that it actually could be *driven* over [with artillery], without taking the preliminary trouble of making a road.'[202]

To implement Lessar's findings, it was still necessary to conquer the Turkmen oasis city of Merv, which stood halfway

between Ashgabat and Herat and between Bukhara and Herat. Merv also separated the Russian forces of Turkestan from those of Transcaspia. Coinciding with Lessar, Lieutenant Alikhanov,[203] a Muslim from Dagestan, spied on Merv and bribed influential leaders.[204] When Great Britain got bogged down in Sudan in early 1884 due to the Mahdi Uprising, Russia jumped into action: General Komarov established a strong outpost in Tejend, 120 km west of Merv, and in February Alikhanov issued Merv with an ultimatum, demanding immediate submission. After brief negotiations, Merv surrendered without a fight on 6 February 1884 and General Komarov quickly expanded the oasis into a military base.[205] Merv's annexation put the lie to the Russians' repeated insistence that they had no intention of occupying Merv (after the conquest of Khiva, the tsar personally and Russia's highest officials had made this assertion more than 30 times).[206] In light of the passivity of the Gladstone government, Charles Marvin had already warned in 1881: 'If we wait till Russia enters Merv and posts Cossacks on the Paropamisus ridge [50 km north of Herat], we shall have to accept, at the dictation of Russia, *her* delimitation of the two empires, with the dishonourable drawback of having to cede the best of India-menacing points [Herat] to her – as the power in possession.'[207] Marvin raised the stakes in February 1884: 'The annexation of Merv, being inevitably attended with the incorporation of the Sarik Turcomans, will extend Russian rule up the Murghab [River] to Panjdeh.'[208] Marvin was right. A year later, after a battle with Afghan troops, Russia captured the Panjdeh oasis about 150 km north of Herat.[209] By comparison, the nearest British base, Quetta, was 800 km away from Herat. Russia took advantage of the fact that Great Britain was preoccupied with Sudan to rapidly push onward to Herat. In May 1884, the Russians occupied the city of Sarakhs, which was halfway between Ashgabat and Herat.[210] Thanks to secure supply routes, Herat was now in reach of armies from Transcaucasia and Turkestan. Colonel MacGregor had already warned, in vain, in 1875: 'If England does not use Sarakhs for defence, Russia will use it for offence.'[211] Now, the vague description in Granville's letter of the Afghan border to the Turkmen was having dire consequences.

The offensive posture of the Russian military was all the more evident when it accelerated the construction of the railway network, which was used primarily for military purposes. It was General Skobelev who, after Lomakin's defeat at Geok Tepe, stressed the need for an immediate expansion of the Transcaspian railway for the rapid transport of troops, artillery, ammunition, and other supplies. As the explorer Henry Lansdell reported in 1893, the engineers of General Annenkov (1835–99) could lay up to 6 km

98. Mountain path on the Afghan side of the Panj River, south of the confluence of the Panj and the Vanj. Since the Anglo-Afghan Agreement of 12 November 1893, the Panj-Oxus and its feeder Pamir mark the northern border of Afghanistan from Zorkul Lake (Wood's Lake) in the east to the town of Kham-i Ali in the west. Photo: 2008.

of track per day on flat terrain.[212] The railway, which was administered by the Ministry of War, started on the eastern shore of the Caspian Sea, where the Russian navy enjoyed exclusive control. It reached Kizil Arvat in December 1881, Ashgabat in 1885, and Merv and Chardju in 1886. A wooden bridge across the Amu Darya allowed for onward travel to Bukhara and Samarkand in 1888 and to Andijan in the Fergana Valley in 1898. Another, purely military line reached the Afghan border in 1898 via Sarakhs near Kushk Post, less than 100 km from Herat. A year later, the railway led up to Tashkent and to Orenburg in 1906. The Transcaspian railway was thereby connected to the European-Russian rail network.[213] From now on, the new rail system fulfilled not only military but also economic purposes. Cotton, for instance, could be transported quickly and inexpensively for processing in the West, and the same was true for cheap industrial products going to Central Asia. In a military conflict over western Afghanistan, Russia already had a significant strategic advantage over Britain with the railway

construction to Ashgabat. As Lord Curzon put it: 'Afghanistan has long been the Achilles' heel of Great Britain in the East. Impregnable elsewhere, she has shown herself uniformly vulnerable here.'[214]

Although Britain responded to the Russian occupation of Merv and Sarakhs by completing the railway line to Quetta in 1887,[215] it was apparent that a paradigm shift had occurred with regard to strategic mobility. Previously, firearms used by infantry pushed back the mobile steppe warriors; and, soon thereafter, maritime powers, which could carry guns and troops around the globe, acquired strategic advantages over the land powers. The railway now ushered in a new era. If they had a railway network, land powers could suddenly transport soldiers and heavy weapons faster and above all in larger numbers than the sea powers. The Russian rail network or the planned German Berlin–Baghdad railway, which was to continue on to Basra on the Persian Gulf, illustrated the land powers' new logistical superiority. If a naval power

lacked an inland rail system at its ports, it was at a disadvantage against a rapidly advancing attacking land power that had such a network. General Roberts, Commander-in-Chief of British India from 1885 to 1893, insisted for this reason that roads and railways should be rapidly built up in India's western provinces: 'We must have roads, and we must have railways. [..] Nothing will tend to secure the safety of the Frontier so much as the power of rapidly concentrating troops on any threatened point... [And] there are no better civilizers than roads and railways.'[216] In order to prevent the construction of a railway controlled by Britain in southern Persia, Russia forced the shah in 1890 to renounce the construction of railways indefinitely.[217] It was solely thanks to the British-Russian rapprochement from 1906/07 that Great Britain was able to prevent a strategic cooperation between the Russian and German railway networks on the Eurasian continent. Despite its superiority in rail transport over Britain's sea transport, Russia was not in a position to use it as a trump card. It not only faced domestic political strife, but the 1904–05 war against Japan broke out at a time when the Trans-Siberian railway, which was started in 1891, only had a single track. After the defeat by Japan and the riots of 1905, Russia was severely weakened.

Russia doggedly pursued the goal of acquiring access to the high seas in the south, be it the Persian Gulf or the Indian Ocean. This goal was confirmed in a 1906 memorandum from the Russian Special Council for Persian Affairs: 'In Persia the aim had been the striving towards an outlet to the Persian Gulf, which idea had included that of building railways in the south.'[218] Another clear indication of Russia's plans to advance to the south was provided by a map produced by the War Department in 1884. It shifted the border with the Turkmen at the latitude of Sarakhs – claimed by Afghanistan in 1881 and recognised at the time by the Russian general staff – around 120 km to the south. This new border was south of the strategically important Zulfikar Pass and south of the Panjdeh oasis.[219] It reduced the distance from the border to Herat from 230 km to 110 km. This new map, which claimed Afghan territory, was based on a secret report that General Petrusevich produced in 1879. In it, he saw the future Russian border south of Panjdeh.[220] Abdur Rahman responded to the Russian provocations – the occupation of Sarakhs and aggressive border change by the War Department – by sending a small force to Panjdeh in the early summer of 1884. Komarov then advanced from Sarakhs

99. The British officer Francis Younghusband crossed the 4,805-m-high Aghil Pass in the years 1887 and 1889, both times in September.[19] The pass is located north-west of the Karakoram Pass and leads to Yarkand. Photo: September 2015.

60 km further south to Pul-i Khatun.[221] The distance between the troops of Russia and the British protectorate of Afghanistan rapidly diminished and a military clash seemed inevitable. It was after the occupation of Merv and Sarakhs that the Gladstone cabinet finally recognised the urgent need to demarcate Afghanistan's north-western frontier. Instead of determining the border together with Afghanistan, it agreed to the Russian proposal of a joint Anglo-Russian Boundary Commission. The Russian proposal soon proved to be a means to gain time. While the British commission, headed by General Sir Peter Lumsden (1829–1918) and Colonel Ridgeway (1844–1930), arrived in Sarakhs in October 1884, the Russian members did not arrive for several months.[222] Before the commission began its work, Russia wanted to at least occupy Panjdeh and probably also Herat. In the words of the British Commissioner Lieutenant Yate (1849–1940), '[the Russians] have led by the nose the Gladstonian Cabinet.'[223]

On 30 March 1885, General Komarov attacked Afghan positions near Panjdeh. Although the Afghans put up a tough resistance, 'two companies of the Afghans were killed to a man in the trenches'.[224] At the same time, the Russians occupied the Zulfikar Pass and immediately threatened Herat.[225] After the death of General Gordon in Khartoum in January 1885 had stirred up the public, the Gladstone government needed to show resolve. It put the navy on alert, and, in India, General Roberts mobilised two army corps. Two days before the fall of Panjdeh, the British government gave Russia notice: 'Any attempt on the part of Russian troops to approach Herat would be equivalent to a declaration of war and would be accepted by Her Majesty's Government.'[226] In other words, an attack on Herat would be answered with attacks on the Kronstadt fortress located off the coast of St Petersburg and on Vladivostok. As in the case with Constantinople in 1878, Curzon's statement from 1907 was once again fitting: 'Frontiers are the chief anxiety of nearly every Foreign Office. [. . .] They are the razor's edge on which hang suspended the modern issues of war or peace, of life or death to nations.'[227] As Russia was not advancing further, at least for the moment, the decision regarding war and peace now lay with Amir Abdur Rahman. He knew that under the Treaty of Gandamak, Britain was obliged to safeguard the territorial integrity of Afghanistan and thus to recapture Panjdeh. But the amir kept his cool. He did not want a Russian-British war inside Afghanistan, which would have brought a great deal of suffering and destruction to his people. It also carried the risk that his kingdom would be divided into a northern Russian half and a southern British one. He was willing to give up Panjdeh, but demanded the return of the Zulfikar Pass,[228] a guarantee of

three districts south-west of Panjdeh, and a large quantity of weapons.[229] Russia, for its part, understood that Gladstone's threat of a global war was genuine. To be sure, Russia could have overrun Afghanistan. But the British navy – with over 700 warships, many of them highly modern and armoured – was clearly superior to the Russian fleet with its 360, in some instances highly obsolete, vessels.[230] The tsar gave in. He stopped the further preparations, evacuated the Zulfikar Pass, and was able to keep Panjdeh. The British-Russian Boundary Commission then proceeded to establish the Afghan border from the pass to the Amu Darya.[231] The border demarcation, which was not ratified until the summer of 1887, was a red line which signalled to Russia that its defiance would mean a global war with Britain. However, London was not prepared to grant Abdur Rahman's reasonable desire to have the demarcation continued from the Amu Darya to the Pamirs – a circumstance that again led to grave Russian-British tensions in the early 1890s.

After Britain had put a halt to the Russian expansion in north-western Afghanistan, the field of operation of the 'Great Game' shifted eastward – first to the Pamirs, and later to Tibet and, indirectly, Manchuria. In the Pamirs, both rivals tried to position themselves in an optimal way. In the summer of 1887, British India encouraged Abdur Rahman to occupy in the Pamirs an area north of the Oxus (Panj) up to the Chinese border.[232] The Chinese border, though, was poorly defined and based solely on a trilingual stone stele from 1759. It stood near Lake Yashil Kul and marked the Chinese territorial claim up to the Alichur Pamir.[233] This course of action was not without risk for Abdur Rahman, as it recalled the former British Council's suggestion that he occupy Panjdeh. His troops were subsequently massacred by the Russians nine months later, while the British stood by ready for battle.[234] This scenario repeated itself in June 1892. The Afghan push into the Alichur Pamir presented a pawn sacrifice for Great Britain with respect to future border negotiations with Russia. Russia also moved forward, and, in 1888, Captain Grombchevsky (1855–1926) arrived with a small Cossack escort in Baltit, the capital of Hunza. With the Mir (ruler) Safdar Ali, he concluded a tentative agreement on the stationing of a Russian post in Baltit and the training of Hunza troops.[235] British India was greatly troubled by the fact that Russia was able to establish an outpost south of the Hindu Kush, as it had counted these areas as part of its own sphere of influence. The young officer Francis Younghusband (1863–1942) was dispatched to the region north of the 5,575-m-high Karakoram Pass in 1889 to learn more about the geography between Hunza and Yarkand, the gateway to Kashgaria. There, in Raskam Valley, he encountered the Russian rival Grombchevsky on 23 October.[236] The Russian carelessly showed Younghusband a map on which the Wakhan and the passes leading to Hunza were marked in red as claimed Russia territory.[237] When Grombchevsky informed Younghusband that he intended to travel further to Ladakh, the Englishman bribed the Russian's Kyrgyz guide to lead Grombchevsky into extremely difficult terrain, 'to cause extreme hardship and loss to the party'.[238] As a result of Younghusband's intrigue, Grombchevsky lost all his pack animals and equipment and barely escaped with his life.

In June 1890, Viceroy Lord Lansdowne (1845–1927, in office 1888–94) sent Younghusband to Kashgar, together with George Macartney (1867–1945) as a translator, to persuade the Chinese authorities to mark out China's territorial claims in the Pamirs as quickly as possible using soldiers, as Ney Elias had recommended

in 1885.[239] In this way, he hoped that Afghans coming from the south and the Chinese marching from the east would peacefully occupy the no-man's land before an imminent Russian advance. But this plan was naive for two reasons: first, it was doubtful whether the Afghan and Chinese soldiers, sent without a surveyor, would be able to peacefully agree upon exactly where the border should be drawn; second, Younghusband, who remained in Kashgar until the end of July 1891, was especially foolish to believe that the all-powerful General Petrovsky would not get wind of his recommendations to forestall Russia militarily. The English officer Ralph Cobbold (1869–1965), who was in Kashgar in December 1897, reported on how Petrovsky had duped Younghusband: 'He [Petrovsky] told me that all the while that

100. The Wakhan Valley in the extreme north-east of Afghanistan.

Captain Younghusband was interviewing the Taotai [District Commissioner] and urging him to dispatch troops to the Pamirs, to complete an effective occupation in anticipation of a Russian advance, the Taotai was keeping Petrovsky daily informed on the purport of Younghusband's proposals, acting on which the Russian agent took steps to render the Russian occupation effective before the Chinese troops were half-way to the Pamirs.'[240] It was through Younghusband's carelessness that the Russian side was first alerted to the fact that Afghan troops had already advanced and that Chinese troops would soon follow.

The Russian governor-general of Turkestan, Alexander Vrevsky, responded quickly. In the early summer of 1891, the Russian Colonel Mikhail Ionov was ordered to occupy six of the eleven Pamirs,[241] along with the side valleys on the northern shore of the Upper Oxus inhabited by Afghan settlers. He was further instructed to displace any Chinese and Afghan garrisons he encountered and to set up new boundary stones. At the site called Soma Tash ('written stone'), where the Chinese stele of 1759 stood, Ionov's battalion met the contingent of the Chinese commander Chang. Ionov ordered Chang to leave Soma Tash immediately and removed the stele, which eliminated China's physical proof of its claim to Alichur.[242] Ionov and his Cossacks then marched south towards the Hindu Kush. They crossed the Pamir and Wakhan rivers, the two headwaters of the Panj River, and then the three passes of Khora Bhort (4,651 m), Baroghil (3,882 m) and Darkot (4,704 m), from which Chitral could be reached, on the one hand, and Yasin and Gilgit, on the other.[243] In Gilgit, however, there was a resident British political agent who managed the district. With this march, Ionov had not only penetrated the British Indian sphere of influence, but he also revealed that there was a potential gateway here for a Russian offensive (albeit without artillery support) against British India. It appeared that the Hindu Kush was no longer an impenetrable shield that could protect India against Russia.[244] On his return to the Pamirs Ionov met Younghusband on 13 August 1891 near Bozai Gumbaz in what is now Afghanistan's Wakhan corridor, some 250 km south of the former Russian border. Younghusband had left George Macartney behind as an unofficial British representative in Kashgar. To Younghusband's astonishment, Ionov showed him a map on which the Russian border not only included the six Pamirs, but also continued further south of the Panj to the ridge of the Hindu Kush near the Khora

101. In the upper Yarkhun valley on the south side of the 3882-m-high Baroghil Pass, leading from the Wakhan River, a feeder of Panj, to Chitral and Gilgit; in the background, middle, stands the 6,872-m-high Koyo Mountain. Photo: 1999.

102. The 4,655-m-high Ak-Baital Pass in the Pamirs of East Tajikistan links Murghab with the Kara Kul Lake and further on with the Kyzyl Art Pass, which leads to Kyrgyzstan. Photo: August 2008.

Bhort Pass, from where a path led to Gilgit.[245] Ionov thereby revealed to Younghusband that he was in Russian territory and had to leave the Pamirs immediately. A short time later, Ionov arrested Younghusband's travel companion, Lieutenant Davison, near Bozai Gumbaz.[246] The apparent expulsion of two British officers from what they believed was Afghan territory, over which British India had established a protectorate since the Treaty of Gandamak of 26 May 1879, and Ionov's crossing of the Afghan passes, created quite a stir in British India and London. The commander-in-chief in India, General Roberts, responded by putting a division on combat alert.[247] British India, however, soon recognised that Bozai Gumbaz was in no-man's land, which eased tensions again.[248]

But the fact that Ionov had closed in on Chitral to within a few hours and Gilgit to within a few days demanded a British response. They had to make sure that the gateways across the Hindu Kush and down into the British sphere of influence were sealed off. Russia had indeed temporarily withdrawn its Cossacks from the Pamirs in the late autumn. However, in order to protect Gilgit, British India occupied the principalities of Hunza and Nagar in the north of present-day Pakistan in December 1891. Due to previous contacts, Hunza and Nagar reckoned with Russian military support.[249] Since Hunza considered itself a Chinese vassal, the British attack was a violation of the Chinese sphere of influence. On the other hand, Russia could have immediately claimed Hunza after seizing Kashgar, which would have thwarted British India.[250] As for Chitral, the principality was incorporated into the British Raj, when intense succession struggles broke out in 1892 after the death of the ruler Aman al-Mulk, who was well disposed to British India, and the British agent in the fortress was under siege.[251] Following Ionov's retreat, the Chinese border troops returned in February 1892. In April, a small Afghan detachment subsequently expelled the Chinese for the second time and took Soma Tash. China then declared that the area could not be defended and should be proclaimed a neutral zone.[252] Yet Ionov returned and commanded the Afghan border guards to leave their posts. Curzon offered his own account of what happened: 'the

Afghan commander, though hopelessly outnumbered, refused and a conflict ensued on June 22, 1892, in which fifteen out of the seventeen Afghans present were slain.'[253] The situation now came to a head. Abdur Rahman declared that he would not only forgo the area from the Panj to the Alichur Pamir, but almost half of the Wakhan up to the 73rd meridian east line of longitude, which would have extended the no-man's land to a length of 165 km.[254] It was foreseeable that Russia would soon rush to fill this vacuum. Meanwhile, Russia consolidated its rule over the Pamir by building the 'Pamirsky Post' fortress near today's town of Murghab in the spring of 1893.[255] Ionov then set up a military base on the Panj River near Khorog in the summer of 1894.[256] Russia had thus conquered all the Pamirs north of the Panj, except for those belonging to China (figs. 1, 88).

Because the agreement of 1872/73 was not only recognised by Russia, but was also used as an argument against Abdur Rahman's

advances into the right-bank areas of Roshan and Shugnan, it was necessary for British India to quickly resolve its grave shortcomings.[257] And this time, unlike in 1872/73, the Afghan amir was involved in the negotiations. British India's primary interest was in keeping Russia away from the Hindu Kush and to avoid leaving a no-man's land in the Pamirs. Abdur Rahman's own concern was largely consistent with this. In addition, he insisted on defensible borders and military security guarantees on the part of Britain. He was also ready to surrender poor, economically insignificant or even costly areas. The amir was aware that, unlike for Herat, the British were not willing to go to war for the right-bank areas of Roshan and Shugnan. After an antagonistic exchange of letters between Abdur Rahman and Lord Lansdowne, Sir Mortimer Durand (1850–1924), the foreign minister of British India, arrived in Kabul on 2 October 1893 to negotiate directly with the suspicious amir. Durand succeeded in convincing the amir to give

103. The Anglo-Russian Boundary Commission, which demarcated the northern boundary of the Wakhan Corridor. Front row, from left to right, Colonel Galkin (Russian General Staff), Monsieur Ponafidine (Russian Councillor of State), Major General M.G. Gerard (British Commissioner), General Povalo-Shveykovsky (Russian Governor of Ferghana and Commissioner), Colonel T.H. Holdich (chief British surveyor); back row, from left to right, Captain E.F.H McSwiney (British Intelligence Officer), Lieutenant Orakolov (Russian interpreter), Surgeon-Captain Dr. A. Alcock (Indian Medical Services), Captain Krutorozhin (commanding the escort of Orenburg Cossacks), Dr. Welman (Russian medical officer). Gerard, Holdich, Wahab and Alcock, *Report on the proceedings of the Pamir Boundary Commission 1896* (1897), p. 1.

up the right-bank areas of Roshan and Shugnan provided that Bukhara ceded Darwaz on the left bank in return. Moreover, Abdur Rahman agreed to retain a narrow strip of land in the Wakhan, which stretched from Ishkashim to the Chinese border, but still needed to be defined on-site. This so-called Wakhan Corridor was to remain demilitarised as a buffer zone to prevent a direct encounter between the troops of British India and Russia. The most momentous passage of the agreement of 12 November 1893 reads as follows: the Amir 'agrees that he will evacuate all the districts held by him to the north of this portion of the Oxus on the clear understanding that all the districts lying to the south of this portion of the Oxus, and not now in his possession, be handed over to him in exchange.'[258] Nonetheless, Abdur Rahman's far-reaching concessions on the Oxus came at a price – one that British India had to pay by making substantial compromises on the Indo-Afghan

104. Carved ancestral figures on the tombs of the Kafirs in Krakal, Bumburet Valley, Kafiristan (Nuristan), eastern Afghanistan. Photo from 1935, German Hindu Kush expedition, Arnold Scheibe estate, DHE 233. Foundation Phototheca Afghanica, Bubendorf, Switzerland.

border.[259] This southern, 2,430-km-long Durand Line forms the border between Afghanistan and Pakistan and, as it runs right through tribal areas of the Pashtuns and Baluchis, ignores ethnic considerations. This international, law-governed Durand Line was not identical with the inner administrative border. Between them, there was a 30 to 150-km-wide and more than 1,000-km-long tribal area with local, autonomous governments.[260] Those Pashtuns now living east of the line within British Indian authority resented this demarcation as a violation of their tribal independence.[261] The line is recognised by only a few of today's Afghan politicians and many of the 49 million Pashtuns have their hopes set on a united Pashtunistan. This unresolved issue is one of the main reasons for the continuing poor relations between Afghanistan and Pakistan.

Although the Russian military tried to torpedo Durand's negotiations with deliberate provocations, the tsar accepted the principles of the British proposals in December. On 11 March 1895, Great Britain and Russia agreed on the demarcation in the Pamirs, albeit without China's consent. The agreement was based on the British-Afghan Treaty of 1893, with the mutual territorial concessions established therein, and determined that the north-eastern border of the Wakhan should extend eastward, from a point just south of Lake Zorkul, along a mountain range to the Chinese border.[262] Although the parallel Sino-Russian border negotiations broke down in early 1894, Russia nevertheless pledged to keep its troops to the west of the Sarikol Pamir. Apart from small provocations – such as the stationing of Cossacks in Tashkurgan, south-east of the Sarikol Pamir, from 1901 to 1917 – Russia maintained the ceasefire.[263] China did not recognise the demarcation in Wakhan until 1963, and the border to Tajikistan until as late as 2002.[264]

The actual border demarcation was carried out by a mixed Russian-British commission, led on the Russian side by General Povalo-Shveykovsky and on the British side by Major General M.G. Gerard and Colonel T.H. Holdich[265] (fig. 103). Between 22 July and 10 September 1895, the commission defined the boundaries and set up the appropriate landmarks. The Panj and its feeder, the Pamir River, were confirmed to be the upper reaches of the Oxus up to Lake Zorkul (Wood's Lake). The border ran southward approximately 20 km from the eastern shore of the lake to the Nicholas Mountains, now called the Wakhan Mountains, and about 100 km along its eastern ridge to the Chinese border. This neutral buffer zone from Ishkashim to the Chinese border forms the 295-km-long and 15- to 65-km-wide Wakhan Corridor, which still belongs to Afghanistan today and separates Pakistan from Tajikistan. The three empires of Russia, China and Great Britain converged at the easternmost tip of the Wakhan Corridor, near the

105. The Joshi (Spring) Festival of the Kalash in Northern Pakistan. The Kalash of the Chitral region are the eastern neighbours of the former kafirs of Nuristan.

5,543-m-high peak Povalo Shveykovsky(Kokrash Kol). As Colonel Holdich described it: 'Here, amidst a solitary wilderness 20,000 feet above sea-level, absolutely inaccessible to man and within the ken of no living creature except the Pamir eagles, the three great Empires actually meet. No more fitting trijunction could possibly be found.'[266] The border agreement of 1895 supplemented that of 1885/87 and defined Afghanistan's northern border with Russia. Although Russia was able to secure large areas in the Pamirs in the agreement of 1895, British India was the real winner: the Russian advance towards the south was halted from Sarakhs in the west to the Taghdumbash Pamir in the east, and the northern side of the Hindu Kush remained demilitarised. As historian Gerry Alder aptly summarises: 'The Pamir [and Panjdeh] disagreement[s] were one of those relatively minor clashes of imperial interests in the pre-1914 years which could conceivably, if mishandled, have so involved the two Powers that honourable withdrawal would have become impossible.'[267] The border remained untouched until the Soviet invasion of December 1979.

Abdur Rahman took advantage of the calm along the external borders to consolidate his power domestically. From 1891 to 1893, he subjugated the Shiite Hazaras of central Afghanistan and settled Ghilzai Pashtuns from southern Afghanistan, who were hostile towards him, in the Hazaras' most fertile valleys. He also deported numerous Ghilzai to the northern regions inhabited by Uzbeks and Tajiks, resulting in a 'Pashtunisation' of north and central Afghanistan. At the same time, he made a significant effort to break the power of the mullahs and feudal lords and to strengthen the central government and the army. Finally, in 1895/96, after the Durand Line had established the boundary between his kingdom and British India, the amir forced the mountain people of Kafiristan (the 'land of the infidels') to embrace Islam, and now called the region Nuristan ('land of light').[268]

8. Kashgaria, Tibet, the Russo-Japanese War and the Anglo-Russian Convention of 1907

After the agreement of 1895, the British-Russian rivalry continued in Persia. It also further smouldered in Kashgaria and commenced in Tibet. For British India, Kashgaria was merely a sideshow and important solely as buffer zone to the difficult passes that led to Hunza and Kashmir. It had also served since Macartney's deployment in 1891 as a listening post for the rumours and goings-on in the Russian general government of Turkestan. For Russia, conversely, Kashgaria was a means of applying pressure against British India and a closed market for low-grade industrial products. Russia was not interested in occupying a poor Muslim country, which had to rely on financial support from the central government, but only in commercial advantages.[269] The low regard British India had for Kashgaria was also evident in Macartney's lack of official status. He was merely 'Special Assistant to the Resident in Kashmir'[270] and had no escort, while his counterpart Petrovsky

maintained a guard of about 60 to 100 Cossacks. Petrovsky, therefore, ignored Macartney, while the Chinese merely tolerated him, as 'China [in Xinjiang] knew she had nothing to fear from British power and nothing to gain from British friendship'.[271] The local Chinese authorities feared Petrovsky and his successors all the more because they pursued a policy of provocation: they initiated or fomented conflicts and then let them escalate as a pretext for deploying additional troops in Kashgar. Nevertheless, Macartney, who was appointed consul only after eighteen years, managed to obtain the release of about 200 British, Indian-born slaves. However, when the new Russian consul Sokov started to register thousands of purportedly Russian citizens from 1910, the Chinese authorities took Macartney's side. Sokov and his secretary Behrens wanted to increase Kashgaria's Russian population to spread Russia's power base. They consequently lured local Muslim merchants by offering them pecuniary and commercial advantages for adopting the Russian nationality. The Chinese governor and district officials feared the loss of substantial tax revenue because Russians were exempt from taxation in Xinjiang. Macartney wrote a critical report, the contents of which prompted Russian foreign minister Sazanov to recall Sokov and Behrens in 1913.[272]

106. Four Indian officers of the 32nd Sikh Pioneers at Khamba Dzong in October 1903. Harvey St George Hume Harvey-Kelly (1880–1946) Archive, private collection. Photo: 1904.

107. The great Kumbum Chörten in the Pelkhor Chöde Monastery of Gyantse, Tibet. During the Anglo-Tibetan War of 1903–4, Tibetans shot from the fortress (Dzong, not seen in the photo) at Younghusband's mission in Gyantse from 5 May to 26 June 1904. Archive Major MacCarthy Reagh Emmet Ray (1867–1906), private collection.

British India's relationship with Tibet – which nominally belonged to China, but where the Thirteenth Dalai Lama (1876–1933) reigned autonomously – was similar to the one with Kashgaria. Himalayan-dominated Tibet was considered a glacis of northern India, which could never fall into the hands of a hostile power such as Russia. The country was poor, the climate harsh, and trading with Sikkim very modest. In addition, both China and the mighty Tibetan clergy wanted to insulate the country from the outside and deny entry to foreigners. After British India and Beijing signed an agreement on a trading post at the border, Tibet, which had not been consulted, steadfastly refused to go along with it. When India increased the pressure on Tibet via China, Tibetan troops crossed the border with Sikkim and advanced about 20 km before they were expelled by British troops in 1888. In 1890 and 1893, India concluded two Tibet-related agreements with China, which Tibet likewise ignored.[273] This essentially banal concern became more important when Lord Curzon, who advocated a Forward Policy, was appointed viceroy in 1899. Curzon suspected that the Dalai Lama's independent posture vis-à-vis his sovereign China hinted at foreign support, namely from Russia. As neither the Tibetan government nor

the Dalai Lama responded to Curzon's two letters and rumours were circulating in Calcutta (modern Kolkata), headquarters of the British Indian government, about alleged Russian agents in Tibet (which even included the Swedish Asia explorer Sven Hedin), Curzon decided to take a more aggressive approach in early 1903.[274]

The starting point of these rumours was the fantastical-sounding plan of the Buryat Russian Bamayev to bring Mongolia and Tibet under Russian control through the construction of a railway from Irkutsk to Kyakhta and then on to Lanzhou in the Chinese Gansu province. Tsar Alexander opposed the plan, but, in November 1893, he agreed to send emissaries to Mongolia under the cover of a trading company as well as young Buryats and Kalmyks to Tibet disguised as monks. Expeditions by Russian explorers such as Tsybikov, Kozlov and Norzunov followed in the succeeding years, to explore Tibet's communication links and resources. These journeys were analogous to the so-called 'private' hunting expedition of British officers to western Tibet. After Tsar Nicholas II (1868–1918, r. 1894–1917) received the Buryat Buddhist monk Agvan Dorjiev (1854–1938), one of the masters of the Dalai Lama, three times from 1898 to 1901, the suspicion grew that he was an agent of the tsar who wanted to lead

Tibet into the Russian sphere of influence. By the same token, the Russian government harboured no serious intentions of converting Tibet into a protectorate. The geographical espionage was rather part of everyday politics. And Tsar Nicholas's involvement went back to the naive vision promoted by the Orientalist Prince Ukhtomsky that he might rise to become patron of all Buddhists.[275]

At the turn of the twentieth century, several military and economic trends emerged which forced the leading colonial power, Great Britain, to rethink and restructure its previous security policies. This, in turn, had important ramifications for Central Asia. While the short First Boer War of 1880/81 had already revealed the striking weaknesses of British troops with respect to the mobile Boers, the Second Boer War (1899–1902) turned out to be an especially costly and protracted affair. Great Britain had to mobilise a disproportionate amount of forces to grapple with the two small Boer republics – a clear sign that the empire and its military were overstretched. The foreign minister for British India, Lord Hamilton, stated soberly in November 1899: 'This war [the Second Boer War] makes self-evident that our Empire is in excess of our armaments, or even of our power to defend it in all parts of the world.'[276] The empire, which consisted of strategically and economically relevant, as well as smaller, secondary colonies, had become too large in relation to the public finances, existing armaments, and the available troops. In addition, the German Empire, whose industry and overseas trade were growing rapidly and which had begun to acquire colonies, threatened to throw the European balance of power out of kilter. In addition, in the area of logistics, the Berlin–Basra railway targeted direct access to the Persian Gulf and the oil resources there by bypassing the Suez Canal.[277] Finally, the German Empire grew inexorably into a world-class military power in the course of a general buildup, especially through the Fleet Act of June 1900, which foresaw the rapid expansion of the German navy. The use of the British navy now needed to be focused on the defence of India and the British Isles, which is why Great Britain needed an ally in the Far East.

Such an ally was found in the emerging industrial and military power Japan, which had humiliated China in the First Sino-Japanese War of 1894–95 and wrested control of Taiwan. On 30 January 1902, Great Britain ended its policy of non-alignment and signed the Anglo-Japanese alliance, which was renewed in 1905 and 1911. Although Article 1 recognised the independence of China and Korea, it also stressed the special concern of Great Britain in China and Japan's interests in China and Korea. Article 2 bound the partners to neutrality if one of the parties went to war with *another* power in connection with Article 1. Article 3 obliged the partners to provide support if a party went to war with *more than one* power.

This meant that in a war between Japan and Russia Britain would be required to stay neutral; Japan, on the other hand, knew that no third power would aid Russia for fear that it would have to conduct a war with both Japan *and* Britain. The treaty extension of August 1905 nullified Article 3 and Article 2 stated in connection with the preamble that any attack by a *single* power on an ally would prompt the immediate entry of the treaty partner into the war. In addition, the scope of the agreement was extended to British India and the sovereignty of Korea was excluded. Britain was thus to enter the war if Russia attacked Japan or its protectorates, and a signal was sent to Russia that an attack on India also meant war with Japan.[278] The change in Great Britain's security-policy strategy, which came to light in 1902 in the British-Japanese alliance, sparked further alliances, including the Anglo-French 'Entente Cordiale' of 1904 and its expansion to the Anglo-French-Russian 'Triple Entente' of 31 August 1907. The latter caused the Central Powers, the German Empire and Austria-Hungary to harbour fears of encirclement. While the Triple Entente, which was signed in St Petersburg on the same day as the Anglo-Russian Convention, undoubtedly created a strong military counterweight to the Dual Alliance between Germany and Austria; it also tied Great Britain to France, which desired a reconquest of the areas of Alsace and Lorraine lost to the German Empire in 1871, and to Russia, whose military weaknesses had been obvious since the Russo-Japanese War of 1904–05. Besides, in the German Empire, the military in the early 1910s increasingly pushed for a rapid start of the war to forestall the alleged threat of complete encirclement. All these factors contributed to the outbreak of World War I. Nevertheless, the world war was not an autonomous fait accompli and could have been avoided. This was exemplified in the winter of 1908/09, when Austria annexed Bosnia-Herzegovina and Russia threatened to intervene because of Serbia, but Britain and France informed St Petersburg that they would not assist Russia militarily, despite the Triple Entente of 1907.[279]

In Asia, the impact of the Anglo-Japanese Alliance was quickly apparent. In the summer of 1903, Curzon sent Colonel Younghusband and the Political Agent Jean-Claude White with a small escort to Khamba Dzong, which lay on the Tibetan side of the border with Sikkim, to force Lhasa to negotiate. When the Tibetans refused for four months to negotiate with the invaders on Tibetan soil, Younghusband reported to Curzon that Dorjiev had delivered an assistance agreement from the tsar to Lhasa. It laid out that Russian weapons would be brought to Lhasa and Cossacks would stay in Tibet. This 'news' had no basis whatever, but was merely, among else, the fabrication of a Scottish missionary called Annie Taylor living in Yatung (today's Yadong) who hoped that a British invasion of Tibet would facilitate her missionary work.[280] Curzon accepted the rumours uncritically, however, and he used them as a pretext to obtain permission from London to carry out a British invasion of Tibet to Gyantse with a 2,600-strong army. Curzon's action shows that so-called 'fake news' was already being exploited for political purposes more than a century ago. The army set out in December 1903 and encountered the Tibetan army at the hot springs of Chumik Shenko near Guru in southern Tibet on 31 March 1904. The Tibetans were equipped with muzzle-loaders and melee weapons while the British had mountain artillery and Maxim machine guns, with which they mowed down about 700 Tibetans within minutes.[281] When the Tibetans – who offered fierce resistance several times even though their Chinese overlords did not assist them – also refused (figs. 106–08) to negotiate in Gyantse, Younghusband marched on Lhasa, from where the Dalai Lama had fled on 30 July.[282]

In Lhasa, Younghusband imposed a severe treaty on the Tibetan regent and the Chinese amban (resident), which went far beyond his instructions from London. Younghusband's excesses concerned Articles 6 and 7, which compelled Tibet to pay reparations over 75 years and transferred southern Tibet's Chumbi Valley to Great Britain as collateral; Article 9, which made Tibet a de facto British protectorate, although it actually belonged to China; and the special agreement to station a political agent in Gyantse, who was authorised at all times to negotiate with the government in Lhasa.[283] There was great irritation in London. Younghusband had not only ignored his instructions, but the reasons for invading Tibet in the first place had vanished into thin air. In Tibet, there were neither traces of Russian weapons nor of Russian Cossacks or agents; nor was there a Russian-Tibetan Friendship Treaty. (The non-existence of Russian arms in Lhasa calls to mind the year 2003, when Iraq's Saddam Hussein allegedly held weapons of mass destruction.) Younghusband was reprimanded and the treaty unilaterally revised.[284] The subsequent British-Chinese Treaty of 1906 confirmed China's sovereignty over Tibet and paved the way for China in the winter of 1909/10 to once again force the Dalai Lama into exile, after he had returned to Lhasa.[285] The political fiasco of the invasion of Tibet was a further indication

108. The 7,206-m-high Nichi-kang-sang Mountain (Nojin Kangtsang) dominates the western climb to the 5,036-m-high Karo La pass, where the invading British Indian army defeated the Tibetans twice on 6 May and 18 July 1904. The fortifications on the west side of the Karo La blockaded the way to Lhasa.[20] Photo probably from mid-July 1904. Archive Major MacCarthy Reagh Emmet Ray (1867–1906), private collection.

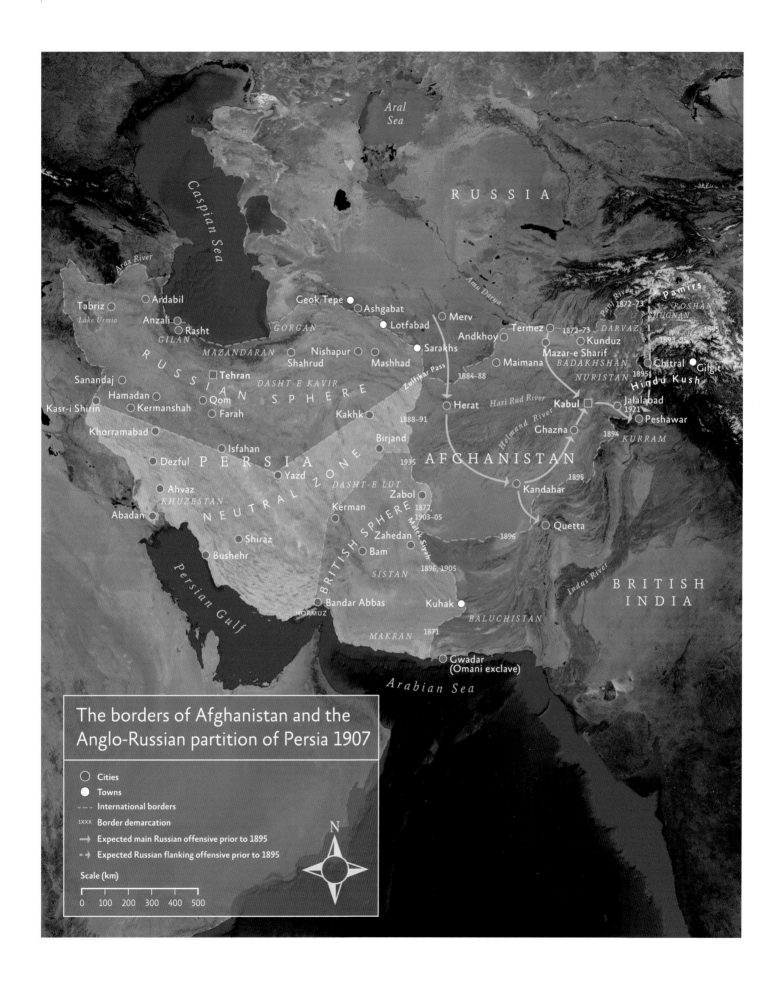

Aral
Sea

Caspian Sea

RUSSIA

Arax River

Amu Darya

Pamirs

Tabriz ○
○ Ardabil
Lake Urmia
Anzali ○
○ Rasht
GILAN
GORGAN

Geok-Tepe ●
● Ashgabat
● Lotfabad
○ Merv

Termez ○ 1872–73
ROSHAN
SHUGNAN
DARVAZ
WAKHAN 1895
1893–95

Pani River 1872–73

MAZANDARAN
○ Nishapur
Shahrud
● Sarakhs
Mashhad ○

Andkhoy ○
○ Kunduz
Mazar-e Sharif
○ Maimana

BADAKHSHAN
NURISTAN 1895
Chitral ● Gilgit
Hindu Kush

Sanandaj ○
□ Tehran
DASHT-E KAVIR

Zulfikar Pass
1884–88

Herat ○
Hari Rud River
Helmand River
Kabul □
Jalalabad
1921

Hamadan ○
Kasr-i Shirin ○
○ Kermanshah
○ Qom
○ Farah

RUSSIAN SPHERE
PERSIA

Kakhk ○
1888–91

AFGHANISTAN
Ghazna ○
1894
KURRAM
○ Peshawar

Khorramabad ○
○ Isfahan
○ Dezful
Yazd ○

Birjand ○
1935
1895

Ahvaz ○
KHUZESTAN
NEUTRAL ZONE

DASHT-E LUT
Zabol ○
1872, 1903–05

Kandahar ○

Abadan ○
Kerman ○
Zahedan ○
Malek Siyah ○

BRITISH SPHERE
Quetta ○
1896

Shiraz ○
Bushehr ○
● Bam

SISTAN
1896, 1905

Indus River
BRITISH INDIA

Persian Gulf

Bandar Abbas ○
HORMUZ

Kuhak ●

BALUCHISTAN

MAKRAN 1871

Gwadar ○
(Omani exclave)

Arabian Sea

The borders of Afghanistan and the Anglo-Russian partition of Persia 1907

○ Cities
● Towns
--- International borders
1xxx Border demarcation
→ Expected main Russian offensive prior to 1895
-▶ Expected Russian flanking offensive prior to 1895

Scale (km)

0 100 200 300 400 500

N

that the era of expansive British imperialism was over and that future efforts would be limited to defending the status quo.

For Russia, on the other hand, the Anglo-Japanese Alliance had drastic consequences. Japan was deeply distressed by the expansion of the Trans-Siberian Railway, which was completed with the Manchurian line and extended over Chinese territory to Vladivostok; by the stationing of 170,000 Russian soldiers in Manchuria; and by Russia's regional penetration. Time was not on Japan's side, as the completion of the Trans-Siberian Railway permitted Russia to mobilise troops on a large scale. Unlike Britain, which issued ultimatums in conflicts and preferred diplomatic solutions, Japan elected to go with the element of surprise. In a similar way as with Pearl Harbor in World War II, Japan suddenly attacked the Russian naval base of Port Arthur (today's Lüshunkou) on 8 February 1904, without making a declaration of war. The Japanese generals were clearly superior to their Russian counterparts and won numerous victories. The conquest of Port Arthur and the land battle near Mukden (Shenyang) were among the most spectacular. The Japanese attack would probably have not taken place without Great Britain's backing in 1902. Russia's involvement in Manchuria and Korea was welcomed by the British prime minister Lord Balfour (1849–1930, in office 1902–5): 'Nothing [could] be better for us than that Russia should involve herself in the expense and trouble of Korean adventure, ... which would be a perpetual guarantee that whenever Russia went to war with another power, no matter where or about what, Japan would be upon her back.'[286] Great Britain remained neutral during the war, though it supported Japan indirectly: invoking the peace treaties of Paris (1856) and Berlin (1878), Great Britain refused to allow the departure of Russia's Black Sea Fleet. For London, it would have represented a *casus belli*. And when Russia decided to send the Baltic Fleet to the Far East, London denied it the opportunity to obtain coal in any British port. Besides this, a serious incident took place on the night of 22/23 October 1904, when nervous units of the Baltic Fleet mistook British trawlers for Japanese torpedo boats on the Dogger Bank, a large shoal in the North Sea. In a state of panic, they opened fire on the harmless fishermen, killing several of them. In the fog, the Russian ships even fired on each other. The British 'Home Fleet' prepared for combat, but war was ultimately avoided when the tsar apologised.

The heterogeneous Russian fleet sailed onward and, on 26 May 1905, suffered one of the most devastating defeats in modern naval history. It occurred in the Strait of Tsushima, which lies between Korea and Japan, against a Japanese fleet superbly led by Admiral Togo. Since a general strike had broken out in Russia shortly before this and hundreds of unarmed demonstrators were shot on 'Bloody Sunday', 22 January 1905,[287] raising fears of a revolution, Russia agreed to a truce. In the Treaty of Portsmouth of 5 September, the enemies agreed to evacuate Manchuria and return it to China. Russia had to pay a high indemnity, recognise the Japanese protectorate over Korea, and cede to Japan the southern half of Sakhalin Island and Port Arthur, including its hinterland (the Liaodong Peninsula). Japan got control over the Russian-built Manchurian railway to Vladivostok and a bridgehead on the Asian continent.[288] The defeat by Japan and the dangers of revolution as well as mutinies in the army brought the expansion of the Russian Empire in Asia to an end. Like Great Britain, Russia sought ways to protect the status quo and to avoid conflicts with its main opponents. With the victory of an Asian power over a European country, the prestige of the 'white man' suffered irreparable damage in Asia, leading to the emergence of nationalist movements in China and India.

The Anglo-Russian rapprochement talks – which started in 1903/04,[289] were then interrupted, and resumed in 1906 – culminated in the Anglo-Russian Convention of 31 August 1907.[290] For the British government, one of the motivations to find a general settlement with Russia concerning Asia was the aborted secret military Treaty of Björkö signed on 24 July 1905 between Wilhelm II of Germany and Tsar Nicholas II of Russia. This defence treaty was directed against Great Britain and Japan. However, it was never ratified by the Russian or German government.[291] The Anglo-Russian Convention defined the respective spheres of influence in Persia, Afghanistan and Tibet, while leaving aside the Bosphorus and the Dardanelles. The three main goals were to avoid accidental conflicts in Asia, to preserve the status quo, and, above all, to reinforce the forces in Europe in the face of the German Empire's threatening military buildup by reducing the forces committed in Asia. It was the growing strength of the Germans which brought the two arch-enemies, Russia and Great Britain, closer together. As for Tibet, both parties recognised the full sovereignty of China and pledged to not exert influence there in any way. 'The Governments of Great Britain and Russia recognize the suzerain rights of China in Thibet. [...] The two High Contracting Parties engage to respect the territorial integrity of Thibet and to abstain from all interference in the internal administration.'[292] Regarding Afghanistan, Russia confirmed that the country was outside its zone of influence and renounced diplomatic contacts with the country. Great Britain committed itself to maintaining the political status quo in Afghanistan and to not occupy or annex any Afghan territory *provided* that the amir met his obligations. For Great Britain, this left open the possibility of military intervention. In addition, Great Britain agreed to refrain from either threatening

Russian possessions in Central Asia or from encouraging the amir to do so himself.[293]

By far the most important part of the agreement concerned Persia. This is because the country was not only significant with regard to the defence of India, but also economically. In 1901, the Englishman William Knox D'Arcy had acquired a 60-year concession for the promotion, sale, and export of petroleum for all of Persia, except the five northern provinces. Four years later, the British Burmah Oil Company took over D'Arcy's financially troubled company to ensure that it did not fall into Russian hands. Although no commercially viable oil deposits had been found yet in Persia, and the navy still used coal, the admiralty had a strategic interest in oil.[294] The convention of 1907 divided Persia into three zones: the northern provinces were assigned to the Russian zone, the southeastern provinces to the British zone, and the central/south-western provinces to the neutral zone administered by the Persian government. The Russian zone ran along 'a line starting from Kasr-i Shirin [on the Baghdad–Kermanshah road], passing through Isfahan, Yazd, Kakhk, and ending at a point on the Persian frontier at the intersection of the Russian and Afghan frontiers'. The smaller British zone traced a line 'going from the Afghan frontier by way of Gažík, Birjand, Kerman and ending at Bandar Abbas'.[295] British interests were safeguarded to the extent that the mostly desert British zone shielded Afghanistan, Sistan and Baluchistan from Russia, while the neutral zone allocated to Persia prevented a Russian advance to the Persian Gulf. Nonetheless, the British consul in Mashhad, Sir Percy Sykes (1867–1945, in office in Mashhad 1905–13) – to whom the convention had been submitted for consideration before its signing – warned that the German Empire could rapidly infiltrate the neutral zone. This, in fact, occurred in 1915.[296]

109. A pair of bullocks help to bring a motor-car offered by the British Indian government to Amir Habibullah through the mountain passes to Kabul. *The Illustrated London News*, 13 May 1905.

Russia, in turn, fortified its protectorate over the northern zone, which also included the capital Tehran, by permanently stationing 12,000–15,000 soldiers there. In addition, Russia exerted considerable influence on the neutral zone by allowing the shah to avail himself of a special Cossack brigade. At the same time, Russia promoted the settlement of Russian citizens in the northern zone, where they enjoyed extraterritorial rights. Since the Russian settlers acquired land on a large scale, this immigration entailed a colonisation of northern Persia.[297] Persia, which was within reach of the Russian army in the north and the British navy in the south, was not consulted. With the signing of the two agreements on 31 August 1907, the 'Great Game' between Russia and Great Britain cooled noticeably, only to then blaze up again after 1917.

Soon after signing the agreement, Persia's importance for Britain increased enormously. In the neutral zone, a large oil field was discovered near Masjed Suleyman, after which the concessionaires founded the Anglo-Persian Oil Company (APOC) in 1909. In the same year, the navy began to fuel new destroyers and submarines with petroleum instead of coal. Petroleum was much more efficient. Ships could now travel twice as fast, required a smaller crew and could be refuelled much faster – even on the high seas. On the other hand, Great Britain had large coal repositories, but no petroleum, and was therefore dependent on the American Standard Oil and Royal Dutch Shell. The First Lord of the Admiralty, Winston Churchill (1874–1965, first time in this office 1911–15) ordered the general conversion of the fleet to oil combustion in the beginning of 1912. Two years later, he acquired a government majority stake in APOC, the future British Petroleum (BP), which enabled him to secure the necessary fuel for the navy. That same year, APOC acquired 50 per cent of the Turkish Petroleum Company, in whose concession area the giant oil field of Kirkuk was later discovered in northern Iraq.[298] The conversion of the navy to petroleum marked the beginning of the strategic orientation of Western industrial powers towards the oil-producing regions of Iran, the Middle East and the Arabian Peninsula, which was extended to Central Asia from 1991. As it turned out, however, the neutral zone continued to represent a bone of contention between Britain and Russia. Russia and Britain agreed, in series of secret assurances from March to April 1915, that after a victorious war Constantinople and the Dardanelles would go to Russia and the neutral zone of Persia with its oil fields would fall to Great Britain.[299] Russia had never been so close to achieving its main strategic objective. But the failed attack on the Gallipoli peninsula in the Dardanelles (25 April 1915 to 9 January 1916) and the October Revolution prevented it once again from becoming reality.

VI

The Drive for Sovereignty – Central Asia between the World Wars

'*We will never allow you to dictate how to run our country and whom to employ in Afghanistan.*'

THE PRESIDENT OF AFGHANISTAN DAOUD rebukes Leonid Brezhnev in the Kremlin in April 1977.[1]

The subjugated states and peoples of Central Asia exploited the geopolitical shocks of World War I to regain their independence. While Afghanistan regained full sovereignty from the British Empire in 1919 and Xinjiang broke away from China with Soviet help, all such efforts within the decaying tsarist empire failed. The Soviet Union captured the regions back militarily that had seceded from Moscow and further extended their empire to Outer Mongolia.

1. Bukhara's and Khiva's Short-lived Independence

In Bukhara, Amir Muzaffar al-Din (r. 1860–85), who had to recognise Russian supremacy, was succeeded by his fifth son **Abd al-Ahad** (r. 1885–1911). Like his father, he ruled domestically independently of Russia. He ruled as an autocratic potentate and viewed the state treasury as his own personal wealth. Government revenue was used to finance the army, the administration and the court. Abd al-Ahad invested only a bare minimum in public infrastructure such as roads and irrigation systems, refusing to spend money on education and health care. Literacy was only at two per cent.[2] At the beginning of the twentieth century, however, new movements emerged that put into question the existing power structures. The Russian defeats by Japan and the unrest in early 1905 gave a big boost to the Muslim nationalists in Russia (who in places paid homage to pan-Turkism), and also in Bukhara. The Persian Constitutional Revolution of 1905–06 and the Young Turk Revolution of 1908 had a similar effect. The guiding force among the nationalists were followers of Jadidism, an Islamic revival movement which arose in Kazan.[3] The Jadids wanted to curb the influence of the oppressive traditionalists and mullahs and restrict Islam to the cultural sphere. They stressed an alternative worldview guided by rational principles of judgement. In short: they sought to align themselves with modernity, while preserving the Muslim cultural heritage.[4] The Bukharian amir initially sympathised with the Jadids. Nonetheless, when he realised that they rejected hereditary dynasties, he took the side of the mullahs in 1909, ordering the reformist school of the local Jadids, established in Bukhara in 1908, to shut its doors.[5] Soon thereafter, the Jadids formed the politically active group of the 'Young Bukharists'.

In January 1910, a conflict that had been smouldering for years between Uzbek Sunnis and Shiite Persians suddenly flared up. As a counterweight to the Uzbek tribal leaders, Abd al-Ahad gave preference to former Persian slaves in his administration. The outrage of the Uzbek majority population over Abd al-Ahad's actions spread throughout the emirate, where massacres erupted among the Shiites which had to be quelled by Russian troops. Russia's engagement in international issues was the only factor that prevented the khanate from being annexed.[6] On the other hand, the standing of Abd al-Ahad's son and successor **Mohammed Alim Khan** (r. 1911–20, d. 1944) was greatly weakened at the time of his accession, which is why he sought the support of the anti-reform clergy (fig. 110). When the Ottoman sultan and caliph Mehmed V (r. 1909–18) declared a jihad against the Allies, including against Russia, on 14 November 1914, Alim Khan took the side of the tsar in demonstrative fashion and donated a large sum to Russia's war chest.[7]

Unlike Bukhara, everyday life in Chorasmia was less affected by the Russian conquest of 1873. Khiva had neither a railway

110. Amir Mohammed Alim Khan of Bukhara (r. 1911–20). Photo: 1911.

connection nor a Russian garrison nor border guards. Moreover, **Sayyid Muhammad Rahim** (r. 1865–1910) and his successor **Isfandiyar** (r. 1910–18) were less greedy than the Bukharian amir. They invested in infrastructure and maintained taxes at a relatively moderate level until 1912. There were also hardly any conflicts with the mullahs, who were less powerful than in Bukhara. Tensions arose instead with the Turkmen Yomut, who revolted as a result of tax reform in the years 1912–13 and 1915.[8]

The impact of World War I on Central Asia was at first apparent in the deterioration of the economic situation. The tsars had imposed a cotton monoculture on the khanates, forcing them to rely on food imports from Russia. The war then caused the demand for cotton – which was needed for the production of ammunition – to skyrocket. At the same time, Russia, which had to feed its large armies, found it increasingly difficult to send foodstuffs to Central Asia. This resulted in a severe undersupply of food. The shipment of tens of thousands of Austrian, Hungarian and German prisoners of war to Central Asia only intensified the problem. In the summer of 1916, the tensions led to a large-scale uprising of the Uzbeks, Turkmen, Kazakhs and Kyrgyz. The tipping point was the decree of 25 June, according to which all able-bodied men of Central Asia, including those of the previously war-liberated peoples, were mobilised and had to serve in work brigades on the frontlines. On 21 July, the Russian governor-general declared martial law, and the uprising was bloodily suppressed by October.[9] But when the February Revolution broke out in Russia on 8 March 1917 (as per the Gregorian calendar),[10] the nationality question emerged once again for Muslims. The new 'Provisional Government' in St Petersburg replaced governor-general Kuropatkin in April with a **'Provisional Executive Committee'**. Simultaneously, workers' and soldiers' councils called 'soviets' were established (as in Western Russia), and, in Central Asia, Muslim groups also formed because Muslims were not represented in the committees and soviets.[11] After the October Revolution, when commanders who were loyal to the old regime began to fight the Moscow Bolsheviks from their own power bases, further anti-Bolshevik territorial dominions developed. In 1918/19, up to ten existed simultaneously east of the Volga.[12]

A severe famine broke out in the emirate of Bukhara in the beginning of 1917, as Russia neither provided food nor paid for the procured cotton. As a consequence, the peasants were unable to buy more seed. Given the glaring weakness of the Provisional Central Government, Mohammed Alim Khan decided it was an opportune time to leave Russia and to restore Bukhara's independence. His renewed freedom to act appears to have prompted him

111. The Sitorai Mokhi Khosa Palace – the 'Palace of Moon-like Stars' – was completed by the Russians in 1911 and known as the summer palace of the khans of Bukhara. Bukhara, Uzbekistan. Photo: 2004.

in April to get rid of the Jadids and Young Bukharists, to seek the support of the clergy and, in the summer, to announce that taxes would be cut in half. Immediately, he gained the broad support of the population. By contrast, in Khiva, the decades-old conflict between sedentary Uzbeks and semi-nomadic Turkmen came to a head again, when the Uzbek Jadids took power and proved unable to stop the plundering raids by Turkmen tribal horsemen. In June, Isfandiyar regained power in a coup, but he and the Cossacks also failed to restore order in the khanate, not least because the soldiers, organised in a soviet, threatened to mutiny.[13] In Tashkent, a power struggle manifested between three groups in 1917: the pro-government Executive Committee was opposed by the Workers' and Soldiers' Soviet (among whose 263 delegates only five were Muslim) and the First Pan-Turkestan Congress of Muslims. The Council of Muslim Scholars, which strove for an Islamised state, soon emerged from the latter. Lastly, the All-Kazakh Congress came into existence in Orenburg.[14]

In Tashkent, the Bolshevik Revolution began earlier, in September 1917, when the soviet made up of Mensheviks[15] and Bolsheviks ousted the Executive Committee. After the violent Bolshevik assumption of power in Petrograd (St Petersburg) on 7 November in the so-called October Revolution, soldiers stationed in Tashkent mutinied. On 14 November, the **Tashkent Soviet of Workers' and Soldiers' Deputies** took power by military coup. This Bolshevik Revolution was a purely Russian affair, from which the local Muslims were excluded. The soviet, in fact, consisted of four Russians, four Jews, a German, a Pole and a Moldavian. When a Muslim group offered government participation to the soviet, it was rebuffed: 'Entry of the Muslims into the supreme territorial organ of revolutionary power is impossible.'[16] In the following months, two developments came to the fore that were diametrically opposed to the aspirations of the Muslims of Central Asia for self-determination. First, in the decision-making bodies of the soviets there was no place for Muslims, or at most they were figureheads. Second, the right of all peoples to self-determination that Lenin and Stalin proclaimed in April 1917, which included secession from Russia, turned out to be pure propaganda.[17] It was clear as early as March 1918 that the proclamations of independence by non-Russian peoples and political entities within the former Russian Empire, such as Bukhara, would be responded to with armed force. The self-determination of colonised peoples proclaimed by Lenin and Stalin only applied outside of the former Russian Empire, primarily to the peoples of the British Empire. The only differences between the imperial colonial policy of the tsars and the policy of the Bolsheviks lay in the greater ruthlessness of the new rulers and in the enforcement of cultural conformity by means of the soviets.

The Muslim and nationalist groups responded quickly to the Tashkent soviet's claim of omnipotence. On 10 December 1917, the Fourth Extraordinary Regional Muslim Congress in Kokand proclaimed the **Autonomy of Turkestan**. Moreover, in Orenburg, the Second All-Kazakh Congress in December 1917 pronounced the autonomous **Alash-Orda** government that was backed by the 'White'[18] Cossack ataman Alexander Dutov (1879–1921). Dutov had occupied Orenburg on 13 November and disrupted the railway line from Moscow to Tashkent. Mohammed Alim Khan of Bukhara, finally, also tried to win international recognition. But when the Bolsheviks succeeded in regaining Orenburg on 31 January 1918, military supplies began to reach Tashkent once again.[19] The Bolsheviks sent units of Red Guards and Armenian Dashnaks[20] to

Kokand, who smashed the Islamic Kokand's autonomy in February/March, sacked the city, and carried out a massacre. Numerous peasants were also shot in Fergana on suspicion of hoarding cotton and foodstuffs – an event that laid the foundation for the later Basmachi Revolt.[21] The massacre of around 14,000 civilians then gave way to a major famine.[22]

The chairman of the Bolshevik **Council of People's Commissars (Sovnarkom)**, a man named Kolesov, then took control of the 600-strong Russian garrison of New Bukhara. On 14 March 1918, he issued Amir Alim Khan with a 24-hour ultimatum. To preempt the arrival of Russian reinforcements for Kolesov, the amir disrupted the railways and telegraph lines to Samarkand and Chardju and expelled the intruders to Samarkand. After this humiliating defeat, the Sovnarkom of Tashkent-Turkestan recognised the independence of Bukhara and made peace on 25 March. This victory over a Bolshevik army represented a major success for the amir, gaining him two years of sovereignty. He proclaimed the independence of Bukhara on 25 June.[23] In Khiva, by contrast, the Uzbek-Turkmen conflict in 1918 led to the murder of Khan Isfandiyar at the hands of Djunaid Khan, the Turkmen leader. Djunaid Khan proceeded to put the brother of the murdered man, **Sayyid Abdallah** (r. 1918–20, d. 1920s), on the throne as a puppet khan.[24] Moscow responded to Kolesov's debacle with a reorganisation of the Tashkent Sovnarkom, whose 26 members now included ten Muslims. On 30 April 1918, Turkestan was declared the **Autonomous Soviet Socialist Republic of Turkestan (ASSRT)**.[25] Shortly thereafter, the revolt of the Czechoslovak Legion suspended[26] the rail connections between Moscow and Tashkent once again and, in mid-July, an anti-Bolshevik government[27] took power in Transcaspia.[28] A White Army then quickly occupied parts of Semirechie. Now, the Soviet Republic of Turkestan was threatened on four sides: from ataman Dutov's Cossacks who had recaptured Orenburg on 3 July,[29] from Semirechie, the Basmachis in Fergana, and Transcaspia. The situation became even more menacing for the Bolsheviks in Turkestan in the summer of 1918, when British, Japanese, French and American troops landed in Vladivostok. Here, the Western Allies pursued the unrealistic plan, in conjunction with the Czechoslovak Legion, of traversing Russia and attacking the German Empire from the east. Japan, however, sought a permanent annexation of East Siberia.[30] Furthermore, the Turkestan economy was facing collapse and, as Colonel Bailey observed in October 1918, 'the [government's] chief source of income was the [banknote] printing press'.[31] In the spring of 1919, the tide turned in favour of the Tashkent Bolsheviks. In late April, the Red Army began to expel the White troops of the monarchist Alexander Kolchak (1874–1920)

112. The madrasah, constructed in 1871, is named after its builder Sayyid Muhammad Rahim Khan II (r. 1865–1910), Khiva, Uzbekistan. Photo: 2004.

from the Volga to Irkutsk. That same month, the British withdrew from Transcaspia, which cleared the way for the Bolsheviks to reclaim Turkmenistan. At the same time, the Red Army pushed forward into Kazakhstan and, by the spring of 1920, eliminated both the Alash Orda government and the White Russians of Semirechie. The foundation of the **Kazakh Autonomous Soviet Socialist Republic (KASSR)** then followed in December.[32]

Despite his victory in March 1918, Alim Khan of Bukhara was in a difficult position. His army was quite large, but poorly trained, and its weapons were obsolete. When the Czechoslovak Legion and Admiral Kolchak cut off the connections to Moscow in the summer of 1918 and the Provisional Trans-Caspian Government emerged, the isolated Tashkent Bolsheviks found it difficult fighting the rebellious Transcaspians. They could only reach the southern front via the railway to Chardju, which went through Bukharian territory. An interruption of the line would have stabilised Transcaspia, which was backed militarily by Great Britain,[33] and put Tashkent even more on the defensive. The amir

not only asked the British for weapons and instructors, but also tried to win them as allies against Tashkent. In December 1918, an envoy of the amir met with General Malleson (1866–1946) in Merv. However, since the world war was already over by this point, and the withdrawal of British troops imminent, the general advised caution against Tashkent.[34] The amir received a transport of 100 camels with arms and ammunition, but no instructors.[35]

The end of the world war and the British withdrawal sealed the fate of Ashgabat, Khiva and Bukhara. First of all, in July 1919, Transcaspia was joined with the **ASSR Turkestan**. Then, the soviets captured Khiva on 1 February 1920 and replaced the khanate in late April with the **Soviet Chorasmia People's Soviet Republic**. The deposed Khan Sayyid Abdallah died in the 1920s in Moscow. Following the British refusal, Alim Khan had contacted the Afghan King Amanullah in July 1919. He opened an Afghan embassy in Bukhara in January 1920 and thus recognised the emirate as a sovereign state. Although Alim sent a delegation to Moscow in June to assure the leading soviets that his intentions were peaceful, General

113. The western city walls of Khiva with the Ata Darwase Gate, Uzbekistan. Photo: 2004.

Mikhail Frunze (1885–1925) attacked Bukhara from three sides at the end of August. Frunze bombed the capital, which suffered major damage, and occupied it on 2 September 1920.[36] The emirate was abolished, and the **Soviet People's Republic of Bukhara** was then founded with the Jadid Faizullah Khojaev (1896–1938) as chairman. The situation of the population deteriorated rapidly in the impoverished city since the stationed Soviet troops demanded free room and board. The new government expropriated private landowners, nationalised undeveloped land and irrigation systems, and promised to provide the poor peasants with land and resources. Alim Khan, however, had already fled into the emirate's mountainous eastern region on 31 August to organise the resistance.[37]

Alim Khan joined the Basmachis' decentralised popular resistance movement, which developed in early 1918 in response to the Soviet massacre in Kokand and Fergana. In May 1920, it founded the **Turkestan Turkic Independent Islamic Republic**, which lasted until the end of 1922.[38] When the Red Army occupied Dushanbe and East Bukharian Faizobod in February 1921, Alim Khan fled

to Kabul. He nonetheless continued to support the resistance movement. In mid-November, the former Turkish minister of war Enver Pasha (1881–1922), who had had a falling out with Mustafa Kemal Atatürk, joined the Basmachi. He was an ardent supporter of pan-Turkism and dreamed of establishing a large Turkish state that would stretch from Constantinople all the way to Kazan, Kazakhstan and Kashgar. After some minor successes, he assumed command. However, his vanity got the best of him – he called himself 'Amir of Turkestan' and 'commander in chief of all Islamic armies, son of the caliph and representative of the Prophet' – which alienated him from some commanders and especially from Alim Khan, who refused to give him any support. After a defeat near Baysun north of Termez and a failed attack on Faizullah Khojaev, he was killed on 4 August 1922 in a skirmish near Baljuan southeast of Dushanbe. By the end of the autumn, the rebellion no longer represented a serious threat for the Soviets. The Basmachi movement enjoyed little support among the Western powers, who were suspicious of their pan-Islamism. The collapse of the movement was also accelerated thanks to the New Economic Policy (NEP) begun by Lenin in 1921, which included a temporary liberalisation of the economy. The economic recovery and amnesty offers to Basmachi fighters effectively pulled the rug out from under the movement.[39]

The ASSR Turkestan had hardly asserted itself when Stalin began to purge the local communist parties and organs of Muslim nationalists. The Muslims were denounced as pan-Islamic and pan-Turkic representatives of a bourgeois nationalism, which pursued national interests instead of devoting itself to class struggle. In Bukhara, for example, 15,000 of the 16,000 party members were excluded, whereupon former officials of the emirate, landowners, wholesalers and clerics all had their political rights revoked.[40] In a further step to destroy the traditional identity-structures and pan-Islamic or pan-Turkic ideas, Stalin decided to dissolve the two republics of Chorasmia and Bukhara as well as the Turkestan ASSR and to create new political entities. The governing criterion for drawing the new internal boundaries was Lenin's definition of a nation as a stable, historically developed community that is characterised by four commonalities: a common language, a contiguous territory, a common economic system, and a common culture.[41] There were three main categories of political entities:

1. The Soviet Socialist Republic SSR of the Soviet Union USSR.
2. The Autonomous Soviet Socialist Republic ASSR within a Union Republic.
3. The Autonomous Soviet Socialist Oblast ASSO within a Union Republic.

In 1924, the following two nation-states and four autonomous entities were established:[42]

1. The **Uzbek SSR,** initially with Samarkand as its capital. The capital was moved to Tashkent in 1930. It included Samarkand, Fergana, central Bukhara and a part of Chorasmia. It lost the Tajik ASSR in 1929 plus the territory of Khujand and obtained the Karakalpak ASSR in 1936.
2. The **Turkmen SSR** with Ashgabat as capital. It included the Turkmen Oblast and western Bukhara.
3. The Kirgiz, as of 1925 **Kazakh ASSR,** within the Russian

114. The wooden Russian Orthodox Ascension Cathedral, constructed at the beginning of the twentieth century in Almaty, Kazakhstan. Photo: 2008.

Federation RSFSR, and with Kyzyl Orda as capital; in 1929 the capital was moved to Alma-ata (Almaty). The ASSR was elevated to a Union Republic SSR in 1936. It replaced the previous republic founded in 1920 and contained the Kazakh Steppes. It lost the Orenburg district in 1925 to the RSFSR and the Karakalpak ASSO in 1930 to the jurisdiction of the RSFSR.

4. The Kara-Kyrgyz, as of 1926 **Kyrgyz ASSR** within the Russian Federation RSFSR with Pishpek (Frunze, Bishkek) as capital. The Kyrgyz ASSR was elevated to a Union Republic SSR in 1936. It included part of the districts of Semirechie, Syr Darya and Fergana.

5. The **Tajik ASSO**, as of October 1924 ASSR within the Uzbek SSR with Dushanbe as capital. It became a Union Republic SSR in 1929. It included the mountainous eastern and south-eastern parts of the former Bukhara People's Republic; in 1929, it obtained the region of Khujand. It included the **Gorno Badakhshan ASSO**. Most Tajik people are Iranophone, yet about 90 per cent are Sunni.

6. The **Karakalpak ASSO** in 1925 within the Kazakh ASSR, as of 1930 within the RSFSR. In 1932 it became an ASSR and was attached in 1936 to the Uzbek SSR with Nukuz as capital. The Karakalpaks live along the Lower Amu Darya.

These internal boundaries, which were finally defined in 1936, became international borders after the collapse of the Soviet Union in 1991. But the demarcation did not run strictly according to ethno-linguistic boundaries, because Moscow wanted to avoid religious or linguistic population centres. This limitation mainly affected the large Iranophone group which was deliberately divided into two parts: the East Bukharians, who were assigned to the mountainous area of Tajikistan, and the urban Iranophones of Samarkand and Bukhara, who constituted the majority of the latter, but were associated with Uzbekistan.[43] The Uzbeks were also torn apart, because the Uzbek majority in the region of Khujand (formerly Leninabad) was assigned to Tajikistan and the strong Uzbek minority of Osh to Kyrgyzstan.[44] In addition, the Uzbek-Tajik, the Uzbek-Kyrgyz, and the Tajik-Kyrgyz borders contained multiple exclaves and, indeed, enclaves that remain a source of tension to this day.

British Troops in East Persia, the Caucasus and Transcaspia, and a German Expedition to Afghanistan – a Revival of the Great Game

The two Russian revolutions of 1917 had a dramatic impact on all the warring parties. The Russian army collapsed[45] and dispersed due to desertions, forcing Lenin to sign the Treaty of Brest-Litovsk with the Central Powers on 3 March 1918, and to revoke the Anglo-Russian Convention of 1907 concerning Afghanistan and Persia. The Soviet withdrawal from the war offered substantial relief to the German Empire on its eastern front and Turkey on its northern front and thus new strategic opportunities in relation to the Allies, especially Great Britain. This was because Russia's absence eliminated three strongholds: in the Caucasus as well as in north-western and north-eastern Persia. As a result, the German Empire and Turkey had a chance to advance to the oil fields of both Khuzestan in south-western Persia and those in Baku, and from there to obtain Caspian cotton. In addition, the Russian withdrawal from Persia gave rise to the possibility of a German-Turkish advance to Afghanistan, which would force Britain to move troops from the Western Front to India.[46] Finally, the attitude of the Turkestan-Bolsheviks vis-à-vis the Central Powers was unclear, specifically as to whether they would remain neutral or sell cotton to the Germans, or even welcome a German-Turkish foray into India. It was equally uncertain how the 40,000 Austrian and German prisoners of war living in Turkestan would behave.[47] Therefore, four small operational teams were commissioned to avert these dangers. They were led by Brigadier General Sir Percy Sykes in southern Persia, Colonel Frederick M.

Bailey in Tashkent, Major General Lionel Dunsterville in Baku and Major General Malleson and Captain Reginald Teague-Jones in Mashhad and Ashgabat.[48]

Brigadier General **Sir Percy Molesworth Sykes** (1867–1945), who had served as consul in eastern Persia since 1894, faced a particularly difficult task. Although Persia had declared itself neutral, four powers conducted war on its territory: the German Empire, Turkey, Russia and Great Britain. When the war began, Russia controlled the northern zone, Great Britain the south-eastern zone plus Ahvaz and Abadan in the south-west, and Persia the south-western and middle or so-called Neutral Zone. To uphold its own security, the Persian government had at its disposal a 10,000-strong 'gendarmerie', headed by Swedish officers, which had been formed as a counterweight to the Russian Cossack brigade. Since the Swedish officers had a pro-German attitude, it was easy for the German consuls and officers to take control of most of the cities in the Neutral Zone and the neighbouring districts and to expel the Allied consuls over the course of 1915. Isfahan was the centre of German power in Persia; other important locations were Kermanshah in the west, Shiraz in the south, and Kerman in the south-east. The British zone of influence was reduced to the oil-rich areas of Ahvaz and Abadan as well as the ports of Bushehr (Bushire) and Bandar Abbas.[49] The situation was also complex because the Allies pursued different objectives: Germany's main enemies were

115. Brigadier-General Sir Percy Sykes (in white uniform) and Commandant Bielomestonov (wearing Cossacks' uniform) with British Indian and Russian officers in Isfahan, September 1916. Sir Percy Sykes, *A History of Persia* (London: Macmillan, 1930), vol. II, photo facing p. 462.

France and Great Britain, and its goal in the Middle East was to access the oil fields and to destabilise India. Turkey's main enemy, on the other hand, was Russia, and its objective was territorial expansion on the Black Sea and the Caucasus in line with a pan-Turkic vision. Russia wanted to conquer Constantinople and the Dardanelles and, over the long term, to control southern Persia. Great Britain's objectives were to protect India and the Persian oil fields and to contain Russian infiltration in the south. Sykes' commission was therefore to secure eastern and south-western Persia, to eliminate Germans and Turks from the Neutral Zone, to free the major routes of bandits, and to halt the creeping Russian advance to the south.

When Sykes landed in Bandar Abbas in March 1916 his 'armed force' consisted of six officers, 20 Indian non-commissioned officers, and 25 Indian soldiers. It also carried weapons, ammunition and money.[50] Thanks to his previous contacts with Persian dignitaries such as Prince Abdol Hossein Farman Farma (1857–1939) and tribal leaders, he managed to quickly form a so-called 'South Persia Rifles' troop, which grew to 3,800 men by the end of 1916. It consisted of tribal warriors, deserting gendarmes, and a reinforcement from India numbering 700 men. Sykes spread the rumour that his force was far larger than its actual size, and initially reconquered Kerman and Yazd. On 11 September he reached Isfahan, which had been seized by Russian troops a few days earlier.[51] Here, Sykes and commander Bielomestonov organised a joint British-Russian military parade to demonstrate the Allies' superiority to the Persians (fig. 115). Sykes' next target was Shiraz, which the Germans had already lost in April, but where riots had broken out. He reached the city on

11 November. Sykes, however, failed to capture the dangerous German agent operating in southern Persia, Wilhelm Wassmuss (1880–1931). The so-called 'German Lawrence' understood better than anyone how to incite whole tribes against the British with gold. After the Russian collapse, the security situation in Persia again deteriorated dramatically. And, in the early summer of 1918, tribesmen of the Kashgai, whom Wassmuss had incited, besieged Shiraz. Sykes' commission was fulfilled by the end of the war. Despite inadequate funds, he succeeded thanks to his network, subterfuge and deception. However, Sykes vehemently opposed foreign minister Curzon's plan to transform Persia into a British protectorate at the beginning of 1919, which ensured that Sykes' military career was brought to an end.[52]

The mission awarded to Colonel **Frederick M. Bailey** (1882–1967) was the most dangerous because it involved gathering intelligence. He was supposed to clarify the attitude of the Bolshevik government in Tashkent toward Great Britain and the Central Powers. If necessary, he was also to convince them not to help the Central Powers or to sell cotton to the Germans, or to allow the freed Austrian prisoners of war passage to Persia, where they would stand at Wassmuss's disposal.[53] The Tibetan-speaking Bailey had previously participated in Younghusband's invasion of Tibet (1903–4) and, from 1905–9, served intermittently in Tibetan Gyantse as a British trade agent. Bailey, Captain Blacker and the consul Macartney, who was returning to England from Kashgar, arrived in Tashkent in August 1918. When the unsuspecting Britons met Commissioner for Foreign Affairs Damagatsky for the first time on 19 August, he revealed that British troops had pushed into Russian Transcaspia. There, they had engaged in skirmishes against Bolshevik troops at Dushak, 170 km east of Ashgabat, on 13 August.[54] This was the first time that the British and the 'Russians' had directly clashed in Central Asia, although 90 per cent of the Soviet troops in Transcaspia were made up of former Austro-Hungarian prisoners of war.[55] As Great Britain and the Soviet Union were in a de facto state of war in Transcaspia, not only was Bailey's mission doomed to failure, but the three Englishmen accused of espionage were in danger of being shot. On 28 August, British and Russian troops collided once again at Kaakha.[56] Whereas Macartney and Blacker managed to escape to India in mid-September, Bailey's capture seemed imminent following an order from Moscow.

Bailey escaped, however, by assuming the identity of an Austrian prisoner of war. He went into hiding on 20 October, first in Tashkent and then in the surrounding mountains. At that time, he still hoped the Bolshevik government would be overthrown. But when he learned of the British withdrawal from Transcaspia and the fall of

116. Major General Lionel Dunsterville (1865–1946) commanded the expeditionary force called 'Dunsterforce' that was intended to operate in the Southern Caucasus. Photo *ca.* 1919. Dunsterville, *The Adventures of Dunsterforce* (1920), frontispiece.

Ashgabat, he decided to flee. Bailey then took on the identity of a Serb and, ironically, enlisted with the Cheka, the Soviet counter-intelligence, to spy on Bukhara's military strength. After he arrived in Bukhara, he interviewed the Indian revolutionary Mahendra Pratap, a member of the former Hentig–Niedermayer expedition.[57] In New Bukhara, Bailey received the following order from the Cheka headquarters in Tashkent: 'Please communicate all information you have regarding Anglo-Indian Service Colonel Bailey.' The Cheka thus knew that Bailey was in Bukhara, but not that he was identical with the new Serbian agent. Bailey escaped and reached Persia on 7 January 1920.[58] Thanks to his courage and presence of mind, he had survived deep behind enemy lines for more than a year. Still, he was unable to influence any decision makers, and the encrypted messages he transmitted were little appreciated. Later, Bailey was a Political Agent for Sikkim and Tibet (1921–28) and plenipotentiary minister for Nepal in Kathmandu (1935–38).

Major General **Lionel Dunsterville** (1865–1946) received far too few resources for his strategically important military mission[59] (fig. 116). From a British perspective, the situation in the South Caucasus was dramatic. The Russian troops posted in north-western Persia had melted away, and the government of the **Transcaucasian Commissariat** was established on 11 November 1917, shortly before the Russo-Turkish ceasefire in early December. Corresponding more or less to modern-day Georgia, Armenia and Azerbaijan, it was quickly attacked by the Ottoman Islamic Army, led by Nuri Pasha, the half-brother of Enver Pasha. The short-term goal of the Turks was to defeat the Transcaucasian state and occupy the oil fields of Baku;[60] the long-term goal was a territorial expansion to Turkestan and thus the realisation of Enver's vision of a pan-Turkic empire. Founded on 22 April 1918, the **Transcaucasian Democratic Federative Republic** collapsed under the weight of the infighting between Armenians, Azerbaijanis and Georgians and the Ottoman attacks after only one month. **Georgia** declared its independence on 26 May 1918, and placed itself under German protection at the Treaty of Poti two days later.[61] The Treaty of Brest-Litovsk had allowed Germany to conclude an agreement with the Central Council of Revolutionary Ukraine and thus to obtain control over the Black Sea. A German column under General Friedrich Kress von Kressenstein landed at Poti, western Georgia, and reached Tbilisi on 19 June 1918 which saved Georgia from a full scale Turkish invasion.[62]

Two days after Georgia, on 28 May, the **Azerbaijan Democratic Republic** likewise emerged as an Ottoman protectorate, and on the same day the first **Republic of Armenia** was proclaimed. Armenia, for its part, was forced to surrender to Turkey on 4 June.[63] The Islamic Army could now go unhindered to the independent city of Baku, where the **Bolshevik People's Commissariat** ruled, headed by the Armenian Stepan Shahumyan (1878–1918). From Baku, however, it was easy to reach Krasnovodsk and the Transcaspian railway, whose auxiliary line extended all the way to Kushk and the Afghan border.[64] This meant that a Turkish advance into Turkestan would be able to

117. The city centre and the Bay of Baku; in the foreground, the three Flame Towers built between 2007 and 2012. Photo: 2016.

free the 40,000 Austrian prisoners of war held there and, in a second operation, this combined force could threaten India via Herat.[65] Another cause for alarm for Great Britain were reports from Major T.S.W. Jarvis, Captain Reginald Teague-Jones (1889–1988) and Colonel Charles Howard Ellis (1895–1975) regarding an agreement that had been reached between Moscow and the Germans. The Soviets agreed to sell to Germany petroleum from Baku and cotton from Turkestan, in the hope that the Germans would hinder their Turkish allies from advancing on Baku.[66] In fact, the rivalry that erupted between Turkey and the German Empire significantly delayed the Turkish attack on Baku.[67] Ultimately, both Germany and Turkey sought their own access to the oil reserves of Baku.

To thwart German or Turkish access to the Baku oil fields, Major General Dunsterville was appointed head of a Caucasus Mission on 14 January 1918 and appointed British representative in Tbilisi, Georgia. The establishment of the German protectorate over Georgia brought this plan to naught, and Dunsterville was instructed to stop the Turkish advance on Baku. Although the more than 30,000-strong Islamic Army, which consisted of two Turkish divisions and as many irregulars,[68] approached Baku quickly in the summer, Lenin strictly forbade Shahumyan from accepting Dunsterville's offer of military aid. Since Dunsterville could not land in Baku without Soviet consent, he worked out plans to destroy its pumping systems, pipelines and oil reserves.[69] At the same time, the British master spy Reginald Teague-Jones was commissioned to travel to Baku and to elicit alternatives to Shahumyan. He arrived in Baku on 10 July and informed the British consul Ranald MacDonell (1875–1941) of the new strategy. On 12 July, Teague-Jones was back in Krasnovodsk, where huge amounts of cotton bales were waiting for shipment to Astrakhan. There, a German delegation had bought whole train loads of cotton. Thanks to a fictitious telegram from Astrakhan to Krasnovodsk, Teague-Jones succeeded in unloading the already full freight ships and turning away further ships arriving from Astrakhan.[70] After a pro-British government took power in Ashgabat shortly thereafter in a coup, no more cotton left Transcaspia. The British had thus temporarily won the 'war for cotton'.[71] In Baku, events unfolded rapidly: on 25–26 July, social revolutionaries, Mensheviks and Armenian Dashnaks over-threw Shahumyan's 'Sovnarkom' and formed the **Centrocaspian Dictatorship**.[72] The commissioners tried to escape, but were picked up and arrested. They were then freed on 14 September, just before Baku fell. However, when they fled back to Astrakhan, the captain steered the ship to Krasnovodsk, where they were arrested once again. The Transcaspian Ashgabat committee sentenced them to

118. Memorial for the British Indian troops killed in action in Baku 1918–19. Baku, photo 2016.

death, and on the night of 19 September, 26 of the commissioners were shot. Only the future Soviet Politburo member Anastas Mikoyan escaped execution due to his youth.[73]

The Centrocaspian Dictatorship asked Dunsterville for military aid, and his vanguard arrived in Baku on 4 August, Dunsterville himself on 17 August. The 'Dunsterforce' mission resembled a suicide mission: 900 British soldiers, some 100 Cossacks and 6,000 battle-averse Armenians faced a whopping force of 14,000 battle-hardened Turks with access to strong artillery. The approaching second, larger Turkish force numbered more than 16,000 men. As Dunsterville and Ellis reported, the Armenians refused to fight, and so the entire burden of defending Baku rested on the shoulders of the British and the Cossacks.[74] When the Turks broke through the defence on 14 September, Dunsterville embarked with his deci-mated troops under the cover of night again to Anzali. The next day, Azerbaijani volunteers marched into Baku, where they slaughtered approximately 15,000 to 20,000 Armenians, partly in retaliation for their own heavy losses the previous March.[75] Although Dunsterville could not hold Baku, he nevertheless prevented the Central Powers from seizing the oil inventories over a period of six weeks. Equally successful as Dunsterville was Commodore D.T. Norris (1875–1937), who reached the port of Anzali on the southern shore of the Caspian

Sea in summer 1918. He proceeded to Baku with Dunsterforce where he requisitioned several coast guard boats and six merchant ships which he had armed. Norris's flotilla controlled the Caspian Sea till May 1919 and successfully prevented the victorious Turks from advancing to Krasnovodsk after their conquest of Baku.[76] Six weeks after Dunsterville's departure from Baku, Turkey surrendered on 30 October and had to commit itself to evacuating its troops from the Caucasus.[77] Another six weeks later, on 17 November, General William Montgomery Thomson (1877–1963) arrived in Baku with the 5,000-strong North Persian Force (for short: 'Norperforce') to restore public order.[78] With these 5,000 men, Dunsterville likely would have been able to prevent Baku's fall and the massacre of the Armenians.

The mission of Major General **Wilfrid Malleson**, referred to as 'Mallmiss', was to restore the British-Russian cordon that shielded Afghanistan. He was also to prevent both a Turkish push towards Afghanistan and a breakout of former Austrian prisoners of war to Persia. When Malleson reached Mashhad in July, however, the main problem had already been resolved: an alliance of the Mensheviks and Social Revolutionaries had overthrown the local Bolsheviks in Ashgabat and seized power on 14 July 1918. The **Transcaspian Ashgabat Committee**, led by the railway worker Fyodor Funtikov, soon controlled the railroad to Merv and Krasnovodsk. It subsequently asked Malleson for help against the expected attacks from Tashkent, as it had only a few (and what is more, unreliable) troops itself. Since Transcaspia now formed a buffer against Bolsheviks and possibly invading Turks, Malleson was given free rein by the British commander in India, General Sir Charles Monro. Should Dunsterville and Norris fail in their mission at Baku, then Malleson had to prevent by all means a Turkish capture of the Krasnovodsk–Ashgabat railway line: 'General Dunsterville [and Commodore Norris were] our first line of defence against the Turko-German plans; our Mission [Mallmiss] was the second.'[79]

Malleson immediately sent a small Indian machine-gun unit, which just barely fended off a Bolshevik attack near Dushak on 13 August. On 28 August, near Kaakha, a larger unit of Punjabi soldiers repulsed a second strong Bolshevik attack after Malleson and the Ashgabat Committee had signed the protocol of an agreement on 19 August (which was never ratified, however). Teague-Jones, who was wounded near Kaakha, was appointed Political Representative in Transcaspia. Malleson, for his part, remained in Mashhad. The committee urged a further advance of the now 900-strong British Indian force to Merv and on to Chardju and the border with Bukhara. Because Great Britain was not officially at war with the Soviet Union and such a foray did not offer strategic advantages, Monro ruled out advancing beyond Merv.[80] The oasis was conquered after heavy fighting on 1 November and the British set up their position near the train station of Bairam Ali.[81] Like the war along the Trans-Siberian Railway, which was occupied by the Czechoslovak Legion, the war in Transcaspia was a railway war with armoured trains. These were armoured with steel and hydraulically pressed cotton and equipped with howitzers, field guns and machine guns. Right at the front were two long wagons, laden with heavy metal pieces, to absorb any mine explosions.[82] While Transcaspia had only two armoured trains, it had enough fuel. The Bolsheviks of Turkestan, on the other hand, had three armoured trains, but had to burn saxaul bushes and dried fish in their fireboxes.[83]

When Turkey surrendered on 30 October and the German Empire capitulated on 11 November 1918, the situation of the British changed abruptly: the German-Turkish danger was not only eliminated, but the strategic basis for 'Mallmiss' disappeared along with it. As a collapse of the unstable and virtually bankrupt Transcaspian government seemed imminent once the British withdrew, Malleson tried to win time. Yet, on 9 and 15 February 1919, London ordered Mallmiss's retreat, which was completed on 14 April.[84] The resurgent Bolsheviks immediately invaded, occupying Merv on 23 May. They then took Ashgabat on 9 July and Krasnovodsk on 6 February 1920.[85] The government in London had recognised that the era of the empire's territorial expansion was now a fading memory. Withdrawal, moreover, would have proven all the more difficult the longer such a military adventure lasted, especially given that there was no realistic alternative post-war scenario in sight.

Whereas Great Britain possessed defensive targets in southern Central Asia and the Middle East to preserve the status quo, the German Empire pursued an offensive strategy. From its perspective, the British Empire had to be destabilised in its colonies in order to bind enemy troops in peripheral regions. Germany also needed raw materials. Its tactics included acquiring new, battle-ready allies, as well as fomenting anti-British riots through propaganda and bribery, and sabotage. The most famous exponents were the agitator Wilhelm Wassmuss and the group led by Captain Fritz Klein, who had specialised in sabotaging pipelines.[86] The **Hentig–Niedermayer expedition**, by contrast, tried to persuade Afghan Amir **Habibullah** (r. 1901–19) to abandon his neutrality, to attack India with his tribal warriors, and to provoke Muslim riots there. Such an action would have a massive impact on western theatres of war. As Lord Kitchener (1850–1916, supreme commander of India 1902–09, and minister of war 1914–16) had estimated, the defence of India would have required pulling out 135,000 troops from the west.[87] The German plan was not entirely unrealistic, as the vast majority of the approximately 330 million Muslims lived under foreign rule, and most of these were in British, Russian and French colonies. The next step was to incite the Muslims of the Empire to revolt against the British in the name of jihad. The mastermind of this anti-British strategy, the diplomat and archaeologist Max von Oppenheim, did not even shy away from recruiting Indian terrorists and suicide bombers.[88] But when the Ottoman caliph declared a jihad against the Allies, it soon became apparent that the Shiite Persians felt that it hardly concerned them. Many of the Arabs living in the Ottoman Empire also were not interested in getting involved in a joint struggle *with* the Turks as they, after all, had been seeking their independence *from* the Turks.

The main actors of this small troop, which originally dated back to an initiative from Enver Pasha,[89] were as follows: the plenipotentiary diplomat and lieutenant **Werner Otto von Hentig** (1886–1984), the military commander and senior lieutenant **Oskar Niedermayer** (1885–1948), and the two Indian revolutionaries **Mahendra Pratap** (1886–1979), the nominal head of the expedition, and the Muslim lawyer **Mohammed Barakatullah** (1854–1927). Von Oppenheim hoped the two revolutionaries would be able to incite unrest and uprisings in India.[90] The missions, which were chaotically organised in Berlin, began inauspiciously. In January 1915, the original mission leader of the earlier military expedition, **Wilhelm Wassmuss**, had a falling out with his team. He left at the end of that month only to then stir up further tribes in southern Persia.[91] In early March, Wassmuss committed an unforgiveable mistake. While on the run after having been arrested by pro-British tribesmen, he left behind the manual for the new German secret code, which fell into British hands.[92] Even worse: he did not report the loss.[93] It was not least thanks to Wassmuss's secret code manual that the British were able to decipher the infamous Zimmermann Telegram of 16 January 1917. This subsequently helped precipitate the United States' entry into the war on 2 April.[94] In March 1915, Enver Pasha – who had originally conceived of the mission – finally revoked Turkish participation in the Afghanistan expedition. He was probably fearful that the German Empire could further strengthen its position in the Neutral Zone, which he wanted to occupy himself.[95] By the end of June, all the expedition's members had arrived in Isfahan.

To reach Herat from Isfahan, the expedition had to use the neutral corridor located between the Russian and British zones.[96] To avoid these areas, Niedermayer and von Hentig selected a marching route across the notorious salt desert of Dasht-i Kevir, despite the summer heat. But the Anglo-Russian cordon was the biggest obstacle. It blocked the way to Afghanistan; its northern half was patrolled by Russian troops, whereas it was patrolled by the British in the south. Niedermayer managed to break through, but only by means of a cunning stratagem. First, von Hentig gave a fictitious letter meant for the German envoy in Tehran to a rather unsuspecting messenger. In it, von Hentig informed the envoy that the expedition would take a north-eastern route.[97] The messenger was

then promptly intercepted by the Russians. As Niedermayer further relates: 'I then detached a camel caravan . . . that we loaded with all kinds of expendable crates, which . . . were filled with stones. It was to be further utilized in the east against the English, who were coming from the south.'[98] Niedermayer then proceeded to divide the main group into the rapid advance group with the key members and weapons and a slower supply column. Shortly before entering the cordon, Niedermayer sacrificed the supply column, sending it to the north-east to lure the Russians away from his position. Niedermayer's 'flying column' then crossed the cordon where the Russian and British zones intersect and reached Afghanistan at night on 19 August. Of the 140 men who had left Isfahan, only 37 made it to Herat.[99] In Herat, von Hentig promised the governor that Afghanistan would receive territories extending from Samarkand to Bombay in the event of a successful joint Afghan-German-Turkish military engagement.[100] The Germans arrived in Kabul on 2 October, where Amir Habibullah placed them under house arrest for three

119. The German Afghanistan expedition in Kabul. Sitting from left to right, Kasim Bey (Turkish captain), Lt. Werner Otto von Hentig (imperial legation secretary and head of the diplomatic mission), Kumar Raja Mahendra Pratap (Indian prince and revolutionary), Oskar Niedermayer (senior lieutenant and head of the military mission), Mohammed Barakatullah (Indian revolutionary). Standing from left to right, Walter Röhr (multilingual Orient merchant and companion of Hentig), Kurt Wagner (captain-lieutenant), Günther Voigt (lieutenant and adjutant to Niedermayer).[21] Photo *ca.* May 1916. Werner Otto von Hentig Archive, vH 038. Foundation Phototheca Afghanica, Bubendorf, Switzerland

weeks. The uninvited guests presented Habibullah with a seemingly intractable problem: Habibullah had declared Afghanistan's neutrality in August 1914, because he knew that an attack on northwest India would not only result in the loss of vital British subsidies, but it would also impose upon him a two-front war against Britain and Russia. On the other hand, the population harboured strong anti-British feelings, while the tribesmen expected rich booty from an India campaign. In addition, both his brother and prime minister Nasrullah (1857–1920) – who was very popular among the Pashtun tribes and had pulled strings in an anti-Habibullah conspiracy in 1909 – and his two sons, Amanullah (1892–1960) and Inayatullah (1888–1946), were pro-German.[101]

When the Germans began a hunger strike to protest their house arrest, the amir relented. He received them on 26 October in the presence of Nasrullah and his two sons. Habibullah listened politely to the delegation, but was only interested in playing for time to see who would most likely win the world war. He stressed that his country was sandwiched between two allied great powers and that the Central Powers were far away. If he decided to enter the war on the side of the Central Powers, he would need weapons, ammunition, money, and large contingents of German and Turkish troops.[102] Von Hentig, however, knew that the latter request was impossible. After all, Enver Pasha was not willing to send a strong enough army to Afghanistan, which would first have to fight its way through Persia.[103] After further negotiations, Habibullah commissioned Niedermayer to modernise the Afghan army. In this task, Niedermayer was aided by Austrian prisoners living in Kabul.[104] They directed the ammunition factory, reorganised the army structures, improved and expanded the officers' school, and had field fortifications erected along the road from Kabul to the Khyber Pass to defend against air attacks.[105] Towards the end of 1915, Nasrullah and Inayatullah attempted to initiate an attack on India behind the amir's back. Nasrullah forged a letter from his brother, in which he promised jihad for the spring of 1916, and sent it to the tribal leaders of the Pashtuns. The letter, however, was intercepted by the British, who had immediately notified the amir. The successful espionage led to two more compromising letters falling into British hands: in November, expedition member Walter Röhr wrote to the German envoy in Tehran that if Habibullah remained neutral any longer 'Perhaps we shall find it necessary to begin organising a coup d'état.' In the second letter, von Hentig wrote to Tehran: 'Perhaps internal revulsion of feeling is necessary here first. We are determined to go to any lengths.'[106] The British viceroy Lord Hardinge (1858–1944, in office 1910–16) quickly told Habibullah about the contents of the letters. Habibullah understood that his German guests were contemplating a coup and would even be willing to get rid of him, presumably in favour of Nasrullah.

To dispose of the German delegation, without provoking the ire of the German Empire, and to appease the pro-German lobby in his court, Habibullah agreed to a treaty protocol that was drafted on 24 January 1916. In the treaty, the Germans recognised the full independence of Afghanistan and committed themselves, without payment, to the supply of 100,000 modern rifles, 300 guns, engineers and officers, as well as £10 million in gold (which corresponded in 2016 to about £1.1 billion).[107] In addition, the German Empire agreed in the event of Afghanistan's entry into the war to return the territories that had been lost to India over the years. In early May, the amir demanded an additional 4 million marks a month (approx. £44 million) and 5,000 German soldiers. The cunning amir, conversely, had committed his country to nothing. He, moreover, insisted the treaty only enter into force *after* being ratified by Emperor Wilhelm II, which would remove any concern of an imminent attack on India. Habibullah had managed to appease both the British and the Germans and the pro-German lobby, without, however, changing his neutral course. The German delegation left Kabul on 21 May, divided into smaller groups. Niedermayer returned to Hamadan via Mashhad and fought on the German-Turkish side in Palestine against Lawrence's military units. From 1924–31, he led out of Moscow three secret German military centres located within the Soviet Union as part of the secret rearmament plan of General Hans von Seeckt (1866–1936) and the associated covert German-Soviet armaments cooperation. The first centre served to train military pilots; the second, to train tank crews; and the third was a laboratory for the production of chemical warfare agents. The aim was to bypass the Versailles Treaty and train future officers of the armoured corps and Luftwaffe in a way that would make it possible to quickly beef up the small, limited Reichswehr into the mass army of the Wehrmacht. During World War II, Major General Niedermayer trained a division consisting of Caucasian and Central Asian prisoners of war and was arrested on 28 September 1944 for making seditious ('*wehrkraftzersetzende*') statements. When the war ended, he escaped from prison and turned himself over to the Soviets, who immediately arrested him. He died in Russian captivity on 25 September 1948.[108] Von Hentig, however, managed to cross the Hindu Kush and reached Kashgaria, where he began to agitate. Expelled to Wuhan at Macartney's prompting, he fled to Shanghai. He then travelled as a stowaway on an American ship to Honolulu, from where he returned to Germany by way of New York. He later worked in the German consular and diplomatic service and died in 1984 at the age of 98.[109]

2. Soviet Centralism in Central Asia

In contrast to tsarist rule, which permitted the Turkic-speaking peoples of Central Asia to retain many of their local peculiarities and was content to exploit the region's raw materials, the Soviet authorities strove for a radical restructuring of the Central Asian societies in order to create a 'classless' society. This gradual restructuring was centrally mandated by the Moscow rulers, and the measures touched on all relevant areas of life such as culture and justice, communication (in written and spoken form), forms of production, and ways of living. As long as the New Economic Policy (NEP) was in effect – which granted the peasants and cattle breeders certain liberties with regard to production until around 1927 – the struggle against Islam was limited to verbal propaganda. It was denounced as an alien religion that oppresses women, keeps its believers in ignorance, and was imposed by Arabs and Persians. What is more, the Muslim belief system, which separates the world into believers and non-believers, made fraternisation with the non-Muslim peoples of the Soviet Union and the establishment of a classless society impossible. To increase the level of education and literacy of the population, public schools were established, which were also open to girls. At the same time, the religious schools and mosques lost their financial support. Due to the rapid increase in literacy, people were no longer dependent on the mullahs to form opinions, but were able to educate themselves through the state media. The increased literacy and diminished influence of the mullahs helped women gain access to the labour market. Besides this, civil marriage was introduced and girls and women were granted equality in inheritance matters. In 1927, the battle lines against religion hardened: the vast majority of mosques and madrasahs were shut down; 'scientific atheism' replaced traditional religious instruction; and sharia courts were prohibited.[110]

The calendar was changed from Muslim to the Gregorian in 1937 to further distinguish the Central Asian societies from their southern, Muslim neighbours Iran and Afghanistan and to step up their Russification. In addition, personal names received the suffix '-ov' for men and '-ova' for women, so that 'Karim', for instance, became 'Karimov'. Nation-building within the Soviet Union also necessitated a modern style of writing. It would be introduced to replace the three previously common scripts: the Persian script for the Tajik language, a modified Arabic script for Turkic languages, and the classical Arabic script for religious subjects. From 1923 to 1928, a modified Arabic script was used. It was then replaced by the Latin alphabet in 1928/29, as the Arab script was considered

the script of the Qur'an. In addition, the Latin alphabet severed the young generation from their Islamic heritage insofar as political boundaries were now writing boundaries with respect to the region's Muslim neighbours. From 1938, the Russification and enforced conformity were intensified, while Russian was elevated to the Soviet Union's common language. Numerous Russian loanwords were absorbed into the Central Asian languages and Russian was used almost exclusively in the exact sciences, medicine and politics. In addition, the teaching of Russian became mandatory in all Central Asian schools. The Cyrillic alphabet was first used for writing down Azerbaijani. From 1939–40, it was used across the Soviet Union for the Buryat, Kazakh, Kyrgyz, Uzbek, Turkmen and Tajik languages, and, a year later, even for Mongolian.[111] After regaining their sovereignty, some Turkic states switched to the new Turkish-Latin alphabet, in slightly modified forms. Today, Turkish-Latin script is used in Azerbaijan and Turkmenistan, while Latin and Cyrillic are used in Uzbekistan and Kazakhstan. Only Cyrillic is used in Kyrgyzstan and Tajikistan.

In 1927, Stalin ended the NEP for two reasons: first, he considered well-off peasants (kulaks), rich cattle breeders, tribal and clan leaders, and village elders to be enemies of international socialism and supporters of a reactionary nationalism. Second, Stalin wanted to speed up the industrialisation of Russia west of the Urals and, in particular, to build up a powerful heavy industry. These goals could only be accomplished by means of corresponding imports from the more highly industrialised West. But the necessary foreign currency could only be procured through the export of agricultural products, primarily grain. This strategy called for a rapid increase in agricultural productivity through mechanisation and state control. The instruments to achieve these objectives were to liquidate the wealthy farmers and cattle breeders throughout the Soviet Union or to deport them to Siberia and Central Asia; to introduce a centralised planned economy; and to collectivise agriculture in terms of the five-year plan from 1929–33. Among the main victims of this approach were the Kazakh and Kyrgyz cattle breeders. The owners of larger herds and the wealthy peasants were deported to Siberia by the tens of thousands, while the herds were confiscated and brought to cooperative collective farms (kolkhozes) or state farms (sovkhozes). Production quotas were then determined for these farms, which they then had to meet. In addition, the semi-nomads were forced to settle down, either in kolkhozes or as factory workers. Rather than submit to the state power, many cattle breeders preferred to slaughter their herds or to escape with them to China, Afghanistan or Iran. Parallel to the collectivisation of cattle herds, grazing land was converted into arable land on a

120. The statue of Lenin in front of the Astrakhan Kremlin; on the left, the grain tower, on the right, the Dormition Cathedral. Photo: 2014.

large scale for the purpose of grain cultivation; in Uzbekistan and Turkmenistan, cotton monoculture was intensified. And, as in the Crimea, entire grain harvests were seized in order to sell them for hard currency abroad. The chairman of the Central Committee of the Crimea ASSR, Mehmet Kubay, protested in the early 1930s as a de facto representative of the Central Asian republics: 'Moscow plunders the Republic of Crimea and exports her natural resources, while leaving no food to the people starving to death.' Stalin responded by having Kubay executed.[112]

For the people of Central Asia, the consequences of the collectivisation policies were disastrous. In Kazakhstan, the quantity of livestock fell by more than 80 per cent. More than one million people died of hunger and disease, and another half million fled to China. Livestock numbers fell by 50 per cent in Kyrgyzstan and Uzbekistan. Since Stalin concurrently exiled non-compliant Russians to Kazakhstan, the Kazakhs became a minority in their own country. Ultimately, the collectivisation of agriculture and the promotion of grain and cotton production represented a redistribution of wealth at

the expense of the rural population of Central Asia in favour of the Russian urban industrial centres.[113] The Soviet economic policies of the 1930s in Central Asia reflected a tightening of the tsars' former colonial policy, for they maximised the exploitation of regional resources and neglected locally added value.

As in the whole of the Soviet Union, in 1936–38, Central Asia became a victim of Stalin's 'Great Purge'. No longer were just the kulaks targeted, but so were suspected opponents of Stalin's political and economic course within the Communist Party, the administration, the officer corps, and general scientific and cultural elite. There were also mass deportations of certain ethnic groups like Koreans,[114] Volga Germans, Ukrainian Poles, Crimean Tatars, and Meskhetian Turks to Central Asia, which only further altered the ethnic composition there. Even earlier, in the 1920s, hundreds of thousands of Russians were moved to Central Asia to build proletarian cells in the context of agricultural mechanisation. As Oskar Niedermayer correctly recognised, the rapid mechanisation and collectivisation of agriculture transformed the peasants into workers, who were also employed in heavy industry and arms manufacture. The hundreds of thousands of tractor drivers and mechanics could be easily retrained as tank drivers. Thus, the mechanisation of agriculture indirectly served the mechanisation of the military.[115] The terror subsided towards the end of 1938, and with the outbreak of the 'Great Patriotic War', which began with the attack of the German Reich on the Soviet Union on 22 June 1941, the ideological coercion loosened. Formerly proscribed local nationalism was revived and the persecution of Orthodox and Muslim clerics put on hold. The anti-Islamic campaigns disappeared, and important mosques were reopened to their original purpose. Suddenly, Marxism, patriotism and religion found common ground. This abrupt change in policy towards Muslim, non-Russian minorities was intended to motivate them to defend the motherland, and also to prevent

the German Reich from winning over these ethnic groups with Islam-friendly policies. The new policy was successful and more than three million Central Asians fought against the Nazis. For example, 1.4 million people from Uzbekistan participated in the war. Of these, 263,000 fell in battle, 133,000 disappeared during the fighting, 396,000 did not return home, and 60,000 were crippled. In addition, 1.2 million Kazakhs and 360,000 Kyrgyz fought at the front.[116]

When the Wehrmacht rapidly pushed into the Soviet Union and severely endangered the arms industry, Stalin took advantage of the existing strategic depth. He moved arms production and other industrial facilities, as well as hospitals and research institutes, behind the Urals to Central Asia and Siberia, beyond the reach of German bombers. Uzbekistan thus received 238 new industrial complexes, including the production of Ilyushin

121. Fishermen on the frozen Aral Sea in western Kazakhstan. Photo: before 2009.

warplanes; Kazakhstan likewise received 140 production facilities and Kyrgyzstan more than 30. The Central Asian railway network played a vital role in bringing soldiers, military equipment and food to the front. Uzbekistan and Kazakhstan became the arsenal of the Red Army. Through this shift of industrial complexes to Central Asia, industrialisation there experienced a dramatic shot in the arm.[117] This relocation eastwards was not limited to industrial plants, however. It also included members of non-Russian ethnic groups: first, from 1939, Poles, Balts and Karelian Finns; then, from 1941, Volga Germans and Romanians; and, from 1943/44, Kalmyks, Chechens, Ingush, Balkars, Crimean Tatars, Karachay-Cherkassians and Meskhetians. In total, between 1939 and 1945, approximately 3.2 million people were affected by these deportations, with a third of them dying of hunger and disease.[118] After 1956, many surviving deportees were allowed to return to their homes.

The continued promotion of agriculture within the scope of the planned economy also led to undesirable ecological developments. As the grain harvests in the Soviet Union were not satisfactory in 1953, Nikita Khrushchev (1894–1971, First Secretary of the Central Committee 1953–64) ordered 3.5 million hectares of pasture to be converted to farmland in Kazakhstan within one year, and then gradually more than 12.5 million hectares. After a short-term yield increase in 1956 and 1958, yields continually declined until 1963. The culprits were poor management in state enterprises, improper use of machinery, droughts, and especially rapid soil erosion due to the omission of regenerative fallow periods. The rapid exhaustion of the soil also caused the average yield of grain in 1963 to be more than 40 per cent less per hectare than in 1953.[119] This failure was one of the reasons that Khrushchev was dismissed in 1964. From an

The shrinking of the Aral Sea

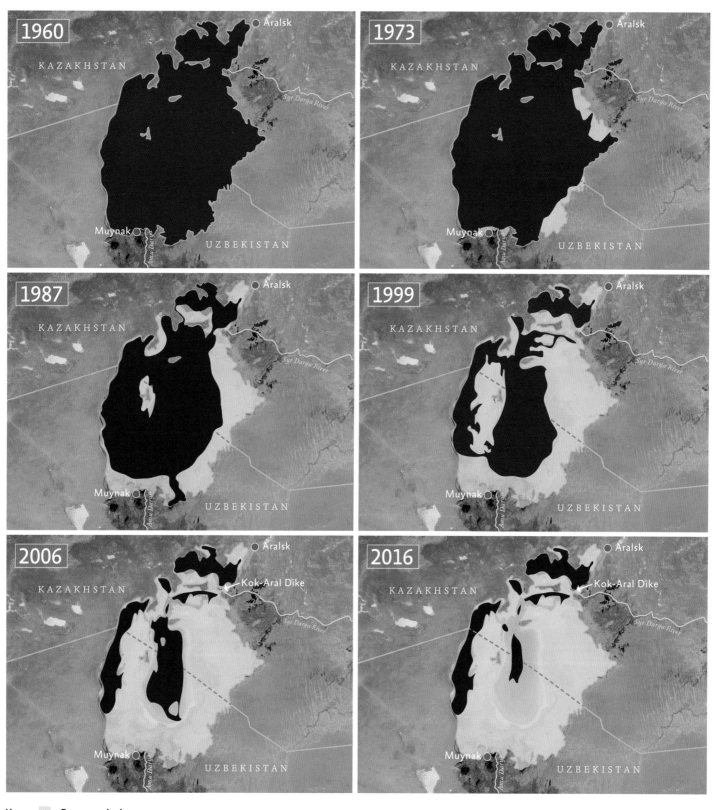

Key:

Former seabed

Coastline in 1960

International boundary

Scale (km)

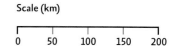

0   50   100   150   200

ecological point of view, even more devastating were the 456 nuclear tests – 116 of which were above ground – that took place from 1949 to 1989 around 160 km east of Semipalatinsk. Today, 18.000 km² – an area almost half the size of Switzerland – is considered to be contaminated by radiation.[120]

Another, likely irreparable ecological disaster was caused by the cotton monoculture in Kazakhstan, Uzbekistan and Turkmenistan. Since cotton plants need a lot of water, Uzbekistan had to take in large amounts of water from the Amu Darya and Kazakhstan likewise from the Syr Darya. The poor quality of open irrigation canals led to large losses as a result of seepage and evaporation. This, in turn, required that additional water be taken from the rivers. Since crop rotation was not practised, there was irreversible soil degradation and salinisation, which was dealt with using ever-increasing amounts of pesticides and chemical fertilisers. The Karakum Canal in Turkmenistan – built from 1954–62 and expanded until 1988 – also withdrew large quantities of water from the Amu Darya in the direction of Ashgabat. However, as the canal was open and lacked a concrete bed, half of the water that passed through it was lost to seepage and evaporation. The consequence of these water withdrawals from the two rivers was the salinisation and desiccation of the endorheic Aral Sea, which has lost about 80 per cent of its area and 90 per cent of its volume since 1960. In 1989, the world's once fourth largest lake separated into two parts, the Great Aral Sea in the south belonging to Uzbekistan, and the Small Aral Sea in the north-east belonging to Kazakhstan. Kazakhstan built a dam in 1992 and 2003–05 to retain the waters of the Syr Darya and thus to save the Small Aral Sea. The measure has been successful from the Kazakh point of view, as they were able to stabilise the Small Aral Sea and decrease the salinity of the water. The fish stocks also rebounded. Meanwhile, the Great Aral Sea has shrunk to a narrow strip of dead water in the west; its former middle and eastern basin is now the newly formed Aral Kum Desert. Today, many former ports and fish factories are located more than 100 km from the water. The Great Aral Sea could only be saved through a massive restriction of the cotton monoculture in Uzbekistan and Turkmenistan, and a significant reduction in water intake of the Karakum Canal. At the moment, neither possibility seems realistic. The drying up of the lake has also had serious health consequences for the Karakalpaks, who live in the former delta of the Amu Darya: the salt dust, which is whirled up by the strong winds and distributed in Karakalpakstan settlements, is highly toxic due to the excessive application of pesticides, herbicides and chemical fertilisers.[121]

3. Afghanistan's Sovereignty, 1919–78

Amir **Habibullah** (r. 1901–19) quickly realised the need to modernise Afghanistan. He ordered the construction of the first modern hospital, the first hydroelectric power station and the first telephone line, and combated illiteracy (98 per cent of Afghans were illiterate) by opening schools for children of all classes and establishing the first Western-type grammar school. He also established the first teacher training college and the first military academy. Habibullah no longer wanted to leave education solely to the mullahs. At the same time, the amir permitted numerous Afghans who had been forced into exile by his father Abdur Rahman to return to Afghanistan. Among them were the families of the Tarzi and the Musahiban brothers from the Muhammadzai Barakzai tribe, who assumed power and conducted government affairs from 1930.[122] The exponents of the two families had differing foreign policy positions: Mahmud Beg Tarzi (1865–1933) was a nationalist and pan-Islamist who had lived in the Ottoman Empire for 22 years; he advocated for the country's rapid modernisation. He was also pro-Turkish and friendly towards Germany, just like Habibullah's sons Amanullah and Inayatullah. On the other hand, the five Musahiban brothers, led by General Muhammad Nadir Khan (1883–1933), were pro-British. Habibullah's first foreign policy test came when Viceroy Curzon issued an ultimatum demanding a revision of the Treaty of Gandamak and the agreement of 21 July 1880.[123] He insisted on even greater control of foreign policy, rigorous restrictions on arms imports, and other concessions. In the event of a renegotiation of the Treaty of Gandamak, Habibullah demanded in return the restoration of the territories that had been ceded to British India. As with Lytton before him, Curzon also responded angrily. In 1901, he aggregated the various semi-autonomous Pashtun areas that had been part of India since 1893 into the North-West Frontier Province (NWFP) and prepared a third invasion of Afghanistan designed to bring the amir to heel.

Curzon's deputy, Lord Ampthill, and his chief negotiator in Kabul, Louis Dane, came up with the solution to the conflict in 1904, when the viceroy was in England.[124] In the treaty dated 21 March 1905, Ampthill accepted Habibullah's counter-proposal, which referred to the agreements of 1879 and 1880, and recognised the preamble, which was non-negotiable for the amir. It read: 'His Majesty... Amir Habibullah Khan, Independent King of the State of Afghanistan...' Here, Britain recognised the independence

122. Amir Habibullah and his entourage on a hunt in the district of Paghman, west of Kabul. Paghman was the Amir's birthplace. In the top row, fourth from left, is Amir Habibullah (r. 1901–19); his son and successor Amanullah (r. 1919–29) is the second from the left. Appearing seventh from the left is Prince Inayatullah, who ruled for just four days in January 1929; second from the right is the moderniser Mahmud Beg Tarzi. In the foreground, middle, stands the future King Nadir Shah, Muhammad Nadir, on a protruding rock (r. 1929–33). Photo *ca.* 1910, Souvenir d'Afghanistan Collection, SdA 2-42. Foundation Phototheca Afghanica, Bubendorf, Switzerland.

of the state of Afghanistan, but retained control of its foreign policy.[125] Habibullah had outmanoeuvred Curzon and London with Ampthill's help. Now, he was no longer a vassal of India, but an independent king. At the outbreak of the world war, Habibullah – against the better judgement of his brother and his sons – declared Afghanistan's neutrality, because he knew that a two-front war against Russia and India would lead to its occupation. After the war, in early February 1919, Habibullah called for the recompense he believed he was due in the form of Afghanistan's unrestricted sovereignty, including in foreign policy matters. The initial response was negative, and Habibullah was murdered by an unknown assailant on 20 February 1919. The assassination was probably undertaken by an alliance between the anti-British traditionalists surrounding Nasrullah and the modernists surrounding Amanullah and Tarzi. On 21 February, **Nasrullah** (1874–1920, r. 21–28 February 1919), with the backing of Inayatullah and most of the tribes, declared himself the new amir

in Jalalabad. **Amanullah** (1892–1960, r. 1919–29), however, then seized the arsenal and the state treasury in Kabul and proclaimed himself amir on 28 February. He had Nasrullah arrested, who died in prison in 1920.[126]

Amanullah subsequently declared the full sovereignty of Afghanistan on 13 April. When Great Britain responded with delaying tactics, he did not hesitate to make the decisive step that von Hentig and Niedermayer had urged Habibullah to make three years earlier. On 3 May 1919, near the Khyber Pass, he attacked India, triggering the Third Anglo-Afghan War. Amanullah had previously written a letter to Lenin on 7 April 1919, in which he said that, on the basis of Lenin's example, he had been able to instill in the Afghan people confidence that the country would win its fight for independence.[127] However, even though the Indian troops returning from Europe had already been demobilised, the amir had severely underestimated the opposing army's firepower. It had rifles with magazines, light Lewis machine guns, hand grenades, armoured vehicles, howitzers and aircraft. After some initial successes, the Afghans suffered a number of setbacks. The bombing of Kabul from the air induced the amir to seek a ceasefire on 28 May, which took effect on 3 June.[128] Amanullah had lost the war, but he won the peace: Great Britain may have emerged victorious from world war, but it was severely weakened and weary of conflict. Afghanistan and Great Britain made peace on 8 August, which was affirmed by the treaty of 22 November 1921. The amir lost the country's previous financial assistance and the possibility of importing weapons via India. He also had to recognise the Durand Line. In return, a letter acknowledged Afghanistan's independence, including in foreign affairs.[129]

Amanullah took advantage of the newly acquired space to manoeuvre in foreign policy to establish diplomatic and economic contacts with foreign countries. At the same time, he soon realised that the British Foreign Secretary Curzon was doing everything he could to limit this freedom.[130] The first state to recognise Afghan independence was the Soviet Union in May 1919. After all, the Bolsheviks were also looking for diplomatic recognition. This was followed in 1921–22 and subsequent years by friendship treaties with the Soviet Union, Iran, Turkey, Italy, France and Germany. But the new superpower, the United States, refused to take up full diplomatic relations with Afghanistan until 1942 in deference to Great Britain. Japan succumbed to similar pressure from the British until 1931. Amanullah had hoped for economic agreements and technology transfers with both countries. The German Weimar Republic initially balked at actively supporting Afghanistan for fear of British reprisals. Curzon's hostile policy towards Afghanistan drove the amir – who felt threatened – straight into the arms of Moscow. The Bolsheviks, for their part, wanted to demonstrate a model example of peaceful relations and build a spy network in Afghanistan directed against India. As the Afghan historian Amin Saikal puts it: 'By 1920 the Kremlin had by and large laid the foundations for its own regional forward policy: first Sovietising the Muslims of Central Asia; afterwards, with their help, Sovietising their brethren in Afghanistan, Iran

123. A caterpillar vehicle Citroën Kégresse P17 with trailer from the French Croisière Jaune expedition drives past the walls of Herat, Afghanistan in June 1931. The Croisière Jaune (4 April 1931–12 February 1932), also referred to as the 'Mission Centre-Asie', was supposed to demonstrate the superiority of Citroën's vehicles. Accompanied by archaeologist Joseph Hackin and the palaeontologist and geologist Pierre Teilhard de Chardin, it also had scientific objectives. The expedition was divided into two parts: the Pamir group travelled from Beirut to Herat, Kabul, Rawalpindi and Srinagar until it reached Gilgit, where the participants marched further on foot to Xinjiang. The China group, on the other hand, drove from Beijing to Ürümqi, where it ran into the turmoil of the Dungan Revolt and was taken hostage for five months by Governor Jin Shuren. Photo: June 1931.

and India. . . . Afghanistan was often described as the "Suez Canal of the Revolution" leading to India,' and, one should add, to the Indian Ocean.[131] However, material developmental aid from Moscow failed to come about, and the Soviet Union also refused to return the oasis of Panjdeh, annexed in 1885. Given that Turkey and Iran also had little interest in getting involved in Afghanistan in consideration of Great Britain, the landlocked country's actual room to manoeuvre remained limited. 'Amanullah was disliked by the British, ignored by the Americans, deceived by the Soviets and incapable of giving credibility to his pan-Islamic stance.'[132] The Weimar Republic alone was prepared to support Afghanistan with technology transfers, which enabled the country to carry out numerous large-scale projects.

Amanullah also modernised the state structures and, in 1923, put into effect Afghanistan's first constitution. The monarchy no longer rested on Allah's will or the consent of the tribal leaders, but on the will of the people. Although Islam was the state religion, all citizens of Afghanistan were equal, regardless of their religion or tribal affiliation. The rights to property, education and a free press were protected; slavery and torture were prohibited. A consultative state council was introduced as parliament – half of its members were elected, half chosen by the amir. In addition, a senate was appointed of preeminent figures. To find and promote a common national identity and story, Amanullah founded the National Museum. He also commissioned France, which was given a 30-year monopoly, with the archaeological exploration and inventory of Afghanistan.[133] He hoped that the archaeological finds would help familiarise all Afghans with a common culture, in reference to which, moreover, the mullahs would not enjoy sole interpretive authority. Nevertheless, the excavations of pre-Islamic Buddhist shrines and figures provoked the wrath of fanatical mullahs, as evidenced by Barthoux's excavations in Hadda in the 1920s.[134]

Although Amanullah's first constitution was moderate, it attracted the ire of Islamic traditionalists, particularly from the Sufi circles of Naqshbandiyya and members of the anti-British Deobandi movement established in India in 1866. The teachings of the Deobandi are strictly Sunni-Hanafi; they condemn any adoption of Western, non-Islamic values and worldviews and propagate a return to the very narrowly defined roots of Islam and the obligation to international jihad. Even though this doctrine disapproves of anti-civilian terrorism, it closely resembles Wahhabism and Salafism.[135] Amanullah was able to quell a first traditionalist-incited rebellion in 1924.[136] But, after a long overseas trip to the Middle East and Europe, which motivated him to further secularise Afghan society, he announced further reforms in July 1928. Intense rioting

then broke out once again in October. In particular, Amanullah's plans for an elected people's parliament, compulsory military service, lifting the veil requirement for women, and granting girls free access to education were a source of outrage.[137] Amanullah, who had declared himself king in 1926, now had to pay the price for not heeding Kemal Atatürk's advice. The Turkish leader had stressed that before one could modernise a backward country, it was necessary to first build a strong and loyal army, a national ideology, a pioneering party, and a popular movement. Yet, all this was missing in Afghanistan. In January 1929, the army disintegrated and an ethnic Tajik, former officer, and bandit leader named Habibullah Kalakani marched on Kabul. To prevent a bloodbath, Amanullah abdicated on 14 January and set his brother **Inayatullah** (1888–1946, 14–17 January 1929) on the throne. He also stepped down after three days, however, at which point **Habibullah Kalakani** (1890–1929, r. 18 January to 13 October 1929) seized power in Kabul. Amanullah and Inayatullah fled into exile.[138]

Although Habibullah Kalakani undid most of Amanullah's reforms and pursued a conservative policy, as a Tajik, he lacked any kind of legitimacy for the Pashtuns. A resistance coalesced around General Muhammad Nadir Khan Musahiban and his two brothers Shah Wali Khan and Hashim Khan. Thanks to British help, Kabul fell to the Musahiban brothers on 15 October 1929. Kalakani was executed and **Nadir Shah** (r. 1929–33) was made the new king. The Pashtun tribe of the Muhammadzai Barakzai consequently regained the powerful monopoly that had been interrupted by Kalakani. Like Kalakani before him, Nadir Shah nullified most of Amanullah's reforms: he reintroduced the veil requirement for women and abolished women's suffrage as 'un-Islamic'. The legal system was again based solely on the Sharia, and the recruitment of soldiers was delegated back to the tribal leaders. The government came to resemble family rule, with Nadir as king and commander, Hashim Khan as prime minister, Shah Wali Khan as minister of war, and Aziz Khan as ambassador in Berlin. In terms of foreign policy, Nadir was actively neutral: he destroyed the last strongholds of the Basmachis in the north and denied any support to the rebels in the great anti-British uprising of the Waziris, Mashuds and Afridis in the NWFP. In remaining on the sidelines here, he essentially recognised the Durand Line. The king was assassinated on 8 November 1933 as part of a vendetta.[139]

The family of the Musahiban agreed to the succession on the same day and established co-rule. Nadir's young son **Zahir Shah** (r. nominally 1933–63, effectively 1963–73, d. 2007) was a ceremonial king and his uncle **Hashim Khan** (in office 1929–46) was prime minister. He was succeeded by his brother Shah

Mahmud Khan (in office 1946–53) who was in turn replaced as premier minister by Mohammed Daoud Khan in 1953 (in office 1953–63, as president 1973–78); Daoud was a son of Aziz Khan. Hashim Khan continued Nadir's conservative socio-religious policy. Just the same, he also invested in the road network and founded Afghanistan's first bank, prompting the emergence of private monopolies. In 1934, he managed a diplomatic coup when he realised Afghanistan's acceptance into the League of Nations. Three years later, Afghanistan signed the non-aggression Treaty of Sa'adabad with Persia, Iraq and Turkey.[140] He also cultivated close economic ties with the Germans. But when the Soviet Union and Great Britain became allies in the summer of 1941 in the war against Nazi Germany, they demanded in September that Hashim Khan (who had proclaimed Afghanistan's neutrality) banish all citizens of the Axis powers, with the exception of a minimal diplomatic service. Hashim knew he had little alternative, for in July the two allies had insisted that neutral Iran expel all Germans to secure the railway that crossed through the oil fields and Persia. When Reza Shah Pahlavi refused, Soviet and British troops invaded on 25 August, forcing the shah into exile. They occupied the country until the end of the war. In November, a *loya jirga* – a national gathering of tribal leaders and dignitaries – sanctioned the expulsion of German, Italian and Japanese citizens.[141] When Hashim Khan fell ill, his brother **Shah Mahmud Khan** (in office 1946–53) replaced him. While he shepherded Afghanistan into the UN in November 1946, he also faced the collapse of the country's historical rival British India in 1947 and the emergence of a new neighbour, Pakistan. Although Britain was among the victors of World War II, it was the real loser over the medium term: both its colonial empire and naval superiority deteriorated and Britain was relegated to a second-rate power. The descent took place not only as a result of the industrial and population-based superiority of the United States and the Soviet Union, both of which were essentially anti-colonial. The new military transport systems of missiles and aircraft, especially of the extremely expensive aircraft carriers, furthermore represented a new, strategically superior paradigm of power enforcement that had global reach.

The partitioning of India took place on 15 August 1947, wherein individual regions and principalities could vote on their future nationality. Premier Mahmud Khan, who declared the Durand Line obsolete with the departure of the British, demanded that the Pashtuns living in the NWFP should be given the choice to opt for a reunion with Afghanistan. But this was rejected by the Election Commission and the NWFP was assigned to Pakistan. Three conflicting positions now emerged that were partly responsible

for the wars in Afghanistan from 1979. First, Afghanistan pushed for a reunification with the Pashtuns living to the east of the Durand Line, which unsettled the Afghan Uzbeks and Tajiks; second, a movement developed among the Pashtuns, which sought an independent state, Pashtunistan; and, third, both scenarios were a threat to Pakistan as its military sought a strategic depth in Afghanistan in the event of war with India. In August 1949, Afridi-Pashtuns proclaimed the Pashtunistan state, which Afghanistan recognised. Fighting subsequently broke out between Afghan and Pakistani border troops. Even worse, Pakistan closed its borders, so that the landlocked country of Afghanistan could no longer import fuel and weapons, or even essential goods.[142] Facing this predicament, the ruling Musahiban family decided to transfer power to the younger **Mohammed Daoud Khan** (1909–78, in office 1953–63); King Zahir remained merely a figurehead.[143]

Even the neutral Afghanistan could not avoid getting caught up in the Cold War (1947–91), which was no longer limited to Europe. Following Stalin's death in 1953, it also spilled over into Asia, Latin America and Africa. The Soviet-American rivalry revived the 'Great Game' once again, this time with global dimensions. And Afghanistan (along with Korea, Vietnam, Cuba, Angola and the Middle East) became one of the main theatres. Daoud first approached the United States with a request for economic and military aid. But the Eisenhower administration only supported states that could be integrated into their anti-Soviet strategy, and, since the end of 1949, it had taken the side of its ally Pakistan in the matter of Pashtunistan. Afghanistan's enmity toward Pakistan also shut it out of the Western-oriented CENTO security pact.[144] After the United States turned him down, Daoud saw no alternative but to conclude a comprehensive agreement with the Soviet Union in January 1955. For Khrushchev, Afghanistan offered the chance to get a foothold in the developing world, to forge a Moscow-Kabul-New Delhi axis, and to attempt taking a step towards the Indian Ocean. Daoud was the first Afghan statesman to disregard the political testament Abdur Rahman uttered on his deathbed in 1901: 'Never trust the Russians.'[145] Daoud's agreement with Russia from 1955 and his obstinate struggle to annex Pashtunistan led to his assassination in 1978 and drove Afghanistan into the intractable civil war that exists to this day.

As a result of Soviet aid, numerous infrastructure projects were implemented, including the expressway leading over the Hindu Kush via the Salang Pass, which the Soviets used to invade the country at the end of 1979. The army was reorganised according to Russian principles, with Russian as a technical military language, and Afghanistan received Soviet weapons, tanks, aircraft and crew at favourable credit terms. The Soviet Union also financed 60 per cent of the incurred costs in the Five-Year Plan from 1956–60. Thousands of officers, civilian specialists and students were trained in the USSR, from where they were easily recruited by the KGB, the secret services and the GRU, the foreign military intelligence agency. The network of agents overseen by the Soviet embassy in Kabul rapidly infiltrated the army, administration and ministries, media and universities. During this time, known Afghan communists were recruited – such as Nur Mohammad Taraki, Hafizullah Amin and Babrak Karmal – who led Afghanistan into the abyss in 1978. Taraki, who had actually been recruited as early as 1951, was like Amin a Ghilzai, whose tribe had lost power to the Durrani in 1738. In 1956, he founded a Marxist group called Khalq ('mass'), whose members were rural Pashtun teachers, students, and civil servants. Amin joined with Taraki. In 1960, the KGB agent Karmal founded a second Marxist group, Parcham ('flag'), whose members were often urban Tajiks.[146] When Daoud attacked the Bajaur region located north of Peshawar in 1960 and again in 1961, Pakistan inflicted heavy losses on the Afghans and sealed off the border. Although Moscow established an air bridge to sustain the Afghan economy, the country suffered enormous damage from the Pakistani blockade. The threat of war loomed, but the Soviet Union was preoccupied with the Cuban missile crisis and wanted to avoid a second confrontation with the US. In March 1963, King Zahir forced Daoud, who had manoeuvred Afghanistan into a dead end, to step down and assumed power himself.[147]

King Zahir (r. 1963–73) pursued the half-hearted strategy of a regulated democratisation of politics and a liberalisation of economy and society. He normalised relations with Pakistan and renounced interfering in the Indo-Pakistani War of 1965 that ended with an Indian victory and the collapse of CENTO, as the US did not rush to Pakistan's aid. In the next Indo-Pakistani War of 1971, Afghanistan also took a neutral position. In 1964, a new constitution went into force which cemented the king's autocratic rule, but barred other family members from taking power, including Daoud. However, as the weak Zahir refused to allow liberal political parties, the parliament continued to be dominated by tribal leaders and religious traditionalists, and, almost inexcusably, he neglected to found his own national political and identity-forming movement. The opposition had no choice but to go underground. It was dominated by two groups: the communists and militant Islamists. The Soviet Union took advantage of the relative political liberalisation. On 1 January 1965, it founded the communist People's Democratic Party of Afghanistan (PDPA), with Taraki as secretary general and Karmal as his deputy. For personal, ethnic and ideological reasons, however,

the leaders of the two factions, Khalq and Parcham, could not bear each other. There was a rupture in 1967. Parcham's followers continued to recruit from within the urban elite; Khalq increasingly strove to attract Pashtun officers.[148] The politically active Islamists rejected the higher clergy's willingness to compromise. In political Islam (e.g. as represented by the Muslim Brotherhood),[149] they saw a revolutionary force that would protect Afghanistan against the 'godless communists' and reorient the country toward the strict Islamic principles of Sharia. Among these early Islamists were the main protagonists of the anti-Soviet guerrillas and the subsequent civil war, such as Burhanuddin Rabbani, Abdurassul Sayyaf, Gulbuddin Hekmatyar, and – somewhat later – the Tajik Ahmad Shah Massoud.[150] In light of the public political stagnation, Daoud found it easy from 1966 to initiate contact with discontented officers and Babrak Karmal's communists. He also had no qualms about provoking unrest, which was fuelled by the famine of 1971–72 and the squandering of foreign subsidies by corrupt officials. With Moscow's approval and the help of the KGB, on 17 July 1973 the Daoud-Parcham conspiracy toppled the king, who happened to be abroad, and announced the monarchy's abolition. The next day, Daoud declared himself President of the Republic of Afghanistan (in office 1973–78).

As soon as he was in power, Daoud continued his aggressive pro-Pashtunistan policy and funded rebel secessionists in northwest Pakistan. The Pakistani prime minister, Zulfikar Ali Bhutto (1928–79, in office 1973–77), then decided to exploit for his own purposes the Islamists who were persecuted in Afghanistan and, like Hekmatyar and Rabbani, had found refuge in Pakistan. He ordered the military's Inter-Services Intelligence (ISI) and Major General Nasrullah Babar, later one of the 'godfathers of the Taliban',[151] to give military training to hundreds of young Afghans. He also appointed Hekmatyar as coordinator with the ISI. In the summer of 1975, Babar sent the trained fighters into Afghanistan to instigate local rebellions. Here, Shah Massoud especially distinguished himself in the Panjir Valley, north of Kabul.[152] The uprisings failed due to a lack of broad support, yet out of fear that Pakistan could provide even more support to the Islamists, Daoud ended his hostile policy towards Pakistan.[153] While the first Pakistani-Soviet proxy war was concluded in 1975, the main players in the imminent 'Great Game' of the second half of the twentieth century had now taken positions: on the one hand, there was the southward advancing Soviet Union; on the other, Pakistan with the United States as an ally. Saudi Arabia joined the latter beginning in 1978. But Daoud sought to free himself from Soviet encirclement. He thus purged the ministries of Parcham members and strove for a rapprochement with the oil-rich Gulf

124. The Buddhist Amarbayas Galant monastery, 'Monastery of Tranquil Felicity', was built on the orders of Emperor Yongzheng from 1727–37 in honour of the Mongolian monk and artist Zanabazar. Amarbayas Galant is one of the few monasteries in Mongolia to have been more or less spared the systematic destruction of the 1930s. Reconstruction began in 1988. Photo: 2001.

States, Iran, Egypt, and the technologically superior United States. Although Daoud had drawn closer to Pakistan, the US remained indifferent. Daoud's contacts with Anwar al-Sadat, however, aroused the ire of the Soviet leadership. Since July 1972, the Egyptian president had been considered a traitor for having expelled Soviet military advisers.

The division was highlighted by a personal quarrel that developed between Brezhnev and Daoud in the Kremlin in April 1977. Brezhnev complained vehemently about the use of Western experts in northern Afghanistan, prompting Daoud to answer coolly in the presence of President Podgorny and prime minister Kosygin: 'We will never allow you to dictate how to run our country and whom to employ in Afghanistan. […] Afghanistan shall remain poor, if necessary, but free in its acts and decisions.'[154] With these words, Daoud summed up the unbowed self-determination of the Afghan tribesmen. At the same time, however, he sealed his own fate. Moscow forced the warring Khalq and Parcham factions to cooperate in the PDPA, once again with Taraki as secretary general and Karmal as his deputy. Hafizullah Amin, who had infiltrated the officer corps, was commissioned to organise the coup, which was scheduled for August 1978. When Daoud had Taraki and Karmal arrested for inciting rebellion on 26 April, Amin, who was only under house arrest, triggered the coup ahead of schedule on 27 April and without consulting with Moscow. It ended the next morning with the shooting of President Daoud and almost his entire family. The rebels quickly asserted themselves: on 1 May, they proclaimed the

Democratic Republic of Afghanistan, with Taraki as chairman of the Revolutionary Council and as prime minister. Karmal, Amin and Major Aslam Watanjar, who had led the tank convoy that attacked the palace, were further appointed as deputy prime ministers. Moscow immediately promised generous economic and military aid.

In retrospect, Daoud, who wanted to modernise Afghanistan and take a neutral path, foundered because of foreign policy misjudgements and an erratic domestic policy. His Pashtunistan policy had devastating consequences. It was not only futile in the face of power relations between Afghanistan and Pakistan, but Afghanistan also made an enemy of its neighbour, which was the only transit country for the import and export of Afghan goods. Due to its lack of infrastructure in its east, Iran was not a logistical alternative. In addition, tensions with Pakistan undermined the possibility of a rapprochement with the US, an ally of Pakistan. Domestically, the king's removal denied Afghanistan a potent national symbol. By the same token, a new identity-forming ideology was also missing that would have embraced the

conservative rural areas. Daoud thereafter underestimated the communists, particularly their ability to infiltrate the administration, military and intelligence agencies. Thus, he gradually lost control over all three. Finally, Daoud proved to be inept and reckless in his rapprochement with the West, especially with Sadat: Sadat was able to free himself from the grip of the Soviets, because he enjoyed the full support of the United States. Egypt was also at a far remove from the Soviet Union. Conversely, the US ignored Daoud's solicitations, while the Soviet Union was essentially in Afghanistan's backyard. At the same time, the Soviets could rejoice, since the establishment of a socialist Afghanistan seemed to extend their sphere of influence across the Hindu Kush. That said, they soon learned otherwise: even though the PDPA controlled Kabul and the army, the hill country had never been exclusively controlled by the central government. On top of this, the Afghan communists proved to be insubordinate, and, in the end, Islam formed the sole beacon around which all the opponents of centralism and foreign intervention would soon converge.

125. The centrally located Sükhbaatar Square in Ulaan Baatar, Mongolia. In the foreground, an equestrian monument in honour of General Sükhbaatar, and in the background, the Blue Sky Tower Hotel built from 2006–11. Photo: 2012.

4. Mongolia as a Pawn of Major Regional Powers

As of the Oath of Dolon Nor of 1691, Mongolia was no longer a political entity.[155] The partitioning of Inner Mongolia into 49 banners and Outer Mongolia into 34, and later 86 banners, resulted in the allocation of the respective territory and population to a specific prince. This so-called 'hoshun' was, in turn, subordinated to the Manchurian administration. Many of the hoshun were highly indebted to Chinese lenders and usurers. Nevertheless, since they were by and large able to freely dispose of the goods within their banner, they pledged them to their creditors who, in this way, were able to establish a monopoly over Mongolian trade and finance in the nineteenth century. The Buddhist church also contributed greatly to the rapid impoverishment of Outer Mongolia. Its clergy was divided into three classes: the very small elite of high-ranking reincarnations, the Khutukhtu; the educated monastery administrators; and the great mass of ordinary lamas, who were little more than temple servants. The economic foundation of the monasteries relied not only on parcels of lands, herds, and donations accumulated through ornate ceremonies, but also on serfs. The church numbered about 113,000 monks, representing 16 per cent of the total population of around 700,000 or one-third of the male population. The majority of ordinary monks probably did not live in the monastery, but with their families. What is more, because the command of celibacy among the Gelugpas was consistently flouted, the monks, especially the itinerant lamas, were mostly responsible for the then rampant venereal diseases. Due to the near-hermetic isolation of Mongolian society, the lack of educational facilities, and the ideological stranglehold of the Buddhist clergy, the Mongols persisted in a state of superstition, ignorance and passive resignation to their fate.[156] Just the same, when the Chinese amban Sando introduced a policy of brisk assimilation in 1910, the highest nobility started to resist. With the consent of the Eighth Jebtsundamba Khutukhtu (1870–1924), they turned to the tsar for help in July 1911. Russia's sole interest, though, was in having a Mongolian buffer zone to China and to the Japanese to secure the narrow Baikal Corridor east of Irkutsk. From Tsar Nicholas to Stalin, the fear prevailed that Japanese troops stationed in Manchuria could cross Mongolia to cut off the Trans-Siberian Railway and isolate Vladivostok from West Russia. Annexing Outer Mongolia was out of the question.[157]

But when the Chinese Revolution erupted on 10 October 1911, the amban's authority also disintegrated in Urga, today's Ulaan Baatar.[158] And on 1 December, the Provisional Government of the Khalkha proclaimed Outer Mongolia's independence. Soon thereafter, on 29 December 1911, a government was formed with five ministries and the Tibetan-born Eighth Khutukhtu Bogd Khan ('holy ruler') was enthroned as head of state.[159] Mongolia was nominally a theocracy, but in fact it was dominated by a few nationalist princes and clerics, whose sphere of influence was limited to eastern Mongolia. Still, the declaration of independence was inherently pan-Mongolian and directed at the Mongols in the west and Inner Mongolia alike. In the west, the Chinese troops stationed in the administrative capital of Uliasutai surrendered without a fight, whereas those in Khobdo (Khovd) capitulated in August 1912 only after a violent struggle. Here, the Kalmyk commander Dambijantsan, referred to as Ja Lama, distinguished himself by his extraordinary cruelty: he saturated the flags of his troops with blood from hearts torn from still-living bodies. The control of the government in Urga over the west remained nominal; the actual rulers were the warlords Dambijantsan, Damdinsuren and Magsarjav. In February 1914, Russian troops arrested Dambijantsan and, in April, occupied the neighbouring province of Uriankhai (today's Tuva region), which they immediately declared a Russian protectorate.[160] But the government in Urga failed to gain international recognition for their independence – with the exception of the controversial Treaty of Friendship and Alliance between the government of Mongolia and Tibet of 11 January 1913.[161]

Neither China nor Russia would accept an independent Mongolia, which could serve as a springboard for Japan to Buryatia and Central Asia. Since securing the Baikal Corridor was a top priority for Russia, it signed a secret treaty with Japan on 8 July 1912 that allocated Outer Mongolia to the Russian and Inner Mongolia to the Japanese zone of influence. This, accordingly, obstructed the realisation of any pan-Mongolian ambitions.[162] Then, Russia and China agreed on 18 November 1913 that Inner Mongolia belonged fully to China and Outer Mongolia could remain politically autonomous domestically, but would stand under Chinese sovereignty.[163] Finally, in the Treaty of Kyakhta of 7 June 1915, Russia forced Mongolia to recognise the Sino-Russian agreement from 1913: China and Mongolia ended all hostilities; Mongolia recognised Chinese suzerainty, and, in return, Russia and China guaranteed Mongolia's autonomy in its internal affairs. Relations with foreign powers, however, were prohibited. Moreover, China could send an amban to the cities of Urga, Uliasutai, Khobdo, Kyakhta and to Uriankhai, while Russia was allowed to station a Cossack guard in Urga.[164] This ended, once and for all, not only the dream of a unified state of all Mongols, but also the genuine self-determination of Outer Mongolia. In Urga, however, the government failed to take advantage of the existing room to manoeuvre internally to enact urgently needed reforms in financial and tax matters, infrastructure, education and health. Even worse, the supreme clergy unscrupulously enriched themselves and had reformist nobles and officials killed. The collapse in 1917 of Russia, the guarantor of Mongolian independence, cleared the way for China to rescind the region's autonomy. The infiltration of Chinese troops began in 1918, and, in the autumn of 1919, the Chinese resident Chen Yi seduced disaffected aristocrats to agree to the nullification of Mongolian self-rule. He also convinced them to consent to the deployment of Chinese troops under the leadership of the pro-Japanese warlord Xu Shuzheng in the face of an impending invasion by the White warlord Grigory Semyonov. Xu seized power and on 17 November forced the government to revoke its own autonomy, which was confirmed in a humiliating ceremony on 20 February 1920.[165] The attempt to establish Mongolia as at least an autonomous state had fallen through, and the region had been reduced to a veritable plaything of foreign powers.

When Xu returned to China, Chen Yi relieved him and launched a comprehensive assimilation programme. This elicited the impotent fury of the nobility, clergy, and the Khutukhtu. At the same time, the Russian Civil War approached the borders of Mongolia. By the beginning of 1920, the Bolsheviks had brought Western Siberia under their control. It was only a matter of time until they succeeded in expelling the White warlord Semyonov from Transbaikalia and his ally Roman von Ungern-Sternberg (1886–1921) from Chita in southern Transbaikalia. Semyonov eluded the Bolsheviks by going eastward. Ungern, however, invaded Mongolia in mid-August 1920 with his small cavalry, which included, among others, 60 Japanese officers.[166] Mongolia thus became entangled in the Russian Civil War. Lenin was not willing to tolerate a pro-monarchist army, backed by Japan, which not only took refuge in a neighbouring state, but was also a potential threat to the Baikal Corridor.[167] A few weeks earlier, on 25 June, agents of the Communist International (Comintern) facilitated the merger of two groups of anti-Chinese nationalists into the Mongolian People's Party (MVP). Even then and until the early 1930s, the People's Party was very heterogeneous: its members were not only officers, officials, and revolutionaries, but also nationalists, nobles, and monks – albeit not workers, as there was no proletariat in Mongolia at the time. The goals of the party were liberation from the Chinese occupiers and the protection of religion and state.[168] The party then sent a delegation to the Soviet Union, to which Damdin Sükhbaatar (1893–1923; fig. 125) and the later dictator Khorloogiin Choibalsan (1895–1952) belonged.

Meanwhile, in the autumn of 1920, Ungern besieged Urga – at first without success. But, then, on 4 February 1921, he expelled the Chinese garrison and occupied the city where he immediately had Jews, alleged Bolsheviks, and Chinese traders killed. The former tsarist officer with German-Baltic roots seized power. On 21 February 1921, he put the Khutukhtu back on the throne as a figurehead and established an arbitrary reign of terror. But Ungern's despotism was short-lived. The Mongols surrounding Sükhbaatar and Choibalsan formed an exile government in Russian Kyakhta. Sükhbaatar then crossed the border to expel the Chinese garrison from Mongolian Kyakhta with his partisans on 18 March. The Provisional Government relocated there immediately and asked the Soviet Union for military aid. In the beginning of July 1921, the Red Army occupied Urga without a fight, and on 9 July, a constitutional monarchy was established. The Khutukhtu was made head of state, Dogsomyn Bodoo prime minister, and Sükhbaatar minister of war.[169] The Soviet troops, the majority of whom consisted of Kalmyks, remained in the country until 1925, not least to prevent counter-revolutionary actions by the Chinese and Japanese. Mongolia, however, had escaped from the Chinese yoke only to be made a protectorate of the Soviet Union. Establishing contact independently with other states remained prohibited. This hybrid state – characterised by a binding link to the Soviet Union and purely nominal Chinese suzerainty – persisted until the plebiscite of October 1945. In retrospect, Ungern did the Soviets a great service with the expulsion of the Chinese: they could then occupy Outer Mongolia and prevent Japanese advances, without having to ever confront China militarily.[170]

The short period of constitutional monarchy, which focused on the consolidation of state structures, met its demise with the death of the Khutukhtu on 20 May 1924. On 26 November 1924, the Third Party Congress decided on the state form of a People's Republic. As for the successor of the Khutukhtu, the leadership proceeded cautiously and did not abolish the institution of Buddhist reincarnations until 1929. Marking the first phase of the People's Republic from 1924 to 1928 was the New Economic Policy and a tolerant attitude towards the Buddhist church. Private companies prospered, and while trade with China dominated, it played a minor role with the Soviet Union.[171] Stalin did away with this relatively liberal policy in the winter of 1926/27, when he demanded the following changes: a purging of the heterogeneous party, especially of its nationalist and clerical elements; an uncompromising fight against the church and feudal lords and their expropriation; and a turning away from foreign states commercially and a radical collectivisation of herds. The Seventh Party Congress of 1928,

126. The Zaisan Monument, built to the south of Ulaan Baatar, commemorates the Soviet soldiers who fell in World War II. In the background, the city of Ulaan Baatar, Mongolia. Photo: 2012.

accordingly, adopted these directives.[172] Although there were neither managers of large enterprises in Mongolia nor agricultural engineers or veterinarians, the cattle breeders were expropriated and their herds collectivised; the system of transport was nationalised; and private trade was banned. The consequences were the same as in Kazakhstan: the cattle breeders living near the Chinese border fled by the tens of thousands to China, especially Xinjiang, and the nomads preferred to slaughter their animals rather than surrender them. Due to a lack of competence, at least a third of all livestock perished within three years. But when serious unrest broke out and the army had to intervene, Stalin found himself forced to stop the collectivisation campaign. Stalin's decision to relent was primarily due to the Japanese aggression against Chinese Manchuria, which Japan occupied in the winter of 1931/32 and converted into the puppet state of Manchukuo on 1 March 1932. On 29 May 1932, the Comintern ordered the reversal of the nationalisation measures and re-privatisation of the nationalised livestock. Since Stalin was infallible, overzealous Mongols were singled out as scapegoats. After the campaign of 1929–32 had eradicated the nobility, the following

campaigns from 1936 – led by Marshal Choibalsan, the 'Mongolian Stalin' – focused on the party, which was purged of nearly all senior members, the officer corps, and the Buddhist church, which was virtually eliminated by 1939. The vast majority of the 800 monasteries were destroyed and about 94,000 monks were displaced to the laity.[173] As the Soviet scholar E.M. Mursajev noted with irony, images of Stalin and Choibalsan then replaced in the nomads' yurts the Buddhist ones.[174]

Japan did not let matters rest with its establishment of the puppet state of Manchukuo. Rather, in February 1936, it established the second Japanese pseudo-state of Mengjiang in the eastern half of Inner Mongolia. It further launched a pan-Mongolian propaganda campaign with the aim of gaining a foothold both to the west, in the direction of Central Asia, and in Outer Mongolia.[175] In response to this threat, Mongolia and the Soviet Union, which had already

▶ **127.** Members of the small Tuvan ethnic group of the Tsaatan, who live mainly from reindeer husbandry. Khövsgöl Aimag, northern Mongolia. Photo: 2011.

sent troops into Mongolia in January 1935, signed a ten-year defence protocol. After a Russian-Japanese border incident in July 1938 south-west of Vladivostok, a further border war with high losses flared up from May to September 1939 along the Mongolian-Manchurian border, near the Khalkyn Gol River. Japan had provoked the conflict, which ended with a Soviet-Mongolian victory, to test the Soviets' willingness to aid Mongolia and the responsiveness of the Red Army. As a result of this defeat, Japan abandoned its expansion plans in north-east Asia. It further signed a neutrality pact with the Soviet Union on 13 April 1941 and decided not to attack the Soviets while on the side of Nazi Germany in the summer of 1941.[176]

The history of the small province of Uriankhai (Tuva) has a similar trajectory to that of Outer Mongolia. After it had been made into a Russian protectorate in 1914, a Chinese amban returned to the region in 1915. From 1917 to 1921, fighting took place in Uriankhai between Bolsheviks and several White groups, until Prince Buyan-Badrakhu founded the People's Republic of Tannu Tuva with the help of the Comintern in August 1921. The state was not officially recognised, however, except by the Soviet Union and, in 1926, by Mongolia. The leader of Tuva was the Buddhist monk Donduk Kuular (1888–1932), who sought close links with Mongolia and fought the immigration of Russian settlers. Although the small republic had only about 60,000 Tuvinians, Donduk Kuular

dared to provoke Stalin in 1926 by proclaiming Buddhism the state religion. Three years later, Stalin had him arrested and initiated a policy of herd collectivisation and cracking down on Buddhism and shamanism. In October 1944, Tuva was transformed into an autono-mous oblast of the RSFSR.[177]

At the end of World War II, Mongolia nominally still belonged to China. In the Sino-Soviet Treaty of Friendship and Alliance of 14 August, 1945, Stalin forced Chiang Kai-shek to agree to a referendum in Mongolia on the question of independence. The referendum took place on 20 October, and the Mongols entitled to vote decided almost unanimously in favour of independence, which was recognised by China on 5 January 1946.[178] Mongolia was now nominally independent, but it remained a de facto Soviet satellite. The extent to which the foreign policy of Mongolia was a function of Soviet foreign policy was exemplified in the relations with China. During the period of Soviet-Chinese cooperation from 1949–59, tens of thousands of Chinese worked in Mongolia, where there was a lack of workers. A Trans-Mongolian Railway was also constructed which connected Moscow to Beijing via Ulaan Baatar. With the onset of the Soviet-Chinese confrontation from 1960–62, Mongolia expelled the country's Chinese guest workers and closed the border with China.[179] Sino-Soviet – and as a consequence Sino-Mongolian – relations did not begin to ease until 1985 under Mikhail Gorbachev.

128. The governor-general of the province of Xinjiang, Marshal Yang Zengxin (in office 1912–28) visited Sven Hedin's expedition in Ürümqi on 18 March. Sven Hedin, *Auf grosser Fahrt. Meine Expedition mit Schweden, Deutschen und Chinesen durch die Wüste Gobi 1927–28* (Leipzig: Brockhaus, 1929), opposite p. 328. The Sven Hedin Foundation, Stockholm.

5. Xinjiang's Autonomy and the Era of Warlords, 1912–44

As in Mongolia, the Chinese Revolution of 1911 had power-political, rather than social, implications in Xinjiang. In the northern region of Ili, the young general and revolutionary Yang Zuanxu rebelled, and in the Tarim Basin, the xenophobic and anti-Manchurian secret society Gelaohui attempted to seize power through the targeted assassinations of government dignitaries. Fears were, in turn, stirred up that Russia could strengthen its Cossack guard to annex Kashgaria. In Xinjiang, therefore, there existed four centres of power: the established government in Tihua (Ürümqi); the republican revolutionaries in Ili; Gelaohui; and the Russian Consulate General. Governor **Yang Zengxin** (1867–1928, in office 1912–28), who was backed by President Yuan Shikai, won the power struggle thanks to the Dungan army of Chinese-speaking Muslims recruited by General Ma Fuxing (1864–1924) (fig. 128). Governor Yang convinced the leading rebels from Ili to form a unity government. Later, he moved them to provincial posts, where he then had them arrested and executed one by one. Afterwards, he weakened Gelaohui, and by the time World War I broke out there was no longer any reason to fear a Russian annexation of Kashgaria.[180] In 1916, Governor Yang rid himself of a group of conspirators from his immediate circle in a rather bizarre manner. First, he had the informant who tipped him off to the threat publicly executed, both to win time and to give the conspirators a false sense of security. A short time later, he invited them to a banquet, where he had three of the ringleaders who were sitting at the table beheaded. He then banished the other conspirators to southern China.[181]

At that time, Xinjiang was completely isolated due to a lack of roads and railways from Central China. Goods transport from Ürümqi to Beijing usually took 120 to 180 days. Travel was fastest from Beijing to the port of Tianjin; from there by ship to Kobe, Japan; from there to Vladivostok; then by train to Irkutsk and Novosibirsk; then with trucks to Barnaul and Kulja, Ili; and, finally, by horse to Ürümqi.[182] Despite this isolation, Governor Yang avoided proclaiming Xinjiang's independence. As the financial subsidies from the central government had failed to transpire since the revolution, he had to expand economic and trade relations with Russia, even though he was highly suspicious of his prodigious neighbour. Xinjiang's trading volume with the Soviet Union was ten times larger than with China, and the province was part of the Soviet economic sphere. Yang attached great importance to

129. Young Uyghur with a 'horn book'. 'The daily lesson of a Muslim boy at the mosque school. The verse from the Koran is written on the shoulder blade of a camel until the student knows his lesson; this verse is then rubbed out and another takes its place.'[22] Photo 1936, The Rev. Claude. L. Pickens Jr. Collection; Harvard-Yenching Library.

equality in diplomatic affairs. When the Soviet Union called for the transfer of Xinjiang's five former tsarist consulates, he successfully countered with a request to establish Chinese consulates in five cities of Soviet Central Asia administered by Ürümqi.[183]

No sooner had Yang stabilised the domestic political situation than the Russian Civil War presented him with a new challenge. Specifically, he had to prevent Xinjiang from becoming drawn into the civil war like Mongolia and Tuva. Yang demonstrated his skilfulness when the defeated White General Boris Annenkov sought protection from the Red Army, which was hard on his heels, in northern Xinjiang in May 1920. By supplying little food to the starving White Army, he forced it to divide into small groups. He subsequently invited Annenkov to Ürümqi, where he then had

130. General Ma Zhongying (1911–37?), a Dungan warlord operating in Gansu and Xinjiang from the later 1920s until 1934. Photo 1933/34: Sven Hedin, *Die Flucht des Großen Pferdes* (Leipzig: Brockhaus, 1939), frontispiece. The Sven Hedin Foundation, Stockholm.

him arrested. At the same time, he expelled the White soldiers to Dunhuang. Finally, Annenkov had to share his prison cell with a Chinese opium addict; when he, too, become addicted to opium in 1924, Yang let the enfeebled White general go. In the case of the White General Bakich, who also invaded northern Xinjiang, Yang allowed the Red Army to fight Bakich on Chinese territory.[184] As Wu Aitchen, the representative of the Chinese Guomindang Party[185] in Ürümqi reported, Yang was proud to have not surrendered a single square metre of Chinese soil. 'These things I have done not with soldiers, for I have none, but with the power of my mind and my pen. I have never troubled to create a large army, for it was clear…that my army could not possibly be bigger than those of my neighbours, and if your army is not the biggest it is safest to have no army at all.'[186]

To increase the self-sufficiency of the province, Yang invested in agriculture and irrigation canals as well as in the gold mines. Because he feared having a proletariat that might be susceptible to Soviet propaganda, he prohibited industrial plants. To prevent cash outflows to China or the Soviet Union, and also to control the flow of funds within the province, he introduced four different local paper currencies: the taels of Ürümqi, Ili, Aksu and Kashgar. He manipulated their exchange rates with each other and with foreign currencies as needed. The Sinologist and Mongolist Owen Lattimore (1900–89), who was in China in the 1920s, praised Yang insofar as he accepted the regional paper money for paying taxes, whereas other warlords rejected their own paper money and insisted instead on goods or silver: 'Every regional potentate issues paper money, the acceptance of which is enforced at the point of a bayonet, while for payment of taxes and of the government receipts only silver is accepted…In Sinkiang there is no such maintenance of blatantly false values,…the government accepts its own paper.'[187] On 7 July 1928 Yang was murdered during a banquet by an ambitious official named Fan Yaonan. But Fan's coup attempt failed because Yang's deputy **Jin Shuren** (1883–1941, in office 1928–33) successfully mobilised loyal troops. Fan was executed the next day, and Jin proclaimed himself the new governor.[188]

Governor Jin, though, lacked Yang's ability to find a balance between the interests of different ethnic groups. This was revealed, for instance, by the incidents in Kumul (Hami), where he sought rapid sinicisation. In Kumul, there was an autonomous Muslim principality, whose khan allegedly descended from Genghis Khan's son Chagatai. When Khan Maqsud Shah died in March 1930, Jin not only abolished the khanate, but he doubled the taxes on all agricultural products. He then confiscated fertile land from Turkish-speaking Muslims, transferring it to Chinese refugees from the neighbouring province of Gansu. Moreover, he granted them a three-year tax exemption. To the expropriated Uyghurs, he not only allocated uncultivated and non-irrigated land on the edge of the desert, but also insisted on the payment of taxes. When a reckless Chinese tax collector provoked riots in the beginning of April 1931, Governor Jin initiated a massacre in Kumul.[189] At the same time, the rebels who fled to the mountains under the leadership of Khoja Niyaz and Yulbars Khan called on the young Dungan warlord Ma Zhongying (1911–37?) for help (fig. 130).

Ma Zhongying was one of five related Wu Ma ('Five Ma') Dungan warlords whose power centres were in the provinces of Qinghai, Gansu and Ningxia. Even before the distress call from Hami, Ma Zhongying had already planned to attack the wealthy oasis, as he had fully plundered his former base in north-west

Gansu. According to the British missionaries Mildred Gable and Francesca French, who were living in Gansu at the time, Ma Zhongying's way of operating 'was the method of the locust and the Hun, and his army was always viewed as a plague. It came, it devoured' and then moved on.[190] Ma's small army of less than 1,000 men unsuccessfully laid siege to Kumul and made a push towards Tihua. After a victory there, Ma continued the siege of Kumul. However, when he was injured in a battle with White troops in the service of Jin, he returned to Gansu. While he recuperated, Generalissimo Chiang Kai-shek (1887–1975)[191] promoted him in early 1932 to commander of the 36th National Army. Chiang presumably wanted to create a counterweight to Governor Jin, who had unilaterally concluded a secret agreement with the Soviet Union to acquire heavy weapons.[192] Ma Zhongying subsequently dispatched his deputy Ma Shiming to the west, along with Khoja Niyaz, to occupy the Turfan Oasis. After their conquest at the end of 1932, Ma Shiming attacked Ürümqi from January until March 1933, which was defended by General Sheng Shicai (1897–1970) and a contingent of White soldiers led by Soviet officers.[193] The Soviet leadership was alarmed by rumours that Ma Zhongying was employing Japanese consultants. It consequently had 2,000 Chinese soldiers – who were fleeing from Manchuria ahead of the Japanese invaders – transported to Ürümqi, where they successfully repulsed Ma Shiming's Dungans. In April, the White mercenaries mutinied against Governor Jin, whereupon **Liu Wen Lung** (in office April–July 1933) was installed as provisional governor and Sheng as commander in chief. **Sheng Shicai** (in office 1933–44) had the upper-hand, however, and forced Liu to resign at the beginning of July (fig. 131). Since Sheng took a decidedly anti-Japanese stance, he enjoyed the confidence of Stalin, which saved him during the next Dungan attack on Ürümqi.[194] Sheng then managed to convince the two ringleaders of the Hami Revolt, Khoja Niyaz and Yulbars Khan, to cross over to the side of the government. The Muslim front was thus effectively broken up into Turkish-speaking Uyghurs and Chinese-speaking Dungans. Sheng pursued in central Xinjiang a policy of reconciliation vis-à-vis the Uyghurs – to the detriment of the Dungans, whose influence he severely constrained.[195]

Local anti-Chinese rebellions also erupted in the south-western Tarim Basin. In Khotan, in March 1933, the three Uyghur Bughra brothers and Sabit Damollah from the Committee for National Revolution (CNR) proclaimed an emirate, the **Khotan Islamic Government**, which soon expanded its sphere of influence to Yarkand and Yangi Hissar. The four founders were influenced by pan-Turkic ideas and Jadidism and sought a purely Uyghur Islamic theocracy. They were decidedly anti-Chinese and anti-communist

and hostile to the Dungans, their Chinese-speaking fellow Muslims, as well as to Christians and Hindus. Those Uyghurs who had been converted to Christianity by Swedish missionaries, and Hindu traders were either executed or forced to convert to Islam. Sheng also lost control in Kashgar: on 2 May, an alliance of anti-Chinese and anti-Dungan Uyghur nationalists and mutinous Kyrgyz mercenaries occupied the city of Old Kashgar. Then, on 3 May, the Dungan General Ma Zhancang, who belonged to Ma Zhongying's 36th National Army and had already conquered Aksu, seized New Kashgar. The military commander under Sheng, Ma Shaowu, and his troops entrenched themselves at his headquarters.[196] In Kashgar, three parties fought each other: government troops, Chinese-speaking Muslim Dungans, and Uyghur-speaking Muslim Uyghurs. Ethnic and linguistic ties were stronger than religious ones. When the Kyrgyz withdrew in early October, power fell to Sabit Damollah, who had been in Kashgar since July. Together with the nationalists

131. Governor-general Sheng Shicai governed in Xinjiang 1933–44 thanks to extensive Soviet military aid; during these years, the province, which was nominally part of China, was little more than a Soviet satellite. Photo 1935. Sir Eric Teichman, *Journey to Turkistan* (London: Hodder and Stoughton, 1937), opposite p. 104.

of Old Kashgar, he proclaimed the **Turkic-Islamic Republic of Eastern Turkestan** (TIRET) on 12 November 1933. It lasted only until 6 February 1934, however, when it was toppled by one of Ma Zhongying's Dungan armies.[197] The short-lived republic – which originally called itself the 'Republic of Uyghuristan'[198] and was not recognised by any foreign state – was not without significance. Specifically, it was the first national state structure created by the Turkic Muslims of Xinjiang which was first and foremost oriented toward ethnic-linguistic and only secondarily religious criteria.[199] The republic was clearly nationalistic and anti-Chinese, as evidenced by Damollah's written proclamation: 'The Dungans, more than the Han, are the enemy of our people. [. .] Yellow Han people have not the slightest thing to do with Eastern Turkestan.'[200]

In December 1933, Ma Zhongying attacked Ürümqi again with a 10,000-strong army. Given the enemy's superior numbers, Governor Sheng requested Soviet intervention, which was quickly granted. The Soviet leadership was concerned about the prospect of Ma Zhongying with his Japanese advisers conquering Ürümqi, and also about the creation of a nationalist-Islamic state in Kashgaria which could establish contacts with Japan and incite disaffected Muslims in Soviet Central Asia. Moreover, the oil fields of Baku would be within reach of Japanese bombers stationed in Kashgar. Stalin would not tolerate a second 'Manchukuo'. At the beginning of January 1934, two Soviet brigades advanced with tank and air support. They ousted Ma Zhongying to Korla,[201] where, on 5 March, he threatened to shoot Sven Hedin if he did not immediately make his car and four trucks, including drivers, available for his escape to Aksu.[202] In April Ma Zhongying reached Kashgar, which his vanguard had occupied on 6 February. Given the hopelessness of his situation militarily, he sent his soldiers to Khotan. After negotiations with the Soviet consul, he went into Soviet exile, where he disappeared around 1937.[203] It appears that Stalin initially kept him as a pawn in order to put Sheng under pressure. Sheng stated: 'It was thought Stalin was keeping Ma as a check upon my own power.'[204] Sheng's troops soon arrived in Kashgar. Nonetheless, in Khotan the military dictatorship of Ma Zhongying's half-brother Ma Hushan was able to survive until 1937.[205] When riots broke out again in Kashgar in the summer of 1937 and Ma Hushan wanted to extend his sphere of influence there, Soviet troops intervened and put down the rebellion. Ma Hushan thus fled to India.[206] The Soviet troops did not return to the Soviet Union, however, but remained stationed in Hami to fend off attacks from Japan or from other Dungan warlords. In exchange for military aid, Stalin secured access to valuable minerals such as gold, tungsten, tin, uranium and manganese, as well as petroleum near Wusu, north of the Tian Shan mountain

range.[207] Xinjiang had thus become a Soviet protectorate whose economy and raw materials were in the service of the Soviet Union. Sheng, though, had no alternative, because his nominal commander, Generalissimo Chiang Kai-shek, was unable to assist him militarily. Domestically, Sheng turned away from the Guomindang concept of the 'Five Peoples of China' (Han, Mongolian, Manchu, Hui, and Tibetan), and recognised 14 ethnic groups in Xinjiang. In doing so, he anticipated Mao's concept of the 56 ethnic groups of China.[208]

Sheng learned just how much he depended on the Soviet Union during his visit to Moscow in 1938, when he asked Stalin for permission to become a member of the Chinese Communist Party after reaching out to Mao Zedong in 1937. Stalin, however, forced him to become a member of the Soviet Communist Party, where he was subject to strict party discipline and, from a Chinese standpoint, was a traitor. Two years later, Stalin compelled him to sign the humiliating 'Tin Mine Agreement' of 26 November 1940, which granted the Soviet Union exclusive mining rights in the tin mines of Xinjiang and far-reaching extraterritorial rights, including an independent Soviet police force.[209] Incensed by Stalin's blackmail, and in light of the rapidly shrinking Soviet financial assistance after the attack from Nazi Germany, Sheng took up relations with Chiang Kai-shek. On 5 October 1942, he turned the tables in spectacular fashion, executing Mao Zedong's brother Mao Zemin, who served as vice finance minister in Xinjiang, and subordinating himself to the Guomindang government. He further banished the Soviets stationed in Xinjiang, hoping that he would also be able to escape his creditor, Russia. Sheng was mistaken, however: the Soviet Union managed to turn the tide of the war in the winter of 1942–43 at Stalingrad, and soon Chiang Kai-shek mobilised large contingents of troops to Xinjiang, making Sheng's dismissal imminent. In the summer of 1944, Sheng desperately tried to switch sides yet again and offered Stalin the opportunity to annex Xinjiang to the Soviet Union. Stalin, though, did not deign to respond to Sheng. Instead, he forwarded the letter to Chiang Kai-shek, who then ordered Sheng to Chungking, China's provisional capital, on 29 August. The era of Xinjiang's autonomy was over.[210]

With Sheng's removal and the appointment of Governor **Wu Zhongxin** (in office 1944–46), the central government took control over Xinjiang for the first time since October 1911. That said, tranquillity did not return to the province. The deployment of 100,000 troops triggered a food crisis and hyperinflation, so that the government no longer accepted its own paper money to settle tax claims and other accounts. It also collected property tax up to 90 years in advance. A deliberately promoted immigration of Han Chinese to Xinjiang for the sake of sinicising the province exacerbated the economic problems. It also aroused the anger of the Uyghurs and Kazakhs, which opened the door for the Soviet Union to once again get a foothold in Xinjiang.[211] In the autumn, two Soviet-sponsored rebellions broke out – one was carried out by Kazakhs living near the Mongolian border; the other, larger one was carried out by Taranchis of Ili. On 15 November 1944, the latter proclaimed the second **Eastern Turkestan Republic** (ETR), which existed de facto until October 1949. The decision to set up a Soviet puppet state in northern Xinjiang had already been taken by the Soviet Politburo, on 4 May 1943.[212] The rebels, in whose ranks

132. Monument in Khotan, Xinjiang. Mao Zedong welcomes a Uyghur farmer to demonstrate the friendship between the Uyghurs and the communist Han Chinese. Photo: 2009.

Soviet officers and soldiers fought out of uniform,[213] achieved rapid territorial gains. This prompted the central government to send General Zhang Zhizong to Xinjiang as a mediator. Since Stalin had concluded a favourable agreement for the Soviet Union with Chiang in August 1945, and the valuable mineral and oil deposits were already controlled by the Eastern Turkestan Republic, Stalin was willing to compromise regarding Xinjiang. When the rebels won a major victory in early September owing to Soviet air support and threatened Ürümqi, he forced them to agree to a ceasefire and, in July 1946, to participate in a unity government under the new governor **Zhang Zhizong** (in office 1946–47).[214]

Officially, Ürümqi assumed control again of the Eastern Turkestan Republic, yet the rebel army remained as a separate entity. Xinjiang was thus divided into two parts: the governing Guomindang party ruled the centre and the south, while the Soviet Union under the guise of the Eastern Turkestan Republic ruled in the north.[215] The reform-minded Governor Zhang, however, was soon stymied by the clashes between Uyghur extremists and intransigent representatives of the central government and resigned in May 1947. His successor was the Uyghur **Masud Sabri** (in office 1947–49). Although he was indigenous, both the conservative Uyghurs in the south and the pro-Soviet Uyghurs in the north rejected Masud Sabri. The unity government collapsed in the autumn, and Sabri was replaced in January 1949 by **Burhan Shähidi** (in office in 1949, for the PRC 1949–55). When communist troops crossed Gansu in the summer of 1949 in the direction of Xinjiang, the Soviet Consul General advised the pro-government commander General Tao to declare Xinjiang's independence. He further promised that Moscow would force Mao to stop his advance to Ürümqi. General Tao, though, surrendered without a fight on 25 September and Governor Shähidi followed suit the next day. Shähidi was then confirmed by Mao, who proclaimed the People's Republic of China (PRC) on 1 October, as government chairman. The problem of a pro-Soviet Eastern Turkestan Republic had already been 'resolved' earlier: Mao had invited its five leading exponents to Beijing, but their plane crashed in Soviet airspace on 27 August. The death of the five Uyghurs was equally auspicious for Mao and Stalin.[216]

The real power, however, lay not with Shähidi but with General Wang Zhen, who reformed Xinjiang according to communist principles. In the course of land reform, landowners were expropriated and their property transferred to poorer farmers, before it was collectivised in stages a few years later. Then, state agricultural and industrial enterprises (bingtuan) were established, which were run by demobilised soldiers and prisoners.

Conceptually, they resembled the military colonies (tuntian) of the Han period. This development gave rise to a massive immigration of Han Chinese. These bingtuan production and construction corps formed a state within a state, as they stood under the authority of neither the respective district authority nor the provincial government, but directly under the army or party leadership in Beijing. At the same time, without Islam being attacked head-on, the Islamic institutions were deprived of their privileges. In 1955, the People's Republic defined its minority policy. While the Soviet Union had chosen the model of a federal union of republics, China opted for the concept of national minorities: they enjoyed a limited amount of autonomy within a specific region, but were subject to the supervision of the Communist Party. All autonomous regions remained an essential part of the People's Republic. The **Uyghur Autonomous Region** was founded on 1 October 1955. It also included thirteen autonomous regions allocated to the thirteen non-Uyghur minorities. **Saifuddin Azizi** (in office 1955–67, 1972–78) was appointed the new government chairman, but the real power resided with party chief and Lieutenant General **Wang Enmao** (in office 1952–68, 1981–85).[217]

The period from 1957 until Mao's death and the fall of the Gang of Four in 1976 was characterised in Xinjiang, as in most provinces of China, by chaos and famine. After the trap Mao set for his critics called the 'Hundred Flowers Campaign' – in which he first called on disaffected citizens to criticise the party leadership and, in a second step, punished them with forced labour camps from the end of February 1957 – he invoked the 'Great Leap Forward' (1958–61). The hasty, unregulated and poorly executed promotion of heavy industry and the neglect of agriculture led to both their collapse and famine, which claimed up to 45 million lives. Although people died by the thousands from starvation in Xinjiang as well, about 2.5 million Han Chinese fled there from 1957 to 1962. This increased the total population from 4.9 million (1953) to approximately 7.5 million – not counting the PLA soldiers. At the same time, 100,000 to 200,000

Kazakhs, whose herds had been confiscated, fled to the Soviet Union. The 'Cultural Revolution' that Mao instigated in 1966 to regain power plunged China into chaos once again and caused civil-war-like conditions. As a result, another 2 million Han Chinese fled to Xinjiang or were sent to labour camps there. As in Tibet, the Red Guards (with Mao's blessing) rampaged against religious places of worship, and mosques were either torn down or converted into pigsties. In Xinjiang, however, not only did bands of Red Guards war against each other, but so did factions of the People's Army. In 1967, Wang Enmao even threatened to occupy the nuclear test site at Lop Nor, if Mao did not allow public order to be restored. This is exactly what happened in the summer of 1968. Wang was dismissed as a 'pawn', then rehabilitated in 1975, and, finally, reinstated in 1981 by Deng Xiaoping as party chief of Xinjiang.[218] The demographics, however, had changed drastically over the first 30 years of communist rule, to the disadvantage of the Uyghurs. Between 1953 and 1982, the total population increased from 4.9 million to 13.1 million and that of the Han people (without PLA soldiers) from 299,000 to just under 5.3 million. While the population of the Uyghurs rose from 3.6 million to 6 million, it decreased proportionally from 73.5 per cent to 45.8 per cent. Factoring in the nearly 3 million Han Chinese migrant workers, the Uyghurs became a minority within their own region.[219]

VII

A Multilateral Great Game in Afghanistan, 1978–92

'First we were invaded by our enemies [the Soviet Union], now we are invaded by our friends [Pakistan].'

Afghan army general **RAHMATULLAH SAFI**[1]

1. External Actors and Divergent Objectives

The communist coup on 27 April 1978 turned Afghanistan into a field of operations for three proxy wars (1978/79–92, 1992–2001, and since 2001) with six major external actors. All of these conflicts were at the same time civil wars. In contrast to the concluded international conflicts in Korea and Vietnam, the one in Afghanistan has continued for nearly 40 years. The complexity of the conflict is due not least to the fact that some actors, such as Pakistan and Saudi Arabia, are still pursuing to this day a dual strategy with different, even contradictory, objectives.

In line with the Brezhnev Doctrine – according to which the Soviet Union has the right to intervene in a socialist state whenever socialism is endangered – the **Soviet Union** wanted to ensure that Afghanistan remained socialist. It also aimed to safeguard the ground it had gained in the direction of the Indian Ocean. In the

late autumn of 1979, however, the Politburo seems to have underestimated the resolve of the United States in responding to the Soviet invasion of Afghanistan. President Carter (in office 1977–81) began to support the resistance fighters via Pakistan, and President Reagan (in office 1981–89) not only expanded on this aid, but accelerated the arms race. In doing so, he followed a strategy paper of the CIA of April 1981, which argued that by intensifying the arms race, the US would put the Soviet Union under pressure since it would overstrain its economy.[2] In fact, the acute economic problems forced Gorbachev (in office 1985–91) to withdraw from Afghanistan and to enact radical reforms, which led to the implosion of the Soviet Union. After the Taliban seized power in Kabul in 1996, Russian foreign policy tried to prevent the spread of militant Islamism to the new republics of Central Asia. It also sought to curb opium and heroin smuggling, which increased dramatically due to the close cooperation between al-Qaeda and the Islamic Movement of Uzbekistan (IMU).[3]

On the other hand, in the context of the Cold War, the **United States** wanted to undo the expansion of the Soviet sphere

133. Group of mujahideen fighters, armed with old rifles, in Kunar province. Photo: 1980.

of influence, stop the Soviet advance which threatened its ally Pakistan, and to inflict on its Soviet nemesis a 'second Vietnam'. In particular, the influential national security adviser to President Carter, Zbigniew Brzezinski, wanted to pay back the Soviet leadership for its massive support of Hanoi and to draw the Soviet Union into a 'Vietnamese quagmire'.[4] The US supported Afghan mujahideen[5] with money and weapons, whose distribution it outsourced to its supposed ally Pakistan. Pakistani President Zia ul-Haq (in office 1977–88), however, pursued a very different, hidden agenda and backed anti-American leaders like Gulbuddin Hekmatyar. Yet the United States had no choice but to depend on Pakistan to supply the mujahideen with weapons because, with the fall of the Shah of Iran on 16 January 1979 and Khomeini's seizure of power two weeks later, it had lost an important ally, Iran, which also bordered on Afghanistan.

The US failed to see that the maxim 'the enemy of my enemy is my friend' can quite well be wrong, especially when the putative friend has the long-term goal of destroying its backer. The US realised much too late that it had indirectly fostered its most dangerous rival: globally active and armed Islamism. After 11 September 2001, the once great rival powers, the United States, Russia and China, found themselves united in the struggle against a new, elusive power practising asymmetric warfare, Islamic extremism – a power which the Saudi-US-Pakistani alliance had cultivated. Islamic extremism is also a byproduct of the Cold War insofar as what the US viewed as an antidote against Marxism later turned on its sponsors. This new great power is a network of ideologies and sympathisers not bound to state borders who share entirely different values from those of the established major powers. Militant Islamism, which also engages in terrorism against civilian populations, epitomises the modern 'inversion of all values'.

Ostensibly, **Pakistan**'s government sought to finally exorcise the latent danger of a Pashtunistan, and with the advance of India's ally, the Soviet Union, it felt pressured on two fronts. President Zia, the army leadership, and intelligence service, however, secretly envisioned installing the radical Islamist Hekmatyar in Kabul to create a Pakistan-led Pakistani-Afghan confederation.[6] Over the medium term, Zia ul-Haq sought to extend jihad to the Soviet Central Asian republics. After Zia's death in 1988 and the Soviet withdrawal in 1989, the military elite and the secret service Inter-Services Intelligence (ISI) broadened Zia's vision. They now not only aimed at a confederation of Central Asian communities, but the creation of a nuclear, Islamic power, led by Pakistan, that could go toe to toe with India as a regional power.[7] This vision was diametrically opposed to US interests, yet the Americans decided

134. Praying mujahid in Kunar province, Afghanistan. Photo: 1980.

to ignore this two-sided game and to continue to support Pakistan. Pakistan recognised only much later that the madrasahs in the north-western tribal areas, which were subsidised with state and Saudi money, had become a haven for anti-government Taliban, who were beginning to encompass the region with terror. The radical Islamists, like the Pakistanis, were thus also double dealing.

India, for its part, sought an alliance with a strong, moderate Afghanistan which was independent of Pakistan and it used the Pashtunistan issue to put pressure on Pakistan. From India's perspective, Afghanistan could never be allowed to degenerate into the hinterland of Pakistan.

Thanks to the nascent oil boom in 1973–74, the **Saudi Arabian** government funded the mujahideen, first of all, to propagate Wahhabism, the Saudi version of an archaic militant Islam.[8] Second, it wanted to get rid of dangerous extremists in the circle of Osama bin Laden and Wahhabi missionaries. The US was largely preoccupied with fighting communism and neglected Afghanistan after the Soviet withdrawal. The Saudis, on the other hand, wanted to promote the breakthrough of Wahhabism in South Asia and later in Central Asia. To be precise: where Saudi Arabia had a clear strategy in Afghanistan, the US had none. Individual members of the wealthy Saudi elite, however, shared the radical vision of the Saudi Osama bin Laden (1957–2011). Afghanistan, accordingly, was to be transformed into a strict Islamic state; used as a base for an international Salafist, al-Qaeda-coordinated jihad,[9] extending from the Hindu Kush across the Caucasus to the Maghreb; and to serve as a springboard for the seizure of power in Saudi Arabia.[10] The ultimate goal of the extremists was the establishment of a supranational, wholly Islamic state, with nuclear-power Pakistan as a close ally.

Iran ultimately pursued more modest goals, namely the protection of the Afghan Shiite Hazara, the securing of its eastern border, and the suppression of increasing opium and heroin smuggling. The leaders of the mujahideen massively expanded the cultivation of the opium poppy after the Soviet withdrawal to finance their private armies. Some of them, like Hekmatyar, ran

135. Arduous route at minus 20 degrees Celsius in the district of Kalafgan, Takhar province, northern Afghanistan. During the Soviet occupation of Afghanistan (25 Dec. 1979 to 15 Feb. 1989) the Soviets and government forces controlled at the most the cities and the national ring road, while the mujahideen were dominant in the remaining regions. Photo: January 2008.

their own laboratories for processing opium into heroin and controlled the smuggling through eastern Iran.[11]

In the end, Afghanistan's mujahideen, who fought against the communist government and went on to fight against the Soviet occupation, accepted any assistance they could get. When they had a falling out after their victory and waged war on each other, this tragic disunity opened the door for radical Islamists to gain a foothold in Afghanistan.

2. Afghanistan's Communist Regime

The Soviet-orchestrated unity government made up of members of the Khalq and Parcham factions quickly broke apart. As Khalq dominated the army elite, Taraki and Amin had little difficulty in expelling and arresting the representatives of Parcham from the government and the administration. In the process, Amin soon became the country's 'strongman'.[12] The new rulers then undertook a radical reconstruction of the Afghan economy and society in the second half of 1978 to convert the extremely conservative feudal society into a socialist one. Amin and Taraki carried out this reorganisation rapidly by decree, without however thinking of the consequences or necessary remedial measures. Three decrees, in particular, aroused the Afghans' anger: Decree 7, which was intended to be emancipatory, stipulated a minimum age for marriage and prohibited the payment of a dowry. This directly intervened in tribal customs and privacy, for it was customary to seal the arbitration of disputes between families or clans through the marriage of minors and the transfer of expensive gifts. When officials began to register girls in the villages, this awakened the fear that the authorities wanted to 'nationalise' the young women. Decree 6 wanted to provide radical relief to farmers regarding mortgage loans and high interest payments, which meant that private credit sources dried up. Finally, Decree 8 was the most controversial: it restricted the ownership of land per family to an area of 30 jarib (6 hectares), while larger plots were confiscated without compensation and distributed to landless peasants. The decree overlooked the fact that larger plots were shared by several families and that six hectares did not suffice to feed a large family. Even worse, the farmers scarcely received any loans and the land distribution policy had ignored the equally important issue of water rights. Although Soviet advisers counselled moderation, Amin tried to push through the measures by force.[13] Often, his 'land reforms' consisted merely in having landlords and wealthy farmers shot.[14]

By the autumn of 1979, the Taraki regime had executed more than 50,000 Afghans.[15] The more power that was concentrated in Amin's hands, the more pronounced his despotic 'Kalashnikov mentality' became. In the summer of 1979, he announced: 'We have 10,000 feudals. We shall destroy them, and the question will be resolved. The Afghans recognise only crude force.'[16]

Despite Soviet loans of over US$14 billion, the internal political situation remained unstable. On the one hand, a relentless struggle for power raged at the centre of government: 'Like two scorpions in a bottle, Taraki and Amin were embarked on a fight to the death.'[17] On the other hand, an uncoordinated, poorly armed resistance flared up in 24 of the 28 provinces, and in Pakistan Islamic groups recruited guerrilla fighters from among the hundreds of thousands of refugees. What is more, as the rebellion of the 17th Infantry Division in Herat on 17 March 1979 demonstrated, the army was showing signs of decay. When the helpless President Taraki asked Brezhnev for a deployment of Soviet troops, prime minister Kosygin refused to shoot at Afghans. The intelligence chief Yuri Andropov further observed that 'Afghanistan is not ready at this time to resolve all the issues it faces through socialism. The economy is backward, the Islamic religion predominates and nearly all the rural population is illiterate.'[18] While Taraki did not officially receive any Red Army soldiers, there was a clear increase in the supply of weapons. Moreover, the Kremlin sent small special units of Uzbeks and Tajiks from Central Asia, who were disguised as 'volunteers' and wore Afghan uniforms.[19] The Kremlin, however, was concerned about Amin's brutal regime. When Taraki visited Moscow in early September, Brezhnev recommended that he depose Amin as prime minister and instead include representatives of the more moderate Parcham political wing in the government. Taraki's chief of staff, Tarun, who was present and also a spy for Amin, warned Amin straightaway. When Taraki flew back to Kabul, Amin unsuccessfully ordered an air defence unit to shoot down the presidential plane. He subsequently had Taraki arrested after a wild shootout at the presidential palace in the presence of the Soviet ambassador on 14 September 1979. Amin finally had Taraki killed on 8 October.[20]

The new Chairman of the Presidium of the Revolutionary Council Amin purged the army and the administration of all Parcham followers, which resulted in thousands of executions and desertions. The government consequently quickly lost control of the rural areas to the various resistance groups. In terms of foreign policy, Amin does not seem to have learned from the fate of President Daoud, whom he ousted. Amin, likewise, made efforts to break away from dependence on Moscow and established contact

136. Abandoned anti-aircraft gun on the outskirts of Faizabad, Afghanistan. Photo: January 2008.

with Pakistan, Iran, the US and even the Islamist Hekmatyar. But he was considered a brutal and unreliable opportunist, who was rejected by the majority of Afghans. No one wanted to take Amin's side, and he possessed only a narrow power base in the army and his own tribe. The Kremlin, for its part, feared that Amin would behave like Sadat in 1972 and switch over to the US camp. Moscow faced a dilemma: either to shrug off the loss of a 'socialist sister state', which contradicted the Brezhnev Doctrine, or to intervene and set up an agreeable government in Kabul. The Soviets chose the latter. In November, the inner circle of the Politburo designated exiled Babrak Karmal as the new president. On 12 December it resolved to remove Amin by force and to install Karmal. The plan's implementation was entrusted to the 'Afghanistan Troika', which consisted of intelligence chief Andropov, defence minister Ustinov and foreign minister Gromyko.[21] Only Kosygin continued to reject the idea of an intervention. After several failed attempts to poison Amin or kill him using sharpshooters, the first Soviet troops crossed the border at Termez on 25 December 1979 and

airborne troops landed in Kabul. Amin was convinced to the very last that these Soviet troops were the military aid that he had long requested. On 27 December, however, special forces stormed the presidential palace. Although the guard put up a strong opposition, Amin was killed and Karmal was declared the new chairman the next day. Eighty thousand Red Army soldiers were stationed in Afghanistan until the end of December.[22] Still, just as Shah Shujah and the British before them simply controlled individual cities, Karmal and the Soviets dominated only urban centres, along with the Ring Road (connecting Kabul via the Salang Pass with Mazar-e Sharif, Maimana, Herat, Kandahar, Ghazni and, again, Kabul), but not the rural areas. Between 1945 and 1979, the Soviet Union intervened twice in another state militarily: in Hungary in 1956 and Czechoslovakia in 1968. For the first time, it was doing so in a Muslim country.

3. The Guerrilla War of the Islamic Mujahideen

A position paper of 26 December 1979 from National Security Adviser Brzezinski to President Carter stated: 'If the Soviets succeed in Afghanistan ... the age-long dream of Moscow to have direct access to the Indian Ocean will have been fulfilled.'[23] The United States was not willing to go along with a Soviet advance to the Indian Ocean, from where the Soviet Union could threaten the oil-exporting countries of the Arabian Peninsula. Equally unacceptable was the threat to the remaining western part of Pakistan, which India had robbed of its eastern half (today's Bangladesh) thanks to Soviet aid in 1971. Brzezinski advised arming the Afghan resistance in coordination with Pakistan and ensuring Pakistan financial and military aid. China would then also be encouraged to

help the mujahideen. All activities and propaganda campaigns were to be coordinated with Muslim states.[24] China also felt threatened by the Soviet advance and quickly began selling replicated Soviet weapons to the Pakistani secret service. The ISI then forwarded them to recognised mujahideen groups.[25] China allegedly even sent armed Uyghurs to Afghanistan to support the mujahideen.[26]

In early 1980, the Soviet Union had two final opportunities to extricate itself from the Afghan quagmire with minimal losses. The commander of the Soviet troops in Afghanistan, Marshal Sokolov, already expressed his concern in January: 'I'm afraid that the Afghan Army is going to melt away and leave us face-to-face with the guerrillas.'[27] The ailing Brezhnev shared this opinion. He wanted to arrange the withdrawal of Soviet troops, yet he allowed himself to be swayed by the Afghanistan Troika, which stressed that President Karmal was dependent upon them.[28] The Americans, who perceived the Soviet invasion as an attempt to reach the Indian

137. US President Reagan meets with Afghans from the eastern Afghan province of Logar at the White House in February 1983. They report on the massacres and torture committed by the Soviets. In clockwise order: Ronald Reagan; Gust Avrakotos (Afghan Task Force Chief for the CIA); the former judge Muhammad Omar Babarakzai; the mujahideen leader Mohammad Ghafoor Yousefzai; the villager Habib-Ur-Rehman Hashemi; the medical student from Kabul Farida Ahmadi; the villagers Mir Niamatullah and Gul Mohammad.[23] Public domain; US Federal Government.

Ocean and the Persian Gulf and thus a threat to the oil fields, proposed neutralising Afghanistan in February. Brzezinski assured the Soviet ambassador in Washington Dobrynin 'that the United States is for a neutral Afghanistan, friendly to the Soviet Union like Finland, but not another vassal like Mongolia'. A Politburo meeting on 10 April rebuffed the American proposal.[29] Nine years later, between 30,000 and 70,000 Red Army soldiers and 1.3 million Afghans were dead, another 5.5 million Afghans had fled abroad, and a further 2 million had been displaced internally. The government, though, controlled only 30 per cent of the territory.[30]

The aversion to the Soviet invaders and their puppet government quickly surmounted most of the internal Afghan tribal disputes and mobilised the majority of Afghans for armed resistance in the name of Islam. But the mujahideen, which initially entered the conflict with guns dating from the time of World War I, needed modern weapons and ammunition, as well as money to feed their families and to recruit and pay other fighters. The main financial backers were the United States and Saudi Arabia. Already on 3 July 1979, President Jimmy Carter had ordered modest financial support to the Afghan resistance fighters, which he expanded in January 1980 in 'Operation Cyclone'. Using these funds, older Soviet weapons were bought from Egyptian and Chinese stocks and shipped to Pakistan.[31] At the same time, the US and China installed two jointly operated listening posts in Xinjiang,[32] and selected Afghan fighters and Pakistani experts were trained in Scotland and in the Federal Republic of Germany.[33] The fact that Saudi Arabia quickly became the largest

contributor to the mujahideen was connected not only with its zeal to spread Wahhabism, but also with the threat to the ruling al-Saud family by radical Wahhabis like Osama bin Laden. After all, on 20 November 1979, the radical Wahhabi and supporter of the international Muslim Brotherhood, Juhaiman Muhammad al-Otaybi (1936–80), had forcibly occupied the Grand Mosque of Mecca and called for the House of Saud's ouster. The incipient guerrilla war in Afghanistan gave the Saudi government the unexpected opportunity to export the radical Wahhabi preachers and violent rebels and hundreds of Muslim Brotherhood members from Egypt, the Middle East and the Maghreb living in Saudi Arabia to Pakistan to fight on the side of the Afghan mujahideen.[34] Later on, the exporting of fanatical fighters and missionaries was carried out once again, this time to the North Caucasus and the Maghreb, where one of the most important foundations of international Islamic terrorism took hold. The Saudi money, which was intermingled with 'donations' from the Gulf States – government and private sources alike – flowed either directly to Pakistan's organisations, particularly the ISI, or to Saudi 'charities', which built hundreds of madrasahs in the Pashtun tribal areas.[35] Here, young Afghan refugees and Pakistanis were indoctrinated with the radical teachings of Wahhabism and Deobandi. The Afghan mujahideen trained in Pakistan and the non-Afghan fighters – the so-called 'Arabs', who came from the Gulf countries, Egypt, North Africa, Somalia, the Middle East, the Caucasus, Bosnia and Xinjiang – brought with them fanatical and intolerant forms of Islam unlike any that had existed before in Afghanistan.

The seven Sunni mujahideen organisations recognised by Pakistan

SUNNI MUJAHIDEEN GROUP	LEADER	ORIENTATION	COMMENT
Hezb-i Islami (Hekmatyar)	Gulbuddin Hekmatyar	Radical Islamist	Until 1994, preferred by Pakistan
Hezb-i Islami (Khalis)	Mawlawi Yunus Khalis	Radical Islamist	Fanatical anti-Shiite, friends with bin Laden
Ittehad al-Islami	Abdul Rassoul Sayaf	Radical Islamist	Pashto-Wahhabi propagandist, preferred by Saudi Arabia
Jamiat-i Islami	Burhanuddin Rabbani, Ismail Khan and Ahmed Shah Massoud	Radical Islamist	Tajik-Afghan representative of the Muslim Brotherhood
Harakat-i Inqilab-i Islami	Mawlawi Mohammad Nabi Mohammadi	Moderate nationalist	Moderate cleric
Jebh-e-Nejat-e Melli	Sibghatullah Mojaheddi	Moderate traditionalist	Naqshbandi Sufi
Mahaz-e Milli-ye Islami	Sayyid Ahmad Gailani	Moderate traditionalist	The ISI crushed the strong guerrilla organisation after 1989

138. Former Taliban fighter in Bamiyan. Photo: 2002.

The US and Saudi Arabian support for the mujahideen was not only motivated by shared interests dating back to 1945, but by their mutual aversion to communism and to Imam Khomeini, who had returned to Tehran from his Parisian exile on 1 February 1979. But while the US had no plan for a post-communist Afghanistan, the Saudis and President Zia ul-Haq had very specific objectives. Zia wanted to turn Afghanistan into a satellite of Pakistan, to get rid of the problem of an independent Pashtunistan, and to later take jihad to Central Asia. In all this, the underlying goal was to eventually make Pakistan a power of great strategic depth on a par with India. The United States provided Zia with the means he required: the Carter, as well as the Reagan, Bush senior, and Clinton administrations, along with the CIA, outsourced the US Afghanistan policy to Pakistan, delivering weapons and money, which the Pakistanis then distributed as they saw fit. President Zia insisted that there could be no contact between Afghan leaders and the CIA except in the presence of an ISI agent.[36] The ISI applied the American and Saudi funds independently and coordinated the activities of the various Sunni factions. As a result, the surrogate

in this proxy war – Pakistan – became more powerful than the sponsor – the United States.

From the dozens of Sunni groups of the mujahideen, there were seven formed by 1981 that were recognised and supported by Pakistan (see table opposite).[37]

Besides Hekmatyar's Hezb-i Islami, these parties formed the loose Islamic Alliance for the Liberation of Afghanistan.[38] Hekmatyar probably remained on the sidelines because of Pakistan's order against having an ALO (a strong umbrella organisation like the PLO). President Zia and the ISI preferred the four radical Islamist parties, which received 70 per cent of the weapons purchased with American and Saudi money, whereby Hekmatyar, who emphatically rejected the West and above all the United States, was especially favoured. Hekmatyar accepted aid from the US for twelve years only to then call for a global war against the Americans.[39] Even more surprising than Hekmatyar's double dealing was the fact that the CIA did not want to acknowledge this danger, despite numerous warnings. In addition to the seven groups that the ISI recognised, there were also standalone parties like that of the independent commander Abdul Haq, who defied the dictates of ISI and was executed by the Taliban in 2001.[40] The smaller Shiite groups financed by Iran received no support from the ISI. From 1981, Hekmatyar's Hezb-i Islami also fought against them, as well as against the Sunni Tajik Shah Massoud. Massoud then concluded a ceasefire with the Soviets that lasted until 1983.[41] The Soviet Union estimated there were 130,000 mujahideen; according to the US, there were 150,000. Still, there were never this many fighting in Afghanistan at one time. What is more, 20–25 per cent of them were non-Afghan 'Arabs'.[42] American intelligence not only neglected to appreciate just how dangerous Hekmatyar was, but it underestimated Osama bin Laden. Bin Laden was initially active as a fundraiser in Saudi Arabia; he then moved to Peshawar in 1984, where he worked closely with the head of the Saudi foreign intelligence service Turki ibn Faisal (in office 1977–2001). Around 1986, bin Laden decided to establish his own global jihadist organisation. To this end, he had artificial caves dug as ammunition depots in the Tora Bora mountains, south of Jalalabad, and expanded the cave and tunnel complex known as al-Masada ('lion's den') into a fortress. Finally, he and the Egyptian jihadist al-Zawahiri, his later successor, founded al-Qaeda al-Askariya ('military camp') at al-Masada in 1988. At the same time, he began to recruit non-Arab extremists for jihad, such as Muslim Filipinos and Burmese Rohingyas.[43] It was bin Laden who most systematically converted the fight against Afghanistan's Soviet occupiers into an anti-Western, globally operating jihad, which also did not shrink from carrying out targeted terror attacks against civilians.

In the beginning, the mujahideen were able to prevent the Soviet troops, who numbered up to 130,000 men, from conquering the rural areas and provinces. To be sure, the Soviets were able to control the strategically vital Ring Road during the day, but at night it belonged to the rebels. Both sides fought with great tenacity, and few prisoners were taken. The Soviet helicopters indiscriminately bombed villages and fired upon fleeing residents. Now and again, captured fighters were thrown out of flying helicopters. The mujahideen, in turn, retaliated by skinning alive captured Soviet

139. The Taliban also used such anti-aircraft guns to shoot at the giant Buddha statues of Bamiyan, Afghanistan. Photo: 2002.

soldiers.[44] The Soviet troops also did not receive any support from the poorly trained, undisciplined, and unmotivated Afghan army, whose soldiers deserted in droves and whose officers repeatedly betrayed to the mujahideen the Soviet operational plans.

Given the lack of progress, the Soviet leadership under the mentally and physically debilitated General Secretary Konstantin Chernenko (in office 1984–85) decided to intensify the war at the beginning of 1984 and to destroy the fighters' living environment. As the British journalist Mark Urban noted, the Soviet strategists were familiar with Mao Zedong's statement 'Guerrillas are like fish, and the people are the water in which fish swim'. They thus decided to dry up the 'fish tank' of the mujahideen. This meant driving out the rural population so that the fighters could no longer turn to it for aid.[45] Low flying Mil-Mi-24 helicopter gunships began to methodically depopulate whole regions by carpet bombing villages and herds, destroying fields and orchards, and dropping light miniature mines, which did not kill people, but nevertheless maimed them. They also used mines in the form of toys such as dolls or stuffed animals to deliberately kill children. At the same time, the Soviets steered clear of attacking the refugee camps in north-west Pakistan, as it might have discouraged rural populations from fleeing there.[46] The Soviet brutalisation of the war, which was now specifically targeted at the civilian population, was effective: the number of refugees fleeing to Pakistan and Iran rose from 750,000/100,000 in 1980 to 3.5/1.7 million in 1984.[47] The Soviet troops slowly gained the upper hand, and the resistance fighters were put on the defensive.

The unfavourable circumstances of the anti-Soviet alliance motivated the CIA and Pentagon in 1985 to supply the mujahideen with modern infrared-guided air defence missiles of the FIM-92 Stinger type, which could be fired from the shoulder. The Stinger missiles had an engagement altitude of 3,000 m and a range of 4,000 m and were intended to break the hitherto unassailable Soviet air superiority. Their success against low-flying helicopters and fighter jets was overwhelming. By mid-1988, the United States had delivered 900 Stinger missiles that were responsible for the crashing of 269 Soviet helicopters and fixed-wing aircraft, resulting in a high hit rate of 30 per cent. The Soviets were forced to adapt their combat tactics. Instead of helicopter gunships, they utilised high-flying jets for widespread bombings, which limited accuracy.[48] The success of the Stinger missiles buoyed the mujahideen, who became more confident that they could force a Soviet retreat. Conversely, the loss of helicopters and aircrafts had a devastating impact on the Soviets' morale. The question loomed among the army leadership as to whether the war was even winnable.

For the new Soviet leader Gorbachev, who wanted to modernise the economically and socially stagnant Soviet Union, the war in Afghanistan was by no means a priority. On the contrary, he decided to withdraw in October 1985. Just the same, he gave the army a year to defeat or at least weaken the resistance so that the Afghan government could then negotiate with the mujahideen from a position of strength. Concurrently, the Afghan army was to be put in a position to fight the insurgents on its own. Since the weak and discredited Babrak Karmal was unsuitable for the upcoming negotiations, Gorbachev forced him to step down in 1986 and replaced him with the head of the KHAD secret police, Mohammad Najibullah (in office 1986–92, d. 1996).[49] On 13 November 1986, the Politburo took stock of the situation and concluded that the war could not be won. Since it would drag on for many more years, it was determined that the Soviets would do well to end the combat mission as quickly as possible. In December, Gorbachev informed President Najibullah – who controlled less than 30 per cent of the remaining population in Afghanistan – about the decision.[50] The following year, the Soviet troops came under further pressure, although they were no longer carrying out offensive operations. The mujahideen received modern French infantry anti-tank missiles of the Milan type, and both the US and Pakistan refused to negotiate on the planned withdrawal.[51] In particular, President Zia refused to negotiate with Najibullah, wanting instead his ouster and the establishment of an Islamic state. The intensity of the extremists' opposition to a rapid return to normalcy in Afghanistan was especially evident when Sayyid Bahauddin Majrooh, the director of a small independent news agency, conducted a survey in 1987. In 106 of the 249 refugee camps, he asked Afghan refugees whom they would prefer as the next ruler of a liberated Afghanistan. Of the more than 2,000 responses, representing all ethnicities and 23 of the 28 provinces, 72 per cent cited King Zahir, whereas only 12.5 per cent wanted a 'pure Islamic state'. When Majrooh published the results, Hekmatyar and other extremists backed by the ISI declared that Zahir's return was out of the question. Moreover, the country's next president would have to be a leader of radical mujahideen. Majrooh was murdered on 11 February 1988, likely by Hekmatyar's camp or the ISI.[52] Three days earlier, Gorbachev unilaterally proclaimed the Soviet withdrawal. It would commence on 15 May and be completed in February 1989, given a successful conclusion by March to the Geneva Accords between the Soviet Union, Afghanistan, the United States and Pakistan (though without the mujahideen). This in fact occurred, albeit not until 14 April 1988.[53] Four months later, President Zia ul-Haq died in a mysterious plane crash, which was variously blamed on the Soviet, as well as the Afghan and Indian, intelligence services.

4. Afghanistan Loses the Peace: the So-called Afghan Civil War, 1989–92

In actual fact, the conditions were ripe for a return of peace in Afghanistan after the Soviet withdrawal. But none of the key parties who fought against the Soviets, however, was ready to negotiate with President Najibullah. Coinciding with the departure of the last Red Army troops from Afghanistan on 15 February 1989, the newly elected President George H.W. Bush (in office 1989–93) signed off on the continuation of the CIA's secret operation in Afghanistan and the financial support of the mujahideen. Before this, though, the State Department had warned about continuing to arm Islamic extremists like Hekmatyar and Jalaluddin Haqqani (a later commander of the Taliban). After the conclusion of the first Gulf War on 28 February 1991, the extremists even received from the United States Soviet T-55 and T-72 main battle tanks which had been captured in Iraq. This enabled them to carry out classic warfare.[54] In Pakistan, chief of staff Mirza Aslam Beg (in office 1988–91) and ISI director Lieutenant General Hamid Gul (in office 1987–89) continued with Zia's Afghanistan strategy of putting anti-US extremist Hekmatyar in place as a vassal of Pakistan. The civilian government, however, was not opposed to negotiations.[55] Unlike the CIA and the ISI, the State Department and the Pakistani Foreign Ministry were in favour of a negotiated settlement. On the Afghani side, Najibullah received large supplies of arms from Moscow, though no military squads, as well as generous financial assistance, which enabled him to buy the 'loyalty' of the army and of individual tribes.

In early 1989, the ISI attempted to force the hopelessly fractious mujahideen leaders to cooperate and form a provisional unity government, the Afghan Interim Government (AIG). It consisted of the leaders of the seven parties, including Hekmatyar, recognised by Pakistan in 1981. The AIG was rejected by most Afghans as a creature of the ISI and only recognised by Pakistan, Saudi Arabia, the United Arab Emirates and Malaysia. Ultimately, the AIG was just a figleaf for Hekmatyar's violent, ISI-controlled installation in the presidential palace in Kabul. As the ISI and Hekmatyar saw it, the greatest obstacle to seizing power in Kabul was not the despised Najibullah, but rather militarily strong, moderate regional leaders such as Ismail Khan in Herat and Shah Massoud in the Panjshir Valley, north of Kabul. The ISI, therefore, refused any delivery of arms to Ismail Khan and paid his commanders to defect to Hekmatyar. In July 1989, Hekmatyar murdered 30 of Massoud's commanders to keep him away from Kabul. As US

diplomat and special envoy to the mujahideen, Peter Tomsen, described it: 'Far from a vehicle for mujahideen political unity, the AIG was fomenting mujahideen disunity.' Thanks to American and Saudi financial assistance, Pakistan's intelligence service and army were able to determine, via their instrument Hekmatyar, that Afghanistan was still far from achieving peace. In this respect, at least, the ISI, Hekmatyar and Najibullah were unified against moderate leaders like Gailani or Massoud.[56] It was, in any case, the deep disunity among the most important leaders of the resistance which relegated them to a pawn of the ISI and paved the way for the Taliban in 1994.

Najibullah's regime, though, had not completely deteriorated yet. Evidence of this could be found in the failed attack on Jalalabad, which lies halfway between Peshawar and Kabul. In early March 1989, under the indirect leadership of Hamid Gul, about 10,000 of Hekmatyar's and Rasul Sayyaf's fighters and 'Arabs' attacked Jalalabad with the aim of taking Kabul and then putting Hekmatyar in power. The city was defended by Afghan troops as well as the Uzbek 53rd Division under General Abdul Rashid Dostum, a mercenary squad financed by Najibullah. When the attackers reached the suburbs, a number of government soldiers surrendered. Arab fighters under bin Laden's leadership proceeded to brutally hack them to pieces, and individual body parts were then sent to the besieged city. This atrocity encouraged the defenders to hold the city at all costs. The attackers were thus forced to retreat in July. Prime minister Benazir Bhutto subsequently dismissed General Gul, who had promised a quick victory.[57] A year later, in October 1990, the ISI and Hekmatyar undertook another attempt to overthrow Najibullah. They planned to bomb Kabul with rockets from the front lines for as long as it took to force Najibullah to surrender. At the last moment, US diplomacy managed to exert enough pressure on Pakistan to put a halt to the action, which spared Kabul a bloodbath.[58] A few days earlier, the US suspended military aid to Pakistan because Pakistan had developed nuclear weapons.[59] The case of the Afghan Wahhabi Jamil al-Rahman demonstrated the intolerance of Hekmatyar and the ISI towards independent dissidents. Al-Rahman once belonged to Hekmatyar's Hezb-i Islami and controlled an area in the valley of Kunar in eastern Afghanistan. When he declared the independence of his small emirate in January 1991, Hekmatyar and the ISI attacked him with artillery and occupied the valley. Al-Rahman was assassinated by an Egyptian member of the Muslim Brotherhood, who had hidden a gun in a hollowed-out Qur'an. The destruction of the tiny Wahhabi emirate sent a signal to the Saudis that the ISI would not accept independent policies of any foreign sponsors in Afghanistan.[60]

It was only owing to the continued Soviet military and financial assistance that President Najibullah was able to remain in power. Despite this aid, however, the pressure on his regime did not abate in the first half of 1991. In the south, the ISI and task forces of the Pakistani Special Services Group (SSG) conquered the important city of Khost east of Ghazna. And, to the north, Shah Massoud took possession of a 500-km-long border strip of the Soviet Union between Kunduz and the Wakhan.[61] Najibullah controlled only 15–20 per cent of the territory. The collapse of the Soviet Union in the autumn of 1991, however, portended the end for Najibullah. After the failed coup against Gorbachev (19–21 August 1991), the Russian leader cut off support to Afghanistan, and on 13 September,

the United States and the Soviet Union signed the 'Negative Symmetry Agreement'. Here, both sides agreed to suspend their financial and weapons aid to the mujahideen, or rather the ISI, and to the Najibullah regime by the end of the year. With the agreement, the United States and the Soviet Union, which was dissolved on 26 December 1991, abandoned the Afghanistan conflict. The agreement, though, did not bring any peace to Afghanistan. Since neither Saudi Arabia nor Pakistan were involved, it was ultimately incomplete. At the end of the Cold War, neither President Bush nor President Yeltsin of Russia was interested in Afghanistan. Pakistan continued with its military activities, endeavouring to establish Hekmatyar as a kind of proconsul in Kabul.[62]

140. Patrician mansion destroyed in the civil war of 1992–96, dating from the beginning of the twentieth century in Kabul, Afghanistan. Photo: 2002.

141. An operational battalion of Russian making in the Panjshir Valley north of Kabul, Afghanistan. Photo: 2002.

Najibullah's days were now numbered, not least because, without advance payment, Russia stopped supplying fuel for the air force or food. Financial aid was also no longer forthcoming. The president, furthermore, could not pay commanders, who were often tribal leaders, for their 'loyalty'. They thus looked elsewhere for a more powerful sponsor. Indeed, in a tribal society like Afghanistan there are no fixed loyalties, either personal or ideological – only tribal connections and respect for Islam are relevant. In December, General Dostum, whose base was located in northern Afghanistan near Sheberghan, broke away. He won Uzbek President Islom Karimov (in office 1991–2016) as a new patron, who immediately began supplying weapons, fuel and other goods. Other commanders and Najibullah's defence minister Watanjar followed Dostum's example. Najibullah had to anticipate that he would be attacked once the snow began to melt in the spring of 1992, both from the north and from the south, and that his air force – his only remaining military advantage at that point – would have to stay grounded due to a lack of fuel. When Dostum seized Mazar-e Sharif, Afghanistan's second largest city, on 17 March and publicly disavowed Najibullah, Najibullah announced the next day that he would resign in favour of a transitional government.[63] Najibullah's foreign minister Abdul Wakil promptly approached Massoud and asked him to rapidly occupy Kabul before Hekmatyar. A race to Kabul thus began between the ISI and Hekmatyar, on the one hand, and Rabbani, Massoud and Dostum, on the other. The UN desperately tried to make a neutral interim solution palatable to the parties. Rabbani, the leader of the radical Islamic party Jamiat-i Islami, categorically rejected the United Nations' efforts on 15 April: 'We will not allow foreigners from anywhere to implement their dirty plans and goals . . . We are waiting for the last strongholds of atheism and infidelity to fall.'[64] The Najibullah regime collapsed the same day, when the allied Massoud and Dostum captured Kabul's Bagram airport. Najibullah sought refuge in the UN compound in Kabul, remaining there until he was brutally murdered by the Taliban on 27 September 1996.[65] Both the victory of the mujahideen over the Soviet Union, the atheistic superpower which soon imploded after its withdrawal from Afghanistan, and the overthrow of its vassal Najibullah gave a tremendous boost to the fighting morale of the international jihadists and to the self-confidence of the Islamic world militarily. The effect of the Soviet defeat on the Islamic world is comparable to the effect that the Russian defeat in 1904/05 at the hands of Japan had on the peoples of Asia. The jihadists had humiliated one of the two secular superpowers in the mountains of Afghanistan. Now, it was time to do the same to the second. Hekmatyar announced in 1992: 'Afghanistan is the graveyard of

142. Father and daughter in the district of Kamdesh, Nuristan province in eastern Afghanistan. Photo: 1992.

the British and the Russians and in-sha'allah it will also become the graveyard of the arrogant Americans. The Afghans will rub the American pigs snout in the ground. . . . We call upon all Muslim nations and communities to rise up to the challenge of the world arrogance, the number one enemy of Islam.'[66]

The capital Kabul, which the war had almost entirely spared, stood on the verge of imminent destruction, as the warring parties were preparing for a first showdown: Massoud and Dostum occupied the city centre and the north-east, Shiite militias the western part of Kabul, and Hekmatyar the southern suburbs. Meanwhile, the ISI tried half-heartedly to compel the seven Sunni groups to form a unity government. The Peshawar Accord, signed on 24 April, was already condemned to failure from the outset because Hekmatyar's heavily armed Hezb-i Islami remained aloof. Under the agreement, Rabbani and Mojaddedi were to alternate

143. Mujahideen hasten with tanks to Kabul during the fall of President Najibullah. Photo: 1992.

as president *ad interim;* Gailani was to be foreign minister, Sayyaf interior minister, Mohammadi minister of justice, Khalis minister of education, and Rabbani also defence minister. Notably missing from this cabinet, however, were Hekmatyar and Shah Massoud – the latter of whom enjoyed considerable prestige for having never left Afghanistan during the Soviet occupation. Rabbani immediately appointed him as defence minister and Hamid Karzai of the Popalzai tribe as vice foreign minister.[67] Despite this agreement, a brutal battle for Kabul raged from 25–28 April, during which the loser Hekmatyar ruthlessly shelled the city with rockets and all parties indiscriminately looted the houses of civilians. Hekmatyar withdrew to the Logar province south of Kabul, whereupon Sayyaf's Wahhabi fighters fought with Shiite militias in murderous street battles. Most of the city was under the control of Massoud and Dostum. Nonetheless, it remained within reach of the rockets of Hekmatyar, who began indiscriminately firing on Kabul with Pakistani missiles in August.[68] The first proxy war on Afghan soil in modern times thus seamlessly transitioned into the second. Chaos spread throughout the country when several leaders of the mujahideen and their fighters switched to banditry, extorting extra taxes and setting up roadblocks, where they demanded payment for passage. Others went into the drug trade.

VIII

Afghanistan Forces the Three Major Powers to Engage in a Joint Struggle against Islamic Extremism

'I do not know the Americans well, but what I do know tells me one thing. They will want revenge, and they will not rest until they get it. The Americans will come to Afghanistan. When they do we must be prepared.'

Afghan warlord **RASHID DOSTUM** to his commanders on 12 September 2001[1]

'We may be fighting the wrong enemy in the wrong country.'

RICHARD HOLBROOKE (1941–2010), US special envoy for Afghanistan and Pakistan[2]

1. The Power Struggle of the Mujahideen, 1992–96

After the Soviet occupier and its vassal Najibullah were defeated, it was not long before the loose partnership of convenience among Afghan resistance fighters disintegrated again along ethnic divides. The Pashtuns rallied around Hekmatyar, Khalis and Sayyaf; the Tajiks around Massoud, Rabbani and Ismail Khan; the Uzbeks around Dostum's Junbesh-e Milli Islami (National Islamic Front) party; and the Shiite Hazaras around the Hezb-e Wahdat alliance. Their sponsors, respectively, were Pakistan, Saudi Arabia and the Gulf Emirates for the Pashtuns, India for the Tajiks, Uzbekistan for the Uzbeks and Iran for the Hazaras. For the Pashtuns and Pakistan, the Tajik Afghans' control of the capital was unacceptable, especially as Massoud would not allow himself to be exploited by the ISI. In the Kabul government, President Rabbani was little more than a figurehead.[3] Massoud actually maintained

power: he not only commanded his own battle-hardened army, but also took charge of the 'useful' units of the former government army. Like Hekmatyar, Massoud was not willing to share power. In February 1993, along with Sayyaf, he expelled the Hazaras from Kabul. He further made sure that General Dostum remained marginalised and did not receive any ministerial posts. The secular general personally disapproved of the fundamentalist rules of conduct that Rabbani and Massoud imposed upon Kabul's liberal citizens. The Tajik Massoud subsequently turned against his Uzbek ally Dostum. First, he undermined the general's efforts against Hekmatyar's Hezb. In a second move, he convinced Ismail Khan to help him attack towards the end of 1993 the six northern provinces under Dostum's control from the south-west and south-east.

Massoud's marginalisation of Dostum had foreseeable consequences. Dostum, indeed, changed sides, concluding a triple alliance with Hekmatyar and the Hezb-e Wahdat. Pakistan promoted the new Hekmatyar-Dostum alliance, for it hoped that

144. The troops of the victorious Northern Alliance withdraw from Kabul in 2002 and are replaced by international peacekeepers of the International Security Assistance Force ISAF. Photo: 2002.

145. Cemetery in Kabul.
Photo: 1992.

146. The Deir al-Aman Palace, the 'Palace of Peace', destroyed during the civil war of 1992–96, outside of Kabul, Afghanistan. The classical palace, designed by the German architect Walter Harten, had been commissioned by King Amanullah in 1928 as a future parliament building. Amanullah was so impressed by the architecture of the German Reichstag during his previous visit to Berlin that he wanted a parliament building in a similar style in Kabul. But Amanullah was overthrown in 1929 and the palace remained empty for a long period. In the 1970s and 1980s, the palace served as a museum and as the headquarters of the defence ministry. Photo: 2004.

a conquest of Kabul would lead to a transit road being opened from Tashkent to Islamabad through the Salang Pass. In return, Massoud enjoyed robust military assistance from India.[4] The triple alliance attacked Kabul on 1 January 1994. Dostum came from the north, Hekmatyar from the south. Nevertheless, Massoud, an outstanding strategist, managed to repel both attacks. Dostum returned to the north, while Hekmatyar continued his futile, albeit extremely destructive, rocket attacks on Kabul. The conflict between the main opponents resulted in a bloody stalemate. In Afghanistan, there was no longer any trace of national unity; the

country was ruled by ruthless warlords and smaller drug barons. The strategy of the Pakistani intelligence to install Hekmatyar as ruler of Afghanistan in Kabul had also clearly failed. At the same time, the Pakistani military leadership realised that a massive military intervention was not on the cards. Any overt action by the armed forces would have compelled the Afghan fighters to join forces against the Pakistani military. Pakistan's generals had thus taken to heart the failure of the Soviets' own incursion.

For Pakistan, the Central Asian republics' independence in 1991 gave the region, and along with it Afghanistan, even greater significance. Where Zia ul-Haq's policy on Afghanistan was primarily determined by strategic and religious-missionary vectors, prime minister Benazir Bhutto (in office 1988–90, 1993–96) and her successor Nawaz Sharif (in office 1990–93, 1997–99) also cast their eye on economic aspects. In the 1980s, trade between Pakistan and Soviet Central Asia was of relatively marginal importance, yet entirely new possibilities opened up for Pakistan from 1991. The Central Asian republics, which were no longer self-sufficient due to the cotton monoculture, were major potential export markets for Pakistani agricultural products. Islamabad, moreover, was highly interested in the import of crude oil and natural gas. The landlocked[5] exporters of fossil carbon – Turkmenistan, Kazakhstan and (to a lesser degree) Uzbekistan – sought export opportunities that were independent from the Russian pipeline network and its restrictions. The focus was on the energy-hungry and emerging countries Pakistan and India as well as access to the Indian Ocean, which would permit export to Japan and Korea, but also to Western Europe. Since the United States put massive pressure on Pakistan and Turkmenistan not to build pipelines through Iran, Afghanistan remained the only possible transit country. Turkmenistan was blocked by the US-Russia power struggle for influence in Central Asia: Russian President Yeltsin insisted that Turkmenistan sell its gas to Russia at rock bottom prices, so that it could then sell this gas to Western Europe at much higher world-market prices. A new 'Great Game of Pipelines' had thus begun in Central Asia. The initiative to build a trans-Afghan pipeline originated with the Argentinian oil company Bridas Corporation, which had promoted natural gas in Turkmenistan since 1992 and was looking for export opportunities. Two years later, Turkmenistan and Pakistan began holding talks, and, on 15 March 1995, both countries signed a memorandum of understanding to build a pipeline with the involvement of Bridas. Since the planned Turkmenistan–Afghanistan–Pakistan pipeline (TAP pipeline) would have to run through southern Afghanistan for geographical reasons, security needed to be guaranteed first and foremost. To this end, Pakistan changed its Afghanistan strategy. No longer would it support Hekmatyar, but rather the Taliban.[6]

The Taliban ('students') were an ultra-Orthodox, Sunni militia recruited from young Afghan and Pakistani Pashtuns, who had been indoctrinated at madrasahs in Pakistan's border region with Afghanistan since the early 1980s. Financed by Saudi Arabia and Gulf emirates, these madrasahs and mullahs taught the puritanical and intolerant doctrines of Wahhabism and Deobandism and prepared the Taliban for jihad. The origin of the Taliban was largely the work of their Pakistani 'godfathers', ISI Brigadier Sultan

Amir Tarrar, called 'Colonel Imam', and Colonel Faizan. In 1988, they founded the Shura (council) of Argestan south of Kandahar, which consisted of ultra-conservative Afghan and Pakistani mullah warriors. They sought to prevent the tribal aristocracy of the Durrani from being reintroduced in their stronghold of Kandahar. Five years later, the third godfather, Interior Minister Nasrullah Babar, recruited and gave militarily training to several hundred Taliban. At the same time, he relocated to Quetta Najibullah's former Khalqi defence secretary, Shahnawaz Tanai, along with hundreds of officers and soldiers of the former government army. In April 1994, a few hundred Taliban along with Arab jihadists, mullah warriors from Kandahar Province, and the soldiers of Lieutenant General Tanai then attacked the Afghan border town of Spin Boldak. The operation proved successful. Afterwards, Babar quickly expanded the new force with the enthusiastic approval of prime minister Bhutto and her coalition partner Fazlur Rahman from the very conservative Jamiat Ulema-e-Islam Party. In the autumn, the Taliban numbered 15,000 men. They were led by about 300 bearded ex-Khalqi officers (who called themselves 'mullahs') and Afghan warrior-mullahs, along with fanatical 'Arabs' and former government soldiers. They had at their disposal helicopters, tanks, artillery, and modern means of communication. Shahnawaz Tanai was head of operations.[7]

The Taliban was thus a colonialist apparatus made up of Afghans, Pakistanis, and 'Arabs' that was formed by the ISI and prime minister Bhutto[8] and funded by Saudi Arabia and the United Arab Emirates (UAE). As former Pakistani finance and prime minister Shaukat Aziz (in office 1999–2007, 2004–07) told the present author, 'we created the Taliban'.[9] Poverty and high unemployment in Afghanistan made it easier for the Taliban to quickly recruit new fighters. In early November 1994, ISI leadership sent a large truck convoy under the command of Colonel Imam to Kandahar, allegedly to deliver relief supplies to Herat. This was merely a pretext. The actual purpose was to install in Kandahar the leader of the Taliban and member of the Hotaki Ghilzai tribe, Mohammad Omar, a.k.a. Mullah Omar (ca. 1960–2013). When the convoy hit an expected roadblock, Colonel Imam called on the Taliban troops waiting in Quetta for help. The campaign of highly motivated, well-trained, and heavily armed Taliban was an unqualified success: in November, they occupied Kandahar and, in December/January, Ghazna and Wardak. The first attack on Kabul failed because of the treachery of a Wahdat leader, who ostensibly joined the Taliban only to then defect to Massoud. Rather than suffer further losses outside of Kabul, the Taliban turned westward. Their conquest of Herat on 4 September 1995 gave them control of all southern and western Afghanistan.[10] Kabul's overthrow was only a matter of time.

The conquest of Herat suddenly made the project of a trans-Afghan gas pipeline a real possibility. What is more, an American-Saudi consortium had formed in the interim that also wanted to construct it. The joint venture consisting of the Californian UNOCAL and Saudi Delta Corporation had already reached a preliminary agreement with the Taliban in 1995. Now a period of intense lobbying began on the part of Pakistan and Saudi Arabia with the Clinton administration. The lobbyists for the new consortium Central Asia Gas Pipeline, 'CentGas', included former Secretary of State Henry Kissinger and former US ambassador to Pakistan, Robert Oakley. The lobbying worked: in April 1996, US Deputy Secretary of State Robin Raphel confirmed that Pakistan did not (!) support the Taliban, except for humanitarian purposes. She further recommended that Massoud and Rabbani come to an agreement with the Taliban. What is more, the American Afghanistan expert Zalmay Khalilzad in October affirmed that 'The Taliban does not practice the anti-US style of fundamentalism practiced by Iran. It is closer to the Saudi model'.[11] This statement actually came after the Taliban had captured Kabul from Massoud on 26/27 September 1996 and immediately started to implement Sharia law, which included restrictions on women's freedom of movement, such as a work and school ban.[12] Regardless, Raphel continued to push the narrative of a relatively benign Taliban. On 1 May 1997, she remarked: 'The Taliban appear to us to be Afghan nationalists rather than radical Islamists with an international agenda.'[13] Bin Laden meanwhile had already returned to Afghanistan in 1996[14] and begun setting up the dreaded 055 Brigade. It consisted of veterans of the anti-Soviet resistance, Pakistanis, Saudis, Egyptians, Chechens, Uyghurs, Uzbeks and Bosnians and formed a sort of al-Qaeda foreign legion. Additionally, bin Laden had officially declared war on the US on 23 August 1996 and, in February 1997, called on all Muslims to kill American soldiers. He repeated this imperative on 23 February 1998: 'To kill the Americans and their allies – civilians and military – is an individual duty for every Muslim.'[15] Notwithstanding these alarm bells, the US applied tremendous pressure on Turkmenistan and Pakistan to break their contract with Bridas Oil and to issue the final tender for constructing the trans-Afghan pipeline to CentGas. The Taliban subsequently reached an agreement with CentGas in January 1998. Russia, Uzbekistan and Iran felt threatened by the United States' support of the radical Taliban. Indeed, they assessed the US and the Taliban to be the biggest risks to the stability of Central Asia and the North Caucasus.[16]

The Russians' suspicions were all the more justified given that the Taliban had been supporting the insurgent Chechens since 1995 and the US vehemently criticised Russia's actions in the First Chechen War (1994–96). Afghan mercenaries fought on the Chechen side in both the First and the Second Chechen War (1999–2000; anti-terrorist operations 2000–09). On the other hand, the Americans encountered numerous Chechens in the ranks of Taliban fighters and their allies in Afghanistan in 2001/02. Pakistan also sought as early as 1996 to stoke the conflicts in Chechnya, for example, through deploying heavily armed extremist 'missionaries'.[17] As a result, the Chechen secessionist war mutated into an international jihad. The career of Ibn al-Khattab (1969–2002), the Saudi Arabian leader of Circassian origin, is paradigmatic: he first fought in Afghanistan, where he met bin Laden and arranged to have Chechen fighters trained at al-Qaeda camps; at the same time, he fought in the Tajik civil war. In 1995, he went to Chechnya, where he commanded a private army made up of Arabs and Turks.[18] Even earlier, around 4,000 Afghanistan veterans of foreign origin were drawn into the Bosnian War (1992–95) in the West, where they contributed significantly to establishing and spreading an extremist and violent form of Islamism.[19] This gave rise in the 1990s to what Vladimir Putin termed an 'arc of instability'[20] – a loosely interrelated, radical Islamist network extending all the way from South-East Asia to Kashmir, Afghanistan, the North Caucasus, Syria, Bosnia and Kosovo, and, more recently, even to terror cells in Western Europe. This 'arc of instability' has its origin in Pakistan and Saudi Arabia.

The terrorist attacks al-Qaeda perpetrated on 7 August 1998 against the American embassies in Nairobi (Kenya) and Dar es Salaam (Tanzania) and the US bombardment of the al-Qaeda camp near Khost (Afghanistan) with cruise missiles put a temporary end to the project of a trans-Afghan pipeline.[21] The cause of the American blindness to the developments in Afghanistan was threefold: first, the US had no long-term policy for Afghanistan, but delegated it to Pakistan; second, the Clinton administration was entangled in the interests of a US-Saudi consortium; and, third, the US not only wanted to contain Iran's influence in South Asia, but to isolate the country as much as possible – a policy that was consistent with the interests of the Saudi regime, Iran's anti-Shiite enemy.

147. Taliban fighters captured in Bamiyan. Questioned by the photographer Helmut R. Schulze, they claimed they were forced by the Taliban to fight; also, they were too poor to buy their freedom with the required US$100.[24] Photo: 2002.

2. The Islamic Emirate of Afghanistan

After the conquest of Kabul, the Taliban proclaimed the Islamic Emirate of Afghanistan with Mullah Omar as amir. Nonetheless, the regime was only recognised by Pakistan, the United Arab Emirates and Saudi Arabia in May 1997.[22] The objectives of the Taliban and their three alliance partners were fairly congruent. The Taliban, specifically, aimed at a 'pure' Islamic state and also supported the Uzbek terrorist organisation Islamic Movement of Uzbekistan (IMU), whose fighters they trained. Pakistan continued to target a regional confederation of Islamic states under Islamabad's leadership, while Saudi Arabia funded extremist and terrorist groups in Central Asia in order to spread Wahhabism.[23] Ultimately, al-Qaeda set its sights on seizing power in Saudi Arabia and propagated an anti-American and anti-Western jihad, which was expressly directed against civilians. The closeness of the ties

between Mullah Omar, bin Laden, and the ISI was revealed after the attacks in Nairobi and Dar es-Salaam. Before striking bin Laden's training camp with cruise missiles near Khost on 20 August 1998, the United States had alerted Pakistan. Lieutenant General Gul, who remained extremely well informed, in turn warned bin Laden, who remained unharmed.[24] When Saudi Arabia, which viewed bin Laden's al-Qaeda as a threat, then demanded that Mullah Omar give up bin Laden for US$400 million, he brusquely refused. Shortly thereafter, Saudi Arabia and the UAE once again severed diplomatic relations with the Taliban regime.[25]

Although Massoud and Dostum had renewed the Northern Alliance in October 1996, the Taliban succeeded in occupying Dostum's northern provinces in May 1997, not least due to support from al-Qaeda and the ISI. Dostum, moreover, was betrayed by two important commanders, who allowed themselves to be bribed and decided to stab Dostum in the back. Dostum was forced to flee to Turkey in exile. The only remaining opponents of the Taliban, who now controlled 80 per cent of Afghan territory, were Massoud and the Hazaras.[26] But the general population was ambivalent toward the Taliban: although they were grateful for the end of the civil war and the return of a certain security, the Deobandi and Wahhabi ideology was foreign to them. They rejected the medieval-like enforcement of Sharia through bodily mutilations – where a person's ears, hands, feet, or head were cut off, depending on the offence – as well as the numerous behavioural proscriptions. TV, cinema, and music were forbidden, for instance, along with the popular pastime of kite flying.[27]

In 1997, tens of thousands of non-Afghan al-Qaeda fighters and Pakistani were in Afghanistan, virtually transforming the country into a Pakistani colony. In all the ministries and in the provinces, there were ISI officers who supported the mullahs, who had no government experience.[28] In 1999, when Mullah Omar began peace talks with Massoud to end the civil war and to even involve non-Pashtun Afghans in the government, General Pervez Musharraf (in office 1999–2008) – who seized power through a coup on 12 October 1999 – brought them to a halt.[29] Musharraf thus prevented peace from coming to Afghanistan.

The cultivation of the opium poppy was among the most important sources of income for the Taliban. Since it supplanted traditional food agriculture, it made Afghanistan increasingly dependent on food imports. Not only was the Taliban here to blame for promoting opium-poppy cultivation, but so is the fact that it is decidedly more lucrative for the farmers than the cultivation of cotton or wheat. In 1999, Afghanistan's annual opium production reached 4,500 tonnes, representing 75 per cent of the total amount produced worldwide.[30] The Taliban's ban on the cultivation of the opium poppy in 2000 only served to restrict the supply, which sent the prices of stored opium soaring.[31] About 60 per cent of Afghan opium was smuggled through Central Asia to Europe and Russia, with the Uzbek IMU responsible for the smuggling from the Afghan border. The IMU, which operated out of Tajikistan and maintained close contacts with Chechen rebels,

148. An Afghan sitting with a prayer chain on two ducts protruding from a destroyed house – a symbol of the destruction in Afghanistan and the anticipation of reconstruction. Photo: 2002.

was an ideal strategic partner for al-Qaeda – ideologically and in commercial terms.[32]

With the conquest of the Hazara territories in northern and central Afghanistan in 1998, 90 per cent of Afghanistan was under Taliban rule. On 8 August the Taliban massacred 8,000 Shiite Hazara civilians in the conquest of the city of Mazar-e Sharif and murdered eleven Iranian diplomats. Iran amassed its troops along the border with Afghanistan, but President Khatami ultimately refrained from taking punitive military action because he wanted to avoid inciting a general Sunni-Shiite conflict.[33] Instead, Iran, along with Russia and India, intensified its military assistance to Shah Massoud, the only leader still putting up fierce resistance in the Panjshir Valley. Even the major offensive from the year 2000, involving regular Pakistani soldiers and officers as well as al-Qaeda brigades, did not manage to defeat Massoud. Massoud appealed in vain to the United States and Western Europe for support. In an open letter to the American people from 1998, he wrote: 'More than 28,000 Pakistani citizens, including paramilitary personnel and military advisers are part of the Taliban occupation forces. […] For many Afghans, regardless of ethnicity or religion, Afghanistan, for the second time in one decade, is once again an occupied country.'[34] US policy makers, however, were preoccupied with the Lewinsky affair and barely paid attention to Afghanistan. Even Massoud's letter of early 2001 to Vice President Dick Cheney went unanswered. Shortly thereafter, on 5 April 2001 – three weeks after Mullah Omar ordered the Buddha statues of Bamiyan to be blown up – Massoud warned the European Parliament in Strasbourg that the conflict in Afghanistan was 'not a civil war but the result of external interference'. He continued: 'If President Bush does not help us, these terrorists will damage the US and Europe very soon.' Massoud was not interested, however, in foreign troops, but rather broad military assistance. Above all, he wanted the US to force Pakistan to end its support of the Taliban and al-Qaeda.[35]

Once in office, President George W. Bush (in office 2001–9) was confronted from April 2001 with numerous warnings from the CIA that bin Laden was planning a large, spectacular attack in the United States, Israel or Western Europe. Some of these even mentioned aeroplane hijackings. Unlike the Clinton administration, Bush and his closest advisers took the warnings very seriously, recognising the extraordinary threat posed by Pakistan. At the same time, they did not know how to motivate the nuclear power Pakistan to carry out a strategic shift, resulting in the loss of valuable time.[36] To get ready for the period after the 11 September attacks on the World Trade Center in New York and on the Pentagon in Washington, bin Laden ordered Massoud and Dostum to be killed. Given that Dostum had returned to Afghanistan in April and with Massoud's help revived the former Northern Alliance, bin Laden wanted to make sure that the US did not have any allies in Afghanistan. While the attack on Dostum and his deputy Lal on 8 September failed, the one on Massoud on 9 September proved successful. Here, two Moroccan members of al-Qaeda, posing as Belgian journalists, detonated a bomb during an interview. It is likely that the Afghan Wahhabi Sayyaf was involved in the assassination.[37] Two days later, nineteen of bin Laden's selected terrorists (including fifteen Saudi nationals) commandeered four aircraft in the United States. They guided two of them into the Twin Towers of the World Trade Center in New York and one into the Pentagon. The fourth, which was to smash into the Capitol Building, was brought down by its passengers east of Pittsburgh. A total of 2,996 people died, including the nineteen terrorists. As Hekmatyar indicated in 1992, bin Laden wanted to lure the United States into invading the country in order to defeat it – as with the Soviets in the 1980s – in the rugged mountain country.[38]

3. The US in Afghanistan and the Fall of the Taliban

President Bush and his team did many things right in the autumn of 2001. Above all, they avoided falling into the trap set by bin Laden with a major attack. First, Bush gave an ultimatum to Mullah Omar to hand over bin Laden in order to deprive al-Qaeda of its leader. 'Bush swore to bring him [bin Laden] to justice. If that failed, he promised, he would bring justice to bin Laden whom he wanted dead or alive.'[39] Mullah Omar immediately refused, which meant war with the Taliban regime. At the international level, Bush invoked Article 5 of the North Atlantic Treaty on 12 September, according to which an armed attack on one NATO member is equivalent to an attack on all members. The other members are thus obliged to come to the attacked partner's aid. Even earlier, on the evening of 11 September, President Putin was the first foreign head of state to assure his support for the US. The American initiative of putting together a broad-based coalition against the Taliban offered Russia the opportunity not only to improve relations with the US, but also to involve it in the fight against international Islamic extremism. Russia had both feared and struggled against Islamic extremism since the early 1990s. In fact, the two rivals had already identified al-Qaeda's terrorism as a common enemy when they brought a joint resolution before the UN Security Council in December 2000.[40] Bush and his Secretary of Defence Rumsfeld

149. An entrance to the Hazrat Ali Mosque in Mazar-e Sharif, Afghanistan. At the time of the photograph, the mosque was reserved for women and children. Photo: 2004.

subsequently requested flyover rights from the Central Asian states and were granted permission to use airports in Uzbekistan, Tajikistan and Kyrgyzstan. Although Putin was concerned about the extent of US influence in Central Asia, he gave his consent on 24 September. He made it clear, however, that Russia would not be sending troops to Afghanistan.[41] Finally, Bush demanded from the reluctant President Musharraf that he closely cooperate with the United States in the planned 'Operation Enduring Freedom – Afghanistan'.[42]

To avoid the making the same mistake as the Soviet Union of conducting a mass invasion, Bush, Rumsfeld and CIA Director George Tenet rejected the plan originally proposed by General Tommy Franks and Central Command[43] to undertake a classic invasion following a six-month preparation period. Instead, they

decided on the following three strategies: first of all, the presumed camps and military installations of al-Qaeda and the Taliban were to be bombed. Since bombing campaigns in a country with little infrastructure have only limited effect, it would be necessary to, secondly, immediately send in ground troops in the form of special CIA and army commandos to track down bin Laden and Mullah Omar and to, thirdly, support anti-Taliban commanders like Dostum. Indeed, within a few days of 11 September, Dostum had already offered the support of his 2,500 fighters.[44] After the fall of the Taliban and the election of a new president, it was expected that a limited number of troops would be able to maintain security in the Kabul region. This unit of the International Security Assistance Force (ISAF) in fact numbered no more than 5,000 men until August 2003.

Even before the bombings began on 7 October, which devastated the small air force of the Taliban, the CIA officer Gary Schroen landed with a small team in northern Afghanistan to initiate contact with Massoud's successor Fahim Khan and Dostum. While Fahim Khan hesitated, Dostum's plan to attack Mazar-e Sharif with his mounted troops and American air support and to establish a beachhead there met with Schroen's approval. On 20 October, a twelve-man strong commando of Green Berets[45] under Captain Mark Nutsch arrived at General Dostum's headquarters. Their joint initiative was a collaboration between modern military technology of the early twenty-first century and medieval warfare. The commando located the Taliban without being detected. Two soldiers with laser markers guided the bombs from bomber aircraft that had been piloted to the area. Then Dostum's mounted warriors killed the surprised Taliban with Kalashnikovs and light anti-tank weapons that were fired from the shoulder.[46] The offensive by Dostum and the commander Atta Muhammad Noor, who was also supported by a US special commando, was successful. Mazar-e Sharif was liberated on 9 November, which caused the Taliban resistance to collapse.

150. A German Tornado multirole combat aircraft starts a reconnaissance flight from Mazar-e Sharif in northern Afghanistan. Photo: 2008.

On 13 November, Fahim Khan's Tajiks occupied Kabul virtually without a fight. At the same time, the Taliban left Jalalabad, while the Hazaras liberated central Afghanistan and Ismail Khan likewise freed the city of Herat.[47] Finally, the Taliban surrendered Kandahar on 8 December. Most al-Qaeda and Taliban fighters, however, were neither killed nor captured, but fled to Pakistan or the mountains: 'The Taliban had disappeared before they could truly be defeated.'[48] Musharraf's promise to close the border with Afghanistan and to prevent fleeing Taliban from entering the country was empty; the border remained permeable. As a result, the US commandos operating in the south-east took few prisoners, while Pakistan merely handed over to US forces fighters or leaders of secondary importance. As the war reporter Carlotta Gall aptly summed up: 'When the [US] invasion took place, the Taliban were pushed into Pakistan, along with al-Qaeda. There was no [Pakistani] anvil, and there was only a[n] [American] hammer.'[49]

Only the northern Afghan city of Kunduz put up fierce resistance. Entrenched there were almost 3,000 Pakistani officers and soldiers, Taliban leaders and al-Qaeda. They were trapped, for Dostum and Atta Muhammad Noor, who besieged the city, had cut off all escape routes to the south. Dostum's Uzbeks would conquer the city within a matter of days. Around 18 November, General Musharraf personally called President Bush and asked permission to evacuate the Pakistanis, since the US controlled Afghan airspace. Bush acquiesced, thereby committing the United States' first error. In the ensuing nights, Pakistani aircraft evacuated around 2,000 ISI and army officers, Taliban commanders, al-Qaeda fighters of different nationalities and Uzbek fighters of the IMU – all dangerous men. It would have been worth interrogating each and every one of them. Dostum was only allowed to take the city after the evacuation was completed.[50]

The second, even more serious, error was committed by General Tommy Franks in southern Afghanistan. Around 13 November, bin Laden had fled to his underground Tora Bora bunker complex in the mountains, while being pursued by a powerful US special commando. Fearing losses, Franks prohibited General James Mattis from sealing off Tora Bora with his marines, and turned to Musharraf to take over the task at the Pakistani border. He also defied CIA director Tenet's urgent demand to quickly deploy additional Special Forces to track down and capture bin Laden. Instead, he directed three minor Afghan commanders of questionable loyalty to capture bin Laden. Despite a canopy of American bombs over Tora Bora, they advanced only slowly and, after ten days, agreed to a ceasefire with the trapped Taliban. As a result, bin Laden was able to flee with his family and followers to Pakistan.

Mullah Omar escaped from Kandahar to Pakistan, allegedly on a motorcycle. He died there from an illness in 2013.[51] In light of General Franks' fear of taking losses, it is difficult to not see a grain of truth in a rather facetious remark by the British General David Richards, 2006/07 ISAF commander-in-chief: 'We inhabit an increasingly risk-averse world in which ignorant people . . . suppose that if wars are properly conducted, in accordance with Health & Safety Executive guidelines, nobody should get killed.'[52] As a result of Franks' aversion to risk and Musharraf's continued duplicity, the military operations missed one of their main objectives. Bin Laden and Mullah Omar were, therefore, able to quietly continue their terrorist jihad from Pakistan. Bin Laden initially lived in the Swat Valley in northern Pakistan; then, from 2004, in Haripur, north of Islamabad; and, from 2006, in neighbouring Abbottabad, where he was killed by US special forces on 2 May 2011.[53] His house was very close to the elite military academy of Pakistan. It is hardly conceivable that neither the ISI or the military leadership of the country knew that he was residing there.

For Musharraf, there were several reasons to not have bin Laden or the Taliban killed. Bin Laden enjoyed respect and sympathy among many Muslims worldwide, and the Taliban were – in Musharraf's own words – 'my strategic reserve and I can unleash them in tens of thousands against India when I want'.[54] The Taliban were furthermore a destabilising factor in Afghanistan, should the new government decide to revive the old Pashtunistan question. And, finally, as long as there is a looming threat of Islamic extremism in Afghanistan, Pakistan – from the US standpoint – remains a front-line state. This earned the country annual military aid payments in the amount of US$1.6–2 billion between 2002 and 2008, along with access to advanced weapons systems. Besides this, there were billions more in undisclosed grants.[55] As former US special envoy to Afghanistan, Peter Tomsen, observed: 'Despite ample evidence that the Pakistani Army was orchestrating Taliban offensives inside Afghanistan, the avalanche of unconditioned American aid to Pakistan continued. From 2002 to 2009, the rising flow of U.S. money to Pakistan paralleled the steady territorial expansion of the Taliban inside Afghanistan.'[56] If there were peace in Afghanistan, this military aid to Pakistan would dry up. Instead, it has proven to be a veritable 'black hole', as many funds have simply been drained away. Musharraf, however, did not consider that his 'guests' might eventually turn against him and Pakistan.

4. The Presidencies of Hamid Karzai and Ashraf Ghani

The collapse of the Taliban threatened to leave a power vacuum in Afghanistan. Although Rabbani, who still viewed himself as the legitimate president of Afghanistan, had returned to Kabul, he was not acceptable to many Afghans or to the international community involved. After all, he was not only a 'man of the past', but a former Islamist. As time was of the essence and elections could not be held right away, it was decided to implement a multi-step procedure: starting with an interim administration, followed by a *loya jirga* – a 'great assembly' representing all tribes and ethnicities – and then a presidential election. Inquiries conducted by the US special envoy James Dobbins and UN delegate Lakhdar Brahimi indicated that the US-preferred moderate Pashtun Hamid Karzai (in office from 2001 to 2014) was agreeable to both the Northern Alliance and many Pashtuns, the ISI, Russia, Iran and Turkey. In early December

at the Bonn Conference, to which no representative of the Taliban was invited, Karzai was appointed chair of a 29-member government committee. A *loya jirga* then confirmed him as president of the transitional government on 13 June 2002. Since Mohammed Fahim commanded the largest Afghan military power, Karzai appointed him vice president and minister of defence. Dostum, however, was sidelined.[57] Karzai won the first democratic presidential election in Afghanistan's history with a clear majority in October 2004. He also won the second presidential election in October 2009, although the vote was overshadowed by a lack of security, low turnout and allegations of manipulation.[58] Pursuant to the Afghan Constitution, Karzai was not allowed to run for a third term of office in 2014. In the first round of voting, the Tajik Abdullah Abdullah, a former companion of Massoud, won the most votes ahead of the Pashtun Ashraf Ghani. The second round, however, was decided in Ghani's favour. The election was in all likelihood rigged. To avoid another civil war, Secretary of State John Kerry brokered a compromise, whereby Ghani was declared president, Abdullah CEO of

151. President Hamid Karzai (in office 2001–14) was the first freely elected president of Afghanistan. Photo: 2002.

152. Patrol of German ISAF troops with light armoured transport vehicles of the Wiesel 1 type in a suburb of Kabul. Photo: 2004.

Afghanistan, and General Dostum first vice president. The power-sharing came into force on 19 September, but the cabinet formation proved extremely difficult. It lasted almost two years, for this was how long the position of defence minister remained vacant.[59] After the return of Hekmatyar from his exile in Pakistan in May 2017, a reshuffling of the cabinet is expected (at the time of writing), as he may insist on his own representation in the government.[60]

After the fall of the Taliban, Musharraf ostensibly cooper-ated with the US, but continued the secret cooperation with al-Qaeda and the Taliban in order to destabilise Karzai's govern-ment. It was not for nothing that Richard Holbrooke (1941–2010),

US special envoy for Afghanistan and Pakistan, noted in the early 2000s: 'We may be fighting the wrong enemy in the wrong country.'[61] Holbrooke's gentle suggestion that neither the Taliban nor Afghanistan was the true enemy of the US was clarified by Peter Tomsen in 2011: 'The epicenter of world terrorism [was] in Pakistan, not Afghanistan; the terrorist sanctuaries in Pakistan are breeding grounds for targeting many nations around the world, Muslim and non-Muslim.'[62] That said, the primary epicentre was located in the Pakistani army leadership and the secret service, not among the people, who strove for peace and prosperity; the secondary epicentre was Saudi Arabia.

More than a year after his escape, Mullah Omar began to speak again in February 2003. He called on all Afghans to jihad against the Americans and threatened all those who collaborated with the United States or the Karzai government with death. Just one month later, a series of murders of pro-government politicians and mullahs, police officers and employees of Western NGOs started in Kandahar province.[63] Omar formed a leadership circle called 'Quetta Shura' to reorganise the Taliban and to carry out attacks in Afghanistan with the active help of the ISI. The Taliban and al-Qaeda divided the Afghan operation areas among themselves. In July 2003, Mullah Omar and Hekmatyar reconciled and joined forces to fight against American troops in Afghanistan and the Karzai government. They speculated that the US invasion of Iraq, commencing on 20 March, would cause Bush to turn his focus away from Afghanistan.[64] The Taliban also cooperated with ordinary bandits. They kidnapped employees of NGOs and sold them to the Taliban, who then extorted ransom from governments, NGOs or the victims' countries of origin.

The number of attacks on foreign soldiers, NGO workers and Afghan police increased dramatically. The wave of murders reached its initial peak in 2006 in southern Afghanistan, especially in Helmand; the British and later American troops then conducted counter-attacks from 2007 to 2010. In 2007, ISAF commander Lieutenant General Eikenberry emphasised before the US Congress that the war would not be won without including the Pakistani safe havens for terrorists.[65] In the following year, the United States was forced to increase its presence to 53,000 troops. When an American commando attacked three houses on Pakistani soil in September 2008, Pakistan took the incident as an excuse to temporarily halt the existing supplies for the ISAF troops via Pakistan. It also issued an order to shoot on American troops should they cross the border. At the same time, the Taliban stepped up their attacks on US supply convoys in Pakistan.[66] The Americans responded to this threat and the interruption of the supply line with drone attacks in the Pakistani border region, and they organised their supplies via Russia and through the three Central Asian states Uzbekistan, Tajikistan and Kyrgyzstan. Despite further reinforcement of ISAF troops, the Taliban succeeded in expanding to the west and north, which provoked a broad British-American counter-offensive in 2010.[67] In the summer of 2011, President Obama announced the gradual withdrawal of American troops and the handover of war operations and their command to the Afghan army. When bin Laden was killed in 2011 by US Special Forces, he was succeeded as the head of al-Qaeda by his deputy Ayman al-Zawahiri. In the spring of 2013, the Afghan army began to

assume responsibility for internal security, even though ISAF forces continue today to advise, train and assist the Afghan forces. On 28 December 2014, NATO formally ended its combat operations; about 13,500 troops officially remained in the country, including 10,000 Americans. These were mostly consultants, air force personnel, and Special Forces. Without American air support, the government army's territorial losses would be significantly greater. There are also about 25,000 military contractors.

In parallel with the withdrawal of ISAF troops, the Taliban and al-Qaeda intensified their activities. By 2016, they gained the upper hand in the southern provinces of Helmand and Uruzgen, as well as in certain places in Faryab (north-west), Bamiyan (central Afghanistan), Nangahar (east) and in Kunduz (north).[68] In the wake of Pakistan's offensive in Waziristan south-west of Peshawar in the summer of 2014 to expel fighters from the Haqqani network[69] and al-Qaeda and Uzbeks of the IMU, these fighters fled to neighbouring Afghanistan by the thousands. Pakistani Taliban then retaliated on 26 December 2014 by slaughtering 147 schoolchildren and teachers in Peshawar.[70] The formation of an Afghan offshoot of the Islamic State (IS) in the winter of 2014/15[71] reflected the emergence of a new militant group that shares similar goals to al-Qaeda and competes with the Taliban for influence, while exceeding it in brutality. The group also engages the Taliban in skirmishes.[72] The appearance of this IS offshoot in Afghanistan will further complicate the peace-finding process. It can be expected that radical Taliban will defect to IS if the moderate wing of the Taliban should ever come to terms with the government. On the part of the insurgents, there is increasingly a lack of representative negotiating partners. About a year earlier, in 2013/14, hundreds of foreign fighters, including Chechens, Uzbeks, Uyghurs, Iraqis and Turks, had set out to Syria and Iraq in order to bolster the ranks of Islamic State.[73]

It was not until July 2015 that the Afghan Taliban announced that Mullah Omar had died in April 2013. They chose Akhtar Mansur (*ca.* 1968–2016) as their new amir. Mansur was amir only for about a year until he was killed by an American drone in May 2016. His successor as the third amir is Hibatullah Akhundzada. In September/October 2016, he approved the resumption of the talks with representatives of the Afghan government that were suspended in 2013. At these discussions, Mullah Omar's brother Abdul Manan Akhun met the Afghan security chief Stanekzai.[74] In September 2016, President Ghani, who is determined to forge the peace process with former adversaries, announced that he had pardoned the former leader of the Hezb-i Islami, Gulbuddin Hekmatyar, within the scope of a peace agreement with the Hezb.[75] Hekmatyar ratified the agreement and returned to Kabul with a heavily armed escort on 4 May 2017.[76] It remains uncertain if Hekmatyar is prepared to cooperate with his former enemies from the Northern Alliance, Vice President Dostum and Governor Atta Muhammad Noor, to find a peaceful solution to the inter-Afghan conflicts.

In Islamabad, in early 2006, President Karzai warned President Musharraf that the Pakistani Taliban could very well turn against their host: 'If anyone thinks that he can train a snake to bite another person, he should know that it is possible at any time for the snake to turn and bite his trainer. Terrorism is something like this example. It is nobody's friend.'[77] Karzai's warning turned into reality in June 2007, when heavily armed Pakistani Taliban entrenched themselves in the Red Mosque of Islamabad near the intelligence headquarters. After an eight-day siege, Pakistani Special Forces stormed the mosque. More than 100 people died.[78] Two years earlier, younger Pakistani Taliban called Tehrik-e Taliban Pakistan (TTP) had allied themselves with al-Qaeda, first, to seize control in Waziristan and, in a second step, to assume power throughout Pakistan. The Afghan Quetta Shura surrounding Mullah Omar remained loyal to Musharraf, but not al-Qaeda. The latter had carried out two unsuccessful attacks on the president in December 2003, because the ISI had arrested two leading al-Qaeda members.[79] This was followed by brazen, bloody attacks on police and army barracks, schools and hospitals, which continue to this day (mid-2017). Pakistan was now no longer simply a Taliban sanctuary, but also a target.[80] Pakistani Taliban of the TTP moreover did not hesitate to kidnap Brigadier Sultan Amir Tarrar, one of the godfathers of the Taliban, and to shoot him to death in January 2011. Figuratively speaking, the ISI had created a tiger, which it believed it could tame; now the tiger turned on its trainer. The revolt of the Pakistani Taliban became even more dangerous for the Musharraf regime when they infiltrated the Swat Valley in 2006, located a mere 130 km north of the capital Islamabad and which they controlled until 2007. They immediately introduced Sharia law, closed the girls' schools, destroyed Buddhist art, and had officials and locals who defended themselves flogged or beheaded.[81] Only now did it become clear to the army leadership that there was a risk that the TTP fighters could penetrate to Islamabad. The army recaptured the Swat Valley in 2009.[82] A tragic irony, however, emerged: Pakistani soldiers and officers had lost their lives against extremists who were sponsored and armed by a small group of senior Pakistani army officers and the ISI.

153. Helicopter observation flight with an open hatch at 50 m ground clearance between Kunduz and Faizabad, northern Afghanistan. Photo: 2007.

5. An Initial Assessment

As of the end of 2017, peace still does not prevail in Afghanistan. The security situation is precarious, and the Taliban, who were defeated in 2001, are once again on the rise in several provinces. By the end of 2017, they controlled about one-third of the national territory[83] – despite US$60 billion in reconstruction aid or the deployment of up to 147,000 soldiers of the NATO-led ISAF (including 100,000 Americans) or, finally, the US$450 billion that has been spent on warfare.[84] The domestic reasons for the present state of affairs include the fact that democracy is a new form of government in Afghanistan and that a sense of national unity is still largely missing. Western-style democracy cannot be imposed at gunpoint, especially in a society that has never tested such mechanisms. Afghans to this day still vote along ethnic and tribal lines, and rarely with regard to an individual party or its respective ideology. In the prevailing rural patriarchal communities, women either relinquish their right to vote to their husbands, or both sexes follow the instructions of the village elders or tribal leader. In addition, the security situation from around 2007 was extremely poor in several southern provinces, and those who wanted to vote were seriously threatened by Taliban fighters.[85] In addition, many warlords and commanders were not willing to cede their regional power to the central government or to surrender their weapons. Therefore, Karzai was forced to make far-reaching compromises when appointing ministers and provincial governors. Apart from longstanding comrades-in-arms and charismatic tribal leaders or commanders, the loyalty of powerful Afghans still needs to be bought with lucrative posts. This, in turn, promotes the spread of corruption and criminal networks. On top of this, President Ghani and CEO Abdullah obstruct each other, which not only makes an efficient government impossible, but also undermines the confidence Afghans have in the government and the state. Since some of these regional potentates and the Taliban are involved in the cultivation of the opium poppy and its processing into opium, it is difficult to fight poppy cultivation. Finally, the economically very weak Afghanistan still depends on external financial assistance,[86] not least because the expanding production of the opium poppy increasingly restricts the cultivation of food.

154. Encounter between an Afghan couple and ambulances of the ISAF in Badakhshan, northern Afghanistan. Photo: 2008.

External reasons are primarily responsible for the continued unsatisfactory situation in Afghanistan, 16 years after the fall of the Taliban. They are listed here in brief:

1. The United States victory over the Taliban did not follow a carefully planned strategy for the economic and political reconstruction of the decimated country and the formation of the Afghan nation. Moreover, the financial resources employed at the outset were inadequate. There was no Marshall Plan for Afghanistan – defeating the Taliban militarily was not enough to stabilise the country. As General Richards rightly criticised, killing Taliban 'is just one weapon in the armoury, along with much speedier reconstruction and development, a political outreach programme, and much else. [...] Employment is key: jobs, jobs, jobs! Much too much development money goes on sandal-wearing initiatives that have no economic impact.'[87] When the Afghans, especially the young men, remain unemployed, they are easy prey for recruiters of the Taliban, who offer them up to US$10 per day.

2. Just a few months after the establishment of Karzai in Kabul, President Bush shifted the foreign policy focus on to Iraq and its alleged production of weapons of mass destruction. As a result, the inner circle of the administration and the army prepared for the coming invasion of Iraq. To be precise, the US took its eye off Afghanistan before it had completed its mission. Later, in 2006, the British Field Marshal Lord Peter Inge asked in the House of Lords: 'Where is the main effort? Is it Iraq or is it Afghanistan? I hope we are not making the mistake of trying to be strong everywhere and ending up being strong nowhere.'[88]

3. Even after the victory, the United States relied on the cooperation of dubious warlords such as Gul Agha in Kandahar, paying them to maintain public order and to prevent the Taliban from returning. But the warlords, who were far away from Kabul, were difficult to keep in check and they took money from both the US and the ISI. These warlords also demanded bribes to guarantee the 'protection' of the foreign professionals involved in the reconstruction of schools, hospitals, electricity and water distribution.[89] Since the coalition led by the United States relied on these former warlords, they neglected the reconstruction of a national army in the early years and thus encouraged corruption.

4. Another fatal mistake on the part of the Bush administration and the Northern Alliance was to veto the broad amnesty proposed by President Karzai for senior Taliban who wanted to lay down their arms and return to Afghanistan, but demanded immunity from judicial authorities. These included the former defence minister of the Taliban and his deputy, the interior minister and even Jalaluddin Haqqani, currently one of the most dangerous Taliban. But Karzai was not allowed to pardon them, and all high-ranking Taliban who fell into American hands were shipped off to Guantanamo. Some of the Taliban who were initially willing to capitulate later played a crucial role in the organisation's rehabilitation, while others were detained by Pakistan without charges.[90]

5. In the first Karzai government, the Tajik faction of the Northern Alliance predominated. It supplied the secretary of defence (Muhammad Fahim), interior minister (Yunus Qanooni), and foreign minister (Abdullah Abdullah). The Pashtuns were under-represented and the Taliban were excluded entirely. Although the US and Pakistan had initially advocated the inclusion of moderate Taliban in the new Afghan government, the Northern Alliance and Russia were strongly opposed. The US had already backed down on 2 November 2001.[91] Karzai was not able to offset the preponderance of Tajiks until August 2003.[92]

6. After three to four years, many Afghans were not only disappointed about the lack of progress in terms of reconstruction, but also angry about the many misguided bombings and drone attacks that killed innocent civilians (e.g. wedding parties). Such unintended killings of civilians could probably have been avoided in targeted commando raids. With justification, an Afghan officer once asked 'if the British Army would be allowed to bomb a house in Northern Ireland because it suspected an IRA gunman inside'.[93] Besides this, individual Afghan informants took advantage of the Americans for the sake of their own personal vendettas or greed. They denounced as 'Taliban' rivals, tribal enemies, or owners of rich fields that they wanted for themselves, leading to their assassination by US drones.[94] The US was hardly in a position to verify information on the ground due to the lack of its own confidants.

7. Another significant reason for the sluggish reconstruction, despite nominally extremely generous aid programmes, was the fact that only a fraction of the money was actually invested locally. Through 2008, 80 per cent of US$35 billion granted from international lenders did not make it into government hands. Instead, these funds either went to corporations, which outsourced the projects to private sub-contractors, who, in turn, outsourced them again to other private sub-contractors. In the process, each company pocketed a profit. The quality of the projects was often poor. Alternatively, the funds went to one of the 341 NGOs working in Afghanistan. Sub-contractors and NGOs used the greater part of the funds for wages of foreigners living in Afghanistan, consulting fees, security, vehicles,

housing rents and international travel expenses, and even for flown-in food and beverages. Added to this were bribes paid to corrupt Afghans. It is estimated that about 40 per cent of the aid money flowed back directly to the donor countries and that a comparable sum went towards financing the expenditures of UN agencies and NGOs as well as external contractors. Ultimately, 'less than 15 percent of the original funding was spent on the intended project'.[95]

8. Individual countries that took part in the ISAF, such as Germany, Spain and Italy, sent troops who did not participate in major offensives, but were only allowed to defend themselves. These troops were not in a position to do very much against the resurgent Taliban.[96]

9. It is also possible that President Bush's refusal to cooperate with Iran in bringing peace to Afghanistan was a mistake, even though the Sunni Pashtuns strongly opposed the Shiite Iranians. Iran, after all, had been engaged in the construction of highways in the Hazara region and to the west of Afghanistan.[97]

10. By far the most important factor in the ongoing crisis was that the Pakistani President Musharraf and his intelligence service continued to play their double game. Just like the top leaders of al-Qaeda, the Taliban who had fled from Afghanistan found refuge again in the tribal areas of north-west Pakistan. Neither Bush nor Obama exerted sufficient pressure on Musharraf and the all-powerful ISI director and later chief of staff Ashfaq Kayani (in office 2004–7; 2007–13) to force them to undertake a fundamental shift in their Afghanistan policy.[98] Instead, the Obama administration pressured Karzai publicly, which he perceived as a humiliation. Relations between Kabul and Washington deteriorated. In this context, an Afghan proverb seems quite apt: 'Through kindness you can even lead an Afghan to hell, but by force you can't even take him to heaven.'[99] There are many indications that the ties between Pakistan's ISI and the dreaded Haqqani network were especially intense. At a Senate hearing on 22 September 2011, the Chairman of the US Joint Chiefs of Staff, Admiral Michael Mullen (in office

155. Two students on the campus of the University of Kabul, Afghanistan. With the fall of the Taliban, girls and women once again had access to schools and universities. Photo: 2004.

2007–14), described the Haqqani network as a 'veritable arm' of the ISI. He further explained that Pakistan's government collaborates with the terrorists and should be punished for it.[100] Mullen's harsh criticism was motivated by the recent assassination of Burhanuddin Rabbani, whom Karzai had recruited for the presidency of the High Peace Council. Karzai had established this council in 2010 with the full support of President Obama to seek a reconciliation with moderate Taliban. Richards, the former ISAF commander in chief, was also convinced of this course of action: 'While we struggle over what to do with ISIS in Iraq and Syria, we can at least help ensure that Afghanistan does not become another part of the so-called caliphate. An accommodation with the Taliban must be part of the solution in Afghanistan.'[101] Rabbani's suicide bomber was an Afghan, but clues relating to the attack's planning pointed to Pakistan.[102]

In 2008, when Karzai once again sought a dialogue with moderate Taliban leaders living in Pakistan, Pakistan had dozens of them arrested to prevent them from negotiating with Karzai.[103] Pakistan thus sabotaged the peace efforts of Karzai and the Obama administration. Peace will not come to Afghanistan without absolute cooperation from all of Pakistan's power brokers, i.e. the government, the army and the secret service. Although certain civilian governments of Pakistan have tentatively tried to end the double game towards Afghanistan, while improving relations with India, they have not been able to prevail against the army. A peace initiative, however, would not only have to involve moderate Taliban and Pakistan, but also Pakistan's economic and financial partners, China and Saudi Arabia. China has substantial investments in both Pakistan and Afghanistan, such as the giant Mes Aynak copper mine near Kabul. The Chinese are thus highly interested in a lasting peace there for economic reasons, and all the more so because it would deny rebellious Uyghurs a refuge or training opportunities.[104] As for Saudi Arabia, it remains uncertain whether royalty and clergy are really prepared to give up on their missionary propagation of Wahhabism and the financing of Islamist extremists.

The New Independence of Central Asian States

'No country can develop its own security by harming the fundamental security interests of others.'

Chinese president **JIANG ZEMIN** (in office 1993–2003)[1]

'There is no Central Asia or other common territorial entity.'

Political historian **S.N. ABASHIN**[2]

1. Non-independent Republics and Regions of the Russian Federation

The independence of the Central Asian republics was the result of the collapse of the Soviet Union, which dissolved on 26 December 1991. The disintegration of the Soviet empire had begun at the latest with the upheavals in the Eastern European member states of the Warsaw Pact in 1989, which had continued in Mongolia in the spring of 1990. The republics in the heartland of Central Asia, however, declared their independence from the fading Soviet Union only reluctantly and only after the failed coup attempt against Gorbachev of 19–21 August 1991. Kyrgyzstan was the first country to do so on 30 August, Kazakhstan the last on 16 December. The relative prosperity of the autonomous republics was largely based on the combination of a command economy and secure markets, as well as subsidies from Moscow. In view of the huge Soviet military arsenal and not least nuclear weapons, the

peaceful transition (a few regional conflicts notwithstanding) of the highly centralised Soviet Union into a number of independent states was nearly miraculous. It was to the credit of presidents George H.W. Bush, Bill Clinton and Boris Yeltsin that they were able to avoid tensions and make the states that had broken away from Russia, such as Ukraine, Belarus and especially Kazakhstan, nuclear free.[3] The worst post-Soviet conflicts were the Tajik Civil War (1992–96) in Central Asia and the Armenian-Azerbaijani conflict over Nagorno-Karabakh (1988–94) in the Caucasus; the Russian-Georgian conflict over Abkhazia (1992–94); the Georgian-South Ossetian conflict (1990–92); the Russian-Georgian War from August 2008; and the two Chechen Wars. The second Chechen War was expanded into an international jihad by Afghanistan veterans, who had been trained and sponsored by al-Qaeda.[4]

In the years 1992–94, President Yeltsin's foreign policy priorities consisted in a rapprochement with the West and the simultaneous neglect of Central Asia, which was considered a financial burden.[5] This explains why the Central Asian republics

156. The two Tuvan shamans Seren Ojun and Darya Kendenova perform a shamanistic ritual at a spring near Kyzyl. Tuva, Russia. Photo: 2002.

157. The 'White Mosque', built in the years 2010–12, in Bolghar south of Kazan, Tatarstan, Russia. The head architect Sergei Shakurov was also involved in the construction of the Kul Sharif Mosque in the Kazan Kremlin. Photo: 2013.

were granted independence without resistance, while a different attitude was adopted towards regions that were either near Moscow or strategically important. The latter included the Republic of **Tuva**, which only had about 310,000 inhabitants and was ruled from 1932 to 1973 by the Stalinist Saltchak Toka. When assaults were made on Russians in 1990, Soviet troops were called in to restore public order. Tuva's declaration of independence in November 1991 was not recognised by the Soviet Union or Russia. Today, it is a republic of the Russian Federation. The approximately 900,000-inhabitant-strong Republic of **Buryatia** is of considerable strategic importance for Russia, as it is crossed by the Trans-Siberian Railway. It proclaimed its sovereignty in 1990, but continued to be an autonomous republic of the Russian Federation. The **Kalmyk** Autonomous Soviet Socialist Republic, with its 285,000 inhabitants, also remained part of the Russian Federation. It is the only political region of Europe where the majority of the population professes Buddhism. Living between the Ural and the Volga are the Muslim Turkic peoples of the Bashkirs and Tatars, who formed the short-lived **Idel-Ural State** in 1917/18. The Red Amy dissolved the republic in late 1918, whereupon it

was replaced by the Bashkir and the Tatar Autonomous Soviet Socialist Republics. **Bashkortostan,** which has just over 4 million inhabitants, declared its sovereignty in October 1990. However, it remained an autonomous republic of the Russian Confederation. This is also true of the Republic of **Tatarstan**, which has 3.85 million inhabitants. The latter proclaimed its sovereignty on 30 August 1990, which the population then affirmed in a 1992 referendum. The relationship of the Republic of Tatarstan to the Russian Federation was contractually arranged in 1994. Tatarstan and Bashkortostan have similar economic structures: both have oil reserves and significant mechanical industries. Tatarstan, in particular, is largely industrialised. It has petrochemical plants and produces helicopters, airplanes and trucks and its largest market is still Russia. However, the special status of Tatarstan ended on 24 July 2017 when the agreement from 1994 expired. It is to be seen if Moscow is prepared to negotiate a follow-up treaty.[6]

158. The Kul Sharif Mosque and its library in the Kazan Kremlin, Tatarstan, Russia. Kul Sharif was the last imam of Kazan before the Russian conquest of 1552; the construction of a mosque, consecrated in 2005, within the Kremlin is a symbol of the peaceful coexistence of Christians and Muslims in Tatarstan. Photo: 2013.

2. The Xinjiang Uyghur Autonomous Region

The Chinese Xinjiang Uyghur Autonomous Region was nominally a part of China from 1912 to 1944, but de facto an autonomous satellite state of the Soviet Union.[7] As already mentioned, the term 'Uyghurs' originated in the late nineteenth century to refer to the Turkish-speaking Muslims of Xinjiang and did not become an official designation until 1934.[8] Of the population of nearly 23 million that was officially counted at the end of 2014, Uyghurs make up about 43 per cent and Han Chinese about 40 per cent. If, however, the close to 3 million seasonal migrant workers, the majority of whom are Han Chinese, are also included, then the proportion of Uyghurs drops to about 38 per cent and that of the Han increases to about 43 per cent.[9] In 1981, Deng Xiaoping slightly pried open the lid on the Pandora's Box in Xinjiang: on the one hand, he spoke out against the secession of the Republic of Xinjiang;

on the other, he advocated greater or genuine autonomy in the region and the self-determination of ethnic minorities.[10] Afterwards, tensions soon developed in the southern half of the province between long-established Uyghurs and Han Chinese immigrants.

Although these tensions were at first social in nature, they soon took on an additional religious character. Paradoxically, it was the Chinese government that initially brought the Uyghurs into contact with extremist Islamic thought. Beginning in 1980, the PLA[11] started training Afghan mujahideen in Pakistan, and, from 1985, it trained hundreds in Xinjiang itself, near Kashgar and Khotan. Specially trained Uyghurs also fought on the side of the mujahideen. They remained in Afghanistan after the Soviet withdrawal, became further radicalised there at local madrasahs, and, in 1996, put themselves at the service of the Taliban by the hundreds.[12] The Karakoram Highway, which connects Xinjiang with Pakistan, ended Xinjiang's isolation. Completed in 1979 and opened to the public in 1986, it has facilitated the spread of radical Islamist ideology among traditionally moderate Sunni Uyghurs.

The victory of the mujahideen over the Soviet Union and its vassal Najibullah stoked the confidence of Uyghur circles and caused them to interweave their political claims to sovereignty with religious demands. The construction of new mosques, funded by Arab states, the spread of Islamist propaganda material, and access to the internet since the late 1990s all contributed to the further radicalisation of Uyghur groups.[13] When the five sovereign '-stan' republics of Central Asia emerged from the wreckage of the Soviet Union in 1991, radicalised Uyghurs in Xinjiang were forced to recognise that they were the only major Muslim ethnic group in Central Asia that did not have their own sovereign homeland. Accordingly, calls for an independent Uyghuristan became louder.[14] As in other Muslim communities, radical Islam developed in the context of a one-party system into the only political alternative.

For China, the possibility of Xinjiang's secession is totally excluded. Not only would such a splitting off significantly undermine national unity, but the region is also of great economic importance. Indeed, since the 1950s and 1960s, when the region was little more than an economic cul de sac, Xinjiang has developed into a prime trading hub with the Central Asian republics. Chinese consumer goods replaced Soviet products there from 1992, and the new republics began to export oil, gas, steel, scrap iron and other metals via Xinjiang to China.[15] Furthermore, Xinjiang has large deposits of raw materials and a strong cotton industry. The region is responsible for a quarter of China's cotton, 40 per cent of which is produced on bingtuan state farms.[16] Of even greater importance are the oil and gas reserves in Xinjiang, which account for about 30 per cent of China's mainland reserves. The first mechanised oil drilling took place in 1909 near Dushanzi, northern Xinjiang, after which oil deposits were discovered in the Tarim and Turfan Basins in the late 1920s. Today, Xinjiang accounts for 13 per cent of China's natural gas and 11 per cent of its oil production. In addition, China imports oil and gas from Central Asia via pipelines running from Kazakhstan to Xinjiang and from there to eastern and southern China. The first oil pipeline between Kazakhstan and Xinjiang was put into operation in 2006, the first natural gas pipeline in 2009.[17]

159. The 12.3m-high-statue of Mao Zedong stands on a 11.7-m-high plinth in Kashgar, Xinjiang, China. It was built during the Cultural Revolution as an expression of the Uyghurs' loyalty to Mao and completed in 1969. Photo: 2009.

Since China's oil imports from the Middle East are mainly shipped through the Strait of Malacca, where they are exposed to the dangers of terrorism, piracy, or a US naval blockade, the oil and gas resources in Xinjiang are of paramount strategic importance.[18] The claim that China has made to supremacy in the South China Sea since 2009 with the so-called 'Nine-Dash-Line' shows that Beijing wants to protect this waterway no matter what.[19] In the East China Sea and in the Yellow Sea, however, Taiwan, Japan, and Korea could disrupt the waterways to north-east China and even threaten the offshore production facilities in the Bohai Bay.[20]

Still, the state implemented programme 'Develop the West' from 2001 that triggered rapid economic growth in Xinjiang and strong immigration from Central China is constrained by stringent environmental barriers. These relate primarily to the quality and availability of water, without which the desert environment of southern Xinjiang is uninhabitable. There are several reasons for the looming ecological crisis: the millions of immigrants and rising living standards in the cities have led to an explosion in water consumption. Also, oil drilling and petrochemical industries are water-intensive, and the expansion of irrigated agricultural land likewise leads to increased water consumption. The crisis is exacerbated by the fact that as water consumption increases, the amount of available water simultaneously decreases. As Xinjiang lies outside the monsoon system, the global temperature rise leads to less rainfall and a pronounced glacier melt, which can dry out the feeder of the Tarim River. The use of machine-made tubewells also lowers the water table and puts the traditional karez water system at acute risk.[21] Desertification is accelerated by the salinisation of annually flooded lands and the traditional felling of poplars and undergrowth for heating, practised at the edge of small oases. Despite large-scale reforestation programmes, the Taklamakan Desert is said to expand every year by around 400 km^2.[22] This strong demographic and environmental pressure fuels the discontent among many Uyghurs. Not only are they increasingly marginalised in the face of growing economic prosperity, but they feel discriminated against with regard to the Han Chinese. This resentment is a breeding ground for Islamic extremism. Just the same, there are no indications that non-Uyghur Muslims in Xinjiang, like the Hui, Kazakh and Tajik, want to secede from China.

The armed struggle of Islamist Uyghur groups began in April 1990 with the Baren Township Riot, south of Kashgar. Here, barely armed insurgents besieged and threw hand grenades at the local government and police buildings. Army units repressed the uprising, which had been organised by the terrorist group Hezb al-Islami li-Turkestan al sharqiah, the East Turkestan Islamic Movement (ETIM).[23] The ETIM is the largest of about 30 militant and separatist Islamist groups in Xinjiang, which have been blamed for around 150 to 200 terrorist attacks and murders (even of moderate clerics) between 1990 and 2009. The unrest reached a climax in the riots of 5–7 July 2009 in Ürümqi, as thousands of Uyghurs armed with batons and long knives preyed on Chinese passers-by. Enraged Chinese then proceeded to set Uyghur shops on fire. According to official figures, 197 people died and 1,721 were injured.[24] However, these riots were hardly motivated by religion or separatist tendencies. In fact, such slogans were completely missing. Rather, they seem to have sprung from a sense of frustration over perceived social and economic injustices and later took on the character of racial unrest. Even the 'modernisation' of the old town of Kashgar that began in the spring of 2009, involving its partial demolition, seems to have played no role

160. Prayer in the Altyn (Golden) Mosque of Yarkand, Xinjiang, China. Photo: 1994.

161. The Buddhist Gandantegchinlen Monastery (Great Place of Complete Joy) to the west of Ulaan Baatar, Mongolia. Built in 1838, the monastery was partially spared the Stalinist destruction wave of the 1930s; it was closed, however, from 1938 to 1944. In the picture, the Migjid Janraisig Temple, where a 5.26-m-high statue of Bodhisattva Avalokiteshvara (Tibetan: Chenrezig), newly built in 1996, is located. Photo: 2001.

in the outbreak of riots in Ürümqi.[25] It remains uncertain whether exiled Uyghurs coordinated the unrest from abroad.[26] Five years later, a group of terrorists who were allegedly tied to the ETIM killed 29 civilians and injured over 140 more in the train station at Kunming,[27] and, on 18 September 2015, more than 50 mostly Han Chinese workers fell victim to a terrorist attack at a coal mine in Aksu.[28]

The ETIM, which is also called the Turkestan Islamic Party (TIP), was founded in 1940 and revived in the late 1980s by Zia al-Din bin Yousef (d. 1990). The organisation, which is funded by the Uyghur diaspora, seeks to bring about Xinjiang's secession from China through violent means, along with the expulsion of all 'infidel' Han Chinese and the introduction of Sharia law. In 1997, Hasan Makhsum (d. 2003) reorganised the group and established a training base in the Tora Bora region, where al-Qaeda and bin Laden had their headquarters. He met with bin Laden several times. Makhsum also maintained close relations with the Uzbek terrorist organisation IMU. At the time, the strength of the ETIM inside Afghanistan was estimated to be anywhere from several hundred to around 2,000 men. After the fall of the Taliban, the ETIM moved its headquarters to Waziristan in north-western Pakistan. Makhsum was killed on 2 October 2003 as part of a Pakistani military operation after China had pressured Islamabad to no longer tolerate his presence on Pakistani soil.[29] Unlike al-Qaeda, ETIM does not have a global orientation; its jihad is rather centred on China. By the same token, this does not prevent Uyghur fighters from fighting in Syria. From Beijing's point of view, the ETIM and similar groups represent the 'three evils' of terrorism, separatism, and religious extremism that must be defeated. It is still difficult to assess how much support such militant separatist organisations have among the wider Uyghur population. In any event, attacks like those of July 2009 have led to great mistrust and a deeper sense of alienation between the Uyghurs and the Chinese.

3. Independent Mongolia

In Mongolia, the transition from a communist one-party state to a multi-party democracy took place peacefully. This was due in no small measure to the general secretary of the Mongolian Communist Party, Jambyn Batmönkh (in office 1984–90). He had replaced his predecessor Yumjaagiin Tsedenbal (in power 1952–84), who resisted the Soviet Union's rapprochement with China initiated in 1982. Buoyed by the fall of the Berlin Wall on 9 November 1989 and the peaceful transition to multi-party systems in countries of the Eastern Bloc, young Mongolian intellectuals founded the Mongolian Democratic Union on 9 December 1989. It organised its first mass demonstration in Ulaan Baatar on 14 January 1990. After further demonstrations and party foundations, around 100,000 people gathered in the central Sükhbaatar Square on 4 March and called for democracy to be introduced. Three days later, leaders of the democracy movement began a public hunger strike. In this political crisis,

the chairman of the Political Bureau, Batmönkh, refused to sign a police deployment order to break up the demonstrations. Instead, he dissolved the Politburo and resigned on 9 March, paving the way for a multi-party system. The first free elections in Mongolia took place on 29 July 1990. Surprisingly, the Mongol People's Revolution Party (MPRP), the successor to the Communist Party, won the general election, which involved four major parties. In the Grand Chamber, it won 60 per cent of the vote and 387 of the 430 seats (83 per cent).[30] As in Eastern Europe, the Soviet troops stationed in Mongolia did not intervene, but gradually withdrew.

The reformer Davaadorjiin Ganbold was the driving force in the new government under prime minister Byambasüren. The political and economic challenges were enormous. From 1989, Mongolia not only lost markets and investors in the wake of the democratic changes in Eastern Europe and the collapse of the Soviet Union, but it now had to pay for much-needed raw materials, fuels and combustibles and spare parts in hard currency. Mongolia was consequently highly dependent on loans from the capitalist world, which

162. In the northern suburbs of Ulaan Baatar, there are extensive yurt settlements. The majority of those who move to the capital are impoverished families from the rural population. Due to a lack of financial resources, they set up their ger (yurt) here or a small house with a corrugated roof. The infrastructure is poor, lacking running water, sufficient electricity, roads, and transportation to the city. Photo: 2012.

forced the government to submit to the instructions of its lenders, including the World Bank, the International Monetary Fund, the Asian Development Bank and USAID. Where Asian 'tiger states' like Singapore, South Korea, Taiwan and Hong Kong had managed in the past to achieve economic growth and prosperity through state-directed economic development, significant investments in infrastructure, technology and education, as well as selective import tariffs, Mongolia's creditors prescribed a market-based shock therapy. This consisted of a poorly designed privatisation of state enterprises and collectivised herds, a release of the consumer price index, and disinvestment in education, infrastructure, social services, health and veterinary activities. The consequences for the general population were disastrous. In 1992, inflation reached 325 per cent and in the following year 183 per cent; at the same time, industrial production in 1992 fell by 24 per cent. In some provinces, more than half of the factories were closed. Despite high per-capita development assistance, the standard of living of many Mongols fell below the poverty line.[31] The international financial institutions made the allocation

and disbursement of loans dependent on the implementation of drastic macroeconomic measures. They thus constituted a kind of illegitimate shadow government, which greatly restricted the elected government's room to manoeuvre. Ultimately, they undermined the sovereignty that the Mongols had struggled for.

This externally imposed economic policy had serious consequences for the majority of Mongolians. To begin with, countless unemployed workers migrated from the cities and turned to livestock farming in the country. But as the workers lacked knowledge of animal husbandry, and since the state no longer invested in feed supplies, the livestock farmers were left vulnerable to the harsh winters.[32] Between 1990 and 1995, the number of nomadic households doubled, while the animal population only increased by about 35 per cent. As a result, fewer than half of all pastoral households had enough animals to survive on over the long term. Just the same, pastureland was damaged due to the sudden increase in the overgrazing of livestock.[33] In a second phase, a rural exodus set in, as impoverished ranchers flocked back to the capital. With

163. A 17-m-high Buddha statue in front of a modern apartment complex in the south of Ulaan Baatar, Mongolia. Photo: 2012.

1.4 million inhabitants, almost half of the country's total population (3.1 million) reside there. In the second half of the 1990s, GDP began to grow again, thanks largely to the sale of raw materials such as copper, gold, silver and cashmere. The growth of the gross domestic product here is tied directly to the respective world market prices.

The first of the two major drivers of growth is the Erdenet copper mine, located north-west of the capital. It is the fourth largest in the world and operated as a Mongolian-Russian consortium. The second driver is the Oyu Tolgoi gold and copper mine in southern Mongolia, where copper has been mined and then processed in China since 2013. Due to the disputes between the major investor Rio Tinto and the Mongolian government – which has wavered between showing friendly and hostile attitudes towards investors – the negotiations were especially challenging. South of Oyu Tolgoi is the huge Avan Tolgoy coal reserve with an estimated deposit of 6.4 billion tons, spread over an area of 1,200 km². The coal is sent to China. As China absorbs 88 per cent of Mongolian exports, 90 per cent of which are raw materials (as of 2014/15), the country is almost completely economically dependent on China and world market prices. It has

to sell its raw materials in order to import fuel and electricity from Russia and cheap manufactured goods from China.[34]

The enforced abolition by international creditors of most import duties and the far-reaching liberalisation of foreign capital transactions has virtually destroyed Mongolia's manufacturing industry. In terms of price, Mongolian private companies simply cannot compete with the government-subsidised Chinese companies. As a consequence, Mongolia has been 'turned into a raw material warehouse for China'.[35] Mongolia has been transformed from an Eastern-bloc exporter of agricultural products and manufactured goods into a China exporter of raw materials. Mongolia will only be able to reduce its dependency on China and world market prices by becoming a processor of raw materials itself. The region's recent economic growth illustrates the dramatic consequences of such dependency: due to a collapse in the price of raw materials, it declined from 17.3 per cent in 2011 to a meagre 2.3 per cent in 2015. At the same time, direct foreign investment fell from US$4.4 billion in 2012 to US$530 million in 2015.[36] To reverse the trend, Mongolia will have to free itself from the tutelage of international financial institutions.

4. The Central Asian Republics

4.1 Central Asia within the Russia-China-US Triangle

Since attaining independence, the 70 million inhabitants of the Central Asian republics are no longer unified. Following the surrender of the Soviet-controlled shared power grid, the slow development of the oil and natural gas pipeline system, and the promotion of local languages, they are now only bound in political and economic terms by their common history. The states are pitted against each other as economic competitors, and there are strong conflicts of interest in the use of critical water supplies. The biggest differences between the five republics lie in their respective raw material reserves. At one end of the spectrum, there are the energy exporters Kazakhstan and Turkmenistan, which have large oil and gas deposits. The former also has significant deposits of uranium, chromite, bauxite and copper, while the latter is furthermore a major cotton producer. At the other end of the spectrum are the poorer, mountainous countries Tajikistan and Kyrgyzstan. They are, on the one hand, energy importers and, on the other, labour exporters. Their most valuable commodity is water (although they cannot freely dispose of it according to their needs owing to the militarily strong agricultural state Uzbekistan) and a significant source of income are the remittances from citizens working abroad. Kyrgyzstan also has significant deposits of gold and rare earth elements. Uzbekistan is positioned between the two poles: while it is a major cotton producer, it also has significant deposits of natural gas, gold, copper and uranium. The country, though, has relatively little petroleum and is a net importer.

At the same time, all five countries share the same fatal handicap, namely geographical centrality. As they are all landlocked (the Caspian Sea is an inland sea), they exist only on the periphery of the international flow of goods. This geographical disadvantage also has a dire impact on both fuel and gas exporters, since they require long pipelines to bring their raw materials to end users and ocean ports. To make matters worse, the existing Soviet pipeline network was geared towards Russia. In the 1990s, Russia greatly underpaid exporters for their raw materials in order to then resell them at high profit margins to Europe. In addition, the United States blocked the construction of pipelines running through Iran, and the poor security situation in Afghanistan through 2017 made building a trans-Afghan pipeline to Pakistan and the Indian Ocean so far impossible. Finally, the insufficient capacity of Central Asia

in the area of oil refining and natural gas liquefaction constitutes a further drawback. Liquefied natural gas (LNG) or compressed natural gas (CNG) can be transported without having to use a pipeline and more conveniently at sea.[37] To this day, the pipelines from Kazakhstan (and Turkmenistan) to China are the only real alternatives to the Russian transport monopoly. Other external similarities between the five republics include their more or less authoritarian regimes, as well as adverse business environments with high entry barriers and business expenses, corruption and legal uncertainty.[38]

Finally, the five states are caught up to varying degrees in the field of tension between geographical neighbours Russia and China as well as the international stakeholders the US and Islamist extremism. While President Yeltsin initially overlooked the Central Asian states, Yevgeny Primakov, head of the Foreign Intelligence Service (1991–96) and Minister of Foreign Affairs of Russia (1996–98), and President Putin recognised – even before the United States – the dangers of Islamic radicalism and the important role of Central Asia in combating it.[39] The presidents of Central Asia, however, had warned about Islamist extremism even earlier still. For the United States, by contrast, Central Asia was only relevant in the early 1990s when it came to ridding Kazakhstan of nuclear weapons, and after 11 September 2001. Apart from a purely military standpoint, the degree of interest waned once again during the invasion of Iraq in 2003. The strategic objectives of the three major powers are not identical and therefore not necessarily exclusive. Russia seeks to retain its historic hegemony, but has too few resources to invest significantly in the new republics. The main Russian instruments are the military Collective Security Treaty Organization (CSTO) and its economic counterpart the Eurasian Economic Community (EURASEC), which was replaced by the Eurasian Economic Union (EAEU) on 1 January 2015.[40] In addition, Russia wants to maintain the already deteriorating pipeline monopoly as long as it can and, like China, to keep Islamic extremism away from its borders, and to nip any separatism in the bud. China also seeks to secure its share of the Caspian fuels and combustibles over the long term, which is why it is investing heavily in local infrastructure. The main tools in China are a differentiated diplomacy that is customised to each country and the Shanghai Cooperation Organization (SCO), which emerged in 2001 from the Shanghai Five, established

---

▶ **164.** Two ministry towers, built in 2004, in the centre of Astana, capital of Kazakhstan. In the background, the Bayterek Tower. Photo: 2012.

Minsk

BELARUS

RUSSIA

Samara

Orenburg

Orsk

Karachaganak

Aktobe

Kiev

Kenkiyak

UKRAINE

Atyrau

Kashagan

Tengiz

MOLDAVIA

Odessa

Astrakhan

Ustyurt

ROMANIA

Novorossiysk

Aktau

Caspian
Sea

Constanta

Black Sea

Bucharest

GEORGIA

Batumi

Tbilisi

Baku

Turkmenbashi

BULGARIA

Samsun

Yerevan

AZERBAIJAN

TUR

Istanbul

Erzerum

ARMENIA

Ashgabat

Ankara

BAKU - TBILISI - CEYHAN PIPELINE BTC

Tabriz

Neka

TURKEY

Izmir

Ceyhan

Tehran

SYRIA

IRAN

CYPRUS

LEBANON

Baghdad

Isfahan

Beirut

Mediterranean Sea

ISRAEL

IRAQ

Bandar Khomeini

Cairo

JORDAN

Bandar Ganaveh

KUWAIT

EGYPT

SAUDI
ARABIA

Kangan

Bandar Abbas

Persian
Gulf

HORM

QATAR

Ishim
Pavlodar
Omsk
ISHIM – ASTANA
RUDNY – ASTANA – ATASU
Astana

Atasu
KENKIYAK – ATASU
ATASU – ALASHANKOU – ÜRÜMQI

KAZAKHSTAN
Lake Balkhash

Dostyk
Alashankou
Ürümqi
Khorgos

...KIYAK – SAMSONOVKA
Syr-Darya River
Turkistan
Almaty
Bishkek
Lunnan
Issyk Kul
Samsonovka
Shymkent
Shagyr
Tekesu
Tashkent
KYRGYZSTAN
Tian Shan

UZBEKISTAN
Taklamakan Desert
CHINA
TAJIKISTAN
Kashgar

Chardju
Amu Darya (Oxus River)
Dushanbe
...ISTAN
...ary

Dauletabad

GWADAR – KASHGAR – ÜRÜMQI PIPELINE

Kabul
Islamabad
AFGHANISTAN

Lahore

Kandahar

TAPI PROJECT
New Delhi

Quetta

PAKISTAN

INDIA

Gwadar
Karachi

Gas and oil pipelines in Central Asia

○ Cities and refineries
— — Existing gas pipelines
- - - Planned gas pipelines
— Existing oil pipelines
- - - Planned oil pipelines

Scale (km)
0   150   300   450   600

N

in 1996. The latter consisted of China and neighbouring Russia, Kazakhstan, Kyrgyzstan and Tajikistan, which earlier belonged to the Soviet Union. The organisation served as a platform to resolve contentious border issues and to demilitarise the borders. Uzbekistan joined the collective in 2001. The SCO wants to ensure the stability of the region and its member states through close cooperation in economic, trade, transport and security issues. They abide by principles pertaining to the members' sovereignty, non-interference in the politics of neighbouring states, and cultural and political diversity. The members of the SCO states thus reject US unilateralism as well as the political guidelines that Western lenders have imposed on Central Asian borrowers, which the SCO deems to be 'values colonialism'.[41] Chinese loans are therefore preferred in particular, because they are not linked to conditions such as the privatisation of state enterprises and land, political pluralism, or the observance of human rights.

For the US, after 11 September 2001, the Central Asian states ultimately transformed from a sideshow into front-line states in the war against the Taliban and al-Qaeda. In this regard, their logistical support seemed critically important. As an institutional tool for the stabilisation of Asian countries and non-NATO members, the US-led NATO launched the 'Partnership for Peace' in 1994, which included all five Central Asian republics. This loose military organisation, though, expressly does not reflect a defence alliance. The mutual assistance requirement applies only to NATO members. In Central Asia, the major powers forged tactical alliances depending on the objective, as for example in the fight against terrorism. The multivector foreign policies of the five republics are the counterpart to the non-exclusive objectives of the major powers. Indeed, they have been used to good effect to play the major powers off against each other. To paraphrase a well-known saying: 'Happiness has many pipelines.'[42]

165. Parade of presidential guard with the Kazakh national flag during the state visit of the German President Roman Herzog in Almaty in April 1995. A steppe eagle is shown on the flag, flying under a sun with 32 rays. The sky-blue colour was considered sacred by the Old Turks and Mongols because it symbolised 'Eternal Heaven'. The basic colour of the flag expresses the Kazakhs' bond with the Turko-Mongolian heritage. Photo: 1995.

166. German President Roman Herzog receives a traditional welcome of bread and salt at the airport of Shymkent, South Kazakhstan, from provincial governor Zautbek Turisbekov. Photo: 11 April 1995.

4.2 Kazakhstan

Kazakhstan was the last Central Asian republic to declare its independence, on 16 December 1991. With an area of 2,724,900 km², it is the largest landlocked country in the world. The sparsely populated country has fewer than 18 million inhabitants, 64 per cent of whom are ethnic Kazakhs and 23 per cent Russian. The head of state of the presidential republic is Nursultan Nazarbayev, who was elected on 1 December 1991 as the only candidate for presi-dent. Similar to Uzbek President Karimov and Turkmen President Niyazov, Nazarbayev had been appointed leader of the regional Communist Party by Gorbachev before independence.[43] While the leaders of Uzbekistan, Tajikistan and Turkmenistan officially supported the anti-Gorbachev coup of August 1991, Nazarbayev and Kyrgyz Communist Party leader Masaliyev refused to recognise the coup leaders and their decrees.[44] Like the other Central Asian heads of state (except for Tajikistan's), Nazarbayev was confronted with Turkey's pan-Islamic and pan-Turkic aspirations. Thanks to Gorbachev's glasnost, Turkey began sending hundreds of Islamic

activists and missionaries to Central Asia as early as 1990, thereby contributing to the re-Islamisation of the region. When the Turkish president Özal proposed the signing of a pan-Turkic declaration in December 1991, Nazarbayev replied: 'Mr. President, we just left the Russian Empire. We do not want to enter another empire now.'[45]

Kazakhstan immediately attracted the attention of the United States after it declared its independence, for the world's fourth largest nuclear arsenal was on Kazakh soil. It not only included 650 tactical nuclear weapons, but also 104 intercontinental ballistic missiles of the R-36M type (NATO code name: SS-18) in fixed silos with ten individually targeted nuclear warheads – the most dangerous weapon of the former Soviet Union – and 40 long-range bombers of the Tupolev Tu-95 type with a range of up to 15,000 km unrefueled. Thanks to Russian-US-Kazakh cooperation, all tactical nuclear weapons were moved back to Russia by May 1992; then, all ICBMs were removed and all silos were destroyed by 1995. This joint achievement of the former rivals was unprecedented.[46] In a next step, the tunnels and bore holes where the underground firings took place

167. A part of the war memorial in Panfilov Park in Almaty, Kazakhstan. The monument honours the Kazakh soldiers who fell in World War II in the defence of Moscow; in particular, it commemorates General Panfilov (1893–1941), who commanded the 316th Infantry Division consisting of Kazakh and Kyrgyz reservists and who, with a small number of soldiers, allegedly destroyed 50 German tanks (other sources speak of 18 tanks) outside of Moscow. The veracity of this episode is greatly debated.[25] Photo: 2005.

at the nuclear test site at Semipalatinsk were demolished and sealed until the year 2000. Just the same, an 18,000-km²-wide area remains contaminated and there is a high incidence of cancer and blood diseases as well as deformities.[47] A delicate bone of contention then concerned the further use of the Baikonur Cosmodrome, the world's largest space port. In 1994, presidents Nazarbayev and Yeltsin agreed that Kazakhstan would lease the space station to Russia on an annual basis for US$115 million, with a term of 20 years. In 2005, the term was extended until 2050.[48] While Kazakhstan had already settled the course of its 6,846-km-long border with Russia in 1992, the negotiations over the 1,533-km-long border with China took somewhat longer. The discussions to resolve the numerous border disputes between the Soviet Union and China had begun in November 1989 and were continued by Russia, Kazakhstan, Kyrgyzstan and Tajikistan after the dissolution of the Soviet Union. The Russian-Chinese border demarcation was laid down in the protocols of 1991, 1994 and 9 December 1999; the Kazakh-Chinese

border demarcation was settled in the agreements of 1994, 1997, 1998, and from May 2002. The agreements also encompassed the establishment of demilitarised zones along the borders and other confidence-building measures.[49]

Nazarbayev's decision to hold off as long as he did before declaring independence is explained by Kazakhstan's geographical location as a border state with Russia. After 1991, more Slavs lived in Kazakhstan – mostly Russians and Ukrainians, who accounted for 43 per cent of the total population – than ethnic Kazakhs. In the northern areas adjacent to Russia, the Slavs were very much in the majority, comprising up to 90 per cent of the population in eight of the nine oblasts.[50] Even the officer corps of the 440,000-strong Soviet force in Kazakhstan was 95 per cent Slavic.[51] The Cossacks in particular were opposed to Kazakh independence and called for splitting off from Kazakhstan should it come to this. What is more, between August and December 1991, leading Soviet politicians threatened to redraw the Russian-Kazakh border if the republic left the Soviet Union. Even after the dissolution of the Soviet Union, Cossacks and Slavs insisted on the country's union with Russia or at least the creation of a largely autonomous Slavic region.[52] Nazarbayev manoeuvred skillfully: he facilitated the emigration of Russians and Ukrainians, even though it meant a substantial loss of expertise; he also offered immediate citizenship to returning ethnic Kazakhs from abroad. Although he rejected the introduction of a Kazakh-Russian dual citizenship, he recognised Russian as a second official language. The measures proved successful. By 2009, the proportion of Slavs decreased to 26 per cent, while that of the Kazakhs rose to 64 per cent.[53] To promote economic development and ethnic intermingling of north and central Kazakhstan, Nazarbayev decided in 1994 to move the capital from Almaty, located in south Kazakhstan, to the inland city of Aqmola. The newly built capital was dedicated on 10 December 1997 and renamed Astana in 1998, which means 'capital' in Kazakh[54] (figs. 164, 168, 184). Although Kazakhstan is a member of the Russian-led Eurasian Economic Union, Kazakhstan's status as a neighbour to Putin's Russia remains uneasy. This was apparent in an ambiguous comment from the Russian President after the occupation of the Crimea: on 29 August 2014, Putin said Kazakhstan had never existed as a state and was merely the outcome of Nazarbayev's policies. Kazakhstan, he further emphasised, was part of the greater Russian world and the majority of Kazakhs desired close relations with Russia. Nazarbayev, on the other hand, was an allegedly prudent president who would never challenge the will of the (supposedly pro-Russian) majority.[55] Putin's warning to Nazarbayev to not pursue a policy that was hostile to Russia was unmistakable.

Thanks to its rich reserves of raw materials and the sensible policies of President Nazarbayev, Kazakhstan is responsible for 60 per cent of the gross domestic product of all five Central Asian republics (173.2 of a total of US$289.3 billion). Also, in terms of per capita gross domestic product, Kazakhstan led as of 2015 with US$10,510, followed by Turkmenistan (US$6,672), Uzbekistan (US$2,132), Kyrgyzstan (US$1,103) and Tajikistan (US$926).[56] The three commodity-producing states owe their reserves not least to the Soviet Union, as the Soviets neglected or even completely ignored the Kazakh, Turkmen and Uzbek natural resources in favour of the more easily exploitable deposits in Western Siberia and Azerbaijan.[57] With 30,000 million barrels[58] (MMbbl) of verified oil reserves, Kazakhstan has the twelfth largest oil reserves in the world. As a producer, it ranked 18th in the world in 2015.[59] Kazakhstan is also 18th with regard to verified natural gas reserves.[60] Kazakhstan's three largest oil and gas fields are the two mainland fields Karachaganak and Tengiz and the giant sea field Kashagan, whose deposit is located at a depth

of more than 4,000 m beneath the Caspian Sea and is accordingly difficult to extract. Discovered in 2000, the field was considered to be the largest new discovery in the oil industry for more than 40 years. Extraction, though, had to be stopped in 2013 only a few weeks after operations began due to technical problems. In the autumn of 2016, extraction was resumed with a modest output of 90,000 barrels of oil per day. Nevertheless, it is surely not profitable with a world market price around US$50 per barrel.[61] As Kazakhstan lacked the capital, know-how, and technical equipment to exploit these deposits, it was forced to sell a majority stake in these exploration and production projects to foreign consortia. Because Kazakhstan was dependent as a landlocked country on the Russian pipeline network, Moscow was able to block any project that displeased it and to insist on Russia's own share from the relevant consortium. This is exactly what happened in May 1994: after Kazakhstan granted a 50 per cent stake to Chevron, 20 per cent to Exxon Mobile, and the remaining 30 per cent to the state company KazMunayGas as part of the Tengiz-Chevroil consortium, Russia proceeded to block the Kazakhstan pipeline from Tengiz to the port of Novorossiysk on the Black Sea. As a consequence, Kazakh oil exports fell by a third compared with 1991. This dealt a severe blow to the Kazakh economy, as many factories that previously manufactured for the Soviet Union had closed that year.[62] To this day, Russia continues to do everything within its power to maintain the highly profitable transit monopoly on oil and gas, while limiting competition with their own oil and gas production. In Milan Hauner's words, 'an oil or gas pipeline valve can be turned off, producing an instant paralysing effect on the consumer countries along the pipeline [and on the producer country], far more quickly and cheaply than a military operation can be prepared and launched.'[63] It was due not least to these kinds of blockades and the financial crisis of 2007/08 that Kazakhstan was forced to sell larger shares in the development of its oil and gas fields. Kazakhstan is estimated to still have 15–18 per cent of the twelve largest domestic fields and to receive about 20 per cent of the profit. China, on the other hand, is believed to now own more than a third of the domestic fields. It is also a stakeholder in KazMunayGas International, which operates in the mid- and downstream business.[64] Kazakhstan is working on reducing its dependence on the Russian distribution network. In the new Caspian Pipeline Consortium, whose pipeline has connected the Tengiz field to Novorossiysk since 2001, Kazakhstan has a share of 19 per cent, the Russian state-owned company Transneft of 31 per cent, Chevron of 15 per cent and Russian Lukoil of 12.5 per cent.[65] Kazakhstan broke the Russian monopoly in 2006 with the 3,000-km-long oil pipeline from Atyrau to the Chinese city of Alashankou. The first natural gas pipeline, the Asia Gas Pipeline, followed in 2009 with the total length of 8,700 km.[66] The second natural gas pipeline was put into operation in 2010 and the third in 2014. Work continues on the fourth.[67] While Kazakhstan can continue to gradually free itself in the natural gas business from the grip of Gazprom (albeit at the cost of dependence on China), more than half of Kazakh oil continues to flow through Russian pipelines. Then again, the Kazakh pipeline to China is also used to transport Russian oil from Western Siberia to China.[68] Russia and Iran oppose the project of a trans-Caspian gas pipeline, which would benefit Kazakhstan and Turkmenistan. The pipeline, in any event, cannot be built without the consent of all the neighbouring states. What is more, Azerbaijan's interest has waned since the discovery of its huge Shah Deniz gas field.[69]

As with all commodity exporters, the question of the sustainability of the relatively high gross domestic product is closely linked to the ability to diversify the economy in areas such as manufacturing, finance and services. Compared to the other republics in the region, Kazakhstan is quite well off in terms of its favourable business climate. Of decisive importance will be the implementation of the state stabilisation fund under Nazarbayev's control.[70] For Kazakhstan, as well as Turkmenistan, the challenge of economic diversification is all the more urgent given that the oil age will not last forever. Alternative energy sources such as hydrogen could slow the demand for oil and, when coupled with a simultaneously expanding offer by countries such as Venezuela and Iran, cause prices to fall. As the former Saudi oil minister Sheikh Zaki Yamani remarked: 'The Stone Age did not end for lack of stone, and the Oil Age will end long before the world runs out of oil.'[71] Kazakhstan managed to build a stable financial industry, which has grown into the leading provider of financial services in Central Asia. In the manufacturing industry, efforts in the pharmaceuticals and the field of fertilisers and pesticides, not to mention petrochemicals, are promising.[72] Kazakhstan has also successfully invested in agribusiness, with a priority being placed on grain. With its 650 mill plants, the country was the world's eighth-largest wheat exporter and second largest flour exporter in 2015. The main markets are Central Asia, Afghanistan, Iran and Russia.[73] As for Kazakhstan's future, the biggest uncertainty lies in the lack of succession planning for the aging President Nazarbayev, born in 1940. The greatest danger is possibly the merger of criminal gangs with Salafist provocateurs, who recruit followers among the low-paid oil and gas workers in west Kazakhstan and carry out terrorist attacks. One such attack took place at the beginning of June 2016, when armed gangs plundered arms businesses and attacked a military base in the industrial city of Aktobe.[74]

4.3 Kyrgyzstan

The state of Kyrgyzstan – which spans an area of 199,951 km[2] and has approximately 6 million inhabitants – declared its independence on 30 August 1991. The history of the young republic has been marked by regional power struggles. The longstanding first secretary of the Kyrgyz Communist Party, Turdakun Usubaliyev (in office 1961–85), enjoyed the support of the east Kyrgyzstan Naryn community. In 1985, Gorbachev replaced him with Absamat Masaliyev (in office 1985–90), who was supported by the west Kyrgyzstan Talas group. In the spring of 1990, violent clashes broke out between the two factions. Bloody unrest then followed in June between local Kyrgyz and the strong Uzbek minority in the south-western region of Osh, resulting in approximately 300 to 1000 deaths. The Uzbeks from Osh fought on the side of the neutral Askar Akayev (in office 1990–2005) from north Kyrgyzstan, who succeeded in winning the support of the Naryn faction. Akayev was appointed Chairman of the Supreme Soviet of the Kyrgyz Soviet Socialist Republic and, in the autumn of 1991, won the first free presidential elections unopposed.[75]

The poor mountainous region was hit especially hard by the collapse of the Soviet Union, as subsidies from Moscow constituted 75 per cent of the state budget. Kyrgyzstan was in urgent need of financial assistance and had to borrow from Russia and the IMF. Because the IMF tied the extension of loans to liberal economic conditions, the government had to end control of the prices of basic goods and privatise state-owned enterprises. This resulted in hyperinflation, the closure of unprofitable companies, and the impoverishment of the general population. A decrease in agricultural production and herd stocks followed. The fact that the country joined the WTO in 1998 did little to change the difficult economic situation. Kyrgyzstan had indeed received plenty of credit, but there was hardly any investment to boost the economy. As a result, the country's debt burden grew continuously.[76]

One of Kyrgyzstan's most important export items is gold. The Kumtor gold mine, though, belongs to the Canadian company Centerra Gold (formerly Cameco Gold Corporation), while the Kyrgyz government itself holds a 32.7 per cent stake. Another significant export activity is the statistically poorly documented, but rapidly growing resale of cheap Chinese products. Kyrgyzstan has 'become a hub for the reexport of Chinese goods to the rest of Central Asia and the CIS'.[77] Just the same, a significant part of this

▶ **168.** The main concert hall, built in 2009 by Italian architect Manfredi Nicoletti, Astana, Kazakhstan. The largest venue of the hall has 3,500 seats. Photo: 2012.

169. The 65-km-long Toktogul Dam in Kyrgyzstan, filled in the 1970s, holds 19.5 km³ of water. The reservoir dams up the Naryn River, a tributary of the Syr Darya. Photo: 2016.

import-export business is conducted within the informal economy. The modest per capita gross domestic product of Kyrgyzstan is US$1,103, almost nine times lower than that of Kazakhstan.[78] At the same time, Kyrgyz consumer prices for domestic products and Chinese imports are lower than comparable Kazakh goods. What is more, the informal economy generates an estimated 40–60 per cent of total economic output. Still, the single most important source of income of Kyrgyzstan are the remittances of Kyrgyz working in Russia – Kyrgyzstan's, and also Tajikistan's, most important 'trade goods' are therefore neither raw materials nor industrial products, but people. The 500,000 to 1 million Kyrgyz working in Russia transfer about US$2 billion home, which constitutes *ca.* 27 per cent of GDP.[79] But as these remittances are often made as cash transfers, they remain untaxed.[80] These transfers are not only of vital economic importance, but have socio-political significance to the extent that they serve as a safety valve against civic unrest. Since the expulsion of hundreds of thousands of Kyrgyz or Tajik from Russia would destabilise both countries and their respective governments,

Moscow possesses a potent political lever. On the other hand, Kyrgyzstan and Tajikistan are more than just dependent on Russia's migration policy; they are also at the mercy of its economic development with respect to the price of oil. When the price of a barrel of crude fell from US$144 to US$34 in 2008 due to the financial crisis, hundreds of thousands of Kyrgyz lost their jobs and were forced to leave Russia. Remittances were consequently cut in half.[81]

Kyrgyzstan shares another feature with the equally mountainous Tajikistan: an abundance of water. In the face of Uzbekistan's economic and military superiority, however, the two mountainous states are hardly in a position to exploit or sell it. Ultimately, the interests of electricity producers Kyrgyzstan and Tajikistan are diametrically opposed to those of the agrarian states of Uzbekistan, Turkmenistan and Kazakhstan, for the use of water for the production of electricity is temporally at odds with its use for irrigation. The upstream mountainous states want to retain the water in their reservoirs in the summer, when relatively little power is consumed. This enables them to use the water in the winter, when the demand for electricity, especially for heating purposes, skyrockets and the reservoirs drain. Conversely, the downstream states, particularly Uzbekistan and Turkmenistan, need large amounts of water in the summer to irrigate the watering-intensive cotton fields and orchards. Yet water that is discharged in the winter causes floods. The end result is that either the agricultural states lack water for irrigation or the mountainous states lack water for electricity. During the Soviet era, these contradictions were remedied by a cross-regional, Central Asian power grid and a coordination office. In the winter, the power producers were only permitted to use a limited amount of water so that the reservoirs were filled to the maximum for the summer irrigation needs downstream. In turn, in the winter and the spring, these agricultural republics were obliged to provide the mountainous states with oil, coal, gas or electricity produced from thermal power plants free of charge. After 1991, Uzbekistan and Kazakhstan left the supraregional power grid. The system of coordinated water management then disappeared and was replaced by a series of bilateral agreements.[82] The downstream states, however, have invoked a UN convention regarding the non-navigational use of international waters from 1997 and flatly refuse to compensate upstream republics for irrigation water. As a result, the two poor mountainous states Kyrgyzstan and Tajikistan bear the extremely high costs of construction and maintenance of dams, even though they cannot use them at their own discretion. Kyrgyzstan controls 70 per cent of the water supply of Uzbekistan, whose president Karimov has repeatedly warned of the possibility of 'water wars', but it can use only 10–15 per cent of its estimated hydroelectric potential due to the unequal power relations. Uzbekistan has interrupted electricity and gas supplies to the two mountain republics more than once during the winter as a warning against increased hydroelectric water use. Kyrgyzstan's situation is further aggravated by the fact that the modernisation and development of antiquated water power plants cannot be accomplished without foreign investors. At the same time, private investors are discouraged by corruption and, above all, by the government's artificial suppression of electricity prices, which hinders profitable power generation.[83]

In Kyrgyzstan, as in the other presidential republics of Central Asia, the difficult economic situation is a breeding ground for corruption. President Akayev may not have fallen prey to corruption during his first presidential term, but from 1996 onward he began to rule in an authoritarian manner and to enrich himself and his immediate family. Personal enrichment first took place by way of monopolies through the sale of fuel and alcohol as well as in the operation of casinos. In total, Akayev allegedly controlled 42 companies through his son and son-in-law, including the

Kumtor gold mine. In a second step, Akayev expanded nepotism even further and sold important or prestigious government posts. Corruption subsequently widened in the middle and lower levels of government.[84] The discontent of the population reached its peak in the parliamentary elections of February 2005. There were voting irregularities, and the alleged election of Akayev's son Aidar and daughter Bermet aroused fears that the soon-outgoing president would nominate one of the two as his successor. The discontent erupted into mass demonstrations, looting, and arson, first in Jalalabad and Osh, and, on 24 March, in Bishkek. Akayev and his family then fled to Moscow. The next day the parliament appointed Kurmanbek Bakiyev (in office 2005–10) interim president, who then won the presidential elections in July by a wide margin.[85]

Akayev's overthrow in the wake of mass demonstrations was a cause of concern for the other Central Asian potentates, particularly Islom Karimov in Uzbekistan. Indeed, it was the third violent overthrow of a president of a former Soviet republic within three years, with all three coups having been sponsored to a greater or lesser degree by externally financed NGOs. US Ambassador Richard Miles and foreign NGOs such as the 'Open Society Institute' (OSI) of the American currency speculator George Soros played an active role during the Georgian 'Rose Revolution' in November 2003, which led to President Shevardnadze's ouster. In Ukraine's 'Orange Revolution' in the winter of 2004/05, which forced a re-run of the presidential elections, American institutions and NGOs like Soros's OSI or the semi-public 'Freedom House' based in Washington and the German Konrad Adenauer Foundation likewise exerted significant influence.[86] And during the Kyrgyz 'Tulip Revolution' in 2005, the very same actors – the Freedom House, OSI, the US embassy – backed the Kyrgyz opposition.[87] It should not be surprising therefore that many Central Asian potentates believe that certain American and Western European NGOs and the US embassies were the masterminds behind some of the disturbances directed against them.

Though Kyrgyzstan does not border on Afghanistan, it has nevertheless been impacted by Islamist terrorism. Specifically, there were internal Uzbek clashes between the government and the militant Islamist terrorist organisation Islamic Movement of Uzbekistan (IMU), which was founded in 1997/98 and has worked closely with al-Qaeda and the Taliban. In 1999, Kyrgyzstan was thrust into the undertow of Islamist terror after the IMU committed six car bombs attacks in Tashkent on 16 February, one of which was aimed at President Karimov. Afterwards, Juma Namangani (1968–2001), the military leader of the IMU built a network of sympathisers, which stretched from the remote mountain region of Tavildara in

Tajikistan to the poorly controlled Batken province in south-western Kyrgyzstan. There are five Uzbek and two Tajik exclaves in Batken. Fighters of the IMU settled there and built a weapons depot. In particular, the two larger exclaves – the Uzbek Sukh exclave with an area of 234 km^2 and the Tajik Vorukh exclave with an area of 97 km^2 – were ideally suited as a base for Islamist operations. The local population was traditionally fundamentalist, and they were out of the reach of Uzbek troops. From Sukh, Namangani could declare an Uzbek 'exile government', whereas the Uzbek army could not intervene without violating Kyrgyz sovereignty.[88] In August 1999, the IMU fighters from Tajikistan invaded Batken, where they abducted Kyrgyz civilians, officials, and officers as well as Japanese geologists. In battles with Kyrgyz soldiers, the Islamists also suffered losses, including, among others, the infamous Chechnya-trained Abduwali Yuldashev.[89] Kyrgyzstan and Japan paid ransoms to free the hostages, and, in the autumn, Russia evacuated around 600 IMU fighters and their families to Afghanistan by helicopter. In the autumn/winter of 2000/01, history repeated itself – this time IMU fighters were also evacuated from their Tajik stronghold in Tavildara.[90] The question remains whether the two Russian air evacuations of IMU fighters were merely intended to free Tajikistan and Kyrgyzstan of their unwelcome guests or whether there were other considerations. In any case, the IMU terrorist operations had severe consequences for Kyrgyzstan and Tajikistan. The enraged Uzbek President Karimov accused the two republics of neglecting the fight against international terrorism. To put them under additional pressure, he further cut off the gas supply to Kyrgyzstan and Tajikistan several times during the winter months, closed the border crossings, and laid mines at the borders.[91] Kyrgyzstan, on the other hand, is able to block the roads leading to the Uzbek exclaves and completely seal them off.[92]

Similar to Uzbekistan, Kyrgyzstan also complied with the United States' desire for an airport permitting troop transport, supply delivery, and refuelling in December 2001. To this end, it provided the Manas International Airport near Bishkek. Like the other Central Asian republics, Kyrgyzstan expected it could free itself from Russia's stranglehold through deeper relations with the United States. These states also hoped that the Bush administration would break with the outgoing Clinton administration's moralising and missionary emphasis on democratic values and human rights. This hope proved to be illusory by 2005 at the latest.[93] The initial annual rent for the air base was very low at US$2 million. For this reason, President Bakiyev negotiated an annual fee of US$17 million in the summer of 2006 and the promise that the US would also provide assistance of US$133 million. The US was willing to negotiate, as President Karimov had ordered it to vacate the Uzbek

Karshi-Khanabad Air Base (K2) by November 2005, which it had used since December 2001. Nonetheless, because the US subsumed the additional assistance under humanitarian programmes that Bakiyev did not want, it was of dubious value. One example here is the work of the Peace Corps, which also serves as an American propaganda tool.[94] To avoid falling behind politically, Russia leased the smaller former Kant Air Base in Bishkek for a period of fifteen years from December 2002. The contract was extended for another fifteen years in 2012.[95] Kyrgyzstan is the only country in the world where there was both an American and a Russian air base from 2002 to 2014 – at a distance of less than 40 km apart.[96]

Despite the Kyrgyz hope of less political corruption, President Bakiyev continued with the kleptocracy of his predecessor. His closest relatives had investments in banks, power supply, department stores, and restaurants, and his family from the south was also allegedly involved in drug smuggling.[97] But the main source of income of both presidents came through the sale of kerosene to the US Air Force, which used the fuel to refill its aircraft onsite, but also for aerial refuelling. President Akayev had organised the kerosene trade via subcontractors, who were controlled by his son and son-in-law. Kerosene purchased from Russia cost US$780 per metric ton (including transportation to Kyrgyzstan). It was then sold to the US Air Force for US$1,263 per ton, resulting in a profit margin of 38.2 per cent. Since the United States bought US$1.857 billion worth of kerosene from 2001 to the end of 2011, the resulting profit was US$709 million – a considerable portion of which was absorbed by the entourages of both presidents.[98] As it is hardly conceivable that the United States was unaware of the huge margins of the Kyrgyz middlemen, the Pentagon must have been actively involved in paying bribes to the ruling families of Kyrgyzstan. The efforts of the State Department to combat corruption in Central Asia thus appear blatantly hypocritical.

When the remittances of Kyrgyz migrant labourers plummeted by 50 per cent in 2008, Bakiyev dangerously wheeled and dealed with both Russia and the United States over the American military base. In February 2009, he announced that he would close the US base and that Russia would transfer a generous aid package, consisting of US$450 million in subsidies and soft loans and US$1.7 billion in credit. At the same time, Bakiyev negotiated with the United States for a continuation of the US base. Moscow had barely paid a first instalment of US$300 million when Bakiyev came to an agreement with the United States in April regarding a yearly lease of US$60 million. The president announced the new deal in July, revealing the duplicitous game he had been playing.[99] Yet Bakiyev's calculation misfired: in the autumn, a campaign began in the Russian press that exposed Bakiyev's corruption and nepotism, and, in early 2010, Russia introduced a fuel export tax to Kyrgyzstan of US$193.50 per tonne. The fuel and transport costs soared immediately in Kyrgyzstan and boosted inflation. This led to mass demonstrations at the beginning of April and to the overthrow of Bakiyev, who fled to Belarus.[100] Simultaneously, a transitional government was put together under interim President Roza Otunbayeva (in office 2010–11). She initiated a constitutional amendment to transform the presidential republic into a parliamentary republic and to transfer more powers to the parliament. The vast majority of the electorate voted in favour of this change in a referendum on 27 June 2010. Shortly thereafter, Otunbayeva had her term extended to December 2011. Under her interim presidency, relatively free parliamentary and presidential elections were conducted. The latter were won by Social Democrat Almazbek Atambayev (in office 2011–17).[101] Since the new

constitution limits the term in power of the president to six years, Atambayev was not allowed to run for the next elections held on 15 October 2017. The more or less fair elections were won by the former prime minister Sooronbay Jeenbekov, Atambayev's candidate. The outgoing president will become Chairman of the Social Democratic Party, a post he already held from 1999 to 2011, thus remaining an influential politician.

The interim government of Otunbayeva was weak, however, and unable to protect the population. In June 2010, severe rioting broke out in the cities of Osh, Uzgen, Jalalabad and Kochkor in south-western Kyrgyzstan between ethnic Kyrgyz and Uzbeks, which lasted a week. In the riots and arson, at least 470 people – mainly Uzbeks – were killed and entire Uzbek neighbourhoods were systematically looted and burned. As a consequence, 400,000 Uzbeks were left homeless and 100,000 fled to Uzbekistan. The unrest was both ethnic and social in nature, stemming from the poorer Kyrgyz, who

170. Monument honouring the fallen on the occasion of the unrest of 2002 in Bospiek Aksy and the revolution of April 7, 2010 in Bishkek. The monument shows a 7-m-high, white-and-black stone block; at the site of the fracture, people are sliding the black block down a slope. The monument symbolises the victory of good over evil. Ala-Too Square, Bishkek. Photo: 2017.

171. German President Roman Herzog (in office 1994–99) and his wife Christiane during a state visit to Uzbekistan in April 1995 together with the Uzbek President Islom Karimov (in office 1991–2016) and his wife Tatiana. Registan Square in Samarkand. Photo: 1995.

have traditionally worked as farmers and livestock breeders as well as in the municipalities. They targeted the large minority of affluent urban Uzbeks who controlled trade and commerce.[102] When the government sent in troops who consisted almost entirely of ethnic Kyrgyz, the troops sided with the Kyrgyz rioters. Order was only restored once Russia consented to Otunbayeva's request for military aid. The outbreak of violence shocked many Uzbeks, especially in the Fergana Valley, and promoted the belief that a strong regime which ensured security and stability in a weak state was more valuable than democratic processes.[103] Kyrgyzstan, in fact, remains a special case politically insofar as it staved off the establishment of a decades-long presidential rule twice and introduced a parliamentary system in 2010. Aside from its gold reserves, the country's vulnerabilities continue to be its lack of raw materials, along with its continued dependence on foreign transfers and, thus, ultimately Russia. The biggest challenges, moreover, lie with Uzbekistan and tensions over controversial water management, drug smuggling, and radical Islamist movements in the impoverished south.

4.4 Uzbekistan

Uzbekistan's 32 million inhabitants make it the most populous country in Central Asia. With a surface area of 448,978 km², however, it is only one-sixth as large as Kazakhstan. The term of First Secretary of the Communist Party of Uzbekistan Sharaf Rashidov (in office 1959–83) was overshadowed by the devastating earthquake of 26 April 1966, which utterly destroyed the old city of Tashkent. After being lavishly rebuilt, the city subsequently developed into the Soviet Union's fourth largest city.[104] When Andropov took power in Moscow in November 1982, he launched an anti-corruption campaign that took aim at the economically important Uzbekistan. Following Rashidov's death – either resulting from suicide or a heart attack – the country's massive misman-agement and a misappropriation of funds in connection with the cotton industry came to light. Although the next secretary general Inamjan Usmankhojaev (in office 1983–88) continued the anti-corruption campaign, he was also accused of corruption after being dismissed. Many young people were so disgusted at the widespread corruption among the party apparatus that they turned to Islam, partly due to the influence of Afghanistan veterans. When violent rioting broke out in Fergana[105] in June 1989, Gorbachev replaced First Secretary Nishanov (in office 1988–89) with Islom Karimov (first secretary 1989–91, president 1991–2016). Uzbekistan proclaimed its independence on 31 August 1991, and Karimov had himself elected president on 29 December.[106]

In a similar way as with Kazakhstan and Kyrgyzstan, Uzbekistan faced the loss of predictable markets and the requirement to pay for Russian goods in hard currency as well as galloping inflation. Besides this, there was an imminent risk of a coup due to radical Islamist groups, which were gaining the sympathies of more and more young men. The instances of corruption caused the communist ideology to lose much of credibility. It had also lost much of its relevance after the collapse of the Soviet Union. Political Islam was thus the only remaining ideological alternative to the status quo. Karimov realised he needed to do everything he could to limit the impoverishment of broad sections of the population, which might make them susceptible to Islamist ideologies. The president decided on a dual strategy of methodically fighting against political Islamism and introducing prudent economic policies. Islamist groups sparked riots in Fergana already in the autumn of 1991, calling for the overthrow of the Karimov government, the establishment of an Islamic state, and the introduction of Sharia law. They included the Islamic Revival Party Uzbekistan (IRPU), the Wahhabism inspired Adolat ('Justice'), and the Islam Lashkarlari Party ('Warriors of Islam').[107] When civil servants were abducted in Fergana in the spring of 1992, Karimov restored order by using Interior Ministry troops and expelling foreign Salafists.[108] Many militants fled to Afghanistan or Tajikistan. A civil war broke out in the latter in May between the ruling neo-communists and Islamic parties of varying degrees of radicalism. When the armed Islamic opposition backed by Afghan mujahideen occupied Dushanbe and the revolution threatened to spill over into Uzbek Fergana, Karimov stepped in. He equipped and trained a brigade loyal to the Tajik regime and provided them with heavy military equipment in their successful attack on Dushanbe, which commenced on 4 December.[109] Karimov's intervention prevented the establishment of an Islamic state north of the Amu Darya River, which would have bordered on Taliban-controlled Afghanistan from 1996. Karimov pursued a strategy of systematically combating political Islamism until his death in 2016. By the same token, he also professed – possibly for political reasons – to being a non-political, tolerant Muslim.

In certain Muslim societies without a parliamentary tradition, it seems that the only alternative to fundamentalism consists in a secular authoritarian regime. Alexey Malashenko formulated the dilemma as follows: 'Experience has demonstrated that Islamism will be impossible to suppress by force alone, while any liberalization would open the way for the Islamists to make use of democratic institutions, especially elections, where they would be able to achieve significant success.'[110] This is the predicament that American and European politicians and NGOs have been slow to recognise; namely, that free elections in some Muslim states can actually lead to an alliance of Islamists gaining power, who then proceed to dismantle democratic institutions. The introduction of parliamentary democracy thus enables a secular regime to be transformed into an Islamist one. For Karimov and his colleagues, the Western slogan 'stability through democratic change' is a contradiction in terms. In their view, abruptly introduced democratic change causes instability. Like the other leaders of Central Asia, Karimov promoted cultural nationalism to affect a state-supported counterweight to political Islam. In each case, a famous real or mythical figure has been unearthed from the past and put on a pedestal such as Amir Timur (Timur-e Lang) in Uzbekistan, Khan Ablai in Kazakhstan, the legendary hero Manas in Kyrgyzstan, and the dynasty of the Samanids and Rudaki in Tajikistan.[111] In Turkmenistan, President Niyazov picked himself instead of a leading figure from the past: in the vein of Kemal Atatürk, he anointed himself 'Leader of all Turkmen' or simply Turkmenbashi.[112]

As a rise in unemployment was the most fundamental threat to the stability of Uzbekistan, Karimov went about modernising the economy cautiously. He was guided by the Chinese synthesis of a fairly free and controlled economy. In this vein, many economic sectors were liberalised, while strategically important segments such as cotton, grain, gold and other metals and natural gas were kept under state control. Today, the cultivation of cotton enjoys the highest priority as an earner of foreign currency and is clearly preferred over the textile processing industry. In addition, grain production was augmented to make Uzbekistan self-sufficient in this area and to put a halt to the spending of foreign currency on the purchase of grain from abroad. Most arable land remained state-owned, for it was feared that a privatisation of land could lead to disputes over water rights and unemployment. Along with the extraction of raw materials, the manufacturing industry was also promoted. For example, Karimov initiated the forming of a joint venture in 1992 with the Korean carmaker Daewoo, whose cars sold well throughout the CIS. After the collapse of Daewoo in 2001, General Motors acquired Daewoo's stake. Twenty-five per cent of GM Uzbekistan currently belongs to the Americans and 75 per cent to the Uzbek state.[113] Overall, Uzbekistan's

172. Cotton harvest south of Tashkent, Uzbekistan. Photo: 2005.

economic output has been impressive: apart from the early 1990s and the period from 2000 to 2002, the country's gross domestic product has grown continuously, from US$9.7 billion in 2002 to US$66.7 billion in 2015.[114] Although cotton is still an important source of foreign currency, the country no longer has the same dependency on cotton production.[115] Cotton exports to the US and Europe also suffered due to boycotts on Uzbek cotton, initiated because the cotton harvest in Uzbekistan is not mechanised, but done manually by 'voluntary' civil servants and students, i.e. adolescents. Since then, Uzbek cotton has only been able to make its way into the processing industry abroad through circuitous routes.[116] Current cotton cultivation has additional challenges, however, including the ongoing threat of salinisation and the poor state of leaking irrigation channels. In addition, Uzbek migrant workers play an important role in Uzbekistan. The approximately 2 million Uzbeks working in Russia contribute remittances of around US$5.7 billion or 10 per cent of GDP (as of 2012), which is an important stopgap to the country's unemployment.[117] Due to complicated regulations, corruption, capital controls, and a

dictated national exchange rate, conditions for foreign investors remain unfavourable.

In the latter half of the 1990s, two foreign-funded organisations emerged out of the numerous Islamist groups in Uzbekistan: Hezb al-Tahrir al-Islami (HTI) ('Liberation Party') and the Islamic Movement of Uzbekistan (IMU). Both groups initially settled in Fergana, as the valley had become a stronghold of Salafist thought since liberalisation in the 1980s. In the early 1990s, Wahhabi and Salafi missionaries from Saudi Arabia, Egypt, Turkey, Pakistan and Afghanistan contributed to the further radicalisation of the densely populated valley. All these groups were motivated by the prospect of introducing Sharia law and the general Islamisation of state and society.[118] The fundamentalist Hezb al-Tahrir Party emerged from the politically active Muslim Brotherhood. Founded in 1953 by a Palestinian, it is active in Egypt, the Middle East, Central Asia and Europe. In Uzbekistan, the party coalesced out of the IRP, Adolat and Islam Lashkarlari factions, which were wiped out in 1992. HTI is organised strictly hierarchically into small cells; its goal is to establish a worldwide Sunni caliphate and the elimination of Shia Islam. HTI explicitly condemns Western values such as democracy, pluralism, the free market economy and human rights. In their view, democracy is relativistic because it equates nonbelievers with believers and prefers the secular state to the Islamic state. HTI considers pluralism blasphemous and atheistic, for it entails the propagation of non-Islamic or atheistic ideas. It suspects that the free market economy will solidify the rule of the hated West and human rights cast doubt on the relations between the individual and Muslim society as they are proclaimed by the Qur'an, while blurring the boundaries between believers and nonbelievers.[119] During the 1990s, the Uzbek HTI became strongly radicalised and a proclamation from June 2001 called for carrying out suicide attacks against nonbelieving civilians: 'There is no difference whether we shall be killing enemy soldiers or . . . destroying their children, women and old men.'[120]

The IMU was founded by the preacher Tahir Yuldashev (1967–2009) and Afghanistan veteran Juma Hojiev (1969–2001) called Namangani. It was more powerful because of its military organisation.[121] Both Yuldashev and Namangani had played a leading role in the riots of February 1992.[122] The original goal was to eliminate President Karimov and to establish an Islamic state. Yuldashev received assistance for the development and financing of the IMU as well as for recruiting, arming, and training its fighters from most anti-Western protagonists in the Afghanistan conflict: the Pakistani Jamiat Ulema-e-Islam Party, closely allied with the Deobandi; Pakistan's ISI; Saudi intelligence; the Taliban; and al-Qaeda. Yuldashev received additional financial support from the Uzbek diaspora, Saudi Arabia, the Gulf States, Turkey, and so-called Islamic charities, which are often controlled by Saudi-Wahhabi clergy or the Saudi royal family.[123] For bin Laden's al-Qaeda, collaborating with the IMU was especially attractive for two reasons: first, because of the geographical location of their base of operations north of Amu Darya, the IMU was an ideal tool for expanding jihad to Central Asia; second, the agent network Namangani had established, which extended from Tajikistan and Fergana to Chechnya, was highly suited for opium and heroin smuggling to Russia and Europe.[124] Al-Qaeda and the IMU effectively constituted a joint venture in international drug smuggling.

After the failed attack on President Karimov in February 1999,[125] which claimed sixteen lives, the IMU carried out robberies and kidnappings in the Batken region.[126] In the summer of 2000, Namangani launched coordinated attacks with hundreds of well-armed fighters in three different directions: the first squad attacked Batken once again, the second the province of Suchandarya in south-east Uzbekistan, and the third to the north

of the capital Tashkent. The government forces were able to kill and drive out the guerrillas only with great difficulty. Few were actually taken captive, as injured IMU fighters were killed by their comrades so that they could not be interrogated by the army.[127] The IMU movement was strong enough to participate in the late summer of 2000 in a major Taliban attack on Massoud. By this point, their fighters were no longer simply Uzbeks, but also Pakistanis and Chechens. In response to these alarming attacks, Karimov closed off the borders with Tajikistan and had them mined. He also interrupted gas supplies to Dushanbe to force the Tajikistan government to take more decisive action against the IMU sanctuaries in Tajikistan.[128] In 2001, the IMU carried out their attacks yet again in Batken. Although Uzbekistan fell into a recession at the same time as the attacks in 2000, the International Monetary Fund closed its office in Tashkent in April 2001.

173. The Middle Ages meets modernity: right, the Kukeldash Madrasah from the 1570s; left, a modern hotel complex, Tashkent, Uzbekistan. Photo: 2004.

Western powers and organisations refused to recognise that international political Islamism had put the stability of the region into acute danger. Even so, the US had already classified the IMU in 2000 as a terrorist organisation.[129]

The attacks on 11 September 2001 fundamentally changed the United States' geostrategic perspective. Suddenly, previously neglected 'undemocratic' countries like Tajikistan, Uzbekistan and Kyrgyzstan were among the front-line states in the war against al-Qaeda and the Taliban regime. Karimov reacted swiftly to the American request to use Uzbek airspace and airforce facilities. By 18 September, two Hercules military transport aircraft of the US Air Force had already landed in Tashkent; and, in October, Karimov made the former Soviet Karshi-Khanabad base (K2) south-east of Bukhara available for an annual subsidy, first of US$50 million and later US$150 million.[130] The IMF was also quick to announce that it would reopen the office it had closed a few months earlier in Tashkent and grant loans to Uzbekistan.[131] In the course of joint operations between US special forces and Afghan commanders of north Afghanistan in November 2001, Namangani and many of his fighters were killed. Yuldashev managed to flee to northern Pakistan. Although the IMU was greatly weakened, it conducted a series of bombings in Tashkent in 2004.[132] It seems that the US not only outsourced the interrogation of captured fighters in Afghanistan to private companies like Blackwater, but also availed itself of Uzbekistan's services.[133]

The 'honeymoon period' between the US and European institutions with Uzbekistan was short-lived. For although the Pentagon needed and appreciated the cooperation of Uzbekistan, the State Department and EU representatives criticised the country's failure to comply with Western standards; for example, in the area of human rights. From 2003 onward, Karimov was disappointed about not being rewarded for his loyalty in the fight against terrorism. Prospective loans from the IMF and the European Bank for Reconstruction and Development (EBRD) were ultimately not granted due to the country's human-rights violations. Moreover, at the annual meeting of the EBRD in Tashkent in May 2003, Karimov was publicly reprimanded by EBRD President Jean Lemierre in front of Uzbek state television cameras. Moreover, it turned out that the numerous scholarships awarded by NGOs to Uzbek students to study in the US or Europe mostly involved the social and human sciences, not the exact sciences, an area in which Uzbekistan had had a lot of catching up to do since the withdrawal of Soviet experts. Karimov responded by concluding an economic and political rapprochement with Russia in August.[134] If one considers the human rights violations in

Saudi Arabia or Kuwait, the United States' double standard in this regard is unmistakable.

In May 2005, riots severely hampered Uzbekistan-US relations. The earlier overthrow of Kyrgyz President Akayev in March, involving Western organisations in the shadows, had unsettled Karimov greatly. On the night of 12 May, armed men stormed a prison in the city of Andijan, Fergana to liberate 23 businessmen who were accused of belonging to the terrorist group Akramiya, a splinter group of HTI. The attackers freed the defendants and hundreds of other prisoners, after which they occupied municipal buildings and took government officials hostage. During the day, thousands demonstrated against the regime. When no negotiated solution with the hostage-takers was in the offing, security forces opened fire. The attackers then proceeded to hold their hostages before them as living shields. According to the government, 187 people died, mostly bandits and terrorists; human rights organisations estimated that between 300 and 500 civilians were killed.[135] A storm of protest arose in the Western media and among NGOs, and, in the United States, the State Department – against the wishes of the Department of Defense – called for an international inquiry into the events in Andijan. Karimov, however, ruled out the possibility that Uzbekistan, as a sovereign state, would tolerate an international commission on its soil. When the United States applied more pressure, the Uzbek Foreign Ministry demanded on 29 July the closure of the American Karshi-Khanabad airbase within the contractual deadline of 180 days. Despite the EU sanctions, the German government remained flexible and was able to retain the Termez airbase.[136]

After the announcement of President Karimov's death on 2 September 2016, Shavkat Mirziyoyev – the incumbent prime minister since 2003 – was appointed interim president. He was then confirmed as president in the presidential elections on 14 December 2016. Uzbekistan's biggest challenges today are to diversify the economy, to improve the investment climate and to provide better legal certainty in order to avoid an impending rise in unemployment.[137] Even before the election, Mirziyoyev declared that he would review the strict regulations in currency trading and seek to improve relations with neighbouring countries.[138] Indeed, since April 2017 regular direct flights between Tashkent and Dushanbe have been restored, the tensions over the Tajik Rogun hydroelectric plant have decreased and progress has been achieved in demarking the mutual border.[139]

4.5 Tajikistan

The mountainous country has a surface area of 143,100 km^2 and 8.6 million inhabitants. With a per-capita gross domestic product of US$926 (only one-tenth of that of Kazakhstan), it is the poorest country in Central Asia. The reasons for this poverty are its mountainous and landlocked geography, proximity to Afghanistan, the lack of raw materials, and the civil war, which lasted from 1992 to 1997. Much like in Afghanistan, the severely rugged geography with highly elevated passes, which are inaccessible in the winter, impeded the formation of a nation-state. Individual regions of contemporary Tajikistan formerly belonged to the khanates of Bukhara and Kokand, to independent princes in the south-east, or to Afghanistan. From the 1870s, they were part of Russia and then its successor state, the Soviet Union. The most important cultural cornerstone of the Tajiks is their language, belonging to the western Persian language group. The vast majority are Hanafi Sunnis, whereas Ismaili Shiites live in Gorno Badakhshan in the east.[140] Towards the end of the Soviet era, five regional power centres formed with their respective stakeholders: in the north with its powerful Uzbek minority the group of Khujand (Leninabad), which was also the main base of the Tajik Communist Party; in the south, in the district of Kulyab, a second, smaller base of the Communist Party; in the capital Dushanbe, a heterogeneous group of reform advocates; and a re-Islamisation took place in the south-west, in the region of Kurgan-Tyube bordering Afghanistan, as well as in Badakhshan in the Pamir Mountains, which likewise borders on Afghanistan.[141] The 1980s witnessed an even more pronounced re-Islamisation of society than in Uzbekistan. It was supported by two factors: at the start of the Afghan War, the Soviet Union deployed a disproportionate number of Tajiks and Uzbeks,[142] who returned disillusioned after their service and turned to Islam. Second, the border to Afghanistan was porous, allowing Islamic missionaries to penetrate the remote southern regions, especially Badakhshan.

One of the early protagonists in the civil war was the former first secretary of the Communist Party, Rahmon Nabiyev from Khujand (in office 1982–85). Due to corruption, Gorbachev replaced him with

174. The Russian Orthodox Nicholas Church in Dushanbe, Tajikistan – a reminder of the strong Russian presence in the capital until the autumn of 2002. Photo: 2008.

175. Destroyed tank from the time of the civil war of 1992–96 on the north side of the 3,201-m-high Saghir Dasht Pass, on the route from Dushanbe to Qala-i Kum, Tajikistan. Photo: 2008.

Kakhar Makhamov (in office 1985–91, also president from 30 November 1990). Nationalist and Islamic fundamentalist forces were already noticeable in 1989, which prompted the Russians to start leaving the country. In February 1990, serious unrest broke out in Dushanbe when Moscow relocated three dozen Armenian refugees there. With help from Soviet special forces, Makhamov succeeded in suppressing the riots incited by nationalists and Muslim fundamentalists. After Makhamov verbally supported the failed anti-Gorbachev coup of August 1991, he had to resign. On 9 September, Tajikistan declared its independence. The appointed interim president Qadruddin Aslonov (7–23 September 1991) dissolved the Communist Party, which led to his downfall on 23 September. The communist Khujandi group appointed Nabiyev

president, who then overturned the order to dissolve the Communist Party. On 6 October Nabiyev resigned in order to participate in the presidential elections in late November, which he won. The interim president during the elections was Akbarsho Iskandarov.[143] The opposition to Nabiyev's neo-communists consisted of the conservative Democratic Party of Tajikistan (DPT), the nationalist Rastakhiz party, the regional, nationalist-conservative La'l-i Badakhshan party, and the Islamic Revival Party of Tajikistan (IRPT). The latter party, which was prone to Islamic fundamentalism, was officially established after 28 October, when the government succumbed to mass demonstrations against the former Soviet law prohibiting political parties with a religious orientation.[144]

Nabiyev first restored the old north–south axis between the communist power centres of Khujand and Kulyab. This move, however, inspired the neglected regions in the south-west (Kurgan-Tyube) and the east (Karategin, Gharm and Pamir) to revolt. In the spring of 1992, the opposition organised mass demonstrations in Dushanbe, which were also joined by radical Islamists and criminals. In response, the government organised counter-demonstrations. The power struggle that ensued on the street was both a confrontation between traditionally more affluent and poorer disadvantaged regions, as well as between secular and religious parties. When the opposition's militia, which was supplied with arms by the Afghan leaders Hekmatyar and Massoud, occupied the presidential palace and the television station in Dushanbe on 5 May 1992, Nabiyev formed an armed national guard with Kulyab supporters. As a result, the power struggle threatened to turn into a civil war. To defuse the situation, Nabiyev initiated talks with the opposition. He set up a coalition government of national reconciliation, which included eight ministers from the opposition. This did not ease the tensions, however. The Khujandis categorically rejected the participation of Islamic fundamentalists in the government and refused to recognise them. Bands of armed Kulyabis advanced on Kurgan-Tyube, a stronghold of the fundamentalists. In June, the country was divided into five power centres: the government maintained only tenuous control in Dushanbe; the neo-communists controlled Khujand and Kulyab, and the nationalist fundamentalists controlled Kurgan-Tyube and the east. The latter received reinforcements in the summer of around 500 to 600 armed Afghan mujahideen. Heavy fighting broke out everywhere, except in the north, and harvests were abandoned in the countryside. The situation escalated further when Islamist militias violently forced President Nabiyev's ouster on 7 September. Akbarsho Iskandarov succeeded him as interim president. The 201st Russian Infantry Division then seized the airport and the access roads from Dushanbe to safeguard the mass exodus of ethnic Russians. In the autumn, secular forces established the People's Front, and, during a parliamentary session in Khujand, appointed Emomali Rakhmonov (in office since 1992) from Kulyab as the new president. Rakhmonov asked the CIS countries for immediate military aid.[145]

For both Russia and Uzbekistan, the prospect of an Islamist government in Tajikistan that maintained close contacts with the Afghan fundamentalists was unacceptable. After all, an Islamist regime north of the Amu Darya threatened to first destabilise Uzbekistan and then all of Central Asia, which would have caused countless more ethnic Russians to flee. Thanks to Uzbek and Russian help, government troops and militias from Kulyab managed to drive out the Islamist militias from Dushanbe and the surrounding areas to the east in December 1992. Rakhmonov continued with the offensives in 1993 and purged Kurgan-Tyube, Gharm and Karategin of Islamist opposition members. They took flight by the hundreds of thousands to either Afghanistan or to the Pamir Mountains, where they were recruited by the IRPT. At the end of March, the first phases of the civil war concluded with 30,000 to 50,000 dead. In the months that followed, Rakhmonov strengthened his position by replacing numerous Khujandis with acquiescent Kulyabis in the government, administration, and the army. President Karimov was enraged by this development, as many leading Khujandis were ethnic Uzbeks. In retaliation, Karimov began to support local warlords in northern Tajikistan.[146]

176. On the south side of the Anzob Pass, north of Dushanbe; in the valley, a tributary of the river Varzob, Tajikistan. Photo: 2008.

177. Gilded statue of Turkmen President Niyazov (in office 1991–2006), known as Turkmenbashi, 'Leader of all Turkmen', near the Independence Monument of Turkmenistan in Ashgabat. Photo: 2014.

In 1993, the four opposition parties joined forces in the United Tajik Opposition (UTO), which was led by Sayid Abdullah Nuri (1947–2006), the leader of the Islamist IRPT. While the Islamists entrenched in Badakhshan increasingly received arms, money and instructors through Hekmatyar, Massoud, the ISI and Saudi Arabia, Russian troops secured the southern border to Afghanistan, west of the Pamirs. Security Minister Viktor Barannikov confirmed that Russia was actually securing its own south-eastern border along the Amu Darya: 'By guarding the Tajik section of [CIS] border, we defend the strategic backbone of Russia.'[147] The open border of Badakhshan and the corruptibility of poorly paid Russian border guards motivated the Afghan warlords to organise the transport of opium and heroin by way of Tajikistan and beyond via Uzbekistan

and Kyrgyzstan, which weakened Tajik society further. Renewed heavy fighting in the summer of 1994 resulted in a stalemate, which was not resolved until the Taliban captured Kabul at the end of September 1996 and Massoud was forced to withdraw his support for the IRPT. Now Taliban commanders threatened to continue jihad beyond the Amu Darya in Tajikistan on the side of the IRTP fighters. Russia's new foreign minister Primakov recognised the danger of an Islamist conflagration and won the support of Iran. The Iranians were indeed sympathetic to the IRPT, but they also feared any further advance of the Taliban and al-Qaeda. With Iran's help, Primakov sought to force the rivals Rakhmonov and Nuri to reach a political compromise. The two leaders, who had had an inconclusive meeting in 1995, signed an agreement on 23 December 1996 that included the establishment of a joint Commission of National Reconciliation, a constitutional referendum, and a new electoral law. This was followed on 27 June 1997 with the signing of the peace agreement that ended the five-year civil war, which had claimed about 100,000 lives and completely decimated the country. The most important element of the deal was a power-sharing agreement, according to which 30 per cent of all state government agencies were to be assigned to the opposition UTO. In 1999, Rakhmonov won the presidential election, not least because the opposition could not agree on a joint candidate, but instead put up three. Rakhmonov's People's Democratic Party won the subsequent parliamentary elections. Soon, it became clear that the IRPT had no alternative economic programme to the People's Party that was either attractive and credible. It was therefore all the easier for Rakhmonov to gradually marginalise the opposition and keep it from power.[148]

The unrest and civil war put the country back by a decade: between 1988 and 1996, both the gross domestic product and industrial production fell by 70 per cent.[149] Tajikistan's ongoing economic crisis was exacerbated by the dictates of the International Monetary Fund. If it wanted to obtain IMF loans, the impoverished and politically weak country was forced to privatise state enterprises and lands. As a result, the still-functioning state farms were broken up, while the small farmers who obtained the acreage were unable to efficiently manage it due to a lack of financial resources.[150] The agricultural sector collapsed so that Tajikistan had to rely on food aid, mainly from Kazakhstan and Russia. Total economic collapse was only prevented by the remittances from the approximately one million Tajiks working in Russia. In 2011, they contributed almost half of the gross domestic product with nearly US$3 billion.[151] Nonetheless, a persistent economic crisis in Russia has caused these transfers to shrink more and more.

Even after the peace agreement, Tajikistan remained dependent on Russia, especially as a guarantor for its internal security and for the integrity of its 1,344-km-long southern border with Afghanistan. What is more, Tajikistan became the primary transit route for arms sales to Massoud, the last warlord still battling the Taliban. Even though the Russian troops numbered 16,000 men – whereby most of the soldiers were ethnic Tajiks and most of the officers Russian – the border remained porous. The transit paths remained open through remote mountain areas for drug smugglers and fighters of the IMU. After lengthy negotiations, Russia and Tajikistan agreed to a phased handover of border control to Tajik security forces, which was completed by 2006. The scaled-back Russian troops withdrew from the border region to their base at Dushanbe. Russia continues to maintain the Okno space observation station.[152]

As a result of 11 September 2001, Tajikistan suddenly gained importance for American warfare. The small country, in turn, had an opportunity to find new Western partners. On 3 November, President Rakhmonov approved the use of Tajik airfields, and, on 6 December, the first French troops landed in Dushanbe. But the progressive withdrawal of US combat troops from Afghanistan and the ending of the German Bundeswehr effort within the framework of ISAF in northern Afghanistan contributed to the deterioration of the security situation, both there and along the southern Tajik border. The need for Russian troops accordingly increased once again. The Russian military presence is contractually regulated until 2042. Its strength will be gradually increased from 7,500 (2015) to 9,000 soldiers by 2020.[153]

The biggest obstacle to a long-term positive economic development is the longstanding poor relations with Uzbekistan, upon which Tajikistan is dependent in multiple ways. Due to its geographic location, routes through Uzbekistan would be ideal for people and goods going abroad. In this regard, Afghanistan is not an option for the foreseeable future, and the Murghab highway in the Pamir Mountains to Kashgar, which opened in 2004, is only useful for trade with China. Furthermore, the road going to Osh, Kyrgyzstan, which also runs through the Pamirs, simply heads into another landlocked country. Nevertheless, the border posts between Uzbekistan and Tajikistan are often closed and the transit fees on the Uzbek side are high. Tajikistan's only international railway lines also pass through Uzbek territory. Finally, Uzbekistan suspended air traffic with Tajikistan from 1999 until April 2017.[154] Despite these obstacles, the country's most serious hindrance to traffic was removed in 2006. Until then, northern Tajikistan was completely cut off during the winter from Dushanbe and the rest of the country, as snow obstructed the 3,400-m-high Anzob Pass. Unlike Saudi Arabia, whose 'development aid' was largely exhausted in Central Asia in the construction of large mosques, Iran made a productive contribution here by financing up to three-quarters of the construction of the Anzob Tunnel at a cost of US$120 million. In this way, it helped promote the Tajik domestic economy.[155]

The dire state of Uzbek-Tajik relations came to light in the spring of 2012, when Uzbekistan announced that it would stop providing gas to the state aluminium company TALCO from 1 April. The closure of the 11,000-employee-strong industrial plant – whose production accounts for 70 per cent of Tajikistan's legal exports – would have had catastrophic consequences. Uzbekistan presumably wanted to force its neighbour to make territorial concessions in the northern border region. This attempt at blackmail failed, however, as Tajikistan had a Chinese coal-gas plant, which converted coal extracted near Dushanbe into gas. When Tashkent realised that the aluminium plant could remain in operation without Uzbek gas, the suspension of deliveries was lifted again.[156]

As with the Uzbek-Kyrgyz tensions, the source of the strained relations lies in the utilisation of Tajikistan's immense water resources.[157] The Soviet distribution system coordinated Tajik water management until 1991. The reservoirs, which were built less for electricity generation than to regulate irrigation, were filled during the winter months and emptied in the summer to irrigate Uzbek and Turkmen cotton plantations. In return, Uzbekistan supplied gas and electricity. After 1991, the central distribution board vanished. Uzbekistan, for its part, then started to demand that the two mountainous republics pay world market prices for gas, oil, and electricity, while expecting to obtain water at the previous levels, on the same schedule, and free of charge. Ultimately, it sought to impose its preferred water management scheme on its two neighbours. At the same time, Kyrgyzstan began at the Toktogul hydroelectric dam to augment electricity production in the winter and thus to discharge water. Tajikistan did the same at Nurek, where the dam is 300 m high. To meet its own electricity needs – TALCO alone consumes 40 per cent of Tajikistan's electricity production – and to be able to export electricity, Tajikistan is now planning to build a second mega-storage plant 100 km north-east of Dushanbe. The Rogun hydroelectric plant is located on the upper reaches of the Vakhsh River. The dam will be 335 m high, the reservoir will hold 11.6 billion cubic metres of water, and the six turbines will supply 13.1 billion kilowatt hours of electricity annually. An agreement to build the dam concluded in 2004 with the Russian aluminium plant RUSAL was abandoned in 2007, when RUSAL proposed – under Uzbek pressure – reducing the dam's height to 285 m. Tajikistan, however, refused. The government decided to finance the project itself and began with the tunnelling work.[158] In July 2014, a report commissioned by the World Bank concluded that the chosen location, dam type, earthquake resistance, and the planned storage capacity were appropriate and realistic. The planned dam thus complies with the international safety standards.[159] President Rahmon officially initiated the construction of the dam on 29 October 2016.[160] If the dam is constructed at the intended height, Tajikistan would control to a large extent the Amu Darya, whose second feeder is the Vakhsh.

178. In the foreground, a monument to the Akhal-Teke horses; behind, to the left, the old palace of President Turkmenbashi and, further left, the new palace, with three domes, of President Berdymuhamedov. Ashgabat, Turkmenistan. Photo: 2014.

179. Mausoleum for President Niyazov (Turkmenbashi), where his parents and two brothers are also buried. Kipchak, Turkmenistan. Photo: 2014.

A second large-scale energy project is near Bokhtar in the south-west of the country, where a large natural gas field was discovered at a depth of 6,000 m. In 2013, a consortium consisting of the British Tethys Petroleum, the French company Total, and the China National Petroleum Corporation, was awarded a permanent licence to extract natural gas until 2038. However, the relative proximity to the Afghan border is problematic, as the terrorist attack of January 2013 near the natural gas field of In Aménas in Algeria demonstrated.[161] Whether Tajikistan can rise to become a major exporter of natural gas to China also depends on the completion of the fourth gas pipeline from Central Asia to China. The 'Line D' is supposed to extend from Turkmenistan via southern Uzbekistan, Tajikistan and Kyrgyzstan to the natural gas hub in Kazakhstan and from there to Xinjiang. The ambitious project, which would have connected the five republics for the first time, was suspended in early 2016 by Turkmenistan, Uzbekistan and Kyrgyzstan. Where Kyrgyzstan argued against the uncertain costs, Uzbekistan opposes entering into a joint venture with Tajikistan, and Turkmenistan fears that a supply of Tajik natural gas from about 2019 would make the planned increase in Turkmen gas deliveries to China impossible.[162] The ultimate completion of the 'Line D', which is so critical to Tajikistan, depends not least on the political pressure that China is willing to exert.

Tajikistan continues to face a number of daunting challenges. In terms of security policy, the resurgent Taliban in northern Afghanistan represent a significant risk, as does the smuggling of drugs and potentially the Islamic state also operating in Afghanistan. The domestic political situation is not yet stable, as the failed uprising of the deputy defence minister General Abduchalim Nazarzoda in early September 2015 confirmed. Afterwards, the IRPT, with whom Nazarzoda sympathised, was prohibited, entailing the risk that moderate Islamists might become radicalised.[163] Other hurdles include the normalisation of relations with Uzbekistan, a reduction of dependence on foreign transfers, the search for a functional *modus vivendi* with moderate Islamists, and the fight against corruption. Tourism, too, has enormous untapped potential in the culturally rich and highly scenic country.

4.6 Turkmenistan

Despite a total land area of 491,210 km², the country only counts about 5.2 million inhabitants, about 90 per cent of whom are Sunni Muslims.[164] Similar to Tashkent, the capital was completely destroyed by a devastating earthquake, in October 1948, and then lavishly reconstructed. Like Nazarbayev and Karimov, the longstanding ruler of Turkmenistan, Saparmurat Niyazov (first secretary 1985–91, president 1991–2006), was appointed by Gorbachev as first secretary of the Turkmen Communist Party. After the failed coup against Gorbachev, Turkmenistan declared its sovereignty, which was ratified in a popular referendum on 27 October. Niyazov was simultaneously elected president with 98.3 per cent of the vote.[165] The president quickly installed an authoritarian regime susceptible to corruption[166] and saw to it that he was surrounded by a strong cult of personality. He named himself Turkmenbashi ('Leader of all Turkmen') and had the port city of Krasnovodsk and airports, canals, schools, the month of January, and much else renamed 'Turkmenbashi'. The other

months and days of the week were renamed as well. He subsequently declared his book *Ruhnama* ('Book of the Soul')[167] to be required reading in schools, universities, administrations, and large companies. The acquisition of a driving licence and an academic title required passing a test on the *Ruhnama*. The book even had to be placed alongside the Qur'an in mosques. In 2004, Niyazov ordered that the prayer leader was to read aloud from the *Ruhnama* at prayer.[168] In the following months, Niyazov closed all rural hospitals, ostensibly to cut costs, fired thousands of employees in nursing, and eliminated one-third of retiree pensions. The president died in December 2006, reportedly of heart failure. Deputy prime minister Gurbanguly Berdymuhamedov (in office since 2006) succeeded him. He hastened to reverse the absurd decrees of his predecessor and to return the pensions to those who were affected. At the same time, Berdymuhamedov retained Niyazov's generous policy of providing citizens with free gas, electricity and water. Beyond this, since 2008 every car owner has received an annual provision of 120 litres of petrol for free.[169] These 'gifts' have

180. The Turkmenbashi Rukhi Mosque, completed by the French construction company Bouygues in 2004, in Kipchak, 15 km north-west of Ashgabat. The name of the mosque means the 'Spirit of Turkmenbashi'. The mosque, with an octagonal floor plan, has seven gates, analogous to the seven gates of Paradise, and the eighth gate is the Qibla, indicating the direction of Mecca. Photo: 2014.

served to help make the continuing authoritarian regime palatable to citizens. Thanks to its foreign policy of 'permanent neutrality' introduced in 1996 and a flexible diplomacy with its own and Afghan Turkmen tribes, the country has been able to keep conflicts in Afghanistan from spilling over into Turkmen territory.

The Turkmen economy rests on two pillars: the cultivation of cotton and the production of natural gas, and (to a lesser extent) petroleum. As nearly 80 per cent of the country is desert, the 850-km-long Karakum Canal (Turkmenbashi Canal) was built from 1954 to 1962. The canal carries water from the Amu Darya to Ashgabat, yet has also contributed significantly to the disappearance of the Aral Sea. Since the canal is open and lacks a concrete bed, almost half of the water is lost to evaporation and seepage. By contrast, the 595-km-long extension to Krasnovodsk (Turkmenbashi) opened in 1986 is largely a closed aqueduct.[170] Turkmenistan's potential wealth lies in its natural gas reserves, which, according to CIA estimates, are the world's fourth largest, after those of Iran, Russia and Qatar. In terms of flow rate, however, Turkmenistan currently ranks only 13th.[171] There are several reasons for this, including a partially outdated pipeline system, too little capacity for liquefying gas to LNG, a lack of technology, and political constraints. The latter include the poor security situation in Afghanistan, which impedes the realisation of a Turkmenistan–Afghanistan–Pakistan–India pipeline (TAPI pipeline),[172] strong US pressure to not do business with Iran, and disputes with Russia over the purchase of Turkmen gas.

Until 1997, Turkmenistan was dependent on the Russian giant Gazprom, the world's largest company in natural gas production and transport. All gas pipelines led to Russia and Turkmenistan was forced to sell its gas at very low prices to the CIS countries, or even to accept barter in lieu of foreign currency. Russia, in turn, then sold the cheaply procured Turkmen gas at world prices to Ukraine and Europe. Of the five Central Asian republics, Turkmenistan is closest to the world's oceans and therefore offers the best opportunity geographically to disrupt Russia's pipeline monopoly. The problem here is not geographical, however, but political in nature. The United States wants to isolate Iran at any price – politically, as well as economically and financially. In 1992, the US thwarted an agreement between Turkmenistan and Iran, in which Iran was to buy Turkmen gas, oil and electricity and subsidise the construction of a pipeline.

181. The Darwaza gas crater, whose name means 'open gate', located 260 km north of Ashgabat, Turkmenistan. The crater, which at first emanated only gas, was formed accidentally during prospecting at the beginning of the 1970s. When the animals of neighbouring farmers died from the gas or fell into the crater, a rancher set the crater on fire in 1973. The crater has burned continuously ever since. Photo: 2014.

The American threats, though, were successful. Ultimately, no international financial institution dared to finance a project that included Iran. The United States, however, could not prevent the construction of a railway line from Mashhad to the border town of Sarakhs, since Iran needed neither loans nor expertise. In May 1996, presidents Niyazov and Rafsanjani ceremoniously opened the railway line between Iranian Sarakhs and Tejen in Turkmenistan. It linked Central Asia's old rail network from the tsarist and Soviet era with Iran's, which is in turn connected to the Turkish network. The century-old tsarist plan to connect Central Asia with the warm-water ports of the Persian Gulf and the Arabian Sea like Bandar Abbas was thus realised, if only to a very limited degree. Kazakhstan and Turkmenistan both have access to the rail network in Pakistan and an opportunity to export their goods to Iran and further to Turkey thanks to the completion in 2009 of the railway line from Bam (Iran) to Zahedan,[173] the border town with Pakistan, and to the line from Uzen (Kazakhstan) via Bereket and Etrek (Turkmenistan) to Gorgan (Iran), which went into operation in December 2014.[174] The Uzen–Gorgan line was financed by Kazakhstan, Turkmenistan, Iran, and the Islamic Development Bank. This enabled Turkmenistan and Kazakhstan[175] to not only disrupt the Russian transport monopoly on land, but also to avoid the dictate of US finance via the IMF and the World Bank. The sovereignty of commodity exporters is also fundamentally determined by the control of the logistics chain.

When presidents Niyazov and Khatami inaugurated a natural gas pipeline from Korpeje, Turkmenistan to Kordkuy, Iran in December 1997, Turkmenistan managed to break through the Russian pipeline monopoly for the first time and to once again bypass US financial restrictions. As the two countries didn't seek loans from the IMF or the World Bank, the United States had no veto power. The mere 200 km pipeline also offered other attractive options. First of all, it would be possible to barter: Turkmenistan could deliver gas to northern Iran and Tehran could sell Iranian gas to a third country on behalf of Turkmenistan.[176] There was the possibility of selling Turkmen and Iranian gas to Europe via Turkey to the extent that the US embargo could be circumvented.[177] In 2000, a second Turkmen-Iranian pipeline was put into operation and then a third in 2010 with a much larger capacity. Owing to the Central Asia-China pipeline leading from Turkmenistan via Uzbekistan and Kazakhstan to China, which was inaugurated in December 2009, China could be won as a new customer. This offered Ashgabat a much-needed alternative to Gazprom and Russia.

As long as Turkmenistan had no real supply alternative to Russia for its natural gas, it was forced to sell its gas cheaply to Gazprom, enabling the Russian company to make big profits. In the words of Berdymuhamedov, 'They [the Russians] robbed us for many years! They were buying our gas for forty dollars and reselling it for three hundred.'[178] In 2007, Turkmenistan increased the pressure and Gazprom finally relented. In order to secure Turkmen gas over the long term, Gazprom committed to buying about 70 billion m³ at international prices.[179] However, when demand and prices declined for natural gas as a result of the financial crisis, Gazprom started to lose money. Although it no longer required Turkmen natural gas, it nonetheless remained obliged to continue importing it. On 9 April 2009, an explosion cut off the Turkmen-Russian pipeline that was most likely caused by Gazprom itself. Suddenly, the volume of procured gas dwindled massively. As a result, Turkmenistan lost approximately US$1 billion in revenue every month until early 2010. In December 2009, Russia and Turkmenistan agreed on a much smaller amount of natural gas, ranging from 10 to 12 billion m³ annually. Without the Central Asia–China pipeline Turkmenistan would have experienced great financial difficulty.[180] Certainly, China and Iran now found themselves in a stronger negotiating position with respect to the import prices. Turkmenistan's own position deteriorated again in January 2016 when Gazprom announced that it would no longer procure any more Turkmen gas. At the same time, it sued Turkmenistan for repayment of US$5 billion for allegedly excessive prices from 2010 onward.[181] The loss of Gazprom hit Turkmenistan especially hard: revenues from the export of natural gas and crude oil fell from US$18.3 billion (2014) to an estimated US$8.9 billion (2016).[182]

In order not to be dependent on China as a purchaser of natural gas, Turkmenistan took the lead in a consortium including Afghanistan, Pakistan and India to realise the earlier project of a Turkmenistan–Afghanistan–Pakistan–India pipeline. Although work began in Turkmenistan in December 2015, the project entails considerable security-related risks, both in Afghanistan and in the tribal areas of Pakistan. Without the inclusion of the Taliban and the tribes on both sides of the Afghanistan-Pakistan border, it will neither be possible to construct the pipeline, nor to operate it safely. It remains doubtful whether the pipeline will be operational by late 2019 as planned, not least because an international investor has not yet been found as of November 2016.[183] Turkmenistan's challenges lie in a looming economic stagnation, the acquisition of new natural gas customers, and the deficits in the education and healthcare sectors inherited from Niyazov.

Outlook

[The fall of the Berlin Wall and the collapse of the Soviet Union] 'led to the assumption that all human divisions were surmountable; that democracy would conquer Africa, the Middle East [and Central Asia] as easily as it had Eastern Europe; that globalization . . . was nothing else than a moral direction of history and a system of security, rather what it actually was, merely an economic and cultural stage of development.'

Author and security expert **ROBERT D. KAPLAN**[1]

The five countries of Central Asia and Mongolia all managed to evolve rapidly from their status as Soviet colonies into stable sovereign states – indeed, in a manner that was largely peaceful, with the exception of Tajikistan. More than a quarter of a century after the Soviet Union's demise, none of these six states belongs to the so-called 'arc of instability' and none is a 'failed state'. Even Afghanistan should not be counted as a failed state, although its government controls only 57 per cent of districts and two thirds of the population, as per late 2017. Some government services work tolerably well and the country was and is still destabilised by heteronomous forces from abroad. Without elucidating the reasons, the differences in the post-colonial development in Central Asia and in Africa remain striking. Crucial for the continued stability in Central Asia were several key factors, including the adoption of established power structures and the general continuation of official staff, which the populations also accepted (with the exception of Tajikistan). The collapse of the Soviet Union hit each of these countries hard economically, but the authoritarian governments succeeded in avoiding acute shortages such as famines, which forestalled the outbreak of social unrest. Afghanistan's dire, externally controlled fate was a prime example for the vast majority of people in Central Asia of the impact of extreme Islamism. Moreover, it demonstrated that parliamentary democracy introduced from the outside cannot *per se* ensure either security or prosperity. Even the allegedly humanitarian-based US military interventions in Kosovo and Iraq made it abundantly clear that democracy may not be imposed with bombs or by means of decree. Indeed, Thomas Hobbes (1588–1679) already observed in *Leviathan* that violent anarchy threatens the social fabric of a society more than an authoritarian regime.[2]

For all the governments of Central Asia (except Mongolia), one of the biggest transnational challenges is the relationship with Islam, especially political Islam. To what extent should Islamic practice and propaganda be tolerated to prevent moderate Muslims from switching to the extremist camp? And where should the red line be drawn when it comes to the intervention of state power? With the exception of the Tajik Civil War and the incidents of 2005 in Andijan, the governments seem to have responded to these concerns fairly effectively. In any event, there have been no developments like the so-called 'Arab Spring', which later spiralled into chaos. The future stability of the region will depend in no small measure on Afghanistan's ongoing political development and Saudi Arabia's foreign policy. Saudi Arabia has invested relatively little in Central Asian infrastructure and industry, but rather focused on the construction of mosques, the propagation of Wahhabism,

and on the funding of banned Islamist groups like the IMU, IRPT and HTI. It is not surprising that the governments of Central Asia are suspicious of Saudi Arabia, which they view – not unlike their perception of the US and NGOs – as a threat to their stability. Each of these actors seeks to impose certain ideas, values and codes of conduct on the governments and the citizens of Central Asia. As the quote above from Robert Kaplan's political analysis *The Revenge of Geography* suggests, however, financial flows, goods and technology can be globalised, but not values and worldviews.

The Central Asian republics have a number of unique strengths that distinguish them from other countries in Asia and Arabia. First of all, they inherited from the Soviet Union a fairly high level of education and a secular world view. This contributed to the fact that Sunni Islam in Central Asia, with the exception of Fergana, has largely remained moderate, in contrast to the Islam of Iran or Saudi Arabia. In addition, women of course – as during the Soviet Union – are integrated into the labour process and the people have a high work ethic. Again, this stands in contrast to Saudi Arabia and some Gulf states. Here most of the locals work in the administration or the service sector, whereas handicrafts or simple manual labour are left to foreign guest workers. Finally, the three republics with rich natural resources also have a functioning agricultural sector, even though up to 80–90 per cent of farming in Uzbekistan and Turkmenistan requires irrigation. Kyrgyzstan and Tajikistan have fewer raw materials, but constitute a 'water tower' for all Central Asia and could in theory export abundant power.

The Central Asian states also struggle with major disadvantages, some of which are geographical in nature, while others are self-inflicted. The latter include their sometimes poor diplomatic relations with each other, limited mutual trade, and the absence of a jointly regulated water management system and compensatory electricity and gas deliveries. There are also protectionist trade barriers, high import and transit duties, restrictions on capital flows and foreign exchange trading, corruption, outdated infrastructure, and relatively high labour costs. All of these factors make it unattractive for European companies to produce or invest in Central Asia, with the exception of business in raw materials.

The most serious handicap is the countries' landlocked geography, as the globalisation of the economy around the world has gone hand in hand with a pronounced 'maritimisation'. Transport by sea makes up 75 per cent of global volume and 67 per cent of the value of world trade.[3] This handicap manifests itself in three ways: commodity producers with access to the world's oceans have a significant price advantage over their landlocked competitors in Central Asia. Kazakhstan and Tajikistan have the further disadvantage that some of their natural resources are located at a great depth and in a challenging geological environment. Secondly, for logistical reasons, Central Asian factories also cannot compete with those in South-East Asian countries that have their own deep-sea ports such as China, Vietnam and Malaysia. Thirdly, plans to revive the ancient Silk Road through Central Asia as a transit route between Europe and China – as the EU TRACECA (Transport Corridor Europe–Caucasus–Asia) project intends – are difficult to realise on a commercially profitable basis. More than 95 per cent of the goods transported between Asia and Europe use the sea routes.[4] The sea has many advantages over land freight. Among other things, it is cheaper and more customer-friendly due to the elimination of

transit and customs formalities and forced bribes. Its primary disadvantage is that it is slower: Transport between Europe and China via Central Asia takes about 17 days by road; with the normal train route about 40 days; and with the still little-used Trans-Eurasia-Express, which crosses Russia and Kazakhstan, 14 to 16 days. Ship transport, however, takes around 30 to 35 days via the Suez Canal and around 45 days via the Cape of Good Hope.[5] As the joint venture of Deutsche Bahn and Russian Railways, the operator of the Trans-Eurasia-Express, shows, the only competitive land route bypasses the Central Asian countries to the south of Kazakhstan.[6] The Trans-Eurasia Express is twice as fast as the route by sea, but three times more expensive. On the other hand, it is much cheaper

182. The oil refinery of Atyrau, Kazakhstan. Photo: 2012.

183. The pyramid in the centre is the Palace of Peace and Reconciliation in Astana, Kazakhstan, which was designed by Foster and Partners and completed 2006. On the left stands the Kazakh National University of Arts, at the right the Palace of Independence. Photo: 2017.

than air freight. The Trans-Eurasia Express is used mainly by the German automotive and machinery industry. For trial purposes, a railway was subsequently opened in January 2016 from Eastern China to Tehran. Bypassing the Caucasus, it crosses Iran and Turkey and could continue on to Russia and Western Europe. This 'Iron Silk Road' project is co-funded by the China-led Asian Infrastructure Investment Bank, established in 2015.[7]

Road traffic within Central Asia is burdened by many obstacles like poor roads, transit duties and formalities, a lack of terminals and refrigeration units, as well as corrupt officials. It is also conceivable that due to expected climate warming the 6,500-km-long North-East Passage through the northern Arctic Ocean will gain in importance. Longer ice-free periods would mean shorter travel times and reduced costs. Such a development would make it

difficult to operate a profitable transit route over land, especially using roads. An important step was achieved in August 2017 when the Russian LNG tanker *Christophe de Margerie* accomplished the journey through the North-East Passage for the first time without the help of an icebreaker. The journey from Hammerfest, Norway, to Boryeong, South Korea, lasted only 19 days, about eleven to sixteen days less than through the Suez Canal.[8]

The future of Central Asia will continue to be dominated by the two regional superpowers, Russia and China. US interest in the region has decreased since its gradual withdrawal from Afghanistan, but also because of the experience that local authorities are 'resistant to learning' about issues relating to democracy. US foreign policy is focused on bringing the situation in Afghanistan under control to a reasonable degree and keeping

Iran isolated. Russia, for its part, has a keen interest in upholding the region's stability in view of its own 15–20 million Muslims and the extended border with Central Asia. It is expected to maintain this security policy focus. In the case of Tajikistan, Moscow demonstrated in tandem with strategic partner Iran that it can force the adversaries in the civil war to arrive at a peace settlement. As for natural gas, Russia is simultaneously a customer and competitor of the resource-rich countries, which regularly leads to conflicts. Finally, in light of Russia's annexation of Crimea and the simmering conflict in eastern Ukraine, Kazakhstan was forced to recognise that Moscow is determined to assert its interests – if necessary, even militarily.

Ultimately, China will remain the most important partner of the Central Asian republics and Mongolia over the medium and long term. The Middle Kingdom not only has an immense appetite for fossil fuels, but it also wants to diversify its sources of supply and import routes. From Central Asia's perspective, business relations with China offer several benefits: China has no territorial ambitions; it adheres to the principle of non-interference in the internal affairs of other states, and it provides loans without conditions relating to reforms and respect for human rights. In short, China lacks the missionary zeal of Western states and institutions. Still, similar to Western or Russian loans, the money from Chinese loans also partly remains within China's own financial system since it is often Chinese companies that carry out the execution of large infrastructure projects.[9] China's economic involvement, though, also holds dangers. Cheap imported manufactured goods from China are increasingly replacing the local products. Simultaneously, Central Asia is running the risk of degenerating into a mere supplier of raw materials. Trade with China, on the other hand, opens up access to new technologies and new opportunities in the services and financial sector such as in logistics, transportation, and legal and translation services.

The future of the Central Asian states will also depend on how skilfully they conduct their seesaw policy between Moscow and Beijing. After all, the history of Turkmenistan demonstrates how greatly dependent a supplier of raw materials can become on its only customer. The Central Asian republics also benefit from the fact that Russian-Chinese competition for raw materials, businesses, and influence in the region is not a zero-sum game. Certainly, in some areas such as security, transport and logistics, the two major powers are pursuing mutual interests and strategies.

If the security situation in Afghanistan and in the tribal areas of north-west Pakistan improves, Central Asia could become part of a huge Beijing-controlled economic zone including China, Mongolia, the Central Asian republics, Afghanistan, Pakistan, and Iran. Here, Iran could also serve as a connecting link to equally resource-rich Azerbaijan and Russia. China is not only investing in Afghanistan, such as in the copper mine Mes Aynak, but is also building the Karakoram Highway into a multi-lane, year-round asphalt expressway that connects Kashgar with Rawalpindi and, ultimately, the port of Karachi. Another 530-km-long expressway will lead from Karachi to the port of Gwadar. China co-financed the port, which opened in 2007, and Beijing maintains a naval base there. This China–Pakistan Economic Corridor (CPEC), which anticipates Chinese investments in the amount of US$45 billion, also includes a future railway line and a natural gas pipeline running parallel to the expressway. China will thus be able to transport both natural gas from Iran and Qatar, as well as goods via the Karakoram Highway.[10] To this end, China is further building a large LNG terminal in Gwadar, where a duty-free industrial zone is also expected to arise. Finally, a branch of the TAPI pipeline has been designated to end in Gwadar, which Turkmenistan could then use to export its natural gas. Obviously, Beijing is also striving for closer relations with Saudi Arabia and Qatar to more fully incorporate these two suppliers of raw materials into its economic system.[11] If this China–Pakistan Economic Corridor actually comes to fruition, China would build a trade and economic empire of unparalleled scope and realise the old Russian dream of extending the empire to the Indian Ocean – without military means. This trade and economic zone, in turn, is part of President Xi Jinping's 'One Belt, One Road Initiative', which he announced in Kazakhstan in September 2013: 'The Silk Road Economic Belt focuses on bringing together China, Central Asia, Russia and Europe; linking China with the Persian Gulf and the Mediterranean Sea through Central Asia and the Indian Ocean.' Backbones of this gigantic project are a maritime and several land routes.

The twenty-first century maritime Silk Road is designed to go from China's coast to Europe through the South China Sea and the Indian Ocean in one route, and from China's coast through the South China Sea to the South Pacific in the other.[12] But, in contrast to TRACECA, the planned land route does not follow only logistical and short-term economic criteria, but also long-term economic and political ones. The southern route is, from a political point of view, the strategically most important one. It does not lead through Kazakhstan and southern Russia, which would be the fastest and cheapest option. On the contrary, it touches all five Central Asian republics and continues via Iran, Turkey, Bulgaria, Romania and the Ukraine to Moscow, and from there via Belarus, Poland and Germany to Rotterdam.[13] This railway route not only leads through very challenging terrain, but it also connects mutually conflicting or even hostile states. 'One Belt, One Road' is not only an attempt to revitalise the ancient Silk Roads, but a large-scale attempt to develop the Eurasian economic zone under the leadership of Beijing. In such a scenario, Central Asia could manage to leave behind the peripheral status it has languished under since the sixteenth century. And China would rise to become the leading power of the Eurasian continent. From a commercial point of view the central railway route via Kazakhstan and the northern one via Mongolia, both linking up with the Trans-Siberian Railway, are more attractive. Since European industrial groups began to move their outsourced production plants from now relatively expensive east China to cheaper north-west China, the central route has the biggest growth potential. However, still unresolved are the issues of different spur widths in China, Russia and Western Europe, and the limited free capacities on the Trans-Siberian Railway. The China–Pakistan Economic Corridor is another element of this transcontinental network. Since the planned maritime route from China to Europe will also touch Vietnam, Singapore, Malaysia, Burma,[14] Calcutta (India), Colombo (Sri Lanka), Mombasa (Kenya) and the Suez Canal (Egypt), this giant transport network will include more than 60 states. President Xi Jinping is cleverly exploiting the recent isolationist tendencies of the US under President Trump to position China as the champion of global free trade.

To further ensure this planned economic and transport zone, China agreed with Russia and Pakistan in December 2016 on removing individual representatives of the Taliban from the UN sanctions list to engage more moderate Taliban in a peace process.[15] It can be expected that Iran will also join in this agreement. These four states share an interest in preventing Islamic State from building up a safe retreat in Afghanistan in the light of its predictable defeat in Iraq and Syria, or infiltrating southern Tajikistan or southern Uzbekistan. This issue is the more vital as

the IS has already established a regional base in the eastern Afghan province of Nangarhar. These four states also oppose a permanent US military presence at the Hindu Kush. If this interest group can establish a basis for talks with the Taliban, the Afghan government would come under intense pressure to enter into this negotiation process. The US Obama and Trump administrations thus seem to have not only lost the initiative to Russia in the Middle East, especially in Syria, but also in this instance to China in Afghanistan and South Asia.[16]

However, on 28 February 2018, Afghan president Ghani proposed peace talks, without preconditions, to the Taliban. As an initial step, he offered a ceasefire, an exchange of prisoners and the recognition of the Taliban as a political party. In return, the Taliban would have to recognise the government and respect the law. At the time of writing, the Taliban had not yet responded. But a week earlier they had endorsed the construction of the Afghan section of the planned Turkmenistan–Afghanistan–Pakistan–India pipeline, including in those regions under their control.[17] In view of the obvious strategic stalemate between the main Afghan adversaries and general war weariness among ordinary Afghans, the timing of Ghani's initiative isn't unfavourable. Within Afghanistan, the main obstacles to peace are the ongoing power struggles within the government and the lack of unified command among the Taliban. Further hindrances are the other Islamist war parties such as the IS and the Haqqani network as well as the numerous war profiteers. At the same time, the most important key to peace is still to be found in Pakistan, to be precise with the army leadership and the ISI who have in the past sabotaged peace initiatives several times. Probably only maximum financial pressure from the US and China could bring these players to heel.

▶ 184. The Bayterek Tower, built in 2010, in Astana, Kazakhstan. The 105-m-high tower symbolises the Tree of Life, in whose crown the mythological bird Simurgh leaves behind an egg. The monument is an allegory for the solidarity of the nations of Central Asia with their cultural heritage, while at the same connoting an optimistic outlook of a self-designed future. Photo: 2012.

Appendix: The Most Important Dynasties of Central Asia from the Sixteenth to the Early Twentieth Century

The Abu'l Khayrids of the Uzbek Khanate, 1500–1598

Muhammad Shahi Beg, called **Shaybani Khan** (r. 1500–1510)

Söyünch (Suyunjuq) Muhammed Khoja (r. 1511–1512)

Köchkünji (Kuchum) Muhammed (r. 1512–*ca.* 1530)

Abu Said Khan (r. 1530–1533)

Ubayd Allah Khan (r. 1533–1539)

Abdullah Sultan I (r. 1539–1540)

Abd al-Latif (r. 1540–1552)

Nawruz Ahmad, called **Buraq Khan** (r. 1552–1556)

Pir Muhammad (r. 1556–1561)

Iskandar Khan (r. 1561–1583)

Abdullah Khan II (r. 1583–1598)

Abd al-Mumin (r. 1598)

Sources: C.E. Bosworth, *The Islamic Dynasties* (Edinburgh: Edinburgh University Press, 1980), p. 155. Svat Soucek, *A History of Inner Asia* (Cambridge: Cambridge University Press, 2000), p. 325.

The Togha-Timurids (Astarkhanids) of the Bukhara Uzbek Khanate, 1599–1785

Jani Muhammad Khan (r. 1599–1603)

Baqi Muhammad Khan (r. 1603–1605)

Wali Muhammad Khan (r. 1605–1611)

Imam Quli Khan (r. in Samarkand and Bukhara 1612–1641/42)

Nazr Muhammad (r. in Balkh 1612–1641/42, 1645–1651, as supreme khan 1641/42–1645)

Abd al-Aziz (r. in Bukhara 1645–1681)

Subhan Quli (r. in Balkh 1651–1681, as supreme khan 1681–1702).

Ubayd Allah Khan II (r.in Bukhara 1702–1711)

Muhammad Muqim Khan (r. in Balkh 1702–1707)

Abu'l Fayz Khan (r. 1711–1747)

Abd al-Mumin (nominal Khan 1747–1748)

Ubayd Allah III (nominal Khan 1748–1756)

Muhammad Rahim Manghit (not a Togha-Timurid, r. 1756–1758)

Abu'l Ghazi (nominal Khan 1758–1785)

Sources: Yuri Bregel, *An Historical Atlas of Central Asia* (2003), pp. 56–60. Svat Soucek, *A History of Inner Asia* (2000), pp. 325f.

The Manghits of the Emirate of Bukhara, 1756–1920

Muhammad Hakim Bey (r. as ataliq 1714–1743)

Muhammad Rahim (r. as ataliq 1743–1756, as khan 1756–1758)

Danial Bey (r. as ataliq 1758–1785)

Shah Murad (r. as amir 1785–1799)

Amir Haydar Töre (r. 1800–1826)

Amir Hussain (r. 1826–1827)

Amir Umar (r. 1827)

Amir Nasrallah (r. 1827–1860)

Muzaffar al-Din (r. 1860–1885, as of 1868 vassal of Russia)

Abd al-Ahad (r. 1885–1911, vassal of Russia)

Mohammed Alim (r. 1911–1917 as vassal of Russia, independent 1917–1920, d. 1944)

Sources: Yuri Bregel, 'The new Uzbek states: Bukhara, Khiva and Kokand: c. 1750–1886', in: Nicola Di Cosmo, Allen J. Frank and Peter B. Golden (eds), *The Cambridge History of Inner Asia: The Chinggisid Age* (Cambridge: Cambridge University Press, 2009), pp. 392–411. Hélène Carrère d'Encausse, *Islam and the Russian Empire. Reform and Revolution in Central Asia* (London, I.B.Tauris, 2009), p. 193. Svat Soucek, *A History of Inner Asia* (2000), p. 325.

The Arabshahids of Chorasmia, 1511–1804

Ilbars Khan I (r. 1511–1525)

Sultan Hajji (r. 1525–?)

Hasan Quli

Sufyan

Bujugha

Avnik

Qal (r. 1539–1546)

Aqatay (r. 1546)

Dost Muhammad (r. 1546–1558)

Hajji Muhammad Khan I (r. 1558–1602)

Arab Muhammad Khan (r. 1602–1623)

Isfandiyar Khan (r. 1623–1643)

Abu'l Ghazi Khan I (r. 1643–1663)

Anusha Muhammad Khan (r. 1663–1685)

Muhammad Aurang (r. 1685–1688)

Ishaq Agha Shah Niyaz (r. 1688–1702)

Arab Muhammad II (1702–?)

Hajji Muhammad II (r. ?–1714?)

Yadigar (1714)

Aurang (r. 1714–*ca.* 1715)

Shir Ghazi Khan (r. 1714/15–1728)

Ilbars II (r. 1728–1740)

Tekir Shah (Nader Shah's governor, r. 1742–1745)

Abu'l Ghazi II Muhammad (r. 1742–1745)

Ghaib (r. 1745–1770)

Abu'l Ghazi III (r. 1770)

Puppet khans of Qungrat leaders Muhammad Amin Inaq (r. 1770–1790) and Avaz Amin Inaq (r. 1790–1804)

Sources: Yuri Bregel, *An Historical Atlas of Central Asia* (2003), pp. 54–60. Svat Soucek, *A History of Inner Asia* (2000), pp. 327f.

The Qungrats of Chorasmia, 1770/1804–1920

Muhammad Amin (r. as inaq 1770–1790)

Avaz Inaq (r. as inaq 1790–1804)

Iltüzer Khan (r. 1804–1806)

Muhammad Rahim Khan Bahadur I (r. 1806–1825)

Allah Quli (r. 1825–1842)

Rahim Quli (r. 1842–1846)

Muhammad Amin (r. 1846–1855)

Abdallah (r. 1855)

Qutlugh Murad (r. 1855–1856)

Sayyid Muhammad (r. 1856–1865)

Sayyid Muhammad Rahim Khan Bahadur II (r. 1865–1910, as of 1873 Russian vassal)

Isfandiyar (r. 1910–18, vassal of Russia)

Sayyid Abdallah (r. 1918–20, vassal of Russia, d. in 1920s)

Sources: Seymour Becker, *Russia's Protectorates in Central Asia. Bukhara and Khiva, 1865–1924* (London: RoutledgeCurzon, 2004). Yuri Bregel, 'The new Uzbek states: Bukhara, Khiva and Kokand: *c.* 1750–1886' (2009), pp. 392–411. Svat Soucek, *A History of Inner Asia* (2000), p. 328.

The Chagataiids of Moghulistan, 1347–1705*

Tughlugh Temür (r. 1347–1363)

Ilyas Khwaja (r. 1363–1365)

Qamar al-Din Dughlat (not a Chagataiid, r. 1365–*ca.* 1390)

Khizr Khwaja (r. *ca.* 1383/90–1399)

Sham-i Jahan (r. 1399–1408)

Muhammad Khan (r. 1408–1416)

Naqsh-i Jahan (r. 1416–1418)

Uways Khan (first reign 1418–21)

Sher Muhammad (r. 1421–1425)

Uways Khan (second reign 1425–1428)

Esen Buqa (r. 1428–1462)

Yunus Khan (r. 1462–1487)

Mirza Abu Bakr Dughlat (not a Chagataiid, r. in Yarkand *ca.* 1481–1516)

Ahmad Alaq Khan (r. in Turfan 1487–1503)

Mahmud Khan (r. in Tashkent 1487–1508)

Mansur Khan (r. in Turfan 1508–1543)

Said Khan (r. in West Moghulistan 1514–1533)

Shah Khan (r. in Turfan 1543–1560)

Abdu'l Rashid (r. in Yarkand 1533–1560)

Abd al-Karim Khan (nominal paramount ruler 1560–1591)

Muhammad Sultan (nominal paramount ruler 1591–1609)

Shuja al-Din Ahmad Khan (r. in Yarkand *ca.* 1610–1618)

Kuraysh Khan (r. 1618)

Abdu'l Latif I (r. 1618–1630)

Sultan Ahmad (r. 1630–1633)

Mahmud Sultan (r. 1633–1636)

Sultan Ahmad Khan (r. 1636–?)

Abdullah Khan (r. *ca.* 1636–1667)

Yolbars Khan (r. 1667–1670)

Abdu'l Latif II (r. 1670)

Ismail Khan (r. 1670–1678)

Abdu'l Rashid II (r. 1679–1682)

Muhammad Amin Khan (r. *ca.* 1682–*ca.* 1694)

Yahya Khoja (not a Chagataiid, r. *ca.* 1694–1695)

Jallad Khanum (not a Chagataiid, r. 1695)

Abkash Khan (nominal rule in Yarkand 1695–1705)

* This list makes no claim to completeness, since rulers succeeded each other quickly and Moghulistan was divided into two or three centres of power. This overview lists only the most important rulers with their sometimes approximate dates.

Sources: Schwarz, Henry G., 'The Khwajas of Eastern Turkestan', in: *Central Asiatic Journal*, vol. 20, No. 4 (Wiesbaden: Harrassowitz, 1976), pp. 266–96. Svat Soucek, *A History of Inner Asia* (2000), pp. 322, 329f.

The Khans of Kazan, 1437/38–1552

Khan Ulugh Mohammad, (r. Golden Horde 1419–1421, 1428–1433, in Kazan 1437/38–1445)

Mahmud bin Ulugh Mohammad (r. 1445–1466)

Khalil bin Mahmud (1466–1467)

Ibrahim bin Mahmud (r. 1467–1479)

Ali bin Ibrahim (first reign 1479–1484)

Muhammad Amin bin Ibrahim (first reign 1484–1485)

Ali bin Ibrahim (second reign 1485–1487)

Muhammad Amin bin Ibrahim (second reign 1487–1495)

Mamuq Khan (r. 1495–1496)

Abd al-Latif (1496–1502)

Muhammad Amin bin Ibrahim (third reign 1502–1518)

Shah Ali bin Allah Yar (first reign 1518–1521)

Sahib Khan Giray (reg. 1521–1524)

Safa Khan Giray (first reign 1524–1532)

Jan Ali bin Allah Yar (r. in Kasimov 1519–1532, in Kazan 1532–1535)

Safa Khan Giray (second reign 1535–1546)

Shah Ali bin Allah Yar (second reign 1546)

Safa Khan Giray (third reign 1546–1549)

Ötemish Giray (r. 1549–1551)

Shah Ali bin Allah Yar (third reign 1551–1552)

Yadgar Muhammad (r. 1552)

Sources: Brian L. Davies, *Warfare, State and Society on the Black Sea Steppe, 1500–1700* (2007), pp. 12–17. Allen J. Frank, 'The western steppe: Volga-Ural region, Siberia and the Crimea', in: Nicola Di Cosmo, Allen J. Frank and Peter B. Golden (eds), *The Cambridge History of Inner Asia: The Chinggisid Age* (Cambridge: Cambridge University Press, 2009), pp. 245–50. Bertold Spuler, *Die Goldene Horde. Die Mongolen in Russland 1223–1502* (Leipzig: Harrassowitz, 1943), pp. 164, 175.

The Khans of the Great Horde and Astrakhan *ca.* 1466–1556

Great Horde, *ca.* 1466–1502

Küchük Mohammad (of Golden Horde, r. *ca.* 1435–1459, since 1433 in Astrakhan)

Mahmud (of Golden Horde, r. 1459–1465)

Ahmad (the former Golden Horde is called the Great Horde from *ca.* 1466, r. 1465–1481)

Murtada Khan (co-ruler, 1481–1498, r. 1499)

Sheikh Ahmed (co-ruler, 1481–1498, r. 1499–1502)

Khanate of Astrakhan, 1502–1556*

Abd al-Karim Khan bin Mahmud Khan (r. de facto early 1490s–1502, de jure 1502–1514)

Jani Beg Khan bin Mahmud (1514–1521)

Husayn (?)

Rapid succession of nominal rulers descending from Ahmad Khan, Mahmud Khan, Murtada Khan and Islam Giray, all more or less depending on Noghai support.

Yamghurchi, a Noghai (1540s–1554)

Dervish Ali (r. 1554–1556)

* This list makes no claim to completeness.

Sources: Allen J. Frank, 'The western steppe: Volga-Ural region, Siberia and the Crimea' (2009), in: Nicola Di Cosmo, Allen J. Frank and Peter B. Golden (eds), *The Cambridge History of Inner Asia: The Chinggisid Age* (Cambridge: Cambridge University Press, 2009), pp. 254f. Samuel Gottlieb Gmelin, *Astrakhan Anno 1770. Its History, Geography, Population, Trade, Flora, Fauna and Fisheries* (1770–84; English translation Washington: Mage Publishers, 2013), pp. 35–51.

The most important Khans and Amirs of the Nogai Horde and their predecessors, 2nd half fifteenth century–*ca.* 1634*

Amir Edigü (warlord of the Golden Horde, d. 1419)

Mansur bin Edigü (r. ?)

Nur al-Din bin Edigü (*ca.* 1426–*ca.* 1440)

?

Musa bin Waqqas (2nd half 15th century)

?

Yusuf Bey bin Musa (r. *ca.* 1536–*ca.* 1555)

Ismail Bey bin Musa (r. *ca.* 1554–1563)

Greater Horde

Ismail Bey bin Musa (r. *ca.* 1554–1563)

Din Achmad bin Ismail (r. 1563–78)

Mirza Urus bin Ismail (r. 1578– *ca.* 1600)

Ishterek Bey bin Din Achmad (r. *ca.* 1600–1618)

At least three competing Khans

Lesser Horde of Azov

Qasim bin Sheykh Mamai (r. *ca.* 1555– *ca.* 1601)

* This list makes no claim to completeness.

Sources: Brian L. Davies, *Warfare, State and Society on the Black Sea Steppe, 1500–1700* (2007), pp. 8, 16. Allen J. Frank, 'The western steppe: Volga-Ural region, Siberia and the Crimea', in: Nicola Di Cosmo, Allen J. Frank and Peter B. Golden (eds), *The Cambridge History of Inner Asia: The Chinggisid Age* (Cambridge: Cambridge University Press, 2009), pp. 241–45.

The Khans of Sibir, 1427–1582/98*

Hajji Muhammad Khan (d. 1428 or 1429)

Abu'l Khayr Khan (r. 1429–68/69)

Ibak Khan (r. *ca.* 1468/69– *ca.* 1494)

Mamuq (Mamat, Muhammad) Khan (r. *ca.* 1494–95, 1496–?)

?

Yagidar Bey (r. ?–1563)

Bey Bulad (co-ruler?)

Küchüm Khan (r. 1563–82, as guerilla leader 1582–98)

* This list makes no claim to completeness.

Sources: James Forsyth, *A History of the Peoples of Siberia. Russia's North Asian Colony 1581–1990* (Cambridge: Cambridge University Press, 1992), pp. 25–27. Allen J. Frank, 'The western steppe: Volga-Ural region, Siberia and the Crimea', in: Nicola Di Cosmo, Allen J. Frank and Peter B. Golden (eds), *The Cambridge History of Inner Asia: The Chinggisid Age* (Cambridge: Cambridge University Press, 2009), pp. 250–53.

The Khans of Crimea, *ca.* 1441–1783

Hajji Giray (r. *ca.* 1441–*ca.* 1466)

Haydar Giray (r. 1456, rebel against his father Hajji Giray)

Nur Devlet Giray (first reign 1466–1468)

Mengli Giray I (first reign 1468–1469)

Nur Devlet Giray (second reign 1469–1471)

Mengli Giray I (second reign 1471–1474)

Nur Devlet Giray (third reign 1474–1475)

Mengli Giray I (third reign 1475)

Nur Devlet Giray (fourth reign 1476–1478)

Mengli Giray I (fourth reign 1478–1514)

Mehmed Giray I (r. 1514–1523)

Ghazi Giray I (r. 1523–1524)

Saadet Giray I (r. 1524–1532)

Sahib Giray (r. 1532–1551)

Islam Giray I (r. as rival Khan 1532–1534)

Devlet Giray I (r. 1551–1577)

Mehmed Giray II (r. 1577–1584)

Saadet Giray II (r. 1584)

Islam Giray II (r. 1584–1588)

Ghazi Giray II (first reign 1588–1596)

Fatih Giray I (r. 1596)

Ghazi Giray II (second reign 1596–1608)

Toqtamish Giray (r. 1608)

Selamet Giray I (r. 1608–1610)

Jani Beg (first reign 1610–1623)

Mehmed Giray III (r. 1623–1628)

Jani Beg (second reign 1628–1635)

Inayet Giray (r. 1635–1637)

Bahadir Giray I (r. 1637–1641)

Mehmed Giray IV (first reign 1641–1644)

Islam Giray III (r. 1644–1654)

Mehmed Giray IV (second reign 1654–1666)

Adil Giray (r. 1666–1671)

Selim Giray I (first reign 1671–1678)

Murad Giray (r. 1678–1683)

Hajji Giray II (r. 1683–1684)

Selim Giray I (second reign 1684–1691)

Saadet Giray III (r. 1691)

Safa Giray (r. 1691–1692)

Selim Giray I (third reign 1692–1699)

Devlet Giray II (first reign 1699–1702)

Selim Giray I (fourth reign 1702–1704)

Ghazi Giray III (r. 1704–1707)

Kaplan Giray I (first reign 1707–1708)

Devlet Giray II (second reign 1709–1713)

Kaplan Giray I (second reign 1713–1715)

Devlet Giray III (r. 1716–1717)

Saadet Giray IV (r. 1717–1724)

Mengli Giray II (first reign 1724–1730)

Kaplan Giray I (third reign 1730–1736)

Fatih Giray II (r. 1736–1737)

Mengli Giray II (second reign 1737–1740)

Selamet Giray II (r. 1740–1743)

Selim Giray II (r. 1743–1748)

Arslan Giray (first reign 1748–1756)

Halim Giray (r. 1756–1758)

Qirim Giray (first reign 1758–1764)

Selim Giray III (first reign 1765–1767)

Arslan Giray (second reign 1767)

Maqsud Giray (r. 1767–1768)

Qirim Giray (second reign 1768–1769)

Devlet IV (first reign 1769–1770)

Kaplan Giray II (r. 1770)

Selim Giray III (second reign 1770–1771)

Sahib Giray II (r. 1771–1775)

Devlet Giray IV (second reign 1775–1777)

Sahin Giray (first reign 1777–1778)

Selim Giray III (third reign 1778)

Sahin Giray (second reign 1778–1782)

Bahadir Giray II (r. 1782)

Sahin Giray (third reign 1782–1783)

Sources: Alan W. Fisher, *The Crimean Tatars* (Stanford: Hoover Institution Press, 1978), pp. 1–69. Josef Hammer-Purgstall, *Geschichte der Chane der Krim unter osmanischer Herrschaft. Aus türkischen Quellen zusammengetragen* (1856, Reprint Charleston: BiblioLife, print-on-demand *ca.* 2012). Neil Kent, *Crimea. A History* (London: Hurst, 2016).

The Timurid Mughal Emperors of India, 1526–1858

Zahir al-Din Muhammad Babur (r. 1526–1530)

Humayum (first reign 1530–1540)

Sher Khan Suri, a non-Mughal Pashtun (r. 1540–1545)

Islam Shah Suri, a non-Mughal Pashtun (r. 1545–1554)

Firuz Shah Suri, a non-Mughal Pashtun (r. 1554)

Muhammad Adil Shah Suri, a non-Mughal Pashtun (r. 1554–1555)

Ibrahim Shah Suri, a non-Mughal Pashtun (r. 1555)

Sikander Shah Suri, a non-Mughal Pashtun (r. 1555)

Humayum (second reign 1555–1556)

Akbar (r. 1556–1605)

Jahangir (r. 1605–1627)

Shah Jahan (r. 1628–1658, d. 1666)

Aurangzeb, Alamgir I (r. 1658–1707)

Bahadur Shah I (r. 1707–1712)

Jahandar Shah (1712–1713)

Farrukhsiyar (r. 1713–1719)

Muhammad Shah (1719–1748)

Ahmad Shah (r. 1748–1754)

Alamgir II (1754–1759)

Shah Alam (1759–1806)

Akbar II (r. 1806–1837)

Bahadur Shah II (r. 1837–1858, d. 1862)

Sources: John F. Richards, *The Mughal Empire* (Cambridge: Cambridge University Press, 2005). Francis Robinson, *The Mughal Emperors* (2007), pp. 112–79.

The Khans of the Northern Yuan Dynasty, 1368–1634

Toghon Temür (r. 1368–1370)

Biligtü Khan Ayushiridara (r. 1370–1378)

Ushkal Khan Tögüs Temür (r. 1378–1388)

Jorightu Khan Yesüder (r. 1388–1392)

Engke Khan?

Elbeg (r. 1393–1399)

Gung Temür Khan (r. 1400–1402)

Örüg Temür Khan (r. 1402–1408)

Öljey Temür Khan (**Bunyashiri,** r. 1408–1412)

Delbeg Khan (r. 1412–1414)

Oyiradai Khan (r. 1415–1425)

Adai Khan (r. 1426–1438)

Toghtoa Bukha (r. *ca.* 1438–1453)

Esen Khan (not a Genghis Khanid but an Oirat Tayishi, ruled de facto 1438/39–1453, r. as khan 1453–1455)

Mar Körgis Khan (r. 1455– *ca.* 1465)

Molon Khan (Tögüs, r. *ca.* 1465–1466)

Mandughul Khan (r. *ca.* 1473–1478/79)

Batu Möngke Dayan Khan (r. *ca.* 1480–1517 or 1524; the later dates 1533 or 1543 are unlikely)

Bodi Alagh Khan (r. ?–1547)

Daraisung Gudeng (r. 1547–1557)

Tümen Jasaghtu Khan (r. 1557–1592)

Buyan Sechen Khan (r. 1592–1604)

Ligdan Khan (r. 1604–1634)

Ejei Khan (did not really reign, d. 1661)

Sources: Christopher Atwood, *Encyclopedia of Mongolia and the Mongol Empire* (2004), pp. 407–10. Veronika Veit, 'The eastern steppe: Mongol regimes after the Yuan (1368–1636)', in: Nicola Di Cosmo, Allen J. Frank and Peter B. Golden (eds), *The Cambridge History of Inner Asia: The Chinggisid Age* (Cambridge: Cambridge University Press, 2009), pp. 162f, 167f, 178, 181. Concerning Esen Khan's reign duration, see chapter III, note 13.

The Khans of the Dzungars, *ca.* 1600–1757

Khara-Khula Tayishi (r. *ca.* 1600–1634)

Erdeni Batur Khong Tayishi (r. 1634–1653)

Sengge Khong Tayishi (r. 1653–1671)

Galdan Boshughthtu Khan (r. 1671–1697)

Tsewang Rabtan (r. 1697–1727)

Galdan Tsering (r. 1727–1745)

Tsewang Dorje Namgyal (r. 1746–1750)

Lama Darja (Dorji, r. 1750–1752)

Dawachi (r. 1753–55)

Amursana (r. as Khan of the Khoit 1755–1757)

Sources: Thomas J. Barfield, *The Perilous Frontier: Nomadic Empires and China, 221 BC to AD 1757* (Cambridge, MA/Oxford: Blackwell, 1992), p. 280. Michael Khodarkovsky, *Where Two Worlds Met. The Russian State and the Kalmyk Nomads, 1600–1771* (Ithaca: Cornell University Press, 1992), p. XIV.

The Kazakh Khans of the unified khanate, *ca.* 1465/70–1718

Giray Khan (d. *ca.* 1480)

Jani Beg Khan, co-ruler (d. 1480)

Burunduq Khan (r. 1480–1511)

Qasim Khan (r. 1511–1519 or 1521)

Muhammad Husayn (Mumash) Khan (r. 1519/21–1523)

Tahir Khan (r. 1523– *ca.* 1529/33)

Birilash (Buydash) Khan (r. *ca.* 1529/33–1534)

Tughum Khan (r. 1534–1538)

Haqq (Aq) Nazar Khan (r. *ca.* 1538–1580)

Shighay Khan (r. 1580–1582)

Tevekkel (Tauekel) Khan (r. 1582–1598)

Ishim (Esin) Khan (r. in Turkistan 1598–1628)

Tursun Mohammad (r. in Tashkent before 1613–1628)

Jahangir Khan (r. 1628–1652)

Batyr (a title, r. 1652–1680?)

Tavke (Tauke) Khan (r. 1680–1718)

After Tavke Khan's death the khanate broke up into three hordes:

The **Junior Horde** *Kishi Zhuz,* abolished by Russia in 1824 (a part of the Junior Horde formed 1801–1845 the **Inner Horde** *Bukey Zhuz*)

The **Middle Horde** *Orta Zhuz,* abolished by Russia in 1822

The **Senior Horde** *Ulu Zhuz,* abolished by Russia in 1848

Sources: Frank J. Allen, 'The Qazakhs and Russia', in: Nicola Di Cosmo, Allen J. Frank and Peter B. Golden (eds), *The Cambridge History of Inner Asia: The Chinggisid Age* (Cambridge: Cambridge University Press, 2009), pp. 363–79. Karl Baipakov and B.F. Kumekov, 'The Kazakhs', in: Chahryar Adle, Irfan Habib and Karl M. Baipakov (eds), *History of Civilizations of Central Asia*, vol. V (Paris: Unesco Publishing, 2003), pp. 89–108. Paul Georg Geiss, *Pre-Tsarist and Tsarist Central Asia: Communal Development and Political Order in Change* (London: RoutledgeCurzon, 2013), p. 114.

The Tayishis and Khans of the Kalmyks, before 1604–1771

Khoo-Örlög Tayishi (r. before 1604–1644)

Daichin Tayishi (r. 1647–1661)

Puntsuk Tayishi (r. 1661–1669)

Ayuka Khan (r. 1669–1724)

Cheren Donduk Khan (r. 1724–1735)

Donduk Ombo Khan (r. 1735–1741)

Donduk Dashi Khan (r. 1741–1761)

Ubashi Khan (r. 1761–1771, d. 1774/75)

Source: Khodarkovsky, Michael, *Where Two Worlds Met. The Russian State and the Kalmyk Nomads, 1600–1771* (Ithaca: Cornell University Press, 1992).

The Afghan Dynasty of the Hotaki Ghilzai, 1709–1738

Mir Ways (r. in Kandahar 1709–1715)

Abd al-Aziz (r. in Kandahar 1715–1717)

Mir Mahmud (r. in Kandahar 1717–1722, in Iran 1722–1725)

Ashraf Khan (r. in Iran 1725–1729, d. 1730)

Husayn Hotaki (r. in Kandahar 1725–1738)

Sources: D. Balland, 'Ashraf Gilzai, the Afghan chief who rules as Shah over part of Iran from 1137/1725 to 1142/1729', in: *Encyclopaedia Iranica* (2011). H.R. Roemer, 'The Safavid period', in Peter Jackson and Laurence Lockhart (eds), *The Cambridge History of Iran: The Timurid and Safavid Periods*, vol. 6 (Cambridge: Cambridge University Press, 1986), pp. 314–17. Mir Hussain Shah, 'Afghanistan', in: Chahryar Adle, Irfan Habib and Karl M. Baipakov, (eds), *History of Civilizations of Central Asia*, vol. V (Paris: Unesco Publishing, 2003), pp. 280–85. Willem Vogelsang, *The Afghans* (Chichester: Wiley-Blackwell, 2008), pp. 221–27.

The Kings and Amirs of the Popalzai and Barakzai of Afghanistan, 1747–1973

Ahmad Shah Durrani (r. 1747–1772)

Timur Shah (r. 1772–1793)

Zaman Shah (r. 1793–1800)

Shah Mahmud (first reign 1801–1803)

Shah Shuja (first reign 1803–1809)

Shah Mahmud (second reign 1809–1818)

Power struggle among the Barakzai brothers, 1818–1826

Dost Muhammad Khan (first reign. 1826–1839)

Shah Shujah (second reign 1839–1842)

Fateh Jang Sadozai (r. 1842)

Shahpur Sadozai (r. 1842)

Akbar Khan (ruled in place of his father Dost Muhammad 1842/43)

Dost Muhammad Khan (second reign 1842/43–1863)

Sher Ali (first reign 1863–1866)

Muhammad Afzal (r. 1866–1867)

Muhammad A'zam (r. 1867–1869)

Sher Ali (second reign 1869–1879)

Yaqub Khan (1879–1880)

Abdur Rahman (r. 1880–1901)

Habibullah (r. 1901–1919)

Nasrullah (r. 21–28 February 1919, d. 1920)

Amanullah (r. 1919–1929, d. 1960)

Inayatullah (r. 14–17 January 1929, d. 1946)

Habibullah Kalakani (an ethnic Tajik, r. 18 January – 13 October 1929)

Nadir Shah (r. 1929–1933)

Zahir Shah (nominal r. 1933–1963, actual r. 1963–1973, d. 2007)

Sources: A. Heathcote, *The Afghan Wars, 1839–1919* (London: Osprey, 1980). Mohan Lal, *Life of the Amir Dost Mohammed Khan of Kabul: with his political proceedings towards the English, Russian, and Persian Governments, including the victory and disasters of the British army in Afghanistan* (London: Longman, 1846). Sir Percy Sykes, *A History of Afghanistan* (1940; reprint, New Delhi: Manoharlal, 2002), Stephen Tanner, *Afghanistan: A Military History from Alexander the Great to the War against the Taliban* (Cambridge, MA: Da Capo Press, 2002). Willem Vogelsang, *The Afghans* (Chichester: Wiley-Blackwell, 2008).

The Khanate of Kokand and the Dynasty of the Ming, early 18th *c.*–1876

Shah Rukh (r. 1709–1721)*

Abdu'l Rahim (r. 1721–1733)*

Abdu'l Karim Bey (r. 1733–1746 or 1750)*

Abdu'l Rahman (*r. ca.* 1750–1751)*

Baba Beg (r. 1751?)*

Irdana Bey (r. 1751–1770)*

Sulayman Shah (r. 1770)*

Narbuta Bey (r. 1770–1798/99)*

Alim Khan (r. 1798/99–1810)

Umar Khan (r. 1810–1822)

Muhammad Ali (Madali, r. 1822–1842)

Sultan Mahmud (r. 1842)

Sher Ali Khan (r. 1842–45)

Murad Bey Khan (r. 1845)

Muhammad Khudayar Khan (first reign 1845–1858)

Mallya Khan (r. 1858–1862)

Shah Murad (r. 1862) **

Muhammad Khudayar Khan (second reign 1862–1863)

Sultan Murad or Shah Murad (1863–1865) ***

Khuda Qul (**Belbakchi Khan**, r. 1865)

Muhammad Khudayar Khan (third reign 1865–1875, vassal of Russia)

Pulad Khan, a Kyrgyz pretender (r. 1875)

Nasir al-Din (r. 1875–1876)

* The dates till 1798/99 are approximate and may differ from one source to another.

** Bababekov says that Shah Murad was a son of Mallya Khan (p. 76); Dubovitskii/Bababekov qualify him as nephew of Mallya Khan (p. 36).

*** Bababekov gives the name Shah Murad for this ruler and identifies him with the previous Shah Murad (p. 76), Dubovitskii/Bababekov name him Sultan Murad and qualify him as son of Mallya Khan (p. 37).

Sources: H.N. Bababekov, 'Fergana and the Khanate of Kokand', in: *History of Civilizations of Central Asia,* vol. V, eds Chahryar Adle, Irfan Habib and Karl M. Baipakov (Paris: Unesco Publishing, 2003), pp. 76f. Yuri Bregel, 'The new Uzbek states: Bukhara, Khiva and Kokand: c. 1750–1886' (2009), pp. 392–411. Victor Dubovitskii with Khaydarbek Bababekov, 'The Rise and Fall of the Kokand Khanate', in: S. Frederick Starr (ed.), *Ferghana Valley. The Heart of Central Asia* (Armonk: M.E. Sharpe, 2011), pp. 29–68. Svat Soucek, *A History of Inner Asia* (2000), p. 326f.

Notes

Introduction

1. Clifford Kinvig, 'Review of *The Scope and Methods of Geography and the Geographical Pivot of History* by Halford Mackinder' (London: International Affairs, vol. 27, no. 4, 1951), pp. 540–41.
2. Shireen Hunter, *Islam in Russia: The Politics of Identity and Security* (Oxon: Routledge, 2015), p. 309.

I.   Descendants of the Genghis Khanids

1. Anthony Jenkinson, *Early voyages and travels to Russia and Persia*, vol. 1 (London: Hakluyt Society, 1886), pp. 85, 87.
2. On the Islamic denominations and early intra-Muslim conflict, see: Christoph Baumer, *The History of Central Asia: The Age of Islam and the Mongols*, vol. 3 (London: I.B.Tauris, 2016), pp. 6–11, 312f.
3. As already mentioned in volume III of the present work, the Mughal dynasty of India (1526–1858), founded by Babur, is not to be confused with the khanate of Moghulistan in East Turkestan (1347–1705). Baumer, *The History of Central Asia*, vol. 3 (2016), p. 342n 135.
4. Yuri Bregel, 'The Abu'l-Khayrids', in: Encyclopaedia Iranica (2009, updated 2011). R.D. McChesney, 'The Chinggisid restoration in Central Asia: 1500–1785', in: Nicola Di Cosmo, Allen J. Frank and Peter B. Golden (eds), *The Cambridge History of Inner Asia: The Chinggisid Age* (Cambridge: Cambridge University Press, 2009), pp. 277–79.
5. Baumer, *The History of Central Asia*, vol. 3 (London: I.B.Tauris, 2016), pp. 267f.
6. Baumer, *The History of Central Asia*, vol. 3 (2016), p. 295. Yuri Bregel, 'Uzbeks, Qazaqs and Turkmens', in Nicola Di Cosmo, Allen J. Frank and Peter B. Golden (eds), *The Cambridge History of Inner Asia: The Chinggisid Age* (Cambridge: Cambridge University Press, 2009), pp. 222f.
7. 'Tayishi' is a Mongolian title of Chinese origin for a tribal leader who was immediately subordinate to the Khan of a tribal union.
8. Bregel, 'Uzbeks, Qazaqs and Turkmens' (2009), pp. 225. Mansura Haidar, *Central Asia in the Sixteenth Century* (Delhi: Manohar, 2002), pp. 66–68.
9. Mirza Muhammad Haidar, Dughlat, *Tarikh-i-Rashidi: A History of the Moghuls of Central Asia*, Trans. D. Ross, (New Delhi: Abi Prints, 1998), vol. 2, pp. 272f.
10. Bregel, 'Uzbeks, Qazaqs and Turkmens' (2009), pp. 226. Allen J. Frank, 'The western steppe: Volga-Ural region, Siberia and the Crimea', in: Nicola Di Cosmo, Allen J. Frank and Peter B. Golden (eds), *The Cambridge History of Inner Asia: The Chinggisid Age* (Cambridge: Cambridge University Press, 2009), p. 253.
11. Baumer, *The History of Central Asia*, vol. 3 (2016), p. 300.
12. Haidar, *Central Asia in the Sixteenth Century* (2002), pp. 103–18. H.R. Roemer, 'The Successors of Timur', in Peter Jackson and Laurence Lockhart (eds), *The Cambridge History of Iran: The Timurid and Safavid Periods*, vol. 6 (Cambridge: Cambridge University Press, 1986), p. 126.
13. Haidar, *Central Asia in the Sixteenth Century* (2002), p. 117. R.D. McChesney, 'The Chinggisid restoration in Central Asia: 1500–1785' (2009), p. 292.
14. Haidar, Dughlat, *Tarikh-i-Rashidi* (1998), vol. 2, p. 162.
15. Haidar, *Central Asia in the Sixteenth Century* (2002), p. 102. R.D. McChesney, 'The Chinggisid restoration in Central Asia: 1500–1785' (2009), p. 280.
16. R.G. Mukminova and A. Mukhtarov, 'The Khanate (Emirate) of Buchara', in: Chahryar Adle, Irfan Habib and Karl M. Baipakov (eds), *History of Civilizations of Central Asia*, vol. V (Paris: Unesco Publishing, 2003), p. 37.
17. E.A. Davidovich, 'Monetary policy and currency circulation under the Shaybanid and the Janid (Astarkhanid) dynasties', in: *History of Civilizations of Central Asia*, vol. V (2003), pp. 427–31. R.G. Mukminova and A. Mukhtarov, 'The Khanate (Emirate) of Buchara' (2003), p. 37.
18. Haidar, *Central Asia in the Sixteenth Century* (2002), pp. 119–21, 130.
19. Haidar, Dughlat, *Tarikh-i-Rashidi* (1998), vol. 2, p. 231.
20. H.R. Roemer, 'The Safavid period', in Jackson and Lockhart (eds), *The Cambridge History of Iran*, vol. 6 (1986), pp. 182–209, 216f.
21. Roemer, 'The Safavid period' (1986), pp. 198, 209, 214.
22. Khwandamir, Ghiyas ad-Din Muhammad, *Habibu al-Siyar* [Beloved of Careers], in *Classic Writings of the Medieval Islamic World*, translated and annotated by Wheeler Thrackston, vol. II (London: I.B.Tauris, 2012), part IV, 523, p. 582. See also: Haidar, Dughlat, *Tarikh-i-Rashidi* (1998), vol. 2, pp. 232–36.
23. Haidar, *Central Asia in the Sixteenth Century* (2002), pp. 133f. R.D. McChesney, 'The Chinggisid restoration in Central Asia: 1500–1785' (2009), p. 293.
24. Khwandamir, *Habibu al-Siyar* (2012), part IV, 524, p. 586. Haidar, Dughlat, *Tarikh-i-Rashidi* (1998), vol. 2, pp. 237–42.
25. Khwandamir, *Habibu al-Siyar* (2012), part IV, 518f, pp. 584f.
26. Khwandamir, *Habibu al-Siyar* (2012), part IV, 524, p. 586.
27. Yuri Bregel, *An Historical Atlas of Central Asia* (Leiden/Boston: Brill, 2003), p. 50. Khwandamir, *Habibu al-Siyar* (2012), part IV, 524f, pp. 586f.
28. Khwandamir, *Habibu al-Siyar* (2012), part IV, 526–29, pp. 587–89. H.R. Roemer, 'The Successors of Timur' (1986), p. 127.
29. Baber, Zehir-ed-Din Muhammed, *Memoirs of Zehir-ed-Din Muhammed Baber*, trans. the late John Leyden and William Erskine (London: Longman et al. 1826), pp. 243–45.
30. Khwandamir, *Habibu al-Siyar* (2012), part IV, 545–48, pp. 595f. H.R. Roemer, 'The Safavid period' (1986), pp. 224f.
31. Bregel, *An Historical Atlas of Central Asia* (2003), p. 52.
32. Bregel, *An Historical Atlas of Central Asia* (2003), p. 52. Haidar, *Central Asia in the Sixteenth Century* (2002), pp. 163–70.
33. The Shia Ismailis inhabiting the Pamir Mountains of Tajikistan are an exception.
34. Haidar, *Central Asia in the Sixteenth Century* (2002), pp. 180–202.
35. Jenkinson, *Early voyages and travels* vol. I, Introduction (1886), pp. i–ii.
36. Date given according to the Julian calendar which was in use in England until 1751. According to the Gregorian Calendar Jenkinson reached Bukhara on 2 January 1559.
37. Jenkinson, *Early voyages and travels* vol. I (1886), pp. 41–91.
38. Jenkinson, *Early voyages and travels* vol. I (1886), p. 88.
39. Jenkinson, *Early voyages and travels* vol. I (1886), pp. 41–94. Kit Mayers, *The first English Explorer. The Life of Anthony Jenkinson (1529–1611) and his adventures on the route to the Orient* (Kibworth Beauchamp: Matador, 2017), pp. 36–131. The

Uzbek raids against Khorasan also made a return journey via Persia impossible.

40 The ruler of Samarkand who invaded Bukhara was probably Baba Sultan, the eldest son of Ahmad Nawruz, who inherited Samarkand in 1556. Jenkinson, *Early voyages and travels* vol. I (1886), p. 93n.2.

41 Bregel, *An Historical Atlas of Central Asia* (2003), pp. 54f.

42 M. Annanepesov, 'Relations between the Khanates and with other powers', in: *History of Civilizations of Central Asia,* vol. V (2003), p. 83. Bregel, *An Historical Atlas of Central Asia* (2003), pp. 54f. Haidar, *Central Asia in the Sixteenth Century* (2002), p. 264.

43 Haidar, *Central Asia in the Sixteenth Century* (2002), p. 262.

44 A. Khan Iqtidar, 'Inter-state relations (c. 1550–1850)', in: *History of Civilizations of Central Asia,* vol. V (2003), p. 330. Haidar, *Central Asia in the Sixteenth Century* (2002), p. 272.

45 Scott C. Levi and Ron Sela, *Islamic Central Asia: An Anthology of Historical Sources* (Bloomington: Indiana University Press, 2010), p. 223.

46 A. Khan Iqtidar, 'Inter-state relations' (2003), p. 333.

47 Haidar, *Central Asia in the Sixteenth Century* (2002), p. 287.

48 J.L. Lee, *The 'Ancient Supremacy.' Bukhara, Afghanistan and the Battle for Balkh, 1731–1901* (Leiden: Brill, 1996), pp. 42–56.

49 Edward Allsworth, *130 Years of Russian Dominance, a Historical Overview: Encounter* (Durham: Duke University Press, 1994), p. 40f.

50 McChesney, 'The Chinggisid restoration in Central Asia: 1500–1785' (2009), pp. 298–302. Mukminova and Mukhtarov, 'The Khanate (Emirate) of Buchara' (2003), pp. 45–48.

51 Lee, *The 'Ancient Supremacy'* (1996), pp. 50–53.

52 Lee, *The 'Ancient Supremacy'* (1996), pp. 57f. Mukminova and Mukhtarov, 'The Khanate (Emirate) of Buchara' (2003), pp. 48f.

53 Lee, *The 'Ancient Supremacy'* (1996), pp. 58–60, tables IV, i–vi. Jürgen Paul, *Zentralasien* (Frankfurt am Main: Fischer, 2012), pp. 357f.

54 Thomas J. Barfield, *The Perilous Frontier: Nomadic Empires and China, 221 BC to AD 1757* (Cambridge, MA/Oxford: Blackwell, 1992), p. 291. Fred W. Bergholz, *The Partition of the Steppe. The Struggle of the Russians, Manchus, and the Zungar Mongols for Empire in Central Asia, 1619–1758* (New York: Peter Lang, 1993), pp. 358–61.

55 Florio Beneveni, *Poslannik Petra I na Vostoke: posol'stvo Florio Beneveni v Persiû i Buharu v 1718–1725 godach* (Moskva: Akademija nauk SSSR. Institut vostokovedenija, 1986), p. 75.

56 Frank J. Allen, 'The Qazakhs and Russia', in: Nicola Di Cosmo, Allen J. Frank and Peter B. Golden (eds), *The Cambridge History of Inner Asia: The Chinggisid Age* (Cambridge: Cambridge University Press, 2009), p. 368. Bergholz, *The Partition of the Steppe* (1993), pp. 361f, 370.

57 See here pp. 103f.

58 After a failed attempt on Nader Shah's life in 1741, he had his son Reza Quli blinded because he suspected his involvement in the conspiracy. Michael Axworthy, *The Sword of Persia. Nader Shah, from Tribal Warrior to Conquering Tyrant* (London: I.B.Tauris, 2006), pp. 238–40.

59 Peter Avery, 'Nadir Shah and the Afsharid Legacy', in: Peter Avery, Gavin Hambly and Charles Melville (eds), *The Cambridge History of Iran: From Nadir Shah to the Islamic Republic,* vol. 7 (Cambridge: Cambridge University Press, 1991), pp. 36–43. E. Eshraghi, 'Persia during the period of the Safavids, the Afshars and the early Qajars', in: *History of Civilizations of Central Asia,* vol. V (2003), pp. 262f.

60 Axworthy, *The Sword of Persia* (2006), pp. 191–93, 221–27. R.G. Mukminova and A. Mukhtarov, 'The Khanate (Emirate) of Buchara' (2003), pp. 394f.

61 See here p. 115.

62 The name Chor Bakr essentially means 'four Bakr'. It refers to the tradition according to which the Imam Sayid Abu Bakr, one of the four Bakr brothers who were supposedly descendants of the Prophet, was buried here around the year 970.

63 For a photo, see: Baumer, *The History of Central Asia,* vol. 3 (2016), fig. 219.

64 On the architecture in Bukhara: Sheila Blair and Jonathan M. Bloom, *The Art and Architecture of Islam 1250–1800* (New Haven: Yale University Press, 1995), pp. 199–204. Haidar, *Central Asia in the Sixteenth Century* (2002), pp. 325–35. Galina Pugachenkova, 'Architecture in Transoxania and Khurasan', in: *History of Civilizations of Central Asia,* vol. V (2003), pp. 479–97, 501.

65 George N. Curzon, *Russia in Central Asia in 1889 and the Anglo-Russian Question* (London: Longmans, Green, and Co., 1889), p. 220.

66 Blair, Bloom, *The Art and Architecture of Islam* (1995), pp. 204–7. Galina Pugachenkova, 'Architecture in Transoxania and Khurasan' (2003), pp. 498–500.

67 Jenkinson, *Early voyages and travels,* vol. I (1886), p. 70.

68 Ebülgâzî Bahadir Khan, Khan of Khorezm, *A general history of the Turks, Moguls, and Tatars, vulgarly called Tartars. Together with a Description of the Countries they inhabit* (London: Knapton et al, 1730; Reprint Bibliolife, 2016), vol. II, pp. 444–51. See also: Theodor Friedrich Julius Basiner, 'Reise durch die Kirgisensteppe nach Chiwa', *Beiträge zur Kenntnis des Russischen Reiches und der angrenzenden Länder Asiens* (St Petersburg: Kaiserliche Akademie der Wissenschaften, 1848), p. 101. Carl Timmermann, *Denkschrift über den unteren Lauf des Oxus zum Karabugas-Haff des Caspischen Meeres und über die Strombahn des Ochus, oder Tedshen der Neueren, zur Balkan-Bay* (Berlin: Reimer, 1845), p. 179. For a longer discussion, see: Alexander von Humboldt, *Asie Centrale. Recherches sur les chaines de montagnes et la climatologie comparée* (Paris: Gide, 1843), vol. II, pp. 226–38. E.M. Mursajew, *Auf unbetretenen Pfaden. Durch Asiens Wüsten und Hochgebirge* (Leipzig: Brockhaus, 1956), pp. 100–109).

69 M. Annanepesov. 'The Khanate of Khiva (Khwarazm)', in: *History of Civilizations of Central Asia,* vol. V (2003), p. 66.

70 Annanepesov, 'The Khanate of Khiva (Khwarazm)' (2003), p. 64. Bregel, *An Historical Atlas of Central Asia* (2003), pp. 52–54.

71 Bregel, 'The new Uzbek states: Bukhara, Khiva and Kokand: c. 1750–1886', in: Nicola Di Cosmo, Allen J. Frank and Peter B. Golden (eds), *The Cambridge History of Inner Asia: The Chinggisid Age*

72 Allsworth, *130 Years of Russian Dominance, a Historical Overview: Encounter* (1994), p. 8. Josef Popowski, *The Rival Powers in Central Asia* (1893; Reprint Quetta: Gosha-e-Adab, 1977), p. 31.

73 The Cossacks were a hierarchical association of cavalries led by an ataman. They were recruited from among escaped Russian and Ukrainian serfs, adventurers and – initially – from Tartars. When they started to settle along rivers from the sixteenth century, they became armed peasants. In the eighteenth century, the Cossacks were gradually absorbed into the Russian cavalry.

74 Bergholz, *The Partition of the Steppe* (1993), pp. 32, 36, 77.

75 Sven Hedin, *Southern Tibet: Discoveries in former times compared with my own researches in 1906–1908* (Stockholm: Lithographic Institute of the General Staff of the Swedish Army, 1917–22), vol. I, pp. 253–59. Peter C. Perdue, *China Marches West. The Qing Conquest of Central Asia* (Cambridge, MA: Belknap Press, 2005), pp. 211f, 306f. Josef Popowski, *The Rival Powers in Central Asia* (1977), pp. 31f.

76 Henry Sutherland Edwards, *Russian Projects against India. From the Czar Peter to General Skobeleff* (London: Remington, 1885), pp. 4–25. Michael Khodarkovsky, *Where Two Worlds Met. The Russian State and the Kalmyk Nomads, 1600–1771* (Ithaca: Cornell University Press, 1992), pp. 157–60. René Létolle Monique Mainguet, *Der Aralsee. Eine ökologische Katastrophe* (Berlin: Springer, 1996). Josef Popowski, *The Rival Powers in Central Asia* (1977), pp. 153f.

77 See below pp. 122, 138f.

78 See below p. 113.

79 Bregel, 'The new Uzbek states' (2009), pp. 398f.

80 Baumer, *The History of Central Asia,* vol. 3 (2016), pp. 247f.

81 The terms Altishahr and Yetishahr were mainly used by Western travellers. See: Ildikó Bellér-Hann, *Community matters in Xinjiang, 1880–1949: towards a historical anthropology of the Uyghur* (Leiden: Brill, 2008), pp. 39f. Paul, *Zentralasien* (2012), p. 239.

82 Haidar, Dughlat, *Tarikh-i-Rashidi* (1998), vol. 2, p. 303.

83 On the history of Moghulistan until the end of the fourteenth century, see: Baumer, *The History of Central Asia,* vol. 3 (2016), pp. 247–49.

84 Hodong Kim, 'The early history of the Moghul nomads: the legacy of the Chagatai Khanate', in Reuven Amitai-Preiss and David O. Morgan (eds), *The Mongol Empire and Its Legacy* (Leiden: Brill, 1999), pp. 302f.

85 Haidar, Dughlat, *Tarikh-i-Rashidi* (1998), vol. 1, p. 58.

86 Haidar, Dughlat, *Tarikh-i-Rashidi* (1998), vol. 1, pp. 60–90. James Millward, 'Eastern Central Asia (Xinjiang): 1300–1800', in: Nicola Di Cosmo, Allen J. Frank and Peter B. Golden (eds), *The Cambridge History of Inner Asia: The Chinggisid Age* (Cambridge: Cambridge University Press, 2009), pp. 260–65.

87 Haidar, Dughlat, *Tarikh-i-Rashidi* (1998), vol. 1, pp. 99–112, vol. 2, pp. 254f, 310–28.

88 T. Choroev, 'The Kyrgyz', in: *History of Civilizations of Central Asia,* vol. V (2003), pp. 110f.

89 Haidar, Dughlat, *Tarikh-i-Rashidi* (1998), vol. 1, pp. 120–37.

90 Haidar, Dughlat, *Tarikh-i-Rashidi* (1998), vol. 2, pp. 384–451, 467.

91 Millward, 'Eastern Central Asia (Xinjiang): 1300–1800' (2009), p. 266f.

92 Taken from: Cornelius Wessels, *Early Jesuit Travelers in Central Asia 1603–1721* (New Delhi: Asian Education Services, 1992), pp. 25f.

93 Baumer, *The History of Central Asia,* vol. 2 (London: I.B.Tauris, 2014), pp. 12–14.

94 George Bishop, *In Search of Cathay. The Travels of Bento de Goes, S.J. (1562–1607)* (Anand: Gujarat Sahitya Prakash, 1998), pp. 116–294. Cornelius Wessels, *Early Jesuit Travellers in Central Asia 1603–1721* (1992), pp. 1–42.

95 Ma Dazheng, 'The Tarim Basin', in: *History of Civilizations of Central Asia,* vol. V (2003), pp. 184f. James Millward, *Eurasian Crossroads. A History of Xinjiang* (New York: Columbia University Press, 2007), p. 86. 'Eastern Central Asia (Xinjiang): 1300–1800' (2009), p. 268. Th. Zarcone, 'The Sufi orders in northern Central Asia', in: *History of Civilizations of Central Asia,* vol. V (2003), p. 774.

96 Ma Dazheng, 'The Tarim Basin' (2003), pp. 184f, 191f. Millward, *Eurasian Crossroads* (2007), pp. 86–88. 'Eastern Central Asia (Xinjiang): 1300–1800' (2009), p. 268.

97 Bergholz, *The Partition of the Steppe* (1993), pp. 251f.

98 Henry G. Schwarz, 'The Khwajas of Eastern Turkestan', in: *Central Asiatic Journal,* vol. 20, No. 4 (Wiesbaden: Harrassowitz, 1976), pp. 276–80.

99 Millward, *Eurasian Crossroads* (2007), p. 96. 'Eastern Central Asia (Xinjiang): 1300–1800' (2009), pp. 268f. Perdue, *China Marches West* (2005), pp. 289–91.

100 Zarcone, 'The Sufi orders in northern Central Asia' (2003), pp. 774f. See below pp. 120f.

101 Ma Dazheng, 'The Tarim Basin' (2003), pp. 192f, 201f. Millward, *Eurasian Crossroads* (2007), pp. 191f. Perdue, *China Marches West* (2005), pp. 199, 222. See below p. 208.

102 Barfield, *The Perilous Frontier* (1992), p. 286.

103 Baumer, *The History of Central Asia,* vol. 3 (2016), pp. 262–73, 279.

104 Baumer, *The History of Central Asia,* vol. 3 (2016), pp. 272f.

105 Concerning the history of Kazan, see also: Michael Khodarkovsky, *Russia's Steppe Frontier. The Making of a Colonial Empire, 1500–1800* (Bloomington: Indiana University Press, 2002), pp. 83–109.

106 Bertold Spuler, *Die Goldene Horde. Die Mongolen in Russland 1223–1502* (Leipzig: Harrassowitz, 1943), pp. 160f.

107 Frank, 'The western steppe: Volga-Ural region, Siberia and the Crimea' (2009), p. 246.

108 The generic term 'Tatars' refers to the Turkic Kipchaks, who in the Middle Ages mixed with the respective local populations and the Mongol conquerors.

109 Baumer, *History of Central Asia*, vol. 2 (2014), pp. 209–13.

110 Andreas Kappeler, *Russland als Vielvölkerreich. Entstehung, Geschichte, Zerfall* (Frankfurt a.M.: Büchergilde Gutenberg, 1992), p. 29. For an older history of the Khanate and its ethnic composition, see: Edward Tracy Turnerelli, *Russia on the borders of Asia: Kasan, the ancient capital of the Tartar khans,* 2 vols (London: R. Bentley, 1854).

111 Baumer, *The History of Central Asia,* vol. 3 (2016), pp. 269f.

112 Frank, 'The western steppe: Volga-Ural region, Siberia and the Crimea' (2009), pp. 247, 258. Khodarkovsky, *Russia's Steppe Frontier* (2002), pp. 83, 203. Bertold Spuler, *Die Goldene Horde. Die Mongolen in Russland 1223–1502* (Leipzig: Harrassowitz, 1943), pp. 166, 175. Michael Weiers, *Geschichte der Mongolen* (Stuttgart: Kohlhammer, 2004), pp. 166, 175.

113 Frank, 'The western steppe: Volga-Ural region, Siberia and the Crimea' (2009), p. 258.

114 Brian L. Davies, *Warfare, State and Society on the Black Sea Steppe, 1500–1700* (London: Routledge, 2007), pp. 5, 9, 13.

115 Baumer, *The History of Central Asia,* vol. 3 (2016), p. 273.

116 Davies, *Warfare, State and Society* (2007), p. 14. Frank, 'The western steppe: Volga-Ural region, Siberia and the Crimea' (2009), pp. 247f. Khodarkovsky, *Russia's Steppe Frontier* (2002), pp. 84–86. Spuler, *Die Goldene Horde* (1943), pp. 191–95.

117 Davies, *Warfare, State and Society* (2007), pp. 5, 8f. Alan W. Fisher, *The Crimean Tatars* (Stanford: Hoover Institution Press, 1978), p. 15. Andreas Kappeler, *Russland als Vielvölkerreich* (1992), pp. 28, 30. On relations between Moscow and Kazan, see also: Janet Martin, 'Muscovite Relations with the Khanates of Kasan and the Crimea (1460s to 1521)', in: *Canadian-American Slavic Studies,* vol. 17, No. 4 (Pittsburgh: University of Pittsburgh, 1983), pp. 435–53.

118 Davies, *Warfare, State and Society* (2007), pp. 14f. Frank, 'The western steppe: Volga-Ural region, Siberia and the Crimea' (2009), p. 208.

119 Davies, *Warfare, State and Society* (2007), p. 40.

120 Christian Noack, 'The western steppe: the Volga-Ural region, Siberia and the Crimea under Russian rule', in: Nicola Di Cosmo, Allen J. Frank and Peter B. Golden (eds), *The Cambridge History of Inner Asia: The Chinggisid Age* (Cambridge: Cambridge University Press, 2009), pp. 303–6.

121 The Streltsy formed a palace guard, which was established by Tsar Ivan around 1550 and rapidly grew into a well-armed professional army. In 1698, Tsar Peter I disbanded the mutinous Streltsy.

122 Davies, *Warfare, State and Society* (2007), p. 12f, 16f.

123 See below p. 42, here below n. 156.

124 Frank 'Russia and the peoples of the Volga-Ural region: 1600–1850', in: Nicola Di Cosmo, Allen J. Frank and Peter B. Golden (eds), *The Cambridge History of Inner Asia: The Chinggisid Age* (Cambridge: Cambridge University Press, 2009), pp. 381–85. Andreas Kappeler, *Russland als Vielvölkerreich* (1992), pp. 31–34, 55.

125 Christoph Baumer, *The Church of the East. An illustrated history of Assyrian Christianity* (London: I.B.Tauris, 2nd edition 2016), pp. 237–40.

126 Allan J. Frank, *Islamic Historiography and 'Bulghar' Identity among the Tatars and Bashkirs of Russia* (Leiden: Brill, 1998), p. 34.

127 Frank, 'Russia and the peoples of the Volga-Ural region' (2009), pp. 376–86. Kappeler, *Russland als Vielvölkerreich* (1992), pp. 33–36. Noack, 'The western steppe' (2009), pp. 328f.

128 Baumer, *The History of Central Asia,* vol. 3 (2016), p. 271f.

129 Frank, 'The western steppe: Volga-Ural region, Siberia and the Crimea' (2009), pp. 253f.

130 Bregel, 'Uzbeks, Qazaqs and Turkmens' (2009), p. 226. Frank, 'The western steppe: Volga-Ural region, Siberia and the Crimea' (2009), p. 253.

131 Frank, 'The western steppe: Volga-Ural region, Siberia and the Crimea' (2009), p. 251. Spuler, *Die Goldene Horde* (1943), pp. 176, 88–247.

132 Spuler, *Die Goldene Horde* (1943), p. 190.

133 Spuler, *Die Goldene Horde* (1943), p. 200–204.

134 Frank, 'The western steppe: Volga-Ural region, Siberia and the Crimea' (2009), pp. 254f.

135 Samuel Gottlieb Gmelin, *Astrakhan Anno 1770. Its History, Geography, Population, Trade, Flora, Fauna and Fisheries* (1770–84; English translation Washington: Mage Publishers, 2013), p. 35.

136 A.A. Kurbatov, *Astrachan Kremlin* (Rostow am Don: I.P. Yutishev 2010), pp. 41–47. M.S. Zaitseva and E.S. Koblova, *Astrakhan Kremlin* (Astrachan: JSC Publishing House Nova, 2011), pp. 6–15.

137 Tsar Peter's efforts in 1701–9 to build a Don-Volga canal failed. The canal was only realised under Stalin and opened in 1952.

138 Gmelin, *Astrakhan Anno 1770* (2013), pp. 40f. See also: Davies, *Warfare, State and Society* (2007), pp. 12f. Fisher, *The Crimean Tatars* (1978), pp. 44f. Khodarkovsky, *Russia's Steppe Frontier* (2002), pp. 115–17.

139 Gmelin, *Astrakhan Anno 1770* (2013), pp. 41–51.

140 Baumer, *The History of Central Asia,* vol. 3 (2016), p. 267.

141 The exact relationship of the almost interchangeable names 'Nogai' and 'Manghit' remains unclear.

142 Frank, 'The western steppe: Volga-Ural region, Siberia and the Crimea' (2009), pp. 241–43.

143 Davies, *Warfare, State and Society* (2007), pp. 8, 16. Allen J. Frank, 'The western steppe: Volga-Ural region, Siberia and the Crimea' (2009), pp. 243f.

144 Khodarkovsky, *Where Two Worlds Met* (1992), pp. 77, 80f.

145 James Forsyth, *A History of the Peoples of Siberia. Russia's North Asian Colony 1581–1990* (Cambridge: Cambridge University Press1992), pp. 25f. Frank, 'The western steppe: Volga-Ural region, Siberia and the Crimea' (2009), pp. 250f.

146 Bruce W. Lincoln, *The Conquest of a Continent: Siberia and the Russians* (Ithaca: Cornell University Press, 2007), pp. 39f.

147 Bergholz, *The Partition of the Steppe* (1993), pp. 22–29. Forsyth, *A History of the Peoples of Siberia* (1992), pp. 29–35. Kappeler, *Russland als Vielvölkerreich* (1992), p. 43.

148 Lincoln, *The Conquest of a Continent* (2007), p. 63. Kappeler, *Russland als Vielvölkerreich* (1992), p. 39.

149 Insofar as the Crimean Tatar Khanate only turned to Central Asia as a second priority and was primarily oriented to the Ottoman Empire, Moscow and Poland-Lithuania, its history will only be concisely summarised.

150 Fisher, *The Crimean Tatars* (1978), p. 3. Frank, 'The western steppe' (2009), p. 256.

151 Fisher, *The Crimean Tatars* (1978), pp. 20–22. Allen J. Frank, 'The western steppe' (2009), p. 256.

152 Lebedynsky cites the year 1441, Fisher 1443.

Alan W. Fisher, *The Crimean Tatars* (1978), pp. 3f. Iaroslav Lebedynsky, *La Horde d'Or. Conquête mongole et 'Joug tatar' en Europe 1236–1502* (Arles: Éditions Errance, 2013), p. 55.

153 Nicola Franco Balloni and Nelia Kukovalska (eds), *The Genoese in Crimea: A Historical Guide* (Kiev: Gorobez, 2009), pp. 82f. Alan W. Fisher, *The Crimean Tatars* (1978), p. 5.

154 Davies, *Warfare, State and Society* (2007), p. 7. Fisher, *The Crimean Tatars* (1978), pp. 8–11, 14, 34.

155 Neil Kent, *Crimea. A History* (London: Hurst, 2016), p. 47.

156 Davies, *Warfare, State and Society* (2007), p. 7.

157 According to Khodarkovsky, between 1600 and 1650 Moscow paid to Crimea 1 million rubles tribute and 5 million rubles ransom. The total corresponded to the cost of founding 1,200 cities, and the lack of these funds hampered the urbanisation of Russia. Khodarkovsky, *Russia's Steppe Frontier* (2002), p. 223.

158 Davies, *Warfare, State and Society* (2007), pp. 20–27. Fisher, *The Crimean Tatars* (1978), pp. 16, 19, 26–28, 40. James Forsyth, *The Caucasus. A History* (Cambridge: Cambridge University Press, 2013), p. 214.

159 Fisher, *The Crimean Tatars* (1978), pp. 38f.

160 Fisher, *The Crimean Tatars* (1978), pp. 42f.

161 Fisher, *The Crimean Tatars* (1978), pp. 16, 29f.

162 Davies, *Warfare, State and Society* (2007), pp. 183–87.

163 The Azov fortress fell again to the Ottomans in 1711, until finally passing into Russian hands in 1739.

164 Fisher, *The Crimean Tatars* (1978), pp. 30f. Neil Kent, *Crimea. A History* (London: Hurst, 2016), p. 50.

165 Fisher, *The Crimean Tatars* (1978), pp. 52f.

166 Fisher, *The Crimean Tatars* (1978), pp. 58–69. Neil Kent, *Crimea. A History* (London: Hurst, 2016), p. 52–57.

167 See Chapters IV and V.

II. The Descendants of the Timurids: the Dynasty of the Mughal in India and Afghanistan

1 John Jourdain, *The Journal of John Jourdain 1608–1617 describing his experiences in Arabia, India and the Malay Archipelago,* ed. William Foster (1905, Reprint New Delhi: Asian Educational services, 1992), p. 224.

2 Baber, Zehir-ed-Din Muhammed, *Memoirs of Zehir-ed-Din Muhammed Baber,* trans. John Leyden and William Erskine (London: Longman et al. 1826), pp. XXVI, LX. This edition will be given in the following notes as Baber, *Memoirs* (1826).

3 Baber, *Memoirs* (1826), p. VI.

4 See above pp. 8–11. Baumer, *The History of Central Asia,* vol. 3 (2016), p. 300.

5 Baber, *Memoirs* (1826), pp. 132–50. Khwandamir, *Habibu al-Siyar* (2012), part IV, 308, p. 494.

6 Baber, *Memoirs* (1826), pp. 140, 156–66, 285.

7 Khwandamir, *Habibu al-Siyar*, vol. II (2012), Part IV, 363, p. 521.

8 Baber, *Memoirs* (1826), pp. 199–208. Khwandamir, *Habibu al-Siyar* ,(2012), part IV, 368–72, pp. 523–23.

9 Baber, *Memoirs* (1826), p. 306.

10 Kenneth Chase, *Firearms: A Global History to 1700* (Cambridge: Cambridge University Press, 2003), pp. 131f. Francis Robinson, *The Mughal Emperors and the Islamic Dynasties of India, Iran and Central Asia* (London: Thames & Hudson, 2007), p. 116.

11 Baber, *Memoirs* (1826), p. 287.

12 Baber, *Memoirs* (1826), p. 304.

13 Baber, *Memoirs* (1826), pp. 304–7.

14 Baber, *Memoirs* (1826), p. 368.

15 The French *Compagnie française des Indes orientales* was only founded in 1664 by Finance Minister Colbert. Iradj Amini, *Napoleon and Persia: Franco-Persian Relations under the First Empire* (Richmond: Curzon, 1999), pp. 10, 16.

16 Bamber Gascoigne, *The Great Moghuls* (New Delhi: Time Books International, 1987), pp. 137–39, 154. John F. Richards, *The Mughal Empire* (Cambridge: Cambridge University Press, 2005), p. 199. Robinson, *The Mughal Emperors* (2007), p. 140.

17 Baber, *Memoirs* (1826), p. 341.

18 The Qur'an does not speak explicitly of the four rivers of Paradise, but simply of the fact that in the 'Gardens of Eternity ... rivers flow' (Qur'an Surahs 2:25, 18:31). But many hadiths mention four rivers flowing out of Paradise.

19 Robinson, *The Mughal Emperors* (2007), pp. 117, 152.

20 Richards, *The Mughal Empire* (2005), pp. 9–12. Robinson, *The Mughal Emperors* (2007), pp. 122–24.

21 In the Third Battle of Panipat on 14 January 1761, the Afghan ruler Ahmad Shah Abdali defeated an army of Marathas, who fought on behalf of the weakened Mughal. Alexander Mikaberidze (ed.), *Conflict and Conquest in the Islamic World* (Santa Barbara: ABC-Clio, 2011), vol. 2, pp. 707f.

22 Robinson, *The Mughal Emperors* (2007), p. 132.

23 Richards, *The Mughal Empire* (2005), pp. 19–25, 39.

24 Baumer, *The History of Central Asia,* vol. 2 (2014), pp. 46–58.

25 Baumer, *The History of Central Asia,* vol. 3 (2016), p. 246, fig. 173, 289.

26 Philippa Vaughan, 'Architektur [Indien: Sultanate und Moghuln]', in: Markus Hattstein and Peter Delius (eds), *Islam: Kunst und Architektur* (Cologne: Könemann, 2000), p. 464.

27 Bianca Maria Alfieri, *Islamic Architecture of the Indian Subcontinent* (London: Laurence King, 2000), pp. 205–22.

28 M. Athar Ali, 'The Mughal empire and its successors', in: *History of Civilizations of Central Asia,* vol. V (2003), p. 313. Richards, *The Mughal Empire* (2005), pp. 35, 47f. Francis Robinson, *The Mughal Emperors* (2007), p. 123.

29 An additional, secondary reason for Akbar leaving Fatehpur Sikri was its problematic water supply.

30 See above pp. 15f. Richards, *The Mughal Empire* (2005), pp. 18, 49f, 112, 114th

31 Richards, *The Mughal Empire* (2005), pp. 55f.

32 Richards, *The Mughal Empire* (2005), pp. 94f.

33 Richards, *The Mughal Empire* (2005), p. 102f. Francis Robinson, *The Mughal Emperors* (2007), p. 146. 'Begum' or 'Begam' is a royal and princely title encountered in Central Asia and India and is the feminine form of the title *beg, bey*.

34 Baumer, *The History of Central Asia,* vol. 3 (2016), p. 303.

35 Baber, *Memoirs* (1826), p. 156. Babur himself wrote a Qur'an in the writing he devised and gave this one-of-a-kind work to the Persian Shah Ismail, his ally against the Uzbeks. The small-format Qur'an is now in the calligraphy museum of the Imam Reza shrine in Mashhad, Iran.

36 Father Monserrate, *The Commentary of Father Monserrate, S.J., on his Journey to the Court of Akbar;* transl. J.S. Hoyland (London: Oxford University Press, 1922).

37 It was the eight-volume polyglot Bible, which was printed 1568–72 by Christophe Plantin in Hebrew, Chaldean, Latin, and Greek. O. Okada, 'Painting in Mughal India', in: *History of Civilizations of Central Asia,* vol. V (2003), p. 595.

38 Blair, Bloom, *The Art and Architecture of Islam* (1995), pp. 287–94. Philippa Vaughan, 'Dekorative Künste [Indien: Sultanate und Moghuln]', in: Markus Hattstein and Peter Delius (eds), *Islam: Kunst und Architektur* (Cologne: Könemann, 2000), pp. 484f.

39 Blair, Bloom, *The Art and Architecture of Islam* (1995), p. 295.

40 Richards, *The Mughal Empire* (2005), p. 173.

41 Richards, *The Mughal Empire* (2005), pp. 121f.

42 See above p. 19 and: Lee, *The 'Ancient Supremacy'* (1996), pp. 50–53.

43 Gascoigne, *The Great Moghuls* (1987), p. 203.

44 Richards, *The Mughal Empire* (2005), pp.133–35, 142, 288f.

45 Robinson, *The Mughal Emperors* (2007), p. 152. Philippa Vaughan, 'Architektur [Indien: Sultanate and Moguls]' (2000), p. 480.

46 Bernier, François, *Travels in the Mogul Empire 1656–1668.* A revised and improved edition based upon Irving Brock's translation by Archibald Constable (1891; Reprint New Delhi: Asian Educational Services, 1996), p. 25. The private gem dealer Jean-Baptiste Tavernier (1605–89), who made six trips to India, reported in detail on the power struggle between Shah Jahan's four sons. Tavernier, Jean-Baptiste Tavernier, *Les six voyages de Jean-Baptiste Tavernier, ecuyer baron d'Aubonne, en Turquie, en Perse, et aux Indes : pendant l'espace de quarante ans, & par toutes les routes que l'on peut tenir, accompagnez d'observations particulieres sur la qualité, la religion, le gouvernement, les coûtumes & le commerce de chaque pais; avec les figures, le poids, & la valeur des monnoyes qui y ont cours* (Utrecht: Guillaume van de Water, Guillaume & Jacob Poolsum, 1712), vol. II, pp. 230–64.

47 Gascoigne, *The Great Moghuls* (1987), pp. 206–20.

48 Niccolao Manucci, *Storia do Mogor or Mogul India 1653–1708.* Transl. by William Irvine (London: John Murray, 1907), vol. I, p. 359.

49 Richards, *The Mughal Empire* (2005), pp. 171–78.

50 Gascoigne, *The Great Moghuls* (1987), pp. 230–38.

51 Robinson, *The Mughal Emperors* (2007), pp. 164f.

52 Richards, *The Mughal Empire* (2005), pp. 200f, 239–42.

53 Laurence Lockhart, 'European contacts with Persia, 1350–1736', in: Peter Jackson and Laurence Lockhart (eds), *The Cambridge History of Iran: The Timurid and Safavid Periods,* vol. 6 (Cambridge: Cambridge University Press, 1986), p. 393.

54 Robinson, *The Mughal Emperors* (2007), p. 179.

III. A Reorganisation of Geography: North Central Asia Becomes a Periphery

1 Isabelle Charleux, *Temples et Monastères de Mongolie-Intérieure* (Paris: Institut national d'histoire de l'art, 2006), p. 86.

2 The chronicles of the Chinese Ming dynasty are virtually the only source for the history of early Northern Yuan. Christopher Atwood, *Encyclopedia of Mongolia and the Mongol Empire* (New York: Facts on File, 2004), p. 407.

3 Baumer, *The History of Central Asia*, vol. 3 (2016), pp. 156, 238f. Edward L., Dreyer, 'Military origins of Ming China', in *The Cambridge History of China, Vol. 7: The Ming Dynasty, 1368–1644, Part I*, ed. Denis Twitchett and John K. Fairbank (Cambridge: Cambridge University Press, 1988), pp. 99–103. Hok-Lam Chan, 'The Chien-wen, Yung-lo, Hung-hsi, and Hsüan-te reigns, 1399–1435', in: *The Cambridge History of China*, Vol. 7, Part I (1988), p. 223. John D. Langlois, 'The Hung-wu reign, 1368–1398', in: *The Cambridge History of China*, Vol. 7, Part I (1988), pp. 128–30.

4 Baumer, *The History of Central Asia*, vol. 3 (2016), p. 262.

5 Atwood, *Encyclopedia of Mongolia* (2004), p. 408. Veronika Veit, 'The eastern steppe: Mongol regimes after the Yuan (1368–1636)', in: Nicola Di Cosmo, Allen J. Frank and Peter B. Golden (eds), *The Cambridge History of Inner Asia: The Chinggisid Age* (Cambridge: Cambridge University Press, 2009), pp. 162f.

6 Barfield, *The Perilous Frontier: Nomadic Empires and China, 221 BC to AD 1757* (Cambridge, MA/ Oxford: Blackwell, 1992), pp. 235–37. Hok-Lam Chan, 'The Chien-wen, Yung-lo, Hung-hsi, and Hsüan-te reigns' (1988), pp. 223–29. Perdue, *China Marches West* (2005), pp. 54–57.

7 Barfield, *The Perilous Frontier* (1992), p. 237.

8 Barfield, *The Perilous Frontier* (1992), pp. 238–42. Perdue, *China Marches West* (2005), pp. 58f. Denis Twitchett and Tilemann Grimm, 'The Cheng-t'ung, Ching-t'ai, and T'ien-shun reigns, 1436–1464', in: *The Cambridge History of China*, Vol. 7, Part I (1988), pp. 316–31. D. Pokotilov, *History of the Eastern Mongols during the Ming Dynasty from 1368 to 1634* (Chengtu: West China Union University, 1947), pp. 47–51.

9 Baumer, *The History of Central Asia*, vol. 3 (2016), p. 177.

10 Frederick W. Mote, 'The Ch'eng-hua and Hung-chi reigns, 1465–1505', in: *The Cambridge History of China*, Vol. 7, Part I (1988), pp. 389f, 400–02.

11 Atwood, *Encyclopedia of Mongolia* (2004), p. 408. Louis Hambis, *Documents sur l'histoire des mongols à l'époque des Ming* (Paris: Presses Universitaires de France, 1969), pp. 34, 36.

12 Veit, 'The eastern steppe: Mongol regimes after the Yuan' (2009), p. 165.

13 The termination of Dayan Khan's reign and death have been reported with wide variations: Ishjamts 1504, which is certainly too early, Atwood 1517 Geiss 1524, Barfield 1533 and Veit 1532 or 1543 and the *Erdeni-tob i* 1543. Atwood, *Encyclopedia of Mongolia and the Mongol Empire* (2004), p. 138.

14 Ssanang, *Erdeni-tobči* (1829), pp. 175–81.

15 Barfield, *The Perilous Frontier* (1992), pp. 243f. Veit, 'The eastern steppe: Mongol regimes after the Yuan' (2009), pp. 166f.

16 Barfield, *The Perilous Frontier* (1992), pp. 277f. Charleux, *Temples et monastères de Mongolie-Intérieure* (2006), p. 28. Michael Khodarkovsky, *Where Two Worlds Met. The Russian State and the Kalmyk Nomads, 1600–1771* (Ithaca: Cornell University Press, 1992), pp. 7f. N. Ishjamts, 'The Mongols' (2003), p. 69.

17 Veit, 'The eastern steppe: Mongol regimes after the Yuan (1368–1636)' (2009), pp. 167f.

18 The banner system was an administrative unit, not linked to the tribes themselves, that was both military and civilian in nature.

19 Barfield, *The Perilous Frontier* (1992), pp. 261f, 275f. Bergholz, *The Partition of the Steppe* (1993), pp. 164–74. Gertraude Roth Li, 'State Building before 1644', in: *The Cambridge History of China, Vol. 9. Part One: The Ch'ing Empire to 1800*, ed. Williard J. Peterson (Cambridge: Cambridge University Press, 2002), pp. 41–63. Ssanang, *Erdeni-tobči* (1829), p. 287. Veronika Veit, 'The eastern steppe: Mongol regimes after the Yuan (1368–1636)' (2009), pp. 178–81.

20 Roth Li, 'State Building before 1644' (2002), p. 65.

21 Geiss, 'The Chia-ching reign, 1522–1566' (1988), p. 475.

22 Barfield, *The Perilous Frontier* (1992), pp. 245f. Perdue, *China Marches West* (2005), pp. 65f.

23 Perdue, *China Marches West* (2005), p. 66.

24 Charleux, *Temples et monastères de Mongolie-Intérieure* (2006), p. 26.

25 Baumer, *The History of Central Asia*, vol. 3 (2016), p. 235.

26 Ssanang, *Erdeni-tobči* (1829), p. 225. English translation from: Veit, 'The eastern steppe: Mongol regimes after the Yuan' (2009), p. 170. See also: Charleux, *Temples et monastères de Mongolie-Intérieure* (2006), p. 38. Perdue, *China Marches West* (2005), p. 66.

27 The two predecessors of Sonam Gyatso, as leaders of the Gelugpa, posthumously received the title of Dalai Lama. Gendun Drup (1391–1474), the successor of the order's founder Tsongkhapa (1357–1419), was honoured as the first Dalai Lama.

28 The title 'Dalai Lama' is accordingly described as 'ocean-like, wise Lama'. The title 'Dalai-yin Khan' has been used among the Mongols since the thirteenth century. Martin Brauen (ed.), *Die Dalai Lamas*, exhib. cat. Völkerkundemuseum Zürich (Stuttgart: Arnoldsche, 2005), pp. 58f. Charleux, *Temples et monastères de Mongolie-Intérieure* (2006), p. 43.

29 Ssanang, *Erdeni-tobči* (1829), pp. 235, 237.

30 Baumer, *The History of Central Asia*, vol. 3 (2016), p. 198. Brauen (ed.), *Die Dalai Lamas* (2005), p. 59. Klaus Sagaster, 'Der mongolische Buddhismus' and 'Das Kloster Erdeni Joo (Erdenezuu)' in: Claudius Müller und Jacob Wenzel (eds), *Dschingis Khan und seine Erben. Das Weltreich der Mongolen*, exhib. cat. Kunst und Ausstellungshalle der Bundesrepublik, Bonn (Munich: Hirmer, 2005), pp. 344f, 348.

31 *The Jewel Translucent Sutra, Erdeni Tunumal Sudur. Altan Khan and the Mongols in the Sixteenth Century.* Edited, translated and annotated by Johan Elverskog (ca. 1607; Leiden: Brill, 2003), pp. 36f.

32 Atwood, *Encyclopedia of Mongolia and the Mongol Empire* (2004), pp. 211, 550. Christoph Baumer and Therese Weber, *Eastern Tibet: Bridging Tibet and China* (Bangkok: Orchid Press, 2005), pp. 75, 175. Charleux, *Temples et monastères de Mongolie-Intérieure* (2006), p. 65. Günther Schulemann, *Geschichte der Dalai-Lamas* (Leipzig: VEB Otto Harrassowitz, 1958), pp. 230–35.

33 The institution of a Khutukhtu (Tibetan Tulku), in which a deceased Buddhist master again embodies himself in his next rebirth, was not invented by the Gelugpa. Rather, it was already employed at the beginning of the thirteenth century by the Order of the Kagyu Karmapa. Baumer and Weber, *Eastern Tibet* (2005) p. 83.

34 Bawden, Charles R. *The Modern History of Mongolia* (London: Weidenfeld and Nicolson, 1968), pp. 53–56. Kyzlasov, L.R., 'The peoples of Southern Siberia in the sixteenth to the eighteenth centuries', in: *History of Civilizations of Central Asia*, vol. V (2003), p. 175.

35 Charles R. Bawden, *The Modern History of Mongolia* (London: Weidenfeld and Nicolson, 1968), pp. 52–55. Charleux, *Temples et monastères de Mongolie-Intérieure* (2006), p. 64. Veit, 'The eastern steppe: Mongol regimes after the Yuan (1368–1636)' (2009), p. 172.

36 The ceremony of 1691, which humiliated the Khalkha princes, was described by eyewitness Father Gerbillon. The princes had to prostrate themselves nine times before the emperor. Antoine-François Prévost d'Exiles, *Histoire générale des voyages ou nouvelle collection de toutes les relations de voyages par mer et par terre*, vol. 7 of 25 (Paris: Didot, 1749), p. 557.

37 Charles R. Bawden, *The Modern History of Mongolia* (London: Weidenfeld and Nicolson, 1968), pp. 71–80. Charleux, *Temples et monastères de Mongolie-Intérieure* (2006), pp. 70, 80–82. Nicola Di Cosmo, 'The Qing and Inner Asia: 1636–1800', in: Di Cosmo et al. (eds), The Cambridge History of Inner Asia: The Chinggisid Age (2009), p. 348. Perdue, *China Marches West* (2005), pp.147–50, 175f, 180–89. Outer Mongolia is roughly equivalent to today's Republic of Mongolia and Inner Mongolia is more or less the same as the area covered by the Inner Mongolia Autonomous Region of China. The division took place for the first time in 1634 and was ratified in 1691.

38 Charleux, *Temples et monastères de Mongolie-Intérieure* (2006), p. 74.

39 Du Halde, Jean-Baptiste, *Description Géographique, Historique, Chronologique, Politique, Et Physique De L'Empire De La Chine Et De La Tartarie Chinoise*; vol. 4 (Den Hague: Scheurleer, 1736), pp. 99, 117.

40 Charleux, *Temples et monastères de Mongolie-Intérieure* (2006), p. 86.

41 This First Changkya Khutukhtu was actually the thirteenth incarnation of an existing line of ancestry of the Gelugpa, active in the north of the Tibetan region of Amdo (today's south-western Gansu). Christoph Baumer, *China's Holy Mountain: An Illustrated Journey into the Heart of Buddhism* (London: I.B.Tauris, 2011), p. 221. Charleux, *Temples et monastères de Mongolie-Intérieure* (2006), p. 80.

42 Baumer, *China's Holy Mountain* (2011), pp. 221f. Michael Henss, 'The Bodhisattva-Emperor: Tibeto-Chinese Portraits of Sacred and Secular Rule in the Qing Dynasty', in: *Oriental Art* (Singapore: Oriental Art Magazine, 2001), vol. XLVII, No. 3, pp. 75–77.

43 The Oirat Dzungars, who likewise glorified the Dalai Lama, were destroyed by Emperor Qianlong in 1756–58. See below pp. 87–90.

44 Bawden, *The Modern History of Mongolia* (1968), pp. 58, 112–22.

45 Bawden, *The Modern History of Mongolia* (1968), pp. 58, 132.

46 Charleux, *Temples et monastères de Mongolie-Intérieure* (2006), p. 80. Peter C. Perdue, *China Marches West* (2005), pp. 279, 440.

47 Henss, 'The Bodhisattva-Emperor' (2001), vol. XLVII, No. 3, figs. 1, 6–9, No. 5, fig. 1.

48 Charleux, *Temples et monastères de Mongolie-Intérieure* (2006), p. 84.

49 See below pp. 201–6.

50 See above p. 40.

51 Forsyth, *A History of the Peoples of Siberia* (1992), p. 40. Bruce W. Lincoln, *The Conquest of a Continent* (2007), p. 55.

52 At the beginning of the seventeenth century, the state fur stocks also served as repositories for the ruble. Bergholz, *The Partition of the Steppe* (1993), pp. 74f, 98.

53 Lincoln, *The Conquest of a Continent* (2007), pp. 45, 63. Kappeler, *Russland als Vielvölkerreich* (1992), pp. 38f.

54 Bergholz, *The Partition of the Steppe* (1993), pp. 16, 98. Lincoln, *The Conquest of a Continent* (2007), pp. 46, 84.

55 Bergholz, *The Partition of the Steppe* (1993), pp. 46f. Forsyth, *A History of the Peoples of Siberia* (1992), p. 37.

56 Bergholz, *The Partition of the Steppe* (1993), pp. 33–36, 78, 80–82.

57 Bergholz, *The Partition of the Steppe* (1993), pp. 33f.

58 Bergholz, *The Partition of the Steppe* (1993), pp. 41–43, 84–96.

59 Bergholz, *The Partition of the Steppe* (1993), pp. 90–93.

60 Bergholz, *The Partition of the Steppe* (1993), pp. 102f, 111, 113, 123f. Forsyth, *A History of the Peoples of Siberia* (1992), p. 96. Jonathan Spence, 'The K'ang-hsi Reign', in: *The Cambridge History of China,* Vol. 9. Part One (Press, 2002), p. 151.

61 Bergholz, *The Partition of the Steppe* (1993), pp. 138f. Forsyth, *A History of the Peoples of Siberia* (1992), pp. 104f. Lincoln, *The Conquest of a Continent* (2007), p. 71.

62 See the next sub-chapter. Bergholz, *The Partition of the Steppe* (1993), pp. 225–30. Forsyth, *A History of the Peoples of Siberia* (1992), p. 107. Lincoln, *The*

Conquest of a Continent (2007), p. 193. Prévost d'Exiles, *Histoire générale des voyages* (1749), vol. 7, p. 447. Spence, 'The K'ang-hsi Reign' (2002), p. 153.

63 Bergholz, *The Partition of the Steppe* (1993), p. 214.

64 Bergholz, *The Partition of the Steppe* (1993), p. 238.

65 Prévost d'Exiles, *Histoire générale des voyages* (1749), vol. 7, p. 447. The garrison of Nerchinsk consisted of 600 additional soldiers. Bergholz, *The Partition of the Steppe* (1993), p. 271.

66 Bergholz, *The Partition of the Steppe* (1993), p. 240–42, 261–64. Perdue offers another account of these events and dates the siege of Selenginsk to early 1689. Perdue, *China Marches West* (2005), p. 166.

67 Prévost d'Exiles, *Histoire générale des voyages* (1749), vol. 7, p. 447. See also : Du Halde, Jean-Baptiste, *Description Géographique,* vol. 4 (1736), pp. 240–318.

68 Perdue, *China Marches West* (2005), p. 168. The tolerance edict was undermined in the years 1705–07 by the papal envoy Maillard de Tournon, when he excommunicated Chinese Catholics who had maintained Confucian rites with the consent of the missionary Jesuits in China. Spence, 'The K'ang-hsi Reign' (2002), p. 123, 158.

69 Prévost d'Exiles, *Histoire générale des voyages* (1749), vol. 7, pp. 490–96.

70 Prévost d'Exiles, *Histoire générale des voyages* (1749), vol. 7, pp. 496–500. The treaty was drafted in Latin, Russian, Chinese Manchurian and Mongolian. In the case of a dispute, the Latin version was binding. Bergholz, *The Partition of the Steppe* (1993), p. 275.

71 Russia exported furs and imported cotton, silk, and tea from China. Lincoln, *The Conquest of a Continent* (2007), pp. 145f

72 Perdue, *China Marches West* (2005), pp. 171f.

73 Perdue, *China Marches West* (2005), p. 250.

74 Lincoln, *The Conquest of a Continent* (2007), pp. 190–95.

75 For the Kalmyks see below pp. 96–100.

76 Perdue, *China Marches West* (2005), pp. 94–102. Khodarkovsky, *Where Two Worlds Met* (1992), pp. 74–77.

77 Perdue, *China Marches West* (2005), pp. 105–7.

78 See above fig. 53 and p. 87 and Peter C. Perdue, *China Marches West* (2005), p. 38.

79 Khodarkovsky, *Where Two Worlds Met* (1992), pp. 88f.

80 James Millward, 'Eastern Central Asia (Xinjiang): 1300–1800' in: Di Cosmo et al. (eds), The Cambridge History of Inner Asia: The Chinggisid Age (2009), p. 270. Perdue, *China Marches West* (2005), pp. 107f.

81 Harald Haarmann, *Universalgeschichte der Schrift* (Frankfurt am Main: Campus, 1998), pp. 510–12.

82 Barfield, *The Perilous Frontier* (1992), pp. 279f.

83 Di Cosmo, 'The Qing and Inner Asia: 1636–1800' (2009), p. 346.

84 See above p. 27.

85 See above p. 81.

86 Barfield, *The Perilous Frontier* (1992), pp. 284f. Bergholz, *The Partition of the Steppe* (1993), pp. 279f. Perdue, *China Marches West* (2005), pp. 151–58.

87 Bergholz, *The Partition of the Steppe* (1993), pp. 290–94, 297. Perdue believes that Galdan was poisoned. Perdue, *China Marches West* (2005), pp. 177–203. Prévost d'Exiles, *Histoire générale des voyages* (1749), vol. 7, pp. 596–601.

88 Barfield, *The Perilous Frontier* (1992), p. 287.

89 Forsyth, *A History of the Peoples of Siberia* (1992), pp. 127, 226f.

90 Bergholz, *The Partition of the Steppe* (1993), pp. 292f. Brauen (ed.), *Die Dalai Lamas* (2005), pp. 81f, 93, 96–98. Perdue, *China Marches West* (2005), pp. 152, 178, 192, 228.

91 Perdue, *China Marches West* (2005), p. 228.

92 The deposed Dalai Lama was probably poisoned as a potential threat. A later legend had it that he was able to escape to the holy mountain of Wutai Shan, where he lived incognito. Christoph Baumer, *China's Holy Mountain* (2011), pp. 281f.

93 Bergholz, *The Partition of the Steppe* (1993), pp. 303f. Brauen (ed.), *Die Dalai Lamas* (2005), p. 103.

94 Bergholz, *The Partition of the Steppe* (1993), p. 299. Khodarkovsky, *Where Two Worlds Met* (1992), pp. 133f. In his report, however, Kangxi's envoy Tulishen writes that he had been instructed by the emperor not to accept such an alliance offer on the part of Ayuka. Sir George Thomas Staunton, *Narrative of the Chinese embassy to the khan of the Tourgouth Tartars, in the years 1712, 13, 14 & 15, by the Chinese ambassador [T'u-Li-Shin], and published by the emperor's authority, at Pekin* (London, John Murray, 1821), p. 10.

95 Bergholz, *The Partition of the Steppe* (1993), pp. 298–301. Khodarkovsky, *Where Two Worlds Met* (1992), pp. 154–56. Staunton, *Narrative of the Chinese embassy* (1821), pp. 147–55, 170–76. China in 1731 and 1732 tried again in vain to win Russia respectively the Kalmyks for a joint attack on Dzungaria. Jin Noda, *The Kazakh Khanates between the Russian and Qing Empires* (Leiden: Brill, 2016) pp. 105–15.

96 Staunton, *Narrative of the Chinese embassy* (1821), pp. 184f. See also: Bergholz, *The Partition of the Steppe* (1993), p. 301.

97 Staunton, *Narrative of the Chinese embassy to the khan of the Tourgouth Tartars* (1821), p. 218.

98 Brauen (ed.), *Die Dalai Lamas* (2005), p. 108. Perdue, *China Marches West* (2005), p. 235. Hugh M. Richardson, *Tibet and its History* (Boulder: Shambala, 1984), p. 49. Bergholz cites 1724 for the expulsion of Dzungars, which is too late. Bergholz, *The Partition of the Steppe* (1993), p. 307.

99 Di Cosmo, 'The Qing and Inner Asia: 1636–1800' (2009), p. 350. Richardson, *Tibet and its History* (1984), pp. 50–52.

100 Perdue, *China Marches West* (2005), p. 238.

101 Perdue, *China Marches West* (2005), pp. 247, 311f.

102 Barfield, *The Perilous Frontier* (1992), p. 290. Allen J. Frank, 'The Qazakhs and Russia', in: Di Cosmo et al. (eds), The Cambridge History of Inner Asia: The Chinggisid Age (2009), p. 368.

103 Khodarkovsky, *Where Two Worlds Met* (1992), p. 186 n. 42.

104 Atwood, *Encyclopedia of Mongolia* (2004), p. 194. Perdue, *China Marches West* (2005), pp. 253–55.

105 Perdue, *China Marches West* (2005), pp. 306f.

106 Owen Lattimore, *Pivot of Asia. Sinkiang and the Inner Asia Frontiers of China and Russia.* (Boston: Little, Brown & Co., 1950), p. 126. Perdue, *China Marches West* (2005), pp. 283–88, 297f.

107 Baumer, *The History of Central Asia*, vol. 2 (2014), pp. 8–14.

108 Millward, *Eurasian Crossroads* (2007), p. 97.

109 See below pp. 207ff. Hodong Kim, *Holy War in China. The Muslim Rebellion and State in Chinese Central Asia, 1864–1877* (2004), p. 68. Millward, *Eurasian Crossroads* (2007), pp. 96, 109f. Perdue, *China Marches West* (2005), pp. 289–92.

110 It is ironic that the concept of a Uyghur identity and nation touted by today's Uyghur nationalists and separatists stems from the Chinese warlord Sheng Shicai and was further used by Mao Zedong. Millward, *Eurasian Crossroads* (2007), p. 208. James Millward and Nabijan Tursun, 'Political History and Strategies of Control, 1884–1978', in: Starr, S. Frederick (ed.), *Xinjiang. China's Muslim Borderland* (Armonk: M.E. Sharpe, 2004), pp. 73, 80. J. Todd Reed and Diana Raschke, *The ETIM. China's Islamic Militants and the Global Terrorist Threat* (Santa Barbara: Praeger, 2010), pp. 6f.

111 Millward, *Eurasian Crossroads* (2007), p. 97.

112 Baumer, *The History of Central Asia*, vol. 2 (2014), pp. 272, 284.

113 In the geological sense, a Pamir is a U-shaped valley in high mountains.

114 See above p. 28.

115 Kim, *Holy War in China.* (2004), pp. 20f. Millward, *Eurasian Crossroads* (2007), pp. 96f, 109f. Perdue, *China Marches West* (2005), pp. 289–92.

116 See below p. 158.

117 David Morgan, *The Mongols* (Malden, MA: Blackwell, 2007), p. 179.

118 Barfield, *The Perilous Frontier* (1992), pp. 300–302. Owen Lattimore, *The Mongols of Manchuria* (London: Allen & Unwin, 1934), pp. 75–84.

119 Baumer, *The History of Central Asia*, vol. 2 (2014), pp. 7, 14.

120 Millward, *Eurasian Crossroads* (2007), pp. 97–105. Perdue, *China Marches West* (2005), pp. 337–52.

121 In older Russian literature until about 1920, the Kazakhs are called 'Kyrgyz', 'Kara Kyrgyz' ('Black Kyrgyz') or 'Kyrgyz Kaisak', even though the Russians realised that these 'Kyrgyz' referred to themselves as 'Kazakhs'. Georges de Meyendorff, *Voyage de Orenbourg a Boukhara, fait en 1820, a travers les steppes qui s'étendent a l'est de la mer d'Aral et au-dela de l'ancien Jaxartes; rédigé par et revu par M. le chevalier Amédée Jaubert* (Paris: Librairie Orientale de Dondey-Dupré, père et fils, 1826), p. 53.

122 On the genesis of the Kazakhs, see above p. 7.

123 Karl Baipakov and B.F. Kumekov, 'The Kazakhs', in: *History of Civilizations of Central Asia,* vol. V (2003), pp .90f, 91n. 7.

124 Baipakov and Kumekov, 'The Kazakhs', pp. 93f. Allen, 'The Qazakhs and Russia' (2009), pp. 363f.

125 S.G. Kljaštornyj and T.I. Sultanov, *Staaten und Völker in den Steppen Eurasiens. Altertum und Mittelalter* (Berlin: Schletzer, 2006), pp. 319f. See also: Baipakov and Kumekov, 'The Kazakhs', p. 95. A. Khan Iqtidar, 'Inter-state relations (c 1550–1850), in: *History of Civilizations of Central Asia,* vol. V, eds Chahryar Adle et al. (2003), p. 333. McChesney, 'The Chinggisid restoration in Central Asia: 1500–1785' (2009), pp. 299f.

126 The chronology of the khans here is uncertain. Allen J. Frank provides no information for the period between 1652 and Tavke's takeover. On the other hand, Baipakov dates Jahangir's reign to 1630–80. For the questionable Batyr period,

Geiss cites r. 1652–80. Baipakov and Kumekov, 'The Kazakhs', p. 96. Frank J. Allen, 'The Qazakhs and Russia' (2009), p. 364. Paul Georg Geiss, *Pre-Tsarist and Tsarist Central Asia: Communal Development and Political Order in Change* (London: RoutledgeCurzon, 2013), p. 114.

127 On the difficulty of precisely dating the emergence of the three Zhuz and defining their territorial expansion, see: Martha Brill Olcott, *The Kazakhs* (Washington DC: Hoover Institution Press, 1995), pp. 10–13.

128 See above p. 87. Baipakov and Kumekov, 'The Kazakhs', pp. 92–96. Khodarkovsky *Russia's Steppe Frontier* (2002), p. 150. Paul, *Zentralasien* (2012), p. 283.

129 Bergholz, *The Partition of the Steppe* (1993), p. 361.

130 Olcott, *The Kazakhs* (1995), p. 31.

131 The Kazakhs were only superficially Islamised and had no mosques in the steppe. They practised ancestor worship and maintained many shamanistic beliefs and rituals. Olcott, *The Kazakhs* (1995), p. 19.

132 The dating of the nominal accession of the Older Horde to Russia is variously represented: Bergholz cites 1734, Baipakov 1738, and Paul 1742. Baipakov and Kumekov, 'The Kazakhs', pp. 98f. Bergholz, *The Partition of the Steppe* (1993), pp. 370–73. Paul, *Zentralasien* (2012), pp. 284f. See also: Khodarkovsky *Russia's Steppe Frontier* (2002), pp. 152f, 163, 204.

133 Nikolaus Rytschkow, *Herrn Nikolaus Rytschkow kaiserlicher russischer Capitains Tagebuch über seine Reise durch verschiedne Provinzen des russischen Reichs in den Jahren 1769, 1770 und 1771* (Riga: Johann Friedrich Hartknoch, 1774), pp. 29–30.

134 Bregel, *An Historical Atlas of Central Asia* (2003), p. 59. Forsyth, *A History of the Peoples of Siberia* (1992), p. 118–23. Kappeler, *Russland als Vielvölkerreich* (1992), p. 44. Popowski, *The Rival Powers in Central Asia* (1977), pp. 33, 57.

135 The number Castle specified of 40,000 is certainly too high. John Castle, 'Journal von der Ao 1736 aus Orenburg zu dem Abul Geier Chan der Kirgis-Cavsack Tartarischen Horda aus freyem Willen und bloß zu dem Besten des Russischen Reiches unternommenen höchst nöthigen und zwar gefährlichen doch glücklich vollbrachten Reise', in: *Materialien zu der russischen Geschichte seit dem Tode Kaisers Peters des Großen. Zweiter Theil, 1730–1741* (Riga: Johann Friedrich Hartknoch, 1784), pp. VII, 3–22, 45, 65f.

136 Baipakov and Kumekov, 'The Kazakhs', p. 98. Bergholz, *The Partition of the Steppe* (1993), pp. 372–75.

137 See above p. 36.

138 Baipakov and Kumekov, 'The Kazakhs', pp. 99f. Bregel, *An Historical Atlas of Central Asia* (2003), pp. 60, 62. Allen, 'The Qazakhs and Russia' (2009), p. 373.

139 Allen, 'The Qazakhs and Russia' (2009), pp. 376–78. 'Russia and the peoples of the Volga-Ural region: 1600–1850', in: Di Cosmo et al. (eds), *The Cambridge History of Inner Asia: The Chinggisid Age* (2009), p. 386.

140 Khodarkovsky, *Russia's Steppe Frontier* (2002), p. 39.

141 See below p. 99f.

142 The southern regions of the Senior Horde were under the control of khanate of Kokand from 1809.

143 Allen, 'The Qazakhs and Russia' (2009), pp. 369–72. Khodarkovsky, *Russia's Steppe Frontier* (2002), p. 182f. Paul, *Zentralasien* (2012), p. 365.

144 Kappeler, *Russland als Vielvölkerreich* (1992), p. 159.

145 See below p. 113.

146 See below p. 138. Ravshan Abdullaev et al, 'Colonial Rule and Indigenous Responses, 1860–1917', in: S. Frederick Starr (ed.), *Ferghana Valley. The Heart of Central Asia* (Armonk: M.E. Sharpe, 2011), p. 33. Victor Dubovitskii with Khaydarbek Bababekov, 'The Rise and Fall of the Kokand Khanate', in: Starr (ed.), *Ferghana Valley* (2011), pp. 33, 45. Alexei Nikolajewitsch Kuropatkin, *Geschichte des Feldzuges Skobelews in Turkmenien nebst einer Übersicht der kriegerischen Tätigkeit der russischen Truppen in Zentralasien von 1839–1876* (Mühlheim am Rhein: C.G. Künstler Wwe., 1904), pp. 11–18.

147 In contrast to the older Russian literature, where the ethnonym 'Kalmyks' means all Western Mongolian Oirats, today it is only applied to the Volga Oirats. As the only Western Mongols, they referred to themselves as 'Kalmyks' (Kalimag, Khal'mag). Atwood, *Encyclopedia of Mongolia* (2004), p. 288.

148 See above pp. 83f.

149 Forsyth, *The Caucasus* (2013), p. 148. Khodarkovsky, *Where Two Worlds Met* (1992), pp.74–80. Paul, *Zentralasien* (2012), p. 251f.

150 On the Buddhism of the Kalmyks, which also contained natural religious ideas, see: Benjamin Bergmann, *Nomadische Streifereien unter den Kalmücken in den Jahren 1802 und 1803* (Riga: Hartmann'sche Buchhandlung, 1804–05), vol. 3, pp. 23–184. Bergmann stayed in Kalmykia in 1802/3.

151 Forsyth, *The Caucasus* (2013), pp. 217, 230.

152 Khodarkovsky, *Where Two Worlds Met* (1992), pp. 80–89.

153 Khodarkovsky, *Where Two Worlds Met* (1992), pp. 66f, 90–95.

154 Khodarkovsky, *Where Two Worlds Met* (1992), pp. 95–99.

155 Khodarkovsky, *Where Two Worlds Met* (1992), pp. 100–33.

156 See above p. 86.

157 Voltaire (François Marie d'Arouet), *Histoire de l'empire de Russie sous Pierre le Grand* (No publisher given, 1763), vol. 2, p. 223.

158 John Bell of Antermony, *Travels from St. Petersburg in Russia, to diverse parts of Asia in two volumes* (Glasgow: Printed for the author by Robert and Andrew Foulis printers to the University 1763), vol. 2, pp. 331–33.

159 Khodarkovsky, *Where Two Worlds Met* (1992), pp. 167f, 173, 183.

160 Khodarkovsky, *Where Two Worlds Met* (1992), pp. 174–83, 189.

161 Khodarkovsky, *Where Two Worlds Met* (1992), pp. 193–96.

162 Khodarkovsky, *Russia's Steppe Frontier* (2002), pp. 141, 216.

163 Khodarkovsky, *Where Two Worlds Met* (1992), pp. 212–30.

164 For an early description of the return, see: Benjamin Bergmann, *Nomadische Streifereien unter den Kalmücken* (1804–05), vol. 1, pp. 141–245.

165 Khodarkovsky, *Where Two Worlds Met* (1992), p. 230.

166 Paul Pelliot, *Notes critiques d'histoire Kalmouke* (Paris: Adrien-Maisonneuve, 1960), vol. 1, p. 38.

167 Mikhailov was a native Persian who was first sold as a child to an Armenian stableman and then to a Russian priest. Later, he fought as Kalmyk dragoon and, from 1770, as a Cossack.

168 Benjamin Bergmann, *Schicksale des Persers Wassilij Michailow unter den Kalmüken, Kirgisen und Chiwensern* (Riga: Hartmann'sche Buchhandlung, 1804), 28f.

169 Nikolaus Rytschkow, *Herrn Nikolaus Rytschkow kaiserlicher russischer Capitains Tagebuch* (1774), pp. 323–409.

170 Pelliot, *Notes critiques d'histoire Kalmouke* (1960), vol. 1, p. 38.

171 Khodarkovsky, *Where Two Worlds Met* (1992), pp. 232–35. Perdue, *China Marches West* (2005), pp. 295–98. A group of Volga-Kalmyks who had travelled to Lhasa for pilgrimage had already in 1705 settled in the region of the Etzin Gol (north-western China) when a Dzungar-Chinese war made their return to the Volga impossible. Henning Haslund-Christensen, *Zajagan. Menschen und Götter in der Mongolei* (Stuttgart: Union Deutsche Verlagsgesellschaft, 1936), pp. 107f.

172 Nikolaus Rytschkow, *Herrn Nikolaus Rytschkow kaiserlicher russischer Capitains Tagebuch* (1774), pp. 418f.

173 Justin J. Corfield, *The History of Kalmykia: from ancient times to Kirsan Ilyumzhinov and Aleksey Orlov* (Victoria: Gentext Publications, 2015), pp. 38–45.

174 Corfield, *The History of Kalmykia* (2015), pp. 81f. The Kalmyks were several times obliged to change their script: in 1924 a modified Cyrillic script replaced their traditional vertical Kalmyk script and in 1930 the former was replaced by the Latin alphabet. And in 1938 the Latin script was superseded by the Cyrillic one. Forsyth, *The Caucasus* (2013), p. 451.

175 Corfield, *The History of Kalmykia* (2015), pp. 87–109. Elza-Bair Guchinova, *The Kalmyks* (Abingdon: Routledge, 2006), pp. 25–40.

IV. Afghanistan until 1837 and the Khanates of Central Asia until the Russian Conquest

1 George N. Curzon, *Russia in Central Asia* (1889), p. 162.

2 The rulers of the Manghits in Bukhara wielded both titles, amir and khan, so that Bukhara could be described as both an emirate and a khanate. Yuri Bregel, 'The new Uzbek states' (2009), pp. 306f.

3 The toponym 'Afghanistan', which means 'the country of the Afghans', emerged in the nineteenth century. The ethnonym 'Afghan' is mentioned for the first time in the Hudud al-Alam, compiled in 982. *Hudud al-Alam: The Regions of the World – A Persian Geography 372 A.H.–982 A.D.,* transl. by V. Minorsky, ed. C.E. Bosworth (Cambridge: Cambridge University Press, 1982), § 10, 16a 48,50, pp. 91.

4 The original text reads: 'Afghanistan is, in terms of geography, barely a country at all.' Robert D. Kaplan, *The Revenge of Geography* (New York: Random House, 2013), p. 245.

5 Mountstuart Elphinstone, *Tableau du royaume de Caboul et de ses dépendances, dans la Perse, la Tartarie et l'Inde, offrant les murs, usages et costumes de cet empire* (1815; abbreviated French translation Paris: Nepveu, 1817), vol. 1, pp. 149–54, 159–63; vol. 2, p. 67.

6 Henry Rawlinson, *England and Russia in the East: A Series of Papers on the Political and Geographical Condition of Central Asia* (London: John Murray, 1875), vol. 369.

7 Mountstuart Elphinstone, *An account of the kingdom of Caubul, and its dependencies in Persia, Tartary, and India: comprising a view of the Afghaun nation, and a history of the Doorannee monarchy* (London: Bentley, 1842), vol. 2, pp. 99–101. A. Heathcote, *The Afghan Wars, 1839–1919* (London: Osprey, 1980), p. 10.

8 Mike Martin, *An Intimate War. An Oral History of the Helmand Conflict, 1978–2012* (Oxford: Oxford University Press, 2014), p. 288. Amin Saikal, *Modern Afghanistan. A History of Struggle and Survival* (London: I.B.Tauris, 2012), pp. 4, 13, 24.

9 Willem Vogelsang, *The Afghans* (Chichester: Wiley-Blackwell, 2008), p. 220.

10 Anonymus, *Der Persianische Cromwel oder Leben und Thaten des Miri-Ways, Fürsten von Candahar und Protectoris von Persien* (no publisher, 1723), p. 92. The alleged field report of the anonymous author from Saxony, which inspired G.P. Telemann to compose an opera, contains so many inaccuracies relating to Mir Ways that it was probably compiled from different sources.

11 Louis Dupree, *Afghanistan* (1973; Oxford: Oxford University Press, 1997), pp. 322–24. Roemer, 'The Safavid period' (1986), pp. 314–17. Mir Hussain Shah, 'Afghanistan', in: *History of Civilizations of Central Asia,* vol. V (2003), pp. 280–83. Vogelsang, *The Afghans* (2008), pp. 221–23.

12 On Tsar Peter's campaign, see see above pp. 98f.

13 Guive Mirfendereski, *A Diplomatic History of the Caspian Sea. Treaties, Diaries and Other Stories* (New York: Palgrave, 2001), p. 14.

14 Peter Avery, 'Nadir Shah and the Afsharid Legacy' (1991), pp. 20–30, 38. Axworthy, *The Sword of Persia* (2006), pp. 97–105, 181–86. D. Balland, 'Ashraf Gilzai, the Afghan chief who rules as Shah over part of Iran from 1137/1725 to 1142/1729', in: Encyclopaedia Iranica (2011). H.R. Roemer, 'The Safavid period' (1986), pp. 326–28. Percy Sykes, *A History of Afghanistan* (1940; reprint, New Delhi: Manoharlal, 2002), vol. 1, pp. 325–38. Willem Vogelsang, *The Afghans* (2008), pp. 221–23.

15 Vogelsang, *The Afghans* (2008), pp. 228f.

16 The original saying of General Nicolls reads as follows: 'We only, in truth, are certain of the allegiance of the people within range of our guns and cavalry.' George Pottinger, *The Afghan Connection. The Extraordinary Adventures of Major Eldred Pottinger* (Edinburgh: Scottish Academic Press, 1983), p. 110.

17 Alexander Burnes, *Cabool: Personal narrative of a journey to, and residence in that city, in the years 1836, 7, and 8* (1843, Champaign: Book Jungle, 2016), p. 274.

18 Stephen Tanner, *Afghanistan: A Military History from Alexander the Great to the War against the Taliban* (Cambridge, MA: Da Capo Press, 2002), pp. 119–22. Vogelsang, *The Afghans* (2008), pp. 229–32.

19 Elphinstone, *Tableau du royaume de Caboul* (1817), vol. 1, pp. 165–67.

20 Rear Admiral Nelson's destruction of the French fleet at Aboukir on 1 and 2 August 1798 made a French advance to the east impossible, if such a plan existed. Iradj Amini, *Napoleon and Persia: Franco-Persian Relations under the First Empire* (Richmond: Curzon, 1999), pp. 8, 11–13, 34–36. Mir Hussain Shah, 'Afghanistan' (2003), p. 292. Pottinger, *The Afghan Connection* (1983), pp. 14f.

21 Mohan Lal, *Life of the Amir Dost Mohammed Khan of Kabul: with his political proceedings towards the English, Russian, and Persian Governments, including the victory and disasters of the British army in Afghanistan* (London: Longman, 1846), vol. 1, pp. 21–23, 27–30.

22 John William Kaye, *History of the War in Afghanistan: from the unpublished letters and journals of political and military officers employed in Afghanistan throughout the entire period of British connexion with that country* (London: Richard Bentley, 1851), vol. I, pp. 641f.

23 Elphinstone, *Tableau du royaume de Caboul* (1817), vol. 1, pp. 1–2, 56–93.

24 Edward Ingram, *The Beginning of the Great Game in Asia 1828–1834* (Oxford: Oxford University Press, 1979), p. 75.

25 Malcolm, John, 'Despatch to Lord Elgin, British Ambassador to the Ottoman Porte, 23 March 1801', published as 'An assessment of the possibility of a Russian invasion of India' in: Martin Ewans (ed.), *The Great Game. Britain and Russia in Central Asia,* vol. I: *Documents* (London: Routledge, 2004), pp. 32–37. Martin Ewans, *Securing the Indian Frontier in Central Asia. Confrontation and Negotiation, 1865–95* (London: Routledge, 2010), p. 7.

26 Harford Jones, 'Letter to Sir Hugh Inglis Bart, November 29, 1802', in: Martin Ewans (ed.) *The Great Game,* vol. I (2004), pp. 49–52.

27 For the text of the Treaty of Finkenstein see: Amini, *Napoleon and Persia* (1999), pp. 102f, 205–8. On 10 May 1807, Napoleon instructed General Gardane to obtain a triple alliance between France, Persia and the Ottomans, and to clarify all the logistical questions which would arise from the advance of a 20,000-strong French army. Napoleon Bonaparte, 'Instructions for General Gardane, 10 May 1807', in: *The Great Game. Britain and Russia in Central Asia,* edited by Martin Ewans, *vol. I: Documents* (2004), pp. 53–56.

28 Amini, *Napoleon and Persia* (1999), pp. 103f.

29 Napoleon soon dissociated himself from the plan of a joint attack on India, while Tsar Paul I gave the seemingly delusional order to Cavalry General Vasily Orlov to attack British India on 12 January 1801. Paul's assassination on 23 March 1801 put an end to the preparations. Tsar Paul I, 'Excerpts from Personal Supreme Rescripts by His Imperial Majesty Paul I to the Ataman of the Don Cossack Troops, Cavalry General Vasily Petrovich Orlov, relating to the Expedition to India, St. Petersburg, 1901', in: Martin Ewans (ed.) *The Great Game,* vol. I (2004), pp. 46–48. Amini, *Napoleon and Persia* (1999), p. 44. Henry Sutherland Edwards, *Russian Projects against India. From the Czar Peter to General Skobeleff* (London: Remington, 1885), pp. 32–38.

30 Kaye, *History of the War in Afghanistan* (1851), vol. I, pp. 637–40. Napoleon's difficult war in Spain

from the middle of 1808 made a French military intervention in Asia impossible. Amini, *Napoleon and Persia* (1999), pp. 158f, 170f, 181. Yorke, Edmund, *Playing the Great Game. Britain, War and Politics in Afghanistan since 1839* (London: Robert Hale, 2012), p. 21.

31 Rose Greaves, 'Iranian relations with Great Britain and British India', in: Peter Avery, Gavin Hambly and Charles Melville (eds), *The Cambridge History of Iran: From Nadir Shah to the Islamic Republic*, vol. 7 (Cambridge: Cambridge University Press, 1991), pp. 385, 387. Popowski, *The Rival Powers in Central Asia* (1977), pp. 81–84.

32 The East India Company forced Ranjit Singh's youngest son, Dalip Singh, to hand over the Koh-i-Noor diamond during the annexation of Punjab in 1849.

33 Lal, *Life of the Amir Dost Mohammed Khan* (1846), vol. 1, p. 107.

34 William Dalrymple, *Return of a King. The Battle for Afghanistan, 1839-42* (New York: Alfred A. Knopf, 2013), pp. XVIf. Lal, *Life of the Amir Dost Mohammed Khan* (1846), vol. 1, pp. 108–19, 145, 153.

35 A. Heathcote, *The Afghan Wars* (1980), p. 18. Lal, *Life of the Amir Dost Mohammed Khan* (1846), vol. 1, pp. 165–72, 226–29. Percy Sykes, *A History of Afghanistan* (1940; 2002), vol. 1, pp. 392–98.

36 Lal, *Life of the Amir Dost Mohammed Khan of Kabul* (1846), vol. 1, pp. 248–50. Percy Sykes, *A History of Afghanistan* (1940; 2002), vol. 1, pp. 398.

37 See above p. 24.

38 For a detailed description of the history of Chorasmia at the end of the eighteenth century, see: Shir Muhammad Mirab Munis and Muhammad Riza Mirab Agahi, *Firdaws al-iqbal. History of Khorezm*, translated and annotated by Yuri Bregel (Leiden: Brill, 1999).

39 Nicolaus von Murawjew, *Des Kaiserlichen Russischen Gesandten Nicolaus von Murawjew Reise durch Turkmanien nach Chiwa in den Jahren 1819 und 1820* (Berlin: Reimer, 1824), part 2, pp. 113f.

40 Bregel, 'The new Uzbek states' (2009), pp. 399f.

41 See below p. 141. Bregel, 'The new Uzbek states' (2009), p. 400.

42 Murawjew, *Nicolaus von Murawjew(s) Reise* (1824), part 1, pp. 118–20, 156f, part 2, p. 73f

43 Murawjew, *Nicolaus von Murawjew(s) Reise* (1824), part 2, p. 74.

44 See above p. 24.

45 Blankennagel, 'Bemerkungen über eine in den Jahren 1793 und 1794 ausgeführte Reise nach Chiwa' in: *Archiv für wissenschaftliche Kunde von Russland*, vol. 18, 1859, pp. 351–83 (Berlin: Reimer, 1859), pp. 352–81.

46 G.S. Vinsky, 'Project concerning the consolidation of Russian trade with Upper Asia through Khiva and Bokhara in the year 1818', in: *The Great Game. Britain and Russia in Central Asia*, edited by Martin Ewans, *vol. I: Documents* (London: Routledge, 2004), p. 68.

47 Murawjew, *Nicolaus von Murawjew(s) Reise* (1824), part 1, pp. 78f, part 2, pp. 9–13.

48 Murawjew, *Nicolaus von Murawjew(s) Reise* (1824), part 1, pp. 95, 107, part 2, pp. 131, 145–49.

49 Murawjew, *Nicolaus von Murawjew(s) Reise* (1824), part 2, pp. 107f.

50 Amini, *Napoleon and Persia* (1999), p. 74.

51 Letter from Wellington to Lord Heytesbury, British envoy in Russia, November 4, 1829. Duke of Wellington, *The Eastern Question. Extracted from the Correspondence of the Late Duke of Wellington* (London: John Murray, 1877), p. 44.

52 For a detailed description of the First Anglo-Afghan War see pp. 123–34..

53 See pp. 129f. The Persian siege army had a unit of alleged 'Russian deserters', who were indirectly led by General Count Simonich, the Russian ambassador in Tehran. A very similar course of action was followed during the Russian annexation of the Crimea in the spring of 2014, when soldiers without national emblems occupied strategic places, and the ensuing battles in the Eastern Ukraine with the participation of so-called Russian 'volunteer units'.

54 Hopkirk, *The Great Game* (1994), pp. 128–30.

55 Pottinger, *The Afghan Connection* (1983), pp. 28–44.

56 Alexander Burnes, *Travels into Bokhara; containing the Narrative of a voyage on the Indus from the sea to Lahore, with presents from the King of Great Britain; and an account of a journey from India to Cabool, Tartary and Persia. Performed by order of the Supreme Government of India, in the years of 1831, 32, and 33*; (London, John Murray 1835), vol. II, pp. 229–81.

57 Melvin M. Kessler, Ivan Viktorovich Vitkevich 1806–39: A Tsarist Agent in Central Asia (Washington: Central Asian Collectanea, 1960), pp. 10–14.

58 Alexander Burnes, *Kabul. Schilderung einer Reise nach dieser Stadt und Aufenthaltes dasselbst, in den Jahren 1836, 1837 und 1838* (Leipzig: T.O. Weigel, 1843), pp. 132–36, 246f, 259–62. Heathcote, *The Afghan Wars* (1980), pp. 19f, 26–31, 42. Pottinger, *The Afghan Connection*. (1983), pp. 52–54. Yorke, *Playing the Great Game* (2012), pp. 26–30, 39.

59 Hopkirk, *The Great Game* (1994), p. 191.

60 Edwards, *Russian Projects against India* (1885), pp. 82–147.

61 James, Abbott, *Narrative of a Journey from Heraut to Khiva, Moscow and St. Petersburgh, during the late Russian invasion of Khiva; with some account of the Court of Khiva and the Kingdom of Khaurism* (London: Allen & Co, 1843).

62 Hopkirk, *The Great Game* (1994), pp. 204f, 213–27.

63 Basiner, 'Reise durch die Kirgisensteppe nach Chiwa' (1848), p. 150.

64 Ewans, *Securing the Indian Frontier* (2010), p. 6. Popowski, *The Rival Powers in Central Asia* (1977), pp. 39f.

65 See above p. 95.

66 Bregel, 'The new Uzbek states' (2009), p. 407.

67 Edward Allsworth (ed.), *130 Years of Russian Dominance, a Historical Overview.* (Durham: Duke University Press, 1994), pp. 56f.

68 See above p. 20.

69 Bregel, 'The new Uzbek states' (2009), pp. 395–98. Ewans, *Securing the Indian Frontier* (2010), p. 54. Paul, *Zentralasien* (2012), pp. 380–82.

70 Meyendorff, *Voyage de Orenbourg a Boukhara* (1826).

71 Garry Alder, *Beyond Bokhara. The Life of William Moorcroft. Asian Explorer and Pioneer Veterinary Surgeon, 1767–1825* (London: Century Publishing, 1985), pp. 343–62.

72 Garry Alder, *British India's Northern Frontier 1865–95* (Longmans, Green & Co., 1963), p. 19. *Beyond Bokhara* (1985), p. 350.

73 Bregel, 'The new Uzbek states' (2009), p. 397.

74 Alexander Burnes, *Travels into Bokhara* (London, John Murray 1835), vol. III, pp. 288–92.

75 Arminius Vámbéry, *Voyages d'un faux derviche dans l'Asie Centrale de Téhéran à Khiva, Bokhara et Samarcand par le grand désert Turkoman* (Paris: Hachette, 1865), p. 133.

76 Vámbéry, *Voyages d'un faux derviche* (1865), pp. 173f. Basiner, 'Reise durch die Kirgisensteppe' (1848), p. 131.

77 Colonel Zalesof, 'Diplomatic Relations between Russia and Bokhara, 1836–1843', in: Shoqan Valikanof and M. Veniukof, *The Russians in Central Asia*, transl. John and Robert Michell (1865; Charleston: Nabu Press, 2016).

78 Hopkirk, *The Great Game* (1994), pp. 201, 230–36, 278f. Joseph Wolff, *Narrative of a mission to Bokhara in the years 1843–1845, to ascertain the fate of Colonel Stoddart and Captain Conolly* (New York: Harper & Brothers, 1845), pp. 194–274.

79 Colonel Zalesof, 'Colonel Ignatief's Mission to Khiva and Bokhara in 1858', in: Martin Ewans (ed.), *Great Power Rivalry in Central Asia, 1842–1880, vol. I: Documents* (London: Routledge, 2006), pp. 36–42.

80 John L. Evans, *Mission of N.P. Ignat'ev to Khiva and Bukhara in 1858*, translated and edited by John Evans (Newtonville: Oriental Research Partners, 1984), pp. 92f.

81 Evans, *Mission of N.P. Ignat'ev to Khiva and Bukhara in 1858* (1984), p. 114.

82 Edwards, *Russian Projects against India* (1885), pp. 159–211.

83 Evans, *Mission of N.P. Ignat'ev to Khiva and Bukhara in 1858* (1984), pp. 12f, 125. See also the following translation: Scott C. Levi and Ron Sela, *Islamic Central Asia: An Anthology of Historical Sources* (2010), pp. 295f.

84 See above p. 82. David MacKenzie, *Count N.P. Ignat'ev: The Father of Lies?* (Boulder: East European Monographs, 2002). pp. 167–200.

85 See below p. 140.

86 See above p. 89.

87 H.N. Bababekov, 'Fergana and the Khanate of Kokand', in: *History of Civilizations of Central Asia*, vol. V (2003), pp. 73f. Victor Dubovitskii with Khaydarbek Bababekov, 'The Rise and Fall of the Kokand Khanate', in: Starr (ed.), *Ferghana Valley* (2011), pp. 30–32. Kim, *Holy War in China*. (2004), pp. 19–22.

88 See above p. 25.

89 Kim, *Holy War in China* (2004), pp. 23, 28f.

90 Irdana Bey had already used the title in a letter in 1763, but not within Kokand. Kim, *Holy War in China*. (2004), p. 21.

91 See above p. 95. Dubovitskii with Bababekov, 'The Rise and Fall of the Kokand Khanate' (2011), pp.33, 37f. Paul, *Zentralasien* (2012), p. 378. Popowski, *The Rival Powers in Central Asia* (1977), p. 41.

92 Paul, *Zentralasien* (2012), p. 379.

93 Kim, *Holy War in China*. (2004), pp. 27–32. Millward, *Eurasian Crossroads* (2007), pp. 113f.

94 Hermann Rudolph Alfred Schlagintweit, *Reisen in Indien und Hochasien* (1880; Reprint Saarbrücken: Fines Mundi, 2006), vol. 4, p. 275.

95 See above pp. 95, 115 and below pp. 138ff.

96 Bababekov, 'Fergana and the Khanate of

Kokand' (2003), pp. 75f. Seymour Becker, *Russia's Protectorates in Central Asia. Bukhara and Khiva, 1865–1924* (London: RoutledgeCurzon, 2004), pp. 17f, 26–28. Bregel, 'The new Uzbek states (2009), p. 407f. Dubovitskii with Bababekov, 'The Rise and Fall of the Kokand Khanate' (2011), pp. 34–38. Kim, *Holy War in China* (2004), pp. 30–32. D. Romanovsky, *Notes on the Central Asiatic Question* (Calcutta: Office of Superintendent of Government Printing, 1870), pp. 10–13, Appendices Xi, XX.

97 Romanovsky, *Notes on the Central Asiatic Question* (1870), pp. 15, 23f, 30–34, 51f, 57, Appendices XXX, XXXIV, LII.

98 Becker, *Russia's Protectorates in Central Asia* (2004), pp. 28–35, 89–91. Dubovitskii with Bababekov, 'The Rise and Fall of the Kokand Khanate' (2011), pp. 34–38.

99 Bregel, 'The new Uzbek states' (2009), pp. 409f. Hélène Carrère d'Encausse, *Islam and the Russian Empire. Reform and Revolution in Central Asia* (London, I.B.Tauris, 2009), p. 38. Alexei Nikolajewitsh Kuropatkin, *Geschichte des Feldzuges Skobelews in Turkmenien* (1904), pp. 39f.

100 Ewans, *Securing the Indian Frontier in Central Asia* (2010), p. 111.

101 John Keay, *The Gilgit Game. The Explorers of the Western Himalayas* (London: John Murray, 1979), p. 159. Ewans, *Securing the Indian Frontier* (2010), pp. 111, 113.

102 See below pp. 154–65.

V. The 'Great Game': Central Asia as a Pivot of Russian and British Expansion Policy

1 Curzon, *Russia in Central Asia* (1889), p. 321.

2 Curzon, *Russia in Central Asia* (1889), pp. 322f. General Skobelev had already expressed an identical opinion in a secret memorandum from January 1878 General M.D. Skobelev, 'Memorandum of Adjutant General M.D. Skobelev about a campaign to India', January 1878, in: Martin Ewans (ed.), *Great Power Rivalry in Central Asia, 1842–1880, vol. I: Documents* (London: Routledge, 2006), p. 442.

3 To better elucidate the political context that shaped the history of Central Asia from the late 1830s, the history of South Central Asia will not be presented in this chapter from a regional perspective, but from the point of view of the two main players, Russia and Great Britain.

4 John William Kaye, *Lives of Indian Officers, Illustrative of the History of the Civil and Military Services of India*, 2 vols. (London: A. Strahan and Co & Bell and Daldy, 1867), vol. II, p. 101.

5 Malcolm Yapp, 'The Legend of the Great Game', in: *Proceedings of the British Academy 111. 2000 Lectures and Memoirs* (London: Oxford University Press, 2001), p. 182.

6 Kaye, *History of the War in Afghanistan* (1851), vol. I, pp. 496–541.

7 Evgeny Sergeev, *The Great Game 1856–1907. Russo-British Relations in Central and East Asia* (Washington: Woodrow Wilson Center Press, 2013), p. 7.

8 Sir George Lacy Evans, *On the Designs of Russia* (1828, Reprint Delhi: Facsimile Publisher, 2016), pp. 17f, 23, 78, 154–70. *On the practicability of an invasion of British India and on the commercial, and financial prospects and resources of the Empire* (1829, Reprint Delhi: Facsimile Publisher, 2016), pp. 79–101. Robert Wilson, *A Sketch of the Military and Political Power of Russia in the Year 1817*, published as *The Great Game. Britain and Russia in Central Asia*, edited by Martin Ewans, vol. IV (1817, Reprint London: RoutledgeCurzon, 2004), pp. VII–X, 111, 144–48.

9 Alois Ritter von Haymerle, *Ultima Thule. England und Russland in Central Asien* (Wien: Verlag von Streffleur's Österreichischen, militärischen Zeitschrift, 1885), p. 85.

10 See above p. 44.

11 See above p. 44.

12 Donald Rayfield, *Edge of Empires. A History of Georgia* (London: Reaktion Books, 2012), pp. 250–59, 269.

13 F. Kazemdazeh, 'Iranian relations with Russia and the Soviet Union', in: *The Cambridge History of Iran*, vol. 7 (1991), p. 334.

14 Muriel Atkin, *Russia and Iran, 1780–1828* (Minneapolis: University of Minnesota Press, 1980), pp. 4, 25, 32f.

15 See above p. 112. Greaves, 'Iranian relations with Great Britain and British India' (1991), p. 389.

16 Edward Ingram, *The Beginning of the Great Game in Asia 1828–1834* (1979), p. 49.

17 Wilson, *A Sketch of the Military and Political Power of Russia* (1817, 2004), p. 197.

18 Hopkirk, *The Great Game* (1994), pp. 114f. Ingram, *The Beginning of the Great Game* (1979), pp. 49f.

19 Neil Kent, *Crimea. A History* (London: Hurst, 2016), pp. 71–75. Nick Megoran and Sevara Sharapova (eds), *Central Asia in International Relations. The Legacies of Halford Mackinder* (London: Hurst & Co., 2013), p. 95, n. 16.

20 Martin Ewans, *Securing the Indian Frontier in Central Asia* (Abingdon: Routledge, 2010), p. 65. Charles Thomas Marvin, *Reconnoitring Central Asia. Pioneering adventures in the region lying between Russia and India* (1885; New Delhi: Asian Educational Services, 1996), pp. 252f. Sergeev, *The Great Game* (2013), pp. 172, 178.

21 Haymerle, *Ultima Thule* (1885), pp. 85f.

22 See below p. 158. Ewans, *Securing the Indian Frontier* (2010), pp. 93–100.

23 Sun Tsu, *The Art of War*, transl. Thomas Cleary (Boston: Shambala, 1988), p. 67.

24 Russian text of the Treaty of Turkmenchay: http://www.hist.msu.ru/ER/Etext/FOREIGN/turkman.htm. Ingram, *The Beginning of the Great Game* (1979), p. 42. Kaye, *History of the War in Afghanistan* (1851), vol. I, pp. 145f. F. Kazemdazeh, 'Iranian relations with Russia and the Soviet Union' (1991), p. 338.

25 Kaye, *History of the War in Afghanistan* (1851), vol. I, p. 146.

26 Atkin, *Russia and Iran* (1980), p. 154.

27 Rawlinson, *England and Russia in the East* (1875), p. 297.

28 Ewans, *Securing the Indian Frontier* (2010), p. 9. Hopkirk, *The Great Game* (1994), pp. 118f. Yorke, *Playing the Great Game* (2012), pp. 22f.

29 Sir John Lawrence, 'Dispatch No. 162 of 23 October 1867', published as 'A case against the 'Forward Policy', October 1867' in: Ewans, *Great Power Rivalry* (2006), pp. 225–35.

30 Ewans, *Securing the Indian Frontier* (2010), p. 9.

31 See above p.109.

32 Twenty years before Conolly, Captain Charles Christie had visited Herat disguised as a horse trader. Kamran Ekbal, 'Charles Christie, Captain (d. 1812), of the Bombay Regiment, an Anglo-Indian officer under the command of Sir John Malcolm', in: Encyclopaedia Iranica (1991, 2011). http://www.iranicaonline.org/articles/christie-captain-charles-d. Peter Hopkirk, *The Great Game* (1994), pp. 39, 41–43, 123–32. C.E. Trevelyan and Arthur Conolly, 'Dispatch No. 24 to Lord Bentinck of 15 March 1831', published in: Ewans (ed.), *The Great Game* (2004), pp. 78–83.

33 Alexander Burnes, *Travels into Bokhara* (London, John Murray 1835), vol. I, 14–150, 195, 250. Lord Ellenborough, 'India Board to Lord Bentinck', 12 January 1830, published as 'The Board of Control of the East India Company expresses concern to the Governor General about Russian designs in Central Asia' in: Ewans (ed.), *The Great Game* (2004), pp. 69–74. Lal, *Life of the Amir Dost Mohammed Khan of Kabul* (1846), vol. 2, pp. 40f, 87–100. Lieutenant John Wood, commanding the steamer *Indus*, proved in 1835 that the Indus was indeed navigable for steamships.

34 See above p. 109.

35 Alexander Burnes, *Travels into Bokhara* (London: John Murray 1835), vol. I, p. 159.

36 See below pp. 131ff.

37 Burnes, *Travels into Bokhara* (1835), vol. I, pp. 298f.

38 See above p. 110.

39 Lal, *Life of the Amir Dost Mohammed Khan of Kabul*, 2 vols. (1846).

40 Burnes, *Travels into Bokhara* (1835), vol. II, p. 141.

41 See above p. 116.

42 Burnes, *Travels into Bokhara* (1835), vol. II, pp. 231–34, 248, 277–80.

43 Burnes, *Travels into Bokhara* (1835), vol. III, pp.115–19.

44 Burnes, *Travels into Bokhara* (1835), vol. III, p. 272.

45 Tanner, *Afghanistan* (2002), p. 156.

46 See below p. 133.

47 Hopkirk, *The Great Game* (1994), p. 168.

48 'Secret Committee's Despatch to Lord Auckland, 25 January 1836', published as 'The Secret Committee of the East India Company's Board of Control prompts and authorizes the Governor-General to initiate the First Anglo-Afghan War', in: Ewans, *The Great Game* (2004), pp. 84f.

49 Sykes, *A History of Afghanistan* (1940; 2002), vol. 1, p. 398.

50 Lal, *Life of the Amir Dost Mohammed Khan of Kabul* (1846), vol. 1, pp. 247–52, 260–62, 278, 293.

51 The Russian troops were camouflaged as alleged 'volunteers' and 'deserters'. George Bruce Malleson, *The Russo-Afghan Question and the Invasion of India* (London: George Routledge and Sons, 1885), p. 24.

52 Heathcote, *The Afghan Wars* (1980), pp. 21f. George Pottinger, *The Afghan Connection. The Extraordinary Adventures of Major Eldred Pottinger* (Edinburgh: Scottish Academic Press, 1983), p. 35.

53 Kaye, *History of the War in Afghanistan* (1851), vol. I, pp. 186f. n. Melvin M. Kessler, *Ivan Viktorovich*

Vitkevich 1806–39: A Tsarist Agent in Central Asia (Washington: Central Asian Collectanea, 1960), pp. 10, 12.

54 On the Russian overtures to local authorities of Kandahar, see: Lal, *Life of the Amir Dost Mohammed Khan of Kabul* (1846), vol. 1, pp. 288–92.

55 See above p. 112.

56 Kaye, *History of the War in Afghanistan* (1851), vol. I, pp. 273f.

57 Concerning the siege of Kabul see: Lal, *Life of the Amir Dost Mohammed Khan of Kabul* (1846), vol. 1, pp. 276–85, 387–91. Kaye, *History of the War in Afghanistan* (1851), vol. I, pp. 202–88. Pottinger, *The Afghan Connection* (1983), pp. 30–45.

58 Burnes, *Cabool* (1843, 2016), pp. 141–45.

59 Gordon Whitteridge, *Charles Masson of Afghanistan: Explorer, Archaeologist, Numismatist and Intelligence Agent* (Bangkok: Orchid Press, 2002), p. 148.

60 Heathcote, *The Afghan Wars* (1980), p. 27. Kaye, *History of the War in Afghanistan* (1851), vol. I, pp. 343f.

61 Lal, *Life of the Amir Dost Mohammed Khan of Kabul* (1846), vol. 1, p. 325.

62 Burnes, *Cabool* (1843, 2016), pp. 275. Kaye, *History of the War in Afghanistan* (1851), vol. I, pp. 175–201. Lal, *Life of the Amir Dost Mohammed Khan of Kabul* (1846), vol. 1, pp. 294–334. Sykes, *A History of Afghanistan* (1940; 2002), vol. 1, p. 406.

63 Lal, *Life of the Amir Dost Mohammed Khan of Kabul* (1846), vol. 1, pp. 266f, 290–92, 338–40, 343.

64 Harold N. Ingle, *Nesselrode and the Russian Rapprochement with Britain, 1836–1844* (Berkeley: University of California Press, 1976), p. 78. Kaye, *History of the War in Afghanistan* (1851), vol. I, p. 200, n. Kessler, *Ivan Viktorovich Vitkevich* (1960), pp. 14–16.

65 Lal, *Life of the Amir Dost Mohammed Khan of Kabul* (1846), vol. 1, pp. 371–78.

66 The manifesto put the blame for the outbreak of war exclusively on Dost Muhammad. Kaye, *History of the War in Afghanistan* (1851), vol. I, pp. 355–59.

67 Both quotes from: Kaye, *History of the War in Afghanistan* (1851), vol. I, p. 363, n.

68 Vincent Eyre, *The military operations at Cabul, which ended in the retreat and destruction of the British army, January 1842. With a journal of imprisonment in Afghanistan* (London: James Murray, 1843), p. 115.

69 Yorke, *Playing the Great Game* (2012), p. 110.

70 Heathcote, *The Afghan Wars* (1980), p. 33. Pottinger, *The Afghan Connection* (1983), pp. 60, 63. Tanner, *Afghanistan* (2002), p. 140. Yorke, *Playing the Great Game* (2012), pp. 30, 32f, 35.

71 Kaye, *History of the War in Afghanistan* (1851), vol. I, pp. 404–30.

72 Kaye, *History of the War in Afghanistan* (1851), vol. I, pp. 442–49. Lal, *Life of the Amir Dost Mohammed Khan of Kabul* (1846), vol. 2, pp. 225–27.

73 Kaye, *History of the War in Afghanistan* (1851), vol. I, p. 461. The Afghanistan expert Charles Masson, alias James Lewis, had already insistently warned in 1835 that Shah Shuja was unpopular among Afghans and that Great Britain's forced installation of him would be doomed to failure. Whitteridge, *Charles Masson of Afghanistan* (2002), pp. 154f.

74 Kaye, *History of the War in Afghanistan* (1851), vol. I, pp. 457–72.

75 Eyre, *The military operations at Cabul* (1843),

pp. 32–34. C.W. Woodburn, *The Bala Hissar of Kabul. Revealing a fortress-palace in Afghanistan* (Chatham: Institution of Royal Engineers, 2009), pp. 2, 5, 16. Yorke, *Playing the Great Game* (2012), pp. 68–71.

76 Lal, *Life of the Amir Dost Mohammed Khan of Kabul* (1846), vol. 2, pp. 358f.

77 Yorke, *Playing the Great Game* (2012), pp. 91f.

78 Eyre, *The military operations at Cabul* (1843), pp. 16–18. Heathcote, *The Afghan Wars* (1980), p. 52. Pottinger, *The Afghan Connection* (1983), pp. 123–34.

79 Eyre, *The military operations at Cabul* (1843). Other contemporary sources include: Kaye, *History of the War in Afghanistan* (1851), vol. II. Lal, *Life of the Amir Dost Mohammed Khan of Kabul* (1846), vol. 2. Lady Sale, *A Journal of the Disasters in Afghanistan, 1841–2* (1843; Reprint Uckfield: The Naval and Military Press, 2005). For modern descriptions see: Dalrymple, *Return of a King* (2013). Patrick Macrory, *Signal Catastrophe. The Story of the Disastrous Retreat from Kabul 1842* (London: Hodder and Stoughton, 1966. Jules Stewart, *On Afghanistan's Plains. The Story of Britain's Afghan Wars* (London: I.B.Tauris, 2011).

80 Eyre, *The military operations at Cabul* (1843), pp. 19–23, 39–52.

81 Eyre, *The military operations at Cabul* (1843), pp. 90–92, 119–26.

82 Eyre, *The military operations at Cabul* (1843), pp. 81f. Yorke, *Playing the Great Game* (2012), p. 113.

83 Osman Khan was temporarily in contact with Mohan Lal. Eyre, *The military operations at Cabul* (1843), pp. 96–118. Kaye, *History of the War in Afghanistan* (1851), vol. II. 83–92.

84 Eyre, *The military operations at Cabul* (1843), pp. 155–57. Kaye, *History of the War in Afghanistan* (1851), vol. II., pp. 151–54.

85 Lal, *Life of the Amir Dost Mohammed Khan of Kabul* (1846), vol. 2, p. 427.

86 The dismissal of Elphinstone was discussed in and outside of the Military Council without result. Lady Sale, *A Journal of the Disasters in Afghanistan* (1843; 2005), p. 120.

87 Pottinger, *The Afghan Connection* (1983), p. 154.

88 Only a few women and young children and a couple of officers who were handed over to Akbar on 9 January as hostages survived captivity. Scattered sepoys (Indian soldiers) were also able to escape. A total of about 100 people survived the destruction of the proud Indus army. In early November 1841, it had a troop strength of 6,000 soldiers and more than 12,000 servants. Eyre, *The military operations at Cabul* (1843), pp. 196–215, 417–26. Lal, *Life of the Amir Dost Mohammed Khan of Kabul* (1846), vol. 2, pp. 429f. Pottinger, *The Afghan Connection* (1983), pp. 154–60, 168. Edmund Yorke, *Playing the Great Game* (2012), p. 141.

89 Only Captain Souter, who had wrapped the regimental flag around himself, as well as four of his soldiers were captured alive. Eyre, *The military operations at Cabul* (1843), pp. 230–33. Pottinger, *The Afghan Connection* (1983), p. 168. Yorke, *Playing the Great Game* (2012), p. 158.

90 Eyre, *The military operations at Cabul* (1843), p. 271. Heathcote, *The Afghan Wars* (1980), p. 67. Lal, *Life of the Amir Dost Mohammed Khan of Kabul* (1846), vol. 2, pp. 441–48.

91 Eyre, *The military operations at Cabul* (1843), pp. 255f, 273–75. Lal, *Life of the Amir Dost Mohammed Khan of Kabul* (1846), vol. 2, pp. 431–36. Yorke, *Playing the Great Game* (2012), pp. 183, 193.

92 Yorke, *Playing the Great Game* (2012), p. 72.

93 Lal, *Life of the Amir Dost Mohammed Khan of Kabul* (1846), vol. 2, pp. 303–70.

94 Heathcote, *The Afghan Wars* (1980), pp. 73–85. Lal, *Life of the Amir Dost Mohammed Khan of Kabul* (1846), vol. 2, pp. 270, 489f. Tanner cites 1845 as the year of Akbar's death, Heathcote and Vogelsang 1847; Sykes reports that Akbar was poisoned in 1846, when he set about overthrowing his father. Sykes, *A History of Afghanistan* (1940; 2002), vol. 2, p. 63. Tanner, *Afghanistan* (2002), p. 201. Vogelsang, *The Afghans* (2008), p. 254.

95 Sir T.H. Holdich at a hearing in 1907. In: Christopher M. Wyatt, *Afghanistan and the Defence of Empire. Diplomacy and Strategy during the Great Game* (London: I.B.Tauris, 2011), p. 160.

96 Pottinger, *The Afghan Connection* (1983), p. 54.

97 Ewans, *Securing the Indian Frontier* (2010), p. 55.

98 M.A. Terentief, *Russia and England in Central Asia* (1876, Reprint, Delhi: Facsimile Publisher, 2016), vol. 2, p. 88. See also: Sykes, *A History of Afghanistan* (1940; 2002), vol. 2, pp. 64f. Stephen Tanner, *Afghanistan* (2002), pp. 254f.

99 Lord Montagu of Beaulieu, 'The North-West Frontier of India', in: *Journal of the Royal Central Asia Society*, vol. XI, No. 2, 1924 (London: Royal Central Asian Society, 1924), p. 137.

100 Terentief, *Russia and England in Central Asia* (1876, 2016), vol. 2, pp. 85–88. For the text of the Anglo-Persian agreement, see: Sir Henry Rawlinson, *England and Russia in the East* (1875), Appendix IV, pp. 388–91.

101 Greaves, 'Iranian relations with Great Britain and British India' (1991), pp. 394f. Sykes, *A History of Afghanistan* (1940; 2002), vol. 2, pp. 65f.

102 Edwards, *Russian Projects against India* (1885), pp. 150, 155.

103 See above pp. 95, 115, 122.

104 D. Romanovsky, *Notes on the Central Asiatic Question* (1870), pp. 2, 6–8.

105 D. Romanovsky, *Notes on the Central Asiatic Question* (1870), p. 10.

106 Sergeev, *The Great Game 1856–1907* (2013), pp. 36, 49.

107 See above p. 82.

108 Kuropatkin, *Geschichte des Feldzuges Skobelews* (1904), p. 19.

109 Becker, *Russia's Protectorates in Central Asia* (2004), p. 17. Ewans, *Securing the Indian Frontier* (2010), p. 18.

110 Jennifer Siegel, *Endgame. Britain, Russia and the Final Struggle for Central Asia* (London: I.B.Tauris, 2002), p. 2f. Becker, *Russia's Protectorates in Central Asia* (2004), p. 10.

111 Malleson, *The Russo-Afghan Question* (1885), pp. 38f.

112 G.M. Cherniaev, 'Memorandum of G.M. Cherniaev sent to Field Marshal Prince Bariatinskii in March 1869', in: Ewans, *Great Power Rivalry* (2006), pp. 247–52. Henry Edwards, *Russian Projects against India* (1885), pp. 262–66, 268–71, 271–93. M.D. Skobelev, 'Memorandum of Adjutant General M.D. Skobelev about a campaign to India', January 1878, in: Ewans, *Great Power Rivalry* (2006), pp. 439–48.

113 Romanovsky, *Notes on the Central Asiatic Question* (1870), p. 61. Seymour Becker, *Russia's Protectorates in Central Asia* (2004), pp. 21f.

114 See above p. 122. Popowski, *The Rival Powers in Central Asia* (1977), pp. 45f. Romanovsky, *Notes on the Central Asiatic Question* (1870), pp. 10–13.

115 See above p. 122. Romanovsky, *Notes on the Central Asiatic Question* (1870), pp. 30–34, 51, 57, appendices XLI, XLV.

116 Ewans, *Securing the Indian Frontier* (2010), Appendix I, pp. 146–49.

117 Kuropatkin, *Geschichte des Feldzuges Skobelews* (1904), p. 29.

118 Kuropatkin, *Geschichte des Feldzuges Skobelews* (1904), p. 39.

119 Becker, *Russia's Protectorates in Central Asia* (2004), pp. 42f, 50f, 56, 77–79.

120 Bregel, 'The new Uzbek states' (2009), p. 409.

121 Becker, *Russia's Protectorates in Central Asia* (2004), p. 67.

122 Rawlinson, *England and Russia in the East* (1875), pp. 271–300.

123 Ewans, *Securing the Indian Frontier* (2010), p. 32. Hopkirk, *The Great Game* (1994), pp. 317f.

124 Becker, *Russia's Protectorates in Central Asia* (2004), pp. 58–62. Ewans, *Securing the Indian Frontier* (2010), pp. 33–36. Popowski, *The Rival Powers in Central Asia* (1977), p. 117f.

125 In February 1838, the Scottish officer John Wood (1812–71) identified Lake Zorkul (called Sarikal in Granville's letter) as the source of the Oxus. As he stood at a fork in the river near the village of Qala-i Panja, he correctly realised that the Wakhan River carried more water than the Pamir. He was persuaded, however, by the locals to follow the Pamir to Zorkul. John Wood, *A Journey to the Source of the River Oxus* (London: John Murray, 1872), pp. 217, 232. In 1886, a local surveyor of Colonel Lockhart identified the Wakhjir-Panj River as the longest affluent of the Oxus River, which N. Curzon confirmed in 1894. George N. Curzon, 'The Pamirs and the source of the Oxus', revised and reprinted from *The Geographical Journal*, July–Sept. 1896 (London: The Royal Geographical Society, 1898), pp. 30–32, 77f.

126 Cobbold, *Innermost Asia* (1900), Appendix D, p. 339.

127 Montagu Gilbert Gerard, et al., *Report on the proceedings of the Pamir Boundary Commission 1896* (Calcutta: Office of the Superintendent of Government Printing, India, 1897), pp. 2f. Ewans, *Securing the Indian Frontier* (2010), p. 43.

128 Alder, *British India's Northern Frontier* (1963), pp. 186, 189, 195.

129 Thomas Edward Gordon, *The Roof of the World: being a narrative of a journey over the high plateau of Tibet to the Russian frontier and the Oxus sources on Pamir* (1876; Reprint Taipei: Ch'eng Wen Publishing, 1971), p. 140.

130 Sir Thomas Douglas Forsyth, *Report of a mission to Yarkund in 1873, under command of Sir T.D. Forsyth with historical and geographical information regarding the possessions of the ameer of Yarkund* (Calcutta: Foreign Dept. Press, 1875), pp. 262–86. Gordon, *The Roof of the World* (1876; 1971), pp. 109–67.

131 Thomas Hungerford Holdich, *The Indian Borderland 1880–1900* (London: Methuen, 1901), pp. 122, 158–60.

132 See below pp. 157f.

133 Ewans, *Securing the Indian Frontier* (2010), p. 44.

134 Cobbold, *Innermost Asia* (1900), Appendix D, p. 340.

135 Malleson, *The Russo-Afghan Question* (1885), pp. 32–35, 99f.

136 Ewans, *Securing the Indian Frontier* (2010), p. 40.

137 Sergeev, *The Great Game 1856–1907* (2013), pp. 144f. Kaufmann had concluded his ultimatum of 18 January 1870 with the threat: 'If I do not receive a satisfactory reply, I will [come and] take it.' Becker, *Russia's Protectorates in Central Asia* (2004), p. 68.

138 Edwards, *Russian Projects against India* (1885), p. 214.

139 Kuropatkin, *Geschichte des Feldzuges Skobelews* (1904), pp. 42f, 66–69.

140 Rawlinson, *England and Russia in the East* (1875), p. 379.

141 Edward Allworth (ed.), *130 Years of Russian Dominance, a Historical Overview* (Durham: Duke University Press, 1994), p. 167. The same arguments are still raised by religious interest groups in Africa and Pakistan against vaccination campaigns.

142 Curzon, *Russia in Central Asia* (1889), pp. 393f. Kappeler, *Russland als Vielvölkerreich* (1992), p. 167.

143 Carrère, *Islam and the Russian Empire* (2009), pp. 40, 50–52.

144 See below p. 175.

145 Franz von Schwarz, *Turkestan, die Wiege der indogermanischen Völker* (Freiburg i.B.: Herdersche Verlagshandlung, 1900), pp. 578–85.

146 Carrère, *Islam and the Russian Empire* (2009), pp. 44f, 49, 73.

147 See below p. 295. The industrialisation of Central Asia began in World War II, when Stalin relocated industrial complexes there. In Central Asia, they were out of range of German bombers.

148 Alder, *British India's Northern Frontier* (1963), p. 44.

149 See below p. 125.

150 Kim, *Holy War in China* (2004), pp. 2–7, 18, 32–48. Millward, *Eurasian Crossroads* (2007), pp. 116f.

151 Kim, *Holy War in China* (2004), pp. 71–97.

152 Svetlana Gorshenina, *Asie centrale. L'invention des frontières et l'héritage russo-soviétique* (Paris: CNRS, 2012), p. 100, n. 16.

153 Kim, *Holy War in China* (2004), pp. 140f. Millward, *Eurasian Crossroads* (2007), pp. 120, 122.

154 Robert Rupen, *How Mongolia is Really Ruled. A Political History of the Mongolian People's Republic 1900–1978* (Stanford: Hoover Institution Press, 1979), p. 7.

155 Alder, *British India's Northern Frontier* (1963), pp. 45, 69.

156 Forsyth, *Report of a mission to Yarkund in 1873* (1875), p. 10. Gordon, *The Roof of the World* (1876; 1971), pp. 29, 87. Kim, *Holy War in China* (2004), pp. 151–54.

157 Owen Lattimore, *Pivot of Asia. Sinkiang and the Inner Asia Frontiers of China and Russia* (Boston: Little, Brown & Co., 1950), pp. 32f, 37f.

158 Alder, *British India's Northern Frontier* (1963), pp. 43f. Hopkirk, *The Great Game* (1994), pp. 337f, 347.

159 George J. W. Hayward, 'Journey from Leh to Yarkand and Kashgar, and Exploration of the Sources of the Yarkand River', in: *Journal of the Royal Geographical Society of London*, vol. 40 (London: John Murray, 1870), pp. 33–166. Robert Shaw, *Visits to High Tartary, Yârkand, and Kâshghar (formerly Chinese Tartary), and Return Journey over the Karakoram Pass* (London: John Murray, 1871).

160 Hayward, 'Journey from Leh to Yarkand and Kashgar' (1870), pp. 38, 117f. The Chang-Lang Pass is not to be confused with the Chang-La Pass further west.

161 Forsyth, *Report of a mission to Yarkund in 1873* (1875), pp. 1f.

162 Sir Henry Trotter, 'The Amir Yakoub Khan and Eastern Turkestan in mid-nineteenth century', in: *Asian Affairs*, vol. IV, No. 4, July 1917 (London: Royal Society for Asian Affairs, 1917), p. 103.

163 The four Pundits of the second Forsyth mission were: 'The Pundit' (Nain Singh), 'A.K.' (Kishen Singh), 'G.K.' (Kalian Singh) and 'the Munshi' (Abdul Subhan). Derek Waller, *The Pundits. British Exploration of Tibet and Central Asia* (Lexington: University of Kentucky, 1990), pp. 147–68.

164 Alder, *British India's Northern Frontier* (1963), p. 218.

165 Gerald Morgan, *Ney Elias. Explorer and envoy extraordinary in High-Asia* (London: George Allen & Unwin, 1971), pp. 173, 200, 205.

166 Morgan, *Ney Elias* (1971), p. 173. *Anglo-Russian Rivalry in Central Asia: 1810–1895* (Oxon: Routledge, 1981), p. 200.

167 Forsyth, *Report of a mission to Yarkund in 1873* (1875), pp. 272, 280f. The information regarding the Murghab River came from the Pundits 'the Havildar' and 'the Munshi'. Ney Elias, however, demonstrated in 1885 that the Panj carried much more water than the Murghab. Morgan, *Ney Elias* (1971), pp. 158, 167.

168 Biddulph revised the notion of the easy passability of the Ishkoman Pass, when he explored its southern side in 1877. Alder, *British India's Northern Frontier* (1963), pp. 111, 118. Keay, *The Gilgit Game* (1979), pp. 87f.

169 Alder, *British India's Northern Frontier* (1963), pp. 8, 11. Younghusband, *The heart of a continent* (1896), pp. 297f.

170 Kim, *Holy War in China* (2004), p. 143.

171 Kim, *Holy War in China* (2004), pp. 164–78.

172 Alder, *British India's Northern Frontier* (1963), pp. 72–79. Clairmont Percival Skrine and Pamela Nightingale, *Macartney at Kashgar. New Light on British, Chinese and Russian Activities in Sinkiang, 1890–1918* (1973; Oxford: Oxford University Press, 1987), pp. 23–26.

173 Percy Thomas Etherton, *In the Heart of Asia* (Boston: Houghton Mifflin, 1926), p. 111.

174 Skrine, *Macartney at Kashgar* (1987), p. 25.

175 Millward, *Eurasian Crossroads* (2007), p. 146.

176 Ewans, *Securing the Indian Frontier* (2010), p. 64. Haymerle, *Ultima Thule* (1885), p. 10. Heathcote, *The Afghan Wars* (1980), p. 95.

177 Ewans, *Securing the Indian Frontier* (2010), p. 64.

178 Vogelsang, *The Afghans* (2008), p. 257.

179 Holdich, *The Indian Borderland* (1901), p. 108. Taline Ter Minassian, *Most Secret Agent of Empire. Reginald Teague-Jones Mastery Spy of the Great Game* (London: Hurst, 2014), p. 67.

180 Alder, *British India's Northern Frontier* (1963), pp. 116f. Ewans, *Securing the Indian Frontier* (2010), p. 64–69.

181 Becker, *Russia's Protectorates in Central Asia* (2004), pp. 96f. Sergeev, *The Great Game 1856–1907* (2013), pp. 181f.

182 Sergeev, *The Great Game 1856–1907* (2013), pp. 183–87.

183 The Martini-Henry rifle was replaced in 1888 by the Lee Metford and Lee Enfield rifles. Yorke, *Playing the Great Game* (2012), pp. 236f, 299.

184 *Treaty of Gandamak*, 26 May 1879 http://www.photheca-afghanica.ch/uploads/tx_fmphototheca/Treaty_of_Gandamak.pdf

185 Holdich, *The Indian Borderland* (1901), pp. 47–49.

186 Lord Frederick Sleigh Roberts of Kandahar, *Forty-One Years in India: from subaltern to Commander-in-Chief*; 2 vols. (London: Bentley, 1897), vol. II, p. 177.

187 Heathcote, *The Afghan Wars* (1980), pp. 116f. Yorke, *Playing the Great Game* (2012), pp. 251–53.

188 Kuropatkin, *Geschichte des Feldzuges Skobelews* (1904), pp. 97–100.

189 Yorke, *Playing the Great Game* (2012), p. 259.

190 Niccolo Machiavelli, *Der Fürst, 'Il Prinzipe'* (1513; Stuttgart: Kröner, 1972), pp. 38, 68.

191 They used to stall after only a few shots. Rodney Atwood, *The March to Kandahar. Roberts in Afghanistan* (Barnsley: Pen & Sword, 2008), p. 87.

192 Roberts, *Forty-One Years in India* (1897), vol. II, pp. 181–309. See also: Atwood, *The March to Kandahar* (2008), pp. 112–15. Heathcote, *The Afghan Wars* (1980), pp. 117–46. Yorke, *Playing the Great Game* (2012), pp. 258–80.

193 Wyatt, *Afghanistan and the Defence of Empire* (2011), pp. 269f.

194 Hopkirk, *The Great Game* (1994), p. 396.

195 Roberts (1897), *Forty-One Years in India*, vol. II, pp. 310–70. See also: Atwood, *The March to Kandahar* (2008), pp. 132–57. Heathcote, *The Afghan Wars* (1980), pp. 147–65. Yorke, *Playing the Great Game* (2012), pp. 280–318.

196 Tanner, *Afghanistan* (2002), p. 213.

197 Kuropatkin, *Geschichte des Feldzuges Skobelews* (1904), pp. 138–190, 194.

198 Sergeev, *The Great Game 1856–1907* (2013), pp. 198f.

199 Marvin, *Reconnoitring Central Asia* (1885; 1996), p. 179.

200 Marvin, *Reconnoitring Central Asia* (1885; 1996), pp. 179, 213–16, 385–400.

201 Marvin, *Reconnoitring Central Asia* (1885; 1996), p. 400.

202 Holdich, *The Indian Borderland* (1901), p. 113.

203 Alikhanov was a major, who was demoted to a soldier because of a duel and then had risen again to lieutenant. Hopkirk, *The Great Game* (1994), p. 411.

204 Before Alikhanov, the Irish journalist Edmond O'Donovan had scouted Merv in 1880/81. First arrested as a Russian spy, he was then elected to the ruling triumvirate. The leaders of Merv, who had heard of the British conquest of Kandahar, believed that the British forces would soon advance to Herat and Merv and drive out the Russians. They ascribed Skobelev's decision to not march on Merv after taking Geok Tepe to the presence of O'Donovan. When the journalist learned that Kandahar would soon be evacuated again, he quickly sneaked off. Edmond O'Donovan, *The Merv Oasis: Travels and adventures East of the Caspian during the years 1879 – 80 – 81 including five months' residence among the Tekkés of Merv* (London: Smith, Elder & Co. 1882), vol. II, pp. 270–88, 353–437.

205 Charles Thomas Marvin, *The Russians at the Gate of Herat* (New York: Charles Scribner's Sons, 1885), pp. 17–45.

206 Ewans, *Securing the Indian Frontier* (2010), p. 84.

207 Marvin, *The Russians at the Gate of Herat* (1885), p. 51.

208 Marvin, *The Russians at the Gate of Herat* (1885), p. 48.

209 See below pp. 157f.

210 Ewans, *Securing the Indian Frontier* (2010), pp. 87f.

211 Marvin, *The Russians at the Gate of Herat* (1885), p. 172.

212 Henry Lansdell, *Chinese Central Asia. A Ride to Little Tibet* (London: Sampson Low et al, 1893), vol. I, p. 83.

213 Alder, *British India's Northern Frontier* (1963), p. 294. Becker, *Russia's Protectorates in Central Asia* (2004), pp. 125–28. Cobbold, *Innermost Asia* (1900), p. 275. Ewans, *Securing the Indian Frontier* (2010), pp. 79, 81.

214 Curzon, *Russia in Central Asia* (1889), p. 356.

215 Ewans, *Securing the Indian Frontier* (2010), p. 84.

216 Lord Montagu of Beaulieu, 'The North-West Frontier of India' (1924), p. 142.

217 Greaves, 'Iranian relations with Great Britain and British India' (1991), p. 409. For the same reason, in 1873, Britain had rejected the plan from Ferdinand de Lesseps, architect of the Suez Canal, to construct a railway from Orenburg and Tashkent to Peshawar. Becker, *Russia's Protectorates in Central Asia* (2004), p. 126.

218 Greaves, 'Iranian relations with Great Britain and British India' (1991), p. 417.

219 Ewans, *Securing the Indian Frontier* (2010), p. 82.

220 Marvin, *The Russians at the Gate of Herat* (1885), p. 50. Hermann Roskoschny, *Afghanistan und seine Nachbarländer. Der Schauplatz des letzten russisch-englischen Konflikts in Zentral-Asien* (Leipzig: Gressner & Schramm, 1885), vol. II, map facing page 336.

221 Holdich, *The Indian Borderland* (1901), pp. 97, 110. Marvin, *The Russians at the Gate of Herat* (1885), pp. 55, 73, 119. Malleson, *The Russo-Afghan Question* (1885), pp. 114f.

222 Holdich, *The Indian Borderland* (1901), pp. 97, 110, 121.

223 Arthur Campbell Yate, *England and Russia Face to Face. Travels with the Afghan Boundary Commission* (Edinburgh: William Blackwood, 1887), p. 322.

224 Yate, *England and Russia Face to Face* (1887), p. 328. Much to the annoyance of the British officers who were present, they were forbidden from assisting their Afghan brothers in arms. Holdich, *The Indian Borderland* (1901), pp. 128, 136.

225 Haymerle, *Ultima Thule* (1885), p. 30. Holdich, *The Indian Borderland* (1901), pp. 126–31.

226 Ewans, *Securing the Indian Frontier* (2010), pp. 96, 100.

227 Bijan Omrani, 'The Durand Line: History and Problems of the Afghan-Pakistan Border' (London: *Asian Affairs*, vol. XL, No. II, July 2009), p. 177.

228 The Zulfikar Pass resembles a canyon more than a mountain pass.

229 Ewans, *Securing the Indian Frontier* (2010), pp. 99, 104.

230 The British naval military strategy demanded that the navy be superior to the two next largest fleets combined. Popowski, *The Rival Powers in Central Asia* (1977), pp. 149–51.

231 In Herat, Holdich had the Musalla, the large mosque and madrasah complex, torn down to get a clear shot at any attacking Russians. Baumer, *The History of Central Asia*, vol. 3 (2016), p. 296, fig. 214. Holdich, *The Indian Borderland* (1901), pp. 142f, 149–63. Yate, *England and Russia Face to Face* (1887), pp. 424–46.

232 Alder, *British India's Northern Frontier* (1963), p. 221.

233 See above p. 89.

234 See above p. 157f.

235 Alder, *British India's Northern Frontier* (1963), p. 160. Ewans, *Securing the Indian Frontier* (2010), p. 120.

236 Sir Francis Younghusband, *The heart of a continent: a narrative of travels in Manchuria, across the Gobi desert, through the Himalayas, the Pamirs, and Chitral, 1884–1894* (London: John Murray, 1896), pp. 185–87, 235–38.

237 Ewans, *Securing the Indian Frontier* (2010), p. 121.

238 Alder, *British India's Northern Frontier* (1963), p. 211.

239 Skrine, *Macartney at Kashgar* (1987), pp. 5, 9, 14, 34.

240 Ralph P. Cobbold, *Innermost Asia. Travel & Sport in the Pamirs* (London: William Heinemann, 1900), p. 67.

241 Cobbold, *Innermost Asia* (1900), p. 32f. The eleven Pamirs are as follows: in China, Kara Köl, Sarikol, Taghdumdash and Mariang; in Tajikistan, Khargush, Rang Köl, Sariz, Alichur, Kalan and Khurd and further west Shewa. Markus Hauser, 'The Pamir Archive: A world of information', in: *Pamirs at the Crossroads*, edited by Andrei Dörre, Hermann Kreutzmann and Stefan Schütte (Berlin: Freie Universität Berlin, 2016), p. 88. The toponym 'Pamir' may stem from the Sanskrit *Upa-Meru*, 'below Mt Meru', or from the Persian *Paya Mihr*, 'throne of Mithra'. Mursajew, *Auf unbetretenen Pfaden* (1956), pp. 252–54.

242 Lord Dunmore saw the stele in the autumn of 1892 in a museum in Tashkent., 7th Earl of Dunmore (Charles Adolphus Murray), *The Pamirs. A narrative of a year's expedition on horseback and on foot through Kashmir, Western Tibet, Chinese Tartary and Russian Central Asie* (London: John Murray, 1893), vol. II, p. 167, note.

243 Garry, *British India's Northern Frontier* (1963), pp. 225f. Hopkirk, *The Great Game* (1994), pp. 466f. Skrine, *Macartney at Kashgar* (1987), pp. 33f.

244 Colonel T.H. Holdich, a senior member of the British Pamir Boundary Commission in 1895, greatly relativised this danger, however: 'There is, indeed, no reasonable probability that any practical method of connecting Russia with India across the Hindu Kush will ever be discovered.' Holdich, *The Indian Borderland 1880–1900* (1901), p. 173.

245 Younghusband, *The heart of a continent* (1896), p. 290.

246 Alder, *British India's Northern Frontier* (1963), pp. 225f. Ewans, *Securing the Indian Frontier* (2010), pp. 122f. Keay, *The Gilgit Game* (1979), pp. 210–12. Skrine, *Macartney at Kashgar* (1987), pp. 33–35. Younghusband, *The heart of a continent* (1896), pp. 288–95.

247 Roberts of Kandahar, *Forty-One Years in India* (1897), vol. II, p. 446.

248 Ewans, *Securing the Indian Frontier* (2010), p. 123.

249 Durand, Algernon, *The Making of a Frontier* (1899, Reprint Karachi: Indus Publications, 1977); pp. 245–65. The English journalist and author Edward F. Knight was eyewitness of the British conquest of Hunza and Nagar. E.F. Knight *Where Three Empires Meet. A narrative of recent travel in*

Kashmir, western Tibet, Gilgit, and the adjoining countries (London: Longmans, Green, 1896); pp. 357–466, 517.

250 Ewans, *Securing the Indian Frontier* (2010), p. 130. Skrine, *Macartney at Kashgar* (1987), pp. 42–45.

251 G.J. Younghusband and Sir Francis Younghusband, *The Relief of Chitral* (1895; Reprint Rawalpindi: English Book House, 1976).

252 Alder, *British India's Northern Frontier* (1963), pp. 234, 238, 250.

253 George N. Curzon, 'The Pamirs and the source of the Oxus', revised and reprinted from *The Geographical Journal*, July–Sept. 1896 (London: The Royal Geographical Society, 1898), p. 46,

254 Alder, *British India's Northern Frontier* (1963), p. 252.

255 Ralph p. Cobbold, *Innermost Asia. Travel & Sport in the Pamirs* (London: William Heinemann, 1930), p. 260.

256 Robert Middleton and Huw Thomas, *Tajikistan and the High Pamirs* (Hong Kong: Odyssey, 2008), p. 430.

257 In a letter of 29 August 1893, the then commander-in-chief in India, Lieutenant General George White, expressed the fear to the Duke of Cambridge, the former commander of the British forces, that Abdur Rahman could put himself under Russian protection: 'It is of great importance to impress the Afghans with the advantage of an English alliance against Russia over the plan of the Amir making direct terms with Russia or perhaps throwing in his lot with her. The Provinces – Roshan, Shighnan & Wakhan – referred to are at the other side of the Hindu Kush and would therefore form an impossible local theatre of War for us.' Private collection.

258 Alder, *British India's Northern Frontier* (1963), p. 330; see also pp. 264–68, 274f.

259 For the entire agreement see: Alder, *British India's Northern Frontier* (1963), pp. 330–33.

260 Ter Minassian, *Most Secret Agent of Empire* (2014), pp. 38f.

261 Andrew M. Roe, *Waging War in Waziristan* (Lawrence: University Press of Kansas, 2010), pp. 84–87.

262 Alder, *British India's Northern Frontier* (1963), Appendix VII, pp. 334f.

263 Skrine, *Macartney at Kashgar* (1987), pp. 124–26, 169f, 238.

264 Ewans, *Securing the Indian Frontier* (2010), p. 140. Middleton and Thomas, *Tajikistan and the High Pamirs* (2008), p. 609.

265 Gerard, Holdich, Wahab and Alcock, *Report on the proceedings of the Pamir Boundary Commission 1896* (1897). See also: Holdich, *The Indian Borderland 1880–1900* (1901), pp. 284–313.

266 Gerard, Holdich, Wahab and Alcock, *Report on the proceedings of the Pamir Boundary Commission 1896* (1897), p. 25.

267 Alder, *British India's Northern Frontier* (1963), p. 285.

268 Tanner, *Afghanistan* (2002), p. 218. Vogelsang, *The Afghans* (2008), p. 268. For a description of Kafiristan prior to its Islamisation see: George Scott Robertson, *The Kafirs of the Hindu-Kush* (London: Lawrence & Bullen, 1896), and for Nuristan prior to the Soviet invasion: Lennart Edelberg and Schuyler Jones, *Nuristan* (Graz: Akademische Druck- und Verlagsanstalt, 1979).

269 Career-hungry officers or consuls occasionally hoped to find a pretext to occupy the province.

270 Skrine, *Macartney at Kashgar* (1987), p. 74.

271 Skrine, *Macartney at Kashgar* (1987), p. 121.

272 Skrine, *Macartney at Kashgar* (1987), pp. 197, 206f, 220f, 232nd.

273 For the text of the treaties of 1886, 1890 and 1893: Hugh M. Richardson, *Tibet & and its History* (Boulder: Shambhala, 1984), pp. 264–68. See also: Alastair Lamb, *Britain and Chinese Central Asia. The Road to Lhasa 1767–1905* (London: Routledge and Kegan Paul, 1960), pp. 174–238. Siegel, *Endgame* (2002), p. 12.

274 Peter Fleming, *Bayonets to Lhasa* (1961; Oxford: Oxford University Press, 1985), pp. 39–48. Lamb, *Britain and Chinese Central Asia* (1960), pp. 241–88.

275 Arash Bormanshinov, 'A Secret Kalmyk Mission to Tibet in 1904', in: *Central Asiatic Journal*, vol. 36, No. 3-4 (Wiesbaden: Harrassowitz, 1992), pp. 174f. Sergeev, *The Great Game* (2013), pp. 252–63. John Snelling, *Buddhism in Russia. The Story of Agvan Dorzhiev, Lhasa's Emissary to the Tsar* (Shaftesbury: Element, 1993), pp. 50–89.

276 Siegel, *Endgame* (2002), p. 14.

277 Great Britain put a halt to the German railway construction to Basra when it concluded an initial protection agreement with the sheikdom of Kuwait in 1899, which was expanded into a protectorate in 1903. Stewart, *The Kaiser's Mission to Kabul* (2014), p. 12.

278 For the text of the two agreements: Siegel, *Endgame* (2002), appendices 4–5, pp. 273–77.

279 On the Triple Entente, see Siegel, *Endgame* (2002), pp. 46, 51.

280 Charles Allen, *Duel in the Snows. The true story of the Younghusband Mission to Lhasa* (London: John Murray, 2004), p. 65, see also pp. 1–3, 19f, 29–33, 196, 287.

281 Allen, *Duel in the Snows* (2004), pp. 104–28. Fleming, *Bayonets to Lhasa* (1985), pp. 72–152. Lamb, *Britain and Chinese Central Asia* (1960), pp. 282–95. Snelling, *Buddhism in Russia* (1993), pp. 108–10. Younghusband, Francis, *India and Tibet* (London: John Murray, 1910), pp. 173–79.

282 Highly interesting are the eyewitness accounts of the invasion of 1903–4: Perceval Landon, *Lhasa. An account of the country and people of Central Tibet and of the progress of the mission sent there by the English government in the years 1903–04*, 2 vols. (London: Hurst and Blackett, 1905). Sir Frederick O'Connor, *On the frontier and beyond. A record of thirty years' service* (London: John Murray, 1931). William John Ottley, *With mounted infantry in Tibet* (London: Smith, Elder & Co., 1906). L. Austine Waddell, *Lhasa and its mysteries. With a record of the expedition of 1903-1904* (London: Methuen, 1906). Sir Francis Younghusband, *India and Tibet. History of the relations which have subsisted between the two countries from the time of Warren Hastings to 1910; with a particular account of the mission to Lhasa of 1904* (London: John Murray, 1910).

283 Fleming, *Bayonets to Lhasa* (1985), pp. 251–55, 268. Lamb, *Britain and Chinese Central Asia* (1960), pp. 302f. Richardson, *Tibet & and its History* (1984), pp. 264–68.

284 Allen, *Duel in the Snows* (2004), pp. 279, 303. Fleming, *Bayonets to Lhasa* (1985), pp. 267–75.

Lamb, *Britain and Chinese Central Asia* (1960), pp. 303–11. Younghusband was indeed appointed Political Agent in Kashmir after his return, but he was not consulted on major issues. He returned to England in 1909, but when the 51-year-old volunteered for military service in 1914, he was dismissed as unsuitable. He was considered a loose cannon. Patrick French, *Younghusband. The last great Imperial adventurer* (London: HarperCollins, 1994), pp. 263f, 270, 290f.

285 French, *Younghusband* (1994), p. 257 Sergeev, *The Great Game* (2013), p. 274. Snelling, *Buddhism in Russia* (1993), p. 126.

286 Balfour, 22 December 1903. Sergeev, *The Great Game* (2013), p. 296.

287 Russia-related dates are given according to the Gregorian calendar.

288 Hopkirk, *The Great Game* (1994), pp. 508f, 513–17. Sergeev, *The Great Game* (2013), pp. 295–301. Wyatt, *Afghanistan and the Defence of Empire* (2011), pp. 140–42.

289 Wyatt, *Afghanistan and the Defence of Empire* (2011), p. 178.dc

290 For the Agreement with respect to Persia and Afghanistan: Stewart, *The Kaiser's Mission to Kabul* (2014), pp. 201–3; regarding Tibet: Richardson, *Tibet & and its History* (1984), pp. 273–75.

291 Sir Percy Sykes, 'Afghanistan: The present position', *Royal Central Asian Journal*, vol. XXVII, No. 2, April 1940 (London: Royal Central Asian Society, 1940), p. 146.

292 Richardson, *Tibet & and its History* (1984), p. 273.

293 Stewart, *The Kaiser's Mission to Kabul* (2014), pp. 202f.

294 Since petroleum has twice the thermic potential as coal, oil was sprayed on the coal.

295 Stewart, *The Kaiser's Mission to Kabul* (2014), pp. 201f.

296 Antony Wynn, *Persia in the Great Game. Sir Percy Sykes, Explorer, Consul, Soldier, Spy* (London: John Murray, 2003), p. 162.

297 Sergeev, *The Great Game* (2013), pp. 237f. Siegel, *Endgame* (2002), pp. 137–39, 186f.

298 Erik J. Dahl, 'Naval Innovation. From Coal to Oil' (JFQ, Winter 2000–01), pp. 50–56. Nikki Keddie and Mehrdad Amanat, 'Iran under the later Qajars', in: *The Cambridge History of Iran*, vol. 7 (1991), p. 208. Siegel, *Endgame* (2002), pp. 178–84. Wynn, *Persia in the Great Game* (2003), p. 149.

299 The Constantinople Agreement, https://en.wikipedia.org/wiki/Constantinople_Agreement Ter Minassian, *Most Secret Agent of Empire* (2014), pp. 50f. Wynn, *Persia in the Great Game* (2003), p. 249.

VI. The Drive for Sovereignty – Central Asia between the World Wars

1 Tomsen, *The Wars of Afghanistan* (2013), p. 110.

2 Becker, *Russia's Protectorates in Central Asia* (2004), pp. 109, 129, 199–203.

3 The Arabic word '*jadid*' means 'new'.

4 The mastermind of the Jadidists, Ismail Gaspraly (1851–1914), strived for a cultural alliance of all Turkic-speaking peoples. Forsyth, *The Caucasus* (2013), p. 315.

5 Becker, *Russia's Protectorates in Central Asia* (2004), pp. 198–208. Carrère, *Islam and the Russian Empire* (2009), pp. 71–88.

6 Allworth (ed.), *130 Years of Russian Dominance* (1994), pp. 196f. Carrère, *Islam and the Russian Empire* (2009), pp. 89f.

7 Becker, *Russia's Protectorates in Central Asia* (2004), p. 208.

8 Becker, *Russia's Protectorates in Central Asia* (2004), pp. 228–34.

9 Allworth (ed.), *130 Years of Russian Dominance* (1994), pp. 208–13. Carrère, *Islam and the Russian Empire* (2009), pp. 119–21. Paul, *Zentralasien* (2012), pp. 389–91. Starr, *Ferghana Valley* (2011), p. 76.

10 According to the Julian calendar, the revolution began on 23 February. It deviated from the Gregorian calendar – which the Bolsheviks introduced on 14 February 1918 – by 13 days in the early twentieth century. The revolution brought the tsarist regime to an end. Tsar Nicholas was forced to abdicate on 15 March 1917 and was shot dead on 17 July 1918. In the present study, the data is reproduced according to the Gregorian calendar.

11 Carrère, *Islam and the Russian Empire* (2009), pp. 122f.

12 Forsyth, *A History of the Peoples of Siberia* (1992), p. 234.

13 Becker, *Russia's Protectorates in Central Asia* (2004), pp. 253–57. Carrère, *Islam and the Russian Empire* (2009), pp. 124–47.

14 R.Y. Radjapova, 'Establishment of Soviet power in Central Asia (1917–24)', in: *History of Civilizations of Central Asia*, vol. VI (2005), pp. 154–58.

15 Unlike Lenin's Bolsheviks, the Mensheviks wanted to give the broad masses a limited say in the socio-political development.

16 Carrère, *Islam and the Russian Empire* (2009), pp. 148–51.

17 Charles Howard Ellis, *The Transcaspian Episode 1918–1919* (London: Hutchinson, 1963), p. 163. Forsyth, *A History of the Peoples of Siberia* (1992), p. 241.

18 The heterogeneous units that fought in the Russian Civil War of 1918–22 against the Bolsheviks were called 'White Armies'.

19 Leonid Mitrokhin, *Failure of Three Missions* (Moscow: Progress Publishers, 1987), p. 75.

20 The Red Guards were forerunners of the Red Army; in Turkestan they consisted of former tsarist soldiers, Austrian and German prisoners of war and Armenian units of the Dashnaks, who were members of the 'Armenian Revolutionary Federation' *Dashnaktsutyun*.

21 See below p. 178. Starr, *Ferghana Valley* (2011), pp. 98f.

22 Michael Sargent, 'British Military Involvement in Transcaspia (1918–1919)', in: Conflict Studies Research Centre, Caucasus Series (Shrivenham: Defence Academy, 2004/2), p. 2.

23 Arthur Swinson, *Beyond the Frontiers. The Biography of Colonel F.M. Bailey, Explorer and Secret Agent* (London: Hutchinson, 1971), p. 175.

24 Becker, *Russia's Protectorates in Central Asia* (2004), pp. 234f, 283f, 262–69. Carrère, *Islam and the Russian Empire* (2009), pp. 148–58. Radjapova, 'Establishment of Soviet power' (2005), pp. 162–65.

25 Carrère, *Islam and the Russian Empire* (2009), p. 159. Radjapova, 'Establishment of Soviet power' (2005), p. 166.

26 The Czechoslovak volunteer units fought until the October Revolution on the side of the Allies. In May 1918, they revolted due to catastrophic conditions and controlled the Trans-Siberian Railway from Penza (west of the Volga) to Vladivostok. Richard H. Ullmann, *Intervention and the War. Anglo-Soviet Relations, 1917–1921* (Princeton: Princeton University Press, 1961), p. 212.

27 Transcaspia was a tsarist and early Soviet administrative unit east of the Caspian Sea. It corresponded roughly to present-day Turkmenistan and south-west Kazakhstan.

28 See below pp. 184f. Ullmann, *Intervention and the War* (1961), p. 315.

29 Mitrokhin, *Failure of Three Missions* (1987), p. 75.

30 Forsyth, *A History of the Peoples of Siberia* (1992), pp. 234–38. Ullmann, *Intervention and the War* (1961), pp. 191–229, 332.

31 Frederick Marshman Bailey, 'In Russian Turkestan under the Bolsheviks', in: *Journal of the Royal Central Asia Society*, vol. VIII, No. 1, 1921 (London: Royal Central Asian Society, 1921), p. 60.

32 Allworth (ed.), *130 Years of Russian Dominance* (1994), pp. 231f, 236–39. Forsyth, *A History of the Peoples of Siberia* (1992), pp. 234–37. Dilip Hiro, *Inside Central Asia. A political and cultural history of Uzbekistan, Turkmenistan, Kazakhstan, Kyrgyzstan, Tajikistan, Turkey, and Iran* (New York: Overlook Duckworth, 2009), p. 40. K. Nurpeis, 'Kazakhstan', in: *History of Civilizations of Central Asia*, vol. VI (2005), pp. 255f. Radjapova, 'Establishment of Soviet power' (2005), p. 168.

33 See below pp. 184f.

34 Ellis, *The Transcaspian Episode* (1963), pp. 141–43.

35 Frederick Marshman Bailey, *Mission to Tashkent* (London: Jonathan Cape, 1946), pp. 237–39. L.V.S. Blacker, *On Secret Patrol in High Asia* (London: John Murray, 1922), pp. 158–61.

36 For photos of the bombed city of Bukhara, see: Rudolf A. Mark, *Krieg an fernen Fronten* (Paderborn: Ferdinand Schöningh, 2013), figs. 20–24.

37 Allworth (ed.), *130 Years of Russian Dominance* (1994), pp. 245f. Becker, *Russia's Protectorates in Central Asia* (2004), pp. 289–95. Carrère, *Islam and the Russian Empire* (2009), pp. 159–77.

38 The term 'Basmachi', used by the soviets, was an insult meaning 'bandits'. Radjapova, 'Establishment of Soviet power' (2005), p. 174.

39 Becker, *Russia's Protectorates in Central Asia* (2004), pp. 289–95. Carrère, *Islam and the Russian Empire* (2009), pp. 303–5.

40 Carrère, *Islam and the Russian Empire* (2009), p. 183.

41 Hiro, *Inside Central Asia* (2009), p. 46.

42 Rafis Abazov, *The Palgrave Concise Historical Atlas of Central Asia* (New York: Palgrave, 2008), maps 37–38. Radjapova, 'Establishment of Soviet power' (2005), pp. 180f. A few cities were renamed, e.g. Pishpek to Frunze, Khujand to Leninabad, Dushanbe to Stalinabad, etc.

43 Lena Jonson, *Tajikistan in the New Central Asia. Geopolitics, Great Power Rivalry and Radical Islam* (London: I.B.Tauris, 2009), pp. 109f

44 Shireen Hunter, *Islam in Russia* (2015), p. 329.

45 The Brusilov Offensive (4 June to 20 September 1916) foreshadowed the Russian collapse, as it proved to be a Pyrrhic victory. The losses of the Russian army amounted to a total of 1 million dead, wounded or captured soldiers, which devastated the troops' morale and triggered mass desertions. Ullmann, *Intervention and the War* (1961), p. 4.

46 The German Hentig–Niedermayer mission (1915–16) will be discussed in the following excursus.

47 The German military attaché in Persia Georg Graf von Kanitz-Podangen and Oskar Niedermayer had already been working on a plan since 1915 to free these prisoners of war and to use them in Persia against the British and the Russians. Mark, *Krieg an fernen Fronten* (2013), pp. 105–9.

48 For the missions of Sykes, Dunsterville and Malleson, see the official report: Frederick James Moberly (ed.), *Operation in Persia, 1914–1919. Compiled by arrangement with the Government of India, under the direction of the Historical Section of the Committee of Imperial Defence by Brig.Gen. F.J. Moberly* (1929; Reprint London: Imperial War Museum, 1987). Also the reports of the main protagonists: Lionel C. Dunsterville, *The Adventures of Dunsterforce* (London: Arnold, 1920). 'Military mission to North-West Persia, 1918', in: *Journal of the Royal Central Asia Society*, vol. VIII, No. 2, 1921 (London: Royal Central Asian Society, 1921), pp. 79–98. Ellis, *The Transcaspian Episode* (1963). Sir Wilfrid Malleson, 'The British military mission to Turkistan, 1918–20', in: *Journal of the Royal Central Asia Society*, vol. IX, No. 2, 1922 (London: Royal Central Asian Society, 1922), pp. 95–110. Sir Percy Sykes, *A History of Persia*, vol. 2 (London: Macmillan, 1930), pp. 451–517.

49 Thomas L. Hughes, 'The German Mission to Afghanistan, 1915–16', in: *German Studies Review*, XXV/3, Oct, 2002 (German Studies Association, 2002), pp. 460f. Ter Minassian, *Most Secret Agent of Empire* (2014), p. 54.

50 Wynn, *Persia in the Great Game* (2003), p.262.

51 Moberly, *Operation in Persia* (1987), pp. 181f, 200–11.

52 Hendrik Gröttrup, *Wilhelm Wassmuss. Der deutsche Lawrence* (Berlin: Metropol, 2013), pp. 248–60. Ter Minassian, *Most Secret Agent of Empire* (2014), pp. 55–62. Wynn, *Persia in the Great Game* (2003), pp. 259–317.

53 Bailey, *Mission to Tashkent* (1946), pp. 26, 40–44. Sir George Macartney, 'Bolshevism as I saw it at Tashkent in 1918', in: *Journal of the Royal Central Asia Society*, vol. VII, Nos. 2–3, 1920 (London: Royal Central Asian Society, 1920), p. 49.

54 The fact that Bailey was ignorant of the British military involvement in Transcaspia was due to the lack of coordination by British India.

55 Blacker, *On Secret Patrol* (1922), pp. 24–26, 139, 223f. Gerald Uloth, *Riding to War* (Stockbridge: Monks, 1993), p 138. Since Austria-Hungary was a multi-ethnic state, these soldiers were recruited from a dozen nationalities.

56 Teague-Jones dates the battle of Kaakha to 28 August 1918, Ellis 26 August. Bailey, *Mission to Tashkent* (1946), pp. 38–40. Ellis, *The Transcaspian Episode* (1963), pp. 31, 52. Swinson, *Beyond the Frontiers* (1971), pp. 13–48. Reginald, Teague-Jones, *The Spy Who Disappeared. Diary of a Secret Mission to Russian Central Asia in 1918* (London: Victor Gollancz, 1990) pp. 107–10. See below p. 185..

57 See below p. 185.

58 Bailey, *Mission to Tashkent* (1946), pp. 71, 82–286. Swinson, *Beyond the Frontiers* (1971), pp. 156–96.

59 Lionel C. Dunsterville, *The Adventures of Dunsterforce* (1920).

60 At the beginning of the twentieth century, the oil fields of Baku met almost half the global demand. Megoran, *Central Asia in International Relations* (2013), p. 104.

61 James Forsyth, *The Caucasus. A History* (Cambridge: Cambridge University Press, 2013), pp. 367–73.

62 Charles Howard Ellis, 'The Transcaspian episode', *Royal Central Asian Journal*, vol. XLVI, No. 2, April 1959 (London: Royal Central Asian Society, 1959), p. 107. Donald Rayfield, *Edge of Empires. A History of Georgia* (London: Reaktion Books, 2012), pp. 328–30.

63 Ellis, *The Transcaspian Episode* (1963), pp. 17f. Ullmann, *Intervention and the War* (1961), p. 303–6.

64 Teague-Jones, *The Spy Who Disappeared* (1990) p. 82.

65 Dunsterville, *The Adventures of Dunsterforce* (1920), pp. 140f.

66 Ellis, *The Transcaspian Episode* (1963), pp. 35, 37. Teague-Jones, *The Spy Who Disappeared* (1990), pp. 52, 62f, 82.

67 Moberly, *Operation in Persia* (1987), p. 348.

68 Alfred Rawlinson, *Adventures in the Near East, 1918–1922* (London: Andrew Melrose, 1923).

69 Ellis, *The Transcaspian Episode* (1963), p. 22. Moberly, *Operation in Persia* (1987), p. 333. Teague-Jones, *The Spy Who Disappeared* (1990), pp. 60f. Ullmann, *Intervention and the War* (1961), pp. 307f.

70 Teague-Jones, *The Spy Who Disappeared* (1990), pp. 62–69.

71 On the strategic importance of cotton, see also: Blacker, *On Secret Patrol* (1922), pp. 6, 20f.

72 Dunsterville, *The Adventures of Dunsterforce* (1920), p. 207. Ullmann, *Intervention and the War* (1961), pp. 309f.

73 Since Stalin and Trotsky launched a political campaign against Teague-Jones in March 1919 and blamed him for the shooting of the Bolshevik commissars, he assumed a new identity and called himself Ronald Sinclair. Sinclair continued to work for British intelligence, and his true identity was only discovered and made public after his death in 1988. Ellis, *The Transcaspian Episode* (1963), pp. 59–62. Peter Hopkirk, *On Secret Service East of Constantinople. The Plot to Bring Down the British Empire* (Oxford: Oxford University Press, 1994), pp. 358–65, 388–99. Ter Minassian, *Most Secret Agent of Empire* (2014), pp. 5, 10, 105–39, 174. Teague-Jones, *The Spy Who Disappeared* (1990), pp. 12, 119–22, 211–16.

74 Dunsterville, *The Adventures of Dunsterforce* (1920), 230f, 235–37, 241–70, 274f, 279f.

75 Hopkirk, *On Secret Service* (1994), pp. 283f, 332–57. Moberly, *Operation in Persia* (1987), pp. 344f, 364f. Teague-Jones, *The Spy Who Disappeared* (1990), pp. 10f. Ter Minassian, *Most Secret Agent of Empire* (2014), pp. 113–15. Ullmann, *Intervention and the War* (1961), p. 310.

76 Malleson, 'The British military mission to Turkistan, 1918–20' (1922), p. 98f. Sykes, *A History of Persia*, vol. 2 (1930), pp. 497f.

77 Afterwards the British occupied Batumi at the Black Sea on 23 December and Tbilisi on 25 December 1918. Mitrokhin, *Failure of Three Missions* (1987), pp. 49, 51.

78 Ellis, *The Transcaspian Episode* (1963), pp. 86f, 121. Moberly, *Operation in Persia* (1987), pp. 420–24. The last British troops left Baku on 19 August 1919.

79 Malleson, 'The British military mission to Turkistan, 1918–20' (1922), p. 99.

80 Moberly, *Operation in Persia* (1987), p. 391.

81 Ellis, *The Transcaspian Episode* (1963), pp. 26f, 30, 52f, 66–80. Sargent, 'British Military Involvement in Transcaspia' (2004/2), pp. 9–15, 19–22. Moberly, *Operation in Persia* (1987), p. 359–62. Teague-Jones, *The Spy Who Disappeared* (1990), pp. 100–11, 157, 189, 196–98. Ter Minassian, *Most Secret Agent of Empire* (2014), pp. 78–88. Ullmann, *Intervention and the War* (1961), pp. 311–20.

82 Blacker, *On Secret Patrol* (1922), pp. 142f. Uloth, *Riding to War* (1993), pp. 139f.

83 Bailey, *Mission to Tashkent* (1946), p. 52. Ter Minassian, *Most Secret Agent of Empire* (2014), pp. 85–87. According to Uloth, the Mensheviks had three armoured trains. Uloth, *Riding to War* (1993), p. 137.

84 Moberly, *Operation in Persia* (1987), pp. 447–51.

85 Ellis, 'The Transcaspian episode', *Royal Central Asian Journal*, vol. XLVI, No. 2, April 1959 (1959), pp. 106–18. *The Transcaspian Episode* (1963), pp. 144–54. Mitrokhin, *Failure of Three Missions* (1987), p. 100. Sargent, 'British Military Involvement in Transcaspia' (2004/2), pp. 26–33. Teague-Jones, *The Spy Who Disappeared* (1990), pp. 201f. Ullmann, *Intervention and the War* (1961), pp. 320–28. J.K. Tod, 'The Malleson Mission to Transcaspia in 1918', *Royal Central Asian Journal*, vol. XXVII, No. 1, January 1940 (London: Royal Central Asian Society, 1940), pp. 45–67.

86 Veit Veltzke, *Unter Wüstensöhnen. Die deutsche Expedition Klein im Ersten Weltkrieg* (Berlin: Nicolai, 2014).

87 Stewart, *The Kaiser's Mission* (2014), p. 77.

88 Hans-Ulrich Seidt, *Berlin, Kabul, Moskau. Oskar Ritter von Niedermayer und Deutschlands Geopolitik* (München: Universitas, 2002), pp. 44–48.

89 The expedition was born from the merger of two different missions: the first military mission was organised by the German General Staff; their original leader was Wassmuss and then Niedermayer. The second mission was the diplomatic mission of von Hentig, which was adopted at the beginning of spring 1915 and stood under the auspices of Emperor Wilhelm II and the Foreign Office. Stewart, *The Emperor's Mission* (2014), pp. 37, 58.

90 Otto Werner von Hentig, *Von Kabul nach Shanghai: Bericht über die Afghanistan-Mission 1915/16 und die Rückkehr über das Dach der Welt und durch die Wüsten Chinas* (Lengwil: Libelle, 2009), p. 10.

91 Mark, *Krieg an fernen Fronten* (2013), pp. 99–101. Oskar von Niedermayer, *Unter der Glutsonne Irans. Kriegserlebnisse der deutschen Expedition nach Persien und Afganistan* (Hamburg: Uhlenhorst, 1925), p. 33.

92 A short time later, Listermann, the German consul in Bushehr, failed to destroy his consular code book before his arrest. Even earlier, on 26 August 1914, the Russians found the radio code of the German navy in the wreck of the SMS *Magdeburg*.

93 A slightly different account of the events is given by C.J. Edmonds, Acting Vice-Consul in Bushehr at that time. Edmonds had arrested Listermann on 9 March 1915 and found in the German consulate two cypher code books. He believes that Wassmuss had managed to get his code book to Listermann and that his book was one of the two cypher dictionaries he, Edmonds, had found. C. J. Edmonds, 'The Persian prelude to the Zimmermann telegram', *Royal Central Asian Journal*, vol. XLVII, No. 1, January 1960 (London: Royal Central Asian Society, 1960), pp. 63–66.

94 Gröttrup, *Wilhelm Wassmuss* (2013), pp. 136–38. Ter Minassian, *Most Secret Agent of Empire* (2014), p. 59.

95 Stewart, *The Kaiser's Mission* (2014), p. 49.

96 For the routes taken by German agents in Persia in 1915–16 see: Moberly, *Operation in Persia* (1987), map 5.

97 Otto Werner von Hentig, *Mein Leben: eine Dienstreise* (Göttingen: Vandenhoeck & Ruprecht, 1962), p. 164. Niedermayer, *Unter der Glutsonne Irans* (1925), p. 95.

98 Niedermayer, *Unter der Glutsonne Irans* (1925), p. 95.

99 Otto Werner von Hentig, *Meine Diplomatenfahrt ins verschlossene Land* (Berlin: Ullstein, 1918), pp. 70–86. Niedermayer, *Unter der Glutsonne Irans* (1925), pp. 95–121. Stewart, *The Kaiser's Mission* (2014), p. 67.

100 Stewart, *The Kaiser's Mission* (2014), p. 68.

101 Hughes, 'The German Mission to Afghanistan' (2002), p. 465. Siegel, *Endgame* (2002), p. 60. Stewart, *The Kaiser's Mission* (2014), p. 70.

102 Niedermayer, *Unter der Glutsonne Irans* (1925), pp. 147–57. Stewart, *The Emperor's Mission* (2014), pp. 71f, 77–81, 89f.

103 Stewart, *The Kaiser's Mission* (2014), p. 68.

104 Emil Rybitschka, *Im gottgegebenen Afghanistan als Gäste des Emirs* (Leipzig: Brockhaus, 1927), pp. 49–53, 56.

105 Hentig, *Mein Leben* (1962), pp. 152f. Niedermayer, *Unter der Glutsonne Irans* (1925), p. 165.

106 Stewart, *The Kaiser's Mission* (2014), pp. 95f. See also: Rybitschka, *Im gottgegebenen Afghanistan* (1927), pp. 54f.

107 This is an approximate indication, which varies depending on the calculation formula; see: http://inflation.stephenmorley.org/ ; http://www.thisismoney.co.uk/money/bills/article-1633409/Historic-inflation-calculator-value-money-changed-1900.html

108 Seidt, *Berlin, Kabul, Moskau* (2002), pp. 179–83, 329–99.

109 Hentig, *Meine Diplomatenfahrt* (1918), pp. 110–245. Hentig, *Mein Leben* (1962), pp. 163–443.

110 Hiro, *Inside Central Asia* (2009), pp. 49f. Paul, *Zentralasien* (2012), pp. 405–7.

111 Allworth (ed.), *130 Years of Russian Dominance* (1994), pp. 81, 257. Hiro, *Inside Central Asia* (2009), pp. 55f. Paul, *Zentralasien* (2012), pp. 467–69. Rupen, *How Mongolia is Really Ruled* (1979), p. 52.

112 Fisher, *The Crimean Tatars* (1978), pp. 144f.

113 Allworth (ed.), *130 Years of Russian Dominance* (1994), pp. 260, 282, 300–302. Hiro, *Inside Central Asia* (2009), pp. 55f. Paul, *Zentralasien* (2012), pp. 409–12.

114 Rupen, *How Mongolia is Really Ruled* (1979), p. 51.

115 Seidt, *Berlin, Kabul, Moskau* (2002), pp. 264, 281.

116 Alimova and Golovanov, 'The evolution of nation-states: Uzbekistan', in: *History of Civilizations of Central*

Asia, vol. VI (2005), pp. 226–32. Hiro, *Inside Central Asia* (2009), pp. 57f. Nurpeis, 'Kazakhstan' (2005), p. 257 Tabyshalieva, Anara, 'Kyrgyzstan', in *History of Civilizations of Central Asia,* vol. VI (2005), p. 279.

117 Hiro, *Inside Central Asia* (2009), p. 59.

118 Philip Boobbyer, *The Stalin Era* (London: Routledge, 2000), p. 130. Forsyth, *The Caucasus* (2013), pp. 534–39. Nurpeis, 'Kazakhstan' (2005), p. 257. http://www.hawaii.edu/powerkills/USSR.TAB1B.GIF

119 Allworth (ed.), *130 Years of Russian Dominance* (1994), pp. 304–6. Hiro, *Inside Central Asia* (2009), p. 234.

120 Hiro, *Inside Central Asia* (2009), p. 237 (Hiro cites a total of 753 nuclear explosions). Paul, *Zentralasien* (2012), p. 481. See also: 'Bulletin of the Atomic Scientists', 28 Sept. 2009, http://thebulletin.org/lasting-toll-semipalatinsks-nuclear-testing. The bulletin estimated 18,000 km^2 to be contaminated; Hiro, by contrast, gave a figure of 300,000 km^2, which seems greatly exaggerated.

121 Renè Létolle and Monique Mainguet, *Der Aralsee. Eine ökologische Katastrophe* (Berlin: Springer, 1996). Paul, *Zentralasien* (2012), pp. 428f, 478f. Hiro, *Inside Central Asia* (2009), p. 192. http://www.nzz.ch/niedergang-und-hoffnung-in-der-wueste-aralkum-1.18103484, dated June 22, 2013.

122 Amin Saikal, *Modern Afghanistan. A History of Struggle and Survival* (London: I.B.Tauris, 2012), pp. 44–48. Vogelsang, *The Afghans* (2008), pp. 270f.

123 See above p. 151.

124 Sykes, 'Afghanistan: The present position' (1940), p. 169.

125 Wyatt, *Afghanistan and the Defence of Empire* (2011), pp. 114–39, 272.

126 Heathcote, *The Afghan Wars* (1980), pp. 169f. Rybitschka, *Im gottgegebenen Afghanistan* (1927), pp. 129–32, 286. Saikal, *Modern Afghanistan* (2012), pp. 57f.

127 Michael Volodarsky, 'First Steps in Soviet Diplomacy toward Afghanistan', in: Yaacov Ro'i (ed.), *The USSR and the Muslim World* (London: Routledge, 2015), p. 218.

128 Heathcote, *The Afghan Wars* (1980), pp. 171–98.

129 Saikal, *Modern Afghanistan* (2012), pp. 63–65. Tanner, *Afghanistan* (2002), p. 219.

130 Nevertheless, Sir Francis Humphreys had already founded the British Legation in Kabul in March 1922. Sykes, 'Afghanistan: The present position', (1940), p. 154.

131 Saikal, *Modern Afghanistan* (2012), p. 69.

132 Saikal, *Modern Afghanistan* (2012), p. 74.

133 Françoise Olivier-Utard, *Politique et archáéologie. Histoire de la Délégation archéologique française en Afghanistan 1922–1982* (Paris: Éditions Recherche sur les Civilisations, 2003), pp. 17–24.

134 Jules Barthoux, *The Hadda Excavations,* vols. I & III, (1930, 1933; Reprint Bangkok: SDI Publications, 2001), I, pp. 2, 12.

135 Saikal, *Modern Afghanistan* (2012), pp. 75f. Vogelsang, *The Afghans* (2008), pp. 278–80.

136 To quash the rebellion of 1924, Amanullah received two British Indian and five Soviet war planes. Christopher M. Wyatt, 'Change and discontinuity: war and Afghanistan, 1904–1924', in: *Asian Affairs,* vol. XLVII, No. III, November 2016 (London: Royal Society for Asian Affairs, 2016), pp. 380f.

137 Vogelsang, *The Afghans* (2008), p. 281.

138 Saikal, *Modern Afghanistan* (2012), pp.88–94. Vogelsang, *The Afghans* (2008), p. 281f.

139 Saikal, *Modern Afghanistan* (2012), pp. 95–106. Vogelsang, *The Afghans* (2008), pp. 284–86.

140 Sykes, 'Afghanistan: The present position', (1940), p. 161.

141 Hiro, *Inside Central Asia* (2009), p. 363. Seidt, *Berlin, Kabul, Moskau* (2002), pp. 318f.

142 Saikal, *Modern Afghanistan* (2012), pp.114–23.

143 Peter Tomsen, *The Wars of Afghanistan. Messianic terrorism, tribal conflicts, and the failures of the Great Powers* (New York: Public Affairs, 2013), p. 89.

144 The Central Treaty Organization included Great Britain, Iraq (until 1958), Iran, Pakistan, Turkey and de facto the United States.

145 Tomsen, *The Wars of Afghanistan* (2013), p. 91.

146 Tomsen, *The Wars of Afghanistan* (2013), p. 92f.

147 Saikal, *Modern Afghanistan* (2012), pp. 130f. Tomsen, *The Wars of Afghanistan* (2013), pp. 94–95.

148 David B. Edwards, *Before Taliban. Genealogies of the Afghan Jihad* (Berkeley: University of California Press, 2002), pp. 46f.

149 The Muslim Brotherhood is a Sunni, politically and religiously conservative revolutionary organisation with roots in the Middle East and Egypt.

150 Amin Saikal, *Modern Afghanistan* (2012), pp. 167f. Tomsen, *The Wars of Afghanistan* (2013), p. 10f.

151 Vyacheslav Belokrenitsky, 'Islamic Radicalism in Central Asia: The Influence of Pakistan in Afghanistan', in: Boris Rumer (ed.), *Central Asia: At the End of the Transition* (Armonk: M.E. Sharpe, 2005), pp. 159, 166.

152 Hekmatyar did not participate in the fighting and remained in Peshawar. His critics believe that he deliberately let the other conservative leaders rush into a disaster to consolidate his own power over the Afghan exiles living in Pakistan. Edwards, *Before Taliban* (2002), p. 236.

153 Hassan Abbas, *The Taliban Revival. Violence and Extremism on the Pakistan-Afghanistan Frontier* (New Haven: Yale University Press, 2014), p. 47. Edwards, *Before Taliban* (2002), p. 76. Saikal, *Modern Afghanistan* (2012), pp. 176f. Tomsen, *The Wars of Afghanistan* (2013), pp. 107–9.

154 Tomsen, *The Wars of Afghanistan* (2013), p. 110.

155 See above p. 75.

156 Charles R. Bawden, *The Modern History of Mongolia* (London: Weidenfeld and Nicolson, 1968), pp. 80–88.

157 Bawden, *The Modern History of Mongolia* (1968), pp. 193f. Robert Rupen, *How Mongolia is Really Ruled. A Political History of the Mongolian People's Republic 1900–1978* (Stanford: Hoover Institution Press, 1979), pp. 5–7, 45, 92.

158 In 1924, Urga was renamed Ulaan Baatar ('red hero') in honour of General Sükhbaatar. The name of Urga was introduced by the Russians; it derived from the Mongol word Örgö ('palace'). Before 1924, the Mongols called the city Da-Khure ('big monastery') Mursajew, *Auf unbetretenen Pfaden* (1956), p. 295.

159 Batsaikhan, Emergent Ookhnoi, *Bogdo Jebtsundamba Khutuktu, The Last King of Mongolia. Mongolia's National Revolution of 1911* (Ulaan Baatar: Institute of International Studies, 2009), pp. 34f, 192. Bawden, *The Modern History of Mongolia* (1968), pp. 193–95.

160 Bawden, *The Modern History of Mongolia* (1968), pp. 196–99. Haslund-Christensen, *Zajagan* (1936), pp. 130–39. Rupen, *How Mongolia is Really Ruled* (1979), pp. 8–10. D. Vasilev, 'The Sayan-Altai Mountain Region and South-Eastern Siberia', in: *History of Civilizations of Central Asia,* vol. VI (2005), pp. 335f.

161 It remains unclear whether Agvan Dorjiev had the competence to sign a treaty for Tibet; presumably Tibet never ratified it. Batsaikhan, *Bogdo Kebtsundamba Khutuktu* (2009), pp. 248–51. Charles Bell, *Tibet, Past and Present* (1924; New Delhi: Asian Educational Services, 1992), pp. 150f, 229f, 304f. Snelling, *Buddhism in Russia* (1993), pp. 150–52.

162 http://encyclopedia2.thefreedictionary.com/Russo-Japanese+Treaties+and+Agreements Bawden, *The Modern History of Mongolia* (1968), p. 199.

163 Bell, *Tibet, Past and Present* (1992), pp. 305f.

164 Batsaikhan, *Bogdo Jebtsundamba Khutuktu* (2009), pp. 290–94. Conceptually, the Kyakhta Agreement resembled the Simla Convention negotiated by Britain, China and Tibet in 1913–14, which provided for the division of the Tibetan-inhabited areas into an Inner and Outer Tibet. China refused to ratify the Convention, however. Snelling, *Buddhism in Russia* (1993), pp. 154f.

165 Atwood, *Encyclopedia of Mongolia* (2004), p. 471. Bawden, *The Modern History of Mongolia* (1968), pp. 204f.

166 James Palmer, *The Bloody White Baron. The extraordinary story of the Russian nobleman who became the last khan of Mongolia* (New York: Basic Books, 2009), pp. 115f.

167 Rupen, *How Mongolia is Really Ruled* (1979), pp. 25f.

168 Bawden, *The Modern History of Mongolia* (1968), pp. 209.

169 Ungern was handed over to the Soviets by his own officers and shot. Bawden, *The Modern History of Mongolia* (1968), pp. 216–35. Palmer, *The Bloody White Baron* (2009), pp. 125–231.

170 Rupen, *How Mongolia is Really Ruled* (1979), pp. 24, 44.

171 Bawden, *The Modern History of Mongolia* (1968), pp. 239–91.

172 Rupen, *How Mongolia is Really Ruled* (1979), pp. 37f, 54, 124.

173 Bawden, *The Modern History of Mongolia* (1968), pp. 301–27, 359–73. Rupen, *How Mongolia is Really Ruled* (1979), pp. 53–59, 124.

174 Mursajew, *Auf unbetretenen Pfaden* (1956,) p. 372.

175 Palmer, *The Bloody White Baron* (2009), p. 239.

176 Forsyth, *A History of the Peoples of Siberia,* (1992), pp. 321f. Rupen, *How Mongolia is Really Ruled* (1979), pp. 45f, 63. Palmer, *The Bloody White Baron* (2009), pp. 239–41.

177 Atwood, *Encyclopedia of Mongolia* (2004), pp. 556f. Forsyth, *A History of the Peoples of Siberia,* (1992), pp. 279–82. Vasilev, 'The Sayan-Altai Mountain Region and South-Eastern Siberia' (2005), pp. 335–38.

178 Ts. Batbayar, 'The Mongolian People's Revolution of 1921 and the Mongolian People's Republic (1924–46)', in: *History of Civilizations of Central Asia,* vol. VI (2005), pp. 370f.

179 Rupen, *How Mongolia is Really Ruled* (1979), pp. 74–86.

180 Millward, *Eurasian Crossroads* (2007), pp. 164–69. Skrine, *Macartney at Kashgar* (1987), pp.173–88, 213–35.

181 Wu, Aitchen K., *Turkistan Tumult* (1940; London: Methuen, 1984), pp. 42–44.

182 Andrew D.W. Forbes, *Warlords and Muslims in Chinese Central Asia. A political history of Republican Sinkiang 1911–1949* (Bangkok: White Lotus Press, 2010), p. 41. Wu, *Turkistan Tumult* (1984), p. 5. Xinjiang's governors reinforced the isolation of the province by means of a sort of visa requirement for citizens of other Chinese provinces. Eric Teichman, *Journey to Turkistan* (London: Hodder and Stoughton, 1937), p. 39.

183 Justin M. Jacobs, *Xinjiang and the Modern Chinese State* (Seattle: University of Washington Press, 2016), p. 72f.

184 Jacobs, *Xinjiang* (2016), pp. 60–62. Millward, *Eurasian Crossroads* (2007), pp. 185f. Wu, *Turkistan Tumult* (1984), pp. 40f.

185 The Guomindang Party, led by Chiang Kai-shek from 1927, was the ruling party of China, but its control over the various autonomous warlords was merely nominal. It was at war with the Japanese invaders from July 1937.

186 Wu, *Turkistan Tumult* (1984), p. 41.

187 Millward, *Eurasian Crossroads* (2007), p. 31.

188 Wu, *Turkistan Tumult* (1984), pp. 45–51.

189 Forbes, *Warlords and Muslims* (2010), pp. 43–51.

190 Mildred Cable and Francesca French, *The Gobi Desert* (London: Virago Press, 1984), p. 223.

191 See note 185 above. Generalissimo Chiang Kai-shek was Head of Government of China from 1927 to 1949 and afterwards of Taiwan.

192 Forbes, *Warlords and Muslims* (2010), pp. 52–62, 106f. Millward, *Eurasian Crossroads* (2007), p. 198. Wu, *Turkistan Tumult* (1984), pp. 66, 71, 75f.

193 See also: Eric Teichman, *Journey to Turkistan* (London: Hodder and Stoughton, 1937), p. 187.

194 Forbes, *Warlords and Muslims* (2010), pp. 70–72, 97–106. Lattimore, *Pivot of Asia* (1950), p. 72. Millward, *Eurasian Crossroads* (2007), p. 195–98. Wu, *Turkistan Tumult* (1984), pp. 71–118.

195 Yulbars Khan became military commander of Kumul, where he met the British envoy Sir Eric Teichman in 1935. Teichman, *Journey to Turkistan* (1937), pp. 85f, 188.

196 Forbes, *Warlords and Muslims* (2010), pp. 73–93.

197 Forbes, *Warlords and Muslims* (2010), pp. 96, 113–16, 123f.

198 Millward, 'Political History and Strategies' (2004), p. 78.

199 Yaqub Beg's emirate is not comparable to TIRET because he came from Kokand and conquered Kashgar from the outside by military means.

200 Joy R. Lee, *The Islamic Republic of Eastern Turkestan and the Formation of Modern Uyghur Identity in Xinjiang* (Manhattan: Kansas State University, 2006), pp. 27f.

201 Forbes, *Warlords and Muslims* (2010), pp. 117–21. Wu, *Turkistan Tumult* (1984), pp. 236f.

202 Ma Zhongying kept his word and sent the car, trucks and drivers back to Hedin intact after using them. *Die Flucht des Großen Pferdes* (Leipzig: Brockhaus, 1939), pp. 111–32, 154–63, 220.

203 Jacobs, *Xinjiang* (2016), p. 104. Forbes, *Warlords and Muslims* (2010), pp. 122–26.

204 Allen S. Whiting and General Sheng Shih-ts'ai, *Sinkiang: Pawn or Pivot?* (East Lansing: Michigan State University Press, 1958), p. 193.

205 In 1936–37, Ma Hushan held the German explorer Wilhelm Filchner captive over the course of seven months in Khotan. Wilhelm Filchner, *Bismillah! Vom Huang-ho zum Indus* (Leipzig: Brockhaus, 1940), pp. 250–91.

206 Forbes, *Warlords and Muslims* (2010), pp. 127–44.

207 Forbes, *Warlords and Muslims* (2010), pp. 136, 145–46. Whiting and Sheng, *Sinkiang* (1958), pp. 56–66.

208 Millward, *Eurasian Crossroads* (2007), pp. 208, 244.

209 Whiting and Sheng, *Sinkiang* (1958), pp. 186–88, 201–8, 218–27, 280–86.

210 Forbes, *Warlords and Muslims* (2010), pp. 157–61. Lattimore, *Pivot of Asia* (1950), pp. 77–81.

211 Forbes, *Warlords and Muslims* (2010), pp. 70–247. Millward, *Eurasian Crossroads* (2007), p. 213.

212 Jacobs, *Xinjiang* (2016), p. 131.

213 Jacobs, *Xinjiang* (2016), pp. 139–41.

214 Jacobs, *Xinjiang* (2016), pp. 148–53.

215 Forbes, *Warlords and Muslims* (2010), pp. 170–96. Millward, 'Political History and Strategies' (2004), pp. 82f.

216 Forbes, *Warlords and Muslims* (2010), pp. 220–22. Millward, *Eurasian Crossroads* (2007), p. 239.

217 Baumer, *The History of Central Asia*, vol. 2 (2014), pp. 7, 14. Jacobs, *Xinjiang* (2016), pp. 174f. Millward, 'Political History and Strategies' (2004), pp. 87–94. *Eurasian Crossroads* (2007), pp. 240f, 246–63.

218 Millward, 'Political History and Strategies' (2004), pp. 94–96. *Eurasian Crossroads* (2007), pp. 265–76.

219 Stanley W. Toops, 'The demography of Xinjiang', in: Starr, *Xinjiang. China's Muslim Borderland* (2004), pp. 244–49.

VII. A Multilateral Great Game in Afghanistan, 1978–92

1 Tomsen, *The Wars of Afghanistan* (2013), p. 446.

2 S. Mahmud Ali, *US-China Cold War Collaboration 1971–1989* (Oxon: Routledge, 2005), pp. 179, 189–200.

3 Ahmed Rashid, *Taliban: Militant Islam, Oil and Fundamentalism in Central Asia* (London: I.B.Tauris, 2000), p. 165.

4 Tomsen, *The Wars of Afghanistan* (2013), p. 143.

5 The word 'mujahideen' is derived from 'jihad' and refers today to those fighting to defend or spread Islam.

6 In Pakistan, the prime minister has only limited authority over the army.

7 Tomsen, *The Wars of Afghanistan* (2013), pp. XIV, 243, 290.

8 In Saudi Arabia, state and religion are not separated, and the state religion is Wahhabi-influenced Islam. The absolute monarchy of the al-Saud family rests on a close alliance with the clerical al-Wahhab family, which holds the most important religious offices. This alliance of the al-Saud with the al-Wahhab goes back to the pact which the local Amir Muhammad ibn Saud (1710–65) of Diriyah, near the modern town of al-Riyadh, entered into with the Hanbali preacher Sheikh Abd al-Wahhab (1703–92) in 1744. Al-Wahhab committed himself to the religious legitimisation of the al-Saud regime and ibn Saud to the exclusive promotion of the Wahhabi doctrine. The founder of the Wahhabi doctrine along with Osama bin Laden and the Egyptian mastermind of the Muslim Brotherhood, Sayyid Qutb (1906–66) invoked the militant lawyer Taqi al-Din ibn Taymiyyah (1262–1368), who cited the principles of *takfir* and *jihad* to legitimise the use of violence. *Takfir* refers to the condemnation of 'bad'; that is, 'non-Wahhabi' Muslims, especially Shiites, who are condemned as apostates; and *jihad*, in this context, denotes the war against the infidels. Ibn Taymiyyah called on Muslims to follow the example of the *Salaf al-saleh* ('pious ancestors'). Al-Wahhab's slogan was: 'One ruler – one religious authority – one mosque'. The Islamic State also invokes al-Wahhab's understanding of *takfir* and *jihad*. Wahhabism can also be interpreted as a 'purging' of Islamic culture of all non-Arab; that is, Iranian, elements. Abdel Bari Atwan, *Islamic State. The Digital Caliphate* (London: Saqi, 2015), pp. 156–58, 202f. Tomsen, *The Wars of Afghanistan* (2013), pp. 184–86.

9 To put it simply, Salafists are non-Saudi Wahhabis. See Note 8.

10 Tomsen, *The Wars of Afghanistan* (2013), pp. XIV, 181f, 519.

11 Panagiotis Dimitrakis, *The Secret War in Afghanistan. The Soviet Union, China and Anglo-American Intelligence in the Afghan War* (London: I.B.Tauris, 2013), pp. 174f. Mike Martin, *An Intimate War. An Oral History of the Helmand Conflict, 1978–2012* (Oxford: Oxford University Press, 2014), p. 56.

12 Tomsen, *The Wars of Afghanistan* (2013), pp. 128f.

13 Edwards, *Before Taliban* (2002), pp. 65f, 83–85. Martin, *An Intimate War* (2014), pp. 42f. Saikal, *Modern Afghanistan* (2012), pp. 190f.

14 Gregory Feifer, *The Great Gamble. The Soviet War in Afghanistan* (New York: Harper Prudentials, 2010), p. 24.

15 Tomsen, *The Wars of Afghanistan* (2013), p.133.

16 Saikal, *Modern Afghanistan* (2012), p. 194.

17 Tomsen, *The Wars of Afghanistan* (2013), p. 144.

18 Dimitrakis, *The Secret War in Afghanistan* (2013), pp. 45–48.

19 Ali, *US-China Cold War Collaboration* (2005), p. 168–70. A former Uzbek fighter verbally described to the author in February 2016 the deployment of Soviet 'volunteers' from Central Asia.

20 Dimitrakis, *The Secret War in Afghanistan* (2013), pp. 50–54. Feifer, *The Great Gamble* (2010), pp. 38–49.

21 Feifer, *The Great Gamble* (2010), pp. 13f, 58f. Artemy Kalinovsky, 'Decision-Making and the Soviet War in Afghanistan. From Intervention to Withdrawal' (Harvard: *The Journal of Cold War Studies*, 2009).

22 Feifer, *The Great Gamble* (2010), pp. 58–81.

23 Ali, *US-China Cold War Collaboration* (2005), p. 172.

24 Ali, *US-China Cold War Collaboration* (2005), p. 173.

25 Ali, *US-China Cold War Collaboration* (2005), pp. 176f.

26 Mohan Malik, *Dragon on Terrorism: Assessing China's tactical gains and strategic losses post-September 11* (Carlisle Barracks: US Army War College, October 2002), p. 5.

27 Feifer, *The Great Gamble* (2010), p. 83.

28 Ali, *US-China Cold War Collaboration* (2005), p. 178. Feifer, *The Great Gamble* (2010), pp. 82f.

29 Tomsen, *The Wars of Afghanistan* (2013), pp. 206f.

30 The official Soviet loss estimate of 13,833 soldiers is much too low. Feifer, *The Great Gamble* (2010), pp. 4, 254f. Saikal, *Modern Afghanistan* (2012), pp. 200f, 346.

31 Dimitrakis, *The Secret War in Afghanistan* (2013), p. 153.

32 Dimitrakis, *The Secret War in Afghanistan* (2013), p. 136.

33 Dimitrakis, *The Secret War in Afghanistan* (2013), pp. 149f.

34 Tomsen, *The Wars of Afghanistan* (2013), pp. 179–81, 191–98.

35 Atwan, *Islamic State* (2015), p. 167. Tomsen, *The Wars of Afghanistan* (2013), pp. 196–98.

36 Saikal, *Modern Afghanistan* (2012), p. 204. Tomsen, *The Wars of Afghanistan* (2013), pp. 10, 17, 246f, 290, 296, 513.

37 Edwards, *Before Taliban* (2002), pp. 235–68. Tomsen, *The Wars of Afghanistan* (2013), pp. XXV–XXVIII, 4, 304, 310f.

38 Edwards, *Before Taliban* (2002), p. 262. Feifer, *The Great Gamble* (2010), p. 98f.

39 See below p. 227.

40 Tomsen, *The Wars of Afghanistan* (2013), pp. XXV, 217, 302, 564, 598, 603.

41 Dimitrakis, *The Secret War in Afghanistan* (2013), p. 165. Tomsen, *The Wars of Afghanistan* (2013), pp. 196, 220f, 243.

42 Tanner, *Afghanistan* (2002), p. 274. Tomsen, *The Wars of Afghanistan* (2013), p. 215.

43 Tomsen, *The Wars of Afghanistan* (2013), pp. 249–51, 366, 381f.

44 Feifer, *The Great Gamble* (2010), p. 109.

45 Tanner, *Afghanistan* (2002), p. 256.

46 Tanner, *Afghanistan* (2002), p. 256f.

47 Feifer, *The Great Gamble* (2010), p. 172. Tomsen, *The Wars of Afghanistan* (2013), p. 213.

48 Dimitrakis, *The Secret War in Afghanistan* (2013), pp. 150, 175f. Feifer, *The Great Gamble* (2010), pp. 209–12. Tanner, *Afghanistan* (2002), p. 267.

49 Feifer, *The Great Gamble* (2010), pp. 185–90. Tomsen, *The Wars of Afghanistan* (2013), pp. 224f.

50 Feifer, *The Great Gamble* (2010), pp. 214–17.

51 Feifer, *The Great Gamble* (2010), pp. 218f.

52 Edwards, *Before Taliban* (2002), pp. 279–83.

53 Four days before the treaty was signed in Geneva, the ammunition and weapons depot in Rawalpindi, operated by the ISI for the mujahideen, exploded. The KGB and KHAD secret services were both suspected as the culprits, along with the ISI itself, which allegedly wanted to cover up the theft of Stinger missiles. The CIA refused to immediately replace the destroyed arsenal. Dimitrakis, *The Secret War in Afghanistan* (2013), pp. 218, 221f, 228. Feifer, *The Great Gamble* (2010), pp. 238f.

54 Dimitrakis, *The Secret War in Afghanistan* (2013), pp. 229–33.

55 Tomsen, *The Wars of Afghanistan* (2013), pp. 250, 290, 294, 335, 344f.

56 Tomsen, *The Wars of Afghanistan* (2013), pp. 255–62, 320–34.

57 Dimitrakis, *The Secret War in Afghanistan* (2013), pp. 223, 232. Brian Glyn Williams, *The Last Warlord: The Life and Legend of Dostum, the Afghan Warrior Who Led US Special Forces to Topple the Taliban regime* (Chicago: Chicago Review Press, 2013), pp. 138f.

58 Dimitrakis, *The Secret War in Afghanistan* (2013), p. 232. Tomsen, *The Wars of Afghanistan* (2013), pp. 404–10.

59 Tomsen, *The Wars of Afghanistan* (2013), pp. 406, 773n.17.

60 Tomsen, *The Wars of Afghanistan* (2013), pp. 367, 386–89.

61 Tomsen, *The Wars of Afghanistan* (2013), pp. 433f.

62 Dimitrakis, *The Secret War in Afghanistan* (2013), p. 233. Tomsen, *The Wars of Afghanistan* (2013), pp. 448–55, 467.

63 Saikal, *Modern Afghanistan* (2012), p. 209. Tomsen, *The Wars of Afghanistan* (2013), pp. 5, 462. Williams, *The Last Warlord* (2013), p. 148.

64 Saikal, *Modern Afghanistan* (2012), p. 210. Tomsen, *The Wars of Afghanistan* (2013), p. 481.

65 Rashid, *Taliban* (2000), pp. 49f. Tomsen, *The Wars of Afghanistan* (2013), pp. 5–14, 481, 540.

66 Tomsen, *The Wars of Afghanistan* (2013), p. 512.

67 In 1994, Karzai had to hastily leave Kabul because of his unofficial contact with Hekmatyar. Bette Dam, *A Man and a Motor Cycle. How Hamid Karzai came to Power* (Utrecht: Ipso facto, 2014), p. 31.

68 Tomsen, *The Wars of Afghanistan* (2013), pp. 14–15, 484–94, 509f. Williams, *The Last Warlord* (2013), p. 151–55.

VIII. Afghanistan Forces the Three Major Powers to Engage in a Joint Struggle against Islamic Extremism

1 Williams, *The Last Warlord* (2013), p. 207.

2 Gall, *The Wrong Enemy* (2014), p. 222.

3 Antonio Giustozzi, *Empires of Mud. War and Warlords in Afghanistan* (London: Hurst & Company, 2009), p. 285.

4 Micheline Centlives-Demont (ed.), *Afghanistan. Identity, Society and Politics since 1980* (London: I.B.Tauris, 2015), p. 84. Edwards, *Before Taliban* (2002), p. 289. Giustozzi, *Empires of Mud* (2009), p. 73. Saikal, *Modern Afghanistan* (2012), p. 222. Williams, *The Last Warlord* (2013), p. 155–58.

5 While Turkmenistan and Uzbekistan border on the Caspian Sea, the latter is a dead end without access to the oceans.

6 After the First Gulf War in 1990–91, the Saudis pressured Pakistan to have Hekmatyar removed because he had supported Saddam Hussein. Centlives-Demont (ed.), *Afghanistan* (2015), p. 97.

7 Tomsen, *The Wars of Afghanistan* (2013), pp. 391, 533–35.

8 It is ironic that a woman educated at the Western universities Harvard and Oxford was partly responsible for the rise of the Taliban.

9 Personal comment on 17 May 2017.

10 Saikal, *Modern Afghanistan* (2012), pp. 222–24. Tomsen, *The Wars of Afghanistan* (2013), pp. 531–38. The oft-repeated tale that the Taliban arose spontaneously in 1994, when Omar Mullah with only 30 men liberated two kidnapped girls and a boy, over whom two local commanders were feuding, belongs to the realm of myth.

11 Steve Coll, *Ghost Wars. The Secret History of the CIA, Afghanistan and Bin Laden, from the Soviet Invasion to September 10, 2001* (London: Penguin, 2004), p. 339.

12 Rashid, *Taliban* (2000), p. 50.

13 Rashid, *Taliban* (2000), pp. 45, 165f, 178f. Tomsen, *The Wars of Afghanistan* (2013), pp. 538, 561.

14 Saudi Arabia had in 1994 deprived bin Laden of his citizenship and expelled him whereupon he lived in Sudan till 1996. Centlives-Demont (ed.), *Afghanistan* (2015), p. 115.

15 Abbas, *The Taliban Revival* (2014), p. 73. Tomsen, *The Wars of Afghanistan* (2013), p. 544.

16 Ahmed Rashid, *Jihad: The Rise of Militant Islam in Central Asia* (New Haven: Yale University Press, 2002), pp. 195, 210. *Taliban* (2000), p. 166.

17 Dimitrakis, *The Secret War in Afghanistan* (2013), p. 237. Hunter, *Islam in Russia* (2015), pp. 339, 356–59.

18 Christoph Bluth, *US Foreign Policy in the Caucasus and Central Asia. Politics, Energy and Security* (London: I.B. Tauris, 2014), p. 144. Carlotta Gall and Thomas de Waal, *Chechnya. Calamity in the Caucasus* (New York: New York University Press, 1998), p. 308.

19 *Neue Zürcher Zeitung*, 7. 11. 2016, p. 13th

20 Hunter, *Islam in Russia* (2015), p. 309.

21 On the disputes concerning a trans-Afghan pipeline, see Rashid, *Taliban* (2000), pp. 157–82.

22 The rump government of Rabbani and Massoud retained Afghanistan's seat in the United Nations. Tomsen, *The Wars of Afghanistan* (2013), pp. 540, 542.

23 Rashid, *Jihad* (2002), pp. 140f, 165f, 173, 176, 224.

24 Tomsen, *The Wars of Afghanistan* (2013), p. 550.

25 Dam, *A Man and a Motor Cycle* (2014), p. 47. Tomsen, *The Wars of Afghanistan* (2013), pp. xvif, 697.

26 Williams, *The Last Warlord* (2013), pp. 173–85, 199.

27 Tanner, *Afghanistan* (2002), p. 284.

28 Carlotta Gall, *The Wrong Enemy. America in Afghanistan, 2001–2014* (Boston: Mariner, 2014), p. 52. Tomsen, *The Wars of Afghanistan* (2013), pp. 541, 555, 571.

29 Gall, *The Wrong Enemy* (2014), p. 50.

30 Centlives-Demont (ed.), *Afghanistan* (2015), p. 137. One of the highest output in opium production occurred in 2007 with 7,400 tonnes, followed by 6,400 tonnes in 2014. In 2017, the output rose to 9,000 tons. https://de.statista.com/statistik/daten/studie/36697/umfrage/produktion-von-opium-in-afghanistan-seit-1990/ *Neue Zürcher Zeitung*, 1 March 2018, p. 7.

31 Martin, *An Intimate War* (2014), p. 108.

32 Rashid, *Jihad* (2002), pp. 165, 229. *Taliban* (2019), p. 243. See also pp. 278f.

33 Marcela Grad, *Massoud. An intimate portrait of the legendary Afghan leader* (St Louis: Webster University Press, 2009), pp. 286f.

34 Coll, *Ghost Wars* (2004), p. 561. Tomsen, *The Wars of Afghanistan* (2013), pp. 555f.

35 Tomsen, *The Wars of Afghanistan* (2013), pp. 555f.

36 Coll, *Ghost Wars* (2004), pp. 564–73.

37 Coll, *Ghost Wars* (2004), pp. 574–76, 582. Williams, *The Last Warlord* (2013), p. 206.

38 Williams, *The Last Warlord* (2013), pp. 54f.
39 Williams, *The Last Warlord* (2013), p. 61.
40 Bluth, *US Foreign Policy in the Caucasus and Central Asia* (2014), p. 45. Lena Jonson, *Vladimir Putin and Central Asia* (London, I.B.Tauris, 2004), 74f.
41 Bluth, *US Foreign Policy in the Caucasus and Central Asia* (2014), pp. 44–47.
42 Saikal, *Modern Afghanistan* (2012), pp. 231, 265.
43 Central Command (CENTCOM) is one of six American regional command centres and responsible for the Middle East, Central Asia and East Africa.
44 Williams, *The Last Warlord* (2013), pp. 63–69.
45 'Green Berets' is the name for members of the elite United States' Army Special Forces Command (Airborne).
46 Williams, *The Last Warlord* (2013), pp. 215–42.
47 Tanner, *Afghanistan* (2002), pp. 295–304. Williams, *The Last Warlord* (2013), pp. 258–60.
48 Tanner, *Afghanistan* (2002), p. 304.
49 Gall, *The Wrong Enemy* (2014), pp. 62f.
50 Tanner, *Afghanistan* (2002), p. 304f. Tomsen, *The Wars of Afghanistan* (2013), pp. 604–7.
51 Tomsen, *The Wars of Afghanistan* (2013), pp. 608–13.
52 General Richards did not have General Franks in mind here, but politicians. David Richards, *Taking Command. The Autobiography* (London: Headline, 2014), p. IX.
53 Gall, *The Wrong Enemy* (2014), pp. 90–92, 242f.
54 Abbas, *The Taliban Revival* (2014), p. 96.
55 Ibrahim Azeem, *U.S. Aid to Pakistan. – U.S. Taxpayers Have Funded Pakistani Corruption* (Harvard: Belfer Center for Science and International Affairs, Harvard University, July 2009), p. 40. Saikal, *Modern Afghanistan* (2012), p. 236.
56 Tomsen, *The Wars of Afghanistan* (2013), p. 627.
57 Dam, *A Man and a Motor Cycle* (2014), pp. 120–24, 153–60, 170–74. Williams, *The Last Warlord* (2013), pp. 266–72.
58 Gall, *The Wrong Enemy* (2014), pp. 197–201. *Neue Zürcher Zeitung*, 3 April 2014, p. 7.
59 Gall, *The Wrong Enemy* (2014), pp. 295–97. http://www.nytimes.com/2014/09/22/world/asia/afghan-presidential-election.html?_r=1
60 See below p. 243.
61 Gall, *The Wrong Enemy* (2014), p. 222.
62 Tomsen, *The Wars of Afghanistan* (2013), p. xvi.
63 Abbas, *The Taliban Revival* (2014), pp. 187, 223.
64 Gall, *The Wrong Enemy* (2014), pp. 67–74.
65 Rashid, *Taliban* (2000), p. 232.
66 Akexander Cooley, *Great Games, Local Rules. The New Great Power Contest in Central Asia* (Oxford: Oxford University Press, 2012), p. 43.
67 Tomsen, *The Wars of Afghanistan* (2013), pp. 620, 634, 658.
68 *Neue Zürcher Zeitung*, 10 September 2016, p. 5; 26 June 2017, p. 5.
69 The terrorist network is led by Jalaluddin Haqqani and his son Sirajuddin. The network has close links to the Taliban and al-Qaeda, but only operates regionally; it is financed through donations from Saudi Arabia and the Gulf States, as well as through the extortion of protection money inside Afghanistan, kidnapping, and smuggling. The network introduced the method of suicide attacks in Afghanistan, which was alien to the Afghans.

70 Gall, *The Wrong Enemy* (2014), p. 298.
71 The Sunni organisation Islamic State, al-daula al-Islamiya, which has been active since 2003, represents a jihadist, Salafist ideology and aims at a supranational caliphate. By 2014, it was called Islamic State of Iraq and the Levant (Greater Syria), ISIS.
72 *Neue Zürcher Zeitung*, 17 February 2016, p. 3.
73 Gall, *The Wrong Enemy* (2014), p. 294.
74 *The Guardian*, 18 October, 2016. https://www.theguardian.com/world/2016/oct/18/taliban-afghanistan-secret-talks-qatar
75 *The Guardian*, 22 September 2016. https://www.theguardian.com/world/2016/sep/22/butcher-of-kabul-pardoned-in-afghan-peace-deal
76 https://www.theguardian.com/world/2017/may/04/afghan-warlord-gulbuddin-hekmatyar-returns-kabul-20-years-call-peace.
77 Gall, *The Wrong Enemy* (2014), p. 132.
78 Gall, *The Wrong Enemy* (2014), pp. 163–70.
79 Abbas, *The Taliban Revival* (2014), pp. 151–59. Rashid, *Taliban* (2000), pp. 225, 239. Tomsen, *The Wars of Afghanistan* (2013), p. 649.
80 Gall, *The Wrong Enemy* (2014), p. 298.
81 *Neue Zürcher Zeitung*, 6 February 2009. *Washington Post*, 9 May 2015. https://www.washingtonpost.com/world/the-taliban-once-ruled-pakistans-swat-valley-now-peace-has-returned/2015/05/08/6bb8ac96-eeaa-11e4-8050-839e9234b303_story.html
82 Abbas, *The Taliban Revival* (2014), pp. 141–50.
83 *Neue Zürcher Zeitung*, 2 November 2016, p. 12.
84 Saikal, *Modern Afghanistan* (2012), p. 244.
85 In most parts of Helmand and Kandahar, the voter turnout in the presidential election of 2009 was between 1 per cent and 5 per cent. Rashid, *Taliban* (2000), p. 234.
86 Abbas, *The Taliban Revival* (2014), pp. 173, 183.
87 Richards, *Taking Command* (2014), pp. 211f.
88 Yorke, *Playing the Great Game* (2012), p. 387.
89 Martin, *An Intimate War* (2014), pp. 111, 124, 138–41, 210f. There are other warlords, such as Atta Mohammad Noor, who also became wealthy, but moreover helped his Balkh province to achieve relative prosperity from 2004. *Neue Zürcher Zeitung*, 10 January 2014.
90 Abbas, *The Taliban Revival* (2014), pp. 81, 117. Gall, *The Wrong Enemy* (2014), pp. 74f, 161.
91 Lena Jonson, *Tajikistan in the New Central Asia* (2009), p. 102.
92 Lena Jonson, *Tajikistan in the New Central Asia* (2009), pp. 102f.
93 Gall, *The Wrong Enemy* (2014), p. 102.
94 Abbas, *The Taliban Revival* (2014), p. 202. Dam, *A Man and a Motor Cycle* (2014), pp. 204–5. Gall, *The Wrong Enemy* (2014), pp. 99f. Martin, *An Intimate War* (2014), pp. 2–5, 125, 133.
95 Tomsen, *The Wars of Afghanistan* (2013), pp. 640, 673. See also: Saikal, *Modern Afghanistan* (2012), p. 263.
96 Rashid, *Taliban* (2000), pp. 229, 232. Tanner, *Afghanistan* (2002), p. 339.
97 Abbas, *The Taliban Revival* (2014), pp. 212–15.
98 Gall, *The Wrong Enemy* (2014), pp. 160, 295. Tomsen, *The Wars of Afghanistan* (2013), pp. 670f, 683.
99 Tomsen, *The Wars of Afghanistan* (2013), p. 674. See also pp. 665, 670, 683, 694.
100 Saikal, *Modern Afghanistan* (2012), p. 261.

101 Richards, *Taking Command* (2014), pp. 194.
102 Gall, *The Wrong Enemy* (2014), p. 261f. Saikal, *Modern Afghanistan* (2012), pp. 267f.
103 Gall, *The Wrong Enemy* (2014), p. 162.
104 Afghanistan also has huge deposits of the light metal lithium. *Neue Zürcher Zeitung*, 16 June 2010, p. 3. Cooley, *Great Games, Local Rules* (2012), p. 84.

IX. The New Independence of Central Asian States

1 Rashid, *Taliban* (2000), p. 232.
2 S.N. Abashin, *Central Asia: How we see it* (2011), in: Alexey Malashenko, *The Fight for Influence. Russia in Central Asia* (Washington: Carnegie Endowment for International Peace, 2013), p. 13.
3 Bluth, *US Foreign Policy* (2014), p. 81. Martha Brill Olcott, *Central Asia's Second Chance* (Washington DC: Carnegie Endowment for International Peace, 2005), p. 71.
4 See above pp. 243f.
5 Lena Jonson, Lena, *Vladimir Putin and Central Asia. The Shaping of Russian Foreign Policy* (London: I.B.Tauris 2004), p. 43.
6 *The Moscow Times*, 25 July 2016. https://themoscowtimes.com/articles/tatarstan-special-status-expires-58483
7 See above pp. 207–10.
8 See above Chapter III.
9 Toops, 'The demography of Xinjiang' (2004), pp. 244–49. https://en.wikipedia.org/wiki/Xinjiang
10 Millward, *Eurasian Crossroads* (2007), p. 278.
11 PLA stands for People's Liberation Army.
12 Yitzak Shichor, 'The Great Wall of Steel: Military and Strategy in Xinjiang', in: S. Frederick Starr (ed.), *Xinjiang. China's Muslim Borderland* (Armonk: M.E. Sharpe, 2004), pp. 149, 158.
13 Millward, *Eurasian Crossroads* (2007), pp. 282, 322–24.
14 J. Todd Reed and Diana Raschke, *The ETIM. China's Islamic Militants and the Global Terrorist Threat* (Santa Barbara: Praeger, 2010), p. 43.
15 Millward, *Eurasian Crossroads* (2007), pp. 289f.
16 Millward, *Eurasian Crossroads* (2007), pp. 299f.
17 Marlene Laruelle and Sebastian Peyrouse, *Globalizing Central Asia. Geopolitics and the Challenges of Economic Development* (London: Routledge, 2015), pp. 174, 176.
18 Millward, *Eurasian Crossroads* (2007), pp. 301f.
19 China has stationed air defence systems and built runways on seven man-made islands. *Neue Zürcher Zeitung*, 16 August 2016, p. 12. http://www.nzz.ch/meinung/kommentare/nach-dem-urteil-zum-suedchinesischen-meer-zittern-vor-china-ld.111104. http://www.nzz.ch/international/asien-und-pazifik/streitfall-suedchinesisches-meer-eine-chinesische-festung-im-ozean-ld.135095.
20 Kaplan, *The Revenge of Geography* (New York: Random House, 2013), p. 210.
21 Baumer, *The History of Central Asia,* vol. 2 (2014), p. 170.
22 Millward, *Eurasian Crossroads* (2007), pp. 311–23. Reed, Raschke, *The ETIM* (2010), pp. 26f. Stanley W. Toops, 'The ecology of Xinjiang', in: Starr, S.

Frederick (ed.), *Xinjiang. China's Muslim Borderland* (Armonk: M.E. Sharpe, 2004), pp. 264–74.

23 Millward, *Eurasian Crossroads* (2007), pp. 325–28. Reed, Raschke, *The ETIM* (2010), pp. 47, 55.

24 Reed, Raschke, *The ETIM* (2010), pp. 35–47, 55–67. https://en.wikipedia.org/wiki/July_2009_%C3%9Cr%C3%BCmqi_riots

25 The resettlement of some 220,000 Uyghurs from the old town into supposedly earthquake-proof apartment blocks on the outskirts did not take place to weaken the culture and identity of the Uyghurs, as is often claimed in the West, but for financial reasons. In China, the land belongs to the state, whereas residents only own their homes. This is why resettlement in provided apartments is legal. The city can then rent out the vacated building area to the highest-bidding real estate company.

26 China puts the blame for the riots on the World Uyghur Congress. Its president Rabiya Kadeer's use of fake photos to prove the alleged brutality of Chinese authorities has undermined her credibility. *Frankfurter Allgemeine Zeitung* FAZ, 10 July 2009, p. 2.

27 https://en.wikipedia.org/wiki/2014_Kunming_attack

28 https://www.theguardian.com/world/2015/oct/01/at-least-50-reported-dead-in-september-attack-as-china-celebrates-xinjiang

29 Abbas, *The Taliban Revival* (2014), p. 108. Millward, *Eurasian Crossroads* (2007), pp. 337f. Reed, Raschke, *The ETIM* (2010), pp.46–54, 68–73.

30 Morris Rossabi, *Modern Mongolia. From Khans to Commissars to Capitalists* (Berkeley: University of California Press, 2005), pp. 7–28.

31 Rossabi, *Modern Mongolia* (2005), pp. 49–73, 104, 109, 246f.

32 The five main livestock animals are horses, sheep, goats, yaks and camels.

33 *Neue Zürcher Zeitung*, 7 August 2009, p. 23.

34 *Neue Zürcher Zeitung*, 12 August 2012, p. 37; 4 May 2013, p. p. 35; 24 March 2015, p. 26. Rossabi, *Modern Mongolia* (2005), pp. 234–37.

35 Rossabi, *Modern Mongolia* (2005), pp. 238, 244f, 249.

36 *Neue Zürcher Zeitung*, 16 July 2016, p. 31. Deutsches Auswärtiges Amt http://www.auswaertiges-amt.de/DE/Aussenpolitik/Laender/Laenderinfos/Mongolei/Wirtschaft_node.html

37 Laruelle, Peyrouse, *Globalizing Central Asia* (2015), pp. 172–85, 259.

38 Cooley, *Great Games, Local Rules* (2012), pp. 134, 155. Werner Hermann and Johannes F. Linn (eds.), *Central Asia and The Caucasus. At the Crossroads of Eurasia in the 21st Century* (Los Angeles: Sage, 2011), pp. 12, 44, 56, 114.

39 Jonson, *Vladimir Putin and Central Asia* (2004), pp. 45, 50f, 63, 65, 81, 127.

40 The EAEU includes Armenia, Kazakhstan, Kyrgyzstan, Russia, and Belarus; Tajikistan is a candidate country. Alexander Cooley, *Great Games, Local Rules. The New Great Power Contest in Central Asia* (Oxford: Oxford University Press, 2012), pp. 56–61. The Commonwealth of Independent States (CIS), founded on 8 December 1991, has lost a great deal of its relevance in recent years.

41 Cooley, *Great Games, Local Rules* (2012), pp. 74–78, 95.

42 Cooley, *Great Games, Local Rules* (2012), p. 9.

43 Hiro, *Inside Central Asia* (2009), pp. 241–48.

44 Allworth (ed.), *130 Years of Russian Dominance* (1994), p. 602.

45 Hiro, *Inside Central Asia* (2009), p. 96.

46 Bluth, *US Foreign Policy* (2014), pp. 81, 115, 122, 202. Hiro, *Inside Central Asia* (2009), pp. 248–51.

47 See above p. 193. http://thebulletin.org/lasting-toll-semipalatinsks-nuclear-testing

48 Jonathan Aitken, *Nazarbayev and the Making of Kazakhstan* (London: Continuum, 2010), p. 147f. Hiro, *Inside Central Asia* (2009), p. 250.

49 Aitken, *Nazarbayev* (2010), pp. 148f. Hiro, *Inside Central Asia* (2009), Rumer (ed.), *Central Asia* (2005), pp. 110, 135–38.

50 Hiro, *Inside Central Asia* (2009), pp. 248, 251. Kaplan, *The Revenge of Geography* (2013), p. 185.

51 Bluth, *US Foreign Policy* (2014), pp. 119f.

52 Hiro, *Inside Central Asia* (2009), pp. 245, 252f. Rumer (ed.), *Central Asia* (2005), pp. 199–202, 250, n.8.

53 https://web.archive.org/web/20100212175154/http://www.stat.kz/p_perepis/Pages/n_04_02_10.aspx

54 Aitken, *Nazarbayev* (2010), pp. 157–70. Hiro, *Inside Central Asia* (2009), pp. 256, 261. Malashenko, *The Fight for Influence* (2013), pp. 31, 104.

55 https://www.theguardian.com/world/2014/sep/01/kazakhstan-russian-neighbour-putin-chilly-nationalist-rhetoric

56 The World Bank, http://data.worldbank.org/indicator/NY.GDP.PCAP.CD, retrieved 23 June 2017. See also: International Monetary Fund, *World economic outlook*, April 2016, retrieved 17 September 2016. http://www.imf.org/external/pubs/ft/weo/2016/01/weodata

57 Laruelle, Peyrouse, *Globalizing Central Asia* (2015), pp. 165, 199.

58 The barrel is a standard measurement, corresponding to 159 litres.

59 OPEC Annual Statistics Bulletin 2016; http://www.opec.org/opec_web/en/publications/202.htm. US Energy Information Administration, *International Energy Statistics,* 2016; http://www.eia.gov/beta/international/data/ Hermann, Linn (eds), *Central Asia and The Caucasus* (2011), pp. 78f.

60 CIA, *The World Factbook*, 2014 Estimate; https://www.cia.gov/library/publications/the-world-factbook/rankorder/2253rank.html. As the neighbouring states continue to feud over the drilling rights, the huge oil and gas reserves in the middle of the Caspian Sea are not included in these figures. If this inland water is defined as a sea, then the neighbouring states would only have rights to the strip of a few nautical miles off their coasts. In this case, the large central area would be considered international waters and the feuding parties would have to come to an agreement about the extraction of the deposits there. If the Caspian Sea is defined as a lake, then the fish stocks and natural resources need to be divided equally.

61 *Neue Zürcher Zeitung*, 7 August 2009, 29 October 2016, p. 35. Olcott, *Central Asia's Second Chance* (2005), pp. 32f.

62 Hiro, *Inside Central Asia* (2009), pp. 253–55.

63 Milan Hauner, 'Russia's Asian Heartland Today and Tomorrow', in: Nick Megoran and Sevara Sharapova, (eds), *Central Asia in International Relations. The Legacies of Halford Mackinder* (London: Hurst & Co., 2013), p. 145.

64 Bluth, *US Foreign Policy* (2014), p. 59. Cooley, *Great Games, Local Rules* (2012), pp. 91f. Hermann, Linn, (eds), *Central Asia and The Caucasus* (2011), pp. 33f. Rumer (ed.), *Central Asia* (2005), pp. 423–27. The oil and gas industry is divided into an upstream business, which deals with the exploration, drilling, and production of raw materials, and a midstream and downstream business, which includes processing, refining, marketing and distribution.

65 Laruelle, Peyrouse, *Globalizing Central Asia* (2015), p. 173.

66 Laruelle, Peyrouse, *Globalizing Central Asia* (2015), pp. 174, 176. The pipeline runs from Turkmenistan through Uzbekistan and Kazakhstan to Xinjiang, southern China and Hong Kong.

67 Malashenko, *The Fight for Influence* (2013), p. 113. The construction of the fourth D pipeline was interrupted early 2016. See below, p. 286. https://en.wikipedia.org/wiki/Central_Asia%E2%80%93China_gas_pipeline#cite_note-br160614-20

68 On the pipelines in Central Asia, see: Hermann, Linn (eds), *Central Asia and The Caucasus* (2011), p. 39. Laruelle, Peyrouse, *Globalizing Central Asia* (2015), p. 174.

69 *The Astana times*, 17 November 2015. http://astanatimes.com/2015/11/turkmenistans-pipeline-strategy-building-a-diversified-export-infrastructure/

70 Hermann, Linn, (eds), *Central Asia and The Caucasus* (2011), pp. 102, 104–6, 122.

71 The Economist, 23 October 2003. http://www.economist.com/node/2155717

72 Laruelle, Peyrouse, *Globalizing Central Asia* (2015), pp. 264–66, 285f, 289.

73 Laruelle, Peyrouse, *Globalizing Central Asia* (2015), pp. 151, 277. http://www.worldstopexports.com/wheat-exports-country/ ; http://www.world-grain.com/Departments/Country-Focus/Country-Focus-Home/Kazakhstan-2016.aspx?cck=1

74 *Neue Zürcher Zeitung*, June 7, 2016, p. 7.

75 Hiro, *Inside Central Asia* (2009), p. 290. Rashid, *Jihad* (2002), pp. 67–69.

76 Hiro, *Inside Central Asia* (2009), p. 297. Olcott, *Central Asia's Second Chance* (2005), pp. 41f. Rashid, *Jihad* (2002), p. 69.

77 Cooley, *Great Games, Local Rules* (2012), p. 86. The border demarcation with China was regulated in the treaties of 1996, 1999, and 2001, respectively. Hiro, *Inside Central Asia* (2009), p. 301. Rumer (ed.), *Central Asia* (2005), p. 136.

78 See above n. 56.

79 Estimates for the 2012. Cooley, *Great Games, Local Rules* (2012), p. 63. Malashenko, *The Fight for Influence* (2013), pp. 6, 92, 136.

80 Hiro, *Inside Central Asia* (2009), p. 304.

81 Hermann, Linn (eds), *Central Asia and The Caucasus* (2011), pp. 147, 158.

82 Regional electricity trade and exchange among the five republics declined by 85 per cent from 1990 to 2008. Laruelle, Peyrouse, *Globalizing Central Asia* (2015), p. 219.

83 Hermann, Linn (eds), *Central Asia and The Caucasus* (2011), pp. XXV, 9f, 26. Lena Johnson, *Tajikistan in the New Central Asia. Geopolitics, Great Power Rivalry and Radical Islam* (London: I.B.Tauris, 2009), pp. 19, 117f. Laruelle, Peyrouse, *Globalizing Central Asia*

(2015), pp. 219f, 230, 236. *Neue Zürcher Zeitung*, 2 October 2008, p. 9; January 22, 2016, p. 5.

84 Hiro, *Inside Central Asia* (2009), pp. 296f, 305f.

85 Hiro, *Inside Central Asia* (2009), pp. 304–7.

86 Laruelle, Peyrouse, *Globalizing Central Asia* (2015), pp. 13, 45, 48. Rumer (ed.), *Central Asia* (2005), pp. 20, 291. https://www.theguardian.com/world/2004/nov/26/ukraine.usa

87 Hiro, *Inside Central Asia* (2009), p. 306. https://www.opendemocracy.net/about. The so-called 'Tulip Revolution' was not actually a revolution insofar as it did not result in a change of government, but merely a change of ruler.

88 Rashid, *Jihad* (2002), pp. 159f.

89 Vitaly V. Naumkin, *Radical Islam in Central Asia: Between Pen and Rifle* (Lanham: Rowman & Littlefield, 2005), p. 92.

90 Rashid, *Jihad* (2002), pp. 164, 172, 178.

91 Rashid, *Jihad* (2002), pp. 161, 177.

92 *Neue Zürcher Zeitung*, 24 January 2013, p. 9.

93 Rumer (ed.), *Central Asia* (2005), pp. 96, 101f.

94 Cooley, *Great Games, Local Rules* (2012), pp. 121f.

95 Jonson, *Vladimir Putin and Central Asia* (2004), p. 96. http://gca.satrapia.com/russia-obtains-military-base-prolongation-in-kyrgyzstan

96 The US base was handed over to the Kyrgyz armed forces in June 2014.

97 Cooley, *Great Games, Local Rules* (2012), pp. 22, 123.

98 Cooley, *Great Games, Local Rules* (2012), pp. 36, 143–46.

99 Cooley, *Great Games, Local Rules* (2012), pp. 3, 58, 67, 124–27.

100 Cooley, *Great Games, Local Rules* (2012), pp. 127–29.

101 Stephan Flechtner and Dagmar Schreiber, *Kirgistan* (Berlin: Trescher, 2015), pp. 79–81.

102 The government charged ousted President Bakiyev and his family with having provoked the riots.

103 Cooley, *Great Games, Local Rules* (2012), pp. 130f. Flechtner, Schreiber, *Kirgistan* (2015), pp. 78f. *Neue Zürcher Zeitung*, 2 July 2010, p. 6; 7 September 2010, p. 7.

104 Hiro, *Inside Central Asia* (2009), p. 126.

105 The Fergana Valley has more than 10 million inhabitants, three-quarters of whom are ethnic Uzbeks; 60 per cent of the territory belongs to Uzbekistan, 25 per cent to Tajikistan, and 15 per cent to Kyrgyzstan, where a significant Uzbek minority lives. Johnson, *Tajikistan in the New Central Asia* (2009), p. 115.

106 Hiro, *Inside Central Asia* (2009), pp. 130–44.

107 Hiro, *Inside Central Asia* (2009), p. 146. Naumkin, *Radical Islam in Central Asia* (2005), p. 58. The internationally operating Islamic Revival Party IRP was founded in 1990 by the North-Caucasian Akhtayev and was very active in the North Caucasus. Forsyth, *The Caucasus* (2013), p. 702.

108 Naumkin, *Radical Islam in Central Asia* (2005), pp. 38, 66. Rashid, *Jihad* (2002), p. 50.

109 Hiro, *Inside Central Asia* (2009), pp. 152, 316f. Johnson, *Tajikistan in the New Central Asia* (2009), p. 112.

110 Malashenko, *The Fight for Influence* (2013), p. 84.

111 On the Samanids and Rudaki see: Baumer, *The History of Central Asia,* vol. 3 (2016), pp. 25–32.

112 Malashenko, *The Fight for Influence* (2013), p. 20.

113 Laruelle, Peyrouse, *Globalizing Central Asia* (2015),

pp. 149, 154–56, 269–72. Olcott, *Central Asia's Second Chance* (2005), p. 120. Rumer (ed.), *Central Asia* (2005), pp. 304f.

114 World Bank: http://data.worldbank.org/country/uzbekistan retrieved 27 November 2016.

115 Olcott, *Central Asia's Second Chance* (2005), p. 50. https://en.wikipedia.org/wiki/Economy_of_Uzbekistan#External_trade_and_investment

116 Laruelle, Peyrouse, *Globalizing Central Asia* (2015), pp. 53, 149. Paul, *Zentralasien* (2012), p. 487.

117 Malashenko, *The Fight for Influence* (2013), pp. 202–4. *Neue Zürcher Zeitung*, 6 Setember 2016, p. 25.

118 Naumkin, *Radical Islam in Central Asia* (2005), pp. 37f, 58–60, 66.

119 Lena Jonson, *Tajikistan in the New Central Asia* (2009), p. 115. Naumkin, *Radical Islam in Central Asia* (2005), pp. 136, pp. 39–247.

120 Naumkin, *Radical Islam in Central Asia* (2005), p. 155. Rashid, *Jihad* (2002), pp. 115, pp. 23–247.

121 The period of establishment is cited as 1996–98.

122 Naumkin, *Radical Islam in Central Asia* (2005), pp. 29, 68–71.

123 Bluth, *US Foreign Policy* (2014), p. 145. Rashid, *Jihad* (2002), pp. 140–42, 154, 166, 224.

124 Rashid, *Jihad* (2002), pp. 144, 154, 165, 173, 176.

125 The responsability of IMU for the attack is sometimes questioned and sought among the United Tajik Opposition, UTO.

126 See above p. 274.

127 Rashid, *Jihad* (2002), pp. 167–72.

128 Rashid, *Jihad* (2002), pp. 173–77.

129 Rashid, *Jihad* (2002), p. 179.

130 Limited military cooperation had already begun between Uzbekistan and the United States in 1999. Hiro, *Inside Central Asia* (2009), pp. 165, 173.

131 Rashid, *Jihad* (2002), p. 184.

132 Bluth, *US Foreign Policy* (2014), p. 146. Naumkin, *Radical Islam in Central Asia* (2005), p. 107f.

133 Cooley, *Great Games, Local Rules* (2012), p. 105.

134 Hiro, *Inside Central Asia* (2009), pp. 183f. Malashenko, *The Fight for Influence* (2013), p. 206. Rumer (ed.), *Central Asia* (2005), pp. 283, 290.

135 'Preliminary findings in the events in Andijan, Uzbekistan, May 13, 2005' (Warsaw: OSCE, 20 June 2005). http://www.osce.org/odihr/15653?download=true

136 Bluth, *US Foreign Policy* (2014), pp. 21, 153. Cooley, *Great Games, Local Rules* (2012), p. 38–40. Hiro, *Inside Central Asia* (2009), pp. 188–90, 413.

137 The lack of legal certainty was revealed, for instance, when the government announced in 2011 that it would end the joint venture with Amantaytau Goldfields, founded in 2003, and nationalise the 50 per cent stake of the English company Oxus Gold. An Uzbek court declared Amantaytau Goldfields bankrupt at the beginning of 2013. http://www.italaw.com/sites/default/files/case-documents/ita0589.pdf ; http://rapsinews.com/judicial_news/20130204/266282267.html

138 *Neue Zürcher Zeitung*, 2 December 2016, p. 5.

139 *Neue Zürcher Zeitung*, 2 September 2017, p. 6.

140 Naumkin, *Radical Islam in Central Asia* (2005), p. 203.

141 Hiro, *Inside Central Asia* (2009), pp. 312, 332.

142 Hiro, *Inside Central Asia* (2009), pp. 129, 314.

143 Hiro, *Inside Central Asia* (2009), pp. 317–24. Hunter,

Islam in Russia (2015), p. 331. Naumkin, *Radical Islam in Central Asia* (2005), pp. 213f. Olcott, *Central Asia's Second Chance* (2005), p. 45f.

144 Naumkin, *Radical Islam in Central Asia* (2005), pp. 214f.

145 Hiro, *Inside Central Asia* (2009), pp. 325–36. Naumkin, *Radical Islam in Central Asia* (2005), pp. 214–22.

146 Hiro, *Inside Central Asia* (2009), pp. 152, 316f, 335–37. Johnson, *Tajikistan in the New Central Asia* (2009), pp. 112f. Naumkin, *Radical Islam in Central Asia* (2005), pp. 223, 227.

147 Hiro, *Inside Central Asia* (2009), p. 340.

148 Lena Jonson, *Tajikistan in the New Central Asia* (2009), pp. 45–48, 89, 96, 147. Naumkin, *Radical Islam in Central Asia* (2005), pp. 227–36.

149 Lena Jonson, *Tajikistan in the New Central Asia* (2009), p. 48.

150 Malashenko, *The Fight for Influence* (2013), p. 156.

151 Laruelle, Peyrouse, *Globalizing Central Asia* (2015), p. 63. Malashenko, *The Fight for Influence* (2013), p. 161.

152 Lena Jonson, *Tajikistan in the New Central Asia* (2009), pp. 49–56, 65f, 79–81.

153 *Neue Zürcher Zeitung*, 8 September 2015, p. 7; 21 January 2016, p. 9.

154 Lena Jonson, *Tajikistan in the New Central Asia* (2009), pp. 85f, 115f.

155 Hiro, *Inside Central Asia* (2009), p. 387.

156 *Neue Zürcher Zeitung*, 12 July 2012, p. 7.

157 See above p. 272.

158 Malashenko, *The Fight for Influence* (2013), pp. 156f. *Neue Zürcher Zeitung*, 7 March 2011, p. 7.

159 *Techno-economic assessment study for Rogun hydroelectric construction project. Executive Summary* (The World Bank, July 2014), pp. 5–6.

160 President Rahmon de-Russified his name in 2007 by removing the Russian suffix '-ov.' Malashenko, *The Fight for Influence* (2013), p. 22.

161 *Oil & Gas Journal*, 5 June 2013. http://www.ogj.com/articles/print/volume-111/issue-5/exploration---development/tajikistan-pamir-pipedream-or-new.html

162 *The Diplomat*, 31 May and 3 June 2016. http://thediplomat.com/2016/05/line-d-of-the-central-asia-china-gas-pipeline-delayed/ http://thediplomat.com/2016/06/chatter-surrounds-turkmenistans-gas-export-plans/

163 *Neue Zürcher Zeitung*, September 8, 2015, p. 7; 10 May 2016, p. 7.

164 Officially, the country has 6.7 million inhabitants: http://www.auswaertiges-amt.de/DE/Aussenpolitik/Laender/Laenderinfos/01-Nodes_Uebersichtsseiten/Turkmenistan_node.html

165 Hiro, *Inside Central Asia* (2009), pp. 193, 199.

166 President Niyazov and his family apparently demanded bribes from international investors and corporations of up to 33 per cent of the project scope. Hiro, *Inside Central Asia* (2009), p. 206. Malashenko, *The Fight for Influence* (2013), p. 187.

167 The Ruhnama is a peculiar mixture of history, rules of conduct, and spiritual guidance.

168 Hiro, *Inside Central Asia* (2009), pp. 205, 215–17, 225. Malashenko, *The Fight for Influence* (2013), pp. 174–76, 182.

169 Malashenko, *The Fight for Influence* (2013), pp. 183f.

170 Hiro, *Inside Central Asia* (2009), pp. 192f.

171 https://www.cia.gov/library/publications/the-world-factbook/rankorder/2253rank.html . http://zentralasien.ahk.de/news/einzelansicht-nachrichten/artikel/bp-turkmenistan-hat-viertgroesste-gasreserven-der-welt/?cHash=f4f14b98bf2f12eb1cd8a21b7ac359e1

172 See above pp. 231ff.

173 Freight transport was first put into operation in 2015. *Railway Gazette* 26 June 2015. http://www.railwaygazette.com/news/policy/single-view/view/pakistan-railways-out-of-intensive-care.html

174 Hiro, *Inside Central Asia* (2009), pp. 200, 211f, 380–82, 388. http://www.railway-technology.com/projects/northsouthtransnatio/ ; http://www.railway-technology.com/projects/northsouthtransnatio/ Until 2015, the cross-border transport of goods to Pakistan remained modest.

175 Kazakhstan had already overcome the Russian pipeline monopoly with its first natural gas pipeline to China in 2006. *Astana Times*: http://astanatimes.com/2015/11/turkmenistans-pipeline-strategy-building-a-diversified-export-infrastructure/

176 Rashid, *Jihad* (2002), p. 219.

177 Hiro, *Inside Central Asia* (2009), pp. 212, 382f, 389, 408.

178 Cooley, *Great Games, Local Rules* (2012), p. 68.

179 In 2008, Gazprom procured around 45 bcm. *EurasiaNet*, 6 July 2016; http://www.eurasianet.org/node/79551

180 Cooley, *Great Games, Local Rules* (2012), pp. 66–68. There had been a severe political crisis between Turkmenistan and Russia already in 2003, when Niyazov refused to extend the agreement on dual citizenship. Those affected were given two months to either voluntarily adopt the Turkmen nationality or, in the absence of an exit visa, to be expelled and forfeit all their belongings. Olcott, *Central Asia's Second Chance* (2005), p. 162.

181 *The Diplomat*, 6 January 2016; http://thediplomat.com/2016/01/russias-gazprom-stops-buying-gas-from-turkmenistan/ *Eurasia Net*, 6 July 2016; http://www.eurasianet.org/node/79551

182 *Neue Zürcher Zeitung*, 19 January 2016, p. 28.

183 *Neue Zürcher Zeitung*, 19 January 2016, p. 28.

X. Outlook

1 Kaplan, *The Revenge of Geography* (2013), pp. 3f.

2 Hobbes, Thomas, *Leviathan* (1651; Ware: Wordsworth Classic, 2014).

3 Laruelle, Peyrouse, *Globalizing Central Asia* (2015), p. 254.

4 Laruelle, Peyrouse, *Globalizing Central Asia* (2015), pp. 250f, 255. As Laruelle and Peyrouse stress, the feasibility studies and profitability analyses by international financial institutions are not unbiased, since these institutions *want* to grant loans.

5 Laruelle, Peyrouse, *Globalizing Central Asia* (2015), pp. 255f. http://www.trans-eurasia-logistics.com/wp-content/uploads/2015/12/Railways_03-15_D_S.3637.pdf; http://www.nieuwsbladtransport.nl/Nieuws/Modaliteiten/Scheepvaart/ArticleScheepvaart/ArticleID/51256/ArticleName/IntweewekenvanChinanaarDuisburg

6 *Neue Zürcher Zeitung*, 16 February 2016, p. 15.

7 *Neue Zürcher Zeitung*, 4 April 2015, p. 6.

8 *The New York Times*, 25 August 2017, https://www.nytimes.com/2017/08/25/world/europe/russia-tanker-christophe-de-margerie.html

9 Laruelle, Peyrouse, *Globalizing Central Asia* (2015), p. 38.

10 DAWN, 20 December 2015, http://www.dawn.com/news/1227664/new-railway-tracks-planned-under-cpec-report. *Neue Zürcher Zeitung*, 23 July 2016, p. 28.

11 *The Diplomat*, 6 June 2015, 2 September 2016, http://thediplomat.com/2015/06/china-qatar-and-rmb-internationalization/, http://thediplomat.com/2016/09/china-and-saudi-arabia-a-new-alliance/

12 The new land Silk Road is primarily conceived as a railway. *Xinhua*, 28 March 2015, http://news.xinhuanet.com/english/2015-03/28/c_134105435.htm. See also http://www.xinhuanet.com/silkroad/english/index.htm

13 *Xinhua*, 24 June 2016; http://news.xinhuanet.com/english/2016-06/24/c_135464233.htm

14 The confrontation between the Burmese armed forces and the Muslim Rohingyas since October 2016 in south-west Burma could lead to a radicalisation of the latter which may endanger the China-sponsored project of constructing a deep-sea harbour at Kyaukphyu in the Rakhine State, Myanmar. The project is of strategic importance for China since it includes the construction of an oil and of a gas pipeline to Kunming, China, thus avoiding the vulnerable Straits of Malacca.

15 *Neue Zürcher Zeitung*, 3 January 2016, p. 4; http://www.nzz.ch/international/asien-und-pazifik/die-rolle-der-taliban-in-afghanistan-die-rueckkehr-des-grossen-spiels-ld.137678

16 The airdrop of a mega bomb (Massive Ordnance Air Blast) ordered by President Trump on 13 April 2017, which destroyed a tunnel complex of the IS in Nangarhar, does not indicate a new American security strategy for Afghanistan.

Captions

1 Clements R. Markham (editor and translator), *Narrative of the Embassy of Ruy Gonzalez de Clavijo to the Court of Timour at Samarcand, A.D. 1403–06* (London: Hakluyt Society, 1859), p. 124.

2 Vaughan, 'Dekorative Künste [Indien Sultanate und Moghuln]' (2000), pp. 475f.

3 Richards, *The Mughal Empire* (2005), p. 13.

4 Vaughan, 'Dekorative Künste [Indien Sultanate und Moghuln]' (2000), pp. 490–93.

5 Charleux, *Temples et monastères de Mongolie-Intérieure* (2006), p. 65. Georg Huth, *Die Inschriften von Tsaghan Baisin. Tibetisch-mongolischer Text* (Leipzig: F.A. Brockhaus, 1894), pp. 20–23, 44, 51, 62.

6 Marylin M. Rhie, Robert F. Thurman, *Wisdom and Compassion. The Sacred Art of Tibet* (San Francisco: Asian Art Museum, 1991), pp. 68, 144f, 267.

7 Müller und Wenzel (eds), *Dschingis Khan und seine Erben* (2005), pp. 348–54.

8 Michael Henss *The Cultural Monuments of Tibet.*

The Central Regions (Munich: Prestel, 2014), vol. I, p. 70.

9 Charleux, *Temples et monastères de Mongolie-Intérieure* (2006), p. 94. Pyotr K. Kozlov, *Mongolei, Amdo und die tote Stadt Chara-Choto. Mit einem Geleitwort von Dr. Sven Hedin* (Berlin: Neufeld & Henius, 1925), pp. 83f

10 Renato Sala and Jean-Marc Deom, *Petroglyphs of South Kazakhstan* (Almaty: Laboratory of Geoarchaeology), pp. 57, 109f.

11 Henss, *The Cultural Monuments of Tibet* (Munich: Prestel, 2014), vol. I, pp. 107, 110.

12 Henss, 'The Bodhisattva-Emperor' (2001), vol. XLVII, No. 3, pp. 3, 5.

13 See: Baumer, *The History of Central Asia,* vol. 3 (2016), fig. 75.

14 Vámbéry, *Voyages d'un faux derviche* (1865), pp. 133f.

15 Carrère, *Islam and the Russian Empire* (2009), p. 38.

16 Leaflet and copyright of the Foundation Phototheca Afghanica, Bubendorf, Switzerland. See also: Ella K. Maillart, *The Cruel Way* (1947; London: Virago Press, 1986), pp. 127f. Rudolf Stuckert, *Erinnerungen an Afghanistan 1940–1946. Aus dem Tagebuch eines Schweizer Architekten* (Liestal: Foundation Bibliotheca Afghanica, 1994), p. 67.

17 Omar Khan, *From Kashmir to Kabul: the photographs of John Burke and William Baker, 1860–1900* (Munich; New York: Prestel, 2002), p. 120.

18 Khan, *From Kashmir to Kabul* (2002), p. 131.

19 Younghusband, *The Heart of a Continent* (1896), pp. 157, 206.

20 Perceval Landon, *Lhasa. An account of the country and people of Central Tibet and of the progress of the mission sent there by the English government in the years 1903–04* (London: Hurst and Blackett, 1905), vol. I, pp. 256–68, vol. II, pp. 84–90.

21 Leaflet and copyright of the Foundation Phototheca Afghanica, Bubendorf, Switzerland.

22 Leaflet Harvard-Yenching Library.

23 https://commons.wikimedia.org/wiki/File:Reagan_sitting_with_people_from_the_Afghanistan-Pakistan_region_in_February_1983.jpg ; https://www.quora.com/Who-is-the-woman-sitting-with-Reagan-and-the-Mujahideen-in-this-picture

24 Helmut R. Schulze, *Afghanistan. Reisen hinter den Horizont* (Heidelberg: Edition HRS, 2008), p. 110.

25 Frankfurter Allgemeine Zeitung from 28 July 2015. http://www.faz.net/aktuell/feuilleton/debatten/luege-ueber-kriegsdenkmaeler-in-russland-empoert-russen-13720292.html

Bibliography

Abbas, Hassan, *The Taliban Revival. Violence and Extremism on the Pakistan-Afghanistan Frontier* (New Haven: Yale University Press, 2014).

Abbott, James, *Narrative of a Journey from Heraut to Khiva, Moscow and St. Petersburgh, during the late Russian invasion of Khiva; with some account of the Court of Khiva and the Kingdom of Khaurism* (London: Allen & Co, 1843).

Abdullaev, Ravshan, Khotamov, Namoz and Kenensariev, Tashmanbet, 'Colonial Rule and Indigenous Responses, 1860–1917', in: S. Frederick Starr (ed.), *Ferghana Valley. The Heart of Central Asia* (Armonk: M.E. Sharpe, 2011), pp. 69–93.

Abdurakhimova, N.A., 'Tsarist Russia and Central Asia', in: *History of Civilizations of Central Asia*, vol. VI, eds Chahryar Adle, Madhavan K. Palat and Anara Tabyshalieva (Paris: Unesco Publishing, 2005), pp. 125–52.

Abliyazov, Kamil Alimovich, *Istoricheskaiya sutba tatar* (Saratov: Nauchnaiya kniga, 2012).

Abuseitova, Meruert, 'The spread of Islam in Kazakhstan from the fifteenth to the eighteenth century', in: Gian Luca Bonora, Niccolo Pianciola and Paolo Sartori (eds), *Kazakhstan: Religions and Society in the History of Central Asia* (Turin: U. Allemandi, 2009), pp. 125–36.

Afghanistan Institute and *Phototheca Afghanica*, Bubendorf, Switzerland. http://www.afghanistan-institut.ch/

Aitken, Jonathan, *Nazarbayev and the Making of Kazakhstan* (London: Continuum, 2010).

Akasoy, Anna, Burnett, Charles and Yoeli-Tlalim, Ronit (eds), *Islam and Tibet: Interactions along the Musk Routes* (Farnham: Ashgate, 2011).

Albrecht, Max von, *Russisch Central-Asien. Reisebilder aus Transkaspien, Buchara und Turkestan* (Hamburg: Druckerei A.-G., 1896).

Alder, Garry, *British India's Northern Frontier 1865–95* (Longmans, Green & Co., 1963).

—*Beyond Bokhara. The Life of William Moorcroft. Asian Explorer and Pioneer Veterinary Surgeon, 1767–1825* (London: Century Publishing, 1985).

Alexander of Malabar, Friar, 'The story of the sack of Ispahan by the Afghans in 1722', 1724, translated by Sir Arnold Wilson, *Royal Central Asian Journal*, vol. XXIII, No. 4, October 1936 (London: Royal Central Asian Society, 1936), pp. 643–53.

Alfieri, Bianca Maria, *Islamic Architecture of the Indian Subcontinent* (London: Laurence King, 2000).

Ali, M. Athar, 'The Mughal empire and its successors', in: *History of Civilizations of Central Asia*, vol. V, eds Chahryar Adle, Irfan Habib and Karl M. Baipakov (Paris: Unesco Publishing, 2003), pp. 299–323.

Ali, S. Mahmud, *US-China Cold War Collaboration 1971–1989* (Oxon: Routledge, 2005).

Alimova, D.A. and Golovanov, A.A., 'The evolution of nation-states: Uzbekistan', in: *History of Civilizations of Central Asia,* vol. V, eds Chahryar Adle, Irfan Habib and Karl M. Baipakov (Paris: Unesco Publishing, 2003), pp. 225–46.

Allen, Charles, *Duel in the Snows. The true story of the Younghusband Mission to Lhasa* (London: John Murray, 2004).

Allworth, Edward (ed.), *130 Years of Russian Dominance, a Historical Overview* (Durham: Duke University Press, 1994).

Alphen, Jan van (ed.), *Schamanismus in Tuva*, exhib. cat. Museum für Völkerkunde Wien (Wien: Museum für Völkerkunde, 1998).

Altan Tobči, trans. and ed. Charles Bawden (Wiesbaden: Harrassowitz, 1955).

Amini, Iradj, *Napoleon and Persia: Franco-Persian Relations under the First Empire* (Richmond: Curzon, 1999).

Amirpur, Katajun, *Schia gegen Sunna. Sunna gegen Schia* (Zurich: Vontobel-Stiftung, 2013).

Amitai, Reuven and Biran, Michal (eds), *Mongols, Turks and Others: Eurasian Nomads and the Sedentary World* (Leiden: Brill, 2005).

Amitai-Preiss, Reuven and Morgan, David O. (eds), *The Mongol Empire and Its Legacy* (Leiden: Brill, 1999).

André, Paul (ed.), *The Art of Central Asia* (Bournemouth: Parkstone Press, 1996).

Andreyev, Alexandre (ed.), *Tibet in the Earliest Photographs by Russian Travellers, 1900–01* (New Delhi: Studio Orientalica, 2013).

Annanepesov, M., 'The Khanate of Khiva (Khwarazm)', in: *History of Civilizations of Central Asia*, vol. V, eds Chahryar Adle, Irfan Habib and Karl M. Baipakov (Paris: Unesco Publishing, 2003), pp. 63–71.

—'Relations between the Khanates and with other powers', in: *History of Civilizations of Central Asia*, vol. V, eds Chahryar Adle, Irfan Habib and Karl M. Baipakov (Paris: Unesco Publishing, 2003), pp. 82–88.

Anonymous, *Der Persianische Cromwel oder Leben und Thaten des Miri-Ways, Fürsten von Candahar und Protectoris von Persien* (no publisher, 1723).

Ashrafyan, K.Z., 'Central Asia under Timur from 1370 to the early fifteenth century', in: M.S. Asimov and C.E. Bosworth (eds), *History of Civilizations of Central Asia*, vol. IV, part 1 (Paris: Unesco Publishing, 1998), pp. 319–45.

Atchinson, J.E.T., *Notes on the Products of Western Afghanistan and of North-Eastern Persia* (Edinburgh: Neil, 1890).

Atkin, Muriel, *Russia and Iran, 1780–1828* (Minneapolis: University of Minnesota Press, 1980).

Atkinson, James, *Sketches in Afghanistan* (London: Graves, 1842).

Atkinson, Thomas Witlam, *Oriental and western Siberia: a narrative of seven years' exploration and adventures in Siberia, Mongolia, the Kirghis Steppes,*

Chinese Tartary, and a part of Central Asia (New York: Harper & Bros., 1858).

Atwan, Abdel Bari, *Islamic State. The Digital Caliphate* (London: Saqi, 2015).

Atwood, Christopher, *Encyclopedia of Mongolia and the Mongol Empire* (New York: Facts on File, 2004).

Atwood, Rodney, *The March to Kandahar. Roberts in Afghanistan* (Barnsley: Pen & Sword, 2008).

Audouin-Dubreuil, Ariane, *Expedition Seidenstraße* (München: Frederking & Thaler, 2003).

Avery, Peter, 'Nadir Shah and the Afsharid Legacy', in: Peter Avery, Gavin Hambly and Charles Melville (eds), *The Cambridge History of Iran: From Nadir Shah to the Islamic Republic*, vol. 7 (Cambridge: Cambridge University Press, 1991), pp. 3–62.

Axworthy, Michael, *The Sword of Persia. Nader Shah, from Tribal Warrior to Conquering Tyrant* (London: I.B.Tauris, 2006).

Azeem, Ibrahim, *U.S. Aid to Pakistan. – U.S. Taxpayers Have Funded Pakistani Corruption* (Harvard: Belfer Center for Science and International Affairs, Harvard University, July 2009).

Baabar, B., alias Bat-Edeniin Batbayar, *History of Mongolia* (Cambridge: The White Horse Press, 1999).

Bababekov, H.N., 'Fergana and the Khanate of Kokand', in: *History of Civilizations of Central Asia*, vol. V, eds Chahryar Adle, Irfan Habib and Karl M. Baipakov (Paris: Unesco Publishing, 2003), pp. 71–81.

Baber, Zehir-ed-Din Muhammed, *Memoirs of Zehir-ed-Din Muhammed Baber,* trans. John Leyden and William Erskine (London: Longman, Rees, Orme, Brown and Green, 1826).

Bailey, Frederick Marshman, 'In Russian Turkestan under the Bolsheviks', *Journal of the The Royal Central Asia Society*, vol. VIII, No. 1, 1921 (London: Royal Central Asian Society, 1921), pp. 49–69.

—*Mission to Tashkent* (London: Jonathan Cape, 1946).

Bailey, Jonathan, Iron, Richard and Strachan, Hew (eds), *British Generals in Blair's Wars* (Farnham: Ashgate, 2013).

Baipakov, Karl, *Drevnjaja i Srednevekovaja Urbanizatsija Kasachstana*, 3 vols (Almaty: Institut arkheologii MON RK; Kazakhstanskoe arkheologicheskoe obshchestvo, 2012, 2013, 2014).

Baipakov, Karl and Kumekov, B.E., 'The Kazakhs', in: Chahryar Adle, Irfan Habib and Karl M. Baipakov (eds), *History of Civilizations of Central Asia,* vol. V (Paris: Unesco Publishing, 2003), pp. 89–108.

Baipakov, Karl and Smagulov, E.A., *The Medieval Town Sauran* (Almaty: Credo, 2005).

Baipakov, Karl, Smagulov, E.A. and Aklhatov, G.A., *The Medieval Jaiyk Site* (Almaty: Credo, 2005).

Bakshi, S.R. and Sharma, S.K. (eds), *Babar. The Great Moghul* (New Delhi: Deep & Deep Publications, 2000).

Balint, Csanad, *Die Archäologie der Steppe* (Vienna: Böhlau, 1989).

Ball, Warwick, 'The archaeology of Afghanistan: a reassessment and stock-taking', in: Juliette van Krieken-Pieters (ed.), *Art and Archaeology of Afghanistan: Its Fall and Survival* (Leiden/Boston: Brill, 2006), pp. 39–48.

—*The Monuments of Afghanistan: History, Archaeology and Architecture* (London: I.B.Tauris, 2008).

Balland D., 'Ashraf Gilzai, the Afghan chief who rules as Shah over part of Iran from 1137/1725 to 1142/1729', in: *Encyclopaedia Iranica*, 2011. http://www.iranicaonline.org/articles/asraf-gilzay-the-afghan-chief-who-ruled-as-shah-over-part-of-iran-from-1137-1725-to-1142-1729

Balloni, Nicola Franco and Kukovalska, Nelia (eds), *The Genoese in Crimea: A Historical Guide* (Kiev: Gorobez, 2009).

Barfield, Thomas J., *The Perilous Frontier: Nomadic Empires and China, 221 BC to AD 1757* (Cambridge, MA/Oxford: Blackwell, 1992).

—*Afghanistan. A cultural and political history* (Princeton: Princeton University Press, 2010).

Barger, Evert, 'Exploration of Ancient Sites in Northern Afghanistan', *The Geographical Journal*, vol. XCIII, No. 5, May 1939 (London: RGS, 1939), pp. 377–98.

—'Some Problems of Central Asian Exploration', *The Geographical Journal*, vol. CIII, Nos 1, 2, January–February 1944 (London: RGS, 1944), pp. 1–17.

Barthold, V.V., *Die geographische und historische Erforschung des Orients mit besonderer Berücksichtigung der russischen Arbeiten* (Leipzig: Otto Wigand, 1913).

—*12 Vorlesungen über die Geschichte der Türken Mittelasiens* (Berlin: Deutsche Gesellschaft für Islamkunde, 1935).

Barthoux, Jules, *The Hadda Excavations*. vols. I and III (1930, 1933) (Reprint Bangkok: SDI Publications, 2001).

Basiner, Theodor Friedrich Julius, 'Reise durch die Kirgisensteppe nach Chiwa', *Beiträge zur Kenntnis des Russischen Reiches und der angrenzenden Länder Asiens*, Fünfzehntes Bänchen (St Petersburg: Kaiserliche Akademie der Wissenschaften, 1848).

Batbayar, Ts., 'The Mongolian People's Revolution of 1921 and the Mongolian People's Republic (1924–46)', in: Chahryar Adle, Irfan Habib and Karl M.

Baipakov (eds), *History of Civilizations of Central Asia,* vol. V (Paris: Unesco Publishing, 2003), pp. 363–71.

Batsaikhan, Emergent Ookhnoi, *Bogdo Jebtsundamba Khutuktu, The Last King of Mongolia. Mongolia's National Revolution of 1911* (Ulaan Baatar: Institute of International Studies, Academy of Sciences, Mongolia, 2009).

Baud, Aymon, Forêt, Philippe and Gorshenina, Svetlana, *La Haute-Asie telle qu'ils l'ont vue: Explorateurs et scientifiques de 1820 à 1940* (Geneva: Olizane, 2003).

Baumer, Christoph, *Traces in the Desert: Journeys of Discovery across Central Asia* (London: I.B.Tauris, 2008).

—*China's Holy Mountain: An Illustrated Journey into the Heart of Buddhism* (London: I.B.Tauris, 2011).

—*The History of Central Asia: The Age of the Steppe Warriors*, vol. 1 of 4 (London: I.B.Tauris, 2012).

—*The History of Central Asia: The Age of the Silk Roads*, vol. 2 of 4 (London: I.B.Tauris, 2014).

—*The History of Central Asia: The Age of Islam and the Mongols,* vol. 3 of 4 (London: I.B.Tauris, 2016).

—*The Church of the East. An illustrated history of Assyrian Christianity* (London: IB Tauris, 2nd edition 2016).

Baumer, Christoph and Weber, Therese, *Eastern Tibet: Bridging Tibet and China* (Bangkok: Orchid Press, 2005).

Bawden, Charles R., *The Modern History of Mongolia* (London: Weidenfeld and Nicolson, 1968).

Beaulieu, Lord Montagu of, 'The North-West Frontier of India', *Journal of the The Royal Central Asia Society*, vol. XI, No. 2, 1924 (London: Royal Central Asian Society, 1924), pp. 136–46.

Becker, Seymour, *Russia's Protectorates in Central Asia. Bukhara and Khiva, 1865–1924* (London: RoutledgeCurzon, 2004).

Bell, Charles, *Tibet, Past and Present* (1924, Reprint New Delhi: Asian Educational Services, 1992).

Bell, John of Antermony, *Travels from St. Petersburg in Russia, to diverse parts of Asia in two volumes* (Glasgow: Printed for the author by Robert and Andrew Foulis printers to the University 1763).

Bell-Fialkoff, Andrew (ed.), *The Role of Migration in the History of the Eurasian Steppe: Sedentary Civilization vs. 'Barbarian' and Nomad* (Basingstoke: Macmillan, 2000).

Bellér-Hann, Ildikó, *Community Matters in Xinjiang, 1880–1949: towards a historical anthropology of the Uyghur* (Leiden: Brill, 2008).

Belokrenitsky, Vyacheslav, 'Islamic Radicalism in Central Asia: The Influence of Pakistan in Afghanistan', in: Boris Rumer (ed.), *Central Asia: At the End of the Transition* (Armonk: M.E. Sharpe, 2005), pp. 152–94.

Bemmann, Jan, Ahrens, B., Grützner, C., Klinger, R., Klitzsch, N., Lehmann, F., Linzen, S., Munkhbayar, L., Nomguunsuren, G., Oczipka, M., Piezonka, H., Schütt, B. and Saran, S. (eds), 'Geoarchaeology in the steppe: first results of the multidisciplinary Mongolian-German project in the Orkhon Valley, Central Mongolia', *Studia Archaeologica Instituti Archaeologici Academiae Scientiarum Mongolicae* (Ulaan Baatar) 30 (2011), fasc. 5, pp. 69–97.

Beneveni, Florio, *Poslannik Petra I na Vostoke: posol'stvo Florio Beneveni v Persiû i Buharu v 1718–1725 godach* (Moskva: Akademija nauk SSSR. Institut vostokovedenija, 1986).

Benjamin, Craig and Lieu, Samuel (eds), *Walls and Frontiers in Inner-Asian History*, Silk Road Studies VI (Turnhout: Brepols, 2002).

Bennison, A.K. and Gascoigne, A.L. (eds), *Cities in the Pre-modern Islamic World: The Urban Impact of Religion, State and Society* (London: SOAS/Routledge, 2007).

Bergholz, Fred W., *The Partition of the Steppe. The Struggle of the Russians, Manchus, and the Zungar Mongols for Empire in Central Asia, 1619–1758* (New York: Peter Lang, 1993).

Bergmann, Benjamin, *Schicksale des Persers Wassilij Michailow unter den Kalmüken, Kirgisen und Chiwensern* (Riga: Hartmann'sche Buchhandlung, 1804).

—*Nomadische Streifereien unter den Kalmücken in den Jahren 1802 und 1803*, 4 vols (Riga: Hartmann'sche Buchhandlung, 1804–5).

Berinstain, Valérie, *Mughal India. Spendours of the Peacock Throne* (London: Thames & Hudson, 1998).

Bernier, François, *Travels in the Mogul Empire 1656–1668*. A revised and improved edition based upon Irving Brock's translation by Archibald Constable (1891; Reprint New Delhi: Asian Educational Services, 1996).

Berry, Scott, *Monks, Spies and a Soldier of Fortune. The Japanese in Tibet* (London: Athlone Press, 1995).

Beurmann, Eduard, *Über Afghanistan* (Darmstadt: Carl Wilhelm Leske, 1844).

Bianchini, Marie-Claude (ed.), *Afghanistan: une histoire millénaire* (Paris: Réunion des musées nationaux, 2002).

Bishop, George, *In Search of Cathay. The Travels of Bento de Goes, S.J. (1562–1607)* (Anand: Gujarat Sahitya Prakash, 1998).

Blacker, L.V.S., *On Secret Patrol in High Asia* (London: John Murray, 1922).

—'Wars and travels in Turkistan, 1918–1919–1920', *Journal of the The Royal Central Asia Society*, vol. IX, No. 1, 1922 (London: Royal Central Asian Society, 1922), pp. 4–20.

Blair, Sheila and Bloom, Jonathan M., *The Art and Architecture of Islam 1250–1800* (New Haven: Yale University Press, 1995).

Blank, Stephen, *Energy, Economics, and Security in Central Asia: Russia and Its Rivals* (Carlisle Barracks: Strategic Sudies Institute, 1995).

Blankennagel, Major, 'Bemerkungen über eine in den Jahren 1793 und 1794 ausgeführte Reise nach Chiwa', in: *Archiv für wissenschaftliche Kunde von Rußland*, vol. 18, 1859, pp. 351–83 (Berlin: Reimer, 1859).

Bloom, Jonathan and Blair, Sheila (eds), *The Grove Encyclopedia of Islamic Art and Architecture*, 3 vols (Oxford: Oxford University Press, 2009).

Blouet, Brian W., 'Mackinder: Imperialism, the Empire of India and Central Asia', in: Nick Megoran and Sevara Sharapova (eds), *Central Asia in International Relations. The Legacies of Halford Mackinder* (London: Hurst & Co., 2013), pp. 39–68.

Bluth, Christoph, *US Foreign Policy in the Caucasus and Central Asia. Politics, Energy and Security* (London: I.B.Tauris, 2014).

Bonora, Gian Luca, Pianciola, Niccolo and Sartori, Paolo (eds), *Kazakhstan: Religions and Society in the History of Central Eurasia* (Turin: Umberto Allemandi, 2009).

Bonvalot, Gabriel, *Du Caucase aux Indes à travers le Pamir* (Paris: Plon, 1889).

Boobbyer, Philip, *The Stalin Era* (London: Routledge, 2000).

Bormanshinov, Arash, 'A Secret Kalmyk Mission to Tibet in 1904', *Central Asiatic Journal*, vol. XXXVI, no. 3–4, 1949 (Reprint Wiesbaden: Harrassowitz, 1992), pp. 161–87.

— 'The Kalmyks in America', *Royal Central Asian Journal*, vol. L, No. 3, June 1963 (London: Royal Central Asian Society, 1963), pp. 149–51.

Borodina, Iraidna, *Central Asia. Gems of 9th–19th Century Architecture* (Moscow: Olanety, 1987).

Bornet, Philippe and Gorshenina, Svetlana (eds), *L'orientalisme des marges: éclairages à partir de l'Inde et de la Russie* (Lausanne: Université de Lausanne, 2014).

Bosworth, C.E. (ed.), *A Medieval History of Iran, Afghanistan and Central Asia* (London: Variorum Reprints, 1977).

—*The Islamic Dynasties* (Edinburgh: Edinburgh University Press, 1980).

Boulger, Demetrius Charles, *The Life of Yakoonb Beg; Athalik Ghazi, and baudelet; Ameer of Kashgar* (London: W.H. Allen, 1878).

Bouillane, Henry de Bouillane de Lacoste, *Autour de l'Afghanistan (Aux frontiers interdites)* (Paris: Hachette, 1908).

Braithwaite, Sir Rodric, 'The Russians in Afghanistan', *Asian Affairs*, vol. XLII, No. II, July 2011 (London: Royal Society for Asian Affairs, 2011), pp. 213–29.

Brauen, Martin (ed.), *Die Dalai Lamas*, exhib. cat. Völkerkundemuseum Zürich (Stuttgart: Arnoldsche, 2005).

Bregel, Yuri, *An Historical Atlas of Central Asia* (Leiden/Boston: Brill, 2003).

—'Uzbeks, Qazaqs and Turkmens', in: Nicola Di Cosmo, Allen J. Frank and Peter B. Golden (eds), *The Cambridge History of Inner Asia: The Chinggisid Age* (Cambridge: Cambridge University Press, 2009), pp. 221–36.

—'The new Uzbek states: Bukhara, Khiva and Kokand: c. 1750–1886', in: Nicola Di Cosmo, Allen J. Frank and Peter B. Golden (eds), *The Cambridge History of Inner Asia: The Chinggisid Age* (Cambridge: Cambridge University Press, 2009), pp. 392–411.

—'The Abu'l-Khayrids', in: *Encyclopaedia Iranica* (20 February 2009, updated 21 July 2011). http://www.iranicaonline.org/articles/abul-khayrids-dynasty

Brenton, Sir Tony, 'Russia and China: An Axis of Insecurity', *Asian Affairs*, vol. XLIV, No. II, July 2013 (London: Royal Society for Asian Affairs, 2011), pp. 231–49.

Bretschneider, Emil, *Mediaeval Researches from Eastern Asiatic Sources: Fragments towards the Knowledge of the Geography and History of Central and Western Asia from the 13th to the 17th Century*, 2 vols (London: Kegan Paul, Trench, Trübner & Co., 1888).

Bubnova, M.A., *Arxeologitcheskya karta Tadjikistana. Gorno-Badaxshanckaya Avtonomnaya Oblast. Zapadnyi Pamir* (Dushanbe: UCA, 2007).

Bugajski, Janusz and Assenova, Margarita, *Eurasian Disunion. Russia's vulnerable flanks* (Washington: Jamestown Foundation, 2016).

Bulag, Uradyn E., *The Mongols at China's Edge. History and the Politics of National Unity* (Lanham: Rowman & Littlefield, 2002).

Burnaby, Fred, *A Ride to Khiva* (1877; Reprint London: Century Publishing, 1983).

Burnes, Alexander, *Travels into Bokhara; containing the Narrative of a voyage on the Indus from the sea to Lahore, with presents from the King of Great Britain; and an account of a journey from India to Cabool, Tartary and Persia. Performed by order of the Supreme Government of India, in the years of 1831, 32, and 33*; 3 vols (London: John Murray 1835).

—*Kabul. Schilderung einer Reise nach dieser Stadt und Aufenthaltes dasselbst, in den Jahren 1836, 1837 und 1838* (1842; German translation Leipzig: T.O. Weigel, 1843).

—*Cabool: Personal narrative of a journey to, and residence in that city, in the years 1836, 7, and 8* (1843, Print on demand, Champaign: Book Jungle, 2016).

Cable, Mildred and French, Francesca, *The Gobi Desert* (1942; London: Virago Press, 1984).

Çağatay, Ergun and Kuban, Dogan (eds), *The Turkic Speaking Peoples: 2,000 Years of Art and Culture from Inner Asia to the Balkans* (Munich/New York: Prestel, 2006).

The Cambridge History of China, Vol. 7. The Ming Dynasty, 1368–1644, Part I, eds Denis Twitchett and John K. Fairbank (Cambridge: Cambridge University Press, 1988).

The Cambridge History of China, Vol. 9. Part One: The Ch'ing Empire to 1800, ed. Williard J. Peterson (Cambridge: Cambridge University Press, 2002).

The Cambridge History of Iran: The Timurid and Safavid Periods, vol. 6, eds Peter Jackson and Laurence Lockhart (Cambridge: Cambridge University Press, 1986).

The Cambridge History of Iran: From Nadir Shah to the Islamic Republic, vol. 7, eds Peter Avery, Gavin Hambly and Charles Melville (Cambridge: Cambridge University Press, 1991).

Cameron, Nigel, *Barbarians and Mandarins. Thirteen Centuries of Western Travellers in China* (Hong Kong: Oxford University Press, 1989).

Carrère d'Encausse, Hélène, *Islam and the Russian Empire. Reform and Revolution in Central Asia* (1966; English translation: London, I.B.Tauris, 2009).

—'Systematic Conquest, 1865–1994', in: Edward Allsworth (ed.), *130 Years of Russian Dominance, a Historical Overview* (Durham: Duke University Press, 1994), pp. 131–50.

—'Organizing and Colonizing the Conquered Territories', in: Edward Allsworth (ed.), *130 Years of Russian Dominance, a Historical Overview* (Durham: Duke University Press, 1994), pp. 151–71.

—'The Stirring of National Feeling', in: Edward Allsworth (ed.), *130 Years of Russian Dominance, a Historical Overview* (Durham: Duke University Press, 1994), pp. 172–88.

—'The Fall of the Czarist Empire', in: Edward Allsworth (ed.), *130 Years of Russian Dominance, a Historical Overview* (Durham: Duke University Press, 1994), pp. 207–23.

—'Civil War and New Governments', in: Edward Allsworth (ed.), *130 Years of Russian Dominance, a Historical Overview* (Durham: Duke University Press, 1994), pp. 224–53.

—The National Republics Lose Their Independence', Edward Allsworth (ed.), *130 Years of Russian Dominance, a Historical Overview* (Durham: Duke University Press, 1994), pp. 254–65.

Carruthers, Douglas, *Unknown Mongolia; a record of travel and exploration in north-west Mongolia and Dzungaria* (1913; Reprint New Delhi, 1994).

Castagné, Joseph, *Les monuments funéraires de la steppe des Kirghizes* (Orenburg: Typografia Turgaïskavo, 1911).

Castle, John, 'Journal von der Ao 1736 aus Orenburg zu dem Abul Geier Chan der Kirgis-Cavsack Tartarischen Horda aus freyem Willen und bloß zu dem Besten des russischen Reiches unternommenen höchst nöthigen und zwar gefährlichen doch glücklich vollbrachten Reise', in: *Materialien zu der russischen Geschichte seit dem Tode Kaisers Peters des Großen. Zweiter Theil, 1730–1741* (Riga: Johann Friedrich Hartknoch, 1784).

Centlives-Demont, Micheline, *Afghanistan. Identity, Society and Politics since 1980* (London: I.B.Tauris, 2015).

Chaliand, Gérard, *Nomadic Empires: From Mongolia to the Danube* (New Brunswick: Transaction Publishers, 2004).

Charleux, Isabelle, *Temples et monastères de Mongolie-Intérieure* (Paris: Institut national d'histoire de l'art, 2006).

Chase, Kenneth, *Firearms: A Global History to 1700* (Cambridge: Cambridge University Press, 2003).

Chavanne, Josef, *Afghanistan. Land und Leute mit Rücksicht auf den Englisch-Afghanischen Krieg* (Wien: A. Hartleben's Verlag, 1879).

Cherniaev, G.M., 'Memorandum of G.M. Cherniaev sent to Field Marshal Prince Bariatinskii in March 1869', in: Martin Ewans (ed.), *Great Power Rivalry in Central Asia, 1842–1880, vol. I: Documents* (London: Routledge, 2006), pp. 247–52.

Chmelnizkij, Sergey, 'Architektur [der Shaibaniden und Khanfürstentümer]', in: Markus Hattstein and Peter Delius (eds), *Islam: Kunst und Architekur* (Cologne: Könemann, 2000), pp. 436–47.

Christian, David, 'State formation in the Inner Eurasian steppes', in: David Christian and Craig Benjamin (eds), *Worlds of the Silk Roads: Ancient and Modern*, Silk Road Studies II (Turnhout: Brepols, 1998), pp. 51–76.

Christian, David and Benjamin, Craig (eds), *Worlds of the Silk Roads: Ancient and Modern*, Silk Road Studies II (Turnhout: Brepols, 1998).

—*Realms of the Silk Roads: Ancient and Modern*, Silk Road Studies IV (Turnhout: Brepols, 2000).

—*Walls and Frontiers in Inner-Asian History*, Silk Road Studies VI (Turnhout: Brepols, 2002).

Cimorelli, Dario (ed.), *Trésors du Bouddhisme au pays de Gengis Khan*, exhib. cat. Musée Guimet (Paris: Silvana Editoriale, 2009).

Clinch, Elizabeth and Nicholas, *Through a Land of Extremes. The Littledales of Central Asia* (Stroud: Sutton Publishing, 2008).

Crosby, Oscar Terry, *Tibet and Turkestan* (New York: G.P. Putnam's sons, 1905).

Chuvin, Pierre (ed.), *Les arts de l'Asie Centrale* (Paris: Citadelles & Mazenod, 1999).

Cobbold, Ralph P., *Innermost Asia. Travel & Sport in the Pamirs* (London: William Heinemann, 1900).

Coene, Frederik, *The Caucasus* (London: Routledge, 2010).

Cohn-Wiener, Ernst, *Turan. Islamische Baukunst in Mittelasien* (Berlin: Ernst Wasmuth, 1930).

Colegrave, Bill, *Halfway House to Heaven. Unravelling the mystery of the majestic River Oxus* (London: Bene Factum Publishing, 2010).

Coll, Steve, *Ghost Wars. The Secret History of the CIA, Afghanistan and Bin Laden, from the Soviet Invasion to September 10, 2001* (London: Penguin, 2004).

Collins, Joseph J., *Understanding War in Afghanistan* (Washington DC: National Defense University Press, 2011).

Compareti, Matteo, Raffetta, Paola and Scarcia, Gianroberto (eds), *Ērān ud Anērān: Studies Presented to Boris Il'i Maršak on the Occasion of His 70th Birthday*, 2003. http://www.transoxiana.org/Eran/

Conolly, Arthur, *Journey to the north of India, overland from England, through Russia, Persia and Affghaunistaun:* in two volumes (1834; Reprint in the US, no date, *ca.* 2015).

Consten, Hermann, *Weidenplätze der Mongolen. Im Reiche der Chalcha*, 2 vols (Berlin: Reimer, 1919).

Cooley, Alexander, *Great Games, Local Rules. The New Great Power Contest in Central Asia* (Oxford: Oxford University Press, 2012).

Corfield, Justin J., *The History of Kalmykia: from ancient times to Kirsan Ilyumzhinov and Aleksey Orlov* (Victoria: Gentext Publications, 2015).

Crossley, Pamela Kyle, 'The Conquest Elite of the Ch'ing Empire', in: Williard J. Peterson (ed.), *The Cambridge History of China, Vol. 9. Part One: The Ch'ing Empire to 1800* (Cambridge: Cambridge University Press, 2002), pp. 310–59.

Curzon, George N., *Russia in Central Asia in 1889 and the Anglo-Russian Question* (London: Longmans, Green, and Co., 1889).

—*Persia and the Persian Question*, 2 vols (London: Longmans, Green and Co., 1892).

—'The Pamirs and the source of the Oxus', revised and reprinted from *The Geographical Journal*, July–Sept. 1896 (London: The Royal Geographical Society, 1898).

Dahl, Erik J., 'Naval Innovation. From Coal to Oil' (Washington DC: National Defense University Press, Joint Force Quarterly JFQ, Winter 2000–01), pp. 50–56. http://www.dtic.mil/dtic/tr/fulltext/u2/a524799.pdf

Dale, Stephen, 'The later Timurids', in: Nicola Di Cosmo, Allen J. Frank and Peter B. Golden (eds), *The Cambridge History of Inner Asia: The Chinggisid Age* (Cambridge: Cambridge University Press, 2009), pp. 199–217.

Dalrymple, William, *Return of a King. The Battle for Afghanistan, 1839–42* (New York: Alfred A. Knopf, 2013).

Dam, Bette, *A Man and a Motor Cycle. How Hamid Karzai came to Power* (Utrecht: Ipso facto, 2014).

Davidovich, E.A., 'Monetary policy and currency circulation under the Shaybanid and the Janid (Astarkhanid) dynasties', in: Chahryar Adle, Irfan Habib and Karl M. Baipakov (eds), *History of Civilizations of Central Asia*, vol. V (Paris: Unesco Publishing, 2003), pp. 427–43.

Davies, Brian L., *Warfare, State and Society on the Black Sea Steppe, 1500–1700* (London: Routledge, 2007).

De Goeje, M.J., *Das alte Bett des Oxus, Amû-Darja* (Leiden: Brill, 1875).

Deasy, Henry H.P., *In Tibet and Chinese Turkestan. Being the record of three years' exploration* (London: T. Fisher Unwin, 1901).

Develin, R.E., *Views in Chitral taken during the advance of the 3rd Brigade of the Chitral Relief Force under the command of Brigadier-General W.F. Gatacre, D.S.O., by Sergeant-Major Develin, R.E., 1895* (London: Maclure & Co. [1896]).

Di Cosmo, Nicola (ed.), *Warfare in Inner Asian History* (Leiden: Brill, 2002).

—'Military aspects of the Manchu Wars against the aqars', in: Nicola Di Cosmo (ed.), *Warfare in Inner Asian History* (Leiden: Brill, 2002), pp. 337–68.

—(ed.), *Military Culture in Imperial China* (Cambridge, MA: Harvard University Press, 2009).

—'The Qing and Inner Asia: 1636–1800', in: Nicola Di Cosmo, Allen J. Frank and Peter B. Golden (eds), *The Cambridge History of Inner Asia: The Chinggisid Age* (Cambridge: Cambridge University Press, 2009), pp. 333–62.

Di Cosmo, Nicola, Frank, Allen J. and Golden, Peter B. (eds), *The Cambridge History of Inner Asia: The Chinggisid Age* (Cambridge: Cambridge University Press, 2009).

Dimitrakis, Panagiotis, *The Secret War in Afghanistan. The Soviet Union, China and Anglo-American Intelligence in the Afghan War* (London: I.B.Tauris, 2013).

Donohoe, Martin Henry, *With the Persian Expedition* (1919, London: Naval & Military Press, undated reprint).

Drew, W.J. and Wheeler, Geoffrey, 'Sinkiang in the modern world', *Royal Central Asian Journal*, vol. LVI, No. 3, October 1969 (London: Royal Central Asian Society, 1969), pp. 42–50.

Dreyer, Edward L., 'Military origins of Ming China', in: Denis Twitchett and John K. Fairbank (eds), *The Cambridge History of China, Vol. 7: The Ming Dynasty, 1368–1644, Part I* (Cambridge: Cambridge University Press, 1988), pp. 58–106.

Dubovitskii, Victor with Bababekov, Khaydarbek, 'The Rise and Fall of the Kokand Khanate', in: S. Frederick Starr (ed.), *Ferghana Valley. The Heart of Central Asia* (Armonk: M.E. Sharpe, 2011), pp. 29–68.

Du Halde, Jean-Baptiste, *Description Géographique, Historique, Chronologique, Politique, Et Physique De L'Empire De La Chine Et De La Tartarie Chinoise: Enrichie Des Cartes Générales Et Particulieres de ces Pays, de la Carte générale & des Cartes particulieres du Thibet, & de la Corée*; vol. 4 (Den Hague: Scheurleer, 1736).

—*The general history of China: Containing a geographical, historical, chronological, political and physical description of the Empire of China, Chinese-Tartary, Corea and Thibet. Done from the French of P. du Halde. The third edition corrected*, 4 vols (London: Printed for J. Watts: And sold by B. Dod, 1741).

Dunmore, 7th Earl of (Murray, Charles Adolphus), *The Pamirs. A narrative of a year's expedition on horseback and on foot through Kashmir, Western Tibet, Chinese Tartary and Russian Central Asie*, 2 vols (London: John Murray, 1893).

Dunsterville, Major General Lionel C., *The Adventures of Dunsterforce* (London: Arnold, 1920).

—'Military mission to North-West Persia, 1918', *Journal of the The Royal Central Asia Society*, vol. VIII, No. 2, 1921 (London: Royal Central Asian Society, 1921), pp. 79–98.

Dupree, Louis, 'Afghanistan in the twentieth century', *Royal Central Asian Journal*, vol. LII, No. 1, January 1965 (London: Royal Central Asian Society, 1965), pp. 20–30.

— 'Afghanistan and the unpaved road to democracy', *Royal Central Asian Journal*, vol. LVI, No. 3, October 1969 (London: Royal Central Asian Society, 1969), pp. 272–78.

— *Afghanistan* (1973; Oxford: Oxford University Press, 1997).

Durand, Algernon, *The Making of a Frontier* (1899, Reprint Karachi: Indus Publications, 1977).

Ebülgâzî Bahadir Khan, Khan of Khorezm, *A general history of the Turks, Moguls, and Tatars, vulgarly called Tartars. Together with a Description of the Countries they inhabit* 2 vols (London: Knapton et al, 1730; Reprint Bibliolife, 2016).

Ekbal, Kamran, 'Charles Christie, Captain (d. 1812), of the Bombay Regiment, an Anglo-Indian officer under the command of Sir John Malcolm', in: *Encyclopaedia Iranica* (1991, 2011). http://www.iranicaonline.org/articles/christie-captain-charles-d

Edelberg, Lennart and Jones, Schuyler, *Nuristan* (Graz: Akademische Druck- und Verlagsanstalt, 1979).

Edmonds, C.J., 'The Persian prelude to the Zimmermann telegram', *Royal Central Asian Journal*, vol. XLVII, No. 1, January 1960 (London: Royal Central Asian Society, 1960), pp. 58–67.

Edwards, David B., *Before Taliban. Genealogies of the Afghan Jihad* (Berkeley: University of California Press, 2002).

Edwards, Henry Sutherland, *Russian Projects against India. From the Czar Peter to General Skobeleff* (London: Remington, 1885).

Ellenborough, Lord, 'India Board to Lord Bentinck, 12 January 1830', published as 'The Board of Control of the East India Company expresses concern to the Governor General about Russian designs in Central Asia' in: Martin Ewans (ed.), *The Great Game. Britain and Russia in Central Asia, vol. I: Documents* (London: Routledge, 2004), pp. 69–74.

Ellesmere, Earl of (ed.), *History of the two Tartar Conquerors of China, including the two Journeys into Tartary of Father Ferdinand Verbiest, in the Suite of the Emperor Kang-Hi* (London: Hakluyt Society, 1854).

Ellis, Charles Howard, 'The Transcaspian episode', *Royal Central Asian Journal*, vol. XLVI, No. 2, April 1959 (London: Royal Central Asian Society, 1959), pp. 106–18.

—*The Transcaspian Episode 1918–1919* (London: Hutchinson, 1963).

Elphinstone, Mountstuart, *Tableau du royaume de Caboul et de ses dépendances, dans la Perse, la Tartarie et l'Inde, offrant les mœurs, usages et costumes de cet empire*, 3 vols (1815; French translation Paris: Nepveu, 1817).

—English edition: *An account of the kingdom of Caubul, and its dependencies in Persia, Tartary, and India: comprising a view of the Afghaun nation, and a history of the Doorannee monarchy*; in 2 vols (London: Bentley, 1842).

Erdeni-tobči: See Ssanang Ssetsen Chungtaidschi.

Eshraghi, E., 'Persia during the period of the Safavids, the Afshars and the early Qajars', in: Chahryar Adle, Irfan Habib and Karl M. Baipakov (eds), *History of Civilizations of Central Asia,* vol. V (Paris: Unesco Publishing, 2003), pp. 247–71.

Espagne, Michel et al. (eds), *Asie Centrale. Transferts culturels le long de la Route de la Soie* (Paris: Vendémiaire, 2016).

Etherton, Percy Thomas, *In the Heart of Asia* (Boston: Houghton Mifflin, 1926).

Evans, John L., *Mission of N.P. Ignat'ev to Khiva and Bukhara in 1858*, translated and edited by John Evans (Newtonville: Oriental Research Partners, 1984).

Ewans, Martin, *Afghanistan. A Short History of its People and Politics* (New York: Harper Perennial, 2002).

—*The Great Game. Britain and Russia in Central Asia*, edited by Martin Ewans, *vol. I: Documents* (London: Routledge, 2004).

—*Great Power Rivalry in Central Asia, 1842–1880*, edited by Martin Ewans, *vol. I: Documents* (London: Routledge, 2006).

—*Securing the Indian Frontier in Central Asia. Confrontation and Negotiation, 1865–95* (London: Routledge, 2010).

Eyre, Vincent, *The military operations at Cabul, which ended in the retreat and destruction of the British army, January 1842. With a journal of imprisonment in Afghanistan* (London: James Murray, 1843).

Fairweather, Jack, *The Good War. Why we couldn't win the war or the peace in Afghanistan* (London: Penguin, 2014).

Farrell, Thomas D., 'The founding of the North-West Frontier militias', *Asian Affairs*, vol. III (old series vol. 59), No. 2, June 1972 (London: Royal Society for Asian Affairs, 1972), pp. 165–78.

Feifer, Gregory, *The Great Gamble. The Soviet War in Afghanistan* (New York: Harper Prudentials, 2010).

Filchner, Wilhelm, *Ein Ritt über den Pamir* (Berlin: Ernst Siegfried Mittler und Sohn, 1903).

—*Bismillah! Vom Huang-ho zum Indus* (Leipzig: Brockhaus, 1940).

Filiu, Jean-Pierre, *From Deep State to Islamic State. The Arab Counter-Revolution and its Jihadi Legacy* (London: Hurst, 2015).

Fisher Alan W., *The Crimean Tatars* (Stanford: Hoover Institution Press, 1978).

—*Between Russians, Ottomans and Turks: Crimea and Crimean Tatars* (Istanbul: ISIS Press, 1998).

Fitzhugh, William W., Rossabi, Morris and Honeychurch, William (eds), *Genghis Khan and the Mongol Empire*, exhib. cat. (Washington: Smithsonian Institution, 2009).

Flechtner, Stephan and Schreiber, Dagmar, *Kirgistan* (Berlin: Trescher, 2015).

Fleming, Peter, *News from Tartary. A Journey from Peking to Kashmir* (London: Jonathan Cape, 1936).

—*Bayonets to Lhasa* (1961; Oxford: Oxford University Press, 1985).

Fleming, Zara and Shastri, Lkhagvademchig (eds), *Mongolian Buddhist Art: Masterpieces from the Museums of Mongolia. Vol. 1, Parts 1&2, Thangkas, Appliqués and Embroideries* (Chicago: Serindia, 2011).

Forbes, Andrew D.W., *Warlords and Muslims in Chinese Central Asia. A political history of Republican Sinkiang 1911–1949* (Bangkok: White Lotus Press, 2010).

Forsyth, James, *A History of the Peoples of Siberia. Russia's North Asian Colony 1581–1990* (Cambridge: Cambridge University Press, 1992).

—*The Caucasus. A History* (Cambridge: Cambridge University Press, 2013).

Forsyth, Sir Thomas Douglas, *Report of a mission to Yarkund in 1873, under command of Sir T.D. Forsyth with historical and geographical information regarding the possessions of the ameer of Yarkund* (Calcutta: Foreign Dept. Press, 1875).

Fourniau, V. and Poujol, C., 'The states of Central Asia (second half of nineteenth century to early twentieth century)', in: Chahryar Adle, Madhavan K. Palat and Anara Tabyshalieva (eds), *History of Civilizations of Central Asia,* vol. VI (Paris: Unesco Publishing, 2005), pp. 29–50.

Frank, Allen J., *Islamic Historiography and 'Bulghar' Identity among the Tatars and Bashkirs of Russia* (Leiden: Brill, 1998).

—'The western steppe: Volga-Ural region, Siberia and the Crimea', in: Nicola Di Cosmo, Allen J. Frank and Peter B. Golden (eds), *The Cambridge History of Inner Asia: The Chinggisid Age* (Cambridge: Cambridge University Press, 2009), pp. 237–60.

—'The Qazakhs and Russia', in: Nicola Di Cosmo, Allen J. Frank and Peter B. Golden (eds), *The Cambridge History of Inner Asia: The Chinggisid Age* (Cambridge: Cambridge University Press, 2009), pp. 363–79.

—'Russia and the peoples of the Volga-Ural region: 1600–1850', in: Nicola Di Cosmo, Allen J. Frank and Peter B. Golden (eds), *The Cambridge History of Inner Asia: The Chinggisid Age* (Cambridge: Cambridge University Press, 2009), pp. 380–91.

Fraser, James Baillie, *J. B. Fraser›s Reise nach und in Khorasan in den Jahren 1821 bis 1822: nebst Nachrichten von den nordöstlich von Persien gelegenen Laendern, und Bemerkungen über den National-Character der Perser, wie über die Regierung und die Macht Persiens*; 2 vols (1825; German translation Weimar: Verl. d. Gr. H. S. pr. Landes-Industrie-Comptoirs 1828–29).

Frechtling, Louis E., 'Anglo-Russian rivalry in Eastern Turkistan, 1863–1881', *Royal Central Asian Journal*, vol. XXVI, No. 3, July 1939 (London: Royal Central Asian Society, 1939), pp. 471–89.

French, Patrick, *Younghusband. The last great Imperial adventurer* (London: HarperCollins, 1994).

Friedman, Victor A., 'The Zaporozhian letter to the Turkish Sultan: Historical commentary and linguistic analysis', *Slavica Hierosolymitana*, vol. 8 (Jerusalem: Magnes, 1978), pp. 25–37.

Fuller, Graham E. and Lipman, Jonathan N., 'Islam in Xinjiang', in: S. Frederick Starr (ed.), *Xinjiang. China's Muslim Borderland* (Armonk: M.E. Sharpe, 2004), pp. 320–52.

Furman, Dimitrii, 'The Regime in Kazakhstan', in: Boris Rumer (ed.), *Central Asia: At the End of the Transition* (Armonk: M.E. Sharpe, 2005), pp. 195–267.

Futterer, Karl, *Durch Asien. Erfahrungen, Forschungen und Sammlungen während der von Amtmann Dr. Holderer unternommenen Reise*, vol. I (Berlin: Reimer, 1901).

Gafurov, B.G., *Central Asia. Pre-Historic and Pre-Modern Times*, 2 vols (1972; English edition Delhi: Dhipra, 2005).

Gall, Carlotta, *The Wrong Enemy. America in Afghanistan, 2001–2014* (Boston: Mariner, 2014).

Gall, Carlotta and De Waal, Thomas, *Chechnya. Calamity in the Caucasus* (New York: New York University Press, 1998).

Gammell, Charlie, 'The Place of Herat in a Modern Afghanistan: Lessons from the March 1979 Uprising', *Asian Affairs*, vol. XLVI, No. II, July 2015 (London: Royal Society for Asian Affairs, 2011), pp. 51–67.

Gammer, Moshe, 'Russia and the Eurasian Steppe Nomads: An Overview', in: Reuven Amitai-Preiss and David O. Morgan (eds), *The Mongol Empire and Its Legacy* (Leiden: Brill, 1999), pp. 483–502.

Gao Yanqing (ed.), *Neimenggu Zhenbao: Treasures of Inner Mongolia*, 6 vols (Hohhot: Inner Mongolia University Press, 2007).

Gascoigne, Bamber, *The Great Moghuls* (New Delhi: Time Books International, 1987).

Geiss, James, 'The Chia-ching reign, 1522–1566', in: Denis Twitchett and John K. Fairbank (eds), *The Cambridge History of China, Vol. 7: The Ming Dynasty, 1368–1644, Part I* (Cambridge: Cambridge University Press, 1988), pp. 440–510.

Geiss, Paul Georg, *Pre-Tsarist and Tsarist Central Asia: Communal Development and Political Order in Change* (London: RoutledgeCurzon, 2013).

Gentiletti, Claude (ed.), *Trésors de Mongolie*, exhib. cat. Musée Guimet (Paris: Réunion des musées nationaux, 1993).

Georgi, Johann Gottlieb, *Beschreibung aller Nationen des russischen Reichs ihrer Lebensart, Religion, Gebräuche, Wohnungen, Kleidungen und übrigen Merkwürdigkeiten* (St Petersburg, C.W. Müller, 1776–80).

Gerard, Montagu Gilbert, Holdich, Thomas Hungerford, Wahab, R.A. and Alcock, M.B., *Report on the Proceedings of the Pamir Boundary Commission 1896* (Calcutta: Office of the Superintendant of Government Printing, India, 1897).

Gillett, Michael, 'Afghanistan', *Royal Central Asian Journal*, vol. LIII, No. 3, October 1966 (London: Royal Central Asian Society, 1966), pp. 238–44.

Gilmour, David, *Curzon* (London: John Murray, 1994).

Giustozzi, Antonio, *Empires of Mud. War and Warlords in Afghanistan* (London: Hurst & Company, 2009).

Gladney, Dru C., 'The Chinese Program of Development and Control', in: S. Frederick Starr (ed.), *Xinjiang. China's Muslim Borderland* (Armonk: M.E. Sharpe, 2004), pp. 101–19.

Gmelin, Samuel Gottlieb, *Astrakhan Anno 1770. Its History, Geography, Population, Trade, Flora, Fauna and Fisheries* (1770–84; English translation Washington: Mage Publishers, 2013).

Golden, Peter B., *Central Asia in World History* (Oxford: Oxford University Press, 2011).

Goldstein, Melvyn C., *A History of Modern Tibet, 1913–51. The Demise of the Lamaist State* (New Delhi: Manoharlal, 1993).

Gorâčeva, Valentina, *Srednevekovie gorodskie zentry i architekturnie ansambli Kirgizii. Burana, Uzgen, Safed-Boulan* (Frunze: Ilim, 1983).

Gordon, Thomas Edward, *The Roof of the World: being a narrative of a journey over the high plateau of Tibet to

the Russian frontier and the Oxus sources on Pamir* (1876; Reprint Taipei: Ch'eng Wen Publishing, 1971).

Gorshenina, Svetlana, *La Route de Samarcande. L'Asie Centrale dans l'objectif des voyageurs d'autrefois* (Genève: Olizane 2000).

—*Asie centrale. L'invention des frontiers et l'héritage russo-soviétique* (Paris: CNRS Éditions, 2012).

Götting, Doris (ed.), *Bilder aus der Ferne – Historische Fotografien des Mongoleiforschers Hermann Consten*, exhib.cat. (Bonn: Deutsch-mongolische Gesellschaft, 2005).

Grad, Marcela, *Massoud. An intimate portrait of the legendary Afghan leader* (St Louis: Webster University Press, 2009).

Greaves, Rose, *Persia and the Defence of India 1884–1892. A Study in the Foreign Policy of the Third Marquis of Salisbury* (London: Athlone, 1959).

—'Iranian relations with Great Britain and British India', in: Peter Avery, Gavin Hambly and Charles Melville (eds), *The Cambridge History of Iran: From Nadir Shah to the Islamic Republic*, vol. 7 (Cambridge: Cambridge University Press, 1991), pp. 374–425.

Green, Sir Henry, *The Defence of the North-West Frontier of India with Reference to the Advance of Russia in Central Asia* (London: Harrison, 1873).

Green, Nile (ed.), *Writing Travel in Central Asian History* (Bloomington: Indiana University Press, 2014).

Grey, C., *European Adventurers of Northern India 1785–1849* (1929; Reprint Uckfield: The Naval & Military Press, no date).

Gröttrup, Hendrik, *Wilhelm Wassmuss. Der deutsche Lawrence* (Berlin: Metropol, 2013).

Grousset, René, *L'empire des steppes: Attila, Gengis-Khan, Tamerlan* (Paris: Payot, 1939). English edition: *The Empire of the Steppes* (New Brunswick: Rutgers, 1970).

Guchinova, Elza-Bair, *The Kalmyks* (Abingdon: Routledge, 2006).

Gumppenberg, Marie-Carin von and Steinbach Udo (eds), *Zentralasien. Geschichte, Politik, Wirtschaft. Ein Lexikon* (München: C.H. Beck, 2004).

Haarmann, Harald, *Universalgeschichte der Schrift* (Frankfurt am Main: Campus, 1998).

Habib, Irfan, 'Colonialism in Central Asia', in: Chahryar Adle, Irfan Habib and Karl M. Baipakov (eds), *History of Civilizations of Central Asia,* vol. V (Paris: Unesco Publishing, 2003), pp. 335–42.

Haidar, Mansura, *Central Asia in the Sixteenth Century* (Delhi: Manohar, 2002).

Halperin, Charles J., *Russia and the Golden Horde: The Mongol Impact on Russian History* (London: I.B.Tauris, 1985).

Hambis, Louis, *Documents sur l'histoire des mongols à l'époque des Ming* (Paris: Presses universitaires de France, 1969).

Hambly, Gavin, *Cities of Mughul India* (New York: G.P. Putnam's Sons, 1968).

—'The Pahlavi autocracy: Riza Shah, 1921–1941', in: Peter Avery, Gavin Hambly and Charles Melville (eds), *The Cambridge History of Iran: From Nadir Shah to the Islamic Republic*, vol. 7 (Cambridge: Cambridge University Press, 1991), pp. 214–43.

Hammer-Purgstall, Josef, *Geschichte der Chane der Krim unter osmanischer Herrschaft. Aus türkischen Quellen zusammengetragen* (1856, Reprint Charleston: BiblioLife, print-on-demand ca. 2012).

Harrington, Peter (ed.), *William Simpson's Afghanistan: Travels of a Special Artist and Antiquarian During the Second Afghan War, 1878–1879* (Solihull: Helion, 2016).

Haslund-Christensen, Henning, *Jabonah. Abenteuer in der Mongolei* (Insel-Verlag, Leipzig, 1933).

—*Zajagan. Menschen und Götter in der Mongolei* (Stuttgart: Union Deutsche Verlagsgesellschaft, 1936).

Hattstein, Markus and Delius, Peter (eds), *Islam: Kunst und Architektur* (Cologne: Könemann, 2000).

Hauner, Milan, 'Russia's Asian Heartland Today and Tomorrow', in: Nick Megoran and Sevara Sharapova (eds), *Central Asia in International Relations. The Legacies of Halford Mackinder* (London: Hurst & Co., 2013), pp. 117–47.

Hauser, Markus, 'The Pamir Archive: A world of information', in: Andrei Dörre, Hermann Kreutzmann and Stefan Schütte (eds), *Pamirs at the Crossroads* (Berlin: Freie Universität Berlin, 2016), pp. 87f. https://www.academia.edu/27962074/The_Pamir_Archive_A_world_of_information

Haymerle, Alois Ritter von, *Ultima Thule. England und Rußland in Central Asien* (Wien: Verlag von Streffleur's Österreichischer militärischer Zeitschrift, 1885).

Hayward, George J.W., 'Journey from Leh to Yarkand and Kashgar, and Exploration of the Sources of the Yarkand River', *Journal of the Royal Geographical Society of London*, vol. 40 (London: John Murray, 1870), pp. 33–166.

Heathcote, T.A., *The Afghan Wars, 1839–1919* (London: Osprey, 1980).

Hedin, Sven, *Southern Tibet: Discoveries in former times compared with my own researches in 1906–1908,* 12 vols (Stockholm: Lithographic Institute of the General Staff of the Swedish Army, 1917–22).

—*Auf grosser Fahrt. Meine Expedition mit Schweden, Deutschen und Chinesen durch die Wüste Gobi 1927–28* (Leipzig: Brockhaus, 1929).

—*Die Flucht des Großen Pferdes* (Leipzig: Brockhaus, 1939).

Heissig, Walther, *Mongolenreise zur späten Goethezeit. Berichte und Bilder des J. Rehmann und A. Thesleff von der russischen Gesandschaftsreise 1805/06* (Wiesbaden: Franz Steiner Verlag, 1971).

—*Die Mongolen. Ein Volk sucht seine Geschichte* (Bindlach: Gondrom, 1989).

—*Religions of Mongolia* (London: Kegan Paul, 2000).

Heissig, Walther and Müller, Claudius C. (eds), *Die Mongolen* (Innsbruck: Pinguin-Verlag, 1989).

Hejazi, Mehrdad and Saradj, Fatemeh M., *Persian Architectural Heritage: Architecture* (Southampton: Architecture WIT Press, 2014).

Helmersen, Gregor von (ed.), *Nachrichten über Chiwa, Buchara, Chokand und den nordwestlichen Teil des chinesischen Staates, gesammelt von dem Präsidenten der asiatischen Grenz-Commission in Orenburg, General-Major Gens* (St Petersburg: Kaiserliche Akademie der Wissenschaften, 1839).

Henss, Michael, 'The Bodhisattva-Emperor: Tibeto-Chinese Portraits of Sacred and Secular Rule in the Qing Dynasty', *Oriental Art* (Singapore: Oriental Art Magazine, 2001), vol. XLVII, No. 3, pp. 2–16, and No. 5, pp. 71–83.

—*The Cultural Monuments of Tibet. The Central Regions*, 2 vols (Munich: Prestel, 2014).

Hentig, Otto Werner von, *Meine Diplomatenfahrt ins verschlossene Land* (Berlin: Ullstein, 1918).

—*Mein Leben: eine Dienstreise* (Göttingen: Vandenhoeck & Ruprecht, 1962).

—*Von Kabul nach Shanghai: Bericht über die Afghanistan-Mission 1915/16 und die Rückkehr über das Dach der Welt und durch die Wüsten Chinas* (Lengwil: Libelle, 2009).

Herfort, Frank, *Imperial Pomp. Post-Soviet High-Rise* (Bielefeld: Kerber, 2013).

Hermann, Werner and Linn, Johannes F. (eds), *Central Asia and The Caucasus. At the Crossroads of Eurasia in the 21st Century* (Los Angeles: Sage, 2011).

Hildinger, Erik, *Warriors of the Steppe: A Military History of Central Asia 500 B.C. to 1700 A.D.* (Cambridge, MA: Da Capo Press, 2001).

Hiro, Dilip, *Inside Central Asia. A political and cultural history of Uzbekistan, Turkmenistan, Kazakhstan, Kyrgyzstan, Tajikistan, Turkey, and Iran* (New York: Overlook Duckworth, 2009).

History of Civilizations of Central Asia, vol. V. *Development in Contrast: from the sixteenth to the mid-nineteenth century*, edited by Chahryar Adle, Irfan Habib and Karl M. Baipakov (Paris: Unesco Publishing, 2003).

History of Civilizations of Central Asia, vol. VI. *Towards the Contemporary Period: from the mid-nineteenth to the end of the twentieth century*, edited by Chahryar Adle, Madhavan K. Palat and Anara Tabyshalieva (Paris: Unesco Publishing, 2005).

Hobbes, Thomas, *Leviathan* (1651; Ware: Wordsworth Classic, 2014).

Hok-Lam Chan, 'The Chien-wen, Yung-lo, Hung-hsi, and Hsüan-te reigns, 1399–1435', in: Denis Twitchett and John K. Fairbank (eds), *The Cambridge History of China, Vol. 7: The Ming Dynasty, 1368–1644*, Part I (Cambridge: Cambridge University Press, 1988), pp. 182–304.

Holdich, Thomas Hungerford, *The Indian Borderland 1880–1900* (London: Methuen, 1901).

Hopkirk, Peter, *Setting the East Ablaze. Lenin's Dream of an Empire in Asia* (London: John Murray, 1984).

—*The Great Game. The Struggle for Empire in Central Asia* (New York: Kodansha America, 1994).

—*On Secret Service East of Constantinople. The Plot to Bring Down the British Empire* (Oxford: Oxford University Press, 1994).

Hu, Richard W., 'China's Central Asia Policy: Making Sense of the Shanghai Cooperation Organization', in: Boris Rumer (ed.), *Central Asia: At the End of the Transition* (Armonk: M.E. Sharpe, 2005), pp. 130–51.

Hudud al-Alam: The Regions of the World – A Persian Geography 372 A.H.–982 A.D., translated and explained by V. Minorsky, ed. C.E. Bosworth (Cambridge: reprint by Cambridge University Press, 1982).

Hughes, Thomas L., 'The German Mission to Afghanistan, 1915–16', in: *German Studies Review*, XXV/3, Oct 2002 (German Studies Association, 2002), pp. 447–76. http://www.jstor.org/stable/1432596

Humboldt, Alexander von, *Asie Centrale. Recherches sur les chaines de montagnes et la climatologie comparée*, 3 vols (Paris: Gide, 1843).

Hunter, Shireen, *Islam in Russia: The Politics of Identity and Security* (Oxon: Routledge, 2015).

Huntington, Samuel P., *The Clash of Civilizations and the Remaking of World Order* (London: Simon & Schuster 1997).

Huth, Georg, *Die Inschriften von Tsaghan Baisin. Tibetisch-mongolischer Text* (Leipzig: F.A. Brockhaus, 1894).

Ides, E. Ysbrants, *Three years travels from Moscow over-land to China: thro' Great Ustiga, Siriania, Permia, Sibiria, Daour, Great Tartary, &c. to Peking* (London: Printed for W. Freeman et al., 1706).

Ingle, Harold N., *Nesselrode and the Russian Rapprochement with Britain, 1836–1844* (Berkeley: University of California Press, 1976).

Ingram, Edward, *The Beginning of the Great Game in Asia 1828–1834* (Oxford: Oxford University Press, 1979).

Iqtidar, A. Khan, 'Inter-state relations (c. 1550–1850)', in: Chahryar Adle, Irfan Habib and Karl M. Baipakov (eds), *History of Civilizations of Central Asia*, vol. V (Paris: Unesco Publishing, 2003), pp. 325–34.

Ishjamts, N., 'The Mongols', in: Chahryar Adle, Irfan Habib and Karl M. Baipakov (eds), *History of Civilizations of Central Asia*, vol. V (Paris: Unesco Publishing, 2003), pp. 209–24.

Jacobs, Justin M., *Xinjiang and the Modern Chinese State* (Seattle: University of Washington Press, 2016).

Jenkinson, Anthony, *Early Voyages and Travels to Russia and Persia*. Edited by E. Delmar Morgan and C.H. Cote, 2 vols (London: Hakluyt Society, 1886).

Jerryson, Michael K., *Mongolian Buddhism. The rise and fall of the Sangha* (Chiang Mai: Silverworm Books, 2007).

The Jewel Translucent Sutra, Erdeni Tunumal Sudur. Altan Khan and the Mongols in the Sixteenth Century. Edited, translated and annotated by Johan Elverskog (ca. 1607; Leiden: Brill, 2003).

Johnson, Rob, *Pulverfass am Hindukush. Dschihad, Erdöl und die Großmächte in Zentralasien* (Stuttgart: Theiss, 2008).

Jones, Harford, 'Letter to Sir Hugh Inglis Bart, November 29, 1802', in: *The Great Game. Britain and Russia in Central Asia*, edited by Martin Ewans, *vol. I: Documents* (London: Routledge, 2004), pp. 49–52.

Jonson, Lena, *Vladimir Putin and Central Asia. The Shaping of Russian Foreign Policy* (London: I.B.Tauris 2004).

—*Tajikistan in the New Central Asia. Geopolitics, Great Power Rivalry and Radical Islam* (London: I.B.Tauris, 2009).

Jourdain, John, *The Journal of John Jourdain 1608–1617 describing his experiences in Arabia, India and the Malay Archipelago*. Edited by William Foster (1905, Reprint New Delhi: Asian Educational services, 1992).

Kaplan, Robert D., *The Revenge of Geography* (New York: Random House, 2013).

Kappeler, Andreas, *Rußland als Vielvölkerreich. Entstehung, Geschichte, Zerfall* (Frankfurt a.M.: Büchergilde Gutenberg, 1992).

Kassimbekov, M.B., *Nazarbayev: A Life Story of the First President of Kazakhstan* (London: Stacey Intl., 2012).

Kauz, Ralph, 'Trade and Commerce on the Silk Road after the End of the Mongol Rule in China, Seen from Chinese Texts', *The Silk Road Journal* 4/2 (2006/07), pp. 54–59.

Kaye, John William, *History of the War in Afghanistan: from the unpublished letters and journals of political and military officers employed in Afghanistan throughout the entire period of British connexion with that country*, 2 vols (London: Richard Bentley, 1851).

—*Lives of Indian Officers, Illustrative of the History of the Civil and Military Services of India*, 2 vols (London: A. Strahan and Co & Bell and Daldy, 1867).

Kazemdazeh, F., 'Iranian relations with Russia and the Soviet Union', in: Peter Avery, Gavin Hambly and Charles Melville (eds), *The Cambridge History of Iran: From Nadir Shah to the Islamic Republic*, vol. 7 (Cambridge: Cambridge University Press, 1991), pp. 314–49.

Kearns, Gerry, 'Imperialism and the Heartland', in: Nick Megoran and Sevara Sharapova (eds), *Central Asia in International Relations. The Legacies of Halford Mackinder* (London: Hurst & Co., 2013), pp. 69–90.

Keay, John, *The Honourable Company. A History of the English East India Company* (London: HarperCollins, 1991).

—*The Gilgit Game. The Explorers of the Western Himalayas* (London: John Murray, 1979).

Keddie, Nikki and Amanat, Mehrdad, 'Iran under the later Qajars', in: Peter Avery, Gavin Hambly and Charles Melville (eds), *The Cambridge History of Iran: From Nadir Shah to the Islamic Republic*, vol. 7 (Cambridge: Cambridge University Press, 1991), pp. 174–212.

Kent, Neil, *Crimea. A History* (London: Hurst, 2016).

Kermani, Navid, *Ausnahmezustand. Reisen in eine beunruhigte Welt* (München: C.H. Beck, 2015).

Kessler, Melvin M., *Ivan Viktorovich Vitkevich 1806–39: A Tsarist Agent in Central Asia* (Washington: Central Asian Collectanea, 1960).

Khan, Omar, *From Kashmir to Kabul: the photographs of John Burke and William Baker, 1860–1900* (Munich; New York: Prestel, 2002).

Khan, Sultan Mahomed, *The Life of Abdur Rahman, Amir of Afghanistan*, 2 vols (London: John Murray, 1900).

Khodarkovsky, Michael, *Where Two Worlds Met. The Russian State and the Kalmyk Nomads, 1600–1771* (Ithaca: Cornell University Press, 1992).

—*Russia's Steppe Frontier. The Making of a Colonial Empire, 1500–1800* (Bloomington: Indiana University Press, 2002).

Khwandamir, Ghiyas ad-Din Muhammad, *Habibu al-Siyar* [Beloved of Careers]', in: *Classic Writings of the Medieval Islamic World*, translated and annotated by Wheeler Thrackston, vol. II (London: I.B.Tauris, 2012).

Kim, Hodong, 'The early history of the Moghul nomads: the legacy of the Chagatai Khanate', in Reuven Amitai-Preiss and David O. Morgan (eds), *The Mongol Empire and Its Legacy* (Leiden: Brill, 1999), pp. 290–318.

—*Holy War in China. The Muslim Rebellion and State in Chinese Central Asia, 1864–1877* (Stanford: Stanford University Press, 2004).

Kimura, Hisao, *Japanese Agent in Tibet. My Ten Years of Travel in Disguise* (London: Serindia, 1990).

Kinneir, Sir John Macdonald, *A Geographical Memoir of the Persian Empire* (1813; Reprint Repressed Publishing, 2013, no location given).

Kinvig, Clifford, 'Review of *The Scope and Methods of Geography and the Geographical Pivot of History* by Halford Mackinder' (London: *International Affairs*, vol. 27, no 4, 1951), pp. 540–41.

Kinvig, Clifford, *Churchill's Crusade: The British Invasion of Russia 1918–1920* (London: Hambledon Continuum, 2006).

Kircher, Athanasius, *Athanasii Kircheri e Soc. Jesu China monumentis, qvà sacris qvà profanis: nec non variis naturæ & artis spectaculis, aliarumque rerum memorabilium argumentis illustrata, auspiciis Leopoldi Primi roman. Imper. semper augusti* (Amstelodami: apud Joannem Janssonium à Waesberge & Elizeum Weyerstraet, 1667).

Kleveman, Lutz, *The New Great Game. Blood and Oil in Central Asia* (London: Atlantis, 2003).

Kljaštornyj, S.G. and Sultanov, T.I., *Staaten und Völker in den Steppen Eurasiens. Altertum und Mittelalter* (Berlin: Schletzer, 2006).

Knight, E.F., *Where Three Empires Meet. A narrative of recent travel in Kashmir, western Tibet, Gilgit, and the adjoining countries* (London: Longmans, Green, 1896).

Knobloch, Edgar, *Monuments of Central Asia: A Guide to the Archaeology, Art and Architecture of Turkestan* (London: I.B.Tauris, 2001).

—*The Archaeology & Architecture of Afghanistan* (Charleston: Tempus, 2002).

—*Russia & Asia. Nomadic and Oriental Traditions in Russian History* (Hong Kong: Odyssey, 2007).

Kohl, Johann Georg, *Reisen in Südrußland*, 3 vols. (1847; Reprint Boston: Elibron Classics, 2008.

Kollmar-Paulenz, Karenina, 'Durch die Kraft des ewigen blauen Himmels: Zur Konstruktion religiöser Identität bei den Mongolen' (13.–frühes 17. Jahrhundert)', *Asiatische Studien* (Bern) 56/4 (2002), pp. 857–77.

Kolmaš, Josef, *Tibet and Imperial China: A Survey of Sino-Tibetan Relations up to the End of the Manchu Dynasty in 1912* (Canberra: Australian National University, 1967).

Kotkin, Stephen and Elleman Bruce, A. (eds), *Mongolia in the Twentieth Century. Landlocked Cosmopolitan* (London: Routledge, 2015).

Kozlov, Pyotr K., *Mongolija i Amdo i mertvij gorod Xara-Xoto* (Moscow: Gosudarstvennoe izdatelstvo, 1923).

—*Mongolei, Amdo und die tote Stadt Chara-Choto. Mit einem Geleitwort von Dr. Sven Hedin* (Berlin: Neufeld & Henius, 1925).

Kradin, Nikolay N., *Nomads of Inner Asia in Transition* (Moscow: URSS, 2014).

Kreutzmann, Hermann, *Pamirian Crossroads. Kirgiz and Wakhi of High Asia* (Wiesbaden: Harrassowitz, 2015).

Krieken-Pieters, Juliette van (ed.), *Art and Archaeology of Afghanistan: Its Fall and Survival* (Leiden/Boston: Brill, 2006).

Krist, Gustav, *Alone through the Forbidden Land. Journeys in Disguise through Soviet Central Asia* (London: Faber and Faber, 1938).

Kurbatov A.A., *Astrakhan Kremlin* (Rostow am Don: I.P. Yutishev, 2010).

Kuropatkin, Alexei Nikolajewitsch, *Geschichte des Feldzuges Skobelews in Turkmenien nebst einer Übersicht der kriegerischen Tätigkeit der russischen Truppen in Zentralasien von 1839–1876* (Mühlheim am Rhein: C. G. Künstler Wwe., 1904).

Kyzlasov, L.R., 'The peoples of Southern Siberia in the sixteenth to the eighteenth centuries', in: Chahryar Adle, Irfan Habib and Karl M. Baipakov (eds), *History of Civilizations of Central Asia*, vol. V (Paris: Unesco Publishing, 2003), pp. 173–80.

Lacy Evans, Sir George, *On the Designs of Russia* (1828, Reprint Delhi: Facsimile Publisher, 2016).

—*On the practicability of an invasion of British India and on the commercial, and financial prospects and resources of the Empire* (1829, Reprint Delhi: Facsimile Publisher, 2016).

Lain, Sarah, 'Strategies for Countering Terrorism and Extremism in Central Asia', *Asian Affairs*, vol. XLVII, No. III, November 2016 (London: Royal Society for Asian Affairs, 2016), pp. 386–405.

Lal, Mohan, *Life of the Amir Dost Mohammed Khan of Kabul: with his political proceedings towards the English, Russian, and Persian Governments, including the victory and disasters of the British army in Afghanistan*; 2 vols (London: Longman, Brown, Green, and Longmans, 1846).

Lamb, Alastair, 'Tibet in Anglo-Chinese Relations: 1767–1842', parts I and II, *Royal Central Asian Journal* (London: Separatum, April 1958).

—'Some notes on Russian intrigue in Tibet', *Royal Central Asian Journal*, vol. XLVI, No. 1, Janury 1959 (London: Royal Central Asian Society, 1959), pp. 46–65.

—*Britain and Chinese Central Asia. The Road to Lhasa 1767–1905* (London: Routledge and Kegan Paul, 1960).

Lamb, Christina, *Farewell Kabul. From Kabul to a more dangerous world* (London: William Collins, 2016).

Landon, Perceval, *Lhasa. An account of the country and people of Central Tibet and of the progress of the mission sent there by the English government in the years 1903–04*, 2 vols (London: Hurst and Blackett, 1905).

Langlois, John D. 'The Hung-wu reign, 1368–1398', in: Denis Twitchett and John K. Fairbank (eds), *The Cambridge History of China, Vol. 7: The Ming Dynasty, 1368–1644, Part I* (Cambridge: Cambridge University Press, 1988), pp. 107–81.

Lansdell, Henry, *Chinese Central Asia. A Ride to Little Tibet*, 2 vols (London: Sampson Low, Marston, and Co., 1893).

Larson, Frans A., *Die Mongolei und mein Leben mit den Mongolen* (Berlin: Kiepenheuer, 1936).

Laruelle, Marlene and Peyrouse, Sebastian, *Globilizing Central Asia. Geopolitics and the Challenges of Economic Development* (London: Routledge, 2015).

Lattimore, Owen, *The Desert Road to Turkestan* (London: Methuen, 1928).

—*The Mongols of Manchuria* (London: Allen & Unwin, 1934).

—*Pivot of Asia. Sinkiang and the Inner Asia Frontiers of China and Russia* (Boston: Little, Brown & Co., 1950).

Lawrence, Sir John, 'Dispatch No. 162 of 23 October 1867', published as 'A case against the "Forward Policy", October 1867' in: Martin Ewans (ed.), *Great Power Rivalry in Central Asia, 1842–1880, vol. I: Documents* (London: Routledge, 2006), pp. 225–35.

—'Dispatch dated 4 January 1869', published as 'The Government of India responds to an invitation to comment on Sir Henry Rawlinson's Memorandum of 1868' in: Martin Ewans (ed.), *Great Power Rivalry in Central Asia, 1842–1880, vol. I: Documents* (London: Routledge, 2006), pp. 237–46.

Leach, Hugh, 'A Ride to Shiwa: a Source of the Oxus', *Asian Affairs*, vol. XVII (old series vol. 73), No. 3, October 1986 (London: Royal Society for Asian Affairs, 1986), pp. 264–76.

Lebedynsky, Iaroslav, *Les Nomades* (Paris: Éditions Errance, 2007).

—*La Horde d'Or. Conquête mongole et 'Joug tatar' en Europe 1236–1502* (Arles: Éditions Errance, 2013).

Leder, Hans, 'Eine Sommerreise in der nördlichen Mongolei im Jahr 1892', in: *Mitteilungen der Kais. Königl. Geographischen Gesellschaft in Wien*, vol. XXXVIII.1 (Wien: R. Lechner, 1895), pp. 26–57.

Lee, J.L., *The 'Ancient Supremacy'. Bukhara, Afghanistan and the Battle for Balkh, 1731–1901* (Leiden: Brill, 1996).

Lee, Joy R., *The Islamic Republic of Eastern Turkestan and the Formation of Modern Uyghur Identity in Xinjiang*, a thesis (Manhattan: Kansas State University, 2006).

Le Fèvre, Georges, *Expédition Citroën Centre-Asie. La Croisière Jaune. Troisième mission Georges-Marie Haardt, Louis Audouin-Dubreuil* (Paris: Plon, 1933).

Létolle, René and Mainguet, Monique, *Der Aralsee. Eine ökologische Katastrophe* (Berlin: Springer, 1996).

Levi, Scott C. and Sela, Ron, *Islamic Central Asia: An Anthology of Historical Sources* (Bloomington: Indiana University Press, 2010).

Lincoln, Bruce W., *The Conquest of a Continent: Siberia and the Russians* (Ithaca: Cornell University Press, 2007).

Lincoln, Frances, Michell, George et al., *Kashgar. Oasis City on China's Old Silk Road* (London: Frances Lincoln, 2008).

Linn, Johannes F, 'Connecting Central Asia and the Caucasus with the World', in: Werner Hermann and Johannes F. Linn (eds), *Central Asia and The Caucasus. At the Crossroads of Eurasia in the 21st Century* (Los Angeles: Sage, 2011), pp. 1–15.

Linschoten, Alex Strick van and Kuehn, Felix, *An Enemy We Created. The Myth of the Taliban-Al Qaeda Merger in Afghanistan* (Oxford: Oxford University Press, 2012).

Lipman, Jonathan N., *Familiar Strangers. A History of Muslims in Northwest China* (Seattle: University of Washington Press, 1997.)

Lockhart, Laurence, 'European contacts with Persia, 1350–1736', in Peter Jackson and Laurence Lockhart (eds) *The Cambridge History of Iran: The Timurid and Safavid Periods*, vol. 6 (Cambridge: Cambridge University Press, 1986), pp. 373–411.

Lunt, James, *Bokhara Burnes* (London: Faber & Faber, 1969).

Ma Dazheng, 'The Tarim Basin', in: Chahryar Adle, Irfan Habib and Karl M. Baipakov (eds), *History of Civilizations of Central Asia,* vol. V (Paris: Unesco Publishing, 2003), pp. 181–208.

Mac Gahan, J. A., *Campaigning on the Oxus and the Fall of Khiva* (1874; Reprint New York: Arno Press, 1970).

Macartney, Sir George, 'Bolshevism as I saw it at Tashkent in 1918', *Journal of the The Royal Central Asia Society*, vol. VII, Nos. 2–3, 1920 (London: Royal Central Asian Society, 1920), pp. 42–58.

MacGregor, Sir Charles Metcalfe, *War in Afghanistan, 1879–80. The Personal Diary of Major General Sir Charles Metcalfe MacGregor*, edited by William Trousdale (Detroit: Wayne State University Press, 1995).

MacKenzie, David, *Count N.P. Ignat'ev: The Father of Lies?* (Boulder: East European Monographs, 2002).

Machiavelli, Niccolo, *Der Fürst, 'Il Prinzipe'* (1513; Stuttgart: Kröner, 1972).

Macrory, Patrick, *Signal Catastrophe. The Story of the Disastrous Retreat from Kabul 1842* (London: Hodder and Stoughton, 1966).

Maillart, Ella K., *The Cruel Way* (1947; London: Virago Press, 1986).

Malashenko, Alexey, *The Fight for Influence. Russia in Central Asia* (Washington: Carnegie Endowment for International Peace, 2013).

Malcolm, John, 'Despatch to Lord Elgin, British Ambassador to the Ottoman Porte, 23 March 1801', published as 'An assessment of the possibility of a Russian invasion of India' in: Martin Ewans (ed.), *The Great Game. Britain and Russia in Central Asia, vol. I: Documents* (London: Routledge, 2004), pp. 32–37.

Malik, Mohan, *Dragon on Terrorism: Assessing China's tactical gains and strategic losses post-September 11* (Carlisle Barracks: US Army War College, October 2002).

Malleson, George Bruce, *The Russo-Afghan Question and the Invasion of India* (London: George Routledge and Sons, 1885).

Malleson, Sir Wilfrid, 'The British military mission to Turkistan, 1918–20', *Journal of the Royal Central Asia Society*, vol. IX, No. 2, 1922 (London: Royal Central Asian Society, 1922), pp. 95–110.

Mänchen-Helfen, Otto, *Reise ins asiatische Tuva* (Berlin: Der Bücherkreis, 1931).

Mandelbaum, Michael (ed.), *Central Asia and the World* (New York: Council on Foreign Relations, 1994).

Manucci, Niccolao, *Storia do Mogor or Mogul India 1653–1708*. Translated with introduction and notes by William Irvine, 3 vols (London: John Murray, 1907).

Mark, Rudolf A., *Krieg an fernen Fronten* (Paderborn: Ferdinand Schöningh, 2013).

Markham, Clements R. (editor and translator), *Narrative of the Embassy of Ruy Gonzalez de Clavijo to the Court of Timour at Samarcand, A.D. 1403–06* (London: Hakluyt Society, 1859).

Marshall, Tim, *Prisoners of Geography: ten maps that explain everything about the world* (New York: Scribner, 2015).

Martin, Janet, 'Muscovite Relations with the Khanates of Kazan and the Crimea (1460s to 1521)', in: *Canadian-American Slavic Studies*, 17, No. 4 (Pittsburgh: University of Pittsburgh, 1983), pp. 435–53.

Martin, Mike, *An Initimate War. An Oral History of the Helmand Conflict, 1978–2012* (Oxford: Oxford University Press, 2014).

Marvin, Charles Thomas, *The Russians at the Gate of Herat* (New York: Charles Scribner's Sons, 1885).

—*Reconnoitring Central Asia. Pioneering adventures in the region lying between Russia and India* (1885; Reprint New Delhi: Asian Educational Services, 1996).

Masson, Charles, *Narrative of a Journey to Kalât, including an Account of the Insurrection at that Place in 1840; and a Memoir on Eastern Balochistan* (London: Richard Bentley, 1843).

Mayers, Kit, *The first English Explorer. The Life of Anthony Jenkinson (1529–1611) and his adventures on the route to the Orient* (Kibworth Beauchamp: Matador, 2017).

McCants, William, *The ISIS Apocalypse. The History, Strategy, and Doomsday Vision of the Islamic State* (New York: St Martin's Press, 2015).

McChesney, R. D., 'The Chinggisid restoration in Central Asia: 1500–1785', in: Nicola Di Cosmo, Allen J. Frank and Peter B. Golden (eds), *The Cambridge History of Inner Asia: The Chinggisid Age* (Cambridge: Cambridge University Press, 2009), pp. 277–302.

—*Central Asia. Foundations of change* (Princeton: Darwin Press, 1996).

McKay, Alex, *Tibet and the British Raj. The Frontier Cadre 1904–1947* (Richmond: Curzon, 1997).

Megoran, Nick and Sharapova, Sevara (eds), *Central Asia in International Relations. The Legacies of Halford Mackinder* (London: Hurst & Co., 2013).

Mehra, Parshotam, *The McMahon Line and After. A Study of the Triangular Contest on India's North-Eastern Frontier Between Britain, China and Tibet, 1904–47* (Madras: Macmillan, 1974).

Menges, Karl H., 'People, Languages, and Migrations', in: Edward Allsworth (ed.), *130 Years of Russian Dominance, a Historical Overview* (Durham: Duke University Press, 1994), pp. 60–91.

Meyendorff, Georges de, *Voyage de Orenbourg a Boukhara, fait en 1820, a travers les steppes qui s'étendent a l'est de la mer d'Aral et au-dela de l'ancien Jaxartes; rédigé par et revu par M. le chevalier Amédée Jaubert* (Paris: Librairie Orientale de Dondey-Dupré, père et fils, 1826).

Meyer, Karl E. and Brysac, Shareen Blair, *Tournament of Shadows. The Great Game and the Race for Empire in Central Asia* (New York: Basic Books, 1999).

Middleton, Robert and Thomas, Huw, *Tajikistan and the High Pamirs* (Hong Kong: Odyssey, 2008).

Mikaberidze, Alexander (ed.), *Conflict and Conquest in the Islamic World*, 2 vols (Santa Barbara: ABC-Clio, 2011).

Mikusch, Dagobert von, *Wassmuss, der deutsche Lawrence: auf Grund der Tagebucher und Aufzeichnungen des verstorbenen Konsuls, deutscher und englischen Quellen und des unter gleichem Titel erschienenen Buches von Christoper Sykes* (Berlin: Büchergilde Gutenberg1937).

Miller, Charles, *Khyber. British India's North West Frontier. The Story of an Imperial Migraine* (London: Macdonald and Jane, 1977).

Mills, Nick B., *Karzai: The Failing American Intervention and the Struggle for Afghanistan* (Hoboken: John Wiley, 2007).

Millward, James A., *Eurasian Crossroads. A History of Xinjiang* (New York: Columbia University Press, 2007).

—'Eastern Central Asia (Xinjiang): 1300–1800' in: Nicola Di Cosmo, Allen J. Frank and Peter B. Golden (eds), *The Cambridge History of Inner Asia: The Chinggisid Age* (Cambridge: Cambridge University Press, 2009), pp. 260–76.

Millward, James and Perdue Peter C., 'Political and Cultural History of the Xinjiang Region through the Late Nineteenth Century', in: Starr, S. Frederick (ed.), *Xinjiang. China's Muslim Borderland* (Armonk: M.E. Sharpe, 2004), pp. 27–62.

Millward, James and Tursun, Nabijan, 'Political History and Strategies of Control, 1884–1978', in: Starr, S. Frederick (ed.), *Xinjiang. China's Muslim Borderland* (Armonk: M.E. Sharpe, 2004), pp. 63–98.

Minassian, Taline Ter, *Most Secret Agent of Empire. Reginald Teague-Jones Master Spy of the Great Game* (London: Hurst, 2014).

Mir I'sset-Uellah, 'Reise nach Mittelasien im Jahr 1812', *Hertha Zeitschrift für Erd-, Völker- und Staatenkunde*. Unter Mirwirkung des Freiherrn Alexander v. Humboldt, besorgt von Berghaus in Berlin und Hoffmann in Stuttgart (Stuttgart und Tübingen: J.G. Cotta'schen Buchhandlung, 1826).

Mirfendereski, Guive, *A Diplomatic History of the Caspian Sea. Treaties, Diaries and Other Stories* (New York: Palgrave, 2001).

Mirza Muhammad Haidar, Dughlat, *Tarikh-i-Rashidi: A History of the Moghuls of Central Asia*, trans. D. Ross, ed. N. Elias (1895; Reprint in 2 vols (New Delhi, 1998).

—*Tarikh-i-Rashidi: a history of the Khans of Mogulistan*, in *Classic Writings of the Medieval Islamic World*, translated and annotated by Wheeler Thrackston, vol. I (London: I.B.Tauris, 2012).

Mitra, Pradeep K., 'The Impact of the Global Financial Crisis and Policy Responses: Central Asia and the Caucasus', in: Werner Hermann and Johannes F. Linn (eds), *Central Asia and The Caucasus. At the Crossroads of Eurasia in the 21st Century* (Los Angeles: Sage, 2011), pp. 135–71.

Mitrokhin, Leonid, *Failure of Three Missions* (Moscow: Progress Publishers, 1987).

Miyawaki, Junko, 'The early history of the Mughal nomads', in Reuven Amitai-Preiss and David O. Morgan (eds), *The Mongol Empire and Its Legacy* (Leiden: Brill, 1999), pp. 290–318.

Moberly, Frederick James (ed.), *Operation in Persia, 1914–1919. Compiled by arrangement with the Government of India, under the direction of the Historical Section of the Committee of Imperial Defence by Brig. Gen. F.J. Moberly* (1929; Reprint London: Imperial War Museum, 1987).

Monserrate, Father, *The Commentary of Father Monserrate, S.J., on his Journey to the Court of Akbar*; translated from the original Latin by J.S. Hoyland and annotated by S.N. Banerjee (London: Oxford University Press, 1922).

Montell, Gösta, 'Mongol life and a journey to Etsingol', *Royal Central Asian Journal*, vol. XXIV, No. 4, October 1937 (London: Royal Central Asian Society, 1937), pp. 605–23.

—*Durch die Steppen der Mongolei* (Stuttgart: Union Deutsche Verlagsgesellschaft, 1938).

Moorcroft, William and Trebeck, George, *Travels in India. Himalayan Provinces of Hindustan and the Punjab, in Ladakh and Kashmir, in Peshawar, Kabul, Kunduz and Bokhara*. Prefaced and edited by Horace Hayman Wilson, 2 vols (1841; Reprint New Delhi: Asian Educational Services, 1989).

Morgan, David, *The Mongols* (Malden, MA: Blackwell, 2007).

Morgan, Gerald, *Ney Elias. Explorer and envoy extraordinary in High-Asia* (London: George Allen & Unwin, 1971).

—*Anglo-Russian Rivalry in Central Asia: 1810–1895* (Oxon: Routledge, 1981).

Morrissey, John, 'US Central Command and liberal imperial reach: "Shaping the Central Region for the 21st Century"', *The Geographical Journal*, vol. 182, No. 1, March 2016 (London: RGS, 2016), pp. 15–26.

Moser, Henri, *A travers l'Asie Centrale. La steppe kirghize – le Turkestan Russe – Boukhara – Khiva – le pays des Turcomans et la Perse* (Paris: Plon, 1885).

Moses, Larry William, *The Political Role of Mongol Buddhism* (Richmond: Curzon Press, 1997).

Mote, Frederick W., 'The rise of the Ming dynasty, 1330–1367', in: Denis Twitchett and John K. Fairbank (eds), *The Cambridge History of China, Vol. 7: The Ming Dynasty, 1368–1644, Part I* (Cambridge: Cambridge University Press, 1988), pp. 11–57.

—'The Ch'eng-hua and Hung-chi reigns, 1465–1505', in: Denis Twitchett and John K. Fairbank (eds), *The Cambridge History of China, Vol. 7: The Ming Dynasty, 1368–1644, Part I* (Cambridge: Cambridge University Press, 1988), pp. 343–402.

Moubayed, Sami, *Under the Black Flag. At the Frontier of the New Jihad* (London: I.B.Tauris, 2015).

Mukminova, R. G., 'The Timurid states in the fifteenth and sixteenth centuries', in: M.S. Asimov and C.E. Bosworth (eds), *History of Civilizations of Central Asia*, vol. IV, part 1 (Paris: Unesco Publishing, 1998), pp. 347–63.

Mukminova, R.G. and Mukhtarov, A., 'The Khanate (Emirate) of Bukhara', in: Chahryar Adle, Irfan Habib and Karl M. Baipakov (eds), *History of Civilizations of Central Asia,* vol. V (Paris: Unesco Publishing, 2003), pp. 33–62.

Müller, Claudius und Wenzel, Jacob (eds), *Dschingis Khan und seine Erben. Das Weltreich der Mongolen*, exhib. cat., Kunst und Ausstellungshalle der Bundesrepublik, Bonn (Munich: Hirmer, 2005).

Müller, Gerhard Friedrich, *Sammlung Russischer Geschichte. Des zweyten Bandes fünftes u. sechstes Stück* (St Petersburg: Kaiserliche Academie der Wissenschaften, 1758).

Munis, Shir Muhammad Mirab and Agahi, Muhammad Riza Mirab, *Firdaws al-Iqbal. History of Khorezm*, translated and annotated by Yuri Bregel (Leiden: Brill, 1999).

Murawjew, Nicolaus von, *Des Kaiserlichen Russischen Gesandten Nicolaus von Murawjew Reise durch Turkmanien nach Chiwa in den Jahren 1819 und 1820* (Berlin: Reimer, 1824).

Mursajew, E. M., *Auf unbetretenen Pfaden. Durch Asiens Wüsten und Hochgebirge* (Leipzig: Brockhaus, 1956).

Nalivkine, Vladimir Petrovic, *Histoire du Khanat de Khokand* (Paris: Ernest Leroux, 1889).

Napoleon Bonaparte, 'Instructions for General Gardane, 10 May 1807', in: *The Great Game. Britain and Russia in Central Asia*, edited by Martin Ewans, vol. I: Documents (London: Routledge, 2004), pp. 53–56.

Naumkin, Vitaly V., *Radical Islam in Central Asia: Between Pen and Rifle* (Lanham: Rowman & Littlefield, 2005).

Nebolsin, P.J. 'Bericht eines russischen Handelsreisenden über Taschkent', *Archiv für wissenschaftliche Kunde von Rußland*, vol. 11, 1852, pp. 570–79 (Berlin: Reimer, 1852).

Niedermayer, Oskar von, *Afganistan* (Leipzig: Karl W. Hiersemann, 1924).

—*Unter der Glutsonne Irans. Kriegserlebnisse der deutschen Expedition nach Persien und Afganistan* (Hamburg: Uhlenhorst, 1925).

Noack, Christian, 'The western steppe: the Volga-Ural region, Siberia and the Crimea under Russian rule', in: Nicola Di Cosmo, Allen J. Frank and Peter B. Golden (eds), *The Cambridge History of Inner Asia: The Chinggisid Age* (Cambridge: Cambridge University Press, 2009), pp. 303–309.

Noda, Jin, *The Kazakh Khanates between the Russian and Qing Empires. Central Eurasian International Relations during the Eighteenth and Nineteenth Centuries* (Leiden: Brill, 2016).

Nourzhanov, Kirill, 'Russia's Asian Heartland Today and Tomorrow', in: Nick Megoran and Sevara Sharapova (eds), *Central Asia in International Relations. The Legacies of Halford Mackinder* (London: Hurst & Co., 2013), pp. 117–48.

Nurpeis, K., 'Kazakhstan', in: Chahryar Adle, Madhavan K. Palat and Anara Tabyshalieva (eds), *History of Civilizations of Central Asia*, vol. VI (Paris: Unesco Publishing, 2005), pp. 247–62.

O'Connor, Sir Frederick, *On the Frontier and Beyond. A record of thirty years' service* (London: John Murray, 1931).

O'Donovan, Edmond, 'Merv and its surroundings', in: *Proceedings of the Royal Geographical Society and Monthly Record of Geography*, vol. IV, no. 6, June 1882 (London.RGS, 1882), pp. 345–57.

—*The Merv Oasis: Travels and adventures East of the Caspian during the years 1879 – 80 – 81 including five months' residence among the Tekkés of Merv,* 2 vols (London: Smith, Elder & Co. 1882).

O'Hara, Sarah and Heffernan, Michael, 'From Geostrategy to Geo-Economics: The "Heartland" and British Imperialism Before and After Mackinder', in: Nick Megoran and Sevara Sharapova (eds), *Central Asia in International Relations. The*

Legacies of Halford Mackinder* (London: Hurst & Co., 2013), pp. 91–116.

Okada, O., 'Painting in Mughal India', in: Chahryar Adle, Irfan Habib and Karl M. Baipakov (eds), *History of Civilizations of Central Asia,* vol. V (Paris: Unesco Publishing, 2003), pp. 585–609.

Olcott, Martha Brill, *The Kazakhs* (Washington DC: Hoover Institution Press, 1995).

—*Central Asia's New States. Independence, Foreign Policy and Regional Security* (Washington: United States Institute for Peace, 1996).

—*Central Asia's Second Chance* (Washington DC: Carnegie Endowment for International Peace, 2005).

—'Rivalry and Competion in Central Asia', in: Werner Hermann and Johannes F. Linn (eds), *Central Asia and The Caucasus. At the Crossroads of Eurasia in the 21st Century* (Los Angeles: Sage, 2011), pp. 17–42.

—'Central Asia's Oil and Gas Reserves: To Whom Do They Matter?', in: Werner Hermann and Johannes F. Linn (eds), *Central Asia and The Caucasus. At the Crossroads of Eurasia in the 21st Century* (Los Angeles: Sage, 2011), pp. 95–134.

Olivier-Utard, Françoise, *Politique et archéologie. Histoire de la Délégation archéologique française en Afghanistan 1922–1982* (Paris: Éditions Recherche sur les Civilisations, 2003).

Olufsen, Ole, *Through the Unknown Pamirs. The Second Danish Pamir Expedition 1898–99* (London: William Heinemann, 1904).

Omrani, Bijan, 'The Durand Line: History and Problems of the Afghan-Pakistan Border' (London: *Asian Affairs*, vol. XL, no. II, July 2009), pp. 177–95.

Omrani, Bijan and Leeming, Matthew, *Afghanistan. A companion and guide* (Hong Kong: Odyssey, 2005).

Otgony, Purev and Gurbadaryn, Purvee, *Mongolian Shamanism*, 2 vols (Ulaan Baatar: Munkin, 2012).

Ottley, William John, *With Mounted Infantry in Tibet* (London: Smith, Elder & Co., 1906).

Palat, Madhavan K., 'The British in Central Asia', in: Chahryar Adle, Madhavan K. Palat and Anara Tabyshalieva (eds), *History of Civilizations of Central Asia,* vol. VI (Paris: Unesco Publishing, 2005), pp. 103–23.

Pallas, Peter Simon, *Bemerkungen auf einer Reise in die südlichen Statthalterschaften des Russischen Reichs in den Jahren 1793-1794,* 3 vols (Leipzig: G. Martini, 1799–1801).

Palmer, James, *The Bloody White Baron. The extraordinary story of the Russian nobleman who became the last khan of Mongolia* (New York: Basic Books, 2009).

Patrikeef, Felix, 'An Elaboration of Empire: Russia's Eastward Expansion and the Imperial Military', in: Craig Benjamin and Samuel Lieu (eds), *Walls and Frontiers in Inner-Asian History*, Silk Road Studies VI (Turnhout: Brepols, 2002), pp. 79–100.

—'The Geopolitics of Myth: Interwar Northeast Asia and Images of Inner Asian Empire', in: David Christian and Craig Benjamin (eds), *Worlds of the Silk Roads: Ancient and Modern*, Silk Road Studies IV (Turnhout: Brepols, 2000), pp. 239–60.

Patrikeef, Felix and Perkins, John, 'National and Imperial Identity: A Triptych of Baltic Germans in Inner Asia', in: David Christian and Craig Benjamin (eds), *Worlds of the Silk Roads: Ancient and Modern*, Silk Road Studies IV (Turnhout: Brepols, 2000), pp. 291–306.

Paul, Jürgen, *Zentralasien*, Neue Fischer Weltgeschichte Band 10 (Frankfurt am Main: Fischer, 2012).

Paul I, Zar of Russia, 'Excerpts from Personal Supreme Rescripts by His Imperial Majesty Paul I. to the Ataman of the Don Cossack Troops, Cavalry General Vasily Petrovich Orlov, Relating to the Expedition to India, St. Petersburg, 1901,' in: *The Great Game. Britain and Russia in Central Asia*, edited by Martin Ewans, *vol. I: Documents* (London: Routledge, 2004), pp. 46–48.

Pelliot, Paul, *Notes critiques d'histoires Kalmouke*, 2 vols (Paris: Adrien-Maisonneuve, 1960).

Perdue, Peter C., 'Fate and Fortune in Central Eurasian Warfare: Three Qing Emperors and their Mongol Rivals', in: Nicola Di Cosmo (ed.), *Warfare in Inner Asian History* (Leiden: Brill, 2002), pp. 369–404.

—*China Marches West. The Qing Conquest of Central Asia* (Cambridge, MA: Belknap Press, 2005).

Petech, Luciano, *China and Tibet in the Early XVIIIth Century. History of the Establishment of Chinese Protectorate in Tibet* (Leiden: Brill, 1972).

Pewzov, Michail, W., *Wo man mit Ziegeltee bezahlt. Bericht über eine Reise durch die Mongolei und die nördlichen Provinzen des Inneren China* (1883; Shortened German translation Leipzig: Brockhaus, 1953).

Pierce, Richard A., *Russian Central Asia 1867–1917. A study in colonial rule* (Berkeley: University of California Press, 1960).

Plattner, Felix Alfred, *Jesuiten zur See. Der Weg nach Asien* (Zürich: Arlantis, 1946).

Pokotilov, D., *History of the Eastern Mongols during the Ming Dynasty from 1368 to 1634* (Chengtu: West China Union University, 1947).

Pomfret, Richard, 'Trade and Transport in Central Asia', in: Werner Hermann and Johannes F. Linn (eds), *Central Asia and The Caucasus. At the Crossroads of Eurasia in the 21st Century* (Los Angeles: Sage, 2011), pp. 43–61.

Popowski, Josef, *The Rival Powers in Central Asia* (1893; Reprint Quetta: Gosha-e-Adab, 1977).

Pottinger, George, *The Afghan Connection. The Extraordinary Adventures of Major Eldred Pottinger* (Edinburgh: Scottish Academic Press, 1983).

Prejevalsky, Nicolay, *Mongolia, the Tangut Country, and the Solitudes of Northern Tibet, with Introduction and Notes by Henry Yule,* 2 vols (London: Sampson Low, Marston, Searle, & Rivington, 1876).

Prévost d'Exiles, Antoine-François (author, translator and publisher), *Histoire générale des voyages ou nouvelle collection de toutes les relations de voyages par mer et par terre,* vol. 7 of 25, translated from the English: John Green, *A new general collection of voyages and travels* published in London 1745–47 (Paris: Didot, 1749).

Prioux, A., *Les Russes dans l'Asie Centrale. La dernière campagne de Skobelev* (1886; Reprint in the US, no date, *ca*. 2014).

Privratsky, Bruce G., *Muslim Turkestan. Kazak Religion and Collective Memory* (Richmond: Curzon Press, 2001).

Pugachenkova, Galina and Khakimov, *Akbar, The Art of Central Asia* (Leningrad: Aurora, 1988).

—'Architecture in Transoxania and Khurasan', in: Chahryar Adle, Irfan Habib and Karl M. Baipakov (eds), *History of Civilizations of Central Asia*, vol. V (Paris: Unesco Publishing, 2003), pp. 477–508.

The Quran, Arabic-German edition, translated by Hazrat Mirz Nasir Ahmad (Rabwah: Oriental & Religious Publishing Corp. Ltd., 1954).

The Quran, translated into French by D. Masson, 2 vols (Paris: Gallimard, 1967).

The Quran, Arabic-English edition, translated by A. Yusuf Ali (Lahore: Sh. Muhammad Ashraf, 1975).

Radjapova, R.Y., 'Establishment of Soviet power in Central Asia (1917–24)', in: Chahryar Adle, Madhavan K. Palat and Anara Tabyshalieva (eds), *History of Civilizations of Central Asia,* vol. VI (Paris: Unesco Publishing, 2005), pp. 185–210.

Rageth, Jürg, et al., *Turkmen carpets: a new perspective: an interdisciplinary study based on radiocarbon dating, dye, mordant, and technical analysis, as well as historical and art historical sources*; 2 vols (Riehen: Jürg Rageth, 2016).

Rashid, Ahmed, *Taliban: Militant Islam, Oil and Fundamentalism in Central Asia* (London: I.B.Tauris, 2000).

—*Jihad: The Rise of Militant Islam in Central Asia* (New Haven: Yale University Press, 2002).

Rawlinson, Sir Henry, *England and Russia in the East: A Series of Papers on the Political and Geographical Condition of Central Asia* (London: John Murray, 1875).

Rawlinson, Alfred, *Adventures in the Near East, 1918–1922* (London: Andrew Melrose, 1923).

Rayfield, Donald, *Edge of Empires. A History of Georgia* (London: Reaktion Books, 2012).

Reed, J. Todd and Raschke, Diana, *The ETIM. China's Islamic Militants and the Global Terrorist Threat* (Santa Barbara: Praeger, 2010).

Rhie, Marylin M., Thurman, Robert F., *Wisdom and Compassion. The Sacred Art of Tibet* (San Francisco: Asian Art Museum, 1991).

Richards, David, *Taking Command. The Autobiography* (London: Headline, 2014).

Richards, John F., *The Mughal Empire* (Cambridge: Cambridge University Press, 2005).

Richardson, David and Sue, *Qaraqalpaqs of the Aral Delta* (Munich, 2012).

Richardson, Hugh M., *Tibet & and its History* (Boulder: Shambhala, 1984).

Rickmer Rickers, Wilhelm, *The Duab of Turkestan. A physiographic sketch and account of some travels* (Cambridge: Cambridge University Press, 1913).

Roberts, Sean R., 'A "Land of Borderlands": Implication of Xinjiang's Trans-border Interactions', in: S. Frederick Starr (ed.), *Xinjiang. China's Muslim Borderland* (Armonk: M.E. Sharpe, 2004), pp. 216–37.

Roberts of Kandahar, Lord Frederick Sleigh, *Forty-One Years in India: from subaltern to Commander-in-Chief*; 2 vols (London: Bentley, 1897).

Robertson, Sir George Scott, *The Kafirs of the Hindu-Kush* (London: Lawrence & Bullen, 1896).

Robinson, B.W., 'Rothschild and Binney collections: Persian and Mughal arts of the book', in *Persian and Mughal Art*, exhib. cat. (London: P&D Colnaghi, 1976).

Robinson, Francis, *The Mughal Emperors and the Islamic Dynasties of India, Iran and Central Asia* (London: Thames & Hudson, 2007).

Rockhill, William W., *Diary of a Journey through Mongolia and Tibet in 1891 and 1892* (Washington: Smithsonian Institution, 1894).

Roe, Andrew M., *Waging War in Waziristan* (Lawrence: University Press of Kansas, 2010).

Roemer, H.R., 'The Successors of Timur', in Peter Jackson and Laurence Lockhart (eds), *The Cambridge History of Iran: The Timurid and Safavid Periods*, vol. 6 (Cambridge: Cambridge University Press, 1986), pp. 98–146.

—'The Safavid period', in: Peter Jackson and Laurence Lockhart (eds), *The Cambridge History of Iran: The Timurid and Safavid Periods*, vol. 6 (Cambridge: Cambridge University Press, 1986), pp. 147–88.

—'The Türkmen dynasties', in: Peter Jackson and Laurence Lockhart (eds), *The Cambridge History of Iran: The Timurid and Safavid Periods*, vol. 6 (Cambridge: Cambridge University Press, 1986), pp. 189–372.

Roerich, Georges de, *Sur les pistes de l'Asie Centrale* (Paris: Geuthner, 1933).

Romanovsky, D., *Notes on the Central Asiatic Question* (Calcutta: Office of Superintendent of Government Printing, 1870).

Rorlich, Azade-Ayse, *The Volga Tatars. A Profile in National Resilience* (Stanford: Hoover Institution Press, 1986).

Rossabi, Morris, *Modern Mongolia. From Khans to Commissars to Capitalists* (Berkeley: University of California Press, 2005).

Roskoschny, Hermann, *Afghanistan und seine Nachbarländer. Der Schauplatz des letzten russisch-englischen Konflikts in Zentral-Asien*, 2 vols (Leipzig: Gressner & Schramm, 1885).

Roth Li, Gertraude, 'State Building before 1644', in: Williard J. Peterson (ed.), *The Cambridge History of China, Vol. 9. Part One: The Ch'ing Empire to 1800* (Cambridge: Cambridge University Press, 2002), pp. 9–72.

Roux, Jean-Paul, *Histoire des Turcs. Deux milles ans du Pacifique à la Méditerranée* (Paris: Fayard, 1984).

—*L'Asie Centrale: Histoire et civilisations* (Paris: Fayard, 1997).

Roy, Olivier, *L'Afghanistan. Islam et modernité politique* (Paris: Le Seuil, 1985).

Roxburgh, David J. (ed.), *Turks: A Journey of a Thousand Years, 600–1600*, exhib. cat. (London: Royal Academy of Arts, 2005).

Rubel, Paula G., *The Kalmyk Mongols. A Study in Continuity and Change* (Bloomington: Indiana University, 1967).

Rudelson, Justin and Jankowiak, William, 'Acculturation and Resistance: Xinjiang's Identities in Flux', in: S. Frederick Starr (ed.), *Xinjiang. China's Muslim Borderland* (Armonk: M.E. Sharpe, 2004), pp. 299–319.

Rumer, Boris (ed.), *Central Asia: At the End of the Transition* (Armonk: M.E. Sharpe, 2005).

Rupen, Robert, *How Mongolia is Really Ruled. A Political History of the Mongolian People's Republic 1900–1978* (Stanford: Hoover Institution Press, 1979).

Ryavec, Karl, E., *A Historical Atlas of Tibet* (Chicago: The University of Chicago Press, 2015).

Rybitschka, Emil, *Im gottgegebenen Afghanistan als Gäste des Emirs* (Leipzig: Brockhaus, 1927).

Rytschkow, Nikokaus, *Herrn Nikolaus Rytschkow kaiserlicher russischer Capitains Tagebuch über seine Reise durch verschiedne Provinzen des russischen Reichs in den Jahren 1769, 1770 und 1771* (Riga: Johann Friedrich Hartknoch, 1774).

Sabloff, Paula W. (ed.), *Modern Mongolia. Reclaiming Genghis Khan* (Philadelphia: University of Pennsylvania, 2001).

Sagaster, Klaus, 'Der mongolische Buddhismus', and 'Das Kloster Erdeni Joo (Erdenezuu)', in: Claudius Müller and Jacob Wenzel (eds), *Dschingis Khan und seine Erben. Das Weltreich der Mongolen*, exhib. cat., Kunst und Ausstellungshalle der Bundesrepublik, Bonn (Munich: Hirmer, 2005), pp. 342–56.

Saikal, Amin, *Modern Afghanistan. A History of Struggle and Survival* (London: I.B.Tauris, 2012).

Sala, Renato and Deom, Jean-Marc, *Petroglyphs of South Kazakhstan* (Almaty: Laboratory of Geoarchaeology, 2005).

Sale, Lady Florentia, *A Journal of the Disasters in Afghanistan, 1841–2* (1843; Reprint Uckfield: The Naval and Military Press, 2005).

Salzmann, Erich von, *Im Sattel durch Zentralasien. 6000 Kilometer in 176 Tagen* (Berlin: Reimer, 1908).

Sanders, Alan K., *Historical Dictionary of Mongolia* (Lanham: Scarecrow Press, 2003).

Sargent, Michael, 'British Milirary Involvement in Transcaspia (1918–1919)', in: *Conflict Studies Research Centre, Caucasus Series* (Shrivenham: Defence Academy, 2004/2), pp. 1–50. https://www.files.ethz.ch/isn/87659/04_apr.pdf

Saruulbuyan, J., Eregzen, G. and Bayarsaikhan, J. (eds), *National Museum of Mongolia* (Ulaan Baatar: The National Museum of Mongolia, 2009).

Sawa, Hisaji (ed.), *Gobi Sabaku [The Gobi Desert]* (Tokyo: Meguro Shoten Shôwa 18, 1943).

Schamiloglu, Uli, 'Tatar or Turk? Competing Identities in the Muslim Turkic World during the Late Nineteenth and Early Twentieth Centuries', in: Ergun Çağatay and Dogan Kuban (eds), *The Turkic Speaking Peoples: 2,000 Years of Art and Culture from Inner Asia to the Balkans* (Munich/New York: Prestel, 2006), pp. 232–43.

Schefer, Charles, *Histoire de l'Asie Centrale par Mir Abdoul Kerim Boukhary. Afghanistan, Boukhara, Khiva, Khoqand depuis les dernières années du règne de Nadir Chah, 1153 jusqu'en 1223 de l'Hégire, 1740–1818 A.D.* (1876; Reprint Amsterdam: Philo Press, 1970).

Schlagintweit, Hermann Rudolph Alfred, *Reisen in Indien und Hochasien: Eine Darstellung der Landschaft, der Cultur und Sitten der Bewohner, in Verbindung mit klimatischen und geologischen Verhältnissen: Basirt auf die Resultate der wissenschaftlichen Mission von Hermann, Adolph und Robert von Schlagintweit, ausgeführt den in den Jahren 1854–1858*, 4 vols (1869–80; Reprint Saarbrücken: Fines Mundi, 2006).

Schulemann, Günther, *Geschichte der Dalai-Lamas* (Leipzig: VEB Otto Harrassowitz, 1958).

Schulze, Helmut R., *Afghanistan. Reisen hinter den Horizont* (Heidelberg: Edition HRS, 2008).

Schuyler, Eugene, *Turkistan. Notes on a Journey in Russian Turkestan, Khokand, Bukhara, and Khuldja*, 2 vols (New York: Scribner, Armstrong & Co., 1876).

Schwarz, Franz von, *Turkestan, die Wiege der indogermanischen Völker* (Freiburg i.B.: Herdersche Verlagshandlung, 1900).

Schwarz, Henry G., 'The Khwajas of Eastern Turkestan', in: *Central Asiatic Journal*, vol. 20, No. 4 (Wiesbaden: Harrassowitz, 1976), pp. 266–96.

'Secret Committee's Despatch to Lord Auckland, 25 January 1836', published as 'The Secret Committee of the East India Company's Board of Control prompts and authorizes the Governor-General to initiate the First Anglo-Afghan War', in: *The Great Game. Britain and Russia in Central Asia*, edited by Martin Ewans, vol. IV (London: RoutledgeCurzon, 2004), pp. 84f.

Seidt, Hans-Ulrich, *Berlin, Kabul, Moskau. Oskar Ritter von Niedermayer und Deutschlands Geopolitik* (München: Universitas, 2002).

Semenov, Petr Petrovich, *Travels in the Tian'Shan' 1856–1857* (London: Haklyut Society, 1998).

Sergeev, Evgeny, *The Great Game 1856–1907. Russo-British Relations in Central and East Asia* (Washington: Woodrow Wilson Center Press, 2013).

Shah, Mir Hussain, 'Afghanistan', in: Chahryar Adle, Irfan Habib and Karl M. Baipakov (eds), *History of Civilizations of Central Asia*, vol. V (Paris: Unesco Publishing, 2003), pp. 273–98.

Shakabpa, Tsepon W.D., *Tibet: A Political History* (New York: Potala Publications, 1984).

Shakespear, Richmond, 'A Personal Narrative of a Journey from Heraut to Ourenbourg on the Caspian in 1840', in: *The Great Game. Britain and Russia in Central Asia*, edited by Martin Ewans, *vol. I: Documents* (London: Routledge, 2004), pp. 95–135.

Shaw, Robert, *Visits to High Tartary, Yârkand, and Kâshghar (formerly Chinese Tartary), and Return Journey over the Karakoram Pass* (London: John Murray, 1871).

Shichor, Yitzak, 'The Great Wall of Steel: Military and Strategy in Xinjiang', in: S. Frederick Starr (ed.), *Xinjiang. China's Muslim Borderland* (Armonk: M.E. Sharpe, 2004), pp. 120–60.

Siegel, Jennifer, *Endgame. Britain, Russia and the Final Struggle for Central Asia* (London: I.B.Tauris, 2002).

Sikorski, Radek, *Dust of the saints. A journey to Herat in time of war* (London: Chatto & Windus, 1989).

Simpson, William, *The Autobiography of William Simpson, R.I.* Edited by George Eyre-Todd (1903; Reprint Oxton: InfoDial, 2007).

Sinha, Sri Prakash, *Afghanistan im Aufruhr* (Freiburg i.B.: HeCHt-Verlag, 1980).

Skobelev, M.D., 'Memorandum of Adjutant General M.D. Skobelev about a campaign to India', January 1878, in: Martin Ewans (ed.), *Great Power Rivalry in Central Asia, 1842–1880, vol. I: Documents* (London: Routledge, 2006), pp. 439–48.

Skrine, Clairmont Percival, *Chinese Central Asia* (London: Methuen, 1926).

Skrine, Clairmont Percival and Nightingale, Pamela, *Macartney at Kashgar. New Light on British, Chinese and Russian Activities in Sinkiang, 1890–1918* (1973; Oxford: Oxford University Press, 1987).

Smagulov, E.A., *Drevnii Sauran* (Almaty: ABDI, 2005).

Sneath, David, *The Headless State. Aristocratic orders, kinship society and misrepresentations of nomadic Inner Asia* (New York: Columbia University Press, 2007).

Snelling, John, *Buddhism in Russia. The Story of Agvan Dorzhiev, Lhasa's Emissary to the Tsar* (Shaftesbury: Element, 1993).

Solomon, Hilel, 'The Anfu Clique and China's Abrogation of Outer Mongolian Autonomy', *The Mongolia Society Bulletin*, vol. 10, No. 1 (Bloomington, 1971), pp. 67–86.

Soucek, Svat, *A History of Inner Asia* (Cambridge: Cambridge University Press, 2000).

Spence, Jonathan, 'The K'ang-hsi Reign', in: Williard J. Peterson (ed.), *The Cambridge History of China, Vol. 9. Part One: The Ch'ing Empire to 1800* (Cambridge: Cambridge University Press, 2002), pp.120–82.

Spuler, Bertold, *Die Goldene Horde. Die Mongolen in Rußland 1223–1502* (Leipzig: Harrassowitz, 1943).

Ssanang Ssetsen Chungtaidschi, *Geschichte der Ost-Mongolen und ihres Fürstenhauses [Erdeni-tobči]*, trans. from the Mongolian and ed. by Issac Jacob Schmidt (St Petersburg, 1829).

Starr, S. Frederick (ed.), *Xinjiang. China's Muslim Borderland* (Armonk: M.E. Sharpe, 2004).

—*Ferghana Valley. The Heart of Central Asia* (Armonk: M.E. Sharpe, 2011).

Starr, S. Frederick and Perdue, Peter C., 'Political and Cultural History of the Xinjiang Region through the Late Nineteenth Century', in: S. Frederick Starr (ed.), *Xinjiang. China's Muslim Borderland* (Armonk: M.E. Sharpe, 2004), pp. 27–62.

Starr, S. Frederick and Tursun, Nabijan, 'Political History and Strategies of Control, 1884–1978', in: S. Frederick Starr (ed.), *Xinjiang. China's Muslim Borderland* (Armonk: M.E. Sharpe, 2004), pp. 63–100.

'State of the Taliban, January 6, 2012. Detainee perspectives. A summary of reflections on the current state of the insurgency, ISAF operational effectiveness, external influences shaping the Taliban, and their views on ending the war and moving forward.' Secret Report ISAF. http://s3.documentcloud.org/documents/296489/taliban-report.pdf

Staunton, Sir George Thomas, *Narrative of the Chinese embassy to the khan of the Tourgouth Tartars, in the years 1712, 13, 14 & 15, by the Chinese ambassador [T'u-Li-Shin], and published by the emperor's authority, at Pekin* (London: John Murray, 1821).

Stein, Sir Aurel, *Innermost Asia: Detailed Report of Explorations in Central Asia, Kan-su and Eastern Iran*, 3 vols (Oxford: Clarendon Press, 1928).

Sternberg, Troy, 'Desert Boundaries: the once and future Gobi', *The Geographical Journal*, vol. 181, No.1, March 2015 (London: RGS, 2015), pp. 61–72.

Stewart, Jules, *Spying for the Raj. The Pundits and the Mapping of the Himalaya* (Stroud: Sutton Publishing, 2006).

—*On Afghanistan's Plains. The Story of Britain's Afghan Wars* (London: I.B.Tauris, 2011).

—*The Kaiser's Mission to Kabul. A Secret Expedition to Afghanistan in World War I* (London: I.B.Tauris, 2014).

Stöllner, Thomas und Samašhev, Zajnolla (eds), *Unbekanntes Kasachstan. Archäologie im Herzen Asiens*, exhib. cat., 2 vols (Bochum: Deutsches Bergbau-Museum, 2013).

Strahlenberg, Philipp Johann von, *Das Nord- und Östliche Theil von Europa und Asia, in so weit solches das gantze russische Reich mit Sibirien und der grossen Tartarey in sich begreiffet* (Stockholm: published by author, 1730).

Strindberg, August, 'Philipp Johann von Strahlenberg och hans karta öfver Asien', in: *Svenska Sällskapet för anthropolpgi och geografi* (Stockholm: Geografiska Sektionens Tidskrift, vol. I, nr. 6, 1879), pp. 1–12.

Stuckert, Rudolf, *Erinnerungen an Afghanistan 1940–1946. Aus dem Tagebuch eines Schweizer Architekten* (Liestal: Fondation Bibliotheca Afghanica, 1994).

Süleymanova, Güzel Valeeva, 'Tatar Art and Culture at the Crossroads of Civilization', in: Ergun Çağatay and Dogan Kuban (eds), *The Turkic Speaking Peoples: 2,000 Years of Art and Culture from Inner Asia to the Balkans* (Munich/New York: Prestel, 2006), pp. 214–31.

Sultan-i-Rome, 'The Durand Line Agreement (1893): – Its Pros and Cons' (2004), http://www.valleyswat.net/literature/papers/The_Durand_Line_Agreement.pdf

Sun Tsu, *The Art of War*, transl. Thomas Cleary (Boston: Shambala, 1988).

Swinson, Arthur, *Beyond the Frontiers. The Biography of Colonel F.M. Bailey, Explorer and Secret Agent* (London: Hutchinson, 1971).

Sykes, Sir Percy, *Thousand Miles in Persia or Eight Years in Iran* (London: John Murray, 1902).

—'Persia and the great war', *Journal of the The Royal Central Asian Society*, vol. IX, No. 4, 1922 (London: Royal Central Asian Society, 1922), pp. 175–87.

—*A History of Persia*, 2 vols (London: Macmillan, 1930).

— 'Afghanistan: The present position', *Royal Central Asian Journal*, vol. XXVII, No. 2, April 1940 (London: Royal Central Asian Society, 1940), pp. 141–71.

—*A History of Afghanistan*, 2 vols (1940; reprint, New Delhi: Manoharlal, 2002).

Sykes, Ella and Sir Percy, *Through Deserts and Oases of Central Asia* (London: Macmillan, 1920).

Syroezhkin, Konstantin, 'Russia: On the Path to Empire', in: Boris Rumer (ed.), *Central Asia: At the End of the Transition* (Armonk: M.E. Sharpe, 2005), pp. 93–129.

Tabyshalieva, Anara, 'Kyrgyzstan', in: Chahryar Adle, Madhavan K. Palat and Anara Tabyshalieva (eds), *History of Civilizations of Central Asia*, vol. VI (Paris: Unesco Publishing, 2005), pp. 271–85.

Tadgell, Christopher, *Islam: From Medina to the Maghreb and from the Indies to Istanbul – Architecture in Context III* (London: Routledge, 2008).

Taki, Victor, *Tsar and Sultan. Russian Encounters with the Ottoman Empire* (London: I.B.Tauris, 2016).

Tanaka, Giichi, *Eingabe an den japanischen Kaiser über eine positive Politik gegen die Mandschurei und Mongolei, eingereicht am 25. Juli 1927 vom Premierminister Tanaka* (Woosung: Tung-Chi Universität, 1932).

Tanner, Stephen, *Afghanistan: A Military History from Alexander the Great to the War against the Taliban* (Cambridge, MA: Da Capo Press, 2002).

Tavernier, Jean-Baptiste, *Les six voyages de Jean-Baptiste Tavernier, ecuyer baron d'Aubonne, en Turquie, en Perse, et aux Indes: pendant l'espace de quarante ans, & par toutes les routes que l'on peut tenir, accompagnez d'observations particulieres sur la qualité, la religion, le gouvernement, les coûtumes & le commerce de chaque pays, avec les figures, le poids, & la valeur des monnoyes qui y ont cours*, 3 vols (Utrecht: Guillaume van de Water, Guillaume & Jacob Poolsum, 1712).

Tchoroev, T., 'The Kyrgyz', in: *History of Civilizations of Central Asia*, vol. V, eds Chahryar Adle, Irfan Habib and Karl M. Baipakov (Paris: Unesco Publishing, 2003), pp. 109–25.

Teague-Jones, Reginald, *The Spy Who Disappeared. Diary of a Secret Mission to Russian Central Asia in 1918. Introduction and Epilogue by Peter Hopkirk* (London: Victor Gollancz, 1990).

Techno-economic assessment study for Rogun hydroelectric construction project. Executive Summary (The World Bank, July 2014). https://www.worldbank.org/content/dam/Worldbank/document/eca/central-asia/TEAS_Executive%20Summary_Final_eng.pdf

Teichman, Sir Eric, *Journey to Turkistan* (London: Hodder and Stoughton, 1937).

Terentief, M.A., *Russia and England in Central Asia*, translated from the Russian by F.C. Daukes, 2 vols (1876, Reprint, Delhi: Facsimile Publisher, 2016).

Thomas, Lowell, *Beyond Khyber Pass* (London: Hutchinson, 1927).

Timkovski, George, *Voyage à Pékin. A travers la Mongolie en 1820 et 1821* (1823, reprint of the French translation from 1827; Édition Kimé, 1993).

Tod, J.K., 'The Malleson Mission to Transcaspia in 1918', *Royal Central Asian Journal*, vol. XXVII, No. 1, January 1940 (London: Royal Central Asian Society, 1940), pp. 45–67.

Tomsen, Peter, *The Wars of Afghanistan. Messianic terrorism, tribal conflicts, and the failures of the Great Powers* (New York: Public Affairs, 2013).

Tomson Glover, J., 'Present-day Kashgaria', *Royal Central Asian Journal*, vol. XXIV, No. 3, July 1937 (London: Royal Central Asian Society, 1937), pp. 437–53.

Toops, Stanley W., 'The demography of Xinjiang', in: Starr, S. Frederick (ed.), *Xinjiang. China's Muslim Borderland* (Armonk: M.E. Sharpe, 2004), pp. 241–63.

—'The ecology of Xinjiang', in: Starr, S. Frederick (ed.), *Xinjiang. China's Muslim Borderland* (Armonk: M.E. Sharpe, 2004), pp. 264–75.

Treaty of Gandamak, 26 May 1879 http://www.phototheca-afghanica.ch/uploads/tx_fmphototheca/Treaty_of_Gandamak.pdf

Tredinnick, Jeremy, Baumer, Christoph and Bonavia, Judy, *Xinjiang: China's Central Asia* (Hong Kong: Odyssey, 2012).

Trench, Charles Chenevix, *The Frontier Scouts* (Oxford: Oxford University Press, 1986).

Trevelyan, C.E. and Conolly, Arthur, 'Dispatch No. 24 to Lord Bentinck of 15 March 1831', published as 'Advice on the likelihood of a Russian invasion of India', in: *The Great Game. Britain and Russia in Central Asia,* edited by Martin Ewans, vol. IV (London: RoutledgeCurzon, 2004), pp. 78–83.

Trotter, Sir Henry, 'The Amir Yakoub Khan and Eastern Turkistan in mid-nineteenth century', *Asian Affairs*, vol. IV, No. 4, July 1917 (London: Royal Society for Asian Affairs, 1917), pp. 95–112.

Turnerelli, Edward Tracy, *Russia on the Borders of Asia: Kazan, the ancient capital of the Tartar khans*, 2 vols (London: R. Bentley, 1854).

Twitchett, Denis and Grimm, Tilemann, 'The Cheng-t'ung, Ching-t'ai, and T'ien-shun reigns, 1436–1464', in: Denis Twitchett and John K. Fairbank (eds), *The Cambridge History of China, Vol. 7: The Ming Dynasty, 1368–1644, Part I* (Cambridge: Cambridge University Press, 1988), pp. 395–342.

Uchtomskij, Esper Esperowitsch, *Orientreise. Orientreise seiner kaiserlichen Hoheit des Großfürsten-Thronfolgers Nikolaus Alexandrowitsch von Rußland, 1890–1891*, 2 vols (Leipzig: Brockhaus 1894, 1899).

Ullman, Richard H. *Intervention and the War. Anglo-Soviet Relations, 1917–1921* (Princeton: Princeton University Press, 1961).

Uloth, Gerald, *Riding to War* (Stockbridge: Monks, 1993).

Valikanof, Shoqan and Veniukof, M., *The Russians in Central Asia: Their occupation of the Kirghiz Steppe and the line of the Syr-Darya, their political relations with Khiva, Bokhara, and Kokan; also descriptions of Chinese Turkestan and Dzungaria,* transl. John and Robert Michell (1865, Print on demand, Charleston: Nabu Press 2016).

Vámbéry, Arminius, *Voyages d'un faux derviche dans l'Asie Centrale de Téhéran à Khiva, Bokhara et Samarcand par le grand désert Turkoman* (Paris: Hachette, 1865).

Vasilev, D., 'The Sayan-Altai Mountain Region and South-Eastern Siberia', in: Chahryar Adle, Madhavan K. Palat and Anara Tabyshalieva (eds), *History of Civilizations of Central Asia,* vol. VI (Paris: Unesco Publishing, 2005), pp. 329–45.

Vaughan, Philippa, 'Geschichte [Indien: Sultanate und Moghuln]', in: Markus Hattstein and Peter Delius (eds), *Islam: Kunst und Architekur* (Cologne: Könemann, 2000), pp. 452–63.

—'Architektur [Indien: Sultanate und Moghuln]', in: Markus Hattstein and Peter Delius (eds), *Islam: Kunst und Architekur* (Cologne: Könemann, 2000), pp. 464–83.

—'Dekorative Künste [Indien: Sultanate und Moghuln]', in: Markus Hattstein and Peter Delius (eds), *Islam: Kunst und Architekur* (Cologne: Könemann, 2000), pp. 484–89.

Veit, Veronika, 'The eastern steppe: Mongol regimes after the Yuan (1368–1636)', in: Nicola Di Cosmo, Allen J. Frank and Peter B. Golden (eds), *The Cambridge History of Inner Asia: The Chinggisid Age* (Cambridge: Cambridge University Press, 2009), pp. 157–81.

Veltzke, Veit, *Unter Wüstensöhnen. Die deutsche Expedition Klein im Ersten Weltkrieg* (Berlin: Nicolai, 2014).

Vereshchagin, V., *Turkestan. Etyudy s natury. Études d'apres nature. Studien nach der Natur. Herausgegeben im Auftrag des General-Gouverneurs von Turkestan* (St Petersburg: Hofkunstbuchhandlung A. Beggrow, 1874).

Vigne, Godfrey T., *A Personal Narrative of a Visit to Ghuzni, Kabul and Afghanistan* (1840; Reprint New Delhi: Manoharlal, 2004).

Vinsky, G.S., 'Project concerning the consolidation of Russian trade with Upper Asia through Khiva and Bokhara in the year 1818', in: *The Great Game. Britain and Russia in Central Asia*, edited by Martin Ewans, *vol. I: Documents* (London: Routledge, 2004), pp. 65–68.

Visser, Philips Christiaan, 'The Karakoram and Turkmenistan Expedition of 1929–1939', *The Geographical Journal*, vol. LXXXIV, no. 4, October 1934 (London: RGS, 1934), pp. 281–95.

Vogelsang, Willem, *The Afghans* (Chichester: Wiley-Blackwell, 2008).

Voigt, Martin, *Kafiristan. Versuch einer Landeskunde auf Grund einer Reise im Jahre 1928* (Breslau: Ferdinand Hirt, 1933).

Vollmann, William T., *An Afghanistan Picture Show: Or, How I Saved the World* (Brooklyn: Melville House, 2013).

Volodarsky, Michael, 'First Steps in Soviet Diplomacy toward Afghanistan', in: Ro'i, Yaacov (ed.), *The USSR and the Muslim World. Issues in Domestic and Foreign Policy* (London: Routledge, 2015), pp. 215–25.

Voltaire (François Marie d'Arouet), *Histoire de l'empire de Russie sous Pierre le Grand*, 2 vols (no publisher given, 1763).

Waddell, L. Austine, *Lhasa and its Mysteries. With a record of the expedition of 1903–1904* (London: Methuen, 1906).

Waldmann, Matt, 'The Sun in the Sky: The Relationship between Pakistan's ISI and Afghan Insurgents' in: *Crisis States Discussion Papers* (London: Destin LSE, 2010). http://eprints.lse.ac.uk/28435/

Waller, Derek, *The Pundits. British Exploration of Tibet and Central Asia* (Lexington: University of Kentucky, 1990).

Ware, Webb, 'The Nushkhi railway and some of the problems on which it bears', *Journal of the The Royal Central Asia Society*, vol. VI, Nos. 1–2, 1919 (London: Royal Central Asian Society, 1919), pp. 44–87.

—'A long arm through the wilderness', *Journal of the The Royal Central Asia Society*, vol. VII, No. 1, 1920 (London: Royal Central Asian Society, 1920), pp. 34–37.

Weiers, Michael, *Geschichte der Mongolen* (Stuttgart: Kohlhammer, 2004).

Weinshtein, Sew'jan, *Geheimnisvolles Tuva. Expeditionen in das Herz Asiens* (Oststeinbeck: Alouette Verlag, 2005).

Weljaminow-Sernow, A.N., 'Historische Nachrichten über Kokand, vom Chane Muhammed Ali bis Chudajar Chan', in: *Archiv für wissenschaftliche Kunde von Rußland*, vol. 16, 1857, pp. 544–62 (Berlin: Reimer, 1857).

—Nachrichten über das Reich Kokand', in: *Archiv für wissenschaftliche Kunde von Rußland, vol. 17, 1858*, pp. 254–75 (Berlin: Reimer, 1858).

Wellington, Duke of (Arthur Wellesley), *The Eastern Question. Extracted from the Correspondence of the Late Duke of Wellington* (London: John Murray, 1877).

Wessels, Cornelius, *Early Jesuit Travellers in Central Asia 1603–1721* (1924; Reprint New Delhi: Asian Education Services, 1992).

Whiting, Allen S. and General Sheng Shih-ts'ai, *Sinkiang: Pawn or Pivot?* (East Lansing: Michigan State University Press, 1958).

Whitteridge, Gordon, *Charles Masson of Afghanistan: Explorer, Archaeologist, Numismatist and Intelligence Agent* (Bangkok: Orchid Press, 2002).

Wiemer, Calla, 'The Economy of Xinjiang', in: S. Frederick Starr (ed.), *Xinjiang. China's Muslim Borderland* (Armonk: M.E. Sharpe, 2004), pp. 163–89.

Wigram, Sir Kenneth, 'Defence in the North-West Frontier Province', *Royal Central Asian Journal*, vol. XXIV, No. 1, January 1937 (London: Royal Central Asian Society, 1937), pp. 73–89.

Williams, Brian Glyn, *The Last Warlord: The Life and Legend of Dostum, the Afghan Warrior Who Led US Special Forces to Topple the Taliban Regime* (Chicago: Chicago Review Press, 2013).

Wilson, Andrew, 'Inside Afghanistan – A background to recent troubles' *Royal Central Asian Journal*, vol. XLVII, No. 3 & 4, July–October 1960 (London: Royal Central Asian Society, 1960), pp. 286–95.

Wilson, Robert, *A Sketch of the Military and Political Power of Russia in the Year 1817,* published in *The Great Game. Britain and Russia in Central Asia,* edited by Martin Ewans, vol. IV (1817, Reprint London: RoutledgeCurzon, 2004).

Wittock, Michel (ed.), *Western Travellers in China. Discovering the Middle Kingdom*, exhib. cat (Brussels: Bibliotheca Wittockiana, 2009).

Wolff, Joseph, *Narrative of a mission to Bokhara in the years 1843–1845, to ascertain the fate of Colonel Stoddart and Captain Conolly* (New York: Harper & Brothers, 1845).

Wood, John, *A Journey to the Source of the River Oxus* (London: John Murray, 1872).

Woodburn, C.W., *The Bala Hissar of Kabul. Revealing a fortress-palace in Afghanistan* (Chatham: Institution of Royal Engineers, 2009).

Woodside, Alexander, 'The Ch'ien-lung Reign', in: Williard J. Peterson (ed.), *The Cambridge History of China, Vol. 9. Part One: The Ch'ing Empire to 1800* (Cambridge: Cambridge University Press, 2002), pp. 230–309.

Wu, Aitchen K., *Turkistan Tumult* (1940; London: Methuen, 1984).

Wyatt, Christopher M., *Afghanistan and the Defence of Empire. Diplomacy and Strategy during the Great Game* (London: I.B.Tauris, 2011).

—'Change and discontinuity: war and Afghanistan, 1904–1924', *Asian Affairs*, vol. XLVII, No. III, November 2016 (London: Royal Society for Asian Affairs, 2016), pp. 366–85.

Wynn, Antony, *Persia in the Great Game. Sir Percy Sykes, Explorer, Consul, Soldier, Spy* (London: John Murray, 2003).

—*Three Camels to Smyrna. Times of War and Peace in Turkey, Persia, India, Afghanistan & Nepal 1907–1986. The Story of the Oriental Carpet Manufactuturers Company* (London: Estate of the late Bryan Huffner, 2008).

Yapp, Malcolm, 'The Legend of the Great Game', in: *Proceedings of the British Academy 111. 2000 Lectures and Memoirs* (London: Oxford University Press, 2001), pp. 179–98.

Yate, Arthur Campbell, *England and Russia Face to Face. Travels with the Afghan Boundary Commission* (Edinburgh: William Blackwood, 1887).

—'Colonel Yate's mission to Herat and the Kushk Valley', *The Scottish Geographical Magazine*, vol. IX, No. 8, August 1893 (Edinburgh: RSGS, 1893), pp. 403–11.

Yeomans, Richard, *The Story of Islamic Architecture* (Reading: Garnet, 1999).

Yorke, Edmund, *Playing the Great Game. Britain, War and Politics in Afghanistan since 1839* (London: Robert Hale, 2012).

Younghusband, Sir Francis, *The heart of a continent: a narrative of travels in Manchuria, across the Gobi desert, through the Himalayas, the Pamirs, and Chitral, 1884–1894* (London: John Murray, 1896).

—*India and Tibet. History of the relations which have subsisted between the two countries from the time of Warren Hastings to 1910; with a particular account of the mission to Lhasa of 1904* (London: John Murray, 1910).

Younghusband, G.J. and Younghusband, Sir Francis, *The Relief of Chitral* (1895; Reprint Rawalpindi: English Book House, 1976).

Yule, Sir Henry (ed. and trans.), *Cathay and the Way Thither: Being a Collection of Medieval Notices of China*, 4 vols (1913–16; reprint, New York: Kraus Reprint, 1967).

Zaitseva, M.S. and Koblova, E.S., *Astrakhan Kremlin* (Astrakhan: JSC Publishing House Nova, 2011).

Zalesof, Colonel, 'Diplomatic Relations between Russia and Bokhara, 1836–1843', in: Shoqan Valikanof and M. Veniukof, *The Russians in Central Asia: Their occupation of the Kirghiz Steppe and the line of the Syr-Darya, their political relations with Khiva, Bokhara, and Kokan; also descriptions of Chinese Turkestan and Dzungaria*, transl. John and Robert Michell (1865; Charleston: Nabu Press, 2016).

—'Colonel Ignatief's Mission to Khiva and Bokhara in 1858', in: Martin Ewans (ed.), *Great Power Rivalry in Central Asia, 1842–1880, vol. I: Documents* (London: Routledge, 2006), pp. 21–86.

Zarcone, Th, 'The Sufi orders in northern Central Asia', in: Chahryar Adle, Irfan Habib and Karl M. Baipakov (eds), *History of Civilizations of Central Asia,* vol. V (Paris: Unesco Publishing, 2003), pp. 771–80.

Zelinskij, A. N., 'Drevnie kreposti na Pamire', in: *Strany i narody Vostoka* 3 (1964), pp. 120–41.

Zhukov, Stanislav and Reznikova, Oksana, 'Economic Ties between Russia and Kazakhstan: Dynamics, Tendencies, and Prospects', in: Boris Rumer (ed.), *Central Asia: At the End of the Transition* (Armonk: M.E. Sharpe, 2005), pp. 417–34.

Ziegler, Gudrun, *Der achte Kontinent* (Berlin: Ullstein, 2005).

Zimmermann, Carl, *Der Kriegs-Schauplatz in Inner-Asien. Bemerkungen zu der Uebersichts-Karte von Afghanistan, dem Punjab und dem Lande am unteren Indus* (Berlin: E.H. Schroeder, 1842).

—*Denkschrift über den unteren Lauf des Oxus zum Karabugas-Haff des Caspischen Meeres und über die Strombahn des Ochus, oder Tedshen der Neueren, zur Balkan-Bay* (Berlin: Reimer, 1845).

Zviagel'skaia, Irina, 'Russia and Central Asia: Problems of Security', in: Boris Rumer (ed.), *Central Asia: At the End of the Transition* (Armonk: M.E. Sharpe, 2005), pp. 71–92.

List of Maps

Satellite imagery © NASA. http://visibleearth.nasa.gov/

Photo Credits

All photos are by the author with the exception of the following:

Bridgeman Images, Berlin, Germany: fig. 110.

British Museum, London, United Kingdom: fig. 4.

Dolya Sergey, Charkiv, Ukraine: fig. 48.

Éditions Glénat, Issy-les-Moulineaux, France: fig. 123.

Etnografiska Museet, Stockholm, Sweden: fig. 39.

Harvard-Yenching University Library, Harvard, USA: fig. 129.

Herfort Frank, Berlin, Germany: figs. 164, 168, 184.

Hormann Christoph, Freiburg, Germany/Imagico.de: figs. 1, 100.

Illustrated London News, London, United Kingdom: fig. 109.

KEYSTONE/MAGNUM PHOTOS/Steve McCurry, USA: figs. 64, 67, 133, 134, 142, 143, 145.

Kreutzmann Hermann, Berlin, Germany: fig. 101.

Kurbatov A.A., Astrakhan Kremlin (Rostow am Don, 2010): fig. 23.

Lujanskij Dimitrij, Bishkek, Kyrgyzstan: fig. 169.

Middleton Robert, Crans, Switzerland: fig. 88.

Municipal Museum of Turkistan, Kazakhstan: fig. 59.

National Army Museum, London, United Kingdom: figs. 80, 93, 94, 96.

Nelson Jimmy, Amsterdam, Netherlands: fig. 127.

Page Warrick, Los Angeles, USA: fig. 105.

Palace Museum Beijing, China: fig. 53.

Paul Getty Museum, Los Angeles, USA: fig. 95.

Phototheca Afghanica, Foundation Bibliotheca Afghanica, Bubendorf, Switzerland: figs. 85, 104, 119, 122.

Rossi & Rossi, London, United Kingdom: front jacket, fig. 46.

Schilling Patrick, Lucerne, Switzerland: fig. 99.

Schulze Helmut R., Heidelberg, Germany: back jacket, figs. 65, 68, 135, 136, 138–41, 144, 146–55, 165, 166, 171, 183.

Sereda Tomas, iStock by Getty Images International, Dublin, Ireland: fig. 182.

Smithsonian Institute. Freer Gallery of Art and Arthur M. Sackler Gallery, Washington DC, USA: figs. 31, 54.

State Hermitage Museum, St Petersburg, Russia: figs. 77, 87.

Sven Hedin Foundation, Stockholm, Sweden: figs. 128, 130.

US Federal Government, public domain, Washington DC, USA: fig. 137.

Weber Therese, Arlesheim, Switzerland: back inner jacket flap, at top.

Weyl Laurent, Argos, Picturetank, Paris, France: fig. 121.

Zanabazar Museum, Ulaan Baatar, Mongolia: fig. 36.

All efforts have been made to name or identify copyright holders. We will endeavour to rectify any unintended omissions in future editions of this work, upon receipt of evidence of relevant intellectual property rights.

Acknowledgements

This book is based on dozens of expeditions and journeys undertaken in the last three decades. My research was successful only thanks to hundreds of kind people in Armenia, Azerbaijan, China, Georgia, India, Iran, Iraq, Kazakhstan, Kyrgyzstan, Mongolia, Pakistan, Russia, Syria, Tajikistan, Tibet, Turkmenistan, Ukraine and Uzbekistan; to all of them I remain grateful. The book itself was produced with the help of several people. Most preferred to remain anonymous; others are briefly acknowledged here, in alphabetical order:

Natalia Boskhaev, Elista, Republic of Kalmykia, Russian Federation, who showed me around in Elista and obtained a permission to photograph prayers and ceremonies inside the *Burkhan Bakshin Altan Sume*, the temple 'Golden Abode of Buddha Shakyamuni' in Elista.

Paul Bucherer-Dietschi, Bubendorf, Switzerland, who let me search in his vast Phototheca Afghanica, Foundation Bibliotheca Afghanica, and put images from his rich archives at my disposal.

Dr Dmitri Voyakin, Almaty, Kazakhstan, who made available scientific literature about recent archaeological discoveries in Kazakhstan.

Helmut R. Schulze, Heidelberg, for interesting and revealing discussions about recent political developments in the new Central Asian Republics and his fascinating photographs.

Håkan Wahlquist, Sven Hedin Foundation, Stockholm, Sweden, for stimulating discussions and the permission to reproduce images taken by Sven Hedin.

Prof Therese Weber, Arlesheim, Switzerland, who accompanied me on numerous expeditions and travels and participated in the research for this more than ten-year-long book project.

Ludmila Zverko, Kazan, Republic of Tatarstan, Russian Federation, who twice showed me Kazan and its surroundings and obtained from the military the permission to photograph the strictly guarded Epiphany celebrations at the Raifa Monastery near Kazan.

Index: Concepts

Humayum Mausoleum, Delhi *46*, 48
Imam Reza, Mashhad 8, 9, 15
Itimad al-Daula Mausoleum, Agra 48
Jahangir Mausoleum, Lahore 48, 57
Khoja Ahmed Yasawi, Turkestan *91*
Niyazov Mausoleum, Turkmenistan *288*
Pahlavan Mahmud Mausoleum, Khiva *22*
Sufi masters' mausoleums 20, 22
Taj Mahal, Agra 48, *54–5*, 57–8
see also architecture
military/warfare equipment:
  Afghanistan 195, 197–8
  aircraft 195, 197, 239, 240, 274, 280
  drones 243, 248
  German Tornado combat aircraft *239*
  helicopter *244–5*
  patrol of German ISAF troops *242*
  the Taliban 233, 240
  see also arms; missiles
minarets 22
  Emin Minaret, Xinjiang *89*
  Kalyan minaret, Bukhara *6*, 20
  'short minaret' Kalta Minar, Khiva *111*
  see also mosques
Ming dynasty of China 25, 63, 65, 68, 70, 71
Ming dynasty of Kokand 19, 119
Ming tribe 19
missiles 197
  anti-tank missiles, Milan type 223
  cruise missiles 234, 235
  intercontinental ballistic missiles 267
  mujahideen and 223
  al-Qaeda and 234
  Stinger missiles 223, 329n53
  see also arms
Moghulistan Khanate 25
monasteries:
  Amarbayas Galant Monastery, Mongolia *199*
  Assumption of the Blessed Virgin Mary, Tatarstan *31, 32*
  Barun-khit Monastery, Mongolia *73*
  Buddhism 65, 68, 70, 72, *73*, 75, 89, *199*, 203, *257*
  destruction of 203
  Erdene Zuu Monastery, Mongolia *68, 70, 71*, 72
  Erdene Zuu Monastery, Altan Stupa and Laviran temple, Mongolia, *69*
  Gandantegchinlen Monastery, Mongolia *257*
  Pelkhor Chöde Monastery of Gyantse, Tibet *167*
  Raifa Monastery, Kazan *34, 35*
  Samye, fortified Buddhist monastery, Mongolia *65*
  Tubten Chokhorling Monastery, Kyzyl, Russia *82*
  see also architecture
Mongol Empire 63, 75
Mongolian Democratic Union 258
Mongols 1, 2, 29, 63, 140
  1640 pan-Mongolian conference 83–4
  Buddhism and 61, 63, 70–3, 75–6, 83, 88, 89, 201, 203
  Chahar Mongols 65
  Dolon Nor allegiance 75, 76, 84, 201
  East Central Asia and 63
  Genghis Khanid Eastern Mongols 63–4, 68, 69, 70
  impoverishment of 90

Khalkha Mongols 75, 81
khoyar yosun alliance 71–3, 75
Manchurian banner system 69
tümen (socio-military units) 68
Uriyangkhad Eastern Mongols 64, 65
Western Mongolian Oirats 25, 63–8, 317n147
Mordvins 29
mosques 188, 190
  Abdullah Khan mosque, Bukhara *5*
  Altyn (Golden) Mosque of Yarkand, Xinjiang *256*
  Badshahi Mosque, Lahore *57*
  Chor-Bakr complex, Bukhara *15*
  destruction of 34, 36, 212
  Friday Mosque of Tilla Kari Madrasah, Samarkand, *21*
  Friday Mosque, Turfan, Xinjiang *89*
  Hazrat Ali Mosque, Mazar-e-Sharif *108–109, 238*
  Id Khah Friday Mosque, Kashgar, Xinjiang *27*
  Jama Masjid/Masjid-i Jahan Numa, Delhi 57, *59*
  Kalyan mosque, Bukhara, *10–11*, 20
  Kul-Sharif Mosque, Tatarstan, Russia 28, *253, 254*
  mihrabs *21*
  Red Mosque, Islamabad 244
  Turkmenbashi Rukhi Mosque *289*
  'White Mosque', Kazan, *253*
  see also architecture; minarets
MPRP (Mongol People's Revolution Party) 258
Mughal dynasty, foundation of 48
Mughal Empire 4, 8, 16, 20, 48, *49*, 103, 106, 311n3
  borders 48, 52
  decline 48, 59–60
  Islamic state/Islamisation of 58–9
  a land power 48
  Peacock Throne 57, 60
  Russia/Indian Mughals land route 24
Muhammadzai-Barakzai dynasty 110
mujahideen 214–17, 222, 328n5
  1991 Negative Symmetry Agreement 225
  AIG (Afghan Interim Government) 224
  banditry and 228
  China and 219, 220
  Deobandis and 220
  financial supporters of 2, 220
  guerrilla war of 2, 217, 219–23
  ISI and 219, 220, 224
  Kabul and 227, 228
  missiles and 223
  mujahideen fighters *214, 228*
  Muslim Brotherhood 220
  opium/drug trade and 216–17, 228
  Pakistan and 2, 219, 220, 221
  power struggle of 230–4
  praying mujahid *215*
  Saudi Arabia and 2, 215, 220, 221
  Soviet Union and 2, 219–20, 222–3, 227
  Sunni mujahideen organizations recognised by Pakistan 220, 221
  training of 220
  US and 2, 215, 219–20, 221, 224, 227
  Wahhabism and 220
  Xinjiang and 254–5
  see also Afghanistan Wars; Islamism; jihad
Muscovy Company 13–14

Muslim Brotherhood 198, 220, 224, 278, 327n149
  use of violence and 328n8
MVP (Mongolian People's Party) 202

N

Napoleonic Wars 1, 100, 125, 131
Naqshbandi Sufi Order 20, 22, 26, 56, 196
  khojas/*khwajas* 26, 119
nationalism 171, 175, 176, 201, 202
  Afghan nationalists 234
  cultural nationalism 277
  Muslim nationalists 174, 179
  nationalist fundamentalists 282
  Russian nationalism 190
  Uyghur nationalists 209, 317n110
NATO (North Atlantic Treaty Organization) 102, 237, 243, 247
  Partnership for Peace 266
NEP (New Economic Policy) 179, 188, 202
NGOs (non-governmental organisations) 243, 248–9, 277, 294
  political disturbances and Western NGOs 273, 280
Nogai Horde/Nogai 14, 19, 29, 31, 32, 33, 36, 39–40, 96, 97
  Greater Nogai Horde 39
  Lesser Nogai Horde 39
Norperforce 184
North-East Passage 296
Northern Alliance 230, 235, 237, 241, 244, 248
Northern Yuan dynasty 63
nuclear power/weapons 252, 261
  Kazakhstan and 267–8
  Pakistan and 215, 216, 224, 237
  see also arms

O

October Revolution, Russia (1917) 148, 172, 175, 176, 180
officers, soldiers, guards:
  Afghan officers and leaders, Kabul *152*
  British Indian and Russian officers, Isfahan *181*
  guards and officers, Yarkand *148*
  Indian officers of the 32nd Sikh Pioneers, Khamba Dzong *166*
  ISAF (International Security Assistance Force) *230, 242*
  Northern Alliance *230*
  soldiers from a British Indian regiment, Peshawar Fieldforce *151*
  Yaqub Khan's commanders and officers *149*
oil and gas 172, 180, 219–20, 261, 331n64
  Afghanistan 233
  Arabian Peninsula 172
  Azerbaijan 270
  Baku 39, 182, 183, 184, 210, 326n60
  Caspian Sea 269, 331n60
  CentGas (Central Asia Gas Pipeline) 234
  Central Asia 172, 261, 294
  China 269–70, 288, 292, 297, 333n14
  CNG (compressed natural gas) 261
  Darwaza gas crater *290–1*
  gas and oil pipelines in Central Asia *264–5*

Gazprom 269, 290, 292, 333n179
'Great Game of Pipelines' 233
Iran 2, 172, 290, 292
Kazakhstan 261, 269–70
Kazakhstan-Xinjiang pipelines 2, 255, 269–70, 288, 333n175
LNG (Liquefied natural gas) 261, 290, 296, 297
Middle East 172
oil refinery of Atyrau, Kazakhstan *295*
Pakistan 233
Persia 172
pipelines 2, 233, 261, 269, 290
Russian Federation 261, 269, 290, 297
Russian pipeline monopoly 261, 269, 290, 292, 333n175
sabotaging of pipelines 185
Tajikistan 288
TAP (Turkmenistan-Afghanistan-Pakistan) pipeline 233
TAPI (Turkmenistan-Afghanistan-Pakistan-India) pipeline 290, 292, 297
trans-Afghan pipeline 233, 234, 261
trans-Caspian gas pipeline 270
Turkmenistan 2, 233, 261, 290, 292
US 233, 290, 292
Xinjiang 255–6
Oirats 25, 26, 63, 64, 77, 80, 83
  Buddhism 75
  Oirat Dzungars 314n43
  Oirat Kalmyks 96
  Western Mongolian Oirats 25, 63–8, 70, 317n147
opium 121
  Afghanistan and 236, 247, 329n30
  IMU and 214, 236–7, 279
  mujahideen and 216–17, 228
  opium and heroin smuggling 214, 216–17, 236, 279
  opium poppy and cultivation of food 236, 247
  al-Qaeda and 214, 236–7
  the Taliban 236
Orthodox Church 34, 142, 190
  forced conversion to 34, 36
  Russian Orthodox Nicholas Church, Tajikistan *281*
  see also cathedrals; monasteries
OSI (Open Society Institute) 273
Ottoman Empire 4, 42, 112, 148
  Black Sea and 42
  Britain and 126
  Constantinople and 41
  Crimea and 29, 41, 96, 182
  defeats and decline of 44
  Europe and 125
  jihad against the Allies 185
  Ottoman Islamic Army 182, 183
  Ottoman protectorates 29, 41, 96, 145, 182
  Russia and 125, 150
Ottomans 13, 23, 33–4
  firearms and 47

P

painting 56, 57
  enthronement of an Uzbek or Kazakh khan, Kazakhstan *93*
  miniature painting 52, 56
  Mughal style 56
  thangka painting *62*
palaces:
  Deir al-Aman, 'Palace of Peace',

Index: People

Index: Places

Praise for *The History of Central Asia*

The Age of the Steppe Warriors, Volume 1

'This is a most impressive book. Dr Baumer has a wide-ranging knowledge of his subject, an extensive on-the-ground acquaintance with Central Asia itself, and an ability to convey that knowledge in a most interesting and comprehensible way. He has a gift for the striking observation. For example, he remarks on a curious parallel between a Central Asian story about a hero's sword having to be thrown into the sea and the rather similar tale about Excalibur, commenting that this is perhaps not merely coincidence: might it have something to do with the Sarmatian soldiers sent by Marcus Aurelius to guard Hadrian's Wall? Another excellent idea is the periodic insertion of "excursuses", on such topics as Roy Chapman Andrews the "dinosaur hunter", the Siberian collections of Peter the Great, and the Amazons. No history of Central Asia, or indeed of anywhere else, can ultimately claim to be "complete". But this one is certainly very comprehensive indeed, far more so than any other recent work of which I am aware. The publication of this volume, and of its successors too, seems to me to be a very valuable enterprise indeed.'
—**David Morgan**, Professor Emeritus of History, University of Wisconsin-Madison, and author of *The Mongols*.

'*The Age of the Steppe Warriors* is as magnificent as it is magisterial. From landscapes and ancient stelae to artefacts of gold, bronze, wood and even textile, the book is filled with images that are in turn fascinating, mysterious and dazzling. For the most part, the photos are of places that are inaccessible to most of us or of artefacts from museums in Russia and Central Asia that few readers will have ever visited... *The Age of the Steppe Warriors* is a beautiful, evocative and thought-provoking book.'
—*Asian Review of Books*

'In an age of specialists, Christoph Baumer is a rare creature: a generalist. Explorer, archaeologist, adventurer, enthusiast, historian, photographer – no one could be better qualified to tackle a subject so vast in time and space. He must be a book lover, for this, the first of four volumes on the subject, is a gorgeous creation, with creamy paper, crisp design and perfect colour pictures... A cultural guidebook on a grand scale... [it] is stamped with his personality... The start of a truly monumental undertaking.'
—*Literary review*

The Age of the Silk Roads, Volume 2

'Christoph Baumer devotes the second book of his four-volume history of Central Asia to the Silk Roads, those extraordinarily significant routes that linked the Eurasian civilizations. He provides an excellent description, focusing on their importance in cultural diffusion. In this well-written survey, Baumer offers the reader a clear portrait of the array of societies that flourished along the Silk Roads. Just as valuable, he emphasizes the means by which religions, methods of governance, and technological innovations spread across Eurasia. He enlivens the text with colorful depictions of rulers, commanders, and voyagers who played notable roles in Silk Roads history. Well-versed in the secondary literature, Baumer provides fine coverage of the Silk Roads' numerous influences on civilizations.'
—**Morris Rossabi**, Distinguished Professor of History, The City University of New York, and Adjunct Professor of Inner Asian History, Columbia University

'It is difficult to fault this remarkable volume. The publishers have created a book of quality with stunning illustrations and lucid maps. It will, I believe, become a standard reference for all who study the complex history of Central Asia and the Silk Road. This is the second volume of Christoph Baumer's projected four-book series on Central Asia and shows its author to be an extraordinary person, whose skills encompass those of an explorer, a historian, an archaeologist and a photographer. Moreover, in each of these exacting disciplines he is no amateur. He displays the rare qualities of both an academic and a man of action. His sparkling prose ensures that the armchair traveller will not nod off. Because of the author's personal engagement this book exudes authority.'
—*Spectator*

The Age of Islam and the Mongols, Volume 3

'This lavishly illustrated book provides a most welcome overview of an often overlooked region during a still more neglected period of history. Addressing the rise of the independent Iranian states that had begun to throw off the Arab stranglehold which descended upon the whole region in the seventh century, Christoph Baumer charts the re-emergence of the Persians and establishment of those Iranian dynastic regimes that succeeded in distancing themselves from the Abbasid caliphs and expanded to the east. This is a hugely ambitious project but Baumer has succeeded in presenting a magnificent vision of medieval Turkestan, combining concise and comprehensive narrative with gorgeous, often startling but always captivating and vivid images. This a remarkable book which maintains the exemplary standards which have earned the author his fully deserved reputation.'
—**George Lane**, Senior Teaching Fellow in the History of the Middle East and Central Asia, SOAS, University of London, author of *Early Mongol Rule in Thirteenth-Century Iran* (2003), *Genghis Khan and Mongol Rule* (2004), *Daily Life in the Mongol Empire* (2009) and *A Short History of the Mongols* (I.B.Tauris, 2018)

'Central Asia history can be confusing for the non-specialist. Into this confusion steps Christoph Baumer with a masterly third volume in his four-volume series on Central Asia, covering the age of Islam and the Mongols. With his consummate professionalism, Baumer cuts through the historical smokescreen and gives a detailed and authoritative account appropriate for both scholar and layman alike. Many have written about Genghis Khan and his successors' national and international military campaigns. But seldom has the prose been lucid and the illustrations so illuminating. In the Great Khan's words, "All the face of the earth from the going up of the sun to its going down [has been] given [to me by God]." Under Baumer's expert guidance and firm hand, historians, religious scholars and the non-specialist can follow Genghis Khan's Islamic predecessors and the Mongols along the surface of the earth.'
—*Spectator*

The Age of Decline and Revival, Volume 4

'Christoph Baumer's highly anticipated *The Age of Decline and Revival* completes his four-volume *The History of Central Asia* and takes the story of this important region up to the present-day. The text is beautifully produced and illustrated, featuring excellent maps, and is informed by a high level of scholarship that comprehensively and uniquely integrates history and archaeology with artistic, cultural and economic developments. Another remarkable aspect of Baumer's work is its inclusiveness, drawing on an extensive range of materials from the Caucasus to China. The series is a must-have for anyone interested in this vast area lying at the very centre of world history.'
—**John E Woods**, Professor of Iranian and Central Asian History, University of Chicago

FINLAND
○ Helsinki
○ Tallinn
ESTONIA
○ Riga
LATVIA
Moscow ○

LITHUANIA
Vilnius ○
○ Minsk
BELARUS
Warsaw ○
POLAND
RUSSIA

Vistula River

CZECH
REPUBLIC
SLOVAKIA
○ Bratislava
Kiev ○
○ Budapest
UKRAINE
HUNGARY

Ural River

K A Z A K

○ Zagreb
Dniester River
CROATIA
ROMANIA
Chisinau ○
Dnieper River
Don River
Volga River
Aral Sea

Sarajevo ○
Belgrade ○
○ Bucharest
Sea of
Azov
*Ustyurt
Plateau*
UZBEKISTAN
BOSNIA AND
HERZEGOVINA
SERBIA
Danube River
Black Sea
*Caspian
Sea*
*Kyzyl K
Deser*
MONTENEGRO
Pristina ○
BULGARIA
GEORGIA
Podgorica ○
KOSOVO
○ Sofia
Tbilisi ○
*Kara Kum
Desert*
ALBANIA
Skopje ○
ARMENIA
Baku ○
TURKMENISTAN
ITALY
MACEDONIA
Yerevan ○
AZERBAIJAN
○ Tirana
Oxur River (Amu D...

GREECE
Ankara ○
T U R K E Y
Ashgabat ○

Athens ○

Tehran ○

M e d i t e r r a n e a n   S e a
Nicosia ○
SYRIA
CYPRUS
Beirut ○
Damascus ○
LEBANON
Baghdad ○
I R A N
ISRAEL
Tigris River
AFGH
Tel Aviv ○
I R A Q
PALESTINE
Amman ○
Euphrates River
Cairo ○
JORDAN

EGYPT
Kuwait City ○
P A
KUWAIT
*Persian
Gulf*
SAUDI
Manama ○
ARABIA
BAHRAIN
QATAR
Doha ○
Riyadh ○
Abu Dhabi ○
Muscat ○
UNITED ARAB
EMIRATES
OMAN

Ural Mountains

Central Asia in the 21st century

○ Modern capitals

N

Scale (km)

0   250   500   750   1000